States of Dependency
Welfare, Rights, and American Governance, 1935–1972

Who bears responsibility for the poor, and who may exercise the power that comes with that responsibility? Amid the Great Depression, American reformers answered this question in new ways, with profound effects on long-standing practices of governance and entrenched understandings of citizenship. *States of Dependency* traces New Deal welfare programs over the span of four decades, asking what happened as money, expertise, and ideas traveled from the federal administrative epicenter in Washington, DC, through state and local bureaucracies, and into diverse and divided communities. Drawing on a wealth of previously unmined legal and archival sources, Karen Tani reveals how reformers attempted to build a more bureaucratic, centralized, and uniform public welfare system; how traditions of localism, federalism, and hostility toward the "undeserving poor" affected their efforts; and how, along the way, more and more Americans came to speak of public income support in the powerful but limiting language of law and rights. The resulting account moves beyond attacking or defending Americans' reliance on the welfare state to explore the complex network of dependencies undergirding modern American governance.

Karen Tani is Assistant Professor of Law at the University of California, Berkeley. Prior to joining the faculty at Berkeley, she received her JD and PhD in history from the University of Pennsylvania and held prestigious fellowships at New York University and the University of Pennsylvania. Her work has appeared in leading journals, including the *Law and History Review* and the *Yale Law Journal*, and has won awards from the American Society for Legal History, the Hellman Foundation, the William Nelson Cromwell Foundation, and the National Academy of Social Insurance. She coedits the *Legal History Blog*, the field's leading source for news and announcements.

Studies in Legal History

Editors

Sarah Barringer Gordon, University of Pennsylvania
Holly Brewer, University of Maryland, College Park
Michael Lobban, London School of Economics and Political Science

States of Dependency

Welfare, Rights, and American Governance, 1935–1972

KAREN M. TANI

University of California, Berkeley

CAMBRIDGE
UNIVERSITY PRESS

CAMBRIDGE
UNIVERSITY PRESS

32 Avenue of the Americas, New York, NY 10013-2473, USA

Cambridge University Press is part of the University of Cambridge.

It furthers the University's mission by disseminating knowledge in the pursuit of
education, learning, and research at the highest international levels of excellence.

www.cambridge.org
Information on this title: www.cambridge.org/9781107076846

First published 2016

Printed in the United States of America

A catalog record for this publication is available from the British Library.

Library of Congress Cataloging in Publication Data
Tani, Karen M., author.
States of Dependency : Welfare, Rights, and American Governance, 1935–1972 / Karen
M. Tani.
New York : Cambridge University Press, 2016. | Series: Studies in legal history
LCCN 2015041408 | ISBN 9781107076846 (hardback)
LCSH: Public welfare – Law and legislation – United States – History. | Social rights –
United States – History. | Social security – Law and legislation – United States –
History. | BISAC: HISTORY / United States / 20th Century.
LCC KF3720 .T36 2016 | DDC 344.7303/2582–dc23
LC record available at http://lccn.loc.gov/2015041408

ISBN 978-1-107-07684-6 Hardback
ISBN 978-1-107-43408-0 Paperback

To Michael B. Katz, in memoriam

Contents

Gallery between pages 150 and 151

Figures and Tables

Gallery images

Acknowledgments

In writing this book about giving and taking, charity and obligation, I have benefited from more support than any scholar is entitled to receive. I am very grateful.

This project owes much to my graduate school advisors and cheerleaders. Annelise Orleck helped me imagine a career as a professional historian and inspired me to write about poverty and inequality. Tom Sugrue welcomed me to graduate school with open arms and invited me to "think big." He continues to remind me, by example, of why historical work is so important, fulfilling, and fun. Sarah (Sally) Barringer Gordon shepherded this project from beginning to end, first as an advisor and later as an editor. Throughout, she has been a generous, tireless mentor and a true and faithful friend. Michael Katz, to whom this book is dedicated, was simply always there – always ready to read, talk, critique, and encourage. I am grateful to him for demanding rigor and precision from his students while never discouraging us from writing, as he did, with passion and empathy. I hope this book would have made him proud.

Numerous colleagues and friends have also devoted time and energy to this project. I am especially grateful to those who commented on the manuscript at my October 2014 book workshop: Sean Farhang, Hendrik Hartog, Laura Kalman, Rebecca McLennan, Reuel Schiller, Jeff Selbin, Jim Sparrow, and Margaret Weir. Less formally, many colleagues at the University of California, Berkeley, provided equally generous support. I am particularly grateful to Kathy Abrams, Catherine Albiston, Cybelle Fox, Kinch Hoekstra, David Lieberman, Joy Milligan, Cal Morrill, Melissa Murray, Phil Rocco, Harry and Jane Scheiber, Steve

Sugarman, Chris Tomlins, and Leti Volpp; to all the members of the law school's Junior Working Ideas Group; and to the members of my wonderful writing group, Charisma Acey, Karen Trappenberg Frick, Carolina Reid, Caitlin Rosenthal, Elena Schneider, Andrea Sinn, and Lisa Trever.

I have been fortunate, as well, to have received support from the broader scholarly community, in forms ranging from generative conversations to detailed line edits. I thank in particular Greg Ablavsky, Kevin Arlyck, Felice Batlan, Bethany Berger, Chris Beauchamp, Ed Berkowitz, Richard Bernstein, Tomiko Brown-Nagin, Margot Canaday, Josh Chafetz, Merlin Chowkwanyun, Erin Delaney, Deborah Dinner, Dan Ernst, Bob Gordon, Alex Gourse, Martha Jones, Amalia Kessler, Jeremy Kessler, Felicia Kornbluh, Jessica Lautin, Sophia Lee, Serena Mayeri, Amy Offner, Bill Nelson, Bill Novak, K. Sabeel Rahman, Gautham Rao, Laura Weinrib, Barbara Welke, Steven Wilf, and Mason Williams. I also benefited from comments received at workshops and conferences, including the Hurst Institute; the Policy History Conference; the Beyond the New Deal Order conference at the University of California, Santa Barbara; the legal history workshops at Harvard University, New York University, Stanford University, the University of Michigan, and the University of Minnesota; the annual meetings of the American Historical Association, the American Society for Legal History, the Law and Society Association, the Organization of American Historians, and the Social Science History Association; and numerous workshops on the University of California, Berkeley, campus.

In writing this book, I have relied heavily on librarians and archivists. I owe great debts to the librarians at the University of California, Berkeley, School of Law, especially Dean Rowan, and at the University of Pennsylvania, as well as to the staffs of the dozens of archives and libraries that I visited. I particularly taxed the National Archives at College Park, where I spent the bulk of my research hours; the Social Welfare History Archives at the University of Minnesota; and the Oral History Archives at Columbia University. I also benefited from access to two private collections of papers and from the reminiscences of their holders. To Frances and David White and to the family of the late Richard Smith: a million thanks.

This project would not have been possible without myriad other forms of assistance. I received financial support from the University of California, Berkeley; the Hellman Foundation; the University of Pennsylvania; the Goleib Fellowship in Legal History at New York University; and the

William Nelson Cromwell Foundation. I am particularly thankful for the funds that supported my research assistants, each of whom I am proud to know: Chan Hee Chu, Luke Diamond, Truc Doan, Gaia Goffe, Nora Krinitsky, Joan Li, Emily Prifogle, Elisa Redish, Meredith Spoto, Maureen St. Cyr, Andrew Talai, Jeremy Varon, and Pauline White Meeusen. My faculty assistants, Stephanie Marple, Stephanie Dorton, and Hailey Anderson, provided invaluable administrative support.

Cambridge University Press has given great time and attention to this book. I am especially grateful to my series editors, Holly Brewer and Sally Gordon; to senior editor Lew Bateman; to copy editor Julie Ericksen Hagen; and to the anonymous readers who reviewed the initial book proposal and manuscript draft.

Parts of *States of Dependency* draw from material that has appeared previously in published journal articles: "Welfare and Rights before the Movement: Rights as a Language of the State," *Yale Law Journal* 122 (2012): 314–83; "States' Rights, Welfare Rights, and the 'Indian Problem': Negotiating Citizenship and Sovereignty, 1935–1954," *Law and History Review* 33, no. 1 (2015): 1–40; and "Administrative Equal Protection: Federalism, the Fourteenth Amendment, and the Rights of the Poor," *Cornell Law Review* 100 (2015): 825–99. I thank the journals for helping me strengthen my work and for permitting me to use portions of it here.

My greatest debt of all is to my family. I owe special thanks to Grandma Yoshi, for helping me feel connected to the "train of history"; to my parents, Paul and Barbara, for their steadfast support; and to my "extended family," Sally and Dan Gordon, for years of writing retreats and good company. I owe the most to my husband, Sean, for living a life of compassion, conviction, and good humor, and for sharing that life with me.

Introduction

Giving is the most dangerous thing in the world – unless, of course, it is well administered.
  – *William E. Royer, welfare director, Montgomery County, Maryland*

The test of a free society will be found in the scope of right and privilege possessed by its weakest elements – those who are under the greatest pressure to surrender their independence.
  – *A. Delafield Smith, assistant general counsel, Federal Security Agency*

When Senator John F. Kennedy declared in 1960 that the nation was entering a promising and perilous "New Frontier" – "a turning-point in history" – Newburgh, New York, seemed to belong in the proverbial dust heap. Once the headquarters for General George Washington and the Continental Army, and a century later a hub for industry and transportation, Newburgh was falling into ruin. Its population was declining, its housing stock decaying, and its economy failing. City Manager Joseph McDowell Mitchell claimed to know exactly whom to blame: the city's hundreds of "chiselers and loafers," "freeload[ing]" migrants, "social parasites," and "illegitimate children." They burned through "taxpayer" dollars, he alleged, bringing in return only crime, blight, and immoral behavior. If Newburgh could simply reassert traditional, local controls over the poor, he insisted, the city would recover its former glory.[1]

On May Day in 1961, Mitchell gave Newburgh's citizens their first glimpse of "home rule" reclaimed, when he summoned all "reliefers" to the police station. Some endured questions about their sexual behavior, drinking, and criminal records, while others waited hours in line. The real blitz, however, occurred on June 20, when Mitchell sent a thirteen-point memo to the city's commissioner of public welfare. Among the changes he ordered were the issuing of welfare "vouchers" rather than cash payments; a monthly review of all Aid to Dependent Children files; a cap on welfare expenditures; and the imposition of strict time limits on relief – strictest of all for those who were "new to the city," such as Puerto Ricans and black migrants from the South. Mitchell also ordered the denial of relief to broad categories of applicants: "all able-bodied adult males" and other "physically capable" persons who refused employment; all applicants who had "left a job voluntarily"; and women who repeatedly bore children out of wedlock. And this, Mitchell promised, was to be "only the beginning."[2]

Mitchell's zeal was not that of a native son. Born and raised in Maryland, he arrived in Newburgh after military tours in North Africa and Germany, a stint in various federal wartime agencies, graduate work in public administration in Southern California, and several years as city manager of a Pennsylvania township. Perhaps that is why his plan appealed not only to his constituents in Newburgh but also to Americans nationwide. While some media outlets protested Newburgh's approach – it was a return to the "Dark Ages," the *New York Times* announced – others deemed the plan "courageous," humane, and even geopolitically astute: "a perfect way to fight and win the cold war." Leaders of other cities large and small wondered whether Mitchell's proposed reforms could help solve their problems. Arizona senator Barry Goldwater, a rising star among conservative Republicans, embraced Newburgh's approach as a national model. And everyone seemed to accept Goldwater's underlying premise: that the country had gotten itself into a "welfare mess."[3]

Looking back on the Newburgh incident, the beginnings of a now familiar story are visible. Although state authorities quickly put a stop to most of Mitchell's plans and Mitchell himself faded from view, his opinions highlighted a broad and deep dissatisfaction with the nation's welfare programs. In the ensuing decade, Mitchell's moralistic, racially coded, and taxpayer-oriented manner of speaking about welfare would become a national trend, even as liberal politicians announced an all-out "war" on the conditions that trapped so many citizens in poverty.[4] As President Lyndon Johnson's administration attempted to bring poor communities out of "the other America" and into the "land of opportunity," state and local welfare policies would codify Newburgh's assumptions, reinforcing a set of laws that already subjected poor recipients to extensive discipline and surveillance. And poor people and their allies would rise up in protest: within just a few more years, a New York welfare rights organization would virtually shut down that city's welfare system, welfare mothers would stop traffic on the Las Vegas Strip, and the National Welfare Rights Organization would amass more than twenty thousand members. In the same period, some of the nation's most brilliant legal minds would turn to "poverty law," helping to convince the U.S. Supreme Court that the poor were being mistreated at the hands of state lawmakers and that welfare recipients possessed a constitutionally protected interest in their public payments.[5]

But if Newburgh was an important harbinger of the events that followed, it is now an equally useful artifact, one that reveals important and understudied changes over time. First and foremost, Newburgh reminds us that local communities had once enjoyed vast discretionary power over the poor, but that in the lifespan of people like Joseph McDowell Mitchell, something dramatic occurred: other levels of government had come to dictate the terms on which public aid would be available to the needy.

local control

This change occurred, in large part, via the Social Security Act of 1935 (SSA). Best known for establishing a mandatory system of retirement saving for individual American workers (Social Security), the act also authorized grants-in-aid for need-based income support ("welfare") for large categories of the poor: fatherless children, the aged, and the blind. By attaching those grants to state rather than local programs, the act ensured that federal and state officials would insert themselves between localities and their needy residents.[6] Local administrative machinery often continued to deliver poor people's benefits, and many localities retained responsibility for "residuals" (those who did not fit into the act's categories), but in general, local administrators in this new era found themselves required to "follow the book" and suffer visits from "higher-ups." The "price" of federal and state support, explained one Kansas writer in 1952, "is a number of rules which for practical purposes take out of the hands of our local people the decision as to who shall get 'relief,' in what form, and how much." Newburgh's call for "home rule" represented both nostalgia for an earlier era, in which poor people looked and acted differently, and a critique of the way that the Social Security Act insulated individuals from the beneficence and scrutiny of their communities.[7]

*local
|
state
|
national*

And yet Newburgh was not just a rallying point for people who romanticized local control. It was also a compelling example for political figures, like Goldwater, who championed states' rights and state sovereignty.[8] These people, too, were responding to a dramatic change over time: the rise of federal grants-in-aid and the corresponding reshaping of federal-state relationships. Between 1900 and 1930, when many

progressive reform efforts bore fruit at the national level, the combined
amount of federal grants to the states rose from $2.8 million annually to
more than $100 million. The increase stemmed from the fact that the
federal government had limited powers but vast funds (thanks to the
institution of the federal income tax), and that influential reformers perceived many problems as beyond the ken of state and local government.
As national policymakers responded to the Great Depression, they continued to rely on the grant-in-aid device, finding in it a way to implement
sweeping reforms while steering clear of a hostile Supreme Court and
appeasing political allies. By fiscal year 1946–47, the estimated annual
total of federal grants to the states exceeded $1 billion. This money
became a significant part of state budgets, creating relationships of dependence and, in some cases, perceptions of coercion. In the early years of the
Depression, federal grants covered less than 2 percent of state and local
expenditures; by 1954, federal grants constituted more than 20 percent of
some states' annual revenue.[9]

Grants for welfare proved particularly remunerative. In 1937, just after
the enactment of the Social Security Act, federal-state aid for highways
($317 million) overshadowed that for welfare ($155 million), but within
just two years the situation was reversed. By 1943, state receipts for welfare
($389 million) were more than double those for highways ($164 million)
and more than thirteen times the receipts for agriculture, an early area of
federal funding. For the fiscal year ending June 30, 1947, grants for the
categorical public assistance programs alone – that is, not including the full
slate of health and welfare programs – constituted 57 percent of the total
federal aid awarded to the states. To the extent that federal funds were
remaking state budgets, public assistance grants now led the way.[10]

The grants came at a cost, however. States received public assistance
grants on a matching basis, meaning a state got nothing if it contributed
nothing, and it got more if it spent more. States responded by spending
their own funds on public assistance and renewing those funds every year,
at the expense of other goals. The nature of public assistance programs
also made it difficult for states to control their outlays. State legislatures
set eligibility requirements but could not control how many people
applied, and claimant expectations, once established, could be difficult
to scale back.

In addition to distorting state budgeting decisions, public assistance
grants brought federal oversight, with all of its historical baggage. There
were rules about how the programs were to operate, who ought to run
them, and how the states were to assure the federal government of their

compliance.[11] An entire federal agency, with offices and agents out in "the field," was dedicated to enforcement.[12] On the eve of the Newburgh controversy, many of these rules had already been the subject of deep federal-state disagreement, and in general the federal government – specifically, federal administrators – had prevailed. This had embittered some state politicians – especially those who perceived federal coercion in other policy arenas, such as the desegregation of public schools and the regulation of labor markets. Federal grants-in-aid were "a mixture of blackmail and bribery," Goldwater declared in his 1960 manifesto, *The Conscience of a Conservative*. "The States are told to go along with the program 'or else.'"[13]

Irritation with federal pressure was not the only element uniting supporters of the Newburgh plan, however. They also objected to the normative content of the rules and procedures that emanated from federal administrators and reached communities via state and local "welfare bureaucrats," as Mitchell called them. Touching on themes that had inspired the followers of the popular political dissidents Huey Long and Father Coughlin in the 1930s and, before them, the Populist movement of the 1880s and 1890s, Mitchell characterized Newburgh's welfare bureaucrats as colonizers from a foreign nation, intent on building their own "empire."[14] The critique contained some truth: since 1939 one of the conditions attached to federal public assistance grants had been the creation of statewide merit systems for the public employees involved with federally subsidized programs. To further encourage professionalization, federal administrators offered training to state and local administrators and subsidized their attendance at social work schools.[15] The result, over time, was a set of state and local welfare administrators who did not always appear to share the values and priorities of the communities they served. As Mitchell defended his thirteen-point plan, he accused local welfare workers of operating according to the "equalitarian," "socialistic," and impractical philosophies they picked up "in the social schools." These philosophies, he said, led welfare workers to dole out cash for "ne'er do wells" to spend on drink, luxury, and ill-considered children – allocative decisions that were then defended as a complex "science" beyond the comprehension of ordinary people. An oft-forgotten part of Mitchell's famous campaign was about "reorient[ing]" the thinking of these welfare workers and questioning their necessity in the first place. Many of those who cheered Mitchell's actions were cheering Newburgh's revolt against the content and size of welfare's "built-in bureaucracy."[16]

They cheered as well Mitchell's brazen recapturing of the language of rights, which had become a staple of liberal politics over the past thirty years and – contrary to historians' conventional wisdom – circulated even within the stigmatized realm of welfare. Mitchell won the nation's attention, he explained, by

challeng[ing] the *right* of social parasites to breed illegitimate children at the taxpayers' expense, the *right* of moral chiselers and loafers to squat on the relief rolls forever, the *right* of freeloaders to make more on relief than when working, the *right* of those on relief to loaf by State and Federal edict, the *right* of people to quit jobs at will and go on relief like spoiled children, the *right* of citizens to migrate for the purpose of becoming or continuing as public charges.

In the face of such claims of entitlement, Mitchell asserted *Newburgh's* rights – its rights to dictate its own future, to conserve taxpayer dollars, and to preserve its traditional way of life. Individuals had rights, Mitchell conceded, but they were the negative rights that lawyer and politician Dean Alfange had set forth in the 1950s in his widely circulated essay "An American's Creed": the right to "seek opportunity, not security"; the right to "prefer the challenges of life" to a state-guaranteed existence; the right to refuse to barter "freedom for beneficence." Mitchell urged poor Americans to look not to the state but "to the ant," the hardest worker in God's kingdom. "Consider her ways," he said, quoting Proverbs, "and be wise."[17]

The resolution of the Newburgh controversy – a resolution that proved at best partial and temporary – is similarly revealing. By 1961, New York's welfare system relied heavily on federal funds; a generation of federal administrative interpretations made clear that these funds hinged on adherence *throughout the state* to the preapproved state "plan." Newburgh's revolt thus put the entire state at risk. No responsible state official could condone Newburgh's actions. At the same time, appearing soft on "welfarism" – a term that connoted fraud, dependency, and high government spending – was sure to alienate important constituencies. Ultimately, state officials turned to the seemingly neutral authority of law. At the urging of Governor Nelson Rockefeller, who wanted neither to betray Republican principles nor to appear to condone discriminatory and inhumane treatment, the state attorney general brought suit against Newburgh and a state court enjoined all but one of Mitchell's new rules. "Newburgh cannot be permitted to secede[] from law," the editors of the *New York Times* explained. Newburgh's error was not, in other words, its obsession with "the undeserving chiseler" but its attempt "to be a law unto itself."[18]

For their part, federal administrators stayed quiet. They had the authority under the Social Security Act to cut off New York's grant, but after twenty-five years of funding the state, its utter dependence on federal money made that solution too harsh – and too dangerous for the federal agency. Such was the lesson of the 1950s, when numerous states attempted to make their programs more restrictive and less appealing, in ways that discriminated against nonwhite applicants and conflicted with established federal policies. Reining those states in had produced damaging charges of federal overreaching and socialistic tendencies. Yet not acting also had costs. By 1961, federal officials understood that they were rapidly losing their credibility as enforcers of welfare law, and with it their ability to bring national authority and expertise to bear on an important policy area. As critics called for a reevaluation of the entire welfare system, federal administrators did little more than promise to study the matter and await Congress's instruction.[19]

Left unresolved in 1961, then, were the questions at the heart of the Newburgh revolt: In a modern nation-state, with a system of divided government, who bears responsibility for those in need? As one journalist put it, "Precisely who is my brother's keeper?"[20] Equally important, and implicit in Mitchell's thirteen-point plan: Who enjoys the power that comes with giving, and how may that power be exercised? When it comes to the poor, where does legitimate power begin and end? These questions had troubled Americans for centuries but had become ever more pressing over the preceding twenty-five years, after the federal government intervened so boldly in the realm of poor relief.[21] These are the questions that poor Americans and their lawyers would ultimately bring to the Supreme Court in the late 1960s, seeking a resolution that neither administrators nor politicians could deliver.

These are the questions, too, that animate *States of Dependency* as it tracks the remaking of American public welfare between 1935, when Congress enacted the Social Security Act, and 1972, when the most radical of the act's possible implications – a national guaranteed minimum income – appeared to expire for good. The book is less about answers, however, than about how diverse groups of Americans searched for answers, drawing on their own experiences of the changes unfolding around them. It is about the lives and deaths of their ideas, alliances, institutions, and laws. It is about the constraints they faced, and the choices they made from within those constraints. And it is about the impact of those choices on fundamental structures and principles of governance, an impact that reverberates today.

In telling this history, *States of Dependency* advances three main arguments, detailed in the sections that follow. In brief, the first argument is about the deployment of rights language in the realm of poor relief during the New Deal. Previous scholarship cast the welfare rights claimants of the 1960s and 1970s as pioneers of a new, deeply controversial way of talking about poor relief. *States of Dependency* shows that the pairing of welfare and rights has another history, grounded less in activism and more in public administration: New Deal administrators spread rights language throughout the nation in an attempt to rationalize and modernize the landscape of public welfare. Over the course of the next three decades, Americans inside and outside of government would translate this rights language from ideas into practice, in complex and sometimes contradictory ways. The second argument is about the role of New Deal public assistance in impelling changes in the respective powers of federal, state, and local governments. Though often described as decentralized and minimally intrusive, New Deal welfare programs helped the federal government develop the robust and extensive administrative machinery that is with us today. Less visibly – and perhaps more importantly – these programs helped states do the same. Localities, meanwhile, lost control over a policy area that had long been their exclusive jurisdiction.[22] The third argument is about the "legalization" over time of American poor relief: its increased reliance on statutory and constitutional law; its incorporation of legalistic procedures; and its eventual turn to courts as the ultimate arbiter of disagreements. Austin Sarat's pithy observation – that for the poor, "the law is all over" – had not always been true. But it became so in the decades after the New Deal.[23]

These three arguments – about welfare and rights, realignments in federal-state-local power, and the legalization of American poor relief – converge to produce a broader intervention: a revised portrait of the modern American state. As previous accounts have suggested, this state is bureaucratized, professionalized, rights-oriented, and centralized, with power concentrated in Washington. It is also, I argue, heavily dependent on state and local government, relatively indifferent toward substantive rights, and tolerant of vast inequality. These latter characteristics are neither accidents nor aberrations. They have not come and gone with changes in political leadership. They are now defining features of American governance.

WELFARE, RIGHTS, AND THE ADMINISTRATIVE
RECONFIGURATION OF CITIZENSHIP

Most scholars associate the concept of welfare rights with the second half of the 1960s: with the broadening of the modern civil rights movement, the establishment of the War on Poverty's Legal Services Program, the flourishing of grassroots welfare rights organizations, and a series of bold pronouncements from the Supreme Court about the constitutional rights of poor citizens. They also associate welfare rights with conservative backlash – with the discourse on wasteful government and "welfare queens" that hung like a cloud over late-twentieth-century social welfare policy, until President Bill Clinton proudly "ended welfare as we [knew] it."[24] In fact, however, the idea of welfare as a right – and the related but distinct idea of welfare recipients as rights holders – has a longer history, one that both helps us understand why rights language appealed to poor Americans and their allies in the 1960s and why rights claims met such fierce resistance from other parts of the polity.

This longer history has been obscured from view by a construct that continues to dominate our understanding of U.S. social welfare provision: the "two-track welfare state." Historically, national-level insurance-based programs – constituting what scholars call the upper track – have been more generous, better administered, and more secure. Old Age Insurance ("Social Security") is the classic example. Payments from these programs have generally been framed as earned rights or entitlements, and white men and their dependents have benefited disproportionately. "Means-tested" programs, in contrast, such as Aid to Dependent Children (ADC) (now Temporary Aid to Needy Families), have historically been less generous and secure, more vulnerable to maladministration, and more stigmatizing. This lower track has disproportionately served women and racial minorities, and its benefits, according to the two-track account, are decidedly *not* rights.[25] Scholars have often noted that when old age and unemployment insurance were brand new, their New Deal designers used welfare as a point of contrast – as the quintessential *non*right against which the superior programs could be defined.[26]

Peering underneath the hood of this two-track welfare state, *States of Dependency* reveals that well before the War on Poverty or the modern welfare rights movement some government officials eagerly introduced rights concepts into the world of welfare. The Social Security Act, we tend to forget, was not just about Social Security; it also authorized matching grants to states for programs of need-based income support. These "welfare" programs encompassed large categories of the poor: dependent (i.e., fatherless) children, the aged, and the blind.[27] Desperate for funds and overwhelmed by their citizens' needs, nearly all states applied for grants – and thereby enabled the federal government to claim an ongoing role in the administration of a jealously guarded local function. "For the first time," to borrow one New Deal administrator's metaphor, "the American people hitched three wild horses, Federal, State and Local governments ... to the same wagon" and set forth on a shared journey.[28] Rights concepts, although nowhere mentioned in the Social Security Act itself, were central to the story of what happened along the way.[29] The task facing New Deal administrators was to reform and supplant what they self-servingly referred to as the "old poor law," a localized, nonuniform system of poor relief with very deep roots. Rights language appeared to be a useful tool for reaching uncomprehending and at times uncooperative state and local officials. The old poor law, federal administrators explained in speeches, guidance documents, and training sessions, understood relief as charity or a gratuity; that is why poor relief could at one time be administered by nonexperts, in a highly discretionary fashion, with little regard for the individual in need. The benefits of the new public assistance programs, in contrast, came to recipients *as a matter of right*, and therefore had to be administered in a more systematic and professional way, with due regard for the recipient's other rights – to fair and equal treatment, to autonomy in his or her spending choices, and to some degree of privacy.[30]

Much of the talk of rights took place out of view of the general public, but it was hardly insulated from Americans' everyday experiences. In the 1940s, as the nation straddled depression and war, the federal government assumed new responsibilities, such as wartime production and price controls, and offered Americans new rights, most notably to political and social security. It also demanded great sacrifices, through a large-scale draft and the first-ever income tax on nonwealthy Americans.[31] The result, by the second half of the 1940s, was an embrace of rights language – which was now tightly tied to the concept of national citizenship – and a simultaneous and deepening anxiety about welfare. A paradigm emerged in which these programs represented tax dollars at work and central-state bureaucracy on the march. These same programs became linked in the public mind to disruptive demographic and cultural changes: the mass migration of African Americans from the South to the North; the increasing number of unmarried mothers and fatherless children; and the abandonment of elderly parents to the care of the state.[32] At the level of actual practice, meanwhile, changes were afoot, even if critics exaggerated their scale: the public welfare system that the New Deal created was more inclusive (albeit still discriminatory), more centralized and bureaucratic, and more capable of seeing and vindicating individual rights.

Attacks on welfare sharpened in the 1950s, just as welfare recipients were beginning to recognize how much the law promised them. Federal public assistance grants were by then a significant source of state revenue, yet if anything, federal authority was under siege. Around the nation, disgruntled state and local politicians blamed federal administrators for importing "collectivist" and "equalitarian" ideas into their communities – such as the "right to welfare" – and constructing a behemoth bureaucracy. Efficiency-touting reformers, such as local chambers of commerce, denounced the growing costs of public welfare and the waste of taxpayer dollars. Open opponents of racial equality, as well as alarmed observers of black geographic mobility, articulated links between race, immorality, and welfare dependency. Federal administrators found themselves on the defensive as one state after another demanded its grant from the federal government but then ignored, challenged, or reinterpreted the conditions attached to the funds. State officials in these places did not want to return poor relief to its pre–New Deal condition – they had become too dependent on federal funds – but neither did they believe they had to accept federal dictates.

In the 1960s, after several states explicitly flouted federal directives regarding their ADC programs and federal administrators failed to stop them, welfare rights claims burst into the federal courts. In some regards, these claims were new: female and nonwhite plaintiffs cast welfare as at once a civil, political, *and* social right, owed to them as free and equal members of a prosperous democratic society.[33] But in many ways these claims were a permutation of the rights language that had long circulated inside the administrative state (in part because former welfare administrators were heavily involved in the litigation): they were about the triumph of federal law over state and local discretion, the sanctity of written rules and uniform standards, and the insistence that poor individuals be allowed a legal identity divorced from local contexts.

The argument, to be clear, is not about back-dating welfare rights as a cause or a movement. The point is that to speak of welfare in terms of rights is not really, or not exclusively, about claiming an individual entitlement to cash. It was, and is, about poor people's relationship to the governing authorities around them – about the meaning of citizenship in a divided polity. When administrators deployed rights language in their

day-to-day work, they implied a type of citizenship that history contradicted and that the structure of their programs belied, but that amassed
genuine supporters over time. Similarly, opposition to the pairing of
welfare and rights has always been about something more than fiscal
prudence or a desire to punish insubordinate black mothers. Though
often cast as a reaction to the excesses of the Great Society or the
liberality of the Supreme Court, such opposition has also reflected a
deeper and older dissatisfaction – a dissatisfaction with the governing
arrangements that the New Deal and its administrators produced.

THE RISE OF FEDERAL AND STATE POWER
AND THE RESILIENCE OF LOCALISM

In relating the long history of welfare rights, *States of Dependency* joins a
raft of recent scholarship on how the national government came to have
such a deep reach into American life and such vast bureaucratic machinery. After centuries of remaining deliberately "out of sight," how did a
strong national government become legitimate? And how did Americans
come to think of themselves as belonging – and beholden – to a national
polity, after devoting their associational energies so steadfastly to local
civic groups, religious organizations, and other place-based communities?
Taxation, conscription, political participation, empire building – these are
all pieces of the puzzle, scholars have shown.[34] Poor relief is an additional
piece, and one that is uniquely revealing. Although often sold by policymakers as a humanitarian imperative and often described by scholars as
simply a tool of labor discipline, poor relief is at bottom a form of
governance. It is a way of ordering relationships within a society, allocat-
ing resources, conveying public values, and strengthening (or weakening)
individual allegiances to the giver. Changes over time in the nature and
administration of poor relief represent changes in governance itself.[35]

   Seen in this light, the Social Security Act's restructuring of American
poor relief is deeply significant: it reflects the existence of an already
empowered national state and suggests an attempt to further strengthen
that state. Through the power of the purse, the federal government insi-
nuated itself between subnational governments and their poor citizens. It
did so subtly at first – so subtly that most poor Americans probably were
not aware of the federal subsidies behind their benefit checks or the federal
bureaucracy peering over the shoulder of their local welfare worker. By
the 1960s, however, the federal government's hand was unmistakable.
Poor Americans came to understand that if they wanted higher welfare

benefits or better treatment from local welfare authorities, they should lobby Congress, file a federal lawsuit, or write to the president of the United States.

And yet I am careful not to treat the federal government as the only level of government that changed during this period. *States of Dependency* is part of an emergent body of scholarship on *intergovernmentality* in twentieth-century U.S. history – scholarship that recognizes the multiple levels of government (and multiple actors at each level) involved in policy-making and administration and analyzes the downstream effects of inter-governmental collaboration.[36] Of particular interest here is the federal government's role in what historian Jon Teaford calls "the rise of the states" – from "spare" governmental units "with little administrative muscle" in the nineteenth century to "dynamic molders of domestic policy and vital providers of government services" by the end of the twentieth.[37] With little comment from contemporaneous scholars, states became enti-ties on which both citizens and the federal government depended.

I argue that the public assistance titles of the Social Security Act of 1935 were crucial to this transition. By offering states conditional grants-in-aid to apply toward relieving certain categories of "unemployables" within their jurisdiction, the SSA not only brought the federal government into the realm of welfare but also indirectly increased states' power. States that wanted federal money could not simply funnel those dollars to the cities, counties, and towns that had traditionally cared for the poor. Via a central state agency – which often had to be created from scratch – states had to assume responsibility for the administration of federal funds, either through supervision of local authorities or through their own state machinery. Other federal requirements demanded uniform, statewide rules and procedures, systems for reviewing local benefit decisions, and personnel standards for local welfare workers. The federal government could not take over the administration of poor relief, but it could incenti-vize states to become stronger, more dependable partners.[38]

Efforts to implement the SSA in its early years show that some states had a long way to go – a reality that proved to be a significant stumbling block for federal administrators. Over time, however, and with federal encouragement, states became the robust, modern govern-mental units that the SSA demanded. Local governments, meanwhile, lost out (even as big-city mayors emerged as major players on the national scene). Local authorities continued to play a vital role in the administration of relief but, increasingly, they had to fight for the discretionary powers that had formerly accompanied that role, such as

the ability to reject outsiders, control benefit levels, and fill administrative positions with political notables. By the 1960s, autonomous
local poor-relief operations were a thing of the past. And although
critics of New Deal welfare programs often harkened back to the good
old days of local control, proposals to restore such control had little
traction. States were not about to dismantle their own central-state
apparatus or the power that came with it.

*language
of localism*

States did, however, use their new capacities, along with the *language
of localism*, to contest the authority of the federal government. After years
of interacting with federal administrators and learning their limits, some
state officials found ways to accept federal money while rejecting the
interposition of the federal government between the states and their
poor citizens, especially their nonwhite citizens. Such strong assertions
of state sovereignty were what welfare rights advocates contested so
fiercely in the 1960s (with only partial success), and what federal anti-
poverty policymakers would increasingly accommodate in the later decades of the twentieth century.

In short, New Deal welfare programs helped change decisively the
American pattern of governance, generally in the direction of centralized
power and large-scale bureaucracy. Along the way, however, they helped
engender political forces and institutions that would temper the ambitions
of national-level authorities and preserve a type of citizenship that, while
uniform in appearance, remained highly variable in experience, especially
for the poor.[39]

THE "LEGALIZATION" OF AMERICAN POOR RELIEF

A third and final argument running through *States of Dependency* is the
notion of the "legalization" over time of American poor relief: statutory
law and implementing regulations remade a localized, patchwork system
of poor relief and put in its place the modern U.S. welfare state. This is not
to say that the older system was without law, merely that the law that
governed it was of a different type: local, customary, flexible, and built
around the idea of public duties rather than individual rights. The new
system was highly legalistic: it employed the language of legal rights,
insisted on written rules, and promised layers of legal process, including
appeals to "higher" legal authorities.[40] In the words of one Indiana
citizen, complaining to the Indiana State Welfare Department about her
family's treatment by a local welfare worker in 1944, "The law, the U.S.
law, says you can't do that."[41]

Much of the new emphasis on legalism came from federal officials: as they administered the Social Security Act, these officials persistently reminded state and local welfare workers that they were part of a new scheme of public provision in which legal processes and legal standards constrained local discretion. Written state and federal laws, not localized moral frameworks, were to guide decisions about public aid. The tissues of law, in other words, were to substitute for the now tenuous and implicitly suspect tissues of community. Those same legal sources gave federal officials the power to punish states that disobeyed (or that tolerated the disobedience of localities); in effect, the states had contracted with the federal government to exchange compliance for federal subsidies.

Americans' growing faith in a particular understanding of the rule of law lent support to federal officials' actions and inspired those officials to rely more and more on legalism. In search of a unifying national creed during and after World War II, American intellectuals seized on the nation's commitment to law, in the sense of both procedural fairness and adherence to the legal outcomes of the democratic process. That commitment, they argued, distinguished America's big government from totalitarian regimes. It also showed that Americans, for all their diversity, shared at least one fundamental value.[42] Thus, when federal administrators spoke to state and local welfare workers in the language of law, they took advantage of powerful resonances.

That did not mean that opposition evaporated – some state and local officials continued to evade federal administrators and disobey their edicts. Increasingly, however, they did so by turning to law. By the late 1940s, some had retained lawyers and crafted alternative interpretations of the Social Security Act and the U.S. Constitution. Using law as a tool, they formally challenged federal officials in agency proceedings and, eventually, in court. Poor people and their advocates did the same vis-à-vis state and local officials, beginning slowly in the late 1930s in state-level administrative proceedings and state court, before bursting into federal court in the mid-1960s.

The result, three decades after the enactment of the Social Security Act, was a divided and in many ways broken system of poor relief, but one in which all parties spoke the language of law. Before the New Deal, written regulations, appeal mechanisms, and the principles of "equal protection" and "due process" were anathema to American poor relief. There was such a thing as legal aid, but the phrase "poverty law" was as yet unthinkable. By the late 1960s, the system had been thoroughly "legalized."

This legalization proved enduring, even as much else changed for the poor. After the heady days of the welfare rights movement, poor Americans found the substance of their rights diminished and their choices constrained. In the words of one scholarly observer, "Law's hard, bureaucratic face ... supplemented, if not altogether replaced, its rights-protecting concerns."[43] To this day, however, poor relief remains a matter of statutes, regulations, and rule books. Critics continue to assail welfare – for its complexity, its inefficiency, its poor fit with American values – but few describe the system as lawless.

RETHINKING THE MODERN AMERICAN STATE

Taken together, the arguments I have outlined help resolve a significant historiographical puzzle. Three decades of "state-building" literature have given us a distinct impression of the modern American state: it is visibly powerful, unapologetically intrusive, and centered squarely in Washington – so much so that some scholars use the terms "the state" and "the federal government" interchangeably. From other historical literatures, however, we learn that well after the New Deal, Americans remained deeply localist in orientation, and that local authorities never relinquished control of some important functions of government, such as education and policing. In our renderings of the mid-twentieth century we thus see both a powerful central state – capable of making war, policing borders, raising money, conscripting and monitoring citizens, and inspiring national feeling – and a halting or laggard central state, with a seemingly underdeveloped presence in major areas of governance and with imperfect claims to the citizens living in the shadows of those areas (most notably, African Americans, children, and the poor). Reconciling these seeming inconsistencies will be the task of the next generation of scholarship. *States of Dependency* begins that work by focusing on one area of apparent lag: poor relief. Instead of treating poor relief as an aberration to be swept under the proverbial rug, *States of Dependency* uses it to construct a more nuanced vision of the modern American state.

About "the state": relative to thirty years ago, when historian William Leuchtenburg claimed the American state as historians' "next frontier," we know a lot.[44] Building on the pioneering work of social scientists Stephen Skowronek, Theda Skocpol, and others, a generation of scholars devoted great care to describing and analyzing "state building" – that is, the construction of those features and capabilities that appear crucial to modern U.S. statecraft.[45] Focusing largely on the period between

Reconstruction and the end of World War I, scholars have chronicled (and continue to chronicle) the development of far-reaching administrative and fiscal capacities, the accumulation of central-state legal authority over citizens and subnational jurisdictions, and the creation of formal institutional ties between the government and the governed.[46] More recently, "state building" studies have moved forward in time, into the 1940s and beyond, to describe how the state grew stronger across all of those dimensions, how it overcame new challenges, and how it legitimized (or failed to legitimize) its newfound authority.[47]

"State building" is in quotes here because other scholars have now looked back in time at the regimes of governance that the modern American state revised, reimagined, and ultimately replaced. Shattering the idea that the United States was ever "stateless," historian William Novak, for example, has reconstructed a coherent regime of governance for much of the nineteenth century. This alternative version of the state – which he dubs "the well-regulated society" – performed much of the work that we associate with modern governance, including vigorous regulation of public health, safety, and morals, but it did so at the local level, through autonomously operating communities.[48]

By clarifying what came before, such accounts helped produce a particular vision of the modern American state. Characteristic traits include centralization of power; vast, translocal regulatory and administrative capacities; a preference for statutory and constitutional law as opposed to the more flexible, community-oriented common law; and robust protections for individual rights, including both rights against government ("negative rights") and rights to government support and action ("positive rights"). Scholars sometimes describe this state as "liberal" because its logic tracks that of modern liberalism (that is, the liberalism that New Dealers claimed in the 1930s, as opposed to the classical liberalism of the previous century): the modern American state intervenes actively in the economy and helps remediate the human tolls of capitalism, while also vigorously protecting individual rights.[49] This "legal-economic and geopolitical hegemon" did not emerge overnight, of course, but most historians agree that it was firmly in place by the 1940s, if not decades earlier.[50]

With consensus, however, comes the puzzle: this image of the modern American state sits uneasily beside evidence from other historical literatures on Americans' day-to-day experiences with public authority in the twentieth century – evidence of the enduring importance of local governance and the limited reach of central-state authority. In the words of federalism scholar Martha Derthick, the founding generation chose "to be both one great nation and many relatively quite small, local communities"; over time, the commitment to local autonomy eroded, but that process was slow – exceedingly slow in some policy areas. Not until the 1960s was there anything like a "comprehensive, generalized system of national scrutiny of state and local government conduct." And that system – imposed from above by Congress and the federal courts – continued to spark resistance.[51] "Despite the pulls of modernity," summarizes historian Thomas Sugrue, despite the "the decline of local political parties" and the dramatic accumulation of federal power, "localism remained surprisingly resilient" in the late twentieth century.[52]

Poor relief – a long-established function of government – is perhaps the clearest example: well after the federal government created a permanent role for itself in providing basic income support, local officials doled out the actual benefits, and, in many places, they continue to do so. Other examples abound, however, and none is trivial. In the twentieth century, Americans witnessed a nationalization of "the politics of crime" and the rules of constitutional criminal procedure, but those changes never brought to policing the sort of centralized control commonly associated with the modern American state. Local officials continued to perform the day-to-day work of street-level law enforcement, and localities continued to foot the vast majority of the bill. We see similar trends in education and land use – policy areas that have been shown to have a decisive impact on Americans' economic prospects and well-being. Throughout the polity, meanwhile, a "localist ideology" has thrived. Local autonomy may be a fiction, but the *idea* of local autonomy – the notion that certain problems and certain people are the natural province of local government – has remained strong and real into the twenty-first century.[53]

States of Dependency paints a picture of the modern American state that incorporates, rather than glosses over, these seeming discrepancies. The book shows how, over the course of three decades – starting at a moment when many scholars believe the modern American state had already arrived – federal government actors and their allies in state and local government and the private sector slowly made over a diffuse, localized system of poor relief. A vestige in many ways of Novak's "well-regulated society," poor relief ultimately became part of a different, more "modern" pattern of governance. But frictions accompanied this transformation, and they did not simply disappear. Rather, they animated a politics that shaped and constrained the broader governing regime.[54]

The result, by the late 1960s, was a system of governance that resembled scholars' image of the modern American state but also had some features that, when judged against that image, seem almost inexplicitly "backwards" or old-fashioned: This state recognized all citizens, even the poorest, as rights-bearing members of the national polity, but limited those rights largely to procedural ones. It left substantive rights to the ebb and flow of politics. As a result, the material promises of citizenship remained thin indeed, and continued to turn on exercises of local discretion. This state relied heavily on federal bureaucracy but equally heavily on state and local bureaucracy, and although it imported professionalism into the other levels of government, it never developed strong tools for controlling subnational administrators. This state championed uniformity, national standards, and equal treatment but also tolerated vast inequality, in both wealth and life chances.[55]

It would be easy to dismiss these seemingly parochial and illiberal traits as temporary flaws in an otherwise sound, newly renovated house, like leaky windows soon to be replaced or graffiti left by a disgruntled neighbor. They are not, this book argues. These traits are bricks, they are mortar. They may not appear in the blueprints, but they are part of the house – part of the state – that Americans built. They are part of the regime of governance that we live with today.

METHOD: A LEGAL HISTORY FOR THE "AGE OF STATUTES"

The history recounted here is the product of two methodological choices. The first was to treat legislation as "a living, breathing force in American politics."[56] Such an approach is vital to the study of the twentieth century. Statutes have always been part of the nation's legal fabric, existing side by side with the slowly accreting common law, but in the first half of the twentieth century, Americans witnessed an "orgy of statute making."[57] Some of these new statutes represented efforts to codify common law principles; many more were part of ambitious new regulatory programs, aimed at everything from consumer goods to the conditions of labor to complex financial instruments. This pattern continued in the second half of the century and became more complex, besides, as new statutes were layered on top of older ones and administrative agencies multiplied.

Given the importance of statutory law to Americans' everyday lives, historians must ask not only how these statutes came to be, but also, as Jeffery Jenkins and Eric Patashnik urge, "What happen[ed] *after* the dramatic moment of legislative enactment?" What happened inside the administrative state, where statutes edged ever closer to meeting their subjects of regulation?[58] This is in some sense the call of the great Willard Hurst, who taught legal historians to look beyond appellate court doctrine to statutes, and to study those laws as they actually operated out in the world. Hurst viewed statutes functionally, however – as responses to the felt needs of society – and evaluated them as such.[59] Today's challenge is to document the way that statutes work in and through society, over spans of decades, as they pass through many hands, encounter new scenarios, and interact with a vast complex of formal and informal laws.

States of Dependency takes up that challenge by focusing on the long and complicated life of the public assistance titles of the Social Security Act, titles that, in turn, spurred hundreds of state public assistance laws and thousands of federal and state administrative regulations. In the course of implementation, all of these laws and regulations required interpretation – not once, but many times over. *States of Dependency* treats these everyday interpretations as significant, understanding that they always mattered to real people and that they often affected the range of possibilities available to future decision makers. In this sense, my method borrows much from the American Political Development tradition in political science and sociology. But it is finer grained, and aims not so much to discern policymaking patterns as to illuminate the workings of a particular form of power (law) in a particularly important era. It is a species of political history, in other words, but one that distrusts the formality and seeming finality of statutes and legal decisions.

A second and related methodological choice was to pay greater attention than most histories do to the activities of a particular layer of legal interpreters: those who occupy that crucial space between official lawmakers and their targets of regulation. In this case, that layer includes federal bureau heads, field agents, and consultants; state and local administrators; government social workers and lawyers; and knowledgeable activists and advocates.[60] Constrained by time, space, money, and the cultural and institutional legacies of the past, how did they carry out their perceived legal mandates? How did they respond to resistance, changed circumstances, and the pressures of their own professional and political communities?

This focus is not meant to devalue the actions of people at the top (appellate judges, state and federal executives, legislators, and so on), nor to neglect the view "from below" (the poor themselves). Borrowing tools from traditional political and legal history, as well as social history, *States of Dependency* relies on voices from throughout the polity. What I want readers to recognize, however, is the power of the people in the middle – those who, on a daily basis, enforced and interpreted sweeping new statutes. Their actions decisively shaped what law meant in practice. And by receiving, translating, and transmitting information from the bottom back to the top, these actors also enabled regular people to influence decision making at the highest levels. We cannot truly understand American life in the "age of statutes" without studying this important layer of action.[61]

These methodological choices go hand in hand with a distinct set of archives. *States of Dependency* relies, first, on documents from across the federal government. These include not only traditional legal-historical sources, such as congressional hearing records and appellate court decisions, but also records from the so-called fourth branch of government: federal agencies (here, the Social Security Board and its subsequent iterations). Federal administrative records provide a window onto day-to-day acts of legal interpretation and enforcement. In this instance, they also informed a second layer of research, into the records of state and local agencies. Although a deep look at welfare administration in every jurisdiction was beyond the scope of this study, I used federal records to locate particularly valuable sites – places where tensions that existed in other parts of the nation surfaced in a more dramatic fashion, prompting actors at all levels of government to articulate assumptions and opinions often left unstated.[62] A third layer of archival research focused on the institutions and actors outside of government that most influenced the world in which government officials operated: the schools that trained them, the professional and civic organizations that shaped their senses of identity and purpose, and the circles of friends they cultivated as they navigated decades-long careers.[63] These sources, too, must be part of a legal history for the age of statutes, for they shaped the boundaries of what was imaginable.

* * * *

What was imaginable? At heart, this book is about competing visions for American poor relief and, by extension, competing visions of American governance. It is about how those visions came together to produce our current order, in which dependency is anathema and dependencies abound. The book showcases the dependency of citizens on government and government on citizens; the dependency of the federal government on state and local administrators, and of state and local governments on federal dollars; the dependency of the poor (especially women, children, and the nonwhite) on their wealthier neighbors; the dependency of those wealthier neighbors on the state, to create and protect what they claim as theirs. The idea of independence has long been central to the study of U.S. history; the reality of dependence, in all its forms, is what demands our attention now.

PART I

1935 to 1949

S tates of Dependency is divided into two parts that loosely track two different eras in public welfare law and administration. **Part I** covers the years between 1935 and 1949, when the general trends in American poor relief were toward uniformity, centralization, professionalization, and the establishment of legal rights. Throughout this period, there was great resistance to these trends. But with Democrats in control of Congress (until 1947) and the executive branch, and courts taking a fairly deferential posture toward agencies, federal administrators of the Social Security Act pursued their goals with relative confidence and freedom. (They faced a very different climate in the decades that followed, as **Part II** argues.)

Chapter 1 centers on the public assistance titles of the Social Security Act of 1935 and connects them with the larger regime of governance that scholars call the "modern American state." Through conditions attached to grants-in-aid, New Deal reformers attempted to achieve a goal far beyond the existing capacity of the federal government: to reorder responsibility for, and power over, poor Americans around the nation. Desperate for resources, states eagerly accepted federal funds. Unfortunately for federal administrators, however, the long tradition of localized poor relief, combined with many states' lack of administrative machinery, meant that little went as planned.

Starting in the late 1930s, Chapter 2 shows, federal administrators turned to the increasingly powerful language of rights to achieve their goals. Owing to the legal and customary bounds of federal power, they had no direct means of influencing local welfare workers and little faith in the efficacy of state supervision, so they reached out indirectly, through speeches at social work conferences, written guides for state field-workers, and allies in social work education. In all these communications they drew on rights language – which gained heft from the nation's confrontation with totalitarianism – to explain the foundation of the public assistance program and to criticize the poor-relief tradition that threatened to overwhelm it. Payments were "entitlements" not "gratuities"; the poor were "claimants" not "paupers." Administrators ascribed to recipients ancillary rights, as well – to payment in cash rather than "in kind," to a confidential relationship with their state and local welfare agencies, and to basic fairness in the consideration of their applications. Proponents of this New Deal–era rights language may have hoped to mobilize rights holders and win for them greater benefits, but their primary aim was to orient local welfare workers toward federal goals and to change those workers' attitudes about their dependent charges. Phrased differently, federal administrators both believed in rights, as did so many people of their time, and used them instrumentally, as a way of implementing their idealized system of governance.

Rights language was useful to federal administrators because of its fuzziness: the word "right" called to mind both dignity and security, and at the same time, seemed incompatible with the methods of private charities and the old poor law, but its precise features were undefined. When various administrators attempted to bring the term into focus in the 1940s, Chapter 3 argues, the schisms in their thinking become apparent. The federal agency's professional social workers, most of whom were women, favored a variant of rights language that emphasized "human need" and rested on universal principles as opposed to positive law. In the tradition of sociological jurisprudence – and in keeping with their search for professional status – they decried what they saw as rigid "legalism" in the face of real suffering. In contrast, the lawyers in the agency, who were predominantly male, used rights language to emphasize the technical requirements of the Social Security Act and rule-of-law values. They were particularly interested in the ideas of due process and equal protection, which they saw as more important than mere money. By the late 1940s, it was clear that these two strands of rights language would have different fates: in the early years of the Cold War, amid a series of scandals over lax local welfare administration and conservative critiques of the growing welfare state, the social work strand suffered while the lawyerly strand thrived.

Although rights language pervaded federal welfare administration in the late 1930s and 1940s, there was no corresponding welfare rights movement on the part of welfare recipients – or at least nothing like the movement of the 1960s and 1970s. Yet contrary to conventional wisdom, Chapter 4 shows, some poor Americans in this earlier era did claim their rights. They did so in thousands of state-level administrative fair hearings, where they contested the decisions of local welfare officials. They also did so in state courts. And although some judges treated their claims with skepticism, many others recognized that welfare recipients had legal entitlements to benefits, as well to fair process. In addition to exploring these early instances of rights claiming, Chapter 4 documents the first modern "welfare rights" case – that is, the first case to frame welfare payments as a civil right in federal court. Here, American Indians proved to be the nation's "first people" once again. With the help of Indian law expert and ex-government lawyer Felix Cohen, reservation Indians sued the federal government for allowing Arizona and New Mexico to exclude them from the states' federally subsidized public assistance programs. Following a political settlement, the plaintiffs withdrew their case, but the litigation presaged the sort of claims that would plague states by the 1960s: claims grounded in federal statutory and constitutional law and built on claimants' awareness of themselves as citizens beyond their local contexts – citizens of state *and* nation.

I

A New Deal for Poor Relief?

The Modern American State and the Endurance of the Local

In 1930, after Mr. Manning lost his job, his wife and children turned to public welfare. The Boston-based family likely first spent down their savings, borrowed on property, and got help from neighbors and relatives. Next they might have turned to the city's network of private and religious charities. Eventually, though – like so many others that year – the Mannings sought "dependent aid" from Boston's Overseers of the Poor.[1] The name "dependent aid" calls to mind the mothers' pensions movement that had swept the nation in the preceding decades (fatherless children and husbandless wives were the quintessential "dependents"). It was in fact Boston's version of "general relief." While a state-run Mother's Aid program supported the city's most respectable poor mothers – usually widows, or women with incapacitated or absent husbands – this municipal program provided limited aid to everyone else. In the 1930s, that included thousands of families like the Mannings, felled by the unemployment of their main breadwinner.[2]

In the spring of 1937, according to the Mannings' case file, the family's fate changed again. Mr. Manning died and the family "was accepted" (whether they applied or were steered, the record does not say) into the Aid to Dependent Children (ADC) program. A more generous version of the Progressive Era Mother's Aid program it replaced, Massachusetts's ADC program targeted the same population and was supervised by the state, but was subsidized by federal funds and subject to federal requirements. It was part of the Roosevelt administration's broad effort to bring "security" – the watchword of the time – to a public suffering the failure of traditional lifelines.

27

ADC proved less secure than the Mannings would have hoped. Within months of the initial grant, as the nation's rebounding economy slid once again into a deep recession, the local worker in charge of the family's case learned from another agency "that there were serious questions about the mother's conduct." An investigation substantiated these reports. Although "the presence of a man visitor" (perhaps a boarder, perhaps a live-in boyfriend or male relative) prevented the caseworker from getting information directly from Mrs. Manning, neighbors confirmed the troubling rumors. The caseworker then returned to the Manning home and confronted the man she found sitting on the stoop. "Who are you," she reportedly asked, "that you should be living in Mrs. M's home?" He refused to answer, so she promptly "put a 'stop' on Mrs. M's check." The agency later informed the family that the children were no longer eligible for ADC; Mrs. Manning would have to reapply to the less desirable municipal relief program.[3]

The location of the Manning family's record adds another layer to the story. It was in the files of the Social Security Board, the federal agency that issued and monitored grants to states for the new ADC programs. Federal agents in the field had funneled this record and others like it back to Washington, DC, as evidence that towns in Massachusetts resisted providing ADC payments to persons who appeared eligible for the new program but failed to meet the high moral standards of the old state Mothers' Aid law. Administrators in the upper echelons of the federal agency debated whether these local acts of resistance placed the state out of compliance with federal law. If so, the state's entire ADC grant might be withheld.

This brief record captures the essence of American social welfare policy at the time. Although resources were scarce, social welfare was a crowded field, filled with overlapping jurisdictions and competing priorities. Traditional poor-relief operations, such as Boston's general relief program, existed alongside innovations from the eras of scientific charity and progressive reform. By the mid-1930s, the question was not whether society recognized an obligation to people like the Mannings, but which level (or levels) of government, which institutions, which agencies ought to care for them, and how that responsibility ought to be carried out. Could the local caseworker condition public assistance on Mrs. Manning's adherence to middle-class notions of sexual propriety? Could the federal agency tell local agencies what to do? What was the state's role? In retrospect, the Mannings' tribulations coincided with a great reordering of power and authority, one institutionalized by the Social Security Act of 1935.

For many scholars and most Americans, the Social Security Act calls to mind the national program of old age insurance that, through decades of expansion and billions of dollars in yearly payments, has monopolized the term "social security." This chapter emphasizes a less appreciated aspect of the act: its efforts to centralize, professionalize, and unify a diffuse system of locally administered poor relief. By offering states conditional grants-in-aid to apply toward relieving certain categories of "unemployables" within their jurisdiction, the SSA not only brought the federal government into the realm of welfare (defined here as need-based income support) but it also indirectly increased states' power.[4] Henceforth states would assert greater responsibility over a function that they had long left to cities, counties, and towns. Under the terms of the act, local governmental units continued to play a vital role in the administration of relief but, increasingly, they had to fight for the discretionary powers that had formerly accompanied that role, such as the ability to exclude strangers, punish deviant behavior, and fill administrative positions with political insiders.

In incentivizing this rearrangement and creating a new legal architecture for American poor relief, the SSA connects to a broader and more fundamental shift: from the regime of governance that legal historian William Novak calls the "well-regulated society" – a locally oriented regime guided by a sense of the "public spirit" and ordered by the common law – to what scholars have labeled "the modern American state." Novak associates the latter with the movement of power from the local level to the center, and with a redefinition of citizenship, from a sense of citizenship that privileged local and associative forms of belonging to one that emphasized the citizen's rights and responsibilities vis-à-vis the nation-state. Both shifts, he argues, were mediated by positive law – statutory and constitutional commitments that delineated where governmental power ended and individual liberty began.[5] The SSA was one such law.

After describing the Social Security Act's modern vision for American poor relief, this chapter turns to the people charged with making that vision a reality. In dialogue with other interested actors – governors, congressional committees, state and local administrators, professional associations – the staff of the newly established Social Security Board gradually decided what every term in the SSA meant. They also decided how to enforce their interpretations, in a context in which they enjoyed the power of the purse but had a limited ability to see and direct what happened at the ground level.[6]

The final part of this chapter details federal administrators' struggles in the face of strong assertions of local authority and thin state supervision. Here, the story connects to a vitally important but under-studied phenomenon in American history: what historian Jon Teaford calls "the rise of the states," from "spare" governmental units "with little administrative muscle" in the nineteenth century to "dynamic molders of domestic policy and vital providers of government services" by the end of the twentieth.[7] The incentives that the SSA created contributed to that change. At the same time, efforts to implement the SSA in its early years show that some states had a long way to go – a reality that proved to be a significant stumbling block for federal administrators.

In short, the modern American state represented in scholarly theory had in some sense arrived by the mid-1930s, but the strength of local institutions, the weakness of the states, and the underdevelopment of federal administrative technologies meant that it would be many years before the new regime uprooted the old one, at least in the crucial and contested realm of poor relief.

THE LONG STRUGGLE TO MODERNIZE RELIEF

In the United States, relief for the poor has taken various forms, including "indoor relief" in almshouses or asylums; "outdoor relief," administered in a person's own home; and the auctioning off of paupers to members of the community, who provided basic necessities in exchange for labor. The precise mixture of methods has varied across time and space. One principle underlay them all, however: poor relief was primarily the responsibility of private charity and local government.

This localist orientation had deep roots. Since the colonial period, Americans had relied on the English framework of "settlement," commonly dated to the Elizabethan era, to determine public responsibility for the poor. A person's place of "settlement" in early America was the geographic unit to which he or she legally belonged, by virtue of long-term residence, birth, or marriage (a wife's status followed her husband's). It was the one place – the only place – obligated to maintain that person in times of need. At their discretion, communities might support residents who lacked settlement, but they did not have to; indeed, they were entitled to expel ("warn out") such persons at any time. States traditionally played a limited role. State statutory law had long set forth the duties of localities, establishing that they should provide for their own, and state courts had often stepped in to adjudicate disputes between local jurisdictions, but states had generally remained aloof from the content and administration of local poor relief.[8]

On the eve of the Great Depression, decades of efforts by scientific charity enthusiasts, public administration experts, and social-justice reformers – not necessarily working together – had initiated important long-term changes in this arrangement, but the effects of these changes were still limited.[9] Most notably, many states had restructured their state boards of charities (themselves a late-nineteenth-century reform) into state welfare departments, with the hope of systematizing and rationalizing the growing realm of public welfare. In most cases, however, these departments merely gathered information and advised policymakers. Reform efforts had also tended to focus on public welfare institutions, such as asylums and almshouses, rather than "outdoor relief."[10] In the words of one reformer, locally administered public relief "remained the great *terra incognita* in the social welfare field": states could attempt to demand information from local officials but, realistically, they could see little and do less.[11] As for direct state contact with the poor, it had increased significantly since the Civil War but remained limited, in the late 1920s, to discrete populations, such as the chronically and mentally ill, orphaned children, victims of natural disasters, and, in a handful of states, those who lacked legal settlement in any local jurisdiction. State aid also tended to take the form of care and shelter (or funding for a private or local entity to administer the same) rather than income support.[12]

In retrospect, state-authorized "pension" programs for widowed or abandoned mothers, the elderly, the blind, and veterans suggested a tectonic shift in the landscape of public relief because state standards and rules generally came along with these benefits. Such programs also pushed back against the notion, popularized by advocates of scientific charity in the late nineteenth century, that all forms of public "outdoor relief" were a baleful influence on the poor. But these pension programs were generally administered at the local level, at the option of the locality, and with a minimum of state supervision and funding.[13] If observers imagined that such innovations would "drag the common garden variety of poor relief along" with them into modernity, they quickly realized that traditional poor relief exerted the stronger pull.[14] Consider, for example, Lyon County, Kansas, whose concerned female citizens had eagerly advocated the adoption of a state mothers' pension law and whose representative in the state senate was largely responsible for getting such a law on the books in 1915. Fourteen years later, local poor relief in Lyon County looked anything but modern. Aid still tended to take the form of groceries, coal, or another family's outgrown clothes, and the distribution of aid depended largely on the opinion of the welfare director, Mrs. George Randolph, who recalled having "no rules."[15]

The federal government's involvement in poor relief was even more limited. Since the early national period, Congress had provided for sick and disabled soldiers and sailors and had issued short-term relief to victims of "disasters," ranging from floods to epidemics to grasshopper plagues. By the turn of the twentieth century, the federal government had also provided aid for discrete categories of federal government dependents, such as American Indians and former slaves. But in general such relief programs constituted the exception rather than the rule: they were limited in scope and scale, and often administered indirectly, through states and voluntary organizations. Broader initiatives – such as Dorothea Dix's 1854 proposal to use resources from the sale of public lands to fund institutions for the mentally ill – foundered against the conviction that general maintenance of the needy was not the business of the federal government.[16]

By the late 1920s, this picture had changed remarkably little. Poverty and unemployment had become national concerns, but the decade's conservative Republican presidents preferred to attack those problems via public partnerships with private groups.[17] In general, to borrow historian Michael Katz's assessment of the period, "public welfare remained an overwhelmingly local responsibility." Yes, the structure of relief giving had become more "rational" and "modern" – as indicated by the transition in some communities from local overseers of the poor to county-level agencies, and by some cities' consolidation of scattered public welfare services into single municipal departments of welfare – but federal and state agencies still "had little or no official relationship with local public outdoor relief."[18]

The endurance of a localized system of poor relief, even in the face of broad trends toward centralized, expert-led government, is no great mystery. "There was no political pay-off [for the state] in being overseer of the poor," explained Frank Bane, who in the 1920s headed Virginia's Board of Charities and Corrections and later led the charge for greater state leadership.[19] Meanwhile, there was every reason to retain local control. Tradition favored it, as did the local politicians who continued to control many state legislatures. Poor relief brought with it opportunities for both distributing patronage and winning votes. Local control also fit with the prevailing logic of poor relief: at a time when relief derived largely from local funds and poverty

often appeared to stem from individual failings (no matter what the
"experts" said about social factors and environments), local authorities seemed best situated to evaluate a petitioner's worthiness.[20] The
"factual basis" of public welfare "is local," explained one former state
commissioner of public welfare in 1928: "It has to do with hearth and
home" – with the "way a father and a mother breed and nurture their
children," with the contents of "the worker's dinner pail," with the
"daughter's conduct at the Saturday night dance."[21]

Last but not least, local poor relief was a relatively low priority for the
people most likely to object to it. As historian Daniel Rodgers has
explained, progressive reformers were less interested in "patch[ing] and
mend[ing] the lives of the poor" than they were in "find[ing] effective
means to keep those who were *not* abjectly poor," such as low-wage
workers and their families, "from being precipitated into poverty's
abyss." Reformers could and did imagine better ways to administer
poor relief, but they had other, more pressing battles to fight.[22]
Moreover, until the Great Depression most reformers simply "assumed
that local governments ... would have to shoulder most of the burden of
welfare governance." This meant working within the existing
framework.[23]

The result, as the nation slid into the Depression's economic free
fall, was a poor-relief system that resembled a crazy quilt, made from a
limited number of fabrics but showcasing "an amazing diversity of
patterns."[24] Some needy persons looked to their county (in the form of
a county board, agency, or court), while others turned to a town,
municipal unit, or parish. In many states, multiple jurisdictions were
in play, with some localities relying on a township system and others
using the county, and often there were wide variations in benefit levels
and administrative practices, even among localities in the same state
and of a similar size.[25] Meanwhile, in almost all areas, and especially
in cities, the boundaries between "public" and "private" were ill-
defined and frequently traversed: it was not unusual to see a private
charity or institution administering public funds, and individuals often
sought assistance from both public and private sources.[26] There were
other places, meanwhile, such as parts of the rural South, where "there
simply was no such thing as public welfare" and little institutionalized
private charity.[27] Amid this diversity, however, was one commonality:
in most areas and for most people, both the federal and state governments were remote presences, at least when it came to the day-to-day
business of economic survival.

FROM FEDERAL EMERGENCY RELIEF TO THE SOCIAL
SECURITY ACT

The Depression overwhelmed every part of this complex system. Local governments went broke as their revenue sources (largely property taxes) dried up. Private agencies, religious charities, and ethnic benefit organizations saw their caseloads rise and their resources fail, despite efforts by local business and community leaders to shore them up. In other words, the "associative" mode of statecraft, which had seemed so promising during and after the First World War, was failing to provide what the public had come to expect. States, too, struggled to respond, even in places with strong executive leadership and the political will to enact sweeping emergency relief legislation. Meanwhile, Americans fell into poverty at staggering rates. In the spring of 1929, nearly three million men and women were unemployed; by the spring of 1931, that figure had grown to eight million.[28] Into that picture entered the federal government, cautiously at first, and then more boldly.

The outlines of the most significant intervention, the Social Security Act of 1935, were actually discernible as early as 1931, when a group of professional social work leaders who supported federal action joined forces with Senators Edward Costigan (D., Colorado) and Robert M. LaFollette Jr. (R., Wisconsin) – powerful, self-identified progressive reformers – and Representative David John Lewis (D., Maryland), a coal miner turned lawyer known for helping to establish Maryland's pioneering workmen's compensation program. After gathering testimony from witnesses with firsthand knowledge of the relief problem (mostly social workers, not coincidentally), the group suggested a program of federal grants-in-aid that it hoped would appear modest. Their draft bill proposed an appropriation of $375 million for poor relief and government-paid work (the National Recovery Act of 1933, by comparison, included an appropriation of $3.3 billion, $400 million of which was set aside for grants-in-aid for public works). Money would be disbursed to states by an existing federal agency and states would do the actual spending.[29]

The suggestion of grants-in-aid was a natural choice. By the early 1920s, Congress had used such grants for highway construction, agricultural research, forest-fire prevention, and child and maternal health care, to name just a handful of tasks.[30] Grants were ideal in areas where state or local government had superior administrative capacities and where federal jurisdiction was murky. Such grants became an even more attractive tool after the Supreme Court – often perceived to be hostile to social and economic

Grants — in — aid

regulation – implicitly ratified the practice in *Massachusetts v. Mellon* (1923).[31] Perhaps most important to those who wanted to bend state law in the direction of reform, grants could be given on a conditional basis, subject to a state's compliance with federal requirements.

Grants-in-aid were not the only option, however, at least not in 1931. Federal loans – which, once given, would be entirely under state control – proved more appealing to key constituencies in Congress: southern Democrats, fearful of federal intervention, and progressive Republicans, who saw the need for a stronger federal response to unemployment but were concerned about increased taxation and an unbalanced federal budget. The Emergency Relief and Construction Act, enacted in the summer of 1932 and signed by a reluctant President Hoover, authorized $300 million for loans to states and cities, to be distributed only upon an affirmation that other resources had been exhausted. Administrative responsibility rested with the recently created Reconstruction Finance Corporation, a temporary government lender modeled after the War Finance Corporation.[32] In the words of one commentator, the scheme allowed the federal government to "play banker but not partner to the states" in their efforts to meet the needs of the poor.[33]

By the end of 1932, the Reconstruction Finance Corporation had distributed only about a quarter of the funds available to it, a result of state governors' inability to convince federal administrators that they had exhausted state and local resources. Meanwhile, the ranks of the unemployed continued to swell, to some 14 million by the fall of that year. Following the election of Franklin D. Roosevelt, the modest program of need-based loans quickly gave way to the system of grants-in-aid that Costigan, LaFollette, and like-minded reformers envisioned. The Federal Emergency Relief Act of 1933, signed into law in May of that year, established a temporary Federal Emergency Relief Administration (FERA) and authorized the agency to distribute to the states $500 million, half in the form of matching grants (that is, grants tailored to the amount that each state chose to spend on relief) and half in grants based on need. Roosevelt immediately appointed Harry L. Hopkins, former executive director and chairman of New York's Temporary Emergency Relief Administration, to head the new federal effort.[34]

Contemporaries recall Hopkins's FERA in much the same way they recall Hopkins himself: energetic, brash, impatient, and dismissive of politics-as-usual, especially when it meant incompetence or needless delay. Within a day of taking office, Hopkins had authorized grants to seven states; by the end of the year, all eligible states and territories had received aid, in amounts totaling $324.5 million overall.[35] During its short lifespan (1933–1935), FERA funneled more than three billion dollars to subnational governments for direct aid and work relief, and it asserted real control over how those funds were administered. Breaking sharply with the past, FERA refused to act on a state's application for a grant until the state created its own state-level relief agency, with a FERA-approved director at the head. FERA further required each state agency to create county-level relief agencies, independent of the existing poor-relief machinery. These demands were consistent with FERA administrators' broader disdain for "political claims to office" and their "low opinion of [state] legislators and elected officials."[36] "The surest way I know to have any relief for the unemployed deteriorat[e] into the most wretched form of outdoor relief," Hopkins once declared, "is to permit every local community to treat these people as they please."[37]

Federal influence continued well after a grant had been issued. Many FERA field representatives "established informal ascendancy over relief administration in their states," using their connection to the federal purse strings to attempt to "improve local practice" and "inculcate new attitudes toward the relief of distress." More dramatically, Hopkins occasionally exercised his power to "federalize" relief in a particular state – that is, to take temporary control of a state's relief operation in order to resolve policy disagreements with state officials or to protect the state relief administration from the untoward influence of party politics. Only Oklahoma, Massachusetts, Georgia, Louisiana, North Dakota, and Ohio experienced "federalization" firsthand. Still, the message was clear. State and local authorities may have administered emergency relief funds, historian Liz Cohen has written, but "everyone knew that the power lay in Washington."[38]

FERA was never intended to be more than a temporary program, however, and FERA administrators were always more concerned with the provisionally unemployed than with the disabled, elderly, and otherwise unemployable clients of traditional poor relief programs (the "chronic cases," as Hopkins put it in a 1934 FERA bulletin).[39] The boldest federal incursion into the historically local realm of poor relief – boldest because of its intended permanency – was the Social Security Act.

Signed into law on August 14, 1935, the Social Security Act provided tens of millions of dollars per year to states, in the form of matching funds, for the relief of large categories of "unemployable" persons: the elderly (Old-Age Assistance [OAA]); dependent children (ADC); and the blind

(Aid to the Blind [AB]).[40] (The "employable poor" and their families were left to state and local programs of general relief, unless they qualified for unemployment insurance or one of the fast-disappearing programs of federally subsidized work relief.)[41] Together, the OAA, ADC, and AB programs were known as "public assistance" and were distinct from the act's now better known old age and unemployment insurance initiatives. Contemporaries understood this suite of programs as consistent with President Roosevelt's promise to quit "this business of relief"[42] – a reference to his administration's by then much-criticized emergency system of direct relief payments – but also responsive to the popular demand for old age pensions and to the gaps left by traditional purveyors of support.[43]

It is worth dwelling on the drafting of the SSA's public assistance titles, for by now historians have tilted so far toward critique – toward a perspective that emphasizes those titles' continuity with a dark and shameful past – that we are prone to downplay the reformist ambitions that animated the legislation, and hence to miss the broad changes in governance that were now sweeping through this policy area.[44]

The Social Security Act was the product, first and foremost, of a set of labor economists, lawyers, public welfare administrators, social workers, and federal department heads whom the Roosevelt administration brought together in the summer of 1934 under the umbrella of the president's Committee on Economic Security (CES). In a context in which ideas abounded about how to relieve the nation's deep poverty – including the increasingly popular and blatantly redistributive plans of activist Francis Townsend and Senator Huey Long (D., Louisiana) – Roosevelt wanted a comprehensive but pragmatic program for his administration to present to the Seventy-Fourth Congress. He hoped that, in just a few short months, the CES would produce one.[45]

Disciplinary divides and prejudices marked the work of the CES and its advisors (economist Eveline Burns, for example, considered the social workers "uninteresting" and impractical), but the group shared a basic outlook.[46] They were a subset of those "social policy tinkerers and inventors, publicists and policy scavengers, policy experts and policy brokers," in the words of historian Daniel Rodgers, that sought to alleviate the pains of industrial capitalism in the decades bracketing the turn of the twentieth century.[47] They had shed the moral fervor of pre–World War I progressivism, and had lost much of that earlier era's confidence in the states to achieve meaningful, large-scale reform.[48] But they retained faith in the beneficent power of government, the value of scientific administration, and the necessity of expertise. When it came to need-based income support – which, despite their primary interest in unemployment insurance and old age insurance, they viewed as essential – their object was not to improve the lot of the poor or rouse community sympathy. Rather, they wanted to modernize public welfare provision in ways that complemented the overall security program. Building on the innovations of the past three decades, they hoped to make traditional poor relief more attuned to the realities of an industrialized capitalist economy, more rational and efficient in its administration, and more consistent with academic understandings of the causes and consequences of poverty, all while staving off democratic pressure for more radical solutions.[49]

Where did this orientation toward poor relief come from? Roosevelt did not want the CES to take the time to engage in months of new research before proposing legislation, which meant that the drafters' own stores of knowledge – ranging from their acquaintance with European social legislation to their personal experiences with public welfare – were crucial. Perhaps most important was the wealth of historical research that had already been conducted by University of Chicago social work educators Edith Abbott and Sophonisba Breckenridge and their students. (Abbott served on the CES's Advisory Committee on Public Employment and Public Assistance, along with her former student Elizabeth Wisner; Edith Abbott's sister and close collaborator, Grace Abbott, was a member of the CES's Advisory Council.) Study after study, often conducted at the state level, documented the origins of existing poor relief operations and the (un)suitability of those operations to twentieth-century life.[50] Many states' poor relief laws, the authors concluded, were vestiges of "a parochial society" – in some instances, actual carryovers from the colonial era.[51] And even where the laws had been amended, they continued to reflect the principles underlying the centuries-old Elizabethan Poor Law. In particular, the authors argued, these laws adhered to the "antiquated" notions of local responsibility for well-settled local residents and lack of responsibility for anyone else who happened to be within local borders. Such parochialism was better suited to "the days of the oxcart and the stagecoach," Edith Abbott complained, than the era of automobiles and radio. Some jurisdictions did, of course, evolve with the times to become models of humane and efficient relief giving, Abbott and her colleagues recognized. But in many others, local responsibility enabled corruption, inadequate standards, and all manner of humiliating and degrading treatment of the poor.[52] This dim assessment of American poor relief, paired with firsthand accounts from FERA administrators, affected how the drafters of the Social Security Act imagined the future. The world that these studies documented cried out for organization, standardization, and expertise. Public assistance must "be administered on a much higher plane than that of the old poor laws," the CES's report to the president concluded.[53]

As for how that lofty goal should be accomplished, the drafters were inclined toward a national solution, although not necessarily toward federal control. (Important members of the CES had cut their teeth on state-level reforms and had no desire to bypass state government.)[54] Grants-in-aid were the favored policy tool. Reports from abroad suggested that grants for poor relief worked well in Germany, which had a federal system and was a perceived leader in social welfare development.[55] Relief loans, the once-obvious alternative, had proven ineffective.

The politics that had made loans attractive to key constituencies in Congress, however, remained alive and well, and would decisively influence the Social Security Act. Most notably, there would be no conditioning of grants on states' adherence to a national standard of need. The CES's suggestion of "a reasonable subsistence compatible with health and decency" – that is, a federally determined "floor" – immediately caught the eye of influential southern Democrats, including Virginia senator Harry F. Byrd and Mississippi senator Pat Harrison.[56] For poorer members of the Union, as the southern states were, this provision raised fiscal concerns: because the Roosevelt administration was committed to a policy of "matching" a portion of what each state spent (rather than simply giving every state a lump sum), a state that lacked the ability to spend would benefit little. More important, however, was the policy's potential impact on Jim Crow, the system of formal and informal rules that preserved the South's racially stratified socioeconomic structure. African Americans could easily be kept ineligible for old age and unemployment insurance (by simply excluding their primary occupations from coverage), but the public assistance titles were based on need, and by any reasonable definition of that term, many African Americans would qualify. And if poor African Americans received adequate assistance from the government, as a national standard would likely require, they might be less willing to work for low wages as field hands and domestic servants. Accordingly, southerners in Congress insisted that states have the power to determine benefit levels. When the Social Security bill emerged from congressional committees, the only limit on payments was an upper one – states could go above it, but the federal government would not match those additional expenditures.[57]

[handwritten margin note: Standard of need]

The drafters also had to abandon dreams of imposing federal personnel standards on state and local public welfare officials. Progressive reformers had long faced resistance from the beneficiaries of political patronage (and struggled with their own indebtedness to party politics), so some congressional opposition was expected. The depth of feeling on the issue, however, resulted from widespread concern about the narrow class of people who would satisfy federal standards. When FERA empowered state and local emergency relief agencies to employ some forty thousand relief workers, it had called for having at least one "trained and experienced" investigator – that is, a professional social worker – on the staff of each local agency.[58] By the time FERA had run its course, these social workers were "thoroughly detested" in Colorado and "anathema" in Pennsylvania. In Georgia, they provoked charges of "pantry snooping," "nosing into ... private affairs," and "exerting excessive and unwarranted control"; in Ohio, they were accused of hounding "helpless people" like a "pack of inquisitors."[59] Ultimately, the SSA gave a federal administrative agency the power to prescribe the general "methods of administration" to which states should adhere, but specifically excluded standards "relating to selection, tenure of office, and compensation of personnel." The implication was that state and local agencies would retain control over what kind of people staffed their operations.[60]

The experts designing the new public assistance titles secured other provisions, however, that fundamentally disrupted the existing poor relief system. First, embracing a controversial practice of FERA and, before it, the Children's Bureau, the SSA implicitly excluded private relief providers from any part in administering the new grants-in-aid.[61] Grants were to go to states. The drafters did not object to voluntary relief efforts, but they believed that public employees, accountable to the public, should administer public funds. This "was just good political science philosophy," explained Frank Bane, then director of the influential American Public Welfare Association.[62] It was also a major power grab. Private providers, such as the Family Service Agency, the Red Cross, and the National Association of Catholic Charities may have been under financial stress, but they remained strong and well established; states were ill prepared to assume those providers' responsibilities.[63] Under the public-funds-to-public-agencies rule, however, states had little choice but to develop the types of "effective, over-all, coordinated," and *permanent* programs that public administration experts favored. "Welfare is an important, respectable, large scale function of government," Bane insisted, "and the states better get themselves set to handle it."[64]

A second and closely related provision (again, borrowed from FERA) permitted federal funds to flow only to states that planned to administer public assistance through, or under the supervision of, a central state ○ organ (the "single state agency" provision). Administering public assistance from Washington, as was the plan with old age insurance, was never really on the table. Progressive reformers had long agreed, however, that "modern" public welfare administration required massing of authority at some kind of center, as a way to minimize the mischief and waste that accompanied extreme decentralization. States were the logical place.[65] (Southern members of Congress raised no objection, suggesting that they considered this sort of "modernization" fully compatible with Jim Crow and therefore unobjectionable.)[66]

A third provision, and another significant break with traditional poor relief, required that every state public assistance plan operate across the state ("it shall be in effect in all political subdivisions"). For political and legal reasons, the SSA's designers could not compel interstate uniformity, but they could address the variability that ○ existed within most states.[67] Such variability stemmed from multiple causes – political patronage, racial discrimination, municipal experimentation, disparate local tax bases – but to the architects of Roosevelt's security program, it necessarily implied an overabundance of local discretion. Discretion, in turn, invited the perpetuation of irrational practices and outdated traditions.

A fourth provision targeted the same problem. By requiring state plans to provide all aggrieved applicants an opportunity for a "fair hearing" at the state level, the SSA created a check on the local officials making first-order decisions about aid payments.[68] Some guarantee of review by an "objective" state administrator would theoretically prevent the denial of relief through local irrationality and ignorance. And when actually demanded, such hearings would also provide state officials valuable glimpses of operations at the ground level.[69]

Complementing the provisions regarding the locus of decision-making power was a set of more substantive conditions, all of which marked a deliberate departure from existing poor relief practices. One condition prohibited states from channeling their grants into the public institutions (poorhouses, orphanages, asylums) that had become favored repositories for the indigent in the nineteenth century.[70] Enlightened thinking in the 1930s held that many institutionalized persons would fare better in their own home or the home of a relative. Reformers also associated institutions with the patronage politics that they abhorred.[71]

Another condition mandated that assistance be in cash rather than "in kind" – again, a significant departure from tradition.[72] "Most of the counties did not give money to welfare recipients," recalled a California social worker. "They gave baskets; they had milk delivered, the welfare department paid the rent directly to landlords." This practice was the norm around the nation.[73] The SSA's money payment requirement reflected the new thinking among some professional social workers about poor people's capacity to become "competent participants in the twentieth-century consumer society."[74] It also responded to the Depression's impoverishment of a broader cross section of the American public: many people in need were perceived, and perceived themselves, as victims of a disaster, rather than as victims of their own malfeasance or irresponsibility. Such people deserved the independence and freedom that came with cash, the drafters believed, and might be demoralized by the receipt of assistance in kind.[75]

A third condition undermined the principle of settlement, which assumed that the "public" was no more than a collection of local communities and that public relief must turn on long-standing community ties. As historian Elisa Minoff has shown, many local communities and some states embraced the concept of settlement with renewed fervor during the Great Depression, using it to disclaim responsibility for newcomers and dissuade further in-migration. The SSA's drafters responded to this impulse by imposing parameters: states that wished to receive federal funds had to guarantee that if a person had spent five of the previous nine years residing in a state, that person could not be excluded from public assistance programs on residence grounds. Place-based understandings of belonging and responsibility thus lived on, but the law encouraged people to think about the state, rather than the town, as their place, and to treat geographic mobility as a fact of modern life.[76]

All told, the "strings" attached to the SSA's tempting bundles of federal cash left much unchanged – too much, from the perspective of some reformers. Most notably, the act left unaided the millions of poor Americans who failed to fit into one of its three prescribed categories. Those individuals were left to the whims of private charity and unreformed (for the most part) state and local programs of general assistance. With the benefit of time, we also see that the new scheme left in place, and helped entrench, race- and sex-based inequalities. By separating "employables" from "unemployables," and by granting so much authority to the states, the SSA cast work as the foundation of citizenship and underwrote the security of white men and their families, while leaving many women and nonwhite Americans vulnerable.[77]

And yet, the act's fundamental changes in public responsibility for the poor were broadly consistent with a sea change in American governance: the rise of the modern American state. Before the enactment of the SSA, multiple institutions, public and private, participated in relief giving. After 1935, the government acquired a "near-monopoly."[78] Before the SSA, relatively few poor Americans expected to receive regular or adequate assistance. They might claim that their settlement in a particular jurisdiction entitled them to aid, but in actuality they were at the mercy of local authorities. After the act, large swaths of this population became eligible for support. That support still issued from local officials, but authoritative state agencies were watching, and state and federal law governed all transactions. In this way, the SSA provided many citizens with a new link to the modern nation-state, even if it remained a tenuous one.

Observers at the time recognized these changes as monumental, even if scholars have since cast them in a different light. "For the first time in our history," remarked Frank Bane, one of the Social Security Act's earliest administrators, "we have hitched three wild horses, Federal, State and Local governments ... to the same wagon." Bane could only watch and wait in the spring of 1936 as, loaded with some of the nation's most pressing problems, that wagon headed "down the road."[79]

THE MACHINERY OF ENFORCEMENT: CARROTS, STICKS, AND AGENCY STRUCTURE

The road looked to be a bumpy one. "Never before," Bane noted, had a program based on grants-in-aid "been projected upon such an extensive scale, immediately affecting so many people and calling for such large expenditures."[80] Despite the magnitude of the task, the Social Security Act's machinery of enforcement was straightforward. Congress created an independent agency, the Social Security Board (SSB), to administer the act and endowed it with one big "carrot" and one big "stick." The carrot was money: the SSB had the power to give federal funds to any state that submitted an appropriate public assistance "plan."[81] The appropriation for the fiscal year ending on June 30, 1936, was relatively modest ($77.5 million) but this figure grew steadily over subsequent years, and was, in any case, a boon to the cash-strapped states.[82] The stick was also money: the SSB had the right to take audit "exceptions" to payments made in violation of the act (that is, it could refuse to "match" these payments). It could also cut off a state's entire grant should the state refuse to correct defects in its plan.[83] Simply stated, the SSA relied almost entirely on monetary incentives, directed exclusively at the states. The same monetary incentives would presumably influence localities, but it was up to the states to keep them in line.

A three-member board sitting atop the agency made all major decisions about how and when to use its enforcement tools.[84] It met, according to one participant, "interminably."[85] Still, the board relied on an extensive support system for making decisions regarding public assistance. Public assistance matters constituted only a fraction of its responsibilities (it also had to administer brand-new schemes for unemployment compensation and old-age insurance), and no board member had significant experience with poor relief.[86] John Gilbert Winant, the chair, had governed New Hampshire for three terms and had served as a member of the CES's Advisory Council, but contemporaries remembered him as not "particularly informed about the problems of social security."[87] The earnest and brilliant Arthur Altmeyer, who had headed Wisconsin's Department of Industrial Relations and had originally come to Washington to serve as assistant secretary of labor, was first and foremost a labor economist. He devoted most of his attention to the Social Security Act's insurance-based programs, which he had helped draft and which he believed would one day swallow most public assistance recipients in their benevolent embrace. Vincent Miles, a former Democratic Party official from Arkansas, had come to the board on the recommendation of the Senate majority leader. A political appointee himself, he was less interested in policymaking than in filling the Social Security Board's field offices with friends of the powerful American Legion.[88] In practice, then, the board depended on those working directly beneath them – the "mezzo-level" bureaucrats, to borrow political scientist Daniel Carpenter's term.[89] This relatively small set of administrators, many of whom remained in place for decades, heavily influenced the way the federal agency used its power over public assistance grants.

Especially important were the top people in the Bureau of Public Assistance (BPA), the division that supervised the new public assistance programs (see Figure 1.1). BPA officials consulted with state officials about plan preparation and advised the board whether to approve state plans. Through representatives in the SSB's regional offices, they also monitored what the states actually did with their public assistance grants and corresponded with state officials about administrative and logistical problems. When a question arose that required the SSB to make a policy

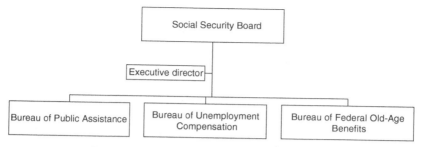

FIGURE I.I. Organizational chart for the Social Security Board: Operating bureaus, 1935. Source: Charles McKinley and Robert W. Frase, *Launching Social Security: A Capture-and-Record Account, 1935–1937 (Madison: University of Wisconsin Press, 1970), 504.*

decision, the BPA often organized materials for the board's consideration and drafted a proposed response.[90]

The BPA's first and long-time director, Jane Hoey, ensured that the bureau exerted maximum influence. Hoey was an Irish-Catholic social worker who had strong familial ties to the Tammany Hall political machine in New York and personal relationships with both Harry Hopkins and the Roosevelts – although "it wasn't on that basis that I came in," she insisted. Particularly relevant to the job was her impressive record of government and charitable service, with stints working for the New York City Board of Child Welfare, the Red Cross, and the Welfare Council of New York. Through those various positions, Hoey had developed definite ideas about how the public assistance program ought to be run.[91] One such idea, a former colleague recalled, was that her slice of the SSB was "an independent agency that should not be subject to any supervision."[92] Hoey developed a reputation for the fierce spirit she brought to her dealings with state governors, whom she regularly attempted to bully, charm, or reason into tweaking their public assistance schemes to her liking. She was persuasive and intimidating, according to contemporaries. At least one governor begged Hoey's superiors not to hold him to anything he promised when "that red-headed blue-eyed Irish gal sat down across the desk" from him.[93]

Despite its title and its assertive director, the BPA was not the final authority on matters relating to public assistance grants. It was technically "coordinate," not superior, to the SSB's five "service bureaus" (see Figure 1.2), meaning that the BPA lacked full control over how the program operated in the states.[94] Two service bureaus in particular

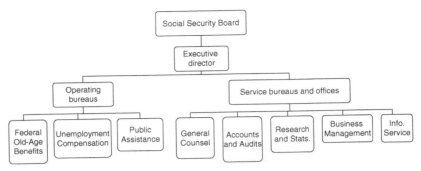

FIGURE 1.2. Organizational chart for the Social Security Board: Operating
and service bureaus, 1935. Source: Charles McKinley and Robert W. Frase,
Launching Social Security: A Capture-and-Record Account, 1935–1937
(Madison: University of Wisconsin Press, 1970), 504–5.

impinged on the BPA's jurisdiction: the Bureau of Accounts and Audits and, to a greater extent, the Office of the General Counsel (GC).[95]

In a scheme that was all about money, the Bureau of Accounts and Audits would appear to be an obvious locus of power, and indeed it had important responsibilities. Accounts and Audits evaluated all state plans for financial sufficiency. After a plan was approved, regional auditors monitored the state's expenditures to ensure that it spent in accordance with the federal act, its own state plan, and the board's policies. The temptation to become de facto policymakers was strong. While out in the field reviewing a local or state agency's expenditures, auditors encountered difficult questions and made decisions on the fly, often neglecting to consult with the BPA. The auditors were not ultimately a threat, however, because the board perceived them as mere "technician[s]." When staff members from the BPA got "very mad" about certain audit exceptions, Arthur Altmeyer recalled, he simply told the accountants that their job was to "check the books," not to "make social decisions."[96] State officials, who had every reason to contest audit exceptions, also helped keep the auditors in check. Ellen Black Winston, for example, North Carolina's longtime commissioner of welfare, directed her staff to "never accede to an audit exception unless [they] ha[d] exhausted all other possibilities."[97]

The Office of the General Counsel was in a stronger position and, as subsequent chapters show, would remain influential for many years. Led for the first few years by Thomas Eliot, a young but cautious lawyer from the Labor Department, the GC's office reviewed state public assistance plans, as well as any proposed legislation that might alter an approved plan; pin-pointed potential "conformity questions"; interpreted the law for the SSB's leadership; and reviewed the BPA's communications to the states. "If I had even a letter that went out to a state," Hoey recalled, it had to be "okayed by the general counsel."[98] Through correspondence with the BPA's regional representatives and its own regional and field attorneys, the GC's office also monitored compliance with federal law at the ground level.[99]

The lawyers did not always get their way – the SSB could ignore their advice and the BPA could drag its heels – but they loudly and persistently voiced their views, often to great effect. General Counsel Tom Eliot "felt that a great number of hostile critics were just waiting, ready to pounce if the board made a single mistake," he recalled in his memoir, making it his "duty to keep the board on the straight and narrow path." Thus Eliot and his assistant attorneys insisted on attending all board meetings, even when they were less than welcome. Arthur Altmeyer, for one, made it clear that "he was not going to be guided too much by lawyers," recalled Assistant GC Jack Tate.[100] (In fairness, Altmeyer was "not enthusiastic about social workers," either, according to Jane Hoey.)[101] The SSB's first executive director, Frank Bane, apparently shared Altmeyer's view. "Social Security was great," Bane's daughter remembers him saying, "until they hired a bunch of lawyers and they told you all of the things that you couldn't do instead of all of the things that you could do."[102]

Bane may simply have been referring to Eliot, whose combination of conservatism, entitlement, and arrogance put off many colleagues (and whose run for Congress a short time later surprised no one), but the comment is evidence of the considerable power that lawyers wielded within the agency. Because of the Social Security Act's complexity, the New Deal's general reliance on law, and the threat posed by a strong and unpredictable Supreme Court (just before the SSA's enactment, the Supreme Court had declared both the National Recovery Act and the Agricultural Adjustment Act unconstitutional), the lawyers' opinions carried weight. As contemporaries and historians have observed, the New Deal was in many ways a "lawyers' deal." The public assistance initiative was no exception.[103]

FEDERAL-STATE COOPERATION

Much of the work described so far took place in Washington, DC, but the states were never far from federal administrators' minds. The entire scheme depended on states' willingness to accept federal money and, with it, the attached conditions. As Bane put it, it was a job of "federal-state relations" – and a challenging one, at that. As one law professor observed at the time, the program of federal-state cooperation that the act summoned into being was "strange to American constitutional law" and "require[d] a new definition of 'federalism.'"[104] For administrators, the basic puzzle was this: How could they get each state to sign on to a program that brought federal power – not on a "temporary" or "emergency" basis, but permanently – into an area that had never been under federal control? The task was further complicated by the disorder that continued to characterize many state welfare operations. In 1934, a survey of forty-eight states found more than 1,000 separate state agencies performing functions within the field of public welfare. The degree to which these agencies supervised local poor relief, and the nature of that supervision, varied immensely from state to state.[105]

Federal officials had several early advantages, however. Although state legislatures had reservations about the new scheme, they recognized that traditional providers of relief had been bankrupted and that their state coffers were next. They were eager to access federal funds. Helen Valeska Bary, who worked for the SSB from its inception, recalled that soon after the act's passage, governors, administrators, and government lawyers "flock[ed] in" from "nearly all the states." They "clamor[ed]" for guidance, Frank Bane agreed.[106] The SSB was happy to oblige. Starting in March 1936, a federal field staff began going out to the states to survey the situation and answer questions. Prior to that time, the SSB distributed instructions on how to prepare a fundable plan and convened a conference in Washington at which Bane gave guidance to representatives attending from forty-two states and territories.[107] The SSB's private-sector allies also helped. In close consultation with the board, the leadership of the American Public Welfare Association drafted and circulated model bills. These were used in more than forty states in 1936 alone. The result was an array of plan submissions that approximated what the SSB wanted. Amateurish plans like Missouri's, which offered "a 'Trouble Department' for handling doubtful cases and an 'Examining Mill' for case review," were the rare exception.[108]

Federal administrators also benefited from the multiple opportunities to influence the states that the Social Security Act created. The first came when states submitted their public assistance plans. To outsiders, this step may have appeared a mere formality: SSB officials wanted to issue grants as soon as possible, and in fact they approved most plan submissions, even deficient ones.[109] In the words of Charles McKinley and Robert Frase, who performed a "capture and record" study of the act's administration between November 1935 and May 1936 (Frase as a member of the board's staff), the board's philosophy was one of cooperation and "flexibility," rather than "coercion." Still, no plan received funding without review and comment by regional and central personnel from the BPA, the GC's office, and Accounts and Audits, and some state plans were rejected. In other cases, the SSB conditioned its approval on subsequent reporting or reform.[110]

Periodic opportunities for review ensured that federal administrators continued to influence state operations. Every quarter, each state looked to the SSB to confirm its expenditures from the previous quarter and approve estimates for the next. At this point the board could – and often did – take the "audit exceptions" noted above, refusing to reimburse the state for payments that were not in conformity with federal rules. These were sharp and financially painful reminders of federal authority.[111] As mentioned earlier, the SSB could also suspend *entire* grants (audit exceptions involved just fractions), a prospect that agency insiders would later refer to as the "nuclear option." In its first four years, the board invoked this power only three times but alluded to it frequently.[112]

Despite the board's considerable leverage, not everything went smoothly. In 1936, Colorado governor Ed Johnson thumbed his nose at federal authority when he submitted an obviously flawed plan and then publicly alerted President Roosevelt to the poor "crippled children" "patient[ly]" waiting for the board to release their "promised benefits."[113] In Ohio, Governor Martin Davey put the SSB to the test when he allowed members of the influential Fraternal Order of Eagles to dominate state and local welfare administration (reprising a previous battle with FERA administrator Harry Hopkins).[114] Challenges from independent-minded state executives would continue over the following decade. Lurking in the background, however, was a more formidable problem: the lack of federal *or* state control over what happened at the local level, where public assistance funds passed into the hands of the poor.

THE IMPORTANCE OF THE LOCAL

"The man or woman in need of help is a citizen of the United States, of the state, of the county, of the township," declared Edith Abbott in 1934, and by extension, "all of these governments ... have some responsibility for promoting and maintaining his welfare." Such was the philosophy of the Social Security Act, and of the modern American state that historians have now sketched. But this philosophy did not map well onto ground-level realities. There, a more astute observation was that of the Saint Paul Community Chest director, Pierce Atwater: "In the main," he wrote in 1937, "citizens of the United States are born and live and die in a local setting."[115] In 1930, the vast majority of expenditures for poor relief – an estimated 91 percent – still came from local funds. That percentage diminished over time, dropping from 82 percent in 1931 to 24 percent in 1933 to between 9 and 11 percent in the last half of the decade, but in dollar amounts, local contributions consistently surpassed 1930 levels. In short, the federal government and the state governments remained relative newcomers to the field – a field that local governments never abandoned.[116]

In fact, the SSA's pragmatic drafters never intended to supplant local poor relief, just to take away the independence of local officials. They envisioned federal-state public assistance programs that would sit atop, and gradually incorporate, the diffuse collection of local agencies that had been tending the poor. On the surface, to be sure, the act emphasized state leadership, but in fact states were allowed to choose between administering their plans directly or merely supervising them. Most states chose the latter, meaning that administration remained at the local level.[117] Writing in 1939, after public assistance programs were up and running around the country, Frank Bane described local communities as "the basis of the whole structure," "both historically and as a matter of practical necessity."[118] Perhaps the most apt characterization, to borrow the words of one state welfare director, was "decentralized centralization."[119]

"Decentralized centralization" turned out to be a complicated strategy. To start, the machinery of local poor relief was still extensive and not at all uniform. In later years the county would seem to be a natural unit for performing welfare functions, but this development was recent enough that in 1932, social welfare experts could characterize counties as "newly discovered territory."[120] In many places, smaller units of government kept their hands in poor relief, making the system even more decentralized than it would appear on any state map. In 1934, Pennsylvania's 67 counties included 425 poor districts and 967 persons legally authorized to administer poor relief. In neighboring Ohio, there were 88 counties, but more than 1,500 local government units with some responsibility for poor relief.[121] In 1937 – well after federal dollars had encouraged reform – a survey of Illinois found more than 1,800 local administrative authorities distributing categorical public assistance, with 41 independent authorities in one county alone.[122]

Moreover, the people running the show at the local level often did not share the worldview that animated New Deal social welfare legislation – a theme running through the records of FERA administrators. Frank Glick, who helped direct the Illinois Emergency Relief Commission from 1933 to 1936, described local relief administrators as "almost invariably without any background of qualification for their task," a description that said little about their inherent ability to do the job but spoke volumes about the wide gap between local personnel and the ideals of public welfare professionals in Washington, DC.[123] Josephine Brown, who headed FERA's Social Service Section and later helped design ADC, agreed. The local poor relief officials she encountered had no special education or training and rarely devoted their full time to the task.[124] They were concerned with keeping expenditures down, she claimed, but otherwise "indifferent." Rather than ascertaining applicants' actual needs, they gave relief on the basis of "hearsay and gossip" and "whatever personal knowledge [they] happened to have, no matter how scanty." Brown also found "ample evidence" of officials using their power to line their pockets and curry political favor.[125] In short, local practices often failed to fit federal policymakers' definition of good public welfare administration.

Local officials' sympathy with the federal view reportedly improved during the two years preceding the enactment of the SSA, when FERA made an effort to secure "trained and experienced" social workers to supervise local relief units, but that effort could do only so much. The emergency relief effort employed some 40,000 persons (not including clerical staff) by October 1934; around the same time, the American Association of Social Workers reported only 8,430 members.[126] FERA and its state-level counterparts made do with the local labor pool, with predictable results. The average local supervisor, federal administrators found, was "a person with great interest" and "a considerable amount of natural ability" but lacking in the enlightened thinking that came (in their view) with formal training.[127] For the tens of thousands of front-line positions, hires tended to be teachers, nurses, and home economists. Federal administrators lamented these workers' lack of exposure to modern public welfare practices: though upstanding members of their communities, they tended to carry with them "the local poor relief traditions and attitudes" of the "colonial and pioneer days."[128]

Local resentment, of federal *and* state authority, was another obstacle. Again, FERA administrators provided ample evidence of this resentment. They had also helped cause it. Particularly in rural areas, FERA administrator Josephine Brown recalled, localities received state-initiated emergency relief efforts as "foreign and superimposed"; places with strong traditions of local autonomy became sites of "conflict and resistance."[129] Years later, another FERA administrator still remembered a warning from an old county judge: "We accept [the directives from Washington]" because people are starving, he told her, "but I just want you to know that the time is coming when we feel that we must again get back into the picture."[130] Michigan's Welfare and Relief Study Commission, which that state's governor appointed in the wake of FERA's demise, received a similar message: "We went along with the set-up for four or five years, but we feel the emergency is over," a county official declared. "We want that which the constitution of this nation says we could have," he continued, "the right to rule ourselves."[131]

These yearnings had much to do with the type of people who assumed responsibility for local relief efforts during the FERA years and who seemed keen to take over all of public welfare thereafter. They were not necessarily outsiders, but neither were they traditional insiders. Often they were young; many were women; and they tended to give the impression that their methods were superior to those of their older, less-educated male predecessors.[132] The sting was worse for those who had themselves fallen on hard times. "Why should these young girls of social prestige" be visitors, one anonymous letter writer inquired of FERA administrator Harry Hopkins in 1935, "when there are women and men who are better qualified intellectually and who have lost everything thru [sic] no extravagance of their own?"[133]

Such resentments continued after the adoption of the Social Security Act. Reports from Michigan, for example, conveyed a "terrific" fear of "imported social workers" at the local level.[134] A detailed study of Illinois noted that county boards "clung to their authority" over pensions for the blind, and that county judges, who had long administered mother's aid, opposed handing over that responsibility to a state agency. Joined by a lobby of more than a thousand township supervisors, those judges helped delay the enactment of ADC in Illinois until 1941.[135] Resistance appeared staunchest in the East and Midwest, where large urban units had long operated independently of state government, but in many parts of the country, Edith Abbott reported in September of 1936, welfare "chieftains" were "determined to hold their cloudy titles to their old local perquisites."[136]

Meanwhile, despite local fears, the people that Abbott hoped would replace the "chieftains" remained few and far between. Tens of thousands of workers were necessary to process applications for the new programs, a need that far surpassed the number of persons that federal administrators considered adequately educated and trained for the job.[137]

THE MISSING LINK: STATE SUPERVISION

These local realities exposed a weakness in the Social Security Act's "New Deal" for American poor relief, and a fundamental stumbling block for the emergent modern American state. Although the act created clear links between the federal agency and the states, it presumed no relationship between the federal and the local. In attempting to address local problems, the best that the SSB could do was use its "carrot and stick" to persuade the state governments to create the sort of machinery that could bring local units into line. Audit local accounts, the board suggested to them; set standards for employees of local units; send state field-workers out to assist local units.[138] Unfortunately for the board, not all states proved willing to implement meaningful schemes of state supervision.[139]

Wisconsin was one of the first states to teach the federal agency this hard lesson. In December of 1935, the state submitted a plan for Old Age Assistance that envisioned county-level administration, via the county judge or county department of welfare. The plan appeared to comply with the federal requirements because a new state Pension Department was slated to supervise the county operations, but everyone knew that county courts, especially in rural areas, would be far more powerful than a newly created state board. Further, Wisconsin's civil service laws did not extend to jurisdictions with fewer than 500,000 people, leaving county officials in charge of both administration and personnel. The plan did give the Pension Department power to reimburse (or not) county expenditures, but it failed to explain how the department would even know, other than through self-reporting by the counties, what was happening out in the field. Ultimately, federal officials approved the plan, hoping for improvement over time. They would be disappointed. Three months later, a board staff member visited the state and learned that the plan was not operating in some of the counties – a fact that state officials characterized as "none of the board's business." Four years later, Wisconsin's agency had yet to establish personnel standards for the county units and suggested that it had no authority to do so.[140]

Disapproving a plan, as happened with Kansas and Massachusetts, was
another potential response to weak promises of state supervision, but an
undesirable one. In 1936, Kansas's plan had passed federal review and
was on its way to board approval when telegrams came in from multiple
local officials. They conveyed their unwillingness to go along with the
arrangement (objecting in particular to a provision requiring financial
contributions from the counties). State officials conceded that they could
not control the counties, and the SSB had to reject the plan.[141] For similar
reasons, the board initially disapproved Massachusetts's ADC submission. Although its plans for OAA and AB programs raised no concerns,
the state insisted that its townships be allowed to administer ADC, as they
had mothers' pensions. In practical terms, this meant that many eligible
children would receive nothing at all. At the time of the plan's submission,
119 townships had no mothers' aid recipients on their rolls; 51 of these
had never participated in the program. The board could not endorse this
degree of local autonomy.[142] It disapproved the plan knowing, however,
that every such decision was both counterproductive and dangerous:
counterproductive because it kept public assistance from taking root
and dangerous because it contributed to the impression that federal
bureaucrats were exactly that – bureaucrats, whose narrow vision
obstructed much-needed relief.

The board took a different tack in Illinois, which presented a plan
similar to Wisconsin's, but the results were similarly discouraging.
Illinois intended to rely almost exclusively on county machinery for the
administration of its public assistance programs, and the state plan
omitted any mention of how it would ensure the competence of local
workers. Such a vast delegation of power signaled to the board that the
state's programs would not operate on the "higher plane" that the act's
drafters envisioned. Yet the SSB appeared to have no basis on which to
threaten disapproval: Congress had explicitly denied the agency the power
to impose its own standards on state and local personnel. Undeterred, the
board decided to interpret the act's "single state agency" provision to
mean that it could disapprove a plan if the proposed *state* agency lacked
power to prescribe local personnel standards (a "strained" argument, in
GC Tom Eliot's assessment, but one that found some support in congressional committee reports). Illinois accepted this interpretation and the
plan moved forward. Within months, however, it was clear that the SSB
had not found its silver bullet. Illinois may have agreed to impose personnel standards on the counties, but the state agency appeared to be little
more than a shell. Seven hundred Illinois residents had by then appealed

the decisions made in their cases and the state agency had no procedure for reviewing the counties' handiwork.[143]

When it came to poor relief, these examples show, some states could ☞ not, or would not, override local authority, no matter how much federal money was on the line. Over time – and with the help of the Social Security Act – states would develop their administrative capacities and thereby "weave the loose threads of [local] government into a stronger fabric of rule."[144] By century's end, historian Jon Teaford could dub local government "the great loser of the 1930s," and state government an underappreciated victor.[145] But as of 1937, that future seemed a long way off. In the meantime, federal administrators would have to find other ways of furthering their goals.

* * * *

"If we would guide by the light of reason," Supreme Court justice Louis D. Brandeis wrote in a famous 1932 dissent, "we must let our minds be bold." Those words failed to persuade the Court's bloc of judicial conservatives to vindicate Brandeis's immediate concern – allowing states to experiment with social and economic legislation – but they distilled the spirit of those who occupied seats of power in and around the Roosevelt administration. Indeed, the quote appears prominently in one of the murals that artist George Biddle painted for the Department of Justice in 1936. Flanked by images of a man in overalls and a gray-haired woman performing manual labor, with a crowded tenement in the background, Brandeis's words reminded federal administrators of the connection between New Deal legislation and the lives it would touch.[146]

The architects of the Social Security Act believed that they were being bold, even as they crafted a scheme that compromised with white supremacists, renounced a national standard of need, and relied on the same local poor relief machinery that they portrayed as mired in parochial thinking. Looking out at a landscape of thousands of autonomous poor relief operations and as many private competitors, the drafters of the Social Security Act laid the groundwork for a more uniform, rule-bound system of public aid, with power centralized at the state and federal levels. In the face of an enduring association between poverty and personal failings, they urged relief givers to presume the capability and competence of the poor. And throughout the nation, they planted ideas about what constituted good public welfare administration, with an emphasis on merit-based hiring, social work expertise, and objective decision making. In short, even though the Social Security Act left much of the existing system of poor relief intact, its creators attempted to alter fundamentally the balance of power between public and private agencies; among federal, state, and local governments; and between the poor and the state.

As soon as the Social Security Act went into effect, however, its administrators came face to face with law as legal philosopher Robert Cover would later describe it: as "the projection of an imagined future upon reality."[147] There was a great distance, as it turned out, between bold legislation and a transformation in the lives of everyday people. Administrators, legislators, judges, and executives at every level of government were left to puzzle through the questions and problems that emerged in the act's wake. Along with influential private and professional groups, as well as many decidedly uninfluential individual citizens, they puzzled over how the federal, state, and local governments ought to interact; over who had authority to make particular decisions; over how to talk about the new public assistance benefits; and over how the recipients of those benefits fit into the political communities around them. In doing so, they puzzled over the larger contours of the modern American state, shaping the ways that it would unfold around them in the decades to follow.[148]

2

Rights as an Administrative Tool

An Appeal to State and Local Bureaucrats

On March 12, 1939, W. B. Hayes wrote a letter to Indiana congressman George Gillie. The letter began with personal touches, meant to signal Hayes's standing and trustworthiness: Hayes recalled a time when the two men had met at the Shrine Temple in Fort Wayne, and noted his own government service as a local postmaster in Garrett. Then on to business: Hayes's mother-in-law, Lulu Brown, had recently applied for Old Age Assistance in DeKalb County and had been rejected, on account of the fact that she now lived periodically with her adult children in neighboring states (Hayes himself resided in Beulah, Michigan). Yet DeKalb County had been her home from 1900 until her husband died in 1937, Hayes explained; she would live there still were it not for her poor health and utter destitution. Invoking the well-established image of the despised foreign pauper – which surely Mrs. Brown was above – Hayes urged Gillie to ensure that she not be treated "as an alien."[1]

It was a letter from a disappearing era, when patronage politics and community reputation played a decisive role in who received aid. The reply, three days later, suggested the broad changes afoot: Congressman Gillie reported that he had consulted with no less than the assistant general counsel of the federal Social Security Board and learned that public assistance was Mrs. Brown's legal right. As a technical matter, residence was mostly a matter of intent, the federal lawyer had explained to Gillie, so Mrs. Brown's travels outside the state did not disqualify her from receiving benefits; she was "entitled" to assistance from Indiana. For Mrs. Brown, in other words, poor relief was no longer a matter of discretion, dependent on community understandings of deservingness and conditioned on rigid adherence to community norms. It was her right. Gillie urged Hayes to pass this message directly to the county authorities and to appeal to Indiana's state welfare agency (a process to which Mrs. Brown was also now entitled) if they did not come around.[2]

Whether Lulu Brown ultimately received the aid she sought, these records do not say, but they do reveal an even more important phenomenon. From the Social Security Board down to the residents of DeKalb County, a new concept was circulating: for large groups of Americans, government assistance was the legal right of all those who met basic eligibility requirements. As Hayes himself would assert in a subsequent letter (in which his tone had changed from supplication to indignation), Mrs. Brown was "fully entitled" by "Law" to relief. Failure to give it to her was nothing less than "an insult upon justice."[3]

Other sources emanating from the federal agency, such as training guides for local welfare workers and policy releases to state agencies, went even further: they enumerated rights apart from the basic guarantee of income support that, with the creation of federal-state welfare programming, were now established in law, such as the right to submit a formal application for assistance, the right to receive fair treatment, the right to spend support payments freely, and the right to keep private one's reliance on the state. Some agency sources went further still, stating that individuals like Lulu Brown had not just *legal* rights but *social* or "democratic" rights – rights to the income, the process, and the freedom necessary "to live as participating members of the community."[4]

This turn to rights language is, in some sense, not surprising: across American history, Hendrik Hartog and others have demonstrated, rights language has been "a relatively stable and permanent social convention." That is because rights are symbolically powerful, invoking associations with freedom and self-ownership; because they appear durable, giving their holders the sense that their interests are secure; and because, despite the appearance of durability, they are constantly vulnerable to "reimagin[ation], repossess[ion], and redistribut[ion]."[5] Rights would have seemed especially malleable in the late 1930s and 1940s, as Americans witnessed the transformation of old rights and the accrual of new ones.

And yet the many references to rights in New Deal–era federal public assistance records *are* surprising, because of their dissonance with conventional accounts of social welfare provision in the United States. According to those accounts, policymakers and administrators did their utmost to attach rights rhetoric and rights practices (automatic and non-fluctuating benefits, minimally invasive procedures) to social insurance. But at the same time, they deliberately denied those trappings to public assistance, predicting and even hoping that public assistance clients would bear the stigma associated with traditional poor relief. Their efforts supposedly succeeded: not until the welfare rights movement, according to the conventional narrative, did Americans use the language of rights to talk about need-based income support, and when they did, federal administrators were not conversant in the dialect. In fact, however, the notion of public assistance as a right and its recipients as rights holders existed in and around the federal agency in its earliest years. It gained currency during the war years as the power of rights rhetoric grew. By the mid-1940s, public assistance administrators at all levels – federal, state, and local – had become familiar enough with the idea to embed it in manuals, use it in casual conversation, and debate its efficacy.

The use of rights language flowed directly from a problem outlined in Chapter 1. The reformers who designed the public assistance titles of the Social Security Act hoped to restructure American poor relief along modern lines, which to them meant centralized programs, run by experts, for the benefit of a free, independent citizenry. The scheme they got, after politicians had their say, operated under federal guidelines and through central state agencies, but left administrative authority largely in local hands. And as federal administrators quickly learned, many local officials (ranging from those who processed and investigated the cases to members of local oversight boards) were accustomed to an older framework, under which public aid was "charity" and those who received it, "paupers." This produced a fundamental disjuncture. Paupers, by definition, sacrificed personal liberty, civil and political rights, and reputation in exchange for material support; at the mercy of their communities, they were quintessentially unfree.[6] This framework directly contradicted federal goals, yet federal administrators had no obvious recourse: the Social Security Act provided a structure for negotiations between the federal government and the states, but federal administrators had no direct power over the local level. A small wrinkle in 1935, this lack of authority had become a major problem by the late 1930s.

As federal administrators toyed with solutions, such as higher standards for local personnel and more explicit regulations for state agencies, they placed more and more emphasis on the concept of rights. Their reasons were many and varied, but at bottom federal administrators hoped that by explaining the new public assistance program in rights terms, they would trigger a shift in the mindset of local welfare workers. A rights framework, after all, was incompatible with old poor-law assumptions. If local welfare workers accepted the notion that assistance should be administered as a right, they were much more likely to adhere, without even trying, to the agency's many technical rules and regulations and to reject the "parochial" practices that the agency aimed to supplant.[7] In other words, federal administrators used rights language not primarily to mobilize rights holders or to demand resources from the state, as has been the focus of an abundant "rights talk" literature.[8] Rather, they used that language as an administrative tool, a substitute for more formal mechanisms of influencing the myriad administrative decisions occurring on the ground.[9]

RIGHTS AS A MARKETING TOOL: SELLING OLD AGE INSURANCE

President Franklin Roosevelt's eloquent declarations of social and economic rights are a hallmark of the New Deal era. Historians of social welfare provision agree, however, that his administration took a more cautious position on support payments to the poor. Prevailing accounts emphasize the Social Security Board's repeated declarations that whereas social insurance benefits were the right of those who qualified, public assistance payments were something less; like traditional poor relief, the payments amounted to a pittance and would be given only after a humiliating confession of dependency on the state. "The benefits contemplated by the Social Security Act may be classified into two groups," SSB chair John Winant explained to the readers of the *Atlantic Monthly* in 1936: public assistance benefits (Old Age Assistance, Aid to the Blind, Aid to Dependent Children) "are based upon the need of the recipient"; Old Age Insurance benefits are "available to an eligible individual as a matter of right." The board took the same message on the road. Federally administered Old Age Insurance benefits "will be paid as a matter of right irrespective of need," read one of board member Arthur Altmeyer's typical speeches, while the benefits paid under state-level assistance programs turned on "proven need" (and all its attendant burdens).[10]

The back story was one of deep fear and a strategic choice: the SSB initially refused to refer to public assistance as a right because it wanted to prevent Old Age Assistance from becoming too popular while Old Age Insurance was still getting off the ground. The risk was real: support for government-funded old age pensions had been on the rise for decades. Dedicated campaigning by the Fraternal Order of Eagles and organized labor produced old age pension schemes in seventeen states by 1932.[11] Several years of Depression living increased that count. Older workers who had lost their jobs discovered that, owing to age discrimination, their plight was rarely temporary. Adult children faced their own economic woes and were unable to support their parents. Around the nation, people banded together in pension associations and annuity leagues, prompting eleven more states to enact old age pension plans over the next two years. Meanwhile, hundreds of thousands of Americans supported proposals for a national plan, such as physician Francis Townsend's call for $200 a month for every citizen over age sixty and Louisiana politician Huey Long's alluring plan for the country to "share the wealth."[12] President Roosevelt's Committee on Economic Security estimated that in 1935 more than one million elderly citizens were in urgent need and that many more were barely better off.[13]

Old Age Insurance (OAI) had been the committee's solution. It was a national program that would be financed by mandatory contributions from employers and employees and that promised to pay to covered earners, on their attainment of age sixty-five, benefits tied to their previous earnings.[14] The need-based Old Age Assistance program (OAA) rounded out the measure: it existed to meet immediate needs (OAI benefits were not scheduled to pay out until 1942) and to provide a modicum of security to elderly citizens whom the insurance-based program excluded, such as domestic and agricultural workers. From most other vantage points, however, the assistance program was the main event and the insurance program the experimental sideshow. Congress focused more on assistance than insurance. The broader public did as well. Those Americans who were aware of the insurance program tended to dismiss it as "the self-interested work of experts," or to view it as part of a general "pension" program for the elderly poor.[15] Meanwhile, enthusiasm for OAA soared. For example, thousands of prospective recipients converged on Missouri's local old age pension boards – 1,500 in Saint Louis alone – on the day the state's enabling legislation went into effect.[16] Enthusiasm for a still more generous Townsend-type alternative may have been even greater. Less than a month after President Roosevelt signed the SSA into law, a group called the Old Age Pension Association, which claimed between fifteen and twenty million members, asked Congress to provide $5.5 billion per year for $30-per-month old age pensions. Around the same time, thousands of "Townsendites," urging even larger sums, descended on Chicago for their first national convention. At the time, the Townsend movement claimed 750,000 dues-paying members in California alone, and more members nationwide, Townsend shrewdly noted, than voted for Hoover in 1932.[17]

With conservative critics gnashing their teeth and competitors scratching at the door, the executives heading the Social Security Board dedicated themselves to establishing a broad constituency for OAI. They embraced rights rhetoric. Thus in 1936, when the SSB reviewed the script for a short public relations film, Altmeyer urged the scriptwriter to use the concept of rights to draw a sharper distinction between the recipients of OAI and those of OAA, and, further, to make the "insured" citizens appear clearly better off: "Show the superior advantages of this spinster lady and self-respecting man getting checks as a matter of right, which perhaps will enable them to go to the seashore or have a hunting lodge, or something like that," he reportedly said. "Emphasize that it is not necessary for them to be 'down and out' in order to get this fixed income."[18] Rights here operated in the same way as the image of the vacation getaway: they distinguished a "superior" program and clientele from an inferior one. Under the rights-based program, Altmeyer hoped to convey, the state asked no questions and thereby left the recipient's self-respect intact, while under the need-based program, the state demanded a demeaning display of destitution, and an especially demeaning peek into the would-be beneficiary's life.[19]

These anecdotes square with the now classic image of America's "two-track welfare state," with an upper track of relatively generous, nationally administered rights-based programs and a lower track of stingy, needs-based programs, often administered at the local level.[20] But records from the "mezzo level" of the Social Security Board – the level just below Altmeyer and the other board members – challenge the notion that rights language marked the divide between public assistance and the superior programs. These records show that in the late 1930s and the 1940s, federal administrators in the Bureau of Public Assistance and the Office of the General Counsel regularly referred to public assistance payments as rights and to public assistance applicants and recipients as rights holders. The following sections explore why these administrators blurred a boundary that, according to the dominant historical interpretation, policymakers carefully marked out and vigilantly patrolled.

RIGHTS LANGUAGE AND PUBLIC ASSISTANCE

Contrary to conventional understandings of federal welfare administration, rights language existed in and around the agency from the beginning. Within the upper echelons of professional social work, from which the BPA drew most of its staff members, the language of rights was familiar.

Those coming from the Catholic Charities tradition, such as BPA director Jane Hoey, imbibed the teaching that a minimum subsistence was a person's natural right; the individual in need thus had a legitimate claim to some of the wealth of those around him.[21] Catholic reformers worked hard to enshrine this ethical obligation in positive law: the influential teacher and clergyman John A. Ryan campaigned for wage and hour legislation, unemployment insurance, collective bargaining laws, and social responsibility for accident, illness, and old age.[22] Hoey, who had been Ryan's pupil at Trinity College, showed her roots when she declared man's "right to these essentials which arise out of his intrinsic nature" and government's "obligation to see that essential human needs are met and that the rights of the individual are protected."[23]

Not everyone involved in relief giving felt this way. When advocates of "scientific charity," such as Josephine Shaw Lowell, burst onto the scene in the late nineteenth century, they had objected to public "outdoor relief" (and nonscientific almsgiving of all kinds) specifically because it tended to create a sense of entitlement in the poor. The "notion that the State is bound to support all who demand assistance" was a "pernicious" one, declared a report from the 1877 meeting of the National Conference of Charities; it led not only to ingratitude and indiscretion on the part of the recipient but also to the broader perpetuation of poverty.[24] The very idea that the poor had a right to charity was a "communistic impression," agreed "child-saving" pioneer Charles Loring Brace in 1875.[25] Such attitudes survived into the twentieth century, dogging (but not defeating) efforts to enact state-level pensions for widowed mothers and the elderly.[26]

By the 1930s, however, the professional social workers with the closest relationship to the New Deal could be heard using the language of rights to describe what they believed to be the most enlightened and desirable social policy. As policymakers puzzled over how to approach the relief problem in the years leading up to the Social Security Act, the American Association of Social Workers (AASW) advocated a national program under which "assistance shall be accorded ... as a *right*," a right protected by process (it "may eventually be claimed in a court of appeal") and exercised freely (it "shall not result in any loss of civil or political rights").[27] Similarly, Harry Hopkins, Roosevelt's influential relief czar, used rights language to explain why state-level widows' pensions represented an "enlightened" model of caring for poor families: Because "widows' pensions in most states took on the character of a 'right,'" he explained in a 1935 article in *Collier's* magazine, they gave recipients "a type of security" and "an independence in the community" unavailable from traditional poor relief or private charity.[28] For similar reasons, he urged Roosevelt to make relief payments for unemployed workers available "as a matter of right" under the new social security program.[29]

Influential professional social workers also used, as negative referent, programs and administrators that *failed* to provide relief as a matter of right. The existing poor relief system "broke the spirits of people" by making them beg for the assistance "which they had a right to ask for and which they should have received at once," declared William H. Matthews, Hopkins's former colleague at the Association for Improving the Condition of the Poor, in 1935. Along similar lines, New York School of Social Work professor (Amy) Gordon Hamilton used rights language to redirect wayward relief caseworkers: each client has "a right... to relief if he needs it," she cautioned in 1934, as well as "a right to handle his own problems" if he so chose. Such statements show that social workers in and around the Roosevelt administration relied on rights language – certainly not exclusively, but substantially. Far from rejecting the pairing of welfare and rights, these prominent social workers used rights language to talk about the extent of society's obligation to the poor, the desired contours of legislation, and the best practices of those tasked with carrying out the law.[30]

Use of rights language in connection with public assistance extended beyond this subset of professional social work, however. Rights language, albeit a different variant, also came from the lawyers hired to advise the Social Security Board and to monitor states' compliance with federal law.[31] One of the first tasks that the SSB gave its Office of the General Counsel was to explicate a provision in the Social Security Act that no one seemed to know much about, and hence no one knew how to explain to the states: the requirement that all state public assistance plans guarantee applicants "an opportunity for a fair hearing" before the state agency that supervised or administered the state's public assistance programs.[32] The SSA's drafters seem to have envisioned an appeal process that would both defuse applicant dissent and encourage objective, uniform decision making at the local level, but they provided little formal guidance, and the provision attracted no attention during congressional review.[33] In 1935, several members of the SSB's growing legal staff devoted their time to identifying the bounds of interpretive possibility. In the process, they began considering the rights that were at stake when claimants contested decisions about their benefits.

Staff attorney Emmett Delaney got to rights through the idea of due process, which he imagined must be implicated in the phrase "fair hearing." Precisely what kind of process was due, Delaney had learned in law school, depended on the right in question. But was a right involved? This turned out to be a tricky question. At that very moment, a system of legal thought grounded in individual rights to contract and property – the jurisprudence that has since borne the name of the Supreme Court's infamous decision in *Lochner v. United States* – was falling out of fashion, and its replacement was not yet clear.[34] Meanwhile, the legal landscape abounded with new forms of government services and benefits, which confounded the traditional boundaries between "public rights" and "private rights," gratuities and entitlements, rights and privileges.[35] Delaney thought about all of these before deciding to simply assume that individual rights of some sort were at stake; he then proceeded to outline appropriate fair hearing procedures.[36] Staff attorney Sue White offered a similar opinion three weeks later. "So long as the funds exist and the laws of a State provide for payments to qualified individuals," some of her case law research suggested, such individuals "have a right" to these so-called "gratuities from the State." "To avail themselves" of that right, she continued, "they may invoke 'due process of law.'"[37]

By April of 1936, the GC's office saw the need to take a firm stance on the issue and informed the agency's leadership that beneficiaries had "vested rights" in their assistance payments (which, in turn, meant that the opportunity for a fair hearing was essential).[38] Internally, the lawyers continued to debate the nature of public assistance payments.[39] But the important point is this: rights concepts were never foreign to New Deal public assistance, even among the administrators who might have been most intent on policing those concepts (the lawyers). In subsequent years, when public assistance programs seemed to be slipping back in time to the old poor law, federal bureaucrats from across the mezzo level would turn to rights language to attempt to reclaim the program for the New Deal.

THE ENDURING PROBLEM OF THE LOCAL

This process of slippage and reclamation derived from the architecture of the Social Security Act. The act used a scheme of "cooperative federalism," in the words of contemporary political and legal theorists, to attempt to restructure and strengthen public provision for the poor: if states would abide by federal requirements, the Social Security Board would pay a percentage of states' payments to needy persons in the designated categories. Several years into the program the board continued to skirmish with state officials over the content of their state plans, but increasingly, inadequate plans were not the board's biggest problem.

"No nation can wisely legislate beyond its capacity to administer," warned SSB executive director Frank Bane in 1939.[40] Having secured landmark public assistance laws throughout the nation (a campaign described in Chapter 1) the SSB became concerned about *states'* capacity. State officials had come to the board with all the right props and promises, including pleasing charts of bureaucratic authority and detailed diagrams of line-and-staff organization, all the way down to the local level. But the truth was, the thinnest dendrites on these organizational charts had far more power than the visual aids implied. The BPA estimated in 1943 that of the 45,000 persons employed in state and local public assistance administration in June of that year, 38,500, or 86 percent, worked in offices established in county, city, and other local government units. States delegated great authority to these units. It was there that applications were processed, needs and resources investigated, and benefits delivered.[41]

State agencies purported to control local administrators, but federal officials expressed increasing uncertainty about the adequacy of that supervision, and increasing concern about the decisions being made at the ground level. "Very good laws and plans" are not self-executing, BPA director Jane Hoey observed two years after the act's adoption; their success depends entirely on "the understanding, sympathy, knowledge, and skill of those who actually come in contact with persons in need." Local workers alone, another experienced public welfare administrator agreed, would decide whether the laws would serve their intended beneficiaries or whether they would instead be "prostituted to ulterior political or personal ends."[42]

These anxieties had a foundation in recent history: public welfare administrators had not forgotten hostile local responses to the Federal Emergency Relief Administration (detailed in Chapter 1). By 1937, however, those anxieties were also grounded in contemporary observation. The SSB's representatives out in the field reported that public assistance workers at the local level ignored, resisted, or simply failed to encounter state authority, while they regularly felt the influence of town and county. Rose McHugh of the BPA's Administrative Surveys Division reported that towns in Massachusetts refused to pay ADC to some families that were clearly eligible. Local officials were administering ADC in the same way that they had administered mothers' pensions – namely, by limiting it to families who had been "settled" in the town for some time and who met local standards of appropriate conduct. (Families deemed ineligible for ADC might receive public aid, but it would be "general relief," a category of public assistance that was not federally subsidized and hence not subject to federal rules.)[43] Similar reports came from the federal officials monitoring public assistance litigation. A court case in Kansas, for example, revealed that a county welfare board – proceeding without the blessing of the state – had made an adult child's automobile ownership grounds for rejecting elderly claimants' Old Age Assistance applications.[44] More general surveys confirmed the trend. In the words of a 1941 BPA Field Division report, establishing state supervision over local operations was "a slow and tedious process"; a history of "local autonomy," combined with community "attitudes and pressures," resulted in "wide variations" in local agency practices.[45]

Other accounts emphasized the political clout of local officials vis-à-vis the states. Local agencies, Michigan's state relief administrator explained in 1937, found state scrutiny "a new and not a welcome" experience.[46] Where local units were powerful, they made their disaffection known. In 1940, when the California state agency attempted to withhold funds from Los Angeles County, to discipline it for neglecting state requirements, the county presented the state legislature with a bill that would deprive the agency of this power. Only federal pressure, a report on the incident implied, prevented the legislature from enacting the bill.[47] Local public welfare authorities in New York "jealously guarded" their autonomy, while in Minnesota, they forcefully urged state administrators to do nothing.[48] So concerned were administrators in Indiana, Utah, and Oklahoma about intruding on local prerogatives that when asked to review local decisions, they took extraordinary measures to resolve disputes through back channels and to dissuade claimants from going forward.[49]

The recordings of state welfare directors, social work educators, and others immersed in public welfare administration convey the problem's deep and tangled roots. Local workers, Georgia public welfare official Wilma Van Dusseldorp explained in 1938, were "in the center of almost overwhelming pressures": they dealt with "hundreds of applicants – each presenting his need according to his conception of his rights," with the county board (itself often rife with "political factions"), and, beyond that, with the "expectations and criticisms" of the broader community.[50] County officials in Alabama impressed one out-of-town visitor with their eagerness to know whether the public funds granted to "Mr. Jones" were going to "Ole Man Jones with the farm across Hokey

Creek," or "Peg-leg Jones who lived on this side of the creek since his wife died last summer."[51] New York City's Welfare Department reportedly received daily batches of letters, signed "Friend," "Citizen," and "Taxpayer," "yelping for the scalp[s]" of clients whom the writers suspected of "chiselling" and other reproachable behavior ("Mr. Jones has a 1937 Chevrolet"; "How come a person on widow's pension can buy diamonds and wrist watches for her children?"; "Mrs. Jones is just like a prostitute").[52] A letter writer in Indiana urged the county welfare department to investigate a woman who fed delicacies to her thirteen cats but allowed her poor old mother to rely on the state.[53] Neighborly concern, these anecdotes suggest, could lead to feeling "constantly under the surveillance of the community," in one administrator's words.[54]

Meanwhile, communities seemed to show little enthusiasm for the information that local welfare workers were supposed to convey to them. As one county worker put it, "National policies and regulations, federally arrived at, leave our communities cold; theories formulated by a remote group of social work royalists are poignantly unreal; practices without roots in local traditions are suspect."[55] It was no wonder that even professionally trained local workers were tempted to administer aid in the "old poor relief" manner – federal administrators' biggest fear.[56]

State agency reinforcement of "good practice" in public welfare likely helped some well-intentioned county directors, but in many locations state agencies could not or would not intervene. Massachusetts, for example, had 355 administrative units dealing with relief in 1938, and local units "adamant[ly] refus[ed] to give up functions even to the next largest subdivision, the county." The existence of so many recalcitrant jurisdictions made state supervision a challenge.[57] In its review of state-level fair hearing records, the GC office's confirmed "a strong parochial influence," well beyond Massachusetts. And to the extent that state agencies might have used fair hearings to clarify state policy, the GC's office found that they often did not, instead deferring to the case-by-case decisions of local boards.[58]

In some instances, this was less a matter of negligence than a matter of uncertainty. From the mid-1930s through the 1940s, debates abounded about the appropriate relationship between state and local welfare agencies, the best manner of exercising state supervision, and the role of local agencies in state policymaking. Martha Chickering and Margaret Watkins, former employees of the California State Department of Social Welfare, seemed to speak for a generation of state welfare administrators when they asked, in a 1945 issue of *Public Welfare*, "How do we know whether it is a good local job?" Often state administrators chose to give their local counterparts the benefit of the doubt rather than attempt to control them.[59]

Federal officials could have brought pressure to bear on these states by cutting off federal grants, but the limits of this enforcement tool became apparent soon after the SSB approved the first round of state plans. In 1937, after hearing whispers that Oklahoma was not supervising its local units, the board sent a task force to investigate. The federal envoys quickly confirmed the rumors. In one county, Executive Director Frank Bane remembered, the task force found that more than 125 percent of all persons sixty-five years and older were receiving OAA grants.[60] "They were giving out [payments] to names of tombstones and that sort of thing," recalled GC Jack Tate.[61] The board suspended Oklahoma's grant. But it was in no one's interest to keep funds from needy individuals. The sanction lasted only as long as it took for Oklahoma officials to arrange, on paper, for improved supervision of the counties. That done, the board quickly reinstated the state's grant and in fact made it retroactive, so that the state lost only a month's worth of federal funds.[62] The lesson was not lost on other states.

Nor did better personnel standards bring adequate understanding of the public assistance programs to local welfare work, although for a time they seemed like the magic bullet. It was common in the early years of the Social Security Act to blame patronage politics for all the problems that federal administrators observed out in the field. "Our government may be one of 'laws and not men,'" one administrator explained, "but men must do the work," and in many states, the spoils system continued to pick those men (and women).[63] Fred Hoehler, a national public welfare leader, counted thirty-eight states that still had a spoils system in 1936. Two years later, the situation was not much improved: there were formal, statewide merit systems in only fourteen states, and some were clearly not working. Elizabeth Wisner, president of the American Association of Schools of Social Work, reported in 1937 that one state civil service commission simply "threw out its merit system" when choosing its commissioner of public welfare, in order to select "the field manager of a cotton growers association." "He lent assistance to [the association's] 40,000 members," the civil service commission explained, "and that is essentially what the [public welfare department] is doing – lending assistance." The public welfare community was likewise outraged when Pennsylvania's merit system failed to protect Philadelphia director

Dorothy Kahn, recent past president of the American Association of Social Workers, from being fired by the local public welfare board. "Crabwise Goes Progress," began the title of one 1937 article on the issue.[64]

Finally in 1939, at the board's urging, Congress amended the SSA to allow the board to prescribe "methods relating to the establishment and maintenance of personnel on a merit basis" (overriding a provision in the original act that had explicitly denied the board this power). Federal administrators and other public welfare professionals were thrilled. Almost immediately, the SSB issued a set of standards to the states to guide them in revising, or, in many cases, creating from scratch, acceptable merit systems. Failure to comply with the standards, the board warned, could result in defunding.[65]

The merit system requirement was, in the short term, a disappointment. Not all state legislatures were convinced that they had the power to impose merit requirements on local employees, much less to delegate that authority to a state agency, so they dragged their feet. A year later, after the GC's office had armed state officials with the firm legal basis that they claimed they lacked, new laws were on the books. But many of these laws reflected "compromise" and "home-rule influence" – for understandable reasons: merit systems were still a foreign concept to most local governments, and they were loath to surrender their traditional prerogatives, especially if it meant placing outsiders in positions of power.[66] In a few states, the issue was so fraught that the legislature would not enact anything, instead foisting the issue onto the state attorney general or supreme court.[67] The resulting state merit systems often appeared to have bite but were paired with toothless enforcement mechanisms.[68]

The deeper problem was that merit requirements were a crude tool for securing the sort of workers that federal administrators wanted, namely those who were skilled in the "science" of public administration, who had a clear understanding of the new assistance programs, and who – if federal administrators were honest with themselves – had some distance from the community in which they would be working. Professional social workers fit the bill, but the Social Security Board was in no position to set the standard so high. Such professionals were relatively few in number and unevenly distributed geographically, and they could often make better salaries elsewhere, especially during the war years. Further, they remained unpopular, often for precisely the reasons that federal administrators seemed to value them so highly.[69]

More realistic standards for education and experience increased the likelihood of getting the type of workers that the board wanted but were no guarantee. Reports from the field indicate that the average worker joining local public assistance staffs in the late 1930s and early 1940s was relatively well educated but had little to no familiarity with social work or public assistance administration.[70] Nor were new hires necessarily well suited to the community: one Goshen County, Wisconsin, worker candidly described herself as "a twenty-two-year-old, city-bred girl" who knew "such things as the Malthusian theory ... and the definition of the Babinsky reflex" but had no idea "what a heifer was."[71] Such workers came to the job, in the tactful words of one staff supervisor, with "at least a few misunderstandings about the agency's function," some misconceptions about "why certain individuals are poor," and "certain reservations about the client's worthiness."[72] Left to their own devices, the reports implied, these workers would not administer but judge – a function that they were decidedly unqualified to do.

RIGHTS LANGUAGE AS AN ADMINISTRATIVE TOOL

Faced with persistent parochialism in administration and states that refused to assert forceful leadership, federal administrators began exploring other options for effectuating the progressive, rational style of aid administration they extolled. Law and custom prevented them from training local employees directly: communications were supposed to go from federal officials to state officials and, at the states' discretion, from states to the local level.[73] But federal administrators could educate local caseworkers indirectly, by channeling messages and materials through appropriate mediators, such as state agencies and schools of social work. This tactic was no secret. Given that the Social Security Act made administration a state and local responsibility, Jane Hoey explained to one social work audience, the Social Security Board's Bureau of Public Assistance relied on "counseling and special services" to achieve adequate programs.[74] By imbuing their guidance with rights language, federal administrators hoped to sever the ties between local welfare workers and traditional poor relief, and at the same time to attach local workers to federal goals.

Starting in the late 1930s, federal administrators opened up at least four indirect means of communicating with local personnel. First, they wrote long statements interpreting particular legal provisions. These were more philosophical than technical, venturing into the history of social responsibility, the causes of dependency, and the psychology of those in need. The agency could not distribute these "circulars" directly to local agencies, but they sent them to state agencies with the hope that state supervisors and field agents would educate the public welfare workers in their orbit.[75]

Second, they offered to help train welfare workers. They were frank about their motives and blunt in their assessment of local skill. As one BPA official told the National Conference on Social Welfare, "The need for in-service training" – which everyone agreed was great – "stands in inverse ratio to the adequacy of professional competency of the staff."[76] From its Educational Division, the BPA created a Division of Technical Training in 1939, headed by former University of Chicago School of Social Service Administration professor Agnes Van Driel. Van Driel's staff wrote guides for states to use in their own training programs, and went so far as to list appropriate reading materials and outline topics to be covered in worker orientation sessions. Division of Technical Training staff also made themselves available as consultants to state agencies. In the division's first year alone, its representatives visited twenty-two states and the District of Columbia, traveling to some jurisdictions multiple times. They further developed their relationships with state and local welfare directors by participating in state and regional social work conferences.[77]

Third, federal administrators took advantage of their strong connections to schools of social work. Most BPA staff members were graduates of such schools and their professional identities were rooted in the training they had received there. Meanwhile, a number of social work educators (Edith Abbott and Sophonisba Breckenridge, for example) maintained tight ties to the federal welfare bureaucracy. They drafted legislation, advised and consulted for federal agencies, and funneled students into government service.[78] Of those on the front lines of public assistance administration – those taking applications, visiting homes, and working with clients – not many had degrees in social work, but social work education still could exert a strong influence on them. Through educated supervisors and agency directors, values and lessons trickled down to the low-level worker. State and local agencies also brought in social work educators as consultants and sent their staffs to occasional educational "institutes." With federal encouragement, some agencies even made funds available for local workers to enroll in social work classes.[79]

Fourth, federal administrators attempted to reach local personnel through professional circuits – for example, through speeches at meetings of public welfare and social work organizations and publications in professional journals. Local welfare workers did not necessarily attend such meetings or read such journals, but higher-ranked state and county personnel did, and they had access to the workers at the ground level. Without other mechanisms of control, federal administrators had to pursue whatever lines of influence they had.

Often they stressed rights, a concept that would have been particularly appealing at this historical juncture. It was a moment when rights not only had traction in the agency but also pervaded the broader cultural and political discourse. Some of the more memorable examples come from the middle and later 1940s – President Roosevelt's "Second Bill of Rights" (1944), the rights-focused report of President Truman's historic Committee on Civil Rights (1947), the United Nations General Assembly's Universal Declaration of Human Rights (1948) – but rights language was in the air years earlier. President Roosevelt, whose sensitivity to the public mood is legendary, used rights language to launch war preparations on January 6, 1941: he called Americans to duty by reminding them of cherished "negative" rights (freedom of religion and speech) and declaring newer "positive" ones (government protection against poverty and insecurity). He made similar pronouncements in the 1930s, when, in the midst of the Great Depression, he urged voters to place their faith in him. Americans, he assured them, had the "right to live."[80] Evidence suggests that many Americans received this message and some parroted it back, in the form of public demonstrations (against the federal government's eventual withdrawal from providing work relief, for example) and in actual declarations of the "'right' to a job."[81]

Around the same time, and surely for some of the same reasons, rights language figured prominently in conversations about dependence and freedom. Americans had long perceived these conditions as incompatible: a formerly enslaved person who depended on his old master for land and farming implements was not truly free; nor was the pauper in the almshouse; nor was the wage earner whose company fed and clothed him. Reliance on another for the necessities of life undermined one's claim to self-government.[82] "When you beg or borrow from the government," explained editors of the Pine Bluff, Arkansas, *Commercial* in 1940, summarizing this traditional line of thinking, "you give up your birthright as a free citizen."[83]

The device of rights seemed to offer a way out of this dilemma. In the 1930s, groups representing organized labor and nonwhite citizens used rights language to seek the protection of the government – arguably a sign of dependence – while maintaining their independence. For example, in the same sentence in which he condemned New Deal relief programs for aiding poor African Americans only on "paternalistic terms," terms that made them "wards," *Chicago Defender* founder Robert S. Abbott urged his readers to fight for government aid. There was nothing wrong with New Deal programs that treated all participants as "full-fledged citizens with guaranteed privileges and respected rights," he wrote in 1934.[84] Labor and civil rights leader A. Philip Randolph used rights language to similar effect in 1941 when he called African Americans to march on Washington to demand fair employment practices. Seeking state protection could be understood as a sign of dependence and yet, by emphasizing rights, Randolph turned it into a campaign for freedom: "We would rather die on our feet fighting for Negroes' rights," he declared, "than to live on our knees as halfmen, as semi-citizens, fighting for a pittance."[85] To speak in terms of rights, in other words, was not just a way of characterizing something as important or sacred; it was a way of making a claim on the government without assuming the posture of the supplicant, the slave, or the ward. This was the chain of meanings and associations that federal administrators relied on as they spread the language of rights into the universe of American poor relief.

To the modern ear, federal administrators used that language somewhat promiscuously, especially given that the word "right" appeared nowhere in the Social Security Act. Public assistance, in federal administrators' telling, was the right of those who were eligible, meaning that state governments had to give it to those who met the statutory requirements. No one could restrict or otherwise interfere with a claimant's payments. All those who sought payment, even those who were not eligible, were also rights holders: they had the right to apply, to receive prompt consideration of their application, and to appeal should they be dissatisfied. Once on the assistance rolls, an individual also had a right to confidentiality: his or her reliance on the state could not be broadcast to the public, or used surreptitiously by enterprising politicians.

But there was a logic behind this multipronged rights language, one that becomes clear when the speakers themselves are brought into focus. Many rights-inflected communications came from Assistant General Counsel A. Delafield ("A. D.") Smith, the lawyer who supervised the GC's public assistance work from 1938 to 1955.[86] Like many of his colleagues, Smith was well educated (Princeton, Harvard Law) and eager to defend the New Deal, but he stood out for being especially "intense" and "dedicated."[87] To make a point during a board meeting, he once walked across the room on his hands (after carefully removing his suit coat, vest, glasses, and all the items from his pockets).[88] On another occasion, the press of work reportedly prompted him to ask his heavily pregnant secretary whether she couldn't "put that off a little while."[89] One of Smith's firmest convictions was that the public assistance programs had a distinct legal and philosophical basis; a second assumption was that many administrators, especially those outside the federal government's employ, failed to understand this basis. He dedicated much of his career to correcting their misapprehensions, often using an easily digestible (or so he thought) language of rights.[90]

A typical example is Smith's 1939 speech to the Annual Meeting of the American Association of Schools of Social Work, the organization most directly responsible for educating future public assistance leaders. Smith characterized the social work notables in the audience, as well as their trainees, as mediators between public assistance laws and the poor. They were the ones, he said, who would "actually reach the individual." As such, it fell to them to explain the new rights (which Smith explicitly labeled "citizenship" rights) that modern social legislation had created. Smith acknowledged that these laws were not as full and generous as some would like ("[a] truly humanitarian code has yet to be drafted"), but celebrated them as a great improvement over what had come before. With social workers' help, he declared – with their commitment to rights – the new legislation could provide many people with unprecedented security.[91]

Similar themes animated a paper that Smith presented at the 1941 meeting of the National Conference of Social Work and later published in the *Social Service Review*, the premier academic journal in the social welfare field. Increasingly, Smith pointed out, government insured the basic security of individuals, both through programs called "insurance" and others not so named. In all programs, however, new rights were created. Smith encouraged his audience to think of these rights as trusts and to think of modern administrative agencies as trust fund managers. Although agencies did not dictate the value of the trusts, their principles and procedures could confirm for claimants that the government's word was good. Welfare workers must remember, he insisted, that modern public assistance programs were designed "to create adequate sanction of these rights, [and] to secure certainty and regularity in their operation."[92] Welfare recipients needed to know this, too: true security, Smith explained in a later publication, "requires the knowledge that what we obtain we obtain as of right."[93] It was a knowledge that local welfare workers were uniquely situated to impart.

Smith hit the same notes when helping to draft federal guidance for states, guidance that would, in turn, influence state-local interactions. In correspondence with the BPA in 1940 about a manual for the bureau's field personnel, Smith suggested introducing the section on fair hearings with an observation about the "new rights" that recent social legislation had created.[94] Smith also suggested an additional section reminding welfare workers "that each individual shall be entitled as a matter of right to the uniform application of the State's criteria of eligibility and standard of need." He wanted to make clear that the SSA generated an "individual right" to "equitable treatment."[95]

In short, Smith was making what he once described as "an appeal for an attitude," an attitude different from what had been the norm.[96] He wanted to show that even though New Deal public assistance might resemble traditional poor relief – in terms of personnel, location, and even payment amounts – a rupture had occurred; a basic divide had formed. On one side was the old poor law, with its haphazard administration, its discretionary payments, and its capricious and condescending "charity mindset." Custom was certainly on this side, and yet, Smith hoped to convey, it was not where an evolved society ought to be. On the other side was the new legislation, based on rational, scientific administration and payments as a matter of right. Smith wanted welfare workers to know that when they dealt with poor individuals in the protected categories, they must stand on the progressive side of the divide, and, further, that they should feel proud of where they stood.[97]

Other federal administrators turned with equal frequency to the language of rights, both to explain the nature of the individual's claim on the state and to clarify how each claimant ought to be treated. At the National Conference of Social Work in 1941, for example, BPA director Jane Hoey called attention to the Social Security Act's guarantees of a fair hearing, cash payment, and confidential public assistance records.[98] The common denominator, she hoped state and local agencies would soon appreciate, was a commitment to the right to assistance and the rights of the individuals who applied for and received aid. Rights were "inherent" in these policy choices, she explained.[99] At the same meeting, BPA field-worker Margaret Leahy reported that such an appreciation was indeed building: she saw "the concept of assistance as a right" gradually overgrowing "the old poor-law traditions" – thanks, she emphasized, to "continuous interpretation and leadership."[100]

A similar message reached state agencies, and through them, local agencies, via a 1944 BPA circular titled "Money Payments," which the

BPA and GC's office created to clarify an apparently befuddling feature of New Deal public assistance. The Social Security Act's requirement that assistance take the form of cash (rather than clothes, food, and so on) could be reduced to a "basic principle," the circular explained: "that assistance comes to needy persons as a right." The point of contrast, again, was old-fashioned poor laws and their "paternalistic" efforts to constrain the spending choices of the poor. Modern public assistance tracked instead a modern notion of citizenship, which by the 1940s included the ability to participate freely in a mass consumption marketplace (or, as the circular put it, in "normal channels of exchange").[101]

Perhaps the most important example of rights language in public assistance administration, however, was Public Assistance Report No. 8, *Common Human Needs: An Interpretation for Staff in Public Assistance Agencies*. The BPA's Division of Technical Training commissioned this report in 1944, after receiving "frequent requests" for training materials. Public assistance supervisors badly needed help "interpreting the basic philosophy of the program," the bureau determined, and frontline workers required such interpretation to "develop constructive attitudes in dealing with people in need."[102] To write the report, the BPA tapped social worker Charlotte Towle, who, like many BPA employees, had close ties to the University of Chicago School of Social Service Administration.[103]

Towle's report stands out among agency publications for drawing explicitly on the insights of psychiatry (Towle was a pioneer in the burgeoning field of psychiatric social work), but like other agency communications, the report also deployed the language of rights in an open attempt to influence the thinking of state and local welfare workers. Without dampening such workers' enthusiasm for providing services to the poor, Towle hoped to convince them to foreground the notion of "sound individualization in a program *based on right*."[104] The aid worker must recognize that, regardless of the applicant's deportment, the worker's own discomfort, or the community's attitude, all eligible persons had a right to financial assistance. All cases must be approached with "genuine conviction as to the applicant's rightful claim on society in time of need." By the summer of 1945, the BPA had distributed five thousand copies of the report to regional public assistance offices, for redistribution to state and local agencies.[105]

That such statements contradicted federal efforts to puff up Old Age Insurance did not dampen public assistance administrators' enthusiasm. In fact, some federal administrators openly questioned that campaign. In a 1937 memo to the board's Informational Service, Leonard Calhoun of the

GC's office warned that "[a] *needy* person may have just as much *right* to assistance under Title I as a qualified individual has to benefits under Title II," payment of contributions notwithstanding. A. D. Smith, Calhoun's colleague in the GC's office, echoed this view in a 1940 article in the *Social Security Bulletin*, the monthly periodical of the Social Security Board. "The function of the State is fundamentally the same in relation to both insurance and assistance programs," he wrote. In both instances the legislation creates "an actual right."[106]

Even more telling, the SSB's leadership did not muffle these statements. Perhaps it was because the intended audience, public welfare professionals, did not overlap with the population that the board's OAI campaign aimed to reach – namely, the regular men and women who might be tempted to press for a more radical alternative. Perhaps, having established a broader base of support for OAI (the inclusion of survivors in 1939 gave it a larger constituency), the board was ready to back away from its earlier position. Perhaps the war made board members hesitant to take any stand that appeared unfriendly to individual rights. In any case, the 1940s witnessed board members tolerating and then cautiously supporting the use of rights language in the administration of public assistance. In 1944, Arthur Altmeyer, no less – the board member who had so insistently pitched the superiority of OAI – declared that both public assistance and social insurance came to recipients as a matter of right.[107]

* * *

By the mid-1940s, references to rights – contrasted inevitably with the stigmatizing gratuities of the old poor law – were a staple of federal agency communications. As one regional attorney commented in a routine internal memo, federal administrators were "striving to establish the principle that, where one meets the requirements of the law, assistance to him is a matter of right rather than a matter of pleasure to be given by the State." Or as she put it in the next sentence, administrators were guarding against "reversion" to the "assistance [as] charity" philosophy.[108] Other professionals working for the federal government spoke in the same language. In other words, this was not simply lawyers speaking in the language they knew best. At their 1944 conference, members of the BPA's regional staff congratulated themselves and other trained social workers for spreading the principle of "public assistance as a right" throughout public welfare administration, and discussed how to overcome the irrational "feelings and attitudes" that prevented local welfare workers from truly embracing the rights concept.[109] By 1946, even a top, politically appointed administrator could be heard referring to "all the work we [in the federal agency] have done ... to convince people that public assistance is a right."[110]

Over time, state welfare records began to reflect this sustained federal effort. The Idaho welfare department's July 1942 "Manual of Policies and Procedures" stated that it was "the legal and democratic right of any person to make application for assistance, to receive equitable consideration of his application and to receive assistance provided he is eligible."[111] Oklahoma's 1944 orientation materials explained that the welfare worker's job was "to see that people eligible under the law get [assistance]," and thereafter to respect the client's spending choices.[112] By the mid-1940s, agency heads well outside of Washington could be heard citing "the right to assistance" as the program's "fundamental premise."[113]

As for whether local, frontline workers actually received this message, some apparently did. When a member of an Indiana county welfare board insisted to a visiting social work professor in 1941 that "no recipient has a legal right to receive this money," it was a good sign that someone had been saying otherwise (perhaps someone like W. B. Hayes, the well-informed son-in-law who appears in this chapter's opening pages). If a poor individual qualified for assistance under state law but "abuse[d] the privilege," the local board member maintained, he "should be relegated to the county [poor] farm as if there were no [State] Welfare Act." But there was a Welfare Act – one that had been tailored to federal specifications – and implicit in the local board member's phrasing was the recognition that a new paradigm came with it.[114]

Other local workers seem to have not only heard the message but also acted on it. In a 1944 session at the University of Pennsylvania School of Social Work, a member of the SSB's regional staff reportedly witnessed a group of Maryland public assistance workers go "wild" when a representative of a private family agency confessed to giving out relief "in kind" rather than in cash. They "all but tore her apart and almost tossed her out the window," leaving her with "a great feeling of inferiority."[115] Even in the Deep South – thought by historians to be the most hostile to modern welfare practices – there is anecdotal evidence of change afoot: to the chagrin of traditionalists, some public welfare workers had started referring to applicants – including African Americans – by the courtesy titles "Mr." and "Mrs.," implying not only dignity but also a rightful claim to public space and public services.[116]

Without more data, of course, we should take the advice of anthropologist James C. Scott and "never assume that local practice conforms with state theory."[117] In this instance, fortunately, we gain much from simply excavating and exploring the "state theory" at work. In the 1930s and 1940s – contrary to much historical writing on this topic – poor relief did not simply limp along on tracks first laid out in Elizabethan England; in this policy realm, as elsewhere, new ideas about governance were taking hold, even as old structures endured. We gain even more from analyzing federal administrators' attempts to impose their theory on reality. Creative and well-intentioned, those attempts were also fraught and messy. And, as subsequent chapters show, they produced a number of unanticipated consequences.

Before turning to those consequences, however, we will examine a tension alluded to in the previous pages, a tension that became apparent as the agency moved from talking about rights to deciding how the government should honor its purported commitments. Within the federal agency, both lawyers and social workers were eager to make poor relief part of a modern system of government, and they both used rights language to that end, but their visions of ideal governance contained important and revealing differences.

3

Rights as a "Live, Motivating Principle"

The Path toward Legalism

On May 15, 1947, shortly after President Truman sounded the opening bell in what would become the Cold War, the Social Security Board's Bureau of Public Assistance announced the theme for that year's series of professional staff meetings: "The Right to Public Assistance."[1] The choice fit the times. Just weeks later, a high-profile commission of the United Nations would begin drafting a Universal Declaration of Human Rights. A presidentially appointed Committee on Civil Rights, meanwhile, was tackling America's widely recognized "Negro problem." And within the world of public welfare, rights language was fast becoming a staple of federal-state communications.

The right to public assistance was also an apt topic for study in 1947 because it seemed so elusive. About a month before the bureau's announcement, prominent social work educator and former government administrator Donald Howard appeared before the National Conference of Social Work with a set of disturbing stories. One was about a public assistance officer who kept on his wall, just opposite the door, "the pictures of six Negroes whom he had helped to 'send over the road'" – by which he meant helped send to prison, presumably for defrauding the agency. The officer posted the pictures because of the "sobering effect" he thought they had on black Americans seeking assistance. Howard described another welfare administrator who wrote complaint letters to himself from a fictitious "Citizens Committee" whenever he saw a public assistance recipient driving an automobile or drinking in a bar. These would be presented to the profligate individual as evidence that the community's sympathy had worn thin. So much the better if the applicant pleaded for reconsideration: the administrator would give him the opportunity to swear "never again [to] visit a tavern or drive a car," after which something might be done to get him back on the relief rolls.[2]

Less disturbing but far more pervasive were the accounts of "grossly inadequate" benefit levels and long waiting times between applications and aid. "Sure, there's a tree that grows in Brooklyn," Howard noted, referencing Betty Smith's popular 1943 novel about a family flourishing amid poverty, but "there are many more that wither and die." America could do better, he stressed, and so could federal aid administrators.[3] The BPA took up the topic of the right to public assistance in the hopes of finally making the concept "a live, motivating principle in the day-to-day job," in the words of BPA director Jane Hoey.[4]

As it turned out, the meetings captured a range of perspectives on this fundamental concept. Hoey, for instance, kicked off the first session by emphasizing every person's "moral" and "economic" rights – "to life, to individual respect and dignity, and to a share in the world's goods"; "to earn a living at an adequate standard"; "to have a home." For her, these had a corollary in government obligation: the "obligation to protect these rights through laws." In contrast, Assistant General Counsel A. D. Smith, a longtime champion of rights in public assistance administration, shuffled the order of right and law: a right may appear to some to be "natural and inalienable," but "no right actually arises," he explained, "until after the legislative body has said it is so." Then came Haskell Jacobs, who worked in the BPA's division of program standards and was trained in both law and social work. He agreed with Smith about the importance of positive law, but noted that statutory commitments were only the beginning. Meaningful rights depended on "an atmosphere of understanding and acceptance on the part of agency workers and the public."[5]

As these quotes suggest, administrative rights language included diverse strains, which tended to track gender and professional lines. After reviewing the increasingly tense relationship between the feminized field of social work and the predominantly male field of law in the years leading up to the New Deal, this chapter outlines the different understandings of rights that circulated within the federal agency during the 1940s. When social workers talked of the right to public assistance and the various rights of the public assistance recipient, they often invoked more than statutory law: they referred to the obligations that all governments owed their subjects and that too few honored – obligations to meet human need, respect human dignity, and acknowledge human interdependence. The word "right" signaled a legitimate but not necessarily a *legal* claim on government. Lawyers' invocations of rights more often emphasized the sense of security and independence that came with a legally cognizable right in a nation governed by law. The lawyers wanted individuals to receive adequate payments, but they were primarily concerned with fair treatment and rational decision making, as promised by positive law.[6]

These disagreements were not simply a manifestation of ongoing professional turf wars.[7] They represented disagreements about the agency's mission and, more broadly, about the regime of governance – the state – that progressive and New Deal reformers had been building. Everyone in the agency agreed about what this state rejected: namely, patronage politics, nonprofessional administration, and nonuniform, unsystematic modes of delivering public goods and services. But what, beyond professionalism and sound public administration, did the modern American state embrace? What were its core commitments? What was its logic?

For a time, diverse views circulated freely within the federal agency, occasionally clashing but generally coexisting. In earlier eras, lawyers appeared to have a monopoly on defining rights (and, arguably, on articulating the principles of legitimate governance). But during the early twentieth century, doctrinal understandings of rights had shifted, and well into the 1940s the future remained uncertain.[8] At this historical juncture, social workers had the opportunity – and through the administration of the Social Security Act, the authority – to advance their own interpretation. Outside the agency, meanwhile, Americans heard capacious pronouncements from their leaders about what government promised: not only freedom of speech and worship but also freedom from fear and want, to borrow language from President Roosevelt's classic 1941 speech. Americans, it seemed, could have it all.

This chapter is about the gradual closing of that era, and about who and what was left standing at the end of the day. Over the course of the 1940s, I argue, social workers struggled to implement their need-driven understanding of rights and, with it, their vision for the modern American state. Their agenda depended on broader uses of federal power and greater financial commitments from all levels of government, at a time when New Deal and wartime interventions had increased suspicion of active, centralized governance. Particularly suspect were government programs – like Aid to Dependent Children – that seemed causally related to an emboldened African American population, no longer confined to the South. Social workers also suffered from a long-established association between women professionals and political radicalism, and from the rise, during the early years of the Cold War, of a robust and incautious anti-communist discourse. By 1947, their stated commitment to a rights-based "socialized state" sounded almost treasonous.

The lawyers' understanding of rights was far less threatening, even though it also implied broad uses of federal power. Whereas the social workers' rights language often seemed to derive from academic theory and an emergent discourse of international human rights, the lawyers' was anchored explicitly in domestic positive law (the U.S. Constitution and the Social Security Act). And if legalistic language had once seemed conservative, even obstructionist, the political milieu of the 1940s gave it a different valence. As Americans confronted totalitarianism abroad, a visibly active state at home, and an energized civil rights movement, "rule of law" values like due process and equal treatment had great appeal. These concepts helped distinguish the United States from its enemies and explain its foreign entanglements, first in World War II and then in the Cold War. Domestically, these concepts helped make government appear less threatening. They also assured the public that even the most virulent political conflicts could be channeled peacefully into the courts (or very courtlike agencies). By the close of the 1940s, the lawyerly vision of rights had embedded itself in the welfare state, providing footholds for a subsequent generation of reformers.

SOCIAL WORKERS AND LAWYERS JOIN THE NEW DEAL

The New Deal and its federal social welfare bureaucracy created new opportunities for both social workers and lawyers, and for perhaps the first time brought them together on a plane of equality. As lawyers flooded into agencies like the National Recovery Administration, the Agricultural Adjustment Administration, and the National Labor Relations Board, social workers found abundant opportunities in the Federal Emergency Relief Administration and the state agencies designed along the same lines.[9] FERA administrator Harry Hopkins (who himself identified as a social worker) cautioned the social work community that he was not out "to develop a great social-work organization throughout the United States," but in fact his agency recruited many social workers and set aside funds to train more.[10]

The Social Security Board – an agency designed to be a permanent feature of American government – offered even greater opportunity, and it was there that lawyers and social workers came together under one bureaucratic roof. Social workers were a natural choice for the Bureau of Public Assistance, the SSB division that implemented the act's public assistance titles. The BPA became even more inviting to social workers when Jane Hoey took the helm. A graduate of a social work school herself, Hoey threatened to resign if the board did not allow her to staff her bureau with her own kind. (She did everything in her power to convince state agencies to do the same, at least for top-tier administrative positions.)[11] Lawyers, meanwhile, were early and "inevitable" additions to the agency, as the board's first executive director put it (somewhat regretfully).[12] The board relied on its general counsel and his staff of about ninety attorneys for everything from defending the Social Security Act's constitutionality to interpreting its complicated and novel provisions.[13]

This joining of lawyers and social workers was significant because to the extent that they worked together prior to the New Deal, social workers were almost always the junior partners (even when, as historian Felice Batlan has shown, social workers were engaged in sophisticated legal practice).[14] Law was "an ancient and honorable profession," in the words of one observer, while social work was "a young and ambitious one" – if it was a profession at all.[15] Among the doubters was education reformer Abraham Flexner, whose bruising speech on the topic at the 1915 proceedings of the National Conference of Charities and Correction (forerunner of the National Conference of Social Work) has become part of social work lore. Like a white knight, legal luminary Felix Frankfurter came to social work's defense – it was a "very definite" profession, he declared – but in doing so, he insisted that social work follow the same developmental path as law, which by then seemed light years ahead.[16] The result was that when social workers and lawyers worked together, as they increasingly did in the era of progressive law reform and "socialized justice," social workers ended up in subordinate and less visible "helping" roles.[17]

This tendency was not simply a result of disparate stages of professional development, however: it also flowed from gendered assumptions about women's capabilities and interests, and entrenched exclusionary practices. By the 1920s women had convinced state legislatures to allow them admission to the bar (a result that the Supreme Court famously refused to mandate in 1872), but the profession remained far from open.[18] In 1920, there were only 1,738 women lawyers in the country, representing less than 1.5 percent of the profession.[19] An additional 3,500 women graduated from law school during the 1920s, but women lawyers continued to encounter discrimination in hiring, pay, and daily practice. Some found a career in law unsustainable.[20] The eminently capable

Sophonisba Breckenridge quit law for want of work, shortly after becoming the first woman to pass the Kentucky bar. Social work, in contrast, was a haven for women like Breckenridge: after obtaining a second graduate degree, a PhD in political science, she became a leader in social work education.[21] By 1920, the social work profession was 66 percent female, a legacy of women's strong presence in charities and settlement houses, and a testament to how well the work fit with traditional assumptions about women's domestic concerns and nurturing instincts.[22] Men, too, chose careers in social work, but owing to their easier paths to managerial and executive positions, their greater opportunities for lateral movement to other professions, and to public questions about the masculinity of male social workers, the typical and archetypal social worker was a woman, the typical lawyer, a man.[23]

In the years leading up to the New Deal, social workers had become increasingly critical of lawyers, and increasingly confident in the value of their own expertise. While they continued to acknowledge the importance of legal precedents and forums, experience had led them to associate courts with antiquated legal categories and outmoded attitudes. As Breckenridge wrote in a 1934 social work text (and surely conveyed to her many students), the administration of the law had become so poor as to be a "travesty on those in distress."[24] Even juvenile courts were a disappointment. In the 1920s, social work leaders in the recently formed Children's Bureau and the Chicago School of Social Service Administration had eagerly tracked the performance of such courts, only to discover that judges privileged legal rules over social needs and favored mass institutionalization over individualized therapeutic treatment. "A judge can destroy in two minutes what a social worker has spent weeks in building up," one report lamented.[25] Social work educators responded by incorporating law into their curricula, ostensibly to facilitate cooperation with lawyers but also to identify the "defects" of judicial administration and devise ways around them.[26]

For their part, lawyers were not much concerned with social workers (which may have given the social workers even more cause for irritation). Lawyers, after all, had long been among the political elite and were accustomed to thinking of themselves as crucial players in America's democratic system. While some elite members of the profession took an interest in the field of social work, most lawyers were either unaware of social workers' presence or conscious only of their capacity for sloppy forays into legal analysis.[27]

It was significant, then, that lawyers and social workers came together as colleagues under the aegis of the Social Security Board. As loyal New Dealers and proud champions of modern public welfare administration, these particular lawyers and social workers wanted many of the same things and shared basic values. And yet it was not surprising when differences in perspective emerged.

THE MULTIPLE MEANINGS OF RIGHTS IN FEDERAL WELFARE ADMINISTRATION

As a discipline and a community, social work has never been either homogenous or harmonious. On some issues social workers from the Midwest, especially Chicago, differed from their eastern counterparts. Chicagoans Edith and Grace Abbott defended the public assistance titles of the Social Security Act when many other social workers mourned Congress's failure to enact a comprehensive welfare program.[28] The Abbotts and their colleagues also preached a more theoretical, policy-oriented form of social work education than the casework-oriented schools in the East. At other moments, a center/periphery divide arose between social workers in the Washington offices of FERA or the SSB and those out in the field. Similarly, administrators of public welfare agencies sometimes felt themselves to be a group apart from those in private agencies. An influential set of administrators split off from the National Conference of Social Work in 1930 for this very reason, forming the American Public Welfare Association. Around the same time, social workers on the bottom rungs of large social welfare bureaucracies made common cause with the broader labor movement and formed "rank and file" organizations.[29]

But among the (predominantly female) social workers at the BPA and those leading other major public welfare agencies, a particular viewpoint dominated. To borrow historian James Leiby's summary, they believed that the ideal expression of public welfare was not social insurance, which relied on earned benefits, but "the assertion of public responsibility, that is, community responsibility" for human need; the recognition "of aid as a democratic right available to citizens who needed it." The end goal, prominent social worker Dorothy Kahn explained in 1941, was "basic maintenance for everyone" – not as a reward for voting for the right party or living in the right place, but rather, as BPA director Jane Hoey put it in 1943, as a matter of "simple justice." It was no accident that Public Assistance Report No. 8, the BPA's popular training document on rights-based administrative practices (discussed in Chapter 2), bore the title *Common Human Needs.*[30]

Because social workers came to rights via needs, they often took care to distinguish rights from *laws*, which in their experience did not guarantee the full extent of what society owed its members.[31] *Common Human Needs* described rights as tied inextricably to human needs but moored only loosely to the letter of the law. Hoey's foreword to the report praised public assistance as a "government service based on human rights," not statutory rights.[32] And for the most part, author Charlotte Towle referred to existing statutes as halfway measures, which aspired toward but did not secure the rights at issue. (The report's opening pages called public assistance laws "the culmination of a democracy's conviction regarding its responsibility for human welfare," but this sentence was a concession to higher-ups in the federal bureaucracy, who had complained that the book lacked "any indication" that the law facilitated, rather than obstructed, constructive encounters between client and worker.) Towle's ideal law would guarantee not only the right "to survive" but also the right "to live in a fuller sense of the word."[33] Notably, BPA personnel criticized consultant Grace Marcus's nearly contemporaneous report for the agency, *The Nature of Service in Public Assistance Administration* (Public Assistance Report No. 10), for discussing assistance as a right without making explicit the "basic human right to maintenance" that was "unrelated to statutes." Marcus's report received only a half-hearted endorsement from the BPA and relatively narrow circulation.[34]

Social workers were also quick to comment when the rights that were guaranteed by law were not guaranteed in practice. "Is there a legal right to relief?" Edith Abbott asked in an article in 1938. (Along with Sophonisba Breckenridge, Abbott ran the Chicago School of Social Service Administration, from which many public welfare workers hailed; she had also helped draft the public assistance titles of the Social Security Act.) The laws providing for relief were "mandatory," so the poor person clearly had a "right" to the benefits laid out in the statute, Abbott wrote in answer to her own question, but no such law could truly be enforced if legislatures failed, as they often did, to provide the necessary funds.[35] Nor, Jane Hoey noted in 1939, could good, progressive laws achieve their goals if "communities . . . clung to older and more restrictive attitudes," as they often did with regard to Aid to Dependent Children.[36] Dorothy Kahn, a former public welfare worker and leader of the American Association of Social Workers, offered an even more pointed critique two years later, when rights language was becoming a staple of federal public assistance administration. "There is much glib talk today," she observed, "about relief and assistance as a 'right.'" Yet a "vast system" – "set up, or at least condone[d]" by social workers – stood in the way of the public assistance claimant. She urged her peers to consider how their own attitudes prevented the poor from exercising their rights.[37]

The lawyers who advised the BPA – most of whom were men with elite northeastern educations – had a different underlying message, even though their views matched the social workers' in many respects.[38] The lawyers readily conceded that the public assistance recipient's rights were ultimately founded in need: under the Social Security Act, need was the measure of the benefit owed.[39] They also shared the social workers' disappointment in the many jurisdictions that failed to treat public assistance payments as rights or public assistance recipients as rights holders. And like the social workers, the lawyers brandished the language of rights in their conflicts with state and local welfare workers. But at bottom the lawyers were less interested in meeting human need than they were in spreading the rule of law – that is, the idea that public welfare was governed by carefully constructed rules, which administrators were required to apply fairly, objectively, and consistently. To lawyers, this was the essence of the New Deal's promise of security. As General Counsel Jack Tate declared in 1946, New Deal public welfare programs would not achieve the goal of "promot[ing] security and independence" unless they were "established as part of the law of the land and ... governed by law."[40]

In some ways, this was a curious position: law's reputation had been much maligned in previous decades, and to some observers law was the New Deal's enemy. Early twentieth-century reformers famously characterized courts as obstructionist, legal doctrine as antiquated, and lawyers as the "hired guns" of "monopoly capitalists." This line of critique continued into the 1930s, as the Supreme Court struck down some of Congress's most prominent attempts to relieve economic distress and reform the economic system. Those whom historians have found invoking "the rule of law" during the 1930s, such as the American Bar Association's Special Committee on Administrative Law, were often anti–New Dealers, bent on revealing the dangers they saw as inherent in powerful independent agencies.[41]

But the world changed quickly in the late 1930s, in ways that caused the "rule of law" to take on a new valence. Antitotalitarianism, a force in American ideology and politics since the 1920s, grew more powerful as the term "totalitarianism" broadened to encompass both fascism and communism.⁴² Abiding anxieties about strong, visible, central-state governance also gained new vitality as President Roosevelt exerted strong executive leadership and New Deal programs touched broad swaths of the population. By 1937, the year of FDR's infamous court-packing plan, major newspapers were discussing the nation's totalitarian potential and Roosevelt's autocratic ambitions. In March 1938, the combination of stunning gains by totalitarian governments abroad and an executive branch reorganization at home prompted such concern that President Roosevelt felt compelled to issue – at one o'clock in the morning – a statement disavowing his interest in dictatorship. Entry into World War II only exacerbated the fears underlying Roosevelt's odd missive. Mass conscription, price regulation, and the creation of dozens of new agencies meant that almost all Americans felt the force of national government in new ways, and had reason to fear its future course.⁴³

Defenders of American government offered the rule of law – or, rather, a notion of this flexible concept – as an antidote to totalitarian impulses and a sign that the United States remained uninfected. In totalitarian regimes, these defenders noted, the despotic government purported to be governed by law but in fact reigned supreme, changing the law at will and ignoring individual prerogatives. In the United States, by contrast, the law alone was sovereign; only democratic processes could change it. Rule of law also called to mind those constitutional checks and guarantees that theoretically protected individuals and minorities from the government. Independent courts, fair judicial processes, and other legal mechanisms assured Americans that their growing state could never become Hitler's Third Reich or Stalin's Soviet Union.⁴⁴

Thus, rule of law, an idea that in 1935 seemed to be antithetical to the New Deal, had by 1941 become its very ethos, at least for the lawyers in the Office of the General Counsel. They could still be heard acknowledging the failings of legal *doctrine* – its "inadequa[te]" response to social facts, its "inept" analogies – but by the early 1940s, the lawyers were going out of their way to portray law, more generally, as the great friend and protector of the New Deal's subjects.⁴⁵ Law allowed poor Americans to come to the government as citizens rather than supplicants; law assured them that "the game had rules," rules that were rational and knowable; law guaranteed that administrative agencies would not become the monstrosities that even New Deal loyalists were coming to fear.⁴⁶ As Assistant GC A. D. Smith explained in a 1941 article in the *Social Service Review* (reprinting a speech he gave to the National Conference of Social Work), law reminded New Deal administrators of the individual rights at issue in even the grandest social program. Thanks to law, "accuracy of reasoning" was always required.[47]

Such statements demonstrate that when the lawyers working for the Social Security Board talked about rights, what they meant sometimes differed from what the social workers meant. Social workers sought to transform basic needs into generally accepted rights (what citizenship theorist T. H. Marshall famously labeled "social rights"). This, to them, was the promise of the New Deal, and a crucial function of the modern American state. They gratefully accepted the law's help but saw legal reform as only the beginning. To the extent that the lawyers wanted to engage in a similar bit of alchemy, their goal was to transform *gratuities* into legal rights. The former were discretionary payments that tended to empower private and locally situated givers; the latter were formal guarantees connecting poor citizens directly to the state. Even more important to them than substantive guarantees, however, was the recognition that poor people were the holders of process-oriented rights ("civil rights," in Marshall's schematic): the rights to fair and equal treatment at the hands of government officials.[48]

These differences were not always salient. Writing in 1939, Smith likened the era to the Christian holy day of Pentecost, when apostles infused with the same spirit spoke "divers tongues."[49] Sometimes, however, these "divers tongues" articulated diverse meanings, with significantly different implications.

THE RIGHT TO A FAIR HEARING: DISPARATE VIEWS

Such divergence was evident in the agency's approach to the Social Security Act's fair hearing requirement ("A State plan for [OAA, ADC, or AB] must... provide for granting to any individual, whose claim... is denied, an opportunity for a fair hearing before [the] State agency [charged with administering or supervising the program]").[50] The drafters of the act inserted this requirement in the hope, apparently, that it would both encourage local officials to adhere to state law, even in the face of popular resistance, and offer public assistance recipients protection against arbitrary and unfair administration.[51] But to the lawyers, the fair hearing provision became much more. It meant, explained A. D. Smith, that "for the first time in social programs," the individual could enter "the sacred administrative precincts" and discern "the whys and wherefores" of official decision making.[52] The poor individual now had "a right capable of adjudication" – even if that adjudication was not in a court of law, Smith continued.[53] In short, the lawyers displayed nothing less than "missionary zeal" on behalf of the fair hearing requirement.[54] The social workers in the agency were less impressed, going so far as to suggest that the fair hearing guarantee was entirely disposable.

That difference of opinion became apparent early – in the spring of 1936 – when the SSB heard rumblings about abolishing or modifying the fair hearing requirement.[55] By this time, the board had issued no regulations on the subject but had signaled to individual states that the fair hearing requirement was no dead letter. Mississippi's lack of a fair hearing provision provoked board comment in December 1935, and inadequate fair hearing provisions were among the board's reasons for rejecting plan submissions from Colorado, Illinois, and California in the spring of 1936.[56] Complaints followed from state and local politicians. Professional state welfare administrators and others with social work backgrounds also protested. Whether because of their experience with juvenile courts, their knowledge of judicial obstruction of progressive reform, or their confidence in their own expertise, social workers were concerned about the "legalism" that fair hearings threatened to bring to the public assistance program. They believed a grievance should be adjusted at the ground level, among parties familiar with the client's situation.[57] Some social workers also suspected, drawing on psychoanalytic theory, that people contested the denial of their applications simply because their situations made them emotionally unbalanced and inclined to nurse grievances. Accordingly, administrators in the BPA suggested an amendment to the act that would substitute "fair review" for the term "fair hearing."[58]

Strong arguments from the agency's lawyers, against the backdrop of a hostile Supreme Court, appear to have prevented the change. The opportunity for a fair hearing was not simply a statutory requirement but a "constitutional" one, insisted then–Assistant GC Jack Tate (he would serve as general counsel from 1937 to 1939 and again from 1940 to 1947). Congress could eliminate all references to hearing or review, he argued, and the courts would still read such a provision into the act, so as to ensure that administrative agencies provided "due process" to public assistance claimants. Showing his roots – Tate graduated from Yale Law School around the time it was becoming a hub for legal realism – he buttressed this constitutional argument with more normative ones. Fair hearings provided not only a safeguard against administrative abuses, Tate explained, but also a mechanism for surveillance and supervision. Through fair hearings, states could see and correct the decisions of local administrators, and through the records of such hearings, the federal government could better determine whether states were complying with their public assistance plans. In other words, fair hearings were both a legal guarantee and a basic feature of sound, socially progressive public administration.[59]

The lawyers' victory was a small one, for although board members appreciated the danger of the Supreme Court, they were less impressed by the innate virtues of legal process. Administrators from the social work tradition, meanwhile, continued to urge the board not to allow fussy, formal procedures to stand in the way of good social work practice. Receiving conflicting advice from its advisors, the board moved slowly. Although states began receiving federal grants in February 1936, the SSB waited until September to offer any guidance on fair hearings to its field staff or to state administrators. And the guidance it ultimately issued was neither strong nor clear.[60]

The result was "wild confusion" out in the states and a wide range of fair hearing practices.[61] Public assistance recipients in Missouri took advantage of the fair hearing opportunity immediately: in 1936, when elderly residents learned that a twelve-dollar cap had been placed on monthly Old Age Assistance grants (state law allowed up to thirty dollars per month), a single county sent the state agency thirty-four appeals. Hearing requests fell to only four in 1937, but the following year, when the state agency mandated that OAA be denied to persons whose relatives had the means to support them, disgruntled applicants filed more than a thousand requests.[62] Filings did not necessary lead to actual hearings, however. The BPA field staff found that Illinois received seven hundred appeals between July 1936 and January 1937 (apparently the result of an organized pension movement) but the state had established only a "tentative" appeal procedure, and no one had ever succeeded in using it.[63] A similar situation existed in Colorado: seven hundred requests for hearings within the first year or so; only ten hearings actually held.[64] In other states, meanwhile, the hearing provision had little discernible impact. Connecticut, for example, recorded only seventeen fair hearings (all in its OAA program) between April 1936 and May 1938.[65]

No one was systematically keeping track of these numbers, but it was clear that most state agencies had no idea what to make of the fair hearing provisions that federal administrators had foisted upon them.[66] According to a 1941 social work masters thesis, many states established hearings machinery "with no conviction and little enthusiasm"; compliance with the federal requirement was "a chore," to be done with minimal expenditures of time, effort, and expense.[67] The BPA reported similar findings. State agencies considered the fair hearing procedure costly and confusing, observed the BPA in October 1937; they preferred to treat appeals as mere "complaints" and make informal redress.[68] Some states, including Oklahoma, simply neglected to inform claimants that they had a right to a fair hearing, lest hearings become "overly prominent."[69] Many states (a 1940 study counted twenty-eight) attempted to achieve similar ends by adding an extra layer of process: a prehearing "adjustment." Only when such adjustment failed could the appellant proceed to a formal hearing.[70]

Anecdotes from the local level confirm these findings. In 1939, the executive director of New York's department of social welfare boasted that the department exhausted all other avenues before providing a hearing, a procedure "so successful" that the department received only five hearing requests in 1938 and 1939 combined.[71] The same director tallied only six requests in 1940, three of which could be attributed to the client's "psychotic attitude."[72] Pierce Atwater, a social welfare administrator and professor in Saint Paul, urged a similar approach: quickly adjust legitimate complaints, he urged administrators, lest the client garner sympathy with the public; if a case becomes "celebrated," turn the spotlight on the complainant and make him defend himself; last, take comfort in knowing that the public was fast becoming "less naïve" about the attention-seeking efforts of the "psychopathic complainant."[73]

The lawyers in the Office of the GC were deeply disturbed by such accounts (which came to them via the agency's regional personnel), but they could do little more than beg – as Assistant GC A. D. Smith often did of BPA director Jane Hoey. Smith understood the bureau's decision to approve underdeveloped state fair hearing procedures, Smith wrote to her in 1939. After all, the federal agency often accepted imperfect plans, with the understanding that federal personnel would guide states toward more appropriate policies over time.[74] But in some states, Smith wrote, "the actuality" was now *worse* than the plan." In addition to the state agencies that attempted to avoid the fair hearing process altogether, there were places where lack of trained personnel prevented any meaningful hearings from taking place, and others where hearings occurred but had no bearing on the agency's ultimate decision. Elsewhere, state agencies failed to follow the most rudimentary legal procedures, such as keeping records and allowing inspection of evidence. Naturally, courts had started to second-guess administrative decision making, Smith continued (hoping to strike a nerve), and more judicial oversight could only bode ill for the BPA's goals. Smith pleaded with Hoey to produce a stronger, more specific directive on fair hearings.[75] Never one to be pushed around, Hoey did nothing. Only months later did Smith procure what he wanted, and only after his office went over Hoey's head to the agency's executive director, Oscar Powell (himself an attorney).[76]

By January 1941, the states at last received a new statement on "the basic principles of fair hearing" – cast now as "mandatory."[77] But monitoring compliance with these principles was the job of the BPA, and its leadership expressed little interest. Stymied again, the lawyers asked the BPA to simply provide *them* with the data – in particular, with copies of fair hearing decisions. Hoey's right-hand woman, Kathryn Goodwin, shot down the request. She noted that the BPA's administrative surveys unit conducted regular evaluations of all aspects of state administration, and the lawyers could consult those if they wished. She also reminded Smith that it was against federal policy to interfere in individual claims. The lawyers cared nothing for "whether John Jones recovered $50," Smith assured Goodwin. He was merely seeking to review the cases that might vindicate – or fail to vindicate – the federal view.[78] (In fact, he had a broader agenda. As he explained to his fellow attorneys, the GC's office hoped to use these decisions to cultivate sound and valuable precedents – a carefully curated common law of public assistance. Like "florist[s] and garden experts," Smith explained, they would "[pick] and disseminat[e] the best," "develop[ing] better species all the time."[79]) Goodwin remained unimpressed, and Smith was left to wonder how he and his colleagues in the BPA had, as he put it, such different commitments to "the growth of rights of a social character."[80]

Ultimately, the lawyers did get some of what they wanted. After Smith raved to Hoey about how "illuminating" he found a survey of fair hearings in Iowa, the BPA agreed to solicit *voluntary* reports from states.[81] More information about what was actually happening out in the states was always better than less, they could agree. But overall, the episode illustrates incongruous perspectives. Lawyers and social workers were both attempting to import rights concepts into the realms of state and local welfare administration. Yet, beyond agreeing that this paradigm rejected the old poor law, they had different understandings of what a rights-based public welfare system looked like. Heading into the 1940s, the lawyers appeared most concerned with giving public assistance benefits the accoutrements of a *legal* right, including especially legal process. The social workers wanted concrete financial commitments – they

actually *did* care whether John Jones received his fifty dollars – and they
resisted the necessary joinder of rights with law.

A MEANINGFUL RIGHT: THE SOCIAL WORKERS' CRUSADE
FOR ADEQUACY AND EDUCATION

By the mid-1940s, after several years of hearing rights talk from the
federal agency, public welfare directors and social work leaders had
begun to echo Dorothy Kahn: If people in need really had a right to
assistance, Kahn asked, then why were they getting so little?[82] Of those
in need, even the most traditionally "deserving" often found that the
"right to assistance" provided a "sub-minimum" standard of living.[83]

Such results flowed in part from the language of the original Social
Security Act, which used a system of matching payments to "enabl[e] each
State to furnish financial assistance, *as far as practicable under the conditions in such State.*"[84] State legislatures decided what was practicable, and
appropriations often did not allow for payments that covered recipients'
basic requirements. In October 1942, when assistance rolls were in fact
declining (presumably allowing for more generous payments), an OAA
recipient in the lowest paying state (Mississippi) received an average of
$9.04 per month ($131.29 in 2014 dollars) with which to purchase food,
shelter, and other necessities of life; a family receiving Aid to Dependent
Children in the lowest-paying state (Texas) received little more, a mere
$10.67 per month. Wartime inflation only exacerbated the problem: as
prices rose, benefit levels did not keep pace.[85] Alert to this reality, social
workers in the BPA continued to boast of the great progress that had been
made since 1935 but also pursued strategies for making the right to
assistance truly meaningful.

High on their agenda was legislative reform: if existing laws did not
support basic human rights, the law should be changed. The impulse fit a
time in U.S. history when millions of citizens were risking their lives for
such rights and when policymakers were crafting ambitious, optimistic
plans for the postwar world.[86] Even before the bombing of Pearl Harbor,
in fact, President Roosevelt's National Resources Planning Board (NRPB)
had expanded on his famous "Four Freedoms" to announce a "new Bill of
Rights" – one that the NRPB proposed to make "real and effective"
through a series of concrete recommendations for legislative and executive
action.[87] It was also an era in which federal agencies "domina[ted] ...
congressional drafting and deliberations" to a degree that would have
been unfathomable just a few decades earlier.[88] That era was quickly

drawing to a close, thanks to bipartisan concerns about Congress's loss of authority. But at least until 1946, when Congress passed the Legislative Reorganization Act, federal administrators had reason to be optimistic about embedding their own preferences in national legislation.[89]

In 1943 and 1945, the leadership of the BPA eagerly supported the Wagner-Murray-Dingell bills, which promised to vindicate at least two items from the NRPB's agenda: "the right to adequate food, clothing, shelter, and medical care" and "the right to security, with freedom from fear of old age, want, dependency, sickness, unemployment, and accident." The bills were most notable, and most controversial, for proposing national health insurance, but they also would have significantly changed the world of poor relief, by replacing the existing categorical public assistance programs (Aid to Dependent Children, Aid to the Blind, Old Age Assistance) with a single, noncategorical income support program. (In other words, the bills proposed to bring federal money and federal standards to the state- and locally dominated realm of "general relief.") Individual payment amounts would necessarily be more adequate under these bills, the drafters believed, because the federal government would be both the source of funds and the administrator, thereby circumventing state-level pressures to keep benefits low.[90]

After these bills failed – victims of conservative gains in Congress, the shifting alliances of southern Democrats, and unflagging opposition from the American Medical Association – government social workers advocated legal reforms that would expand existing programs, ADC being their main concern.[91] (The OAA and Aid to the Blind programs were generous by comparison and were not ripe for expansion; OAA, in fact, appeared likely to shrink, as Congress continued expanding the Old Age and Survivors Insurance program.) The 1946 amendments to the Social Security Act – drafted by the agency – raised the ceiling on matchable payment amounts from $18 for one child in a family to $24, and from $12 for each additional child to $15. States that wanted to offer more generous ADC benefits now had an added incentive, and states that had been paying more than the previous maximum matchable amount were encouraged to continue. A change in the matching formula pushed in the same direction: under the terms of the 1946 amendments, the federal government promised to pay two-thirds of the first $9 of the average monthly ADC benefit; the remainder (up to the federal maximum) would be matched at the previous one-half rate. This was a boon to the poorest states (which also tended to award the most meager benefits) – a recognition of the fact that when they spent a dollar of their own money, it hurt more than when a richer state did the same.[92] Combining these two changes, the maximum federal contribution per month increased by 50 percent, from $9 for the first child and $6 for each additional child to $13.50 and $9, respectively (i.e., from $15 to $22.50 for a family with two children). The Republican-controlled Eightieth Congress enacted similar changes in 1948, raising the maximum federal contribution per month to $16.50 for the first child and $12 for each additional child (i.e., to $28.50 for a family with two children).[93]

Monetary incentives had never been enough, however, as the BPA well knew. In 1947, at one of the staff meetings on the topic of the right to public assistance, BPA staff member Vocille Pratt called attention to a case in which an eleven-year-old ADC recipient "was found to be suffering from active tuberculosis and rheumatic heart disease" – a full eight years after her state had purportedly committed to meeting her needs. A year after the 1946 amendments, the child's state still capped ADC payments at fourteen dollars per month for the first child (about $149 per month, or $4.80 per day, in 2014 dollars).[94] What did the right to assistance mean in this context?

Such questions led the BPA to seek expansion of the ADC program through administrative measures as well as legislative reforms. In 1944, via State Letter 43 (state letters were the most formal type of guidance document that the BPA issued, prior to the creation of the *Handbook of Public Assistance* in 1946), the BPA informed state welfare agencies that the federal government would now match payments made to unborn children – a significant reinterpretation of the phrase "dependent child." The same state letter encouraged states to eliminate requirements that prevented children from receiving timely aid, such as some states' requirement that the caretaker first pursue legal action against an absent father, or the policy that no aid should flow until after a demonstrated period of continued parental absence. State Letter 46, issued three months later, urged states to eliminate all eligibility restrictions that were based on the "suitability" of the applicant's home or "fitness" of the caretaker. Subsequent BPA communications encouraged state agencies to strengthen their commitment to adequate payments and to demand sufficient appropriations from state legislatures.[95]

All the while, the BPA continued to focus on community education and interpretation. "We [in the Bureau] have come to the same conclusion as the man in the street," Jane Hoey wrote to her regional directors in 1946: "The right [to assistance] is a right that has little meaning unless the needy individual secures the amount of money that the law establishes he is entitled to."[96]

A lawyer reading this statement might jump immediately to legal solutions, but the BPA stressed attitudinal changes at the ground level. In the words of one of the era's most prominent social work educators, the "enforceable legal right to assistance" was "not the point"; the community's *perception* of a right was what got results.[97] Heading into the second half of the 1940s, the BPA dedicated significant energy to affecting that perception. After circulating five thousand copies of its text *Common Human Needs* (1945), which described public assistance as a "program based on right," the BPA commissioned two more printings. These were distributed to state and local welfare workers, as well as to schools of social work education. BPA representatives followed up with state agencies in person, to divine how they were approaching the subject of rights in staff development programs. The goal, explained the chief of the BPA's Technical Training Division in 1947, was a staff that was not only "familiar with and in accord with the agency's philosophy, policies and procedures," but also "competent in the use of agency machinery to make rights real."[98]

THE PROCEDURAL TURN: FAIR HEARINGS AS DUE PROCESS

Agency lawyers did not oppose social workers' education- and adequacy-oriented efforts to vindicate the right to assistance, but at bottom they had a different understanding of the value and significance of rights. Yes, rights brought material benefits, but the claimant derived just as much or more, A. D. Smith argued, from the *legal process* that came with the rights. The mere fact that a claimant could "execute" his rights (that is, turn them into authoritative legal judgments) demonstrated that he was not a "ward" of the state, but a "free citizen."[99] Translated into day-to-day bureaucratic activities, this meant that the lawyers continued to grumble about the BPA's lack of enthusiasm for their fair hearing project.[100]

Much to the lawyers' delight, however, the winds outside the agency were shifting in their favor. As historian Edward Purcell has explained, the rise of totalitarianism abroad led to a crisis among America's intellectuals. In previous decades, many had embraced a worldview that privileged social scientific research and particularized observations of human behavior ("scientific naturalism"; in law, legal realism). They believed that this type of knowledge, not higher law or timeless ethical principles, ought to dictate policy choices and legal contests. The rise of European dictator-ships in the 1930s, along with mounting evidence of the dysfunction of American democracy, made this position uncomfortable. During the war, those who embraced scientific naturalism faced charges of nihilism, moral relativism, and the destruction of American civilization. The critics did not win the day, however. Intellectuals coalesced around a theory of democ-racy that was "broadly naturalistic and relativistic" while also celebrating the American way. With brilliant sleight of hand, they cast moral cer-tainty, which they cleverly labeled "philosophical absolutism," as the handmaiden of political absolutism; they championed relativism (rephrased as open-mindedness) as a hallmark of a free and democratic society.[101]

A consequence of this shift was a growing devotion to legal and political process. Americans, according to this theory of democracy, did not always agree on substantive values, but they agreed to settle their disputes via a time-tested set of procedures, which were "characterized by openness, negotiation, accommodation, and compromise." The natural result of this common commitment, theorists argued, was that the deci-sions reached were generally respected; government officials did not have to – did not even *think* to – enforce their will with an iron fist.[102]

The administrators in the upper echelons of the federal social welfare bureaucracy were attuned to these developments. They had trained under leading intellectuals, and through their academic publications and con-ference papers, they actively participated in the ideological shifts that Purcell identifies. As federal administrators, they were also implicated in one of the most visible manifestations of the procedural turn: the move-ment through Congress, starting in 1939 and culminating in 1946, of a comprehensive administrative procedure bill. The bill originated with the American Bar Association (ABA) and the 1938 report of its Special Committee on Administrative Law. Authored by Roscoe Pound – once a famous critic of legal formalism, but now an equally sharp critic of the world built on its ashes – the report denounced the "administrative absolutism" of the New Deal agencies and called for stringent legislative and judicial oversight. Had the report emerged in 1933, when the ABA assembled the archconservative committee, it likely would have died a quiet death. By the late 1930s, however, totalitarian advances, adminis-trative inefficiencies, and Roosevelt's vastly increased presidential power had created a more favorable climate. In 1940, congressional Republicans managed to pass legislation based on Pound's proposals (the Walter-Logan Bill), by tapping into some New Dealers' now greater appreciation for "democratic processes." Roosevelt promptly exercised his veto, but astute observers – including Roosevelt himself – knew that a process-oriented "reining in" of the administrative state was only a matter of time. Procedure, historian Joanna Grisinger explains, had become *the* means for parties to "talk about bureaucracy" and, by extension, crucial terrain on which to attack and defend the substance of the New Deal.[103]

Logically, then, the mid-1940s were ripe for the lawyers to raise the volume of their requests for legal procedure and add rhetorical flourish. "The test of a free society," A. D. Smith declared in a 1946 issue of the *Social Security Bulletin*, "will be found in the scope of right and privilege possessed by its weakest elements – those who are under the greatest pressure to surrender their independence." Subjecting the United States to that test, Smith proclaimed deep disappointment. Not only did this leading democracy continue to treat public assistance as a "gratuity," contingent on good behavior or other "irrelevances," Smith wrote, but it had allowed the entire "welfare field" to remain largely cut off from law and legal interpretation. (Smith, of course, revered the Social Security Act, but noted its impotence in the face of "traditional attitudes and conceptions.") The answer, he maintained, was to double down on the nation's commitment to "procedure and principle" – to his understanding of the "rule of law."[104] Smith made the same point negatively: invoking economist and philosopher Friedrich Hayek, whose antistatist, anti-"planning" ruminations had by then achieved wide distribution in the United States, Smith warned that the downfall of a great society could come from a failure to recognize and safeguard individual rights.[105] Smith was in truth well to the left of Hayek (for one, Smith "always felt that government did very good work," his son recalled). Nonetheless, he was not above admonishing his peers in public welfare administration that "the search for security without legal rights" would lead directly to the sort of "serfdom" that Hayek foretold.[106]

The same intellectual, political, and cultural currents that prompted Smith to slather his writings with antitotalitarian, prodemocratic rhetoric led BPA officials to soften toward the lawyers' fair hearing project. The head of the BPA's Special Standards Section, in a statement she drafted for state agencies in 1945, described fair hearings as tightly bound up with the concept of "assistance as a right"; she further linked them to the "right to democratic process" and "the maintenance of democratic government."[107] Similarly, staff members in the BPA's Plans and Grants Section conceded that local workers needed a "wider understanding" of the fair hearing provision, which they agreed was an essential safeguard of the right to assistance.[108] BPA director Jane Hoey, too, seemed to develop a new appreciation for legal process around 1945, boasting to social work educator Edith Abbott of the "great deal of work" that the BPA had done in the fair hearing area over the previous two years.[109]

This is not to say that administrators at the state and local level suddenly embraced the idea of fair hearings. Reports indicated that some state agencies continued to fend off hearing requests through discouragement and delay; others performed "sham" hearings; still others dutifully applied federal directives but bungled (in the federal view) the required procedures.[110] Nor did all federal administrators fall immediately into line. In February 1945, BPA staffers complained that the lawyers were "reduc[ing] in significance" the right to assistance by associating it so closely with hearings.[111] Likewise, in November 1945 the lawyers protested a draft of the BPA's handbook that described the fair hearing standards as a "recommendation" rather than a "requirement." (They demanded a rewrite.)[112] Meanwhile, some lawyers turned their noses up at BPA gestures of cooperation. Having these social workers explain fair hearings to state agencies was like "us[ing] persons unskilled in chemistry to set up a 'carbon cracking' plant," sniffed one regional attorney in 1944.[113]

Despite the squabbling, a shift was discernible by the end of 1946. Whether because of the lingering shadow of totalitarian government, the enactment of the Administrative Procedure Act, or the many other demonstrations of the nation's ostensible commitment to process, the BPA leadership moved a long way toward the lawyers' position. By year's end, BPA staffers were eagerly revising the fair hearing standards in recognition of the developmental lag in this area.[114] They continued to characterize hearings as "informal" proceedings, but in a nod to the lawyers, their new draft standards emphasized that constitutional due process was at issue.[115]

The BPA also moved forward with a plan to publish annotated fair hearing decisions – another lawyerly scheme that the bureau had previously thwarted. As Jane Hoey explained to her regional directors in October 1946, these decisions would not only dispel state and local "misapprehension[s]" about the process but would also show how hearings "safeguard[ed]" claimants' exercise of all their other rights.[116] Editorial comments in one edition of the decisions affirmed "the value of the hearing process in protecting the rights of applicants and recipients."[117] Comments in another noted that hearings were "part and parcel of orderly, responsible administration of a public program in a democracy."[118] Yet another edition drew the conclusion that hearings served both the individual claimant and "the nation-wide program," by clarifying its foundational commitment to due process.[119] The right to assistance and the right to fair process, these annotations implied, were inextricably connected.

A. D. Smith and the other attorneys were surely behind some of these celebratory remarks, but by the late 1940s the fair hearing provision had true devotees among the social workers. Bernard Scholz of the BPA's Division of Standards and Program Development published a glowing tribute to fair hearings in a 1949 issue of the *Social Security Bulletin*, describing them as a "fundamental democratic safeguard" and "the touchstone of the whole [public assistance] program." Scholz, who had previously worked in state welfare programs in Pennsylvania, Iowa, Illinois, and Maryland, lauded the states that embraced hearings, for by doing so they signaled their acceptance of claimants' legal rights.[120] The BPA leadership, while never conceding that the lawyers were the natural or appropriate interpreters of the fair hearing provision, seconded Scholz's claims.[121] Top BPA administrators were "anxious to get [his article] into print as soon as possible," so as to broadcast the bureau's views to state and local public assistance staffs.[122]

THE EQUAL PROTECTION PRINCIPLE: TOWARD UNIFORMITY AND EQUAL TREATMENT

A second change that affected the agency's priorities over the course of the 1940s was a growing national interest in, and anxiety about, equal treatment. Like due process, the notion of equal protection was a key component of the lawyers' vision of sound, modern governance. And it was somewhat in tension with the social workers' vision. Social work, after all, was based largely on individualized assessment – on diagnosing clients' problems and developing tailored solutions. Any requirement of uniform treatment was potentially problematic.

By the mid-1940s, however, there was no denying the appeal of the equal protection principle or the power of its advocates. As the Roosevelt administration edged closer to entry into World War II, influential African Americans, backed by a potent black press, had resolved to pursue a "double victory" – against fascism abroad and racism at home. In 1941 A. Philip Randolph famously threatened to summon a hundred thousand black Americans to march on Washington for "a massive display of internal dissent," at a time when the president required national unity.

Roosevelt was sufficiently concerned to issue the antidiscrimination mandate that Randolph demanded (Executive Order 8022, forbidding racial discrimination by defense contractors). Occurrences that Randolph never would have wished for kept racial inequality in the headlines: the 1942 shootings of seven black soldiers at Fort Dix, New Jersey, after a dispute over their use of an off-base pay phone; the 1943 "zoot suit riots" in Los Angeles, during which mobs of white soldiers and sailors attacked young black and Latino males; and the black insurrection that broke out in Harlem after residents heard that the police had killed a black veteran. To borrow the apt summary of historian Thomas Sugrue, "wartime America was boiling with racial conflict," and central to this conflict was the promise, as yet unrealized, of equality.[123]

After the war ended, the focus on equality intensified. Black Americans demanded equal rights, galvanized by the assurances made to them during the war and outraged by the discrimination they continued to encounter. Postwar confrontations with totalitarianism, now embodied by an aggressive and rapacious Soviet Union, shone an even brighter light on the nation's commitment to equality. Believing that vulnerable nations hung in the balance and that Soviet propagandists were eager to capitalize on any misstep, federal officials could not afford to appear complacent about racial inequality.[124] In December 1946, following a wave of racial violence in the South, President Harry Truman appointed what would become a historic Committee on Civil Rights. The committee's widely circulated report, titled *To Secure These Rights*, declared "essential" not only the right to safety and security of the person, but also the right to equality of opportunity.[125] In contemporaneous appearances, Truman reinforced his commitment to equality. In June 1947, he became the first president to give a live address to a meeting of the National Association for the Advancement of Colored People (NAACP). Standing on the steps of the Lincoln Memorial, he asserted that there was "no justifiable reason for discrimination because of ancestry, or religion, or race, or color" and assured his national audience that the government would vigilantly defend his position.[126] Not long after, Truman ordered the establishment of a permanent Fair Employment Practices Commission and the desegregation of the military. Less public actions suggested a shallower commitment to black Americans, but there is no doubt that these highly visible gestures and pronouncements helped cement equality as a postwar American value.[127]

The Supreme Court, too, was demonstrating a new enthusiasm for equal treatment. In 1944, just eleven years after rejecting a challenge to an all-white primary, the Supreme Court ruled eight to one that such primaries violated the Constitution.[128] In 1948, the Court took another bold step, holding that the Fourteenth Amendment protected individuals against even private discrimination, should that discrimination depend on the courts for enforcement. The ruling directly addressed racially restrictive covenants, a crucial tool in the battle to "defend" all-white neighborhoods, but also called into question other Jim Crow practices.[129] Additional decisions from the period struck down, on equal protection grounds, practices that states used for selecting juries, admitting students to law school, and licensing the use of state resources. The Court hesitated only where claims of racial discrimination intersected with concerns of national security (as in the infamous *Korematsu* decision).[130]

The strong pronouncements coming from the executive and judicial branches vindicated arguments that federal agency lawyers had long been making, for if due process was a favorite topic among the lawyers in the 1940s, equal protection was of similar concern. Just as they saw the Social Security Act's fair hearing provision as an expression of constitutional due process, they saw in the act's references to statewide uniformity ("A State plan must ... be in effect in all political subdivisions of the State") an incorporation of the constitutional right to "equal protection of the laws." "Implicit" in this provision, Smith attempted to convince the BPA in 1940, was the notion that "uniform[]" and "equitabl[e]" assistance was "a matter of individual right." (The use of the word "equitable" seems to have been a gesture of good will toward social workers. Equitable decision making, after all, was fully compatible with casework. In other writings aimed at different audiences, Smith used the words "equal" and "equality.")[131]

Smith's statutory interpretation was a stretch – the drafters appeared to be concerned with statewide *participation* in public assistance programs (that is, no local holdouts), not equality as such – but Smith nonetheless urged BPA officials to spread his view in the states. In other writings from the early 1940s, such as a 1941 article in the *Social Service Review*, Smith highlighted the "equal-protection-of-the-law" questions that routinely emerged in welfare administration. Could a state exclude a person on account of time already spent on the relief rolls? Or because the person's parents were aliens? Could a state exclude Indians? Since these were all instances in which an agency treated one category of persons differently from others, they all called for equal protection analysis.[132]

The lawyers' references to equal protection grew more frequent over time, and their tone more forceful. During the war years, they insisted that dedication to the equal protection principle is what made the nation great. Unfortunately, Americans were not living up to their commitments; unfairness and irrationality pervaded public assistance. In his 1946 speech to the field staff, General Counsel Jack Tate complained about state laws that excluded children from ADC because of parental desertion, or because the children lived with a relative of a different religious faith, or because they were not "legitimate." The wrong went beyond penalizing innocent children, Tate said. He criticized all those laws and practices that treated one individual worse than another because of behavior, or living conditions, or some other "irrelevant" factor.[133] These were "of course plainly unconstitutional," Tate opined.[134]

At first glance, this argument would seem to mirror those that poverty lawyers advanced in federal court two decades later. Indeed, Tate referred to some of the very practices ("suitable home" laws, moralistic behavior requirements) that welfare rights organizations would target for judicial evisceration. But Tate and his colleagues had little confidence in the judiciary. As Tate conceded in his 1946 speech, "no close legal precedents" supported his views, and none would likely be forthcoming. Historically, courts had not given searching consideration to matters "described as charitable or eleemosynary," and although the legal landscape was changing fast, Tate believed that it was up to administrators, not judges, to vindicate poor Americans' right to equal treatment.[135]

Over time, the other top administrators in the agency came around to the same view. In September 1946, BPA director Jane Hoey and Social Security Commissioner Arthur Altmeyer explicitly recognized the Social Security Act's inclusion of an "equal treatment" mandate, a development that the lawyers considered "significant and gratifying."[136] Thereafter, the agency pursued two new initiatives: (1) a press for uniform statewide standards of need (that is, intrastate equality of treatment, at least when it came to assessing poor people's basic requirements), and (2) a legislation-oriented campaign for greater recognition of the equal treatment principle. Behind the scenes, meanwhile, the lawyers continued to use their understanding of the Equal Protection Clause to evaluate states' compliance with federal law (a phenomenon discussed more fully in Chapter 6).[137]

The push for statewide uniformity stemmed entirely from administrative convictions, not legislative will. Nonetheless, in conversations with state officials, federal administrators cited the 1946 amendments to the Social Security Act as a basis for their actions. (As noted, those amendments increased the federal share of the cost of public assistance, enabling states to be more generous.) According to Arthur Altmeyer, the amendments embodied a desire "to reduce the disparity in assistance granted between recipients within a State so that recipients in equal need [would be] treated equally" – at least that is how he explained the new law to a meeting of state welfare commissioners in the fall of 1946. In the short term, the federal agency asked state agencies to "evaluate the extent to which State-wide standards of assistance are now in effect in your State."[138] In the longer term, federal administrators confronted states with a new requirement: to keep their plans in conformity with the Social Security Act and continue receiving federal funds, each state now had to provide what had previously been only recommended: a clear statement – applicable throughout the state – about what its citizens needed (that is, budgets that set forth essential items and their cost), as well as uniform procedures for determining whether an individual applicant was in need.[139]

Around the same time, the BPA and the GC's office announced "a new attempt" to protect recipients' rights, this time by attaching federal funding to the states' incorporation of "the overall principle of equality of treatment and equal protection" in their public assistance laws. The campaign began at the state level. "Wherever appropriate," Jane Hoey directed her regional directors, they were to recommend to state officials ways to strengthen "statutory provisions affecting the right to assistance and equitable treatment of individuals." (Note again, however, the use of "equitable" rather than "equal.") A. D. Smith issued similar calls to his regional attorneys, reminding them that when they encountered state public assistance litigation they should "miss no opportunity" to characterize social programs as creators of "legal rights" to which "the usual legal guarantees of due process and equal protection" applied.[140]

Many state legislatures, of course, did not want to build enforceable guarantees of equal treatment into their public assistance laws, lest they disrupt long-established social hierarchies and undermine the local economies that relied on those hierarchies. Thus the lawyers went a step further in early 1948, recommending an amendment to the Social Security Act that would explicitly reference the constitutional guarantee of equal protection; states that refused to abide by this guarantee would be deemed out of conformity with the act and ineligible for federal funds. (This was hardly a pie-in-the-sky idea: only months before, Truman's Committee on Civil Rights had explicitly recommended that Congress condition "all federal grants-in-aid and other forms of assistance" on the absence of discrimination and segregation.) Predictably, the proposal began with A. D. Smith, who raised the idea at that year's meeting of the agency's regional attorneys. But General Counsel Alanson Willcox (a longtime lawyer for the Social Security Board and now Jack Tate's successor) was so enthused that he passed it on to administrators at the very top of the federal social welfare bureaucracy, whom he knew were concerned about the appearance of discrimination in the federal programs. (The 1939 reorganization of federal agencies had placed the Social Security Board under the jurisdiction of a new umbrella entity, the Federal Security Agency, and inserted another level of authority between Social Security leadership and the president.)[141]

Because public assistance benefits were "so widely conceived as 'gratuities,'" Willcox explained to these senior officials, "[t]he too common thought is that the State may give to one and withhold from another in its unfettered discretion" – a practice that violated the nation's "democratic pledge of equality." Smith's proposal promised to remedy the problem, without imposing "any bureaucratic controls." It simply withheld grants until State laws guaranteed their commitment to equal protection; should states subsequently violate their pledge, Smith envisioned a judicial resolution, rather than an administrative one.[142] Willcox made progress: within a year, a similar provision appeared before Congress as part of the Social Security Administration's proposed revision of the Social Security Act.[143]

The provision did not become law. In retrospect, it is clear that the agency's proposal was caught in a larger power struggle: one between bureaucrats, who "had become the primary makers of law and policy in the modern state," and Congress, which in the mid-1940s had started to reclaim its authority.[144] At the time, however, it appeared that agency lawyers had not "fully or properly briefed" Social Security Commissioner Altmeyer on the provision's "real significance," leaving him to blunder before the House Ways and Means Committee. The committee also apparently had reservations about involving the federal courts. When offered a substitute provision designating judicial review of fair hearings as the mechanism for protecting claimants' rights to due process and equal protection, the committee rejected it out of concern for the "multitude of [court] suits" that might follow.[145] Given some of the Supreme Court's recent civil rights decisions, members of the southerner-dominated committee had reason to fear the sort of judicial precedents that might result.[146] Still, the proposal itself was suggestive: offered to Congress as an official recommendation of the Social Security Administration, it shows the increasingly good fit between a lawyerly interpretation of the right to public assistance and the broader political milieu.

THE DANGERS OF "SOCIALIZED" RIGHTS

Support for the lawyers' interpretation of rights in public assistance did not have to mean a dwindling of support for the social workers' interpretation. Indeed, the same antitotalitarian impulses that buttressed lawyerly calls for due process and equal protection could support the social workers' goals. As Jane Hoey wrote in 1941, "the only convincing answer to the tenets and attainments of totalitarianism" was for democratic government to provide the same material benefits and a better way of life. Social rights, in other words, were a "defense program."[147] By the late 1940s, the social workers could also claim to have the international community on their side. Article 22 of the Universal Declaration of Human Rights, adopted by the United Nations General Assembly at the end of 1948, declared that every person – "as a member of society" (not citizen of a nation) – had the right to social security and was entitled to realize "the economic, social and cultural rights indispensable for his dignity and the free development of his personality." Article 25 went further, stating that every person had "the right to a standard of living adequate for the health and well-being of himself and of his family, including food, clothing, housing and medical care and necessary social services."[148]

Domestically, however, this brand of rights language encountered increasing opposition, for as much as the postwar period was a time of liberal imagination and hope, it was also a time of conservative resurgence, anticommunist fervor, and hostility toward empowered women. On March 21, 1947, shortly after announcing the confrontational foreign policy doctrine associated with his name, President Truman ordered the creation of a loyalty program for federal employees. Many public and private employers followed suit. That same year, Congress overrode Truman's veto and enacted the Taft-Hartley Act, which prevented members of the Communist Party from serving as union officers and signaled a broader disaffection with the power of organized labor. Accompanying fears of Communist subversion were deep anxieties about men's and women's roles, sparked by the realities of women in the workforce, gay men in the military, and sex outside of marriage. The result was a rededication to the traditional model of heterosexual male supremacy, as epitomized by the male-headed nuclear family.[149]

Together, these changes made social workers particularly vulnerable and helped delegitimize their proposals. Unlike lawyers, social workers had a unionized rank and file that was open to charges of Soviet sympathy. In places such as New York City, with large, left-leaning social service unions, social workers quickly grew accustomed to suspicion and harassment, carried out under the guise of ferreting out security risks. Social work's demographic profile – it remained predominantly female – also left it open to attack. Gender stereotypes cast women as soft and irrational, and therefore particularly vulnerable to communist influences.[150]

All these themes are visible in an episode from late 1947, when conservative civic leaders in Baltimore stumbled on one of the BPA's widely circulated statements on the right to public assistance, *Common Human Needs*. The occasion was an investigation of Baltimore's welfare program, which appeared to have more residents on the rolls, and more employees on the payroll, than the booming economic times called for. After finding what it expected, the self-proclaimed Commission on Governmental Efficiency and Economy (which was not, in fact, a municipal agency) issued a report charging the Baltimore Department of Welfare with wasting taxpayer resources and encouraging dependency. The report also accused the federal government of leading the city's agency astray, citing several sentences from *Common Human Needs*. A reference to the "socialized state" was particularly damning, as were discussions of the public welfare worker's role in convincing the "client" of his "right" to relief.[151]

Within months, newspapers around the country had picked up the story, often pairing it with references to the upcoming presidential election. Under the headline "Pour Out Cash, Staffs Told," the conservative *Chicago Tribune* reported that the "New Deal administration" was "deliberately ... swelling federal relief rolls on the eve of the 1948 presidential campaign." "Now It's Relief for Everyone," declared a nationally syndicated news column: "'Tax and tax; spend and spend; elect and elect.' Who said the new deal is dead?" The *Press* in Logansport, Louisiana, reported that "orders" had gone out to local welfare workers "not to be too critical of an applicant, but rather to HELP HIM GET ALL HE CAN FROM THE FEDERAL GOVERNMENT." Each article named *Common Human Needs* as the source of its information.[152]

Media attention only increased after President Truman's surprise reelection victory, as his administration put in motion plans for the "Fair Deal" that he had promised voters. Opponents of national health insurance, a key component of Truman's legislative program, used *Common Human Needs* to tar the entire federal social welfare bureaucracy, with special attention devoted to its head, Federal Security Administrator Oscar Ewing. (The Federal Security Agency, which now housed the federal government's various social welfare programs, would presumably coordinate any new health initiatives; after joining the agency in 1947, Ewing had assumed a leading role in selling Truman's proposal.) The American Medical Association, in particular, was so relentless that by 1951 it had goaded Ewing into ordering the destruction of all the remaining copies of *Common Human Needs*, along with the printing plates.[153]

As for Charlotte Towle, the author of *Common Human Needs*, she was never invited to consult for the government again. (Had she been formally employed by the agency, she almost surely would have been terminated or pressured to quit.) In 1954, she was even denied a passport.[154] To government social workers, the message was clear much earlier than that: rights language that implied substantive commitments, as opposed to merely procedural ones, was dangerous.

* * *

By the end of the 1940s, intraagency interpretations of the right to public assistance had moved in several distinct directions – toward due process and equal treatment, away from guarantees of an adequate living. And yet it would have been difficult at that juncture to predict the precise implications for American poor relief. Many components of the New Deal remained intact, and despite Republican gains, New Deal liberals still occupied positions of power throughout government. Going forward, federal administrators might have moved the concept of a decent standard of living back to center stage, following, perhaps, in the footsteps of Great Britain. But that did not happen. As concerns mounted about the cost of public assistance and the insidious influence of communism, the rule of law remained central to the agency's work. Federal administrators focused on whether states were complying with their legal obligations and whether they were treating the poor fairly and equally, not on whether they provided citizens with the means for a humane existence.

Before moving forward in time, however, we turn to a related set of questions: how did poor beneficiaries understand these programs? Did those who turned to public assistance hear and embrace the rights language filtering through the administrative state? We know from historian Liz Cohen and others that over the course of the 1930s, many Americans rethought their relationship to government. As private charities, ethnic institutions, and industrial employers failed them, they welcomed the government into their lives as job creator, mortgage backer, savings protector, insurance provider, and relief giver. Working-class Americans, in particular, came to view these services as entitlements: "Rather than feeling like beggars," Cohen writes, "workers felt they deserved benefits as citizens."[155] To what extent was this attitudinal change visible among public assistance claimants, who were subjected to the most onerous and invasive application procedures and who had the most tenuous connection to the world of work? Did the poorest clients of the New Deal recognize denials of their rights and pursue vindication? And if so, what were the implications for community, state, and nation? These are the questions to which Chapter 4 turns.

4

Claiming Welfare Rights

Fair Hearings, State-Court Claims, and a Forgotten Federal Case

"Dear Sir and to Whome is Implicated in Wellfare of the Real need of those in a Pitifull condition," began one 1941 letter to a state welfare department in the Midwest, "I need help."[1] This humble petition, which resonates so well with dominant characterizations of welfare recipients in this era, stands in sharp contrast to the rights language documented in the preceding chapters, a language that federal administrators pumped deliberately and determinedly into public welfare operations around the country. The juxtaposition raises a question: When the New Deal restructured American poor relief – ushering in statewide public assistance programs with clear eligibility requirements and explicit procedural protections, all tethered to federal and state statutes – did poor individuals adjust their own posture accordingly? Did they assert the various welfare rights that federal administrators insisted they had? We have long assumed that they did not – that although poor Americans actively applied for public assistance, and accepted it when offered, they rarely made the sort of claims on public authority that we associate with rights; when they did, the standard story continues, government officials quickly and firmly put them in their place.

Poverty law scholars are largely responsible for crafting and spreading this narrative, starting with Social Security Board lawyer A. D. Smith and continuing with welfare rights advocates and theorists Edward Sparer and Charles Reich, from whom so many subsequent scholars borrowed.[2] One of their prime examples is the colorful case *Wilkie v. O'Connor* (1941), involving an Old Age Assistance claimant from Seneca County, New York, who "insist[ed]" on "sleep[ing] under an old barn, in a nest of rags" reachable only by "crawl[ing] upon his hands and knees." Local officials offered David Wilkie more "suitable living quarters" and even an increase in his monthly assistance payment, but he refused to abandon his chosen abode. Finally the county welfare department revoked his grant.³ Wilkie responded by bringing a mandamus action in the county court: his monthly OAA check of $24.50 was a "reward" for a life well lived, he claimed; the county welfare commissioner was obligated to give it to him. The county court disagreed, as did the state court to which Wilkie turned next. The appellate judges were in fact so bemused that, despite finding Wilkie to be improperly before the court – grounds for dismissing the suit outright – they issued a written opinion refuting his "fallacious" arguments. The payments he had received were "charity," and in accepting it, he consented to adhere to "the standards and conventions of civilized society." "One would admire his independence," the judges noted, "if he were not so dependent."⁴ Subsequent scholars cited this case for the proposition that until the 1960s, courts treated welfare as a "privilege," not a "right." As administrative law expert and civil libertarian Walter Gellhorn explained in 1968, a welfare recipient before a court in this earlier period was little different from a "beggar" seeking alms from passersby: he had "no demands he could enforce."⁵

Gellhorn's statement may have been true to his own experience – he worked as a regional attorney for the Social Security Board from 1936 to 1938 – but there was in fact more to the case of David Wilkie. "Dave," as he was known around town, believed that "it just ain't constitutional" for the welfare department to question his choice of sleeping quarters. In his fifty-some years working as a horse trainer, he explained to a local newspaper, he had mainly slept in the stalls with the animals; why should he "pay money out of [his] allowances" for "a steam-heated room, hot and stuffy," where he found it impossible to get comfortable? "I'm not goin' to do it and they can't make me," he averred. Appellate court judges might have found such statements absurd, and yet Wilkie's lawyer, Ernest G. Gould, was no less than the "dean" of the county bar association, and Wilkie's local paper documented his views with respect, describing him as "venerable" and a "self-made man."⁶

How many David Wilkies were out there? How many individuals asserted their legal rights to public assistance – that is, to material support – or claimed the rights attached to public assistance – for example, to due process – in the era before the welfare rights movement? This chapter begins as close as possible to the ground level, with an investigation of surviving fair hearing records. These records show, first, that every year hundreds and sometimes thousands of people chose not to accept the

decisions of local welfare officers. Claims making was unequal, however –
a second important finding: Old Age Assistance claimants dominated
appeals proceedings, although clients of the other programs (Aid to the
Blind, Aid to Dependent Children) also appear in the records. Third,
appellants' neighbors and family members were often involved, suggesting that claims making was not merely the hobby of querulous or legally
sophisticated individuals; rather, it engaged entire households and communities. Given the limited availability of hearing transcripts, we cannot
gauge the extent to which hearing seekers used rights language, but we do
know, simply by their actions, that these individuals were aware of their
procedural rights, that they believed the government owed them something more than what they were getting, and that they were comfortable
turning the power of their state government against local officials. If the
availability of fair hearings was part of what made the modern American
state "modern," the traces of these hearings help us understand which
Americans bought in, and why.

Some people went further, still, appealing agency decisions to the
courts. In some instances, as in David Wilkie's case, judges behaved as
conservatively as New Dealers feared they would, characterizing statutory
entitlements as no different from the centuries of poor-relief payments
that had preceded them. But in many other cases, judges affirmed, and
indeed, helped explain, the crucial differences between New Deal public
assistance and traditional poor relief. They held that public assistance was
governed by written rules and procedures, that payments were not subject
to the whims of local officials, and that those who satisfied eligibility
requirements had a legal entitlement to government support.

To be clear, these findings do not support the conclusion that public
assistance claimants always, or even often, received what they were due.
Nor do they suggest that having legally recognized rights gave poor
Americans greater security. If state legislatures could create a legal entitlement to public assistance, the Idaho Supreme Court noted, they could also
impose more burdensome eligibility conditions, decrease payment
amounts, or eliminate the entitlement altogether.[7] Public assistance
remained "a gratuity of the sovereign" and "a creature of the statute," a
Missouri Court of Appeals agreed.[8]

But these cases are historically important. They show us not only the
existence of welfare rights claims but also how rights claiming changed
over time as litigants, lawyers, and courts mapped new territory. This
chapter's discussion of state court cases emphasizes three developments,
all of which show poor people reaching beyond their local contexts to

claim a new kind of citizenship. The first was the establishment, in the late 1930s and early 1940s, of the principle that the legal right to welfare was based on each claimant's individual need, as measured by state statutes and regulations, *not* on party affiliation or traditional metrics of worthiness. The second development, starting around the mid-1940s, was the appearance of due process–type arguments: Had local administrators given each claimant's case full and adequate consideration? The third, of approximately the same vintage, was the emergence of equal protection claims: Had legislators acted fairly when they ratcheted up eligibility requirements and thereby disentitled some recipients, or when they imposed higher burdens on some applicants than others? Few and far between, these cases say little about how most poor Americans understood government support, but they are a testament to the institutional and ideological groundwork that reformers had laid in previous decades. They also show incremental changes in what some people (and their lawyers) found imaginable – a precondition for more dramatic social and legal change.

The best evidence of this shift in imagination is the appearance in the late 1940s of a new type of welfare rights claim, one that bore many of the hallmarks of the welfare rights litigation of the 1960s and 1970s. Following its overview of state-level fair hearings and court cases, this chapter offers a rich account of a single federal court action: *Mapatis v. Ewing* (1948). This was a civil rights–inflected case, brought in the hope of making state welfare programs more inclusive. Like the elderly citizens who pioneered welfare rights litigation in the late 1930s, the *Mapatis* plaintiffs had an exceptional relationship to the polity and some powerful allies in government: they were American Indians[9] living on reservations in the Southwest who, despite their state and national citizenship, had been denied public assistance in the states where they resided. With the help of former federal government lawyer Felix S. Cohen, an expert in Indian law, and with covert assistance from federal welfare administrators, the Indian plaintiffs demanded what the Social Security Act and the Constitution promised them. Unlike their white, elderly counterparts in other parts of the country, however, these claimants met fierce and determined resistance from state officials, a result of racial bias, cultural distance, and Indians' refusal to exchange the attendants of sovereignty for the meager benefits of state citizenship.

Owing to a political settlement, the case disappeared before it could establish a place in the judicial record books, but it stands as an important landmark in the history of American poor relief. If fair hearing records and earlier cases showed that claimants had started to understand welfare benefits as something more than local charity – something approaching an entitlement owed to them by their state government, *Mapatis* demonstrated the realization that welfare benefits also implicated federally protected rights, and therefore national citizenship. These rights were potential weapons in a long struggle – a struggle by excluded and marginalized groups to expand what legal historian Barbara Welke calls the "borders of belonging" at the state and local levels.[10]

FAIR HEARINGS

Legal scholarship often associates rights with courts. But in the 1930s, and escalating dramatically in the 1940s, *agencies* became key mediators between citizens and government. It was there that citizens often exercised their rights, which themselves had grown in importance over the past decades (to become "the coin of [the] realm," in historian James Sparrow's words).[11] This marriage of rights and agencies followed directly from the era's sweeping new statutes, which demanded more from citizens and gave them more in return. These same statutes often entrusted agencies with enforcing the new bargains. In the context of public assistance, claimants looked first to local agencies to give them what the law promised. If dissatisfied, they could then appeal to a state agency – at least in theory. As Chapter 3 noted, states receiving grants under the Social Security Act were required to offer fair hearings, but many seemed less than eager to hold up their end of the bargain. Apart from a stretch in the second half of the 1940s, the federal agency also did relatively little to monitor states' performance or otherwise gather information (much to the chagrin of the agency's lawyers).

Patchy as they are, existing findings yield many insights and in general confirm the existence of a nontrivial amount of claims making in fair hearings. One particularly rich vein is in the reports that the federal agency compiled at the height of its interest in due process. Between the beginning of 1945 and the end of 1947, the agency collected data from fifty-four agencies in forty-five jurisdictions (most states, plus Alaska and the District of Columbia).[12] The states reported the number of appeals they received in each public assistance category and the number of appeals they actually held (see Table 4.1). They also reported on the nature of the claims and the results.

Perhaps the most important insight to draw from the reports – one that flatly contradicts scholarly assumptions about poor people's use of

TABLE 4.1. *Fair hearing data reported to the federal agency, January 1945–June 1947*

	Jan.–June 1945	July–Dec. 1945	Jan.–June 1946	July–Dec. 1946	Jan.–June 1947
Jurisdictions reporting	42	42	43	43	43
Appeals received	4,092	2,610	2,404	2,976	2,954
Appeals pending and received		3,833	3,227	3,952	4,089
OAA		3,483 (91%)	2,800 (87%)	3,479 (88%)	3,475 (85%)
ADC		264 (7%)	328 (10%)	357 (9%)	486 (12%)
AB		86 (2%)	109 (3%)	116 (3%)	128 (3%)
Appeals disposed of (by hearing or otherwise)		3,005	2,248	2,848	2,712
OAA		2,792 (93%)	1,918 (85%)	2,513 (88%)	2,323 (86%)
ADC		162 (5%)	254 (11%)	255 (9%)	300 (11%)
AB		51 (2%)	76 (3%)	80 (3%)	89 (3%)
Appeals disposed of by hearing		1,752	1,147	1,776	1,697

Note: The January–June 1945 report could not be located in the archive. Data come from the July–December 1945 report, which refers to figures from the previous report. The agency received similar data for the July–December 1947 period, but I could not locate the report in the archive, nor could I find a summary of the results.

Sources: Bureau of Public Assistance, "Appeals and Fair Hearings in Public Assistance, Statistical Analysis, July–December 1945," Box 79, GC Correspondence on PA, HEWR; Bureau of Public Assistance, "Appeals and Fair Hearings in Public Assistance, Statistical Analysis, January–June 1946," Box 79, GC Correspondence on PA, HEWR; Bureau of Public Assistance, "Appeals and Fair Hearings in Public Assistance, Statistical Analysis, July–December 1946," Box 79, GC Correspondence on PA, HEWR; Bureau of Public Assistance, "Appeals and Fair Hearings in Public Assistance, Statistical Analysis, January–June 1947," Box 79, GC Correspondence on PA, HEWR.

the fair hearing process – is that every year during this period, thousands of Americans contested the decisions of local welfare officers. There were at least 6,702 appeals filed in 1945 and 5,380 in 1946. Data from the first six months of 1947 suggest a similar total for that year (and again, these figures do not include all jurisdictions). Based on the very limited data from previous years, it is unclear whether these figures were high, low, or average.[13] A conservative estimate, however, suggests at least a thousand appeals per year between 1938 and 1944. We know that Missouri alone received 1,384 fair hearing requests between 1938 and the end of 1940. Wisconsin counted 1,723 fair hearing requests between 1936 and 1940 (and another 950 between 1941 and 1948). Reports from Illinois were more modest – 196 appeals filed between July 1, 1939, and April 30, 1942 (and most in Cook County) – but the basic point stands: poor individuals in various jurisdictions knew about and pursued their fair hearing rights.[14] This was so despite the inattention, incompetence, and affirmative discouragement of at least some state and local agencies.[15]

Reports show that claimants contested all types of decisions. They filed appeals when their local agency rejected or failed to act on their applications or suddenly discontinued benefits. Claimants who satisfied eligibility requirements appealed decisions regarding payment amounts, hoping for more. The specific basis for the vast majority of appeals, especially involving OAA, was disagreement about the extent of the claimant's need: in light of the claimant's resources – including property, family support, income, and so on – did he or she really need state support? If so, how much? Need, however, was just one eligibility factor: OAA claimants could be rejected because they were not old enough, or in some states, because they refused to agree to reimburse the state from their estate after death. Claimants for Aid to the Blind could be turned away because their eyesight was too good. An Aid to Dependent Children claimant could be denied assistance for failing to prove that a child lacked parental support or, in some states (despite federal discouragement), for failing to establish the "fitness" of the caregiver or the "suitability" of the home. In all three programs, claimants could be rejected on residence grounds, an eligibility factor that seemed straightforward but, in an age of increased mobility, proved to be surprisingly complex. All of these requirements surfaced in fair hearings.[16]

Looking beyond the number and type of complaints, important dividing lines emerge in the demography and geography of claims making, suggesting wide variations in claimants' interest in and ability to pursue administrative appeals. Most strikingly, Old Age Assistance programs produced far more hearing requests than did the programs serving dependent children and the blind. Numerically, that makes sense: of the various public assistance programs, OAA served vastly more people than AB or ADC. The Social Security Board estimated that more than two million people – or about 20 percent of the age-eligible population – received OAA by 1945. Looking cumulatively at the years 1940–48, that percentage never fell below 20 percent, whereas the proportion of children receiving ADC never exceeded 3 percent.[17]

However, OAA claimants not only filed more appeals; they also appealed at higher rates, especially relative to ADC claimants. Between July 1945 and December 1946 (the period for which the reports include appeal rates), OAA claimants appealed from decisions to reject their applications at a rate of approximately 11 appeals per 1,000 rejections. AB claimants appealed at a similar rate, about 10 per 1,000, but the rate for ADC was far lower: 2 appeals for every 1,000 rejections. Decisions to discontinue grants produced similar figures: OAA claimants appealed about 11 out of every 1,000 cases closed (not counting cases closed because of the death of the recipient). The rate for AB was comparable, 12 per 1,000, but for ADC it was far lower: 2 per 1,000.[18]

These rates likely reflected elderly Americans' strong claims on the polity. As a group, they wielded considerable power in the 1930s, a result of the organized pension movements that proliferated during the Depression. Elderly Americans voted, and politicians vied for their favor. OAA claimants, especially men, also enjoyed a more enduring claim on the government than the women eligible for ADC. To be sure, women played a vital role in producing vigorous, upstanding citizens – an impetus behind Progressive Era mothers' pensions. But their need appeared more transient (it would diminish when their children reached adulthood or when they tied themselves to a male breadwinner), and, with the exception of widows, more suspect. Members of the OAA population, by contrast, could cite their years of hard work and independence, as well as their lifetime of service to family, community, and nation. The fact of the Depression, and its popular characterization as a natural disaster, allowed them to argue that their destitution stemmed not from poor planning or a faltering work ethic, but from circumstances outside their control. AB recipients could make similar arguments: the physical disability at the root of their dependency was no fault of theirs.[19]

The relatively low ADC appeal rates also likely reflected poor mothers' recognition of just how much they stood to lose by initiating an appeal. An anecdote from Guernsey County, Ohio, is suggestive: in 1948, an ADC administrator – who also happened to be a juvenile court judge – threatened claimants with the removal of their children if they appealed his benefit decisions to the state agency.[20] Not many ADC administrators personally enjoyed such power, but poor mothers' entanglement with the child-protective arm of local government surely made them vulnerable in ways that OAA and AB claimants were not.[21]

Numbers of fair hearings varied not only from program to program but also from jurisdiction to jurisdiction, precluding broad generalizations about how poor Americans interacted with state and local agencies or how they understood the public assistance programs to which they applied. The state data collected between 1945 and 1947 reveal wide variations both in how frequently claimants filed hearing requests and in the treatment they received after they initiated the process. Of the thirty-eight states that sent the federal agency complete fair hearing reports for all their programs in the 1945–47 period, the total number of fair hearing requests ranged from fewer than 50 in eleven states (with three states reporting fewer than 5) to 500 or more in the ten states on the other side of the spectrum, with one state receiving more than 7,000 requests (see Table 4.2). Scattered reports from previous years document the same kind of variation.[22]

Textual records, such as the reports compiled by federal regional attorneys, suggest an additional note of caution: these numbers appear to reflect the tactics of state and local officials, and might therefore be an especially poor indicator of the attitudes and desires of claimants. In Utah, a state that received fewer than twenty-five fair hearing requests in the three-year period noted above, the state welfare department reportedly "discourage[d] all applications for hearings, particularly when the applicant bases his hearing on a disagreement with policies or procedures of the department." John Anderson, an OAA applicant from Utah's San Pete County, received the hearing to which he knew he was entitled only after writing multiple letters to the state welfare department and ignoring state officials' request that he first "see if his difficulties [could] be ironed out" locally.[23] In Montana, where fair hearing numbers were similar to Utah's, the state's official rules (as of 1945) informed claimants that they could appeal to the state welfare department only after seeking county-level reconsideration.[24] Claimants who pushed on to the state level found little to recommend the process. In the separate hearings of claimants Alva Manker and John Broadus, the Montana welfare department called for an increase in the claimants' welfare grants, but promptly undermined its

TABLE 4.2. *Number of hearing requests received in 38 states, January 1945–December 1947*

Number of hearing requests received, 1945–47	Number of states	States
Fewer than 5	3	Delaware, Nevada, South Dakota
5–24	4	Alabama, Montana, South Carolina, Utah
25–49	4	Arizona, Florida, Pennsylvania, Rhode Island
50–99	7	Colorado, Connecticut, District of Columbia, Idaho, Iowa, Mississippi, North Dakota
100–199	6	Illinois, Kansas, Maine, Michigan, Nebraska, West Virginia
200–299	4	Arkansas, Kentucky, Minnesota, Virginia
300–499	0	
500–999	5	California, Georgia, Louisiana, Ohio, Oklahoma
1,000–1,499	4	Indiana, Missouri, Texas, Washington
More than 7,000	1	Massachusetts

Note: All of the listed states sent in data for all of their programs during the period under study with the exception of Massachusetts, which neglected to send in its AB data for one of the six-month reporting periods.
Source: "Hearings in Public Assistance, January 1945–December 1947," *Social Security Bulletin* 11, no. 9 (September 1948): 18.

own decision after a local welfare board complained about the claimants' proclivity for "gambling and alcoholic beverages." State officials assured the local board that it could later "arbitrarily" decrease the grants to sums "that these men c[ould] wisely expend."[25]

Moving from measures of fair-hearing activity to a more qualitative assessment of what occurred in the fair hearing setting (made possible by the federal agency's short-lived publication of selected fair hearing decisions, as well as correspondence from federal regional attorneys), several valuable insights emerge. First, although many claimants were highly deferential and allowed officials to guide them through the process, the structure of the proceedings offered opportunities for claimants to "tattle" on their local caseworkers and to speak for themselves, rather than through a caseworker's notations on a standardized form. It is hard to generalize about what happened in the years before 1945, when records are sparser, but in the second half of the 1940s some claimants took advantage of these opportunities.

Consider the Maude Stark case from 1948, in which seventy-year-old Stark sought a higher OAA grant. At the start of her hearing, she answered the referee's questions obediently and concisely. But as the conversation moved toward the itemized budget that Stark's caseworker used to calculate her grant, Stark spoke more freely: "Right here is a good time to ask you," she stated, turning the tables on her interrogator, "why it is that you won't allow me, ... you can only give me $63.55, and that is not adequate." "I need other things," Stark continued, expressing the sort of consumer entitlement that Americans had come to associate with full citizenship, such as an occasional trip to the theater or the opera. "I have not seen a picture costing twenty-five cents for over three months," she protested. Instead, she sat at home with her cats (which she had to have, she explained, on account of the rats). "I am not dead," Stark reminded the hearing referee.[26]

As the proceeding went on, Stark also revealed a second reason for her appeal, one that was less about need or loneliness and more about fairness. Back in January of 1947, the local agency had accidentally issued her an additional check, which she understood to be for special clothing items that she had discussed with her caseworker; the agency later blamed Stark for its error, going so far as to maker her execute a "confession of judgment" in which she admitted to misleading local officials. "That is why I am boiling mad," she told the referee. "I still don't understand why I was considered a liar." The narrative prompted a response from the assistant attorney general, who had attended the hearing as a representative of the state. "Your character remains unimpugned," he assured Stark.[27] We have no way of knowing how common Stark's behavior was, but at a minimum her transcript broadens our historical imagination about what was possible in these administrative spaces and how some claimants understood fairness and justice in the welfare context.[28]

We can extract a similar lesson from the multiple hearing records in which claimants resisted restrictions on their behavior – restrictions that we might have presumed were simply accepted as the price of dependency. Consider the 1948 appeal of Frank Freeman. Freeman had been receiving OAA but was removed from the rolls after he transferred his farm to his four adult children. State regulations often treated such transfers with suspicion, on the theory that elderly citizens would try to "have their cake and eat it too" – that is, pass on wealth to future generations and receive support from the state. Freeman did not see it that way: he reasoned that he was simply repaying his children for all the medical bills and main-tenance costs they had covered, and for the eight years they had spent tending to their ailing mother, Freeman's wife. He could not understand how compensating his loyal children led to the cancellation of his grant. "If I was entitled to it in the first place I ought to be now," he told the hearing referee.[29] Texas appeal F-866 (the source does not disclose the claimant's name) suggests similar sentiments, although no transcript sur-vives. The appellant, a mother of two children, had been removed from the ADC rolls in January of 1946 after she followed the advice of her child welfare worker and placed her "feeble-minded" son in an institution. Shortly thereafter she reconsidered, feeling the child would do better in her care. When the local agency refused to support her choice (by rejecting her ADC application), she appealed to the state welfare board.[30] In both cases, the appellant prevailed, suggesting that in at least some places, for some people, fair hearings provided genuine opportunities for dissent and redress.

A final theme that emerges from surviving records is the involvement of the broader community in the enterprise of claims making, suggesting that simply tallying the fair hearing requests will understate the societal impor-tance of the phenomenon. Doctors, neighbors, relatives, and local old-age pension organizations helped claimants understand their rights and articulate them before state agencies. The adult children of OAA clai-mants figure particularly prominently in hearings, for they understood their parents' rights as bound up with their own. Consider the 1941 hearing of William Blank, who had been denied assistance because of the resources of his adult daughter (and whose family physician helped him file an appeal). When state welfare authorities urged the daughter, Mary Smith, to exhaust her own savings in supporting her father, Smith reacted with indignation. "As an American, I think I have some rights"; where was the "justice," she asked, in mortgaging her own security for her father's?[31] Smith was not alone: adult children often adhered to their positions even in the face of attempts to shame or discipline them. "We do not often have a case where there is as much income in the family as there appears to be here," the director of the New Jersey Division of Old Age Assistance pointedly informed the adult daughter and son-in-law of OAA claimant Henrietta Litter during a 1945 hearing. Why should the taxpayers have to support her? The children were unfazed. "She [Litter] is entitled to O.A.A. to the maximum amount," the son-in-law replied.[32]

In summary, the fair hearing opportunity required by the Social Security Act was not uniformly available, nor was it uniformly used.

The uneven distribution of fair hearings across states and across claimant groups reminds us that even after the New Deal ostensibly unified American poor relief, that system remained rife with inequality. At the same time, the fair hearing requirement was hardly the "dead letter" that scholars have assumed. Every year, there were poor claimants who used the administrative appeals process to contest benefit decisions. In doing so, they and their families strengthened their ties to state government, helped rein in the power of local officials, and participated in a broader reconceptualization of poor relief – from something resembling charity or a gratuity to something that could be demanded as a matter of right.

STATE COURT LITIGATION

The twenty-five years before the modern welfare rights movement witnessed not only administrative claims by welfare recipients but also a surprising amount of what I call welfare rights litigation. I define such litigation to include cases in which a participant or would-be participant in a federally subsidized state public assistance program advanced a legal claim against a government official or agency in order to receive public support or to vindicate some other legal right attached to public assistance, such as the right to a fair hearing.[33] Key-word searches in a database of case reporters – a crude but useful measurement – turned up 117 reported welfare rights cases from the years 1935 to 1960 (see Table 4.3).

As I did in the previous section, here I look first to the aggregate data. I show that welfare recipients *did* go to court before the 1960s, but their ability to do so varied, depending on their location, resources, and presumed worthiness of government support. I then offer a more qualitative assessment of the courts' decisions, emphasizing the ways in which judges and litigants conceptualized New Deal–era public assistance programs. At a time when federal administrators were deploying rights language to welfare agencies around the nation, such language also appeared in court, we will see, albeit in forms that were tightly tethered to state (as opposed to federal) law and that almost invariably emphasized the conditional nature of the rights.

Before turning to what we can learn from these first-generation welfare rights cases, a word on what we cannot. The numbers surely underrepresent how frequently individuals went to court. The database used here contains all "reported" (published) decisions of the fifty states, from their date of statehood to the present, but reported cases represent a narrow

TABLE 4.3. *Number of reported welfare rights cases, 1935–1960*

Program	1935–40	1941–45	1946–50	1951–55	1956–60	Total
Old Age Assistance (OAA)	28	43	11	14	8	104
Aid to Dependent Children (ADC)	0	2	0	2	3	7
Aid to the Blind (AB)	1	3	2	1	0	7
Aid to the Permanently and Totally Disabled (est. 1950)	n/a	n/a	n/a	0	1	1
TOTAL	29	48	13	17	12	117[a]

Note: To identify cases, I used the electronic database Westlaw, which includes the full text of all reported federal and state cases. I searched federal and state cases in 1935–60 for the terms: "old age assistance," "old age security," "aid to dependent children," "aid to the blind," "aid to the permanently and totally disabled," and "public assistance" /s "social security act" (where "/s" signifies "in the same sentence"). A research assistant read all the cases and identified those in which a recipient or would-be recipient of a federally subsidized state-run public assistance program sued a federal, state, or local agency or official to assert a claim related to their participation in that program. Cases resulting in multiple reported opinions (e.g., by an intermediate appellate court and then by a state supreme court) were counted only once.

[a] Two of the cases involved both OAA and AB and hence appear twice in the table. These cases were counted only once when calculating the total.

slice of all litigation. Some cases disappear before a judge or jury reaches the merits – for example, through settlement – thus leaving the state nothing to report. In addition, states generally do not publish decisions by courts "of first instance" (also known as trial-level courts), the bodies responsible for the bulk of day-to-day judicial work. Today, states often publish the decisions of their intermediate appellate courts (the level before the state supreme court), but in the period under question not all states had such courts. For the most part, then, my findings include only cases in which (1) the nonprevailing party could and did appeal the initial court's decision, (2) the appellate court (intermediate or supreme) produced a written opinion, and (3) the jurisdiction chose to report the opinion.[34] The geographical spread of the reported cases (see Table 4.4) is potentially misleading for the same general reason. Alaska, for example, did not have an intermediate appellate court until 1980, which means that no welfare rights case from that jurisdiction would appear in the data unless the case made it to Alaska's supreme court. Many states fit the same profile.[35]

TABLE 4.4. *Reported welfare rights cases by state, 1935–1960*

	Court of first instance	Intermediate appellate court	State supreme court	Total
Alaska	–	–	0	0
California	–	6	4	10
Colorado	–	–	1	1
Connecticut[a]	1	–	0	1
Delaware	0	–	0	0
Florida	·	–	0	0
Hawaii	–	–	0	0
Illinois[a]	–	1	4	5
Indiana	–	0	0	0
Iowa[a]	–	–	1	1
Kansas	–	0	0	0
Kentucky	–	–	3	3
Louisiana	–	0	0	0
Maine	–	–	0	0
Massachusetts	–	–	2	2
Michigan[a]	–	–	0	0
Minnesota[a]	–	–	2	2
Mississippi	–	–	0	0
Missouri[a]	–	63	7	70
Montana	–	–	1	1
Nebraska	–	–	0	0
Nevada	–	–	0	0
New Hampshire	–	–	0	0
New Jersey	0	0	0	0
New York	0	2	0	2
North Dakota	–	–	0	0
Oklahoma	–	–	2	2
Oregon	–	–	0	0
South Dakota	–	–	1	1
Utah	–	–	1	1
Washington[a]	–	–	13	13
West Virginia	–	–	0	0

Note: Excluded are states that explicitly insulated state welfare department decisions from judicial review throughout the period. Dashes signify that a state did not report decisions of that particular court. Cases that resulted in multiple reported decisions are counted only once, in the category of the higher court.

[a] State explicitly provided for judicial review of public assistance determinations.

Anecdotal evidence from federal agency records and elsewhere confirms the incompleteness of the case set described in Table 4.4. We know from such evidence that in 1940, for example, an attorney went to a county court in Wisconsin to seek higher grants for five OAA recipients, apparently at the behest of a local pension organization.[36] Official reports from Wisconsin document no such cases – just as the case reports from Kansas include no mention of Mary Okimoto, who in 1939 sued the Wyandotte County Board of Social Welfare after it suspended ADC payments to her three children on "suitable family home" grounds.[37] Similarly invisible is Eva Roberson of Franklin County, Illinois, another mother of three. She went to court in 1949, state and federal administrative correspondence shows, when her local welfare board determined that she had not made a sufficient effort to secure child support from her former husband and suspended her family's payments.[38] The list could go on. The point is that these cases and surely many others never made it into the published record.[39]

With these caveats, a few notable patterns stand out. Of the 117 cases, all came from state courts. (The 1948 *Mapatis v. Ewing* case, discussed later in the chapter, was a federal court case, but the plaintiffs abandoned it before it went to trial, leaving no trace in case reports.) The dominance of state court cases accords with how most claimants probably understood public assistance in this era. To all appearances, it was something that came from the state legislature, via local officials. Only the savviest individuals would have been aware of the extent of federal government involvement. Naturally, then, claimants turned to state rather than federal court. It is possible that some claimants considered the latter, on the theory that their cases raised questions of federal law (a point of entry into federal court), but there they would have encountered a $3,000 "amount in controversy" requirement ($10,000 after 1958) – likely an insurmountable hurdle.[40] Creative claimants might have avoided this obstacle by invoking the 1871 federal Civil Rights Act (subjecting to civil liability "every person" who, acting "under color" of state law, deprives another person of the "rights, privileges, or immunities" secured to him or her by "the Constitution and laws"), but again they would have encountered difficulty: judges at the time treated this law as an exceedingly narrow passage into federal court, available only when the plaintiff claimed racial discrimination by state actors.[41]

All but 13 of the 117 cases involved Old Age Assistance, which is also not surprising. The same factors that made OAA claimants more likely to request fair hearings made them more likely to seek judicial redress. In addition, OAA claimants had better prospects than AB or ADC claimants for attracting lawyers. With the backing of pension societies and adult children, and with the prospect of years of state-funded income support, elderly citizens were able to reward attorneys for taking their cases, either with cash or good public relations. Based on the biographies of the lawyers who repeatedly appeared in these cases, OAA claimants tended to attract top local talent, including men who had been or would go on to be judges and legislators.[42]

A less intuitively clear feature of the case set is its geographical distribution (see Table 4.4). Looking at the sample as a whole, Missouri courts are responsible for a disproportionate number of decisions: of the 104 reported OAA cases, 65 were in Missouri, and the state also produced 5 of the 7 reported ADC cases. The rest of the cases tended to be in states to the North and West, such as Illinois, California, and Washington. Eastern states reported only 5 cases, all involving OAA: 1 in Connecticut, 2 in Massachusetts, and 2 in New York. None of the reported cases was in the South, with the exception of 3 cases in Kentucky (1 in each category).

To some extent, this distribution is an artifact of the reporting system. Connecticut and New York, for example, would be unrepresented had they not chosen to report some decisions of their lower courts. At the other extreme, Missouri appears to have taken an unusual interest in reporting decisions from its intermediate appellate courts: Illinois reported a comparable number of supreme court decisions relating to welfare rights and yet far fewer intermediate appellate level decisions, suggesting that Missouri was simply publishing more of its appellate docket.

Beyond that, the seventeen states that reported cases correlate loosely with the existence of judicial review provisions in state laws. This was a time, legal historian Reuel Schiller has noted, when the relationship between courts and agencies was in flux. It was clear that agencies had undertaken much of the day-to-day work of governance, but it was not clear when and how courts would review their work or what remedies they might provide. The first state-level administrative procedure act was not adopted until 1941, by North Dakota; five years later a federal Administrative Procedure Act was on the books, but only nine states had followed North Dakota's lead.[43] Without such uniform guidance, agency-specific judicial review provisions mattered greatly. As of 1937, only seven states explicitly authorized claimants to appeal the decisions of state welfare departments to the courts: Connecticut, Illinois, Iowa,

Michigan, Minnesota, Missouri, and Washington.[44] Twenty-one states
said nothing, arguably leaving open the path to court via common law
actions (such as a writ of mandamus, a damage action in tort, or a request
for a declaratory judgment), but, as Schiller notes, the relevant common
law doctrines would have brought with them a "mind-numbing" array of
legal standards and considerable uncertainty.[45] Eighteen states specifically characterized the decisions of state welfare departments as final.[46]

State-specific political circumstances also surely mattered. Missouri's
abundance of cases appears to be related to its powerful and organized
old-age pension lobby and, relatedly, the overinclusiveness of the state's
OAA program during its first few years, when political boss Tom
Pendergast of Kansas City controlled Missouri's Democratic Party and
milked New Deal programs for all possible patronage opportunities.
Subsequent reinvestigations of OAA cases – urged by federal officials
and ordered by Governor Lloyd Stark (ally-turned-enemy of the
Pendergast machine) – resulted in the removal of some 7,500 elderly
citizens from the rolls. Many then turned to the open arms of the courts.[47]
Washington and California had similarly strong pension movements,
which appeared to affect elderly citizens' attitudes toward OAA. As
early as 1938, the director of the Washington State Department of
Welfare complained that "the clients aren't what they used to be": "No
longer do they supplicate for charity, pleading 'worthiness' in their own
behalf," he observed. "Today they assert their rights as human beings and
as members of the body politic – their worthiness is their own business."[48]
The distribution of AB cases appears to reflect similar factors: California,
the source of three of the seven reported AB cases, was on the front line of
efforts by blind persons to organize for public assistance and other rights.
Illinois, the source of two cases, was one of the first states to enact a
pension-type law for blind citizens.[49]

But even if reported cases cannot reveal all that we would like to
know – such as how frequently poor Americans attempted to assert
their legal rights in court – they still have much to offer. These cases tell
us about which legal claims poor individuals thought to make, and when.
They also show us how courts responded. Here, it matters greatly that all
the cases included here were officially "reported": because of their availability and precedential effect, such cases were more likely than unre-
ported cases to shape the imaginations of judges and litigants. In the
sections that follow, I trace five developments: (1) the establishment of
the basic idea that welfare benefits could be an entitlement; (2) the clar-
ification that the entitlement was based primarily on need, as opposed to

traditional markers of deservingness; (3) the unbundling of the rights of individual claimants from the obligations of their family members; (4) the articulation of the right to a fair hearing (and the corresponding obligation to seek one before turning to the courts); and (5) the emergence of arguments about equal protection.

Welfare as a Statutory Entitlement

Many scholars have credited the welfare rights cases of the late 1960s with first establishing the legal concept of welfare as an entitlement – that is, with the idea that large categories of individuals had an enforceable right to government assistance, based on their fulfillment of statutory criteria.[50] They cite the Supreme Court case *Goldberg v. Kelly* (1970) for the proposition that "welfare benefits 'are a matter of statutory entitlement for persons qualified to receive them.'"[51]

In fact, numerous state court cases recognized this concept of entitlement well before the 1960s. Claimants began asking state courts to do so almost as soon as New Deal public assistance programs went into operation – people like seventy-two-year-old Houston C. Price of Neosho, Missouri. A lifelong Missourian, with the exception of a few years spent in "Indian Territory," Price found himself "completely broken down" in 1937 and unable to work. He and his wife survived on the five or so dollars per month that she earned through sewing and the fifty per month that she received from a son-in-law. It was enough, Price conceded, to keep them in a "fairly" comfortable two-bedroom apartment – which is why the State Social Security Commission found Price ineligible for OAA. Undaunted, Price pursued the matter in local court and won. Affirming that decision, a state appeals court focused entirely on the eligibility conditions in the state OAA statute – specifically, on the meaning of "without means of support." Surely, the court held, the legislature did not intend for donations from relatives, a transaction outside the realm of the market, to be treated like a person's wages or real estate when assessing "means of support." Pairing this interpretation with the uncontroverted facts, the court found that Price was entitled to assistance.[52]

Joanna Bernard Conant, a seventy-eight-year-old widow and longtime resident of Washington State, went to court with a similar story. In 1937, when she applied for OAA, she lived with her adult daughter and son-in-law, who also provided her with food and clothing. The State Department of Social Security found her ineligible because, although she met the age requirement and although she had she had no income or property to her name, she admitted to receiving all the support she needed from her family. Like Price, however, Conant prevailed in court. Need was the statutory basis for OAA payments, and needy she was, the Washington Supreme Court explained. If she "were compelled to beg from door to door ... her need would be no greater than if compelled, as she now is, to accept" the "gratuitously bestowed" support of her kin. The "law is plain," the court continued: where an applicant met the statutory conditions, as Conant did, the state had a legal duty to support her, and Conant had a legal right to claim that support.[53]

This holding had startling implications, as dissenting justice John Sherman Robinson was quick to point out. For one, the state now owed Conant more than $400 in retroactive payments. The award of back payments was indeed important, for it helped solidify the idea of welfare as a legal right – and in this, Washington was not alone. A 1945 lawsuit by the California State Board of Social Welfare against Los Angeles County (for refusing to give three claimants lump sums for previous months of erroneous nonpayment or underpayment) resulted in a similar holding: as soon as the applicant became entitled to aid, the California Supreme Court explained, an abstract government obligation "became a debt due."[54] The Illinois courts reached a similar conclusion. The state's modern public aid programs, appellate judge George W. Bristow explained in the Aid to the Blind case *Creighton v. Pope County* (1943), were crafted to differentiate beneficiaries from "paupers"; they "import[ed] respect to the recipient and implie[d] duty and obligation upon the state."[55] Eligible claimants did not have "contractual rights," the state Supreme Court later cautioned, when Pope County appealed from the judgment against it, but they did have "vested" rights – such that they were entitled to accrued but unpaid benefits and could seek a court's aid "in coercing a county to perform its statutory duty."[56]

Welfare as an Individual Right, Based on Need

The dissenting justice in *Conant v. State* (1938), the landmark Washington OAA case, was concerned about the majority's decision for another reason, as well: the decision guaranteed Joanna Conant thirty dollars a month, the state's statutory minimum, even though everyone agreed that her family would continue to supply her "all the necessaries of life." Justice Sherman predicted – presciently – that federal officials would refuse to support this interpretation of the law, leaving the state on the hook for a vastly expanded pool of OAA recipients but without the benefit of federal subsidies; eventually, this would result in lower payments across the board, to the detriment of the truly needy.[57]

Federal administrators were, indeed, watching, and although they did not object to the idea of public assistance as the legal right of those who qualified (indeed, they were eager to see their state and local counterparts accept this precept), they threatened to withdraw federal funds if states continued to disregard "gratuitous support actually made available to an applicant."[58] In other words, they insisted that state and local administrators not depart from means testing. Their main worry was a judicially created "pension" for *everyone* over the age of sixty-five. This would obviate the need for federal Old Age Insurance (Social Security), which the federal government had sold to the public as a pension and which remained politically vulnerable. (It was not until 1940 that anyone who had paid into the system began receiving benefits.) In response to federal warnings, the state legislatures in both Missouri and Washington quickly took action, clarifying that eligibility for OAA turned on "actual need" – or as one Missouri newspaper translated it, "bread and butter," not just "birthdays." The courts promptly fell into line.[59]

This emphasis on "actual need" mattered greatly for people on the ground. For many elderly citizens, it was the difference between receiving something from the state and receiving nothing. For those who received something, it was the difference between reporting income and property holdings, a relatively impersonal task, and offering up every transaction of love and obligation, a much more intimate accounting. But the assurance of an onerous and invasive application process should not obscure an important contemporaneous development: even after it became clear that OAA was not "a matter of right" for all elderly citizens, disappointed claimants went to court and won decisions that affirmed their *individual* status as rights holders. They may not have belonged to an age-based class of "pensioners," these decisions made clear, but many had strong and real claims on the state. As a Missouri appellate court explained in 1945, the state OAA law was not just a device for excluding particular elderly people from the state's beneficence; for eligible individuals, it created an "affirmative" obligation – an obligation to provide them with a "reasonable subsistence compatible with decency and health."[60]

Consider the case of Saul Hooks of Saint Louis. Physical disabilities had caused him to lose his most recent job, on a Works Progress Administration project, and he had not worked since. At age sixty-nine, he believed he was entitled to support from the state. The local welfare department disagreed, on account of the basic necessities he received from his adult son, Richard, and Richard's common-law wife, Glendora. At a hearing before Missouri's State Social Security Commission, Hooks (with the help of his lawyer) painted a bleaker picture, tinged with allusions to servitude. His meals consisted of whatever Richard and Glendora did not finish; he did not eat at their table. He owned but one pair of trousers, which did not fasten, and no coat or "top shirt"; his shoes had holes and his underwear was patched; his sole pair of socks had worn out months before the hearing. He enjoyed going to church, he testified, but refused to darken the church door in such shabby attire. Richard testified that he could not afford to do any better for his father: he had a decent job with a railroad company but could barely keep up with his own expenses. The commission was apparently unmoved, but the trial and appellate courts found a way to justify the payments Hooks sought. The commission's "desire to conserve the State's funds" was "very proper," the Saint Louis Court of Appeals recognized in 1942, but surely, the court reasoned, the legislature did not intend to deny assistance to someone living in such indisputably poor conditions.[61]

The technical legal basis for the court's holding was that the commission's decision was not supported by "substantial evidence," a standard of review that had fast become a staple of administrative law.[62] But cases like Hooks's sent a more general message. Although the state legislature had designated OAA a "gratuity," explained Judge Hopkins Shain of the Kansas City Court of Appeals in 1941, the law gave specific individuals "a right to that gratuity."[63]

On the basis of such pronouncements – and of the as yet uncertain meaning of "substantial evidence" – many other elderly citizens turned to the courts, especially in Missouri. And although few of their cases received the sort of scrutiny that Hooks's case received, claimants continued to invite judges to consider the humblest details of their lives: their quarts of blackberries, number of hogs, and pairs of overalls; the costs of their doctor's visits and the specifics of their ailments; the spare dollars they received on birthdays and holidays. Notably in the age of Jim Crow, even a "colored" citizen – Gasconade County's William S. Nichols – appears in the court records, questioning the State Social Security Commission's denial of his appeal.[64] In short, nothing about the process of means testing, however intrusive and degrading, prevented these individuals from believing that they had legal rights and asking courts to vindicate them.

Individual Rights and Family Obligations

William Nichols ultimately lost his case, for the same reason that thousands of claimants found their OAA benefits denied or revoked: state administrators determined that his adult daughter and son-in-law were using a portion of the son-in-law's earnings to furnish him with the "necessities of life."[65] The courts affirmed many such decisions, even when the cases involved upstanding claimants, and even when the costs fell on the most pitiable of relatives: sons and daughters who had their own sons and daughters to care for, or who were themselves elderly and frail.[66] Consider the case of sixty-seven-year-old Amos M. Hardy, a man who had all the traditional markers of deservingness: he had once operated a small store in southwestern Missouri, an occupation that allowed him to fulfill all the responsibilities of the male breadwinner, but he had lost one arm and injured the other in a train accident. Now, felled by old age and misfortune, he and his family relied in part on the thirty-seven dollars per month that a son in the military sent home and the small amounts that his wife earned through laundry work. But it was his eldest daughter, nineteen-year-old Ada Bell, who covered the bulk of the family's expenses, through her paychecks from a telephone company. In light of Ada Bell's contributions to the household, the State Social Security Commission had refused to place Hardy on the OAA roll. The court acknowledged the hardship imposed on the young woman but left the commission's decision undisturbed.[67]

All of these cases, however – even the ones that left plaintiffs empty-handed – subtly strengthened the notion of poor citizens as rights holders. They did so by disentangling poor claimants from their private domestic contexts and articulating their bond with the state. The cases spoke at length about household resources and expenses, but the legal claim belonged to one person. The disposition of the claim depended not on the vitality and endurance of the household, not on the opportunities that relatives forewent or the dreams they deferred, but on the claimant's immediate needs and resources.[68]

This was so even in cases where the elderly plaintiffs were far from autonomous agents, such as eighty-three-year-old Minnie Dunnavant, who mentally was "just like a child," or Louise Gaeckler, who displayed no understanding of her own financial affairs. In Gaeckler's case, her son-in-law attempted to use the legal proceedings to advance his own claims and "contention[s]" – about the house he had never purchased and the nerves he frayed as he "ke[pt] the wolf from the door." But the case ultimately turned on Gaeckler's needs and Gaeckler's resources, including those that she chose to accept from her willing relatives.[69]

The word "choice" may seem inapt: it suggests that people like Louise Gaeckler, "penniless" and "in broken health," could have chosen not to rely on family and instead have turned to the state. But in fact some people did just that. When courts affirmed their choice, the concept of welfare as a legal entitlement gained further ground. Consider, for example, OAA recipients Parker and Isa Gray of Los Angeles County, California. Their names entered the court records not via a welfare rights case but through the county's action against their adult daughter, Gretta La Fuente, to recover the cost of payments made to the Grays between October 1937 and February 1939. La Fuente had the means to support her parents, the county claimed, and ought to remit the cost of their maintenance. A public school teacher with a teenage son of her own to support, La Fuente offered a creative argument in her defense: she owed nothing to the county because her parents were never, in fact, eligible for OAA; they were never eligible because she had offered to care for them in her home, obviating their need for public assistance. It was not her fault that her parents refused her kindness (they had "never gotten along" with this particular daughter, the Grays explained). The California Supreme Court rejected La Fuente's clever argument – and in doing so, underscored her parents' rights. California's OAA law created an "entitlement" to those who satisfied specific eligibility requirements – of age, need, residence, and so on. The legislature might have excluded those who refused to accept help from relatives, but it had not, leaving people like the Grays free to claim state support instead. In the same discussion, the court distinguished OAA from traditional poor relief: The latter required "pauperism," a word that connoted utter destitution and degradation. The state's OAA law, by contrast, was concerned with more than basic survival; it also attempted to accord beneficiaries "dignity," "independence," and "happiness of mind."[70]

As the facts of these cases suggest, a more legalistic, rights-conscious relief system coexisted uneasily with traditional ideas about family responsibility. In the *La Fuente* case, the recognition of the Grays' right to public assistance came in the context of upholding their adult daughter's obligation (owed in this case to the state) for their maintenance. When the Grays claimed benefits, they invited the state to deploy its coercive machinery against their kin. (In this, California was not exceptional; many states had relative-responsibility laws on the books, although enforcement mechanisms and procedures varied widely.)[71] In many other cases, elderly citizens attempted to claim their new rights but were unable to do so because of their children's insistence, however grudgingly, on providing for them. Adult children often endured "unnecessary hardships," the Missouri Supreme Court observed, "rather than incur the public odium which might attach to them if they refused to support their parents and thus made them eligible for state assistance."[72] For elderly citizens who were fortunate enough to live in the orbit of family, rights and relatives were not always compatible.

In the longer term, however, rights survived and the notion of family obligation shifted. What relatives once understood as a private duty many came to interpret as a public tax, to be grudgingly paid or skillfully avoided.[73] Consider the 1945 appeal of seventy-eight-year-old Ada Achor, who had lived with her two adult sons since the death of her husband in 1919. County welfare officials removed her from the OAA rolls on learning that another member of the household, her granddaughter, was receiving a salary of twenty dollars per week – twice what her father made as a farm laborer. The commission affirmed this decision, but the trial-level and appellate courts disagreed. Though it may "seem strange" and "unjust from a moral viewpoint," the appeals court explained, the granddaughter contributed "not one cent ... to the family budget or to her grandmother." The commission acted arbitrarily and unreasonably, therefore, in treating these wages as a resource.[74] The more often relatives behaved in this manner, the less stigma they attracted and the more valuable and important the elderly citizen's legal claim on the state became.

Rights *against* Government: The Right to Fair Process

The cases described thus far have been about the right to receive public assistance. That is, they were affirmative claims to government support. Entangled in some of these claims was a quintessential negative right, detachable from the question of eligibility: the right to fair treatment or, in the Constitution's language, "due process."

Whether the Constitution's due process guarantees even covered recipients of public benefits was, until the 1960s, a live question.[75] That had not stopped federal administrators, however, from importing those guarantees into the public assistance context (as discussed in Chapter 3), nor did it stop claimants from making process-based arguments in court. Alva M. Bowen of Grays Harbor County, Washington, was one. Sometime after getting on the OAA rolls, Bowen came to believe that his assistance grant of thirty-four dollars per month was six dollars short. On June 7, 1941, he formally requested a fair hearing from the state Department of Social Security, and when that hearing did not happen in the statutorily prescribed period (thirty days), Bowen went to court. The tactic worked. After a hastily convened hearing, the department increased Bowen's grant, thereby mooting the lawsuit. Affirming the importance of due process, the local court ordered the department to pay Bowen's substantial legal fees (seventy-five dollars).[76]

The right to a fair hearing did not always translate into material benefits, however. Indeed, that right made it harder for some claimants to cash in on the law's promises: when plaintiffs sued without first seeking a hearing, courts increasingly cited the "failure to exhaust administrative remedies" as grounds for dismissing their case, even when the state's administrative machinery was of dubious value. Consider the 1940 case of George M. Thompson of Pawnee, Oklahoma: he was on the state OAA roll, receiving eleven dollars per month, until the county welfare department learned of the occasional gifts he received from his two adult daughters (a sixty-five-cent shirt, two suits of underwear, a pair of blankets) and terminated his grant, reasoning that the daughters were willing and able to support him. "There was no use," the director of the county assistance board informed Thompson, in asking for a redetermination or further investigation. Undeterred, Thompson sought, and won, a writ of mandamus from a local court, ordering the Oklahoma Public Welfare Commission to reinstate his benefits. But the State Supreme Court overturned the order: having failed to exhaust his statutorily prescribed remedy – a fair hearing before the State Commission – Thompson had no right to file suit.[77] The irony did not escape dissenting justice Fletcher Riley: the real exhaustion, he noted, would be Thompson's, as, despite his "clear legal right to relief," he spent his waning months pursuing a pointless administrative appeal.[78]

Hearings, even inadequate ones, were not necessarily pointless, however, for they sometimes provided courts with clever process-based arguments for ordering state agencies to reconsider their decisions – one more reason why the judicial articulation of welfare rights mattered in this "pre–welfare rights" era. This was the gist of a series of opinions from the Missouri appellate courts in the mid-1940s: it was clear by then that courts should not engage in the business of fact-finding, and if the state agency's factual findings substantially supported its decision, the decision should stand. In some cases, however, such as that of William Rosebraugh of Rolla, Missouri, this level of deference threatened to lead to unpalatable results, and the courts used arguments about fair treatment to demand a second look. Plagued by "hardening of the arteries, eye trouble, and a right hernia," eighty-two-year-old Rosebraugh relied heavily on the kindness of his son-in-law, a laboratory technician, and his daughter, a wartime mess hall supervisor. To make ends meet, the daughter also rented out rooms in the family home, relegating her father to sleeping on a davenport and moving her own marital bed to the basement. On discovering these income streams in early 1944, county authorities cancelled Rosebraugh's OAA payments, and the State Social Security Commission upheld the county's decision (even though the daughter had by then lost both her job and the renters). The Springfield Court of Appeals, to which Rosebraugh turned next, seemed sympathetic to Rosebraugh – or, more precisely, to his middle-class daughter and son-in-law, who, the court emphasized, had "a right to a 'reasonable subsistence compatible with decency and health' within the sphere of [their] environment and station in life." To reverse the commission, however, the judges had to find firmer legal ground. Ultimately, they emphasized process: in basing Rosebraugh's OAA grant on a family budget that did not match the family's actual expenses, such as the twenty-six dollars the family spent each month on tithing, the commission had acted "arbitrar[ily] and unreasonabl[y]."[79]

The same court reached a similar judgment in the case of sixty-eight-year-old Edgar L. Foster. Unable to work after being gored by a cow, Foster attempted to provide for himself and his nearly blind wife by keeping a small amount of livestock and subletting some farm acreage. Foster's OAA application was denied on the basis of a monthly budget that a county employee named "Mrs. Wallace" had prepared, using a state-issued set of "'standard' family expenses." "The actual facts of an individual case should govern over a theoretical estimate," Judge William L. Vandeventer scolded. A decision that relied on the caseworker's budget in the face of an applicant's "positive and uncontradicted evidence" as to his actual requirements was "arbitrary and unreasonable." Prevented from ruling on the substance of the case, in other words, the judge characterized the administrative decision-making process as unfair.[80]

Skepticism about the "highly theoretical" judgments of female caseworkers unacquainted with hard-scrabble Missouri farm life seems to have animated some of the court decisions. ("Buildings and fences require constant repairs," chided Judge Floyd Sperry of the Kansas City Court of Appeals, when he saw that a female caseworker's budget included no allowance for the "nails, shingles, lumber, staples, wire, etc." needed to maintain an OAA applicant's farm.[81]) The point, however, is that by scrutinizing the way the state agency reached its decision – its process – judges were able reach outcomes that felt fair to them. Process-based decisions, in turn, helped establish that even those who did not satisfy statutory eligibility conditions had enforceable rights to fair and accurate application determinations. Such pronouncements further removed poor Americans from the legal category of "pauper" and constructed them instead as claimants – individuals whom the state might owe.

The Emergence of Equal Protection

By the end of the 1940s, poor plaintiffs had begun to advance one additional type of welfare rights claim – one that bore a stronger resemblance to the claims associated with the modern welfare rights movement. Citing the equal protection guarantee of the U.S. Constitution, they challenged prevailing ideas about who was entitled to government aid and who was not. In other words, they went beyond demanding a fair, individualized consideration from state and local administrators to demanding fair treatment for entire groups.

To appreciate the novelty of this approach, consider one of first reported uses of an equal protection argument in a welfare rights case: it occurred in 1942, and came not from the mouth of a poor claimant but from a state attorney general in Kentucky. At the center of the case was fourteen-year-old Mamie Ray. Mamie's father, adjudged mentally "unsound" in 1937, resided apart from the family in a state institution; Mamie's mother, Viola, claimed to suffer from "physical infirmities" that left her unable to support her daughter. In short, Mamie Ray was a perfect candidate for the state's recently created Aid to Dependent Children program. On the advice of the state attorney general, however, the commissioner of welfare refused to approve her application, citing concerns about the constitutionality of the state ADC law. With the help of lawyers Anna H. Settle, president of the Consumers' League of Kentucky, and Richard P. Dietzman, former chief justice of the Kentucky Court of Appeals, young Mamie became the face of this legal dispute.[82]

In defense of the commissioner's position, Attorney General Hubert Meredith called the court's attention to the "invalid classification" at the heart of Kentucky's ADC law: in defining "dependent children," the legislature had included only needy children who lived with a close relative, thereby excluding another class of children who were "equal in their dependency." In essence, Meredith argued, the legislature had granted "a special or exclusive privilege," one that could not stand. Meredith's motives in making this equal protection argument – which threatened to deprive *all* dependent children of support – are unclear. Based on his previous actions, such as seeking an injunction against the overzealous Kentucky Highway Patrol and publicly denouncing a suspiciously well paid state librarian, he was likely concerned with wasteful spending and corruption. (As an outspoken critic of the existing gubernatorial administration, he may also have been attempting to embarrass a political rival.) Fortunately for Mamie Ray, Meredith failed: the Kentucky Supreme Court found the classification unobjectionable.[83]

In retrospect, the *Meredith* case occupies an important breach in the history of equal protection jurisprudence. Meredith asked for an interpretation that harkened back to the early decades of the twentieth century – the so-called *Lochner* era – when courts assumed a "night watchman" role over a burgeoning regulatory state. Courts used the doctrines of equal protection and due process to ensure that "class interests" – which generally meant the working class and its allies – did not use their political strength to achieve unfair advantage. By 1942, however, the tide had turned. The U.S. Supreme Court had famously abandoned the night watchman posture, at least when it came to social and economic legislation; state courts had followed a similar course, evaluating most state legislation under a highly deferential standard. The exception, going forward (and not yet obvious to lawyers or litigants), would be legislation involving "discrete and insular minorities." Over the course of the next decades, African Americans, women, and others would slowly win more rigorous standards of review from the courts, restoring to the Equal Protection Clause some of its original promise.[84]

We can see litigants grasping for this more robust Equal Protection Clause in the federal court case *Mapatis v. Ewing* (1948). The litigation left barely a mark on the judicial record books but its history is worth recounting in depth, for the case foretold the future of welfare rights litigation. Here, the line between welfare rights and civil rights blurred; claimants harnessed the power of the federal government and its lawyers against the authority of the states, and state officials developed sophisticated arguments of their own to preserve what they saw as the implicit terms of the New Deal.

MAPATIS V. EWING: THE FIRST FEDERAL WELFARE RIGHTS CASE

It is only fitting that a group of American Indians, along with two federal government lawyers, were behind *Mapatis v. Ewing*, the first welfare rights case to be advanced in federal court. Such cases probe the nature of the relationship between the state and federal governments, as well as the meaning of citizenship – concepts that American Indians had long informed, and often unsettled. Federal government lawyers, meanwhile, were expert in the technologies of federal regulation, the evolving jurisprudence of the federal courts, and the levers of power in Washington. Together they called on the courts to remedy the policies and practices that kept Indians from obtaining much-needed public benefits in their home states of Arizona and New Mexico.[85]

The backdrop for these exclusionary practices was Indians' ambiguous status vis-à-vis the American government. What rights did they enjoy? What obligations did they owe? And who was responsible for enforcing such promises? The nation's founding documents provided incomplete and contestable answers. Interactions with eastern tribes informed the content of the U.S. Constitution, but the document itself did not purport to govern them, much less the tribes in the West.[86] Indians' relationship to the federal and state governments was continually negotiated and became more complex as the legal space designated "Indian country" came into being. Federal courts developed relatively simple doctrines to govern disputes, but their rulings were difficult to enforce, and their judgments rested on characterizations (such as "alien nation," "ward," "dependent domestic nation") that were themselves contradictory and unstable.[87] The legal status of Indians in the Southwest was particularly complex: under the terms of the Treaty of Guadalupe Hidalgo (1848), Mexican citizens in the ceded territory – including Pueblo Indians – became U.S. citizens; the same history created uncertainty as to whether the Pueblos were "Indians" for purposes of federal protection and regulation.[88] Even after the enactment of the Indian Citizenship Act of 1924, which declared "all noncitizen Indians born within the territorial limits of the United States" to be U.S. citizens, there was vast confusion. Lewis Meriam, head of the Institute for Government Research and author in 1928 of the influential Meriam Report on the status of American Indians, pointed to one family, living on the grandfather's allotment of tribal land, in which some members were "exclusively wards of the nation," others were "free and independent citizens of the state and county," and others – including a "little child of mixed Indian and white blood" – were the subject of fierce intergovernmental disputes. Invoking a well-worn phrase, Meriam offered this as an example of "the Indian Problem."[89]

Administrators of the Social Security Act encountered their own version of the "Indian Problem" when they discovered that the 1935 act provided no guidance on whether states must include Indians in their federally subsidized public assistance programs or whether responsibility for their support remained with tribal governments and the federal Bureau of Indian Affairs (BIA). This was not a trivial question. Although Indians comprised less than 0.5 percent of the nation's population in 1930, making for modest fiscal stakes, they had long been entangled (and had often purposely entangled themselves) in power struggles between the state and federal governments.[90] As a source of guidance, the act's legislative history was as barren as its text. In the words of one agency lawyer, the record contained only "ominous silence."[91]

After another agency lawyer raised concerns about the Fourteenth Amendment, the board decided to give vague but threatening responses to state inquiries (discrimination might trigger "serious questions") – and for the most part, that sufficed.[92] States that approached the BIA received a similar, if more forceful, response. Interior Department solicitor (and former NAACP legal strategist) Nathan Margold insisted that the Social Security Act offered no legal shelter to states contemplating exclusion – a message that his agency conveyed to North Dakota and Montana.[93] Those states and others (for example, California, Idaho, Oklahoma, Utah, Washington, Wisconsin, and Wyoming) ultimately did not attempt to exclude Indians, "wards" or otherwise, from their programs.[94]

Arizona and New Mexico, however, would not submit so easily. These states had distinct histories and were not always natural allies, but by 1935 they shared several important characteristics.[95] In both states the federal government was a major landowner, and its agencies, a regular and not entirely welcome presence. Both also had relatively large American Indian populations: Indians represented 13.2 percent of Arizona's population and 8.7 percent of New Mexico's in 1930, giving the two states 10 and 7 percent, respectively, of the nation's total Indian population. Moreover, the major Indian communities in the region – the Navajo (Diné), Apache, and Hopi – had remained on reservation land rather than dispersing into non-Indian communities.[96] State officials there demanded to know why they should have to care for people who, in Arizona senator Carl Hayden's words, did not pay taxes and chose to reside in "primitive conditions" on federal reservations.[97]

Eventually, both states submitted public assistance plans that satisfied the Social Security Board and thereby allowed federal funds to start flowing, but in practice the states continually excluded Indians from their programs.[98] In November 1938 none of New Mexico's 28,941 Indians received public assistance; in Arizona, home to 43,726 Indians, a mere 15 were on the assistance rolls and all lived on the Colorado River Indian Reservation, which straddled the Arizona-California border. A year later, according to Social Security Board records, New Mexico continued to deny assistance to reservation Indians and was aiding at most two dozen nonreservation Indians; Arizona had no Indians at all on the rolls.[99] Yet by all accounts, Indians in these states suffered extreme poverty. In 1940 the average per capita annual income among the Navajos, for example, was a mere $82 (compared with a national average of a $575 and a regional average of $399).[100]

Historian Ira Katznelson has diagnosed the Roosevelt administration with a condition of "pragmatic forgetfulness with regard to racial matters," and the Social Security Board was no exception.[101] Despite evidence of discrimination, the board's leadership agreed "to let sleeping dogs lie," according to Senator Hayden. Hayden was then already a dozen years into his long stint on the powerful Senate Appropriations Committee, making the board's decision very pragmatic indeed. "Make no inquiries of any kind," Hayden instructed his state's anxious commissioner of social security and welfare in October 1939, and "there will be nothing for us to worry about." Hayden also did what he could to ensure that the metaphorical dogs kept sleeping. In May 1940, when entrepreneurial BIA field agents urged Navajos to apply for state public assistance – in hopes, Arizona officials suspected, of creating "test cases" – Hayden colluded with Indian Affairs commissioner John Collier to make the matter go away.[102]

Such maneuvers became increasingly difficult as American Indians – much like African Americans, Latino Americans, and women – seized on the rhetoric and demands of wartime to claim their rights as citizens. In early 1941, an attorney contacted the BIA on behalf of several tribes and demanded to know whether Indians in Arizona were entitled to public assistance benefits. That same year, representatives of eight Indian communities – the Mojave, Chemehuevi, Hualapai, Maricopa, Pima, Cocopah, Papago, and Supai – paid a visit to Arizona governor Sidney Osborn and claimed that if they were citizens enough to be drafted, they should be citizens enough to vote and to receive old-age assistance. By the spring of 1943, nearly forty Indians on the Gila River Reservation, home to the Pima and Maricopa communities, had filed old-age assistance applications with their county public welfare board and appeared "determined to have the matter brought to a head."[103] Neither Arizona nor New Mexico changed its ways, however. State officials stood especially firm with regard to reservation Indians. In the mid-1940s, it was Arizona's policy to take applications from reservation Indians but reject them "wherever possible." New Mexico's state welfare agency, though more progressive than Arizona's in all other respects, rejected applications outright, citing the federal government's overarching responsibility as well as language barriers, insufficient resources, and jurisdictional deficiencies.[104]

Around 1946, as Indian veterans of World War II returned home to a still vastly unequal Southwest, Indian activists discerned an advantage in working with and through the Social Security Board, which had finally started to crack down on the states. That spring, the board had sent stern warnings to both Arizona and New Mexico, informing them that the SSB had evidence of discrimination and was prepared to impose financial sanctions should the states not change their practices.[105] The National Congress of American Indians (NCAI), a recently formed pan-Indian organization, gave the board further ammunition by encouraging reservation Indians in Arizona and New Mexico to apply for public assistance and then closely tracking the applications. Drawing on insiders' knowledge of government bureaucracy – most of the NCAI's founding members had ties to the Bureau of Indian Affairs – the NCAI then forwarded evidence of inaction to allies at the Social Security Board.[106]

In 1947, this strategy seemed to be working. Caught in the act, state officials defended rather than denied their discriminatory actions, even in the face of widely publicized exposés of the dire need on the Navajo reservation. "The Indian reservation might as well be Canada," Arizona governor Daniel Garvey explained to a local newspaper, "because they do not permit the officers of the state to go there in carrying out their duties"; the Indians' true status was as "wards" of the federal government – or, as New Mexico governor Thomas J. Mabry suggested, "neglected 'prisoners of war.'" "The plight of these people is not of the state's doing," insisted Arizona senator Ernest McFarland.[107] In the wake of such statements, the Social Security Board summoned representatives from both states to Washington, DC – an unusual and ominous signal.

The subsequent negotiations would bring the NCAI and its allies one step closer to a lawsuit. On the advice of their congressional delegations, officials from the two states refused to concede responsibility for reservation Indians but offered to "process" Indian applications – that is, to accept and review applications, and then turn them over to the BIA for payment out of BIA reserve funds. Social Security Board officials agreed to the deal, perhaps because they saw a game-changing reform just around the bend: Congress appeared likely to pass a Marshall Plan–type "rehabilitation" program for the Navajos, and if the Navajos' economic status improved, the states' insistence on excluding reservation Indians from their public assistance programs should, in theory, weaken.[108] Before that could happen, however, the deal fell apart. By the spring of 1948, the BIA claimed to have run out of funds, leaving the states with assistance applications on their books but no expected reimbursements. State officials stalled, shuttling papers from one office to another and holding Indians' applications for "further study."[109]

Enter Felix S. Cohen, the nation's preeminent authority on Indian law and the architect of the "Indian New Deal" (a legislative attempt to restructure tribal governance and thereby win for American Indians both greater autonomy from the U.S. government and more secure rights). Cohen had recently left the Interior Department and was spoiling for a fight. That he chose this one is, on first glance, unusual. Unlike many of his contemporaries, Cohen resisted the notion that Indians must assimilate into non-Indian political communities; he treated tribal legal claims as legitimate and important. But he also believed Indians had individual rights as citizens of their respective states and the United States.[110] In 1948, Cohen joined the legal campaign to vindicate Indian voting rights in Arizona and New Mexico, which continued to deny Indians the franchise – in the former, because they were "wards," and in the latter, because they were "not taxed."[111] For the same reason, Cohen threw his considerable energy into the public assistance battle, which he likely learned about through his former Interior Department colleague James Curry, then general counsel to the NCAI. In the words of Cherokee politician and celebrity Will Rogers Jr., an NCAI ally, the Indians in the Southwest were suffering "starvation without representation," a condition, he said, that ought to offend all Americans.[112]

While Rogers and other Indian advocates aroused public sympathy, Cohen and Curry attempted to convince the Social Security Board to wield the "power of the purse" and intervene. On July 7, 1948, on behalf of the NCAI, the All-Pueblo Council, the Jicarilla Apache Tribe, and the San Carlos Apache Tribe, Cohen and Curry petitioned the board for a hearing to determine whether Arizona and New Mexico were in conformity with the Social Security Act. Formal hearings themselves were rare, a last step before the board applied the harsh sanction of complete defunding. More rare still was an attempt by an outside party – Cohen and Curry styled themselves as amici curiae (friends of the court) – to influence the SSB's decision making.[113]

When the hearing mysteriously disappeared from the board's calendar – mere months before the contentious 1948 elections and shortly after the

Democratic Party's adoption of a liberal civil rights plank prompted a revolt by conservative white southerners – Cohen and Curry went from being "friends" of the agency to adversaries. On September 21, 1948, Cohen, Curry, and Arizona attorney Royal D. Marks filed *Mapatis v. Ewing* in federal court, alleging that federal officials had deprived eight Pueblo and Hualapai plaintiffs, and others like them, of their civil rights. One of the plaintiffs was blind, another was the mother of six children, and the rest were elderly. All were in need. They claimed that through "misrepresentations, misappropriations . . . of public funds, and interference with the normal administrative procedures" of the Social Security Board, high-ranking officials had conspired with Arizona and New Mexico to deprive reservation Indians of the equal protection of the law. The object of the alleged conspiracy, they charged, was political power: by preventing the board from taking action against the states, the defendants hoped to assure a Democratic victory that fall.[114]

Poor Indians paid the price, according to the complaint: an estimated 802 Indians in New Mexico and 922 in Arizona were eligible for public assistance – they were, after all, state citizens, even if they resided on reservations. But "no known Indian" in New Mexico and only three in Arizona had ever received benefits – benefits that were terminated once administrators became aware of the recipients' Indian blood. As a result, the plaintiffs charged, more than eighty-two Indians in New Mexico and Arizona had died of starvation or malnutrition in the past five years. The plaintiffs themselves were "in dire distress," and yet state officials had either denied or refused to act on their applications. The plaintiffs asked the court to stop the defendants from obstructing the board's promised conformity hearing.[115]

Had the *Mapatis* litigation moved forward to trial, the federal government defendants would have been in an interesting position: the plaintiffs' legal arguments mirrored those that the Social Security Board's own lawyers had long asserted in internal correspondence.[116] The case never made it that far, however. In early 1949, as the Navajos endured a winter of unprecedented severity and the Red Cross airlifted supplies to the reservation, the board finally held formal hearings to determine whether it could legally issue federal funds to the two states that denied public assistance payments to Indians.[117] Tellingly, the board invited Felix Cohen and James Curry to file amicus briefs – an unprecedented gesture.[118]

At this point, cracks in the states' united front became apparent. During the hearings, New Mexico officials defended their actions but also acknowledged "social and humanitarian" concerns. The chair of New Mexico's Department of Welfare, Ruth Falkenburg Kirk, had personally publicized the Navajos' plight and, in private correspondence, suggested that she would have supported the NCAI campaign had the governor not "told [her] to lay off." Outside the hearing, state officials assured the board that they "want[ed] to do the right thing for Indians"; the "problem," they averred, was simply "too big for [the] state."[119]

Arizona officials conceded nothing and fought fiercely – an outgrowth, perhaps, of the racism that continued to organize everyday life in the state, or perhaps a reprise of the recent battle with federal authorities over the Colorado River. (In 1934, outraged by the unfavorable terms of the Colorado River Compact, state officials had forcibly obstructed the construction of the Parker Dam.)[120] Before the Social Security Board, Arizona's commissioner of public welfare, Harry Hill, characterized Indians as undeserving and the federal government as overbearing. Arizonans' generosity could hardly be expected to extend to "a class of people who have contributed nothing ... to the welfare of the state or its progress," Hill insisted. The state's resistance to the board's questionable legal interpretation was also entirely natural, Hill explained: time and again, the federal government "dangl[ed]" money before the state, exploiting its "helplessness" in order to usurp state power. If the federal agency won Indians' inclusion among assistance beneficiaries, Hill warned, "further encroachments" would be "only a matter of time." Back home, Arizona officials primed the public for a fight, warning that federal government sanctions would halve the funds available for "white residents."[121]

For all this bluster, by February 1949 Arizona and New Mexico were prepared to compromise. Two developments impelled their retreat. First, the Social Security Board disclosed its lack of sympathy for the states' position. (And, as Harry Hill complained to a local newspaper, federal administrators functioned as "judge, jury and prosecution" in this proceeding.) Second, Congress took up the Navajo-Hopi Rehabilitation Act, a bill devoted to raising standards of living and building "self-reliant communities" on the Navajo and Hopi reservations. The act fell short of 100 percent federal financing for Indian welfare, but it would funnel ninety million dollars toward helping the states' poorest tribes.[122]

In late April, as this legislation moved through Congress, state officials met with representatives from the Social Security Board in Santa Fe. (Unbeknown to them, President Truman would later veto the Navajo-Hopi Rehabilitation Act.) There, they formally agreed to treat Indian public assistance applications the same as all others and to spend their own funds on Indian claims. The BIA, with money from a special congressional appropriation, agreed to pay two-thirds of every Indian's determined need; the remaining third would be paid like any other claim, through a combination of state funds and federal "matching" funds. In total, nonstate sources would provide 90 percent of the financing.[123]

The Santa Fe Agreement, as it became known, did not satisfy some Indians. Just months earlier, David Johnson Sr. had informed the NCAI that his people, the Pima-Maricopa Indians, did "not want to be handled separately or even set apart in [a] separate class"; remembering, perhaps, decades of struggles over federal treaty agreements, he insisted that his people receive equal treatment under the existing law. Felix Cohen and his clients, however, saw the agreement as a victory. As soon as the states began to cut benefit checks, he asked the court to dismiss the *Mapatis* case. As he explained to Roger Baldwin, director of the American Civil Liberties Union (ACLU) and an ally in the Indian voting rights cases, the litigation had achieved its goals: it forced politicians to cease interfering in the federal agency's enforcement work and thereby promoted Indian civil rights.[124]

***

The *Mapatis* litigation, although cut short by a political settlement, is a fitting coda to the scattered fair hearing records and state court cases discussed in this chapter. Like those decisions, it shows us how welfare rights claims circulated in and around the administrative state in the 1930s and 1940s. It shows us what some claimants believed they deserved and how they understood their ties to the political communities around them. It shows us the resistance that claimants faced, especially when they appeared "undeserving," and the perseverance and luck that they needed in order to receive vindication from state agencies and courts.

The *Mapatis* litigation also sets up the chapters that follow, by demonstrating how a savvy group of plaintiffs, with the help of knowledgeable lawyers and sympathetic federal administrators, could turn federal grants-in-aid into a powerful legal and political tool in their dealings with state and local officials. This insight helps us understand why some state and local officials began to resist and undermine the idea of welfare rights so vigorously in the 1950s, and why litigants turned to the federal courts in greater numbers as soon as they had the opportunity.

Gallery

FIGURE 1. Members of the Social Security Board, November 12, 1937. Seated (*left to right*) are commissioners Mary M. Dewson, Arthur J. Altmeyer (chairman), and George E. Bigge; Acting General Counsel Jack B. Tate and Executive Director Frank Bane stand behind. Harris & Ewing Collection, Library of Congress.

FIGURE 2. Bureau of Public Assistance director Jane Hoey, August 18, 1936 or 1937. Hoey was in charge of administering the Social Security Board's public assistance programs from 1936 until 1953. A social worker by training, Hoey filled her bureau with like-minded professionals. Harris & Ewing Collection, Library of Congress.

FIGURE 3. Old Age Assistance claimants, November 1941. State-run Old Age Assistance programs, subsidized by the federal government, aided more than 2.2 million people in the fall of 1941, including Mr. and Mrs. Jucius Catlan of Greene County, Georgia (shown here). But the states remained free to set benefit levels, and payment amounts varied widely. In the Catlans' region, the Deep South, average monthly payments per recipient were less than $10 in 1941; in the West, average payments were as high as $36.51. (Bureau of Public Assistance, "Changes in Public Assistance, 1940–42," *Social Security Bulletin* 5, no. 12 [1942]: 50, and "Public Assistance," *Social Security Bulletin* 5, no. 1 [1942]: 49.) Photograph by Jack Delano. Farm Security Administration/Office of War Information Collection, Library of Congress.

FIGURE 4. Aid to Dependent Children propaganda photo, created between 1940 and 1946. Despite federal administrators' best efforts, the welfare program for poor children and their caregivers fell under suspicion in the 1940s as critics noted the increasing proportion of nonwhite children and never-married mothers on the rolls. Farm Security Administration/Office of War Information Collection, Library of Congress.

FIGURE 5. David Wilkie, Seneca Falls, New York, May 1940. When the Seneca County Welfare Department reduced Wilkie's Old Age Assistance grant on account of his refusal of "suitable living quarters," Wilkie filed suit in state court. "'Dave' of Seneca Falls Fights for Right to Sleep under Barn," *Syracuse Herald-American*, May 12, 1940. Onandaga Historical Association, Syracuse, N. Y. Reprinted with permission.

FIGURE 6. General Counsel Alanson Work Willcox, undated. After brief stints in private practice and at the Treasury Department, Willcox joined the Social Security Board's Office of the General Counsel. Like many of the board's midlevel bureaucrats, he worked for the Social Security Board or its umbrella agency, the Federal Security Agency (later the Department of Health, Education, and Welfare), through multiple administrations—in Willcox's case, those of Presidents Roosevelt, Truman, Kennedy, and Johnson. U.S. Department of Health and Human Services.

FIGURE 7. Welfare advocate Elizabeth Wickenden, March 6, 1962. Wickenden's long career working to improve public welfare spanned the New Deal and the War on Poverty. In the early 1960s, in response to a wave of discriminatory state policies, she and her network of administrators, academics, philanthropists, lawyers, and social welfare workers created the field of poverty law. Michigan League for Public Policy. Reprinted with permission.

PART II

1950 to 1972

By 1950, federal administrators and their allies had achieved remarkable successes in their battle to make poor relief part of a more modern (as they understood it) pattern of governance. But changes in the political climate now made their previous tactics less effective. Those changes emboldened political enemies, new and old, and ultimately encouraged a different set of liberal reformers – outside of the administrative state – to pick up where New Deal administrators had left off.

Chapter 5 follows the federal-state public assistance program into the early 1950s, when restive state politicians, not recalcitrant local officials, were federal assistance administrators' biggest problem. With federal encouragement, most states had developed the administrative machinery and supervisory capabilities that they lacked in the 1930s. In the meantime, statutory reforms, administrative practices, and socioeconomic changes had caused the number of public assistance recipients to grow and their perceived deservingness to wane. But federal administrators, many of whom had been in place since the mid-1930s, continued to push their New Deal vision. With the Depression over and more conservative leadership in Congress, some state officials pushed back: throughout the early Cold War period, they questioned federal policies, disobeyed federal agency mandates, and, with increasing confidence, advanced their own interpretations of federal law, sometimes even attempting to drag the federal agency into court. I document these trends by examining several of the states that, for varying reasons, posed the most serious challenges to federal administrators between 1950 and 1954. They are not the states that scholars might expect. To date, studies of postwar welfare "backlash" have tended to focus on the Deep South and have invoked race as the key explanation for that backlash. The episodes detailed – involving Arizona, Indiana, and New York – invite a more nuanced interpretation in which race figures importantly, but so, too, do concerns about federal overreaching, suspicions of bureaucratic governance, long-simmering resentments of the New Deal, and Americans' growing sense of themselves as "taxpayers."

By the mid-1950s, public assistance had become entangled in the postwar politics of racial equality, female sexuality, and urban change. Many states proposed restrictive amendments to their welfare laws, hoping to prune unwed, nonwhite mothers from their welfare rolls and to monitor tightly those who remained. With Congress and many public welfare professionals bent on "rehabilitating" the poor, and with new Eisenhower appointees at the head of the agency, there appeared to be little space for notions of poor peoples' rights. And yet, as I argue in Chapter 6, rights language and rights claims endured. Critics of the emergent rehabilitation paradigm fretted about its cost in terms of individual rights and began developing the notion of rights *against* well-intentioned, professionally trained bureaucrats. On the ground, meanwhile, poor individuals continued to claim their rights, both before state and local agencies and in court. And in the day-to-day world of federal-state welfare administration, federal officials adhered to the legal interpretations that they had developed in the 1940s – interpretations that emphasized due process and equal treatment. By confronting state officials with the technical requirements of the Social Security Act and the Constitution, federal administrators prevented many state schemes from becoming law. Ultimately, however, Chapter 6 is about the limits of administrative enforcement. In the wake of *Brown v. Board of Education*, a Supreme Court decision that gave greater urgency to concerns about federal coercion, federal administrators often compromised the very rights that they had long deemed vital.

Chapter 7 opens in 1960, when federal administrators became embroiled in a nationally publicized dispute with Louisiana over that state's discriminatory "suitable home" policy (the policy was explicitly aimed at lowering the number of "illegitimate" children receiving ADC, most of whom were African American). The so-called battle of Newburgh (discussed in the introduction) followed shortly thereafter. The result was a thorough reappraisal of New Deal public assistance programs. Under intense scrutiny, federal administrators continued to enforce their understanding of the Social Security Act and the Constitution, but with greater caution. Outside the agency, meanwhile, old New Dealers, younger liberal lawyers, and a coalition of academics and activists took up some of the work that had previously fallen on the agency's shoulders. An emergent poverty law network, led by Elizabeth Wickenden, extrapolated from agency precedents and recent civil rights cases to develop and broadcast arguments about the rights of the poor. Lawyers and their clients – who themselves had begun to organize – then took those arguments to federal court.

Chapter 8 covers the events of the next eight years, when, according to the conventional narrative, Americans witnessed the spectacular rise of welfare rights and its equally spectacular demise. I place these events in a longer arc: in my telling, poverty lawyers and the modern welfare rights movement, along with their remaining allies in the federal agency, encouraged the Supreme Court to articulate a set of governing principles that had in fact already gained much ground within the world of federal-state welfare administration – that the poor were national citizens, that national citizenship carried with it rights against abusive state and local welfare practices, and that income support was both a crucial resource for poor Americans and a legitimate government function. The establishment of these principles mattered to many actors, not just the poor. Other judicial decisions, however, clarified their limits. National citizenship did not bring with it a right to a minimally adequate standard of living, the Supreme Court held, nor did citizens have a right to federally (as opposed to state and locally) administered benefits. Contemporaneous legislative choices, such as the failure of President Nixon's Family Assistance Plan and the move to grant states greater control over their Aid to Dependent Children programs, made the implications of the Court's decisions crystal clear.

5

States' Rights against Federal Administrative Enforcement

Contesting Dependency

In the fall of 1938, the two-year-old Indiana State Department of Public Welfare was filled with optimism. Staff of the department's new division for information and public relations had launched a massive campaign of "interpretation" to explain the department's good work, logging some sixty thousand miles within the state in a single year ("twice around the world and more than a third of the way 'round again!" boasted the department newsletter). Through films and radio scripts, exhibits at county fairs, "literature kits" given out to interested groups, and carefully produced "human interest" stories designed for local newspapers, department employees cheerfully spread the word.[1]

Just twelve years later, in 1950, the outlook was much darker. Despite the department's earnest "Know Your Welfare Program" slideshow, despite its stated commitment to "building windows and turning on lights so that everyone . . . can see and know what we are doing," public welfare in Indiana was under siege.[2] The charge, ironically, was that the Public Welfare Department had concealed its operations from public view, and forced local welfare agencies to do the same, by requiring that the identities of public assistance recipients be kept confidential. Conservative state politicians, aided by powerful allies in the local media, conjured images of liberal bureaucrats frittering away taxpayer dollars behind an "iron curtain of secrecy," a convenient and evocative Cold War reference.[3] Hiding behind the principle of client confidentiality, these critics alleged, the department had encouraged welfare fraud, aided socialism, and attempted to build a behemoth centralized bureaucracy. When the department countered that it was simply obeying an established requirement of the Social Security Act – on which Indiana's generous federal

155

assistance grants hinged – critics took the fight to Washington. There they confronted federal welfare administrators and, when stymied, convinced Congress to nullify the offending provision of federal law.

This bit of political maneuvering stands in stark contrast to how such actors had resolved their differences in the past. And it was not an isolated incident. Around the same time, officials in Arizona and New York also rebelled against federal administrative authority. Following Indiana's challenge to federal mandates, Arizona sued federal administrators for refusing to tolerate the state's long-running discrimination against American Indian public assistance claimants – discrimination, not coincidentally, that federal administrators helped expose in the 1940s. New York, which had been the model for so many New Deal programs, developed a similarly adversarial relationship with the federal agency. Frustrated by federal efforts to impose uniform eligibility standards and a more robust merit system across their large state, and embarrassed by a welfare scandal in New York City, New York officials set out to expose the federal agency's untoward influence on their ability to govern. In all three instances, state officials went beyond merely vocalizing disagreement with the federal agency. Instead, they openly challenged the claimed legal basis for the agency's actions and actively sought to undermine the agency's legitimacy.

Together these episodes illustrate the broader intergovernmental tensions that simmered in the wake of the New Deal and began to boil at midcentury. Critics at the state level signaled that they accepted some aspects of the system of governance that the New Deal had enshrined, such as generous federal subsidies, subtle augmentation of state (over local) power, and the powerful signals of inclusion directed to white, working men and their families. But they began publicly and vigorously to contest others, including the new system's seeming insensitivity to state and local contexts; its glorification of professional education and expertise; and its tendency to infuse welfare administration with concepts like equality and rights – concepts that had not been part of the original bargain and that appeared to be producing expensive and disruptive consequences.[4]

These tensions burst into view so vividly around 1950 for at least four reasons. First, with the Depression and World War II over, Americans were deciding which of that previous era's dramatic changes ought to be undone – cast off as artifacts of an exceptional time – and which represented the new "normal." There is no doubt that when it came to traditional poor relief, a vast restructuring had occurred: local governments continued to issue aid to their citizens, but state and federal involvement had increased immensely, via the sharing of personnel, information, and, most important, money. So far, federal money had also come with federal directives – about who ought to be aided, who ought to be hired, and many things in between. But did it have to? For those who questioned either the fact or the substance of federal edicts, the time had come, in the 1950s, to press their case. State officials now had fifteen years' experience with New Deal public assistance – more than enough time to learn the proclivities of federal administrators and to master the technical requirements of the Social Security Act. With the economy seemingly on track and many of the elderly poor now cared for by Old Age Insurance, the desperation that had characterized earlier state interactions with the federal government had also diminished.[5]

A second reason for the emergence of federal-state welfare conflicts was the powerful intersection in the second half of the 1940s of federal government power and attacks on white supremacy, which, in turn, produced national political realignments. For much of the 1930s the political leadership of Jim Crow states (that is, those states with the greatest, though by no means the only, stake in white supremacy) had welcomed the growth of federal government power: it brought the region resources, technology, and infrastructure, while leaving the racial hierarchy untouched.[6] The representatives of Jim Crow states were similarly supportive of the United States' entry into World War II, which promised to further augment federal power. With a secure hold on Congress, they had little to fear. These defenders of white supremacy were ever alert to the possibility of subversion, however, and by the early 1940s they perceived worrisome signs, ranging from Supreme Court decisions on segregation and voting rights to President Roosevelt's establishment of the wartime Fair Employment Practices Committee (FEPC) to a budding alliance between black Americans and the labor movement. By the end of the decade, white supremacy appeared to be in genuine danger, at least to its most ardent proponents. As Congress considered a permanent FEPC and President Truman loudly proclaimed his commitment to civil rights, southern Democrats responded by tempering their support for New Deal programs, especially those that might advantage civil rights activists. And although they continued to support expansive federal power, they forged alliances with Republicans, who were much more skeptical. Republicans, for their part, learned the value of speaking not only in terms of free enterprise and efficiency but also of states' rights.[7] With the New Deal coalition fracturing, federal welfare administrators had to tread carefully.

Disaffected state officials, meanwhile, found that they could tap into a rich vein of anxiety about federal power.

Political opportunity also resulted from a third circumstance: the gathering momentum of what historian Kim Phillips-Fein has labeled "the businessman's crusade against the New Deal." With ever-greater sophistication and organizational support, "ordinary businessmen" sought "to undo the system of labor unions, federal social welfare programs, and government regulation of the economy that came into existence during and after the Great Depression."[8] At midcentury, their cause had broader appeal than ever before. By then, the country had ample experience with robust, highly visible government interventions. And although many Americans had reaped the rewards of those interventions, they were also more alert than ever to the attendant dangers. Friedrich von Hayek's *The Road to Serfdom* (1944), for example – popularized in condensed form in *Reader's Digest* – cast centralized government planning as a natural antagonist to democracy and individual liberty.[9] So did enterprising politicians, such as Arizona Republican Barry Goldwater. To support the "Truman New Deal," Goldwater reminded voters during his 1952 Senate race, was to allow "federal bureaus and federal agencies to take over an ever increasing portion of your life."[10]

The most worrisome danger that anti–New Dealers brought to light, however, was the drain on the workingman's wallet. The need to finance the war had made many more Americans feel like taxpayers, via the broadening of the federal income tax ("from a class tax to a mass tax," in historian Molly Michelmore's words); after the war the federal government showed no signs of returning to a narrower tax base. Anti–New Dealers encouraged Americans to understand their new taxpayer identity in a particular way: as giving them a right to question government and a responsibility to keep it in check. Government "handouts" – such as public assistance programs – were a favored target of scrutiny. (By contrast, the invisible handouts that nonpoor Americans and corporations received through the tax code received little attention.)[11] Politicians and journalists in this period railed against disability claimants who were in fact perfectly capable of working, such as the Seattle factory technician rumored to have quit his relatively well paying job after finding that a trifling arm injury entitled him to receive more in disability from the government than he was earning, and the Tennessee man who could allegedly see well enough to hunt squirrels but was collecting fifty dollars per month in Aid to the Blind.[12] Even the perennially popular Old Age Assistance program was vulnerable. Critics noted with disapproval the elderly claimants who shrewdly hid or gave away property in order to qualify for aid, who relied on the "taxpayers" rather than on their well-to-do children, and who stopped working to "retire" on the public's dime (a sensitive issue, given that average monthly OAA payments were then almost twice as much as average monthly Social Security checks).[13] "Under the present standards set up by the State and Federal governments," complained the Tioga County (New York) Board of Supervisors in 1950, "the relief client lives better and is clothed better, sees more movies and has more recreation than many of the people who pay taxes."[14]

A particularly resented type of "relief client" – and a fourth reason for the unprecedented confrontations over New Deal welfare policies at midcentury – was the recipient of Aid to Dependent Children. Traditionally, poor mothers had turned either to marriage or the labor market for financial support. Like so many gendered traditions, however, this one showed signs of stress in the 1940s. The ADC rolls had grown steadily since 1935, owing to overall increases in the nation's population, to women's rising fertility rate, to higher rates of divorce and separation, and, truth be told, to some states' practice of shifting recipients of "general assistance" (a state and local burden) onto federally subsidized public assistance rolls. But that did not stop critics from blaming liberal federal welfare policies.[15] Observers also noted that the racial composition of ADC recipients had changed: whereas African American children comprised 14 percent of the ADC population in 1937–38, that figure had risen to 30 percent in 1948. This change was the result of several factors, including federal antidiscrimination pressures; black women's greater likelihood of being divorced, separated, or widowed; and – crucially – white women's increased access to another, more secure income-support program, Old Age Insurance, via the 1939 inclusion of survivors of covered wage earners.[16] But whatever the cause, the change hit a nerve. In an age of deep anxiety about gender roles and the nuclear family, women receiving ADC for their children appeared to embrace sex and childbearing while rejecting the institution – marriage – meant to protect, control, and reward them. Black single mothers raised special concern: their behavior showed that they had not only reclaimed their own reproductive capacity, once a cherished asset of southern slaveholders, but had also chosen to rely on the government rather than to work for low wages in fields and whites' homes.[17]

These developments came together at midcentury to encourage some representatives of state government to voice their dissatisfaction with federal-state welfare administration – and with it, their dissatisfaction with the broader regime of governance it represented. They were alert to the dangers of federal grants and conflicted about their dependency on federal aid, they made clear. They were also now prepared to test the boundaries of federal bureaucratic control.[18] And while the rebellious stances of Indiana, Arizona, and New York were not the nationwide norm, these states would ease the way for states in the Deep South in the late 1950s, when a new crop of racially discriminatory policies became a subject of federal concern.

INDIANA: PROFESSIONALS AND BUREAUCRATS BEHIND AN "IRON CURTAIN OF SECRECY"

At first glance, the battle in Indiana over "welfare secrecy" was a purely local matter, the result of a unique confluence of Indiana-specific circumstances. One was an incident in Elkhart County: prosecutor David Russell Bontrager asked local welfare authorities for a list of ADC recipients, to determine whether the children's fathers were fulfilling the terms of their court-issued support orders, a matter of both moral and fiscal significance. The welfare agency's rebuff – citing federally mandated confidentiality requirements – still rankled months later, when Bontrager won election to the state senate and was in a position to do something about it.[19] This roughly coincided with a second incident, in Indianapolis, involving the Stockholm Peace Petition and its circulation by two employees of the Indiana State Welfare Department. (The petition sought to ban use of the atomic bomb and, according to the U.S. attorney general, was the handiwork of America's enemies.)[20] Coming shortly after the outbreak of the Korean War, the petition's circulation was scandalous, and it prompted further inquiry. Within weeks, the conservative *Indianapolis Star* claimed to have found "relief recipients driving late model automobiles" and "heading for Florida with the birds for seasonal vacations," as well as "race-track habitués," "broods of illegitimate children," and "people holding down well-paying jobs."[21] *Star* reporter Lester Hunt, the author of most of the exposés, tied this state of affairs directly to the department's insulation from public scrutiny – a point on which state senator Bontrager readily agreed. "Rip the mask off the welfare department," Bontrager promised a local civic group, and "the flies" would "drop off the relief rolls." By January of 1951, he had proposed a bill mandating public lists of the names and addresses of welfare recipients, along with the amount of assistance they received.[22]

Thus began Indiana's nationally publicized showdown with federal welfare authorities – a showdown that Bontrager and other Indiana Republicans welcomed. After steadily supplanting private charity, Bontrager claimed, the Federal Security Agency was now using its power over federal funds to prevent local citizens from examining "the cancerous growth" that was "eating the heart out of" their government. This was just another instance of "taxation without representation," Bontrager declared, and the time had come for "a little Boston Tea Party."[23]

Like the historical Boston Tea Party, Indiana's uprising resonated well beyond the local level because of its connection to the broader trends just outlined. To start, it had everything to do with the New Deal and the way it had seemed to gain ground at the expense of state and local politicians. Consider the origins of the offending confidentiality requirement: by 1939, the Social Security Board had spent several years attempting to persuade state and local welfare departments to keep welfare records confidential. The board objected to how politicians used recipient lists to solicit votes, as well as to how the free flow of information supported old poor law–style discipline and surveillance (for example, the practice of supplying taverns with lists of relief recipients, to prevent them from spending the money on drink). Without a firm legal basis for their objections, however, federal administrators were on shaky ground – which is why they convinced Congress to add language to the Social Security Act. The 1939 amendments explicitly conditioned states' grants on their agreement to safeguard client information. This same set of amendments required the establishment of merit systems for state and local welfare workers – a clear and deliberate effort to professionalize the public welfare sector.[24]

States responded as expected, by bringing their formal rules into conformity with federal law. But both within government and outside of it, people continued to find welfare records irresistible.[25] Around the country, prosecutors sought names of children receiving ADC so that grand juries might investigate the spending habits of their caregivers and the whereabouts of their fathers.[26] Private parties and specialized courts sought to use welfare records as proof in insurance litigation, workmen's compensation evaluations, personal injury disputes, and rape prosecutions.[27] Wherever federal administrators learned of such cases, they objected, maintaining that if the inquiry did not relate to the administration of public assistance, not even the Government Accounting Office or the Internal Revenue Service should have access to claimants' confidential information.[28] Arthur Altmeyer himself, the head of the Social Security

Administration, sent Indiana's Department of Public Welfare a stern letter in early 1947, warning that should state authorities subpoena welfare records in the course of prosecuting unrelated criminal charges, Indiana's federal grant would be in jeopardy.[29] Thus Prosecutor Bontrager's local welfare department was in a difficult position when he demanded information about families on the ADC rolls. A former judge, Bontrager wielded power in his northern Indiana town, but the federal government was even more powerful, and the entire state's federal funding hung in the balance.[30]

Indiana's battle over welfare secrecy intersected, as well, with broader concerns about the security of white supremacy and the government's apparent subsidizing of out-of-wedlock childbearing. Indiana, a state with a well-deserved reputation for hostility to African Americans, now found that its ADC rolls were blacker than the median nationwide.[31] In June 1948, nonwhite children in the United States received ADC at 2.8 times the rate of white children. In Indiana, the nonwhite rate was 4.3 times the white rate (around 63 of every 1,000 nonwhite children in Indiana received ADC, compared with around 15 of every 1,000 white children).[32] Russell Bontrager's sudden interest in the fathers of dependent children was no coincidence, nor was the *Indianapolis Star*'s reference to the "broods of illegitimate children" profiting from the state welfare department's misfeasance.

And then there were the left-leaning women welfare workers, the first hint of trouble at the welfare department, according to the *Star*. Larue Spiker and Mary Louise Gilbert, the two alleged subversives, embodied the perceived connections among gender, social work, political radicalism, and government bureaucracy. The link between women and welfare work was by then well established, and the subject of some resentment. "If that woman worker comes out here again," read a letter sent to the Indiana State Welfare Department in 1937, "i'll run hur thru with a sord and throw er over me shoulder an kary er to the woods"; "i've no use for shemales."[33] But by midcentury, the stakes had grown higher: women social workers and feminized, egg-head bureaucrats had become the personification of a creeping federal "welfare state," a term just coming into vogue.

The image derived its power in part from popular suspicions of experts. There was a saying, often attributed to Mark Twain, that an expert was just an ordinary fellow from another town. Trained social workers in this era were often "ladies" rather than "fellows," and thanks to federal merit-system requirements, they had made significant inroads in the field of public welfare. Once in place, moreover, they seemed to make a point of distinguishing themselves from the sort of decision makers who filled other public posts. The social work lexicon was "bewilder[ing]," filled with unnecessarily "abstruse and esoteric terminology," complained one concerned layperson; "mumbo-jumbo double-talk," griped another.[34] Critics accused social workers of manufacturing a "wilderness" just so they could "guide the ignorant lay people like Moses through [it]."[35]

To what end? Status was one goal, critics alleged, but as the Orwellian "double-talk" reference implies, there was another: to those who were concerned about the growth of centralized state power and the expansion of the federal government into "private" realms, the social workers staffing state and local welfare operations looked like the handmaidens of a threatening new regime. Thanks to merit systems, these workers were not as beholden to local party politics. (In a state like Indiana, still dominated by traditional party organizations, this was no small matter.)[36] Their loyalties instead seemed to lie with national professional organizations and with Washington. These were precisely the "little bureaucrats" that southern senators had warned of in their campaign against a permanent Fair Employment Practices Committee in 1946: "Clothed with all the power and majesty of the Federal Government," these "snoopers and busybodies, smellers and agitators," would "walk into a man's castle" and, on the pretense of doing good, tell him exactly what to do.[37]

The claim was overstated but not entirely spurious. Many professional social workers, including those in prominent public welfare positions, admired President Franklin Roosevelt's "second bill of rights" of 1944, with its promise of adequate housing, medical care, education, and income support. The achievement of these rights, they understood, required greater federal government intervention. Thus they supported President Truman's plan for national health insurance, as well as the expansion of the social insurance program and the raising of existing public benefit levels. At the rank-and-file level, especially in big cities, public welfare workers belonged to some of the nation's most radical unions.[38]

Opponents of a more robust welfare state, such as the powerful American Medical Association, used these connections to tar the entire federal social welfare bureaucracy (including, by association, its local outposts) as soft, idealistic, and dangerously vulnerable to communist subversion.[39] Against the backdrop of the early Cold War and the federal government's own loyalty and security initiatives, public welfare workers found their patriotism questioned and their motives impugned. Were they really interested in helping the poor, critics asked, or were they using their position and expertise to build a socialist state from the inside out?[40] In Indianapolis, *Star* reporter Lester Hunt traded on these associations when, in the midst of the controversy over welfare secrecy, he noted with alarm the number of non-Hoosiers on the state welfare department's payroll. He gave an equally sensationalist cast to the fact that the department had sent more than a dozen "proteges" to college, some going as far away as California.[41] All this when, in the words of one *Star* reader, a "good widow with just ordinary horse sense and experience with life's problems" could do the work just as well.[42]

To say that Indiana's uproar over welfare secrecy resonated with broader themes is not to say that it could have developed anywhere, however. There was one final circumstance that transformed the local scandal into a national controversy: an ongoing crusade among Indianapolis businessmen against the perceived excesses of the New Deal. In 1946, five years before the confidentiality controversy, two members of the Indianapolis Chamber of Commerce openly opposed the location of a proposed Department of Commerce field office in the city. They deemed it a waste of taxpayer money and a symbol of federal control.[43] The following year the Indiana state legislature passed a resolution decrying *all* federal aid and urging the state's representatives in Congress "to fetch our county courthouses and city halls back from Washington's Pennsylvania Avenue." "Indiana needs no guardian," the legislature resolved, and would fight Washington's "adopti[on]" effort by resisting all "subsidies, doles and paternalism." Grants-in-aid, claimed another proposed resolution, were simply "an entering wedge" for federal encroachment. [44]

This was not just talk, at least for Indianapolis's "anti-aiders," as one journalist dubbed them. Between 1946 and 1954, civic leaders there prevented the Department of Commerce from awarding the city a $50,000 annual grant; convinced Congress to withhold hundreds of thousands of dollars in federal flood-control aid; cut off thirty-two schools from the federal school lunch program; and developed an urban renewal program that relied on local dollars rather than federal "slum clearance" money. Future targets included federal "handouts" for infrastructure and education. In short, powerful forces in Indiana politics were already attuned to the coercive potential of federal grants and organized to resist it.[45]

This alignment helps explain why, in 1950 and 1951, the *Indianapolis Star* not only pounced on the issue of welfare secrecy, but also persistently articulated links to federal overreaching. The fight over confidentiality, explained the paper's editors in February 1951, was "a fight to throw off the heavy hand of Federal control" and the "system of government" that it represented. It was also a critique of federal bureaucrats and their ideology. Since when was government support a "right"? Since when did a "new class of professional givers" – social workers – choose who enjoyed the right and who did not?[46] The *Star* punctuated these points with allusions to other noble battles: the federal confidentiality requirement as a modern Stamp Act, welfare workers as foreign agents.[47] It did not take long for readers to join the chorus. "Patrick Henry never said, 'Give me liberty or give me Federal aid,'" griped John I. Niblack, a superior court judge from Marion County, in a letter to the editor.[48] Even the *Indianapolis News*, a rival paper, could not resist chiming in. Employing what would become a signature move in post–World War II conservative rhetoric, the *News* reframed a protection for minority rights as a violation of the rights of an innocent (taxpaying) majority. The dispute over welfare records, *News* editors declared, was about whether the federal government could deny the people of Indiana their constitutionally guaranteed "right to see how their tax money is spent."[49]

Within days, more distant newspapers picked up the story and placed it in the same context. The *Atlanta Constitution* blamed Georgia's "nauseating welfare abuses" – such as that of the wealthy attorney who insisted that the state should support his aging mother – on the federal government, for "virtually prohibiting adequate investigation of applicants."[50] "The socialistic burocrats [*sic*] in Washington" had "forced" the confidentiality provision upon the states, explained the conservative *Chicago Tribune*, "as part of the price of federal aid."[51] To such critics, Indiana was on the front line of a larger struggle – against social work professionals, federal government dominance, and New Deal social and economic regulation.

The controversy would divide Indiana politicians and eventually spread all the way to Washington, DC. Democrats in the state legislature agreed that "being bossed" by the Federal Security Agency was tiresome, as was "yielding to every whim of a social worker."[52] But they also understood the stakes: money. Senator Bontrager's bill conflicted with the confidentiality provision of the Social Security Act, jeopardizing the $20 million in federal funds that Indiana received annually for its public assistance programs. The subsequent vote fell along party lines. Indiana governor Henry Schricker lined up fellow Democrats to vote against the bill; the Republican-controlled legislature passed it anyway and then overrode the governor's veto.[53]

The Federal Security Agency was, indeed, watching. As was their custom, federal administrators gave state officials time to remedy the discrepancy with federal law, but Indiana's Republican legislators stood firm, daring the agency to act. On May 15, 1951, the federal agency held a formal hearing on the matter, and in late July, when Indiana officials still had not backed down, Federal Security Administrator Oscar Ewing – a native Hoosier, no less – announced that the law "compelled" him to cut the state off.[54]

Historically, this tactic had worked well for federal administrators. But Indiana Republicans were not willing to back down so fast, especially given the moral support they were receiving from other jurisdictions. Between January and September of 1951, at least five other state legislatures – in Alabama, Florida, Illinois, Oklahoma, and Tennessee – passed laws that would have opened up the welfare rolls and thereby violated the federal confidentiality requirement. Unlike Indiana, they gave themselves an exit, either by choosing to accept their governor's veto (as Indiana Republicans refused to do) or by using a savings clause, but their message was clear: the Federal Security Agency, not the states, should change its ways. At their annual gathering that fall, the nation's governors signaled their agreement, unanimously resolving that acceptance of federal money should not preclude a state from publicizing information about relief recipients. There was support from Congress, as well. In a series of House and Senate bills, congressmen from Illinois, Virginia, and New York joined Indiana's representatives in proposing legislation to nullify the Social Security Act's confidentiality provision.[55]

These congressmen – who, in retrospect, epitomized the important affinity between conservative Republicans and southern Democrats – used the welfare secrecy issue to gesture toward everything that was wrong with New Deal public assistance, and with federal-state relations more generally. "The weapon of shame" had long been a part of the state and local arsenal, Illinois senator Everett Dirksen, a Republican, observed. Who were these federal bureaucrats to revoke it, especially when the consequences were so dire for state and local governments?[56] Democratic representative Burr Harrison of Virginia sketched a picture of vast sums of taxpayer money lining the pockets of "shameless cheats" and encouraging "improvidence and illegitimacy." Concealing this from public view – and thereby enabling "extravagant, inefficient and socialistic [welfare] administration" – was a familiar cohort of old New Dealers. From their perches in distant Washington, Harrison implied, federal administrators were aggressively expanding their purview, sowing the seeds of socialism, and doing everything in their power to avoid scrutiny.[57]

As Indiana's crusade against welfare secrecy rose to the national stage, two men became the conflict's public face. One was Federal Security Administrator Oscar "Jack" Ewing, a distinguished lawyer (formerly in private practice with Supreme Court Justice Charles Evan Hughes) and nationally known Democratic politician. The other was William Jenner, a grassroots Republican who was then the junior senator from Indiana. In 1951 Ewing was probably best known for serving as "the peripatetic barker for the Truman welfare state," in the words of the *Saturday Evening Post* ("Apostle in chief of the handout state," in the harsher judgment of the *Cleveland Plain Dealer*) – a reference to his futile attempts to sell President Truman's proposal for national health insurance.[58] Jenner had by then earned a national reputation of his own, mostly for his hard-line anticommunist stance and his loyalty to Senator Joseph McCarthy. But his real ambition, according to one colleague, was to become governor.[59] As Indiana officials confronted the possibility of "going it alone" on poor relief, Jenner searched for a way to both let the state have its federal funds and reject the strings tying those funds back to Washington. Ewing, meanwhile, faced a barrage of criticism for using federal money "to force compliance with his dictatorial will." "Can this one man take millions of dollars in taxes from the citizens of this state and deny them the right to know how the tax money is spent?" asked Muncie's *Star Press*. "If he can, the people of every other state have lost a large measure of the liberty guaranteed to them by the Constitution of the United States [and] are already on the road to dictatorship and serfdom."[60]

By late September 1951, earlier efforts to amend the Social Security Act had stalled in committees, and Indiana officials had failed to convince a federal court to intervene (a tactic that Arizona officials would try for themselves, in a different context, soon after).[61] But Jenner had one last trick up his sleeve, made possible by the urgent need to finance the Korean War. During a night session on September 29, 1951, immediately prior to the final vote on the contentious Revenue Act of 1951, Jenner succeeded in adding to the act his standard language on the confidentiality of welfare records.[62]

This proved to be the winning move. In their discussion on the Revenue Act, conferees for the House and Senate decided to retain Jenner's rider, probably because it promised to win Republican support in the House for what was essentially a tax increase. Removing any ambiguity, the conferees also specified that Indiana would be entitled to receive its federal public assistance grant in the future, and, further, that the federal government owed Indiana the payments that Federal Security Administrator Ewing had withheld.[63] On October 20 President Harry Truman signed the bill into law. He lamented the "unwarranted publicity, and personal indignity and unhappiness" that might result for aid recipients, but, as Jenner predicted, the president did not derail the needed revenue legislation.[64]

The *Indianapolis Star* was quick to claim "a complete and smashing victory" – not, revealingly, a victory over welfare fraud, but over "Oscar Ewing and the Federal government." This had been the plan all along, the *Star*'s managing editor insisted: conservative critics "raised a rumpus" in Indiana to force a change in the federal law and thereby show the American people how to "throw off the socialistic shackles of a power-hungry [federal] bureaucracy." Less celebratory coverage prevailed elsewhere, but the press nonetheless presented the Jenner Amendment as a victory by the states over the federal bureaucracy – "perhaps the most notable victory," claimed one conservative news outlet, "since the arrival of the New Deal."[65]

At the ground level, these laws turned out to have little discernible impact. Journalists made use of the new provisions, and some people checked up on neighbors, tenants, debtors, and family members, but county auditors' offices were not overrun with hordes of the merely curious.[66] The head of Indiana's Welfare Department reported that in one county, only one person requested to see the list: an old woman who wanted to make sure she was on it.[67] Nor was there conclusive evidence that the law deterred "chiselers." Indiana's welfare rolls did decline in the wake of the secrecy battle, but no one could say whether the law caused the change. The numbers were trending downward well before the controversy, and some states that preserved client confidentiality reported greater declines than Indiana.[68]

It was also not clear immediately after the enactment of the Jenner Amendment that "intergovernmental relations" had changed. The following February, federal Bureau of Public Assistance director Jane Hoey felt sanguine enough to send a little poem about the episode to former SSB executive director Frank Bane, then head of the Council of State Governments. After describing the persecution of "Federal minions" and the "painful" acts of the governors, she concluded: "Then fill up the papers with misery in ink / And after the States have quaffed the drink / The Federals will rescue – or let them all sink!!" In short, the states had acted out, but they still needed federal money to run their welfare programs; so long as that imbalance existed, "the Federals" would be the ultimate decision makers. The *Indianapolis Times* reached the same conclusion: the hard-won legal reform "obviously does not end the possibility that funds may again be blocked for some other reason – or whim – of a Washington bureaucrat."[69]

And yet Indiana's fight against confidentiality made a lasting impression on those "Washington bureaucrats." Using anti-communist and anti-statist rhetoric – the same rhetoric that Senator Joseph McCarthy employed in his ruthless red-baiting – Indiana officials voiced the suspicion that New Deal public assistance programs did not represent objective, value-neutral progress in the realm of social welfare; these programs were themselves premised on a hidden ideology, and a dangerous one at that. The confidentiality battle was also, in retrospect, a "turning point" in the relationship between state officials and the federal social welfare bureaucracy.[70] The Jenner Amendment not only weakened the threat of federal withholding, it also suggested to state policymakers that through "backdoor attack[s]" they could change the federal law in ways that directly contradicted federal agency preferences.[71]

ARIZONA: COERCED INCLUSION OF AMERICAN INDIANS

Like Indiana, Arizona has not figured prominently in histories of post–World War II welfare policy. Yet Arizona, with support from neighboring New Mexico, was involved in one of the fiercest contests in the history of the federal-state public assistance programs. Also like Indiana, Arizona forced federal administrators to do what they hoped to avoid in the early 1950s: engage in public, politically charged showdowns in which they not only became the face of a controversial welfare state but also appeared to be keeping money from desperately poor citizens.

Arizona differed from Indiana in many other regards, however – a sign that hostility to federal welfare administration was not a regionally specific phenomenon. Like other western states, Arizona had joined the union relatively late (1912) and had a correspondingly different relationship with the federal government: in Arizona's path to statehood, there was never a time when the federal government's presence was weak, invisible, or dwarfed in significance by local government. Federal bureaucrats battled and then tended to the region's American Indians, developed public infrastructure, policed the state's southern border, and managed massive tracts of federally owned land.[72] The sort of federal interventions that deeply disrupted many state governments during the Depression and World War II were, to Arizona, not so new. Arizona differed from Indiana, too, in its formal politics: at midcentury, Arizona was still a one-party (Democratic) state, and that party was not a political machine.[73] Nothing that federal welfare administrators did, in other words, particularly threatened the political status quo at the state or local level.

And yet federal welfare authorities *were* threatening, in ways that energized Arizona's own growing cohort of anti–New Dealers and struck a chord with many others. If the fight with Indiana was ostensibly about how welfare recipients should be treated once they were on the rolls, the fight with Arizona was about the very terms of inclusion: who was entitled to a spot on the rolls and who would have to scrape by in some other way. The population in question was deeply controversial. The federal government had long accorded special status to American Indians and denied states jurisdiction over them and their land. In practice, however, states often mistreated the Indians in their midst while allowing the federal government to shoulder the cost. When federal administrators forced a different arrangement on Arizona – one in which the state had to treat Indians as citizens but was denied the authority that generally accompanied beneficence – they revealed the full and dangerous extent of national power. Federal authorities thus further exposed themselves to criticism, both from race-conscious southern Democrats and from conservative Republicans.

As discussed in Chapter 4, Arizona's dispute with federal administrators unfolded over a period of fifteen years. Since the enactment of the Social Security Act in 1935, Arizona and New Mexico had insisted that American Indians, especially those living on reservations, did not need to be included in state public assistance programs. This was because reservation Indians were subject to federal protection, exempt from state taxation, and beyond the reach of state jurisdiction in most other regards, state officials explained. Barely beneath the surface, however, were long histories of discrimination and acute concerns about cultural and racial difference. The two states' welfare laws did not explicitly exclude Indians – which is why federal administrators initially approved their applications for federal grants – but in practice, state and local officials did everything they could to avoid making payments to poor Indians, while counting on powerful Arizona senator Carl Hayden to protect the states' interest in Congress.

That strategy worked for about a decade, at which point the states' exclusionary practices attracted the attention of the National Congress of American Indians, the leadership of several tribes, and former government lawyers James Curry and Felix Cohen. With the help of this coalition, reservation Indians applied for assistance and documented the rejections and evasions that followed. The evidence they collected, along with stark facts about rates of starvation and mortality on Indian reservations in the Southwest, eventually formed the basis of a civil rights case filed in federal court (*Mapatis v. Ewing*), in which the Indian plaintiffs demanded that federal administrators defund the two recalcitrant states. The evidence also became ammunition in federal administrators' subsequent negotiations with the states. Those negotiations culminated in an April 1949 conference in Santa Fe, New Mexico: there, representatives from the two states agreed to treat Indians' public assistance applications the same as all others. As a concession, the federal government agreed to subsidize those payments more heavily, via a special congressional appropriation to the Bureau of Indian Affairs.[74]

This settlement satisfied the *Mapatis* plaintiffs, or at least their lawyers, but not the political leadership of the two states – which is why in May 1949, not two weeks after the Santa Fe conference, New Mexico congressmen Antonio M. Fernández appeared before the House Subcommittee on Indian Affairs to suggest adding new language to the then pending Navajo-Hopi Rehabilitation Act. Framed as a "Marshall Plan" for two of the poorest tribes in the Southwest, the act proposed to devote $90 million to the creation of "self-reliant communities on the Navajo and Hopi reservations.[75] As part of this "rehabilitation" program, Fernández proposed, Congress should deem members of the affected tribes to be subject to "all of the laws" in the state in which they resided. No more claiming the benefits of state citizenship – such as public assistance – while simultaneously refusing to be governed by state authority. Was it not, after all, Congress's intention "to make the Indians self-supporting and into good individual American citizens"? "I do not think that we are going to get very far," Fernández warned, "unless they are sooner or later made subject to the laws of the State."[76]

The proposal may have derived from Fernández's own, immigrant-oriented conception of citizenship: prior to running for Congress, he had served as president of the famously assimilatory League of United Latin American Citizens (LULAC). But the proposed amendment also fit with western politicians' long history of using legal jurisdiction to capture reservation resources, human and otherwise. In this case, one local newspaper reported, the chief concerns were "protect[ing] ballot boxes, supervis[ing] elections, and ... guard[ing] the State Social Security checks from forgery and altering" – in other words, constraining Indians from enjoying and exercising the very citizenship rights that they had only recently won. As passed by the House, the Fernández Amendment also included a provision requiring reservation schools to follow state curricula. In short, the amendment would ensure that Indians' rights were paired with state power – the power to surveil, police, and punish.[77]

The specific implications for public assistance became clearer as the Fernández Amendment wound its way through the legislative process. The House and Senate conferees added to the amendment, now Section 9 of the proposed Navajo-Hopi Rehabilitation Act, a rider that memorialized the Santa Fe Agreement but named the Social Security Administration, rather than the unreliable Bureau of Indian Affairs, as the source of the additional federal funds. When Arizona or New Mexico processed a claim from a reservation Indian, the rider provided, the Social Security Administration would match the state payments at a higher than usual rate. (The formula was complicated, but in one example the federal agency would pay $46 of a $50 welfare payment, or 92 percent.) Thus, in the final version of the proposed law, the federal government's extension of state jurisdiction over American Indians and the states' acceptance of public welfare obligations were rolled together into an implicit quid pro quo, with ironclad assurances of federal financial support.[78]

The states' jurisdictional grab doomed the act, however, and set the stage for an even more dramatic confrontation between state officials and federal administrators. Although members of the Navajo Tribal Council voted to support Section 9, they quickly changed their minds. In the press, former commissioner of Indian Affairs John Collier loudly denounced the "sinister" changes to the original legislation. The American Civil Liberties Union, NCAI, and others joined him in urging President Truman to veto the bill, and Truman obliged. He agreed that state jurisdiction was the "logical consequence of our policy" (that is, the policy of Indian assimilation and the termination of tribal members' special status) but maintained that such jurisdiction must be accepted voluntarily, "in the orderly course of social and economic integration."[79]

It was one thing to be stymied by the president and another to be thwarted, continually, by unelected federal bureaucrats. That was exactly how some Arizona officials characterized what occurred over the following years. New Mexico had by this point accepted its responsibility for reservation Indians, perhaps because in the most recent fiscal year, 1950–51, it had spent a mere $41,335 in state funds on Indian public assistance payments.[80] But some Arizona officials, especially members of the state's upstart Republican Party, were eager to reopen the "Indian question."

The impulse reflected both the resolve of federal bureaucrats, insistent that Arizona not slip back into old habits, and trends in state and national politics. Following their 1948 confrontation with the Social Security Administration, Arizona officials almost immediately encountered similar pressure from the U.S. Children's Bureau over discrimination in the state's federally subsidized program for crippled children.[81] State officials also skirmished with federal administrators over the terms of the 1949 Santa Fe Agreement. (Arizona had attempted to back out the following year, when Congress finally enacted a Navajo and Hopi Rehabilitation Act.) "We are shocked," declared Arizona governor Howard Pyle in 1951, after receiving yet another defunding threat from the Social Security Administration, by "how completely we are subject to the whims of the Federal Government."[82] Given the liberal enthusiasm for Indian rights in recent years, when Eleanor Roosevelt, no less, condemned the lack of "decency and justice" afforded to "the first citizens of this country," Pyle was probably not actually that shocked.[83] But his rhetoric hit all the right notes for a different political constituency: the conservative, anti–New Deal Republicans who had maneuvered him into office. For a politician like Pyle – as for future Republican presidential nominee Barry Goldwater, who had managed Pyle's 1950 gubernatorial campaign – defending state sovereignty was a top priority. So, then, was taking a tough stance against the federal bureaucrats who had been pushing the state around.

A golden opportunity arrived in the form of a 1950 amendment to the Social Security Act, authorizing matching grants for state-run programs of Aid to the Permanently and Totally Disabled (APTD). (As noted in Chapter 3, liberal reformers had by this time lost their bid to replace the existing categorical public assistance programs with a single federally administered income support program; they turned instead to expanding the welfare state piece by piece, in this case by extending aid to another particularly sympathetic subset of the unemployable poor.) As with the act's original programs, a state that wanted the generous federal subsidy submitted an APTD "plan"; the federal agency checked the plan against federal requirements and, if appropriate, approved.[84] For Arizona, the process was the perfect vehicle for a test case: in the spring of 1952, following the Arizona legislature's lead and in the wake of Indiana's momentous dispute with federal administrators, the state's public welfare agency sought federal participation in a plan that denied assistance "to any person of Indian blood while living on a federal Indian reservation." Federal administrators, aware of Arizona's desire to test its rights, dutifully played their part: they promptly disapproved the plan, and Arizona filed suit in federal court (*Arizona v. Hobby*). Finally, Arizona officials hoped, a court of law would curb the federal agency's authority.[85]

The ensuing arguments before the district court bear examination not because they reveal Arizona officials' "true" motivations, but because they show a new degree of legal sophistication and confidence on the part of state officials, and an utter lack of deference to federal administrators. As in Indiana, prominent spokespersons for the state refused to accept that the federal agency was the ultimate arbiter of the Social Security Act's meaning.

Appearing before the district court to argue against the federal government's motion to dismiss the case, Arizona lawyer Kent Blake emphasized two points. The first was the federal government's history of responsibility for their Indian "wards." The state had no problem with Indians living in "regular communities" and assuming all the attendant responsibilities, Blake noted. The state's issue was with reservation Indians – and not because of race, he hastened to add, but because they "enjoyed" a "peculiar and privileged status." The federal government maintained them on lands held in trust, provided them with hospitals and schools, and shielded them from the reach of state law. In case after case, the Supreme Court had told the states to keep its hands off these federal charges. How, then, could the federal agency demand that Arizona treat them as full-fledged state citizens? Blake's second point was less about federal power and more about federal *agency* power – or lack thereof. Under the Social Security Act, Blake argued, federal administrators had no right to disapprove Arizona's plan. Once a plan satisfied the terms of the law – which Blake insisted Arizona's did – their only function was to open the cash drawer.[86]

Assistant U.S. attorney Ross O'Donoghue, joined by two longtime Social Security Administration lawyers, defended the agency's right to deny funds to Arizona and insisted that the state's plan did *not* meet the statutory requirements. Invoking administrative interpretations of the principle of equal protection (discussed in Chapter 3), O'Donoghue also raised the Fourteenth Amendment: the state's plan favored Arizonans without Indian blood and Arizonans not living on reservations, and neither group had a "proper" relationship to the goal of meeting the needs of the disabled.[87]

The court also heard from former Interior Department lawyer Felix Cohen, who represented three amici curiae: the Hualapai Tribe, the San Carlos Apache Tribe, and the Association on American Indian Affairs (a liberal, New York–based group of philanthropists and anthropologists). The renowned Indian-law expert remained a thorn in Arizona's side, but much else had changed in the years since the *Mapatis* litigation. For one, Cohen had been the target of a hard-fought campaign by the new Indian Affairs commissioner (and former director of the Japanese American internment camps), Dillon S. Myer. Shortly after taking office, Myer announced new regulations for tribes' choice of legal counsel. The stated concern was to prevent self-dealing by lawyers such as Cohen and Curry, but critics perceived an underlying desire to quash civil rights activism and control tribes' use of the Indian Claims Commission. (Critics also hinted at the influence of certain Democratic congressmen who were "annoyed" at Cohen and Curry over the Republican gains that their Indian voting cases had produced.) With help from the American Bar Association, the NCAI, and other allies, the accused attorneys defeated the regulations, but the fight was long and bitter.[88]

A second and related development since Cohen's earlier skirmish with Arizona was the Truman administration's increasingly aggressive campaign to encourage Indian assimilation by terminating the services and legal arrangements that ostensibly stood in their way. Termination policies, Kenneth Philp has shown, had broad appeal: they "reflected the conservative and nationalist mood of the Cold War era" and "resonated with the ideologies of individualism and capitalism." But in the early 1950s, termination took a turn that disturbed many Indians and their advocates. As Myer tightened the BIA's grip on tribes, Congress considered proposals to give states civil and criminal jurisdiction in Indian country without tribal consent. This inflamed Cohen: although some tribes had reason to welcome state jurisdiction, he had witnessed the prejudices that Indians encountered at the state and local level. In Arizona, he predicted, Indians could anticipate "raids" on their property, businesses, hospitals, and schools should the federal government withdraw its protection.[89]

Cohen's argument in *Arizona v. Hobby* was, therefore, all the more striking, for in that case he argued passionately for Indians' ability to participate in state-run programs. As in the *Mapatis* case, he invoked the constitutional principle of equal protection. Appearing before the district court on February 20, 1953, he painted a picture of Indian and white citizens living side by side, as did some residents of the Hualapai reservation. Could one receive public aid and the other be denied? If the case involved "Negroes," Cohen noted, invoking recent NAACP victories (and inviting an analogy that has long troubled federal Indian law), the answer would surely be "no." As for Indians' unique relationship with the federal government – which he vigorously defended elsewhere – Cohen denied its relevance. This case was about whether Arizona could establish a program that "exclud[ed] from its scope, say, Republicans, Catholics, or Jews, or Democrats," and then demand that the federal government fund the lion's share of the cost.[90]

Cohen failed to convince Judge Henry Schweinhaut, former head of the Civil Rights Section at the Department of Justice, that Arizona intended to discriminate on the basis of race – a sign, perhaps, that the connection between welfare rights and civil rights was not yet intuitive. Nonetheless, Schweinhaut agreed with the Social Security Administration's refusal to approve the state's plan. Arizona legislators had presumed, perhaps understandably, that the federal government owed the Indians more than Arizona did and had treated them differently on that basis. But Arizona had also accepted a federal grant, conditioned on the state's granting a similar "gratuity" to its own citizens, including Indians. In his view, the Social Security Administration "could not, constitutionally, or under the terms of the statute, itself" approve a plan such as Arizona's.[91]

Had Arizona officials not appealed this unfavorable decision, they might have preserved a small victory for others butting up against federal administrative authority. The trial court accepted without question its right to adjudicate the dispute, thereby creating a precedent for other states to challenge federal agency decisions. Arizona, after all, was hardly alone in resenting the federal welfare bureaucracy. But Arizona refused to let Judge Schweinhaut have the last word, and in May 1954 an appellate court vacated his decision – on grounds that were decidedly unfavorable to the state. "The purpose of this suit," explained Judge David Bazelon of the U.S. Court of Appeals for the D.C. Circuit, "is 'to reach money which the government owns,'" and since the federal government – the "sovereign" in this context – had not consented to being sued, the case had to be dismissed.[92]

For a suit intended to vindicate *state* sovereignty, it was a disappointing end. On paper, at least, Arizona was now formally required to give Indians the material benefits of citizenship – that is, not only political rights but also affirmative rights to government support – while the state's coercive and regulatory powers on Indian land remained tightly constrained. Of broader importance, the appellate court's decision appeared to close off an important avenue of redress for state officials concerned about the high-stakes decisions of federal welfare administrators. Sympathetic eyes were watching, however, and would remember Arizona's determined stand in years to come.

NEW YORK: ENFORCING UNIFORMITY, UNDERMINING LOCAL CONTROL

Across the country in New York, state officials shared Arizona's frustration. In the early 1950s – building on Indiana's victory – they, too, confronted federal administrators over what they characterized as federal overreaching. In this instance, the conflict was resolved without Congress or the courts, but the mere fact of New York's defiance is noteworthy. To Arizona officials, negotiating aggressively with the federal government was a long and glorious tradition and also a natural reaction to American Indian civil rights gains. To the anti–New Dealers who had seized control of Indiana's state legislature, it was part of an effort to roll back intrusive federal government regulations and thwart the development of a collectivist welfare state. New York, by contrast, had been the darling of the New Deal and an apparent model of enlightened governance. Key New Dealers hailed from the state, including "relief czar" Harry Hopkins, Secretary of Labor Frances Perkins, and President Roosevelt himself; New York's responses to the Depression had provided the templates for many national-level reform and recovery initiatives. At midcentury, however, New York officials found themselves subject to the coercive side of one of those very reform programs. Their spirited resistance reminds us that the principles of governance that many New Dealers took for granted were, when implemented, disruptive and controversial, even in the seemingly liberal Northeast. As the public face of that implementation, federal welfare administrators were at the eye of the storm.

At issue in the federal agency's dispute with New York were three principles that New Dealers had deemed essential to modern American governance: uniformity, centralization, and professionalization, all of which tended to come at the expense of local authority and all of which had been built into the Social Security Act. By innovating in these directions prior to the New Deal (New York was one of the first states to adopt a merit system for public employees, for example), New York had managed to reflect the pinnacle of modern statecraft while also allowing its many subjurisdictions to wield considerable control over poor relief, a cherished local government function. By the late 1940s, however, nearly every state in the union had (or had at least agreed to) a more uniform, more centralized, and more professionalized public welfare edifice than New York's – thanks, in large part, to the oversight of federal administrators. With the New Deal programs well established and World War II no longer stopping the clock on meaningful reform, federal administrators were getting impatient with the Empire State.

As in Indiana, a welfare scandal helped bring the conflict to the surface. It began in 1947, with the New York Society for the Prevention of Cruelty to Children (SPCC) and its docket of child neglect cases. Part philanthropic organization, part law enforcement agency, the SPCC presented 488 cases that year to New York City's Children's Court, including the seemingly routine case of a heavy-drinking Bronx man whose neglectful actions had left his four children homeless the previous November.[93] Sensational information came to light, however, during the hearing: in December 1946, the New York City Welfare Department had paid the family the exorbitant sum of $500 for one month's rent and food (the equivalent of more than $6,000 in 2014 dollars). The figure was so high, a department spokesperson subsequently explained, because in the midst of the city's severe housing shortage, the only living quarters that could be found for the family were in a Manhattan hotel. Subsequent investigation revealed that as of May 21, 1947, the municipal Welfare Department was maintaining thirty-seven families in similar accommodations.[94]

By the end of the month, the department had moved all the families out of hotels and Municipal Welfare Commissioner Edward Rhatigan had gone on a publicity offensive, emphasizing the inadequacy of the city's housing resources and the modesty of the so-called luxury hotel suites.[95] But the damage was done. New York's state legislature had recently increased the state's share of local relief expenditures – to a historic high of 80 percent – and state officials were anxious about where the money was going. The New York State Social Welfare Board (a policy-setting body consisting of lay citizens appointed by the governor) announced a full-scale investigation.[96] Neither Rhatigan's resignation nor a mayoral-level inquiry could stop it.[97]

That state-level investigation, conducted by a committee of the State Social Welfare Board, produced a dismal picture of the city's relief system. Particularly damning was the public testimony of Bernard Shapiro, supervisor of social work for the New York State Department of Social Welfare and a former employee of the New York City Welfare Department. On looking into the families maintained in hotels between September 1946 and May 1947, Shapiro found that one woman had been indicted for grand larceny and was using her hotel room "as a front for a gambling establishment"; another woman had entertained men in her room "while her children roamed the lobby." And then there was "Madame X," an attractive California divorcée who wore a mink coat to her relief interview and had reportedly received $60,000 in settlement money before moving to New York with her illegitimate child. The men were no better, Shapiro reported: they included an alcoholic, a "bigamist," and a man who refused a hernia operation that would have allowed him to return to work. Such findings were not aberrations, Shapiro suggested, but rather the inevitable results of a "client is always right" attitude on the part of municipal welfare authorities.[98]

Within days, the infamous mink coat had been produced for public inspection (the State Social Welfare Board went so far as to hire a fur expert to assess its value), and the new municipal welfare commissioner, Benjamin Fielding, had checked into the hospital, suffering from "exhaustion."[99] But the investigation was far from over. The director of the New York State Bureau of Public Assistance testified that fewer than 10 percent of the 200 cases she had sampled from a welfare center in Queens satisfied the eligibility rules. A caseworker for that center anecdotally confirmed these findings and added that he received "nil" by way of supervision. The testimony of another local employee, medical social worker Dorothy Pickett, reinforced popular suspicions about the relationship between professional social work and an ever-expanding welfare state: asked why men who refused to work were nonetheless deemed eligible for relief, Pickett cited "psychogenic" factors, which she defined as "slight abnormalities in reactions to normal situations."[100]

Such testimony allowed State Commissioner of Social Welfare Robert Lansdale to point fingers. He charged local workers with engaging in "poor man's psychoanalysis" and building "rapport" with clients at the expense of accurate eligibility determinations.[101] Defenders of the city's welfare department were, in turn, quick to shift the blame back to the state. Social worker Dorothy C. Kahn, executive director of the Welfare Council of New York, responded to Lansdale's criticisms by pointing to state officials' staggering failure to uncover the alleged abuses. The recent "orgy of publicity" was merely an attempt to direct attention away from the state's *supervisory* laxity, she alleged.[102] Municipal officials echoed this critique in March 1948, when the State Board of Social Welfare announced the results of its investigation. If conditions were truly as bad as alleged, then *state* officials had been "plainly derelict" in their duties.[103]

With the distance of time, it is clear that the scandal had revealed a fundamental problem with public welfare in New York State: in some ways, the state had adopted a thoroughly modern system, with substantial state financing, a central state agency, and clear lines of authority running from the state agency to local departments. But in practice, local welfare operations were largely autonomous, just as they had been before the New Deal. In many cases, local welfare agencies hired their own people and set their own standards of need, and although they spent state money, they rarely encountered state supervision. Local welfare commissioners also tended to be politically connected, and they used their influence to maintain broad discretion over the administration of all forms of poor relief.[104]

It was in this context that state officials began shifting blame to federal authorities – even though many of the problem cases actually came from New York's nonfederally subsidized "home relief" program. In January 1948, lawyer and leading Republican Henry Root Stern, chairman of the New York State Board of Social Welfare, told an audience at the Women's City Club that federal agency training materials were to blame for the local welfare crisis. He cited in particular *Common Human Needs*, the Bureau of Public Assistance report that had come to national attention during a recent relief scandal in Baltimore. Such materials encouraged local workers to place ineligible persons on the relief rolls, Stern explained, in violation of good state policies. "There is only so much money to go around," Stern warned – and taxpayers would tolerate only so much indulgence.[105]

The state board's official report – the culmination of its 1947–48 investigation – made the same point: "Over the years," it said, federal administrators had formulated polices "with little or no participation" by state officials and then circulated them widely at the local level, where they "materially influenced" local workers. In theory, that influence was limited to the administration of the federally subsidized programs, but the very same workers often administered home relief. The views of federal administrators were thus thoroughly implicated in New York City's welfare disaster. Had federal officials minded their own business, the report implied, a different approach might have prevailed – at least if Stern and other members of the state board had had their way.[106] In short, criticizing the federal agency had become a useful way of deflecting attention from the contradictions embedded in New York's public welfare program.

Unfortunately for the federal agency, its actions over the next few years played directly into the hands of those who found a convenient scapegoat in a snoopy and overbearing federal bureaucracy. In 1948, as federal administrators in Washington advocated an unprecedented expansion of the welfare state, federal regional officials investigated New York City's public assistance cases and came down hard – on the state. In nearly a quarter of the cases sampled, their review concluded, the individual's eligibility for assistance "was seriously in question." On the basis of this finding, federal administrators demanded reimbursement from the state for the misspent funds. They also insisted on tighter state oversight of the city, regular progress reports, and a systematic state review of all of the city's ADC and OAA cases.[107]

At the same time, federal officials continued to press New York about two sources of federal-state disagreement. The first was the so-called uniformity issue. As Chapter 1 explains, many of the drafters of the Social Security Act understood local variation and local discretion as fundamentally antimodern – a recipe for inefficiency, corruption, and arbitrary decision making. That is why one of the conditions of federal funding was that a state program be "in effect in all political subdivisions of the State, and, if administered by them, be mandatory upon them." Administrators interpreted this language to mean that programs must operate "uniformly" across the state: the same procedures should be used, the same eligibility rules should apply, and so on. By the 1940s, however, they were also insisting on uniform standards for determining need – in the form of written guidance from the state on what items should be factored into individual grants, and hence on what constituted a decent standard of living in the state.[108]

With public assistance already up and running in the states, it had been difficult for federal administrators to insist on adherence to their new understanding of "uniformity." So they waited until the federal law changed. In the fall of 1946, when Congress increased the matching rate to the various public assistance programs, federal administrators announced a quid pro quo: now that states had more federal money available to them, it was time for the states to provide explicit, uniform, statewide standards of need and to ensure that local welfare departments adhered to those standards. New York, with its dozens of autonomous welfare districts, was one of the states that had proven most resistant – and most savvy – in its response to federal pestering. By 1948, a federal BPA representative reported, the New York State Welfare Department had provided local agencies with "extensive guide material" on standard setting, but so extensive was the "maze" of state recommendations that federal administrators found it "impossible to identify and isolate" what the department actually regarded as its statewide standards. Meanwhile, each local agency determined for itself what to do – which was precisely what the state department intended.[109] Around the same time as the New York City relief scandal, federal officials signaled that they were prepared to take a firmer stance[110]

The second long-standing source of disagreement was New York's merit system for state and local welfare workers. Pursuant to the Social Security Amendments of 1939, federal funding for public assistance was conditioned on "the establishment and maintenance of personnel standards on a merit basis" (that is, a civil service system for state and local employees administering public assistance). This meant salary scales, job classifications, competitive examinations, procedures for promotion and separation, qualification standards, and a system for evaluating workers' training and experience. At the time the amendment was enacted, fewer than two dozen states had merit systems in place for their employees, and only about half of those systems covered public welfare employees. Within a year, every state that accepted federal funds had promised to place state and local public assistance workers (with the exception of top policymakers and executives) under a merit system.[111]

For those states that had never had a civil service system, the impact of this small amendment was revolutionary: it not only raised personnel standards in public assistance but also encouraged states to adopt merit systems for other public employees.[112] The professional social workers who attracted such ire in Indiana were a tangible result of this reform. In New York, which already had a merit system (albeit one with many holes), the effect was the opposite. When asked to comply with the new amendment, New York officials essentially promised to do more of what it was already doing, by extending the state's existing civil service system to the forty-four counties and one township that had thus far excluded public welfare workers from coverage.[113] The emptiness of that promise soon became apparent: state officials permitted hundreds of local welfare positions, including dozens of director and deputy director positions, to remain exempt from the merit system, allowing for political appointments. Certain "provisional" employees – temporary employees hired outside merit system procedures – occupied their posts for years. This followed directly from local welfare districts' continued opposition to hiring people from outside their own districts and from a failure to offer regular civil service examinations, an omission that state officials did little to correct.[114]

Federal officials tolerated this state of affairs during the 1940s because wartime personnel shortages gave New York a valid excuse for noncompliance, but they never lost sight of the issue.[115] And when Congress enacted the Social Security Amendments of 1950, authorizing grants for Aid to the Permanently and Totally Disabled, the federal agency seized the occasion to at last bring New York into line.

Like most states, New York was quick to see the advantage of the new program. Disabled citizens were in many cases already receiving public aid, in the form of state or locally funded general relief. By shifting those citizens to the new APTD program, states could receive federal matching payments of up to thirty dollars per individual. From city cases alone, New York City welfare commissioner Raymond Hilliard calculated, the state stood to gain $7 million per year. By December of 1950, New York's sixty-six local public welfare districts had shifted 25,000 citizens into the new category, and state officials were looking forward to a hefty reimbursement from the federal government.[116]

Collecting that windfall would not be so simple, however. Before the funds would flow, federal administrators had to approve New York's APTD plan (which had gone into effect prior to receiving federal agency review). In November 1950 federal officials warned the New York State Board of Social Welfare that unless its plan provided for a mandatory statewide standard of need, no federal money would follow for APTD (the state calculated that it was already owed $1.75 million). The state's other funding would be in jeopardy as well, starting with its ADC funding for the next quarter – some $8.25 million. Federal officials also asked that the state at last remedy the deficiencies in its merit system, which at the time exempted more public assistance workers than in all the other states combined.[117] In short, the federal agency was using New York's desire for APTD to take issue with the administration of *all* of New York's other federally subsidized programs – and to finally bring those programs into conformity with federal law.

State officials were outraged, or so they said. New York's welfare system was one of the best-run and most generous in the nation, they insisted. They noted, too, that New York was a large state, with varying conditions and costs of living. Any standard of need that suited New York City would, by definition, not suit a rural upstate county, making the very idea of a statewide standard "harsh" and "impersonal." As for personnel practices, everyone knew that New York had the oldest civil service law in the country. "No state in the Union," declared State Welfare Commissioner Robert Lansdale, "[w]as more completely committed in principle and practice to the merit system in government employment."[118] Unstated, but surely on the minds of Lansdale and the state board's members, were New York's powerful local welfare directors. In states with a tradition of local autonomy, one "Washington authority" told a reporter in 1952, "the localities would like us to put the money on the stump and run."[119] Local officials in New York had long been accustomed to just such a process, and they fought the change now demanded from on high.

These complaints circulated far afield. As the Indiana and Arizona examples show, a new era was dawning in federal-state relations, and the states had something to gain by visibly standing up to federal welfare administrators. In Indiana, it was the possibility of making a dent in a feminized, tax-sucking federal welfare state. In Arizona, it was the prospect of resolving the "Indian problem" on favorable terms – that is, of getting as much federal money as possible while also circumscribing the rights of citizens who continued to elude the state's control. In New York it was the appearance of putting up a good fight against uniformity, centralization, and professionalization – even as state officials tacitly embraced all of these forces, along with the growth of state power that came with them.

New York's dispute with the federal government played out as if according to script. After conferring with Lansdale, the New York State Board of Social Welfare issued two resolutions strongly condemning the actions of the Federal Security Agency. The board directed Commissioner Lansdale to submit an amended plan to the federal agency but to refuse to adopt any provisions that went beyond "the methods and principles" currently governing public assistance administration in New York State. For their part, federal administrators attempted to resolve the disagreement quietly, through private negotiations. By late December, despite the heated rhetoric, New York had orally agreed to the federal agency's terms. In return, the federal agency back-dated its approval of New York's APTD program, allowing the state to receive federal matching funds for the bulk of its APTD expenditures that fall. The federal agency also agreed to continue issuing grants for ADC. Nine months later, an official federal-state "truce" was announced.[120]

In the press, however, Governor Thomas Dewey used the controversy to assail "aggressive" uses of federal power and "pettifogging bureaucracy." A powerful operative in the Republican Party and a vocal critic of the Truman administration, Dewey insisted that Congress had never authorized the federal agency to "impos[e]" these two "demands" (uniform statewide standards and merit system requirements), both of which augmented the power of federal administrators at the expense of poor citizens and their representative governments. The uniformity requirement treated people in need "as mere numbers of members of a herd," Dewey explained, rather than as "citizens of the community in which they live," while the civil service demands "presume[d] to override" the considered judgment of the state legislature. The Republican-dominated state legislature echoed Dewey's sentiments in February 1951 with a resolution asking Congress to overrule the federal agency. Was "Mr. Ewing" "going to have his way" again? asked a columnist for the *Knickerbocker News*, referencing the dust-up in Indiana. Or would New York show that it, too, would rather "secede from the federal program" than "be intimidated by a bunch of bureaucrats"?[121]

Secession was not a realistic option – indeed, by April 1951, New York had officially bowed to the bureaucrats and was accepting federal funds. But state officials did find a way to register their concern, via the high-profile commission that Governor Dewey appointed to investigate the matter.[122] The Kelley Commission – named for its chair, Nicholas Kelley (son of social-welfare crusader Florence Kelley) – ultimately authored a report that captured exactly how much critics of New Deal public assistance had learned in the early 1950s.

Much of the commission's 1952 report, importantly, was about law – and since three of the five members of the Kelley Commission were lawyers, its legal analysis was entirely credible. The commission examined the Social Security Act, its subsequent amendments, and various related appropriation acts, including their legislative history, and concluded that the federal agency had no sound basis – only "mere legal technicalities" – for the demands it had made on New York State. The observation was not without merit: trained at the high point of legal realism, federal agency lawyers probably would have admitted the existence of multiple interpretive possibilities and further admitted to choosing the ones that aligned with their vision. The commission's next observation, however, had more bite: the commission accused federal administrators of enjoying an "overpowering" and implicitly illegitimate "bargaining advantage" in their dealings with the states: money. Phrased differently, federal administrators were not experts (or at least were not the sort of experts that should be trusted), but they nonetheless had the ability to impose their views on the states. Tapping into the same lines of thought that had informed the Administrative Procedure Act (1946), the report concluded by recommending that Congress provide a "method by which any State may test in court its rights to receive grants-in-aid" before being cut off by the federal agency. States, in other words, deserved the same kind of appeal rights that the Social Security Act already accorded individual claimants and that Congress had given to regulated entities elsewhere in the administrative state. [123]

This seemingly modest suggestion reflects a major development: state officials in New York and elsewhere no longer questioned the basic architecture of New Deal public assistance – federal funding was a given, and the Social Security Act was the touchstone for all conversations – but they were eager to renegotiate the balance of power within this system and were demanding the institutional machinery to do so. Placing a formal check on the authority of federal grant makers was an ideal first step.

* * * *

The early 1950s witnessed the "beginning of a revolution ... against big growing public assistance programs imposed by the federal government," recalled the director of a prominent state welfare department some thirty years after the fact. "The introduction of social work into the program, the necessity for uniform standards throughout the state, the establishment of the merit system – all of these things they resisted."[124] This chapter has examined who "they" were and why they rose up at this historical moment.

By the late 1940s, federal administrators had succeeded in imposing a set of core ideas about proper administration and good welfare practice, reaching across the nation and down to the grassroots. This set of principles was broadly familiar, even if subject to caricature and misunderstanding: the ideal welfare administrator was a professionally trained social worker – which, practically speaking, often meant someone from outside the local community. Equally important, an applicant for relief was not first and foremost a member of the community with a defined position in a social hierarchy, but was rather an individual, whose need alone was determinative. Modern, rational, uniform administration took precedence over preserving the social order and conserving taxpayer dollars. Local variation in the administration of assistance was, by definition, suspect.

Federal administrators had enforced these principles by attaching them to multimillion-dollar federal grants. "With money goes power," Ohio governor Frank Lausche reminded the attendees of the 1951 Governors' Conference, and "[w]ith power goes control." Lausche proposed that states help local governments raise revenue, thereby allowing them to resume some of the functions that they had traditionally carried out.[125] But as this chapter has demonstrated, other critics took a different tack. "Must it always be that he who pays the piper calls the tune?" Massachusetts governor Christian A. Herter wondered aloud several years later.[126] State officials in Indiana, Arizona, and New York helped people like Herter think to ask that question. These three states eagerly accepted federal funds – which they increasingly characterized as simply their own state dollars, repackaged – but attempted to reject and under-mine federal controls.

They did so in ways that would become increasingly common in the next decade. Confronted by a historically excluded group that was now attempting to redeem the promises of the New Deal, officials in Arizona went on the offensive: they enacted a state law that they knew conflicted with federal administrative interpretations, hired lawyers to defend their position, and hoped that the federal agency had grown too weak to stop them. In years to come, as African Americans made ever more assertive claims to citizenship, states in the Deep South and elsewhere would do the same.

In Indianapolis – where the right-wing John Birch Society would soon be founded – anti–New Deal conservatives also used the law in resisting the federal government. "Able lawyers" approved of Indiana's resistance, the *Indianapolis Times* emphasized, and "any American who can read" could see that federal administrators' interpretation of the Social Security Act "directly contradict[ed] the spirit, if not the letter, of the Constitution."[127] Indiana conservatives' real innovation, however, was to take advantage of national political realignments to force a change in federal law. The climate was right, they showed, to begin chipping away at statutes that had long seemed untouchable.

New York's resistance was subtler, but arguably more damaging to federal authority in the long run. In acceding to federal authority, state officials in fact augmented their own power vis-à-vis local government, but their loud objections – often voiced in the language of localism – hid that power from view. Anger that might have been directed toward the state was instead directed toward the federal government. "Unhampered by the rules Washington imposes as a price for this 'aid,'" one sympathetic local welfare worker explained in 1952, "we could … take care of our own at a fraction of the present cost. We would make sure that no one was cold or went hungry, as we have always done."[128] Most state officials were not, in fact, about to disassemble their welfare bureaucracies and restore power to the local level, but they benefited from such romanticized visions of the past.

Heading into the Eisenhower years, these three templates of resistance remained an underutilized resource, but state administrators and executives were talking among themselves, formally and informally – and astute Washington observers detected a change in the wind.[129] In the words of Eveline Burns, one of the original drafters of the Social Security Act, the days had passed when proponents of social welfare could concentrate solely on Washington, securing the policies they favored by attaching new conditions to states' grants. "In the years ahead," she counseled in 1953, "we would be wise to direct more of our efforts toward the state legislatures and to public opinion within the states."[130]

6

Rights against the State(s)

Questioning Rehabilitation, Resisting Restriction

On June 27, 1954, Andrew Wade IV and his wife, Charlotte, returned from an evening out just in time to see an explosion rip through a large section of their new house. The Wades were shaken but not entirely surprised. They were the first black family to move into an all-white neighborhood on the outskirts of Louisville, Kentucky, and they had done so at a particularly inauspicious time: on May 17, within days of their move, the Supreme Court had issued its controversial decision in *Brown v. Board of Education*. A barrage of threats and harassment followed for the Wades, beginning with shattered windows and culminating in the bombing – a depressingly familiar pattern to black Americans who challenged the color line. More unusual, in the Wades' case, was the criminal proceeding that followed, in which a local prosecutor rejected the possibility of segregationist terrorism and instead pointed the finger at local civil rights activists: they planted the bomb, the prosecutor alleged, as part of a communist-inspired plot to fuel racial tension.[1]

On the surface the story had little to do with public welfare, and yet federal welfare officials were following it closely.[2] Two lesser-known defendants in the ensuing sedition prosecution had caught their eye: Mary Louise Gilbert, a Louisville social worker, and her roommate, Larue Spiker, described in the press as "an unemployed factory worker." Prior to the bombing, under the auspices of the Women's International League for Peace and Freedom, both women had sent letters to the Wades' new neighbors urging tolerance – which in 1954 Louisville was enough to place them under a cloud of suspicion. Four years earlier and 114 miles north, in Indianapolis, federal administrators remembered, these very same women had fallen under a similar cloud – and had ultimately helped spark a national controversy over federal-state welfare administration.[3] That this remote connection merited attention from high-level federal agency officials speaks to the importance of what happened in Indiana in the early 1950s, when conservative Republicans, flanked by southern Democrats, encouraged Indiana officials to defy the federal welfare agency and risk the state's multimillion-dollar federal grant, a game of chicken that ended with Congress nullifying the offending provision of the federal law (the Social Security Act's confidentiality requirement). It also gives a sense of the climate surrounding New Deal public assistance programs in the mid-1950s. This was an era of "massive resistance" to federal desegregation mandates, continued fear of communist subversion, conservative executive leadership, and deep anxiety about the survival of normative family structures.

From existing scholarship, we know some of the implications for public welfare. We know, for example, that the far-reaching welfare state envisioned by President Roosevelt's National Resources Planning Board fell out of the realm of political plausibility, and with it, liberals' hopes for broad, universal social rights. We know that existing social welfare programs survived and some even grew – thanks to well-placed New Deal administrators and Democratically controlled Congresses – but that for one major program, Aid to Dependent Children, the New Deal goal of providing income support for unfortunate families shifted to a postwar goal of rehabilitating deviant ones.[4] In the states, meanwhile, we know that many legislatures took an increasingly restrictive approach to public assistance. Responding to criticisms of fraud, waste, and bloated government, they amended OAA laws to lower benefit levels, ratchet up eligibility requirements, and demand that applicants look first to their relatives for support. For ADC, punitive and work-centered reforms abounded. In what some scholars refer to as the first "backlash against welfare mothers," states enacted laws that discouraged and denied claims by mothers who were "employable" (that is, who could be serving as local low-wage labor), who had given birth to illegitimate children, and who were unmarried but sexually active.[5] None of these developments would appear to bode well for the rights language and rights claiming discussed in Part I.

And yet rights survived this era of rehabilitation, restriction, and retrenchment. By looking beyond legislatures and politically appointed policymakers to the day-to-day administration of public benefits, this chapter shows how. I emphasize three welfare-related contexts in which rights endured: in the conversations occurring among welfare professionals, where the rehabilitation paradigm prompted concerns about overzealous bureaucrats; in the claims making of poor individuals, unconvinced that they should now abandon what the New Deal had promised them; and in the actions of federal administrators as they attempted to combat an unprecedented wave of discriminatory state-level welfare restrictions.

Rights thus continued to play an important role in conversations about poor relief and the modern American state more generally, but that role had started to change. In the past, I have argued, rights had often surfaced as an explanatory or hortatory tool – a way of helping Americans think differently about the polities around them and their relationships to those polities. In this era, rights appeared in more familiar forms: as a chit – that is, as a means of claiming material benefits from the state – and as a shield – a source of protection from government authorities who demanded too much from needy individuals and deferred too little to their personal choices.

These rights articulations, both by poor claimants and by federal administrators, were not always successful. More to the point, rights had complex repercussions for federal administrators' original vision of modernized poor relief. By the end of the 1950s, the emphasis on claimants' legal rights, combined with the example-setting resistance of states such as Indiana, Arizona, and New York, had indirectly resulted in some of the most insidious state welfare laws of the twentieth century. In the Deep South, especially (although not exclusively), federal administrators ultimately felt compelled to approve welfare reforms that were punitive and discriminatory – and deliberately so. The modern American state, it was becoming clear, *had* invited the poor into a different relationship with the polities around them – but that relationship was not necessarily more generous or respectful.

RIGHTS AGAINST THE REHABILITATIVE STATE

Standing before the January 1952 meeting of the American Public Welfare Association (APWA), association director Loula Dunn predicted that the year ahead would be "difficult." The statement "summarized the mood of the entire conference," according to one observer. To some extent, the meeting's mood reflected America's seemingly perilous place in the world: the Korean War was then in its second year, and atomic weaponry was a topic of daily conversation. The main concern, however, were the persistent attacks on the APWA's very enterprise. Thanks in part to a flurry of welfare "scandals," investigations of public welfare departments had become an "occupational disease," to use the words of a leading social work journal.[6] The 877 conference attendees, many of whom were state and local public welfare officials, could only speculate as to what was causing such vitriol. Some emphasized welfare's "public relations" problem: welfare workers had simply failed to "sell" legislators and communities on the importance of their work. Others wondered "whether public welfare spokesmen had not antagonized the public by putting too much emphasis on assistance as a right." Hanging over the entire conference was the previous year's battle over the confidentiality of public welfare records, which had been a blow to professional welfare workers' philosophy and stature.[7]

By the fall, the future looked darker still. The election of a Republican president, Dwight D. Eisenhower, ended two decades of executive support for "comprehensive social welfare," and although Eisenhower was surely friendlier to New Deal programs than the Republican runner-up, Robert Taft, the welfare community was "worried as hell" about the fate of the federal social welfare bureaucracy.[8]

Changes did indeed follow. During Eisenhower's first year in office, President Roosevelt's astutely titled Federal Security Agency became the Department of Health, Education, and Welfare and was tethered more tightly to the White House via its elevation to cabinet-level status. Top positions changed hands: Arthur Altmeyer, a member of the original Social Security Board and thereafter the social security commissioner, retired. Jane Hoey, the longtime head of the Bureau of Public Assistance went less gracefully – only after the new administration reclassified her civil service position and removed her from it.[9] Eisenhower replaced those New Deal stalwarts with Republicans John Tramburg and Jay Roney, respectively, both of whom who had served as directors of state welfare departments in the Midwest. At the very top of HEW, Oscar Ewing's post went to Texas "Democrat for Eisenhower" Oveta Culp Hobby. The former first lady of Texas had an impressive résumé (she directed the Women's Army Auxiliary Corps during World War II) but brought to HEW no experience with public welfare and no obvious sympathy for either its practitioners or recipients.

Outside the federal agency, meanwhile, antiwelfare rhetoric continued. After publishing a series of negative articles, including "The Relief Chiselers Are Stealing Us Blind," the popular magazine *Saturday Evening Post* finally offered public assistance some good press in 1952, complete with large photos of clean, smiling white families.[10] But to those engaged in public welfare work, attacks on the "welfare state" still seemed to consume "thousands of gallons of ink and millions of cubic feet of air."[11] Worse, the attacks appeared to be working. In the words of one social work professor, even informed, educated members of the public had come to see "something nefarious" in federally supported welfare programs.[12]

Never a homogenous group, some members of the social welfare community urged a retreat from the methods and principles that so inflamed critics, while others insisted that the public would eventually see the light. Many agreed, however, on the wisdom of devoting more attention to the nonmonetary, or service-related, aspects of the public assistance program, for three reasons. First, public welfare workers had often observed that money alone was not the answer to the complex, interrelated problems of their poor clients.[13] The nation's growing interest in psychology after World War II, especially prevalent among social workers, reinforced this thinking: many poor clients would remain poor, psychology taught, unless they received treatment for the disorders that had landed them in poverty in the first place.[14] Second, focusing on the concept of social service gave public welfare workers a way to emphasize their professional skills. Although most did not have graduate degrees in social work, they believed their jobs entailed much more than filling out forms and cutting checks; they resented the notion, cited in Chapter 5, that a "good widow with just ordinary horse sense" could do the job.[15] Those welfare workers who had invested in graduate education were even more anxious to counter that opinion, lest outsiders encroach on or devalue the professional sphere they had fought so hard to create.[16] And third, a focus on services appealed to those welfare workers who were genuinely concerned about the behavior and dependency of their clients. Rehabilitative services aimed not only to restore the poor to normalcy but also to transform them – into the independent, productive citizens of American liberal imagination.[17]

At one point in the program's history, such a heavy emphasis on services would have been, if not taboo, at least officially disfavored. The Social Security Act of 1935 mentioned services in the provisions addressing maternal and child welfare, but not in the public assistance titles. Those spoke of the "money payment," which federal administrators interpreted as a rejection of the notion that poor people required counseling or oversight. And although they often acknowledged the value of social casework, federal administrators urged state and local welfare workers to focus on fair, efficient, and objective determinations of eligibility. Clients with difficult problems could always be referred to private agencies.[18]

In the 1940s, however, the boundary between public assistance and casework blurred. As prosperity returned after the Depression, the structural understanding of poverty that prevailed in elite policymaking circles in 1935 became less persuasive, opening more space for discussion of poor people's personal flaws. At the same time, private social agencies – the traditional home of social services – edged closer to public welfare. War-related problems, including relocation, civil defense, and juvenile delinquency, allied private organizations with public agencies and encouraged a "cross-fertilization" of philosophy and technique.[19] As discussed in Chapter 3, the federal agency's Bureau of Public Assistance was in fact already "seeded" with professional social workers, men and women who had attended school alongside their private-agency peers and received the same training in casework.[20] As these administrators tried to sell state and local agencies on the virtues of a similarly credentialed staff (one prong of their campaign to elevate standards and drive out parochialism), they naturally found themselves highlighting the unique services that social workers could offer. By the mid-1940s, the BPA had drafted guidelines on the place of services in public assistance administration, and welfare professionals routinely discussed the issue in their publications and at their conferences.[21] By the end of the decade, social services had made their way into the federal agency's formal recommendations to Congress.[22]

If the emphasis on the nonmonetary aspects of public assistance was a long time coming, it had also become pragmatic, as evidenced by the champion it found in Wilbur Cohen, perhaps the most influential mezzo-level bureaucrat of his time. The former special assistant to Arthur Altmeyer had been demoted in the agency's transition to Republican leadership, but he was too valuable to be forced out.[23] From his new position as director of HEW's Division of Research and Statistics, Cohen functioned as a key strategist for a cohort of loyal New Dealers. The group's maneuvers were based on Cohen's recognition that President-elect Eisenhower did not, in fact, seek to roll back the New Deal, and that he might even be willing to extend existing programs if he believed that the nation could thereby achieve long-term savings.[24] Programs framed as "rehabilitative" were thus ideal: they allowed Eisenhower to support humanitarian measures while promising to wean Americans off government support. Eisenhower's HEW appointees might, of course, propose their own reforms, but Cohen thought it unlikely. "Mrs. Hobby," as the new HEW secretary was somewhat derisively known, struck the old-timers as "cautious" and "uncertain." She had ideological preferences, to be sure, but seemed unsure about how they mapped onto the substance of the department's programs.[25]

Seizing the opportunity, Cohen and his allies at HEW and in the APWA drafted amendments to the Social Security Act that reflected Eisenhower's interest in rehabilitation but also quietly advanced New Deal goals. On the social insurance side, they helped convince Congress in 1954 to "subsidize the disabled worker's social security piggy bank," thereby laying the groundwork for a full-fledged disability insurance program.[26] On the public assistance side, in 1956, they won federal matching funds for the costs states incurred in providing social services to public assistance clients.[27] The Bureau of Public Assistance encouraged states to take advantage of the new funds and even outlined the myriad underlying problems – from "deviate sexual practices" to "unwholesome neighborhood influences" – that they might choose to address in the near future.[28]

Many public welfare workers welcomed the new approach. At the January 1958 APWA conference, administrators celebrated public welfare's improved "sale-ability" following the 1956 amendments. Preventative and restorative services gave public welfare workers a positive "new story" to tell "John Q. Citizen," one attendee applauded. People who once sought to "make trouble" for public welfare, reported a Maui County, Hawaii, administrator in the summer of 1957, now marveled at the "varied and complex services" offered by the local welfare department. The opportunity to provide services even boosted morale, according to the head of New York's Bureau of Public Assistance. Her staff "d[id] not expect to eradicate poverty or desertion or chronic illness in the next 10 years," she acknowledged, but with "new vision and new courage," they were "finding joy in the process."[29]

Such sunny statements, however, masked a tension that was clear to anyone who had worked in public welfare in the past decade: rehabilitation coexisted uneasily with the federal agency's previous emphasis on rights. This is evident from the strained attempts to connect the two. Yes, the client had a "right to self-determination," explained social work professor Helen Perlman in 1951, but it was up to social agencies to decide what level of client decision making was "realistically feasible." Writing in 1957, BPA staff member Susan Tollen celebrated the Social Security Act for "preserving the full legal status of its beneficiaries," but simultaneously characterized welfare recipients as "people in failure" who required professional assistance to climb back to self-sufficiency.

Other public welfare professionals attempted to square the circle by celebrating clients' newfound "right" to rehabilitative services.[30]

Yet a true belief in the rights of welfare recipients *did* contradict the project of rehabilitation. Renowned social worker Grace Marcus articulated the point as early as 1944, when the BPA hired her as an outside consultant. Unless services were completely optional, Marcus noted in a memo to the agency, they conflicted with the foundational notion of assistance as a right. Even the process of evaluating an applicant's need – a first step in establishing eligibility – was perilous, for it might lead the public welfare worker to treat the applicant as "a helpless baby" rather than a competent, rights-bearing citizen. Public welfare agencies must not use "economic helplessness" as an excuse for foisting unwanted services on the poor, Marcus warned.[31]

Assistant General Counsel A. D. Smith raised similar objections in 1946, when there was talk within the agency of forging a statutory link between public assistance and professional social work. While he appreciated the services that social workers provided, Smith wrote to BPA director Jane Hoey, tying that work to assistance payments would support "the view that poverty is a basis of public wardship." Wasn't this the very view that the agency was trying to "quash"? Smith raised the point more frequently and publicly as the rehabilitation paradigm gained ground. "The ultimate purpose" of social programs, Smith maintained in a 1949 article in the *Harvard Law Review*, "should be to see that individuals come to regard [them] as affirmations of worth, and not as testimonials of personal inadequacy." Thus social welfare statutes should always be framed in terms of the individual's "legal rights," Smith contended, rather than as mandates to authorities "to 'administer' forms of service or relief."[32]

Such concerns ultimately impelled Smith, after his retirement, to publish *The Right to Life* (1955), an eccentric, philosophical text that he distributed to colleagues in social work schools, law schools, and other federal and state agencies, and that would ultimately inform welfare rights theory in the 1960s.[33] On the one hand, Smith celebrated social work: he dedicated his opus neither to his wife, who quietly supported all his endeavors, nor to his sons, who endured his frequent instructions on how to "attack" life, but to "Those Esteemed Members of the Social Work Profession By Whose Counsel I Have So Greatly Profited and Whose Abiding Faith in Their Fellow Man Exemplifies My Philosophy."[34] And indeed, their influence comes through in the text's many references to human interdependence and human needs. On the other hand, Smith's longstanding commitment to legal rights in public welfare also emerges stronger than ever. Particularly troubling to him, by 1955, were administrative practices that invited welfare workers to judge "the ethical base of [the client's] individual right" or "the scope of his individual prerogative." If social workers intended to provide rehabilitative services, Smith warned, these should be completely separate from any "authoritative" judgments about eligibility or ineligibility.[35]

Smith's former colleague in the GC's office, Alanson Willcox, sounded the same note of caution in a 1957 article on "patterns of social legislation" (Willcox was then general counsel of the American Hospital Association; he would return to HEW to serve as GC under Kennedy.) "The power of the purse is great," Willcox wrote, and "by paying people to do things or not do them," it had become possible "to control their actions as effectively as by threatening to send them to jail." Government administrators thus had to be vigilant, he continued, "lest, out of zeal to better people's lot, we impose on them patterns of behavior in matters in which ... government ought not meddle."[36]

Willcox believed that administrators were "avoiding this danger fairly well."[37] Alan Keith-Lucas, an English immigrant who worked in private and public welfare agencies in Ohio and Louisiana before becoming a professor of social work at the University of North Carolina, was much less sanguine.[38] From this outsider-insider position, Keith-Lucas attacked "the presuppositions underlying modern social work practice" – and thus animating much of public welfare administration. The notion that those who needed state assistance were "sick" and "c[ould] only be made well through the help of a class of trained, objective, neurosis-free practitioners" was dangerous, Keith-Lucas argued in a 1953 article. In practice, it resulted in "well-intentioned infringements of personal liberty" and, perhaps eventually, "a benevolent or paternalistic dictatorship."[39]

Keith-Lucas made these arguments even more powerfully in *Decisions about People in Need* (1957), a widely reviewed empirical study of cases from two states' ADC programs. Many thousands of times per day, Keith-Lucas calculated, public welfare workers in the United States made decisions that meant "the difference between health and sickness," the "continuance or severing of family ties," and even "life and death." So great was the welfare worker's power, he found, and so dire the clients' need, that clients often unquestioningly accepted welfare workers' findings and demands, at the expense of personal rights and freedoms. Rights and rehabilitative casework, in other words, were incompatible. "The

American people ... must make up their mind," Keith-Lucas declared; "they cannot have both."[40]

There was another solution, however – one that these authors hinted at but did not fully develop: to preserve their free and equal status in an era of rehabilitation, poor people needed stronger rights *against the state*, including its most well-intentioned and expert deputies. Welfare rights theorists would elaborate on this theme in the 1960s, as subsequent chapters will show. For the purposes of this chapter, however, the point is this: the rehabilitative turn in public welfare policy did not augur a fundamental change in governance theory to a paradigm in which welfare recipients were no longer subjects of law or holders of legal rights. To the contrary, the emphasis on rehabilitation helped some policymakers, professionals, and academics see in rights a new and different value for the poor.

The rest of this chapter moves from ideas to practice: it documents the various ways in which administrators, claimants, and lawyers kept a rights framework alive and then examines the consequences of their actions. As we will see, the Eisenhower years were an important learning period for those who opposed the concept of rights in welfare. Increasingly, they deployed rights language of their own, emphasizing the rights of taxpayers against "tax eaters," and of states against the federal government.

THE ENDURANCE OF CLAIMS MAKING

Since the Social Security Act in 1935, federal administrators had expended great energy attempting to explain federal requirements to state and local agencies, often using the language of rights. Under the old locally controlled systems of poor relief, they believed, payments to the needy were nothing more than charity. The administrators used rights language to explain how federally subsidized public assistance was different – how it encompassed different assumptions and values – and why it required different procedures and personnel.[41] By midcentury, federal administrators were still making such pronouncements, and it was possible to discern an effect on at least some state administrators.[42] As one state public welfare supervisor explained to new trainees, applicants to public programs were "not begging"; they were "merely presenting to us their statement that they come within a group that has certain rights set up by law."[43]

By the time Eisenhower took office in early 1953, critics of the federal welfare bureaucracy had been complaining about such statements for a few years – and not just about the existence of such statements, but about their influence. In investigating its state welfare department in 1951, the Tennessee legislature had decried department officials' embrace of the federal concept of assistance as a "matter of right."[44] Articles in the popular press echoed these concerns. "Only a few years ago people applying for help would slip in here quietly and hope no one saw them," one Kansas caseworker told a writer for *Reader's Digest* in 1952. "Now they search the regulations to see how they can qualify, and demand relief as a right." The article connected this attitude directly to federal laws and "Washington thinking."[45]

Similar comments pervaded a set of November 1953 hearings before the Subcommittee on Social Security of the House Committee on Ways and Means, chaired by the conservative Nebraska Republican Carl Curtis. Curtis used the hearings, which were ostensibly about the proposed extension of the Old Age and Survivors Insurance Program, to put pointed questions to state-level welfare experts about the concept of "public assistance as a matter of right." Unfailingly, the witnesses testified that their state public assistance programs granted only conditional statutory rights, not "vested," inherent, or "absolute and constitutional" rights – and yet many citizens believed otherwise.[46] Robert French, executive director of the Public Affairs Research Council of Louisiana, testified that to both Louisiana state legislators and their constituents, public assistance was "very much ... a right."[47] *Thoughtful* citizens realized that income support was "not a matter of right," Minnesota's commissioner of public welfare testified, but the general "frame of mind" was otherwise. He recounted the story of "a rather well-to-do manufacturer" who insisted that his father was "entitled" to Old Age Assistance and who told local welfare workers to "mind [their] own business." Even members of the state legislature were known to share such views, the commissioner lamented.[48] If federal administrators had once urged constant affirmation of "public assistance as a matter of right," these state administrators now found themselves constantly explaining that it was *not*.[49]

Chairman Curtis likely handpicked these witnesses in an effort to garner support for his own vision for the welfare state. Each one character-ized public assistance as "government charity" or a "duty upon society," not an individual right. New Jersey's commissioner of Institutions and Agencies suggested that, going forward, Congress should prohibit the federal agency from propagating its "abstract philosophies," such as "the client must always be paid in cash, or it is his right and you must convince people of his right." States ought to decide such questions for themselves, he asserted.[50] An administrator from Curtis's home state went a step further, urging Congress to shift all elderly citizens into the federally administered and funded Social Security program and return responsibility for the other public assistance populations to the states, to handle as they pleased. The United States Chamber of Commerce, not coincidentally, had offered the same proposal, and Curtis himself would echo it in the coming months.[51]

But if Curtis manufactured support for the notion of a "right to assistance" run amok, he did not manufacture the real instances of rights claiming that continued to make their way into state administrative hearings and state court, sometimes in forms that would have been unfathomable just twenty years prior. Consider the McCoy case from Jackson County, Missouri. Louis McCoy, age fifty, was an army veteran, a recent widower, and, as of late 1952, a recipient of ADC on behalf of his seven adolescent children. McCoy could not work full-time, he claimed, because he was needed at home. When the local welfare department reconsidered its decision to put McCoy on the rolls, he appealed to the State Welfare Department and then sued the state agency in court. This effort failed – the judges could not get past their belief that, at seventeen, McCoy's eldest daughter was surely capable of watching the other children while he went to work – but the claim itself is noteworthy. McCoy was an "able-bodied man," the record emphasized, the type of person who historically had the weakest claim to public support, and yet he unashamedly claimed an entitlement to ADC. He claimed it not simply in a paper application, but in an administrative hearing and two judicial appeals.[52]

Similarly revealing is the California case of Harrlet Jane Bertch and fellow members of Christ's Church of the Golden Rule. The elderly claimants had given all their worldly possessions to the church and placed themselves entirely in its service and care. The maneuver seemed to harken back to older days, when religious institutions tended to their own and elderly citizens relied on private bonds to keep themselves out of the dreaded poorhouse. But then Bertch and her colleagues applied for OAA. Their applications reportedly "incensed" the state welfare director, and placed the California State Social Welfare Board in a difficult position: evidence showed that the church was not meeting the claimants' needs, but also that they had accepted this standard of living, and that any benefits they received from the government would go directly into church coffers.[53] Complicating matters was the fact that the church was the latest in a series of enterprises headed by Arthur L. Bell, a "suave and handsome" Christian Scientist who had gotten rich by selling the elderly dreams of a "socialized Utopia" and conspiracy theories about the bombing of Pearl Harbor, and who, by 1950, was navigating various criminal charges.[54] When the state's Social Welfare Board denied the church members' OAA claims, lawyer Howard Crittenden Jr. (who also represented Bell in his criminal cases) alleged interference with their religious freedom and denial of the equal protection of the laws. The California Supreme Court ultimately dodged both allegations by finding a statutory basis for reversing the welfare board, but, again, the claims themselves are revealing. Not only did these citizens have a statutory right to assistance, their lawyer argued, they also had *constitutional* rights, which would be violated if the state denied their claims.[55]

Across the country in Polk County, Iowa, a third such case emerged, and like the others, it suggests the endurance of a rights framework, even amid a rehabilitative turn. The case began in the summer of 1955, when Pearl B. Collins's monthly ADC grant dropped from a generous $253.89 (on account of her six children and her own and her spouse's physical inability to work) to $175, the cap established by a new state law.[56] Represented pro bono by lawyers E. W. McNeil and Neill Garrett – former president of the Iowa Bar Association and former special assistant to the attorney general, respectively – Collins appealed the decision to the Iowa State Board of Social Welfare and then sued the board when the hearing did not go her way. Her main argument was grounded in the equal protection guarantee of the state constitution: the "family cap" law discriminated against her children by according more favorable treatment to children of similarly needy but smaller families.[57] The argument worked, both at the trial level and, in 1957, before the Iowa Supreme Court. "As to paupers and indigent persons there is no common law or constitutional duty resting upon the state to provide support," Justice Norman Hays noted; nevertheless, having created a statutory right for a class of citizens, the legislature was not free to add an "unreasonable or arbitrary subclassification."[58] Beneath the legal jargon was a holding that had major implications: Pearl Collins and her husband would decide how many children to have, and the state would quite literally support their choice.

Evidence of what was happening at the ground level is harder to come by, but there are hints that Pearl Collins was hardly the only ADC recipient who felt entitled to something more from the government – either more money or better treatment. According to historian Premilla Nadasen, poor women in Boston had already begun to organize, building the informal networks that would soon lead to the formation of Mothers for Adequate Welfare. Throughout the 1950s, one member of that group recalled, women who lived in the same neighborhood would occasionally "go together directly to the local field office and quarrel with the welfare office supervisor" about the kind of treatment they received. Sometimes they would even "go straight to the central office and try to get an appointment with the Director." Similarly, historian Lisa Levenstein has documented African American women's "deliberate and assertive" use of ADC and the municipal courts in the 1950s in Philadelphia. Her subjects claimed public resources while also attempting to preserve their privacy and autonomy.[59]

The point of these anecdotes, taken together, is not that the rights framework thrived in public welfare in this period. Conservative politicians were systematically attacking it, while many authorities simply remained unconvinced that the giving of welfare implicated any kind of right. In the words of the dissenting justices in *Collins*, ADC payments were a "gratuity, a bounty from the state," a "mere privilege."[60] The point is that even in these fraught years for New Deal public welfare programs, and in spite of a shift in emphasis, rights concepts and rights claims survived. Neither the rehabilitation discourse of elite Washington policymakers nor the "welfare backlash" manifesting in the media and in state legislatures tells the full story.

"STEMMING THE TIDE": PROTECTING RIGHTS BY POLICING STATE LAW

These observations are not meant to trivialize the phenomenon of welfare backlash: Around the country, a wave of behavioral requirements and other eligibility restrictions emerged in state policymaking settings as lawmakers reacted to perceptions of fraud and immorality, and to the growing presence of nonwhite Americans on the welfare rolls. But when seen from the perspective of day-to-day administration, even the welfare backlash suggests the endurance of rights. Federal administrators – in particular, the lawyers – were monitoring all these proposed laws, and although many restrictive and de facto discriminatory measures became law on their watch, they also consistently articulated the rights of poor citizens. By describing potential rights violations as "conformity questions" – that is, issues that might trigger a withdrawal of federal funds – they helped prevent some of the worst proposals from becoming law (although, as we will see, that tactic had a price).[61]

By the 1950s, agency lawyers had been engaged in this work for some time. Like their colleagues throughout the agency, they wanted to ensure that New Deal social welfare programs took root in the states, not to obstruct them.[62] Within this framework, however, they tracked and discouraged practices that they saw as violations of assistance recipients' rights. For example, in prior years, federal lawyers had carefully monitored states' use of legal guardianship, a practice traditionally used to assign fiduciaries to manage the interests of minors, the mentally ill, and other legally "incompetent" persons.[63] Starting in the early 1940s, some states authorized guardians for public assistance recipients who spent their grants on nonessential items; others denied assistance unless and until the applicant petitioned for such a guardian. Once in place, guardians were to manage their charges' spending and provide regular reports to the state or local agency.[64] In other words, they were a mechanism for keeping tabs on the "undeserving poor," while purporting to comply with a federal government framework that insisted on cash payments. Federal administrators could have turned a blind eye to this practice – the Social Security Act said nothing about guardianship, and the most relevant language could easily have been interpreted to allow such arrangements.[65] Instead, agency lawyers pushed back. "Obviously," wrote General Counsel Jack Tate to his boss, Federal Security Administrator Paul McNutt, in 1941, "the assistance group should not be singled out in this manner for loss of civil rights because they are poor."[66] In regular messages to state agencies and state congressional delegations, the lawyers insisted that states should not appoint guardians to public assistance recipients unless otherwise warranted under the state's general guardianship statute, and only after the state had observed its regular legal procedures.[67]

Similarly, federal agency lawyers had long looked out for and discouraged laws that conditioned payment on an applicant's behavior, such as the 1943 Utah bill that tied ADC payments to the mother's acceptance of state-selected employment, the 1948 Missouri bill that required the mother to file a nonsupport action against the father of her needy child, and the 1944 Rhode Island bill that would have obligated some recipients to expend part of their payment on medical services.[68] Without much statutory support, the lawyers informed state agencies that "the Social Security Act did not contemplate the use of assistance as a means of controlling behavior."[69] If states wanted to prohibit particular conduct – such as excessive alcohol consumption, or the purchase and display of luxury items, or nonmarital procreation – they should use their general police power and amend their criminal code, not their social welfare laws.[70]

A final example from these earlier years is the federal agency lawyers' objection to "suitable home" laws – later to become a favored means among states for weeding illegitimate children from the ADC rolls. Although the original Social Security Act did not impose a suitable home requirement, evidence suggests that members of Congress intended to allow states to incorporate such provisions into their own laws (some notion of "suitability" was often part of the mothers' pension laws on which states modeled their ADC programs).[71] By the mid-1940s, however, federal lawyers routinely objected to such requirements. As they saw it, state and local administrators tended to use "suitability" as a means of achieving goals unrelated to alleviating need. This was especially apparent when a state's definition of "unsuitability" did not line up with its general protective statutes – for example, when the state was willing to deem a home "unsuitable" for public support, but not so "unsuitable" that the state would take responsibility for the needy child.[72]

Whether because they were naturally inclined to adhere to precedent or because of the long tenure of key figures in the GC's office, the lawyers did not revise these interpretations as the years went on. But two developments made their job more difficult after 1953: more conservative leadership at the top of the federal agency and, in the wake of federal school desegregation efforts, a determined effort by states to control their ADC programs, as a way of both challenging federal power and influencing the behavior of black citizens.

On the first point: although lawyers made important first-order judgments about states' conformity with federal law, ultimate authority rested with politically appointed administrators, such as the commissioner of the Social Security Administration. Charles Schottland, who occupied this post from 1954 to 1958, was generally considered a friend to New Deal public assistance and was himself a lawyer, but he proved reluctant to give teeth to some of the agency's long-standing legal interpretations. His most recent experience had been in state administration, and as a result he tended to see the agency lawyers as unduly "rigid." He dismissed the money payment principle, for example, as seeming "wonderful" – until a "senile old man ... lost his check" and found himself "starving to death because he couldn't handle his cash."[73]

Schottland's boss posed a potentially greater challenge. HEW secretary Oveta Culp Hobby was a newcomer to public assistance, unschooled in the institutional history that underlay the lawyers' interpretations. Ideologically, she was miles away from the old New Dealers. While in office, she opined that functions like welfare ought to be "left to the

States," and that grants-in-aid – a necessary evil – ought to be administered with a "minimum" of federal "supervision and control."[74] She also opposed the president's order to desegregate schools on U.S. army bases and moved slowly when called on to oversee federal distribution of the Salk polio vaccine, lest she allow "socialized medicine," as she put it, to enter "by the back door."[75] (Her eventual replacement, Marion B. Folsom [1954–58], had a greater appreciation for HEW's programs; in the early 1930s he was one of the few business leaders who supported the Roosevelt administration's old-age insurance program.)

Finally, Parke Banta, the top lawyer at HEW after 1953, was considerably more conservative than his predecessor, Jack Tate. He was also in no way a "New Deal lawyer" – the first holder of his office for whom that was true. Whereas previous general counsels came from academia, prestigious northeastern law firms, and other New Deal agencies, Banta's experience was entirely at the state and local levels: as a county prosecutor and school board member, head of the Missouri State Social Security Commission (1941–45), a Republican member of the House of Representatives (1947–49), and chairperson of the Missouri State Chamber of Commerce's committee on legislation.

The only saving grace, for those who had been in the agency longer and remained loyal to its original goals, was that "a number of [the Eisenhower appointees] were ridiculously ignorant about what they were supposed to be doing," recalled Deputy Social Security Commissioner William Mitchell. "Mrs. Hobby would never touch anything that hadn't been through [Assistant Secretary] Rufus Miles's hands and through the hands of the general counsel," Mitchell explained. And Banta, he said, "usually ... wouldn't touch anything that hadn't been through the counsel in charge of that particular program and the assistant general counsel."[76] In other words, key decisions were open to influence by mezzo-level administrators, many of whom had joined the agency in a more liberal administration.

Even more important than the changes in federal leadership, however, was states' determination to go their own way in the administration of ADC, a program that had by now become entangled in the public mind with the image of an immoral, unproductive, husbandless black woman. Gone were the days when state officials approached New Deal social welfare programs "with open minds and open hearts and open eyes and ears," lamented one longtime federal administrator.[77] As the bitter battles described in Chapter 5 demonstrate, state officials had grown more skeptical. They also now had at their disposal capable state bureaucracies and proven tactics of resistance, including foot dragging, political maneuvering, finger pointing, and feigned ignorance. More and more states turned to these tactics in the mid- and late 1950s. They did not object to a permanent system of federal funding – that part of the modern American state was now firmly established – but they were determined not to let the federal government control their relationships with the thousands of families that now sought ADC. They enacted laws that tested the limits of the Social Security Act or knowingly crossed the line into illegality, and then they stood their ground.

Not all of the new state measures were ADC-specific. Some reflected a general concern with welfare abuse and a corresponding desire to have more control over all categories of the dependent poor. For example, Montana, North Carolina, and Alabama proposed to appoint special guardians for assistance recipients, Washington sought to disqualify recipients who cashed their checks in bars or cocktail lounges, and New York introduced policy to allow county commissioners to decide what living arrangements were in the client's "best interest."[78]

Many other measures, however, demonstrated unease about the current ADC population. One concern – less pronounced in the program's early days – was that many women receiving ADC for their children were not working and really ought to be. Thus legislatures in Washington, Missouri, Florida, Georgia, New Mexico, South Carolina, Tennessee, Mississippi, and the District of Columbia entertained proposals to condition ADC on a mother's willingness to accept suitable employment.[79] Other proposed laws stopped shy of work requirements but insisted on rehabilitative treatment, a sign that for some poor people, social services were not just another facet of the state's beneficence but a price of admission.[80]

The behavior that most concerned legislators, however, was not mothers' refusal to work but their nonmarital sexual activity and childbearing. Wisconsin, California, and South Dakota attempted to require welfare workers to report misconduct or immoral behavior by ADC mothers.[81] The California proposal would have made the birth of a second illegitimate child automatic grounds for the mother's referral to the probation department, to determine whether her home was fit for children (if not, removal to a foster home would follow).[82] ADC grants, in these schemes, became a means of surveillance, and the information gathered from such surveillance, an invitation to other arms of the state to intervene in recipients' lives. A proposal to require claimants to submit to fingerprinting before they could receive benefits would have served the same purpose, tethering them to a rapidly growing criminal justice system.[83] Similar proposals targeted the fathers of dependent children. Illinois, Virginia, and Washington entertained proposals to condition ADC benefits on a mother's agreement to file nonsupport paperwork.[84] Another proposal in Illinois would have gone a step further, requiring the mother to establish the paternity of the child before receiving aid.[85] Mississippi, Tennessee, and Georgia entertained the same idea.[86] Most prevalent of all, however, were efforts to remove the products of illicit sex from the rolls: twenty-one states, representing all regions of the country, considered proposals to deny ADC to children born out of wedlock.[87] Related proposals allowed such children to receive aid only if the mother committed not to put the state in that position again. Lawmakers in Alabama considered tying aid to the mother's promise to cease "illicit" relationships.[88] Like-minded legislators in Delaware wanted more than mere words, proposing that mothers of multiple illegitimate children request sterilization in exchange for benefits.[89]

These measures ostensibly applied to all ADC recipients, but lawmakers often targeted black, unwed mothers. As the historian Elaine May and others have demonstrated, reconstructing the white, middle-class, nuclear family and containing women's sexuality were postwar social and cultural imperatives. Unwed black mothers, by their mere existence, undermined both goals.[90] These women attracted additional censure because historically they had worked for low wages on farms and in homes, and now, critics alleged, they were making a "business" out of childbearing, at public expense.[91] A Missouri legislator, for example, described with alarm a woman "who quit a job as a maid because she could draw more from the state for her six children." The "production of illegitimate children is one of the best jobs" in the county, complained a representative of the Illinois Agricultural Association to state lawmakers. Such statements are difficult to square with the notoriously low payment levels in many states. But, as one North Carolina critic explained, women could still make a profit by combining ADC with "prostitution, and perhaps bootlegging."[92] Growing civil rights demands provided a final reason to target black ADC mothers: by equating African Americans' disproportionately high illegitimacy rates with immorality, and by highlighting the burden they placed on the tax-paying public, segregationists saw an opportunity to undermine claims to equal rights.[93]

As some public welfare and civil rights advocates argued at the time, and as historians later documented, statistics on illegitimacy and race were dubious. In some states, lawmakers manipulated marriage rules to make

African American unions illegitimate.[94] Around the country, government officials and service providers supported white, unwed mothers in maternity homes and helped them legitimize their babies through adoption, while they discouraged black mothers from doing the same.[95] In the 1950s, however, state officials contended that they were well within their rights when they refused to support illegitimate children and when they subjected poor, unwed mothers to additional policing and regulation.

The states were also responding to complaints from their "taxpaying" constituents (a category that excluded poor people, despite their contributions to public coffers). As historian Molly Michelmore has argued, all Americans in the 1950s benefited from government largess, but some of the most common forms of that largess – tax breaks, subsidized employer benefits, Social Security payments, and so on – were not visible; taxpayers were left to wonder where their hard-earned dollars were going, and they saw only welfare.[96] Popular characterizations of ADC in this period support her conclusions. With the amount of money that the state spent on welfare every year, calculated the Los Angeles *Mirror* in 1959, Los Angeles could be operated "tax-free for two years – with enough leftover to send every taxpayer here a refund check." The same article cited outrageous examples of welfare abuse, all at the taxpayers' expense: a woman whose twenty-two illegitimate children had enabled her to collect $50,000 in welfare payments ("tax free!"); another mother whose eight children were found living in squalor while she filled her wardrobe with "plenty of new dresses and shoes, paid for by taxpayers."[97]

Against this onslaught of new and innovative state-level actions, federal lawyers raised the sorts of objections they had honed in the 1940s. These objections prevented some proposals from becoming law, especially when filtered through a state attorney general or respected state welfare director. A 1951 Georgia law that limited ADC payments to covering one illegitimate child per family became void after Georgia attorney general Eugene Cook – who in future years would staunchly defend his state's stance on segregation – learned of the "serious constitutional questions" it raised.[98] When Georgia legislators later considered imposing criminal sanctions on mothers who applied for ADC if they had illegitimate children, an appearance from a knowledgeable state welfare department official reportedly made all the difference.[99] And in 1955, when North Carolina considered prohibiting payments to families with more than two illegitimate children, the federal Bureau of Public Assistance informed the state welfare department that the bill would likely violate both the Social Security Act and the Constitution, a message that state welfare director

Ellen Winston conveyed directly to Governor Luther Hodges.[100] Federal administrators sent similar messages in response to bills in South Dakota, Alabama, Delaware, and Illinois, and although many factors may have prevented the bills from becoming law, it is notable that none of them did.[101]

These tactics were not always received kindly, however, and may ultimately have done more harm than good to the federal administrators' cause. Carl Harper, the regional attorney for the Deep South, knew this better than anyone. A Yale-educated lawyer who had been with the agency from its early years (that is, an archetypal New Deal lawyer), Harper "deplore[d]" what he saw as attempts to "predicat[e] eligibility for assistance on the surrender of constitutional rights." This was the very concern that A. D. Smith and others raised in their critiques of the "rehabilitative turn" in public welfare. But as a southerner, he understood what the federal agency was up against when it came to the states.[102] By the mid-1950s, he noted, the disputed welfare bills shared the floor with proposals to outlaw desegregated baseball and impeach members of the U.S. Supreme Court.[103] Harper also reported, in the late 1950s, that the phrase "conformity question" (meant to suggest the possible withdrawal of federal funding) simply did not scare states in his region the way it used to. State officials responded by asking for specific legal citations and bright-line rules – requests that presaged counterattack, not cooperation.[104] "We cannot continue to stem the tide" this way, Harper warned his colleagues in Washington.[105]

COMPROMISING RIGHTS IN THE FACE OF "MASSIVE RESISTANCE"

Harper was right: with increasing frequency state legislatures ignored federal objections, and in the face of this rising tide, federal administrators struggled to respond. Withdrawing a state's welfare grant had never been an ideal "stick": it punished poor Americans while also straining relationships with the states and exposing the agency to criticism. Starting around 1955 – in the era of "massive resistance" to federal civil rights mandates – the cost was higher than ever. By the end of the decade, direct attacks on state laws were a rarity. Weak, circuitous legal interventions, usually with the state welfare agency, became the norm.

HEW's response to Mississippi's 1955 attack on illegitimacy among welfare recipients is illustrative. When the Mississippi legislature attached a rider to its 1955 appropriation act (and subsequent appropriation acts)

prohibiting assistance payments to a child whose mother had an illegitimate child after she was placed on the assistance rolls, federal lawyers
warned that the state had established an "unreasonable classification" of
doubtful validity, and thus was placing its federal grant at risk. (The
choice of language itself was an artful dodge: although the state legislature
did this within days of the Supreme Court's *Brown v. Board* decision, the
federal lawyers made no mention of race; the unreasonable classification
to which they objected was the distinction between a needy child who had
no siblings, or had only legitimate siblings, and an equally needy child
whose sibling or siblings were illegitimate.) Agency leaders chose not to
take formal action, however – not yet. Instead, they negotiated with the
state public welfare agency over how it would choose to interpret the new
state legislation.[106]

At first, the Mississippi Department of Public Welfare claimed that the
rider was simply a "suitable home" restriction of the sort that federal
officials had by then grudgingly approved in other states. The fact that an
illegitimate birth constituted decisive evidence of unsuitability was beside
the point, state officials maintained. Subsequently, the state agency conceded some ground, agreeing that an illegitimate birth would be just one
factor in a multifactor evaluation. Continued pressure convinced the state
agency to allow an affected mother to be reinstated if she convinced the
local agency that she had ceased "illicit relationships" and was "maintaining a suitable home."[107] At that point, the federal agency approved
the amended state plan.

The changes that federal administrators negotiated had little meaning
for the families that the law targeted, however, and Mississippi set a
precedent for other states in the region. Federal officials' hands were tied
several years later when Florida and Alabama sought to go just as far –
much to the frustration of regional attorney Carl Harper. Through
"minor change[s] in wording" and "thin verbal camouflage," Alabama
and Florida achieved results that were "exactly what we have in years
passed told the Georgia, Tennessee and Mississippi agencies would not be
consistent" with federal law, Harper griped.[108]

By the late 1950s, in short, the federal agency's legal arguments had lost
the influence they once had on state legislatures, especially in the Deep
South.[109] Federal agency attorneys now attempted to nullify, undermine,
or retard state laws at the implementation stage. These rearguard actions
were ineffectual, however: audits of the state programs documented ram-
pant racial discrimination in the administration of ADC.[110] Public assistance in the 1950s was undeniably much more rule-bound and legalistic

than any scheme of poor relief that had come before, but – building on the examples of Indiana, Arizona, and New York – states had learned how to circumvent the rules that they did not like. Increasingly, they did so by claiming that their interpretations of federal law were just as valid as the federal agency's.

Federal lawyers, meanwhile, had become so accustomed to compromise that in one breath they could deride a welfare bill as a blatant attempt to exclude black families, and in the next find that, technically, the law met federal requirements.[111] The lawyers' strategy also frequently backfired, as when they inadvertently helped states stay within the bounds of the law while achieving discriminatory and punitive ends, or when one state adopted a second state's federally approved law (an uncomfortable situation for an agency that preached treating like things alike) without also adopting the countervailing state regulations that federal administrators had painstakingly negotiated to accompany it.[112] Decades of attempting to police rights violations thus culminated in the sort of policies that made welfare rights all but illusory for many poor Americans.

7

Welfare Rights outside the Courts

The Administrative Origins of Poverty Law

In the summer of 1960, as the country prepared for a landmark presidential election, the federal agency's proverbial chickens came home to roost. Using Mississippi's federally approved "suitable home" law as a template, Louisiana amended its Aid to Dependent Children law to prohibit payments to any woman who had a child out of wedlock after receiving a check from the welfare department, unless and until she presented proof that she had "ceased illicit relationships" and was "maintaining a suitable home for the child." A law enacted in the same legislative session denied welfare benefits to an illegitimate child if the mother of that child had two or more older illegitimate children.[1] State attorney general Jack Gremillion sharpened the laws by giving them retroactive effect. The result, as intended, was a purging of the state's ADC rolls: 22,500 children lost their benefits. The vast majority (an estimated 98 percent) were African American.[2] This, too, was intentional: historians now recognize these laws as part of a "segregation package," designed to countermand federal integration orders, retaliate against African Americans for their civil rights demands, and undermine state politicians who had blunted or deflected segregationist demands.[3]

As poor mothers struggled to provide for their families, local churches, community groups, and civil rights organizations mobilized. Taking the lead, the Greater New Orleans branch of the National Urban League (NUL) pressured state officials to repeal the law, raised and distributed funds, called on the Department of Health, Education, and Welfare to intervene, and assembled a network of supporters.[4] The campaign even developed an international component: Operation Feed the Babies attracted national headlines when a group of concerned British women airlifted supplies into New Orleans. The next step, activists warned, was an appeal to the United Nations International Children's Emergency Fund, America's reputation be damned.[5]

The incident produced memorable reactions. Newly elected governor Jimmie Davis, whose victory at the polls owed something to his popular "hillbilly" music and much to his segregationist campaign promises, labeled the affected mothers a "bunch of prostitutes" who ran "baby factories for money." He dismissed reports of starvation as the handiwork of the opportunistic, New York–based civil rights organizations "poised like carrion crows" over the state.[6] Editorials in major newspapers condemned Louisiana. The *New York Times* called its approach "mean" and "uncivilized"; the *Chicago Defender* described the abrupt terminations as "not only unjust, but criminal."[7]

A less memorable but more significant aspect of the Louisiana "suitable home" controversy – chronicled in more detail later in this chapter – was what it meant for HEW, and for federal-state welfare administration more generally. As the 1950s went on, HEW officials had found it ever more difficult to police state and local welfare operations for violations of federal law. The early 1960s brought more obstacles, despite the return to power of more liberal agency leaders. Although accusations of socialism had died down, the agency continued to field charges of promoting immorality, tolerating fraud and inefficiency, and constraining state and local governments from pursuing sensible policies. Criticism of ADC was especially acute, even after a slate of welfare reform measures in 1962 ostensibly transformed the troubled program. Meanwhile, the agency was quickly becoming involved in the fraught politics of desegregation, owing to its role in administering federal grants for hospitals and schools. With southern Democrats at the helm of powerful congressional committees, it was an uncomfortable position indeed. Amid these pressures, federal welfare administrators grew more cautious, even as they continued to scrutinize state laws and policies and to object to those that undermined the rights of the poor.

Allies outside the agency, including a sizeable cohort of former federal administrators, were not so constrained. Indeed, knowledgeable citizens appeared to have more routes than ever for contesting policies that they considered illegal or unwise. Galvanized by Louisiana's actions, a network of public welfare professionals, social welfare advocates, and civil rights activists began to explore their options. First, they sought to influence the "conformity" hearing that HEW convened on the Louisiana case. From there, they moved toward the federal courts, which in the later years of Chief Justice Earl Warren's tenure were doing more than ever to vindicate the rights of unpopular minorities vis-à-vis state and local governments. Reported welfare rights cases remained few and far between in the early 1960s, but a growing coalition of welfare rights advocates, led by lobbyist and policy analyst Elizabeth Wickenden, was laying the groundwork for a more comprehensive attack. Between 1961 and 1963, Wickenden reached out to liberal legal academics, developed an infrastructure for gathering and disseminating information, and drew on her informants throughout the federal-state welfare bureaucracy to compile a catalogue of practices that abused welfare recipients' statutory and constitutional rights and were thus ripe for challenge. She was, in other words, a "network entrepreneur," to use historian Steven Teles's term: someone who built ties among individuals and "facilitate[d] the diffusion of ideas," thereby "reduc[ing] the transaction costs of political activity."[8]

A result of this entrepreneurship was the birth of what lawyers and legal scholars came to know as "poverty law," a field of knowledge and practice dedicated to enforcing the rights of low-income Americans and reforming the law in their favor. Poverty law and the people who were attracted to it in the early 1960s became the foundation for the strategic litigation campaign associated with the modern welfare rights movement, a campaign that would eventually appear to revolutionize the structure and practices of American poor relief. By recovering the spadework of the previous years, this chapter shows how and why that turn to litigation occurred and argues for the importance of previous decades of legal-administrative maneuvering.

THE LOUISIANA "SUITABLE HOME" BATTLE AND THE EMERGENCE OF OUTSIDE ADVOCATES

At the time Louisiana's actions made national headlines, HEW personnel had in fact known about the state's suitable home policy for months. Internally, some had expressed concern. "The public assistance titles of the Social Security Act must be read and administered in the light of Constitutional limitations," insisted HEW attorney Myron Berman in August 1959. The agency was obligated to "determine the reasonableness of a[ny] State plan classification," he continued, referring to the Fourteenth Amendment's Equal Protection Clause, and to cut off funds where a classification was "constitutionally obnoxious."[9] Laws that classified children on the basis of the "sins of their parents" had long raised red flags.[10]

By May of 1960, however, HEW had issued only a vague warning to state officials. The agency remained silent in July, when the Louisiana agency began to implement the new laws, and in August, when a delegation from "Queen Mother" Audley Moore's Universal Ethiopian Women of New Orleans attempted to raise the matter with President Eisenhower.[11] As part of a Republican administration, HEW may have suffered from what one observer dubbed "election paralysis": Richard Nixon, the Republican vice president, and Senator John F. Kennedy were engaged in a close contest for the presidency, and Nixon needed southern support.[12] Another possible explanation for federal administrators' slow response was their incredulity that Louisiana administrators would actually follow through on the legislature's designs. Governor Jimmie Davis's predecessor, Earl Long, was no civil rights champion, but he and his powerful politician kin (brother Huey and nephew Russell) had been less prone than other politicians in the region to segregationist fanaticism.[13] In the late 1950s, as state officials in Mississippi, Georgia, Alabama, and Florida tested the control they could exert over black citizens under the guise of protecting their states' poor children, Louisiana's welfare operation appeared to be above the fray and in expert hands. The state's commissioner of public welfare, Mary Evelyn Parker, was a trained social worker who had recently chaired the White House Conference on Children and Youth. Just two years earlier, American Public Welfare Association director Loula Dunn had praised Louisiana's welfare program for its relative progressiveness and capable leadership.[14]

Federal officials finally began to exert meaningful pressure on Louisiana in the early fall, around the same time that a federal judge ordered school desegregation in New Orleans – a fact that surely colored how state officials perceived federal authority.[15] On September 1, 1960, BPA director Kathryn Goodwin (Jane Hoey's longtime assistant, now promoted to Hoey's old post) informed Parker that the state's new ADC laws raised "serious concern" in Washington: the seemingly automatic closure of many cases and the drastic reduction in the total caseload had prompted federal officials to wonder whether the state's actions were "consonant with the spirit and letter of the Social Security Act" – a thinly veiled reference to the prospect of defunding. Parker defended her agency. She noted that her staff had given federal officials notice of the challenged legislation and that the state was only following Mississippi's federally approved path. As for the 22,500 children removed from the rolls, Parker assured Goodwin that local offices were accepting reapplications and recertifying many cases. Revoking the state's grant, she reminded Goodwin, would only result in hardship for the 55,000 children whom the state continued to support.[16]

Such exchanges were by then standard fare in federal-state public assistance administration, but two related developments were more remarkable: the extensive and organized lobbying of the federal agency by concerned civil rights and welfare organizations, and the response from the top of the administrative hierarchy. By mid-September, the voices crying for HEW to take action in Louisiana had grown in strength and number. The National Social Welfare Assembly (NSWA), a council of leading social work and social welfare organizations, was the most significant addition to the chorus. The group's September 30, 1960, petition to HEW secretary Arthur Flemming (Marion Folsom's successor) not only bore the names of the nation's most reputable charitable organizations but also carried the imprimatur of agency insiders. According to the petition, "persons familiar with the provisions of the Social Security Act and their implementation under law over the years" believed that the agency had "ample authority" to find Louisiana in violation of federal law and perhaps also the Constitution.[17]

The knowledgeable persons who signed the petition were giants in the field: former BPA director Jane Hoey and former Social Security commissioner Charles Schottland, to name just two. But Flemming surely recognized the fingerprints of a figure with even greater influence in Washington, DC. The moving force behind all the NSWA's policy positions was Elizabeth Wickenden, an old New Dealer who had deep and comprehensive knowledge of public welfare policy, a legendary work ethic, and influential liberal friends. "Wicky," as she was known around town, cut her teeth in Harry Hopkins's Federal Emergency Relief Administration, where she ran the program for the thousands of "transients" who roamed the country searching for work during the Depression. Following FERA's demise, she moved with Hopkins to the Works Progress Administration and quickly became "indispensible" to Aubrey Williams, Hopkins's second-in-command. Wickenden's star rose higher still when Williams became executive director of the National Youth Administration: Williams promised her that he would eventually formalize her vital role in the new agency with the title deputy director. The title never came – a story familiar to many of Wickenden's female contemporaries – but the connections that she cultivated made her powerful for decades to come. Those were the years in which Wickenden and her husband, Arthur ("Tex") Goldschmidt, grew close with future Supreme Court justice Abe Fortas and his wife, Carol, and when she befriended future president Lyndon Johnson. In the 1930s and after, as she transitioned to a career as the Washington representative for various social welfare groups, she also developed close relationships with high-ranking administrators in the federal Social Security Administration, such as Wilbur Cohen and Arthur Altmeyer.[18] It was Altmeyer – retired but still following the work of his old agency – who brought the Louisiana situation to her attention.[19]

That Louisiana piqued Wickenden's interest is no surprise. As historian Landon Storrs has demonstrated, Wickenden was a "left feminist": part of a cohort of "women and men who pursued a vision of women's emancipation that also insisted on class and racial justice" during the decades bracketing the mid-twentieth century. In addition to advocating for left-liberal causes such as labor and consumer rights, social insurance, and international peace, left feminists fought against "racial and sexual discrimination in employment, ... the exclusion of female and minority-dominated occupations from the Fair Labor Standards and Social Security Acts, and ... the poll taxes that disproportionately disfranchised minorities and women." To the extent that the political climate allowed, they also practiced what they preached, through nontraditional and two-career partnerships.[20] Wickenden thus had several reasons to object to Louisiana's suitable home law. Locked out of the social insurance programs that supported many white families, poor black mothers in Louisiana not only received meager benefits but also experienced stringent oversight and punishment for violating moral commands, all at the expense of their children. Louisiana's actions also bore a resemblance – faint at first glance, but striking on deeper examination – to a practice that Wickenden had condemned since her FERA days: the use of state residency requirements to deny public assistance to otherwise eligible applicants. Wickenden viewed such requirements (which the Social Security Act limited but allowed) in the same way that a previous generation of welfare reformers viewed the old poor-law principle of settlement: as an "embarrassing anachronism."[21] Louisiana's moralistic behavioral requirements fit the same mold, as outmoded and unjust as the use of scarlet letters.

Amid these pressures, Secretary Flemming took the unusual step (unusual for the Eisenhower years) of publicly criticizing a state's welfare administration. Louisiana's welfare policies had aroused the "conscience of the country," Flemming declared on September 23, 1960. An investigation would follow, and the state's entire $22 million public assistance grant was in jeopardy. On October 3, the agency went further: Social

Security commissioner William Mitchell (Flemming's direct subordinate) announced a date for a formal "conformity" hearing. Sixteen HEW investigators fanned out across Louisiana to gather evidence.[22]

Wickenden and her allies only ratcheted up their advocacy work, however. Drawing on the successes of the NAACP Legal Defense and Educational Fund, they treated the upcoming hearing like a judicial appeal and began preparing "friend of the court"–style (amicus) legal briefs to submit to the agency. Multiple groups in fact seem to have taken up this tactic around the same time, demonstrating the broad appeal of litigation to left-liberal organizations, but it was Wickenden who ultimately over-saw the efforts. In early November, as she plotted the legal strategy of the NSWA, she learned that the federal agency's former (and future) general counsel, Alanson Willcox, had already prepared a brief for the American Civil Liberties Union. She was aware of a similar effort by civil liberties lawyer Shad Polier (the husband of Wickenden's friend Justine Wise Polier), for the Child Welfare League of America. At her instigation, the groups were soon pooling advice and resources.[23]

In an earlier era, when Indian law expert and former federal govern-ment lawyer Felix Cohen sought to intervene in a conformity hearing on behalf of Indians on reservations in the Southwest, federal administrators had been sympathetic but not overtly helpful. (Behind the scenes, as Chapter 4 notes, it was a different story.) Now agency insiders rushed to aid the amici. Their eagerness reflected their alienation – literal, in some cases – from the Eisenhower administration, their frustration with state intransigence, and their eagerness to see federal law enforced. Jane Hoey circulated a memo on the pertinent sources of legal authority – drawing, no doubt, on her years of correspondence with the prolific and persistent A. D. Smith. (True to form, she cited not only the Social Security Act and the Constitution but also the aspirational language of the Declaration of Independence and the United Nations' Declaration of Human Rights.)[24] Arthur Altmeyer retrieved quotes from the Social Security Act's legislative history.[25] In addition to Alanson Willcox, at least two other former staff attorneys from HEW's general counsel's office offered time and advice.[26] Regional attorney Bernice Bernstein, one of Wickenden's close friends and a longtime agency employee, received correspondence and was likely involved behind the scenes.[27]

On November 14 and 15, 1960, after one postponement of the hearing and several weeks of failed negotiations, Louisiana officials arrived in Washington, DC, to defend their law. (Back in New Orleans, the state's resistance to federal desegregation mandates was also coming to a head, as four black girls, flanked by federal marshals, walked into two all-white public elementary schools in Orleans Parish.) The first day of arguments traveled ground that federal administrators and state officials had now traversed for nearly twenty-five years: Ed Yourman of HEW's general counsel's office made the case that Louisiana had violated the Social Security Act – and, he implied, the Fourteenth Amendment – by enacting a "wholly unreasonable and capricious" eligibility requirement and by implementing the law in a manner that denied ADC recipients their right to a fair hearing. BPA director Kathryn Goodwin supported Yourman's argument with testimony about the arbitrary differentiations in treatment that investigators observed on the ground. Louisiana responded in kind. Former governor Robert F. Kennon, appearing as counsel for the state, conceded that Louisiana's "drastic" actions had been a departure from its usual "[Grade] A performance" on welfare matters, but he insisted that Congress had never prohibited laws of this nature. In fact, he noted, HEW had approved a similar law in "a neighbor state" (Mississippi).[28]

Reading the winds, perhaps, or simply realizing that they could make concessions while still vindicating the intent of the state legislature, Louisiana officials took a different tack on the second day. To the apparent surprise of HEW officials, state welfare commissioner Mary Evelyn Parker testified that her agency had now made substantial revisions to its policies. Although the offending law remained on the books, the state agency had implemented fair hearing procedures for affected claimants and re-enrolled 60 percent of the families who had lost their benefits. Parker promised that local workers would review the cases of all families that had not yet reapplied for aid. As to "suitability" determinations – the ostensible basis for removing thousands of black children from the ADC rolls – the agency committed to helping mothers make their homes appropriate for their children, and, where that failed, to find placements for the children elsewhere.[29]

Louisiana's savvy response ultimately allowed HEW to avoid the amici's powerful arguments. The amicus briefs bear note, however, because of what they signified about the state of welfare policy and administration in 1960. Since 1935, the public assistance titles of the Social Security Act had received close study from the federal agency and its state-level counterparts, but few others had entered the fray. Cases had occasionally gone to court, but both judges and litigants had generally taken a narrow approach and grounded the issues entirely in particular provisions of state law. With just a handful of exceptions, meanwhile, lawyers and legal academics did not study the law of public assistance. Established doctrine, after all, suggested that public assistance was in the nature of a gift or gratuity, which implied that there was little to discuss: the government gave and took at its pleasure.

The picture looked different in 1960, thanks to the diffusion of agency lawyers into nongovernmental work and their years of exchange with public welfare professionals. With the lawyers' encouragement and assistance, four different groups – the ACLU, the Child Welfare League of America, the National Urban League, and the Family Services Association of America – ultimately submitted legal briefs regarding Louisiana's compliance with the Social Security Act. Not all emphasized the same points (the National Urban League, for example, focused more on racial discrimination), but together they made one thing clear: sharp, organized, and legally knowledgeable people were watching.[30] And they did not want a behind-the-scenes political compromise, as in the cases of Arizona and New Mexico in 1949. They wanted reasoned legal analysis and an authoritative decision – the kind they could use to hold other states to account.

HEW released its decision on January 16, 1961, four days before the inauguration of John F. Kennedy as president. Social Security commissioner Mitchell, to whom Secretary Flemming had delegated the decision, began by noting HEW's deep concern about states' uses of suitable home requirements. He also noted, disapprovingly, that Louisiana's main interest did not appear to be protecting children but rather "controlling illegitimacy and disciplining parents." But he could not ignore the "many precedents and analogies" (a reference to HEW's compromises with other Deep South states) that had been established during the past quarter century of public assistance administration. Those precedents left him "no practical alternative" but to find that the federal law permitted "a true suitable home eligibility requirement." This did not mean that Louisiana had acted lawfully – state officials' "overzealous interpretation and implementation" of the laws "clearly" violated the Social Security Act – but in light of the state agency's recent corrective actions, Mitchell was "constrained to conclude" that no conformity issue existed. HEW would not revoke Louisiana's grant.[31]

If Mitchell's decision was a disappointment to the amici, the announcement that Secretary Flemming issued to accompany the decision was a vindication. A native New Yorker and a Washington insider since the 1930s (apart from stints as a university president in Ohio), Flemming was not sympathetic to Louisiana's actions. He was also in a good position to follow his conscience: after Kennedy's victory in the 1960 election, Flemming was a "lame duck" with no aspirations of remaining in his post and hence very little to lose by alienating southern segregationists. Still, the easier path would have been to stay out of it, especially after HEW general counsel Parke Banta flatly refused to entertain defunding as a valid legal option. (Banta said "he wouldn't know how to go about" defending such a decision, Flemming recalled.)[32] Unsatisfied, Flemming consulted a few lawyers who had been with the agency longer, including Wickenden's friend Bernice Bernstein. A New Deal lawyer of the same vintage and caliber as Alanson Willcox, Jack Tate, and A. D. Smith, Bernstein was intimately familiar with the agency's position on suitable home policies, its broader commitment to equal protection, and the legal groundings for all of the agency's work: she had been around when these principles were first articulated and she used them often in her dealings with states. Armed with Bernstein's expertise, Flemming ordered Commissioner Mitchell to issue the technical ruling on the conformity question, but he also issued firm new guidance to the states on the meaning of federal law.[33]

The Flemming ruling, as it came to be known, read like the writings of A. D. Smith during the height of his equal-treatment crusade. (Smith had by this time retired to western Massachusetts.)[34] The Social Security Act gave states the discretion to impose *"reasonable* conditions of eligibility," the secretary began. Some conditions, by implication, were not reasonable. Conditions that denied aid to a child solely because of the conduct of his or her caretaker – such as Louisiana's suitable home condition – fit that description because they aimed primarily to correct the adult's behavior, not to meet the child's need. States were free, of course, to regulate their citizens' conduct, but they were not free, Flemming scolded, to use the ADC program to impose higher standards on the poor.[35] Flemming might in fact have gone a step further: he believed that the Fourteenth Amendment's Equal Protection Clause, not simply the Social Security Act, mandated this conclusion. But he received a stern warning from Assistant Secretary Rufus Miles about the dangers of weighing in on a constitutional question that the courts had not yet considered. Constitutional questions that implicated racial discrimination, Miles cautioned, were especially fraught.[36] Ultimately, Flemming seems to have concluded that he did not need to cite the Constitution to make his point. His ruling gave states until July 1, 1961, to rid their plans of "suitable home"-type requirements. Flemming also promised, even as he turned over the agency's reins to Kennedy appointee Abraham Ribicoff, that specific federal regulations would follow.[37]

Historians who have studied the Flemming ruling and the ensuing amendment to the Social Security Act have seen no great gain: the price of congressional approval was additional language that deferred the effective date of the Flemming ruling from July 1, 1961 to September 1, 1962.[38] During that time, suitable home laws in Louisiana and elsewhere served their intended purpose. In Florida, for example, researchers found that a suitable home policy affected 17,999 ADC cases between July 1, 1959, and June 30, 1961, resulting in a caseload drop of 13.7 percent and a significant decrease in the proportion of nonwhite families on the rolls. More than 7,000 of the affected families withdrew from the ADC program before their cases were officially discontinued or their applications rejected, and of these families, only 6.6 percent had reapplied for aid by the end of the two-year period. In short, even as states phased out their suitable home policies, those policies sent strong and lasting signals of discouragement to the targeted families.[39]

Still, Elizabeth Wickenden found the resolution of the Louisiana episode energizing. In 1959 she had complained of feeling "exasperate[ed]" with her role as an analyst and lobbyist for the NSWA. "I am beginning to think all this 'Let's rally round and write our Congressman' sort of thing is mesmeristic," she confided in Wilbur Cohen. Her work on the Louisiana case suggested a tantalizing new route for achieving change: "Legal process," Wickenden discovered, could be both "an instrument ... for protecting the rights of this peculiarly disadvantaged group [the poor]," and, "more significantly[,] for effecting a more equitable and protective application of welfare law and policy."[40] Before long, she and her allies would be extending their ambitions beyond agency proceedings and into federal courts, taking on the policing role that federal administrators were increasingly unable to pursue.

GETTING OUT OF THE WELFARE MESS: LOCAL ACTIVISM AND THE 1962 PUBLIC WELFARE AMENDMENTS

In the wake of the Flemming ruling, it became clear that Wickenden and like-minded advocates would have many more occasions to question states' legal treatment of the poor, for although the ruling settled the immediate dispute, it did not address the broader problem of intransigent state officials, weak federal administrative enforcement, and a politically unpopular welfare program. Many Americans had come to view the ADC program, in particular, as big, expensive, and the almost exclusive province of nonwhite, never-married women. Increasingly, they were also concerned about its effect on future generations. The notion of a "culture of poverty," a term coined by ethnographer Oscar Lewis, had by then migrated into popular discourse, joining anecdotes about multigeneration ADC families and long-term efforts to defraud the welfare system. Twenty-five years earlier, Americans had been relatively comfortable with the idea that some citizens depended on government support and would do so for many years – for their lifetimes, in the case of the elderly and the blind, and for the span of child's growth into adulthood, in the case of widowed or deserted mothers. For the latter, that comfort had now turned to deep unease.[41]

There were signs, too, that welfare recipients were stirring, in ways that fed popular anxieties. Case reports suggest that the number of state-level welfare rights cases had declined (they would increase again in the middle of the decade), but anecdotal evidence hints at a rising discontent and a growing sense of entitlement. An Erie County, New York, caseworker reported with alarm the suspiciously "well-furnished home" in which he found one new applicant and the applicant's insistence that the caseworker refrain from looking inside the rooms without a search warrant. "I know my rights," the applicant reportedly said.[42]

Around the country, in fact, there were signs that ADC recipients in particular were pushing back against local administrative practices – practices that, in an earlier era, they would have accepted. Consider, for example, Eula Henderson of Contra Costa County, California. In March 1958, Henderson informed her county welfare worker that she would soon have a sixth child in the house and that the child's father – whom she identified as William Roberts – did not intend to supply financial assistance. Thereafter, Henderson received ADC for the child, Cassandra, and cooperated with the county as it pursued (and ultimately dropped) a child support action against Roberts. The following year, however, after discovering that Henderson was living with an ex-boyfriend who may have been Cassandra's real father, the county reversed course and cut off Cassandra's benefit. A county worker then asked Henderson, as a condition of her daughter's reinstatement, to take a lie detector test regarding Cassandra's paternity. Rather than submit, Henderson pursued a hearing before the state agency. The 1960 judgment in her favor became the subject of a years'-long dispute between the county and the state.[43]

In Chicago, another poor mother of six children, Flossie Monroe, took a similarly courageous stance. In the early hours of October 29, 1958, a group of Chicago police officers forced their way into her apartment, ostensibly in aid of a murder investigation but without a warrant. They rousted her and her family out of bed, ignoring her protests that she was naked, subjected the family to physical and verbal abuse, and ransacked the family home. Despite the close ties between law enforcement and the local welfare department, from which the family received ADC benefits, Monroe and her husband sued the individual police officers for violating their civil rights – resulting eventually in the well-known Supreme Court decision *Monroe v. Pape* (1961).[44]

ADC recipients were also starting to wield power collectively. In Cuyahoga County, Ohio, starting in the late 1950s, recipients and their allies in churches, social service agencies, and civil rights organizations responded with alarm to the county's reduction of grant amounts (to 80 percent of what the county itself considered the minimum standard). Between 1957 and 1961, at least two short-lived groups – Mothers' Campaign for Welfare and Cleveland Mothers – formed to challenge the cuts. The names of these groups suggest a tried and true strategy, one that had worked for Progressive Era advocates of mothers' pensions and would be deployed again by the National Welfare Rights Organization: as producers and caretakers of the next generation of future citizens, mothers had an honorable and legitimate claim on public funds. Conditions in Los Angeles generated similar collective efforts: in 1958, the Welfare Action and Community Organization emerged from welfare recipients' common negative experiences with caseworkers. The group aimed to register voters and change the philosophy of the local welfare department. There were traces of less formal organizing, as well. A local welfare worker reported that families in some areas of Los Angeles would "hold meetings" and "figure out ways of increasing their monthly checks." "Some families on relief know more about the laws than we do," the worker noted.[45] By 1961 there were enough groups in Los Angeles that local leaders decided to establish a "legislative body" of sorts – the Los Angeles County Welfare Rights Organization – to coordinate interactions with the county's board of supervisors.[46]

These scattered acts of resistance show that concerned "taxpayers" were not the only ones dissatisfied with the government's treatment of the poor. Such resistance also sets the stage for the nationally dramatized incident with which this book began.

Newburgh city manager Joseph McDowell Mitchell had had enough with the entitled poor, he declared in June of 1961, as he unveiled a dramatic thirteen-point plan to reform the local welfare system. All the points ostensibly aimed at reducing costs, but their true focus was making public aid less available and desirable to able-bodied men and women, mothers of illegitimate children, and individuals "new to the city" (that is, nonwhite migrants). The plan also sought to restore local control over welfare administration by placing more supervisory and decision-making power in the hands of politically accountable local officials. All of this might have been fine had Newburgh been funding its own aid programs. However, like all the nation's local welfare operations, Newburgh now benefited directly from federal money, filtered down to the local level through central state agencies and attached to hundreds of federally influenced state rules. Mitchell knew all this; he simply dared those other levels of government to say no.[47]

Major media outlets hungrily tracked the ensuing standoff between Mitchell and New York state officials. National politicians, civil rights groups, public welfare professionals, and regular citizens all weighed in, as Newburgh became a "miniature of the troubled welfare canvas" across the urban North.[48] Local governments may have lost the clout they had enjoyed earlier in the century, but they could still start national firestorms. By August of 1961, Newburgh had done just that. In the short time that it took state officials to suppress Newburgh's revolt, critics of public welfare had already called for a reevaluation of the nation's entire welfare system.[49]

As for federal administrators, they did their best to distance themselves from the incident, portraying it as a state-local dispute.[50] HEW secretary Abraham Ribicoff's years as a Connecticut state legislator, state representative, and governor had sensitized him to the poisonous politics of ADC, and he was not eager to weigh in on Newburgh's plan.

In fact, though, he was already working on welfare reform. Ribicoff had come to his cabinet post acutely aware of how "annoyed" state and federal legislators were with "welfare problems," which is why in the late spring of 1961 he and Wilbur Cohen (who returned to the agency on Kennedy's election) assembled a committee of experts, the Ad Hoc Committee on Public Welfare, to study federal-state welfare programs and issue formal recommendations. Agency leaders were also in close contact with Elizabeth Wickenden, who had received funding for a similar project via her connections at the Field Foundation (a liberal philanthropic organization focused on civil rights and social welfare), as well as with George Wyman, a respected state welfare administrator whom Ribicoff appointed as a consultant.[51]

The so-called Battle of Newburgh gave these reform efforts a sense of urgency as, throughout the summer and fall, media outlets used the incident to explore a broader "welfare mess." "The Growing Scandal in

Relief" made the cover of *U.S. News & World Report* in September 1961, sharing space with the nation's escalating nuclear arm's race with Soviet Russia. Were mothers finding it "profitable" to have children but remain unwed? asked the author, revisiting a familiar critique. And what about "the racial factor"? The article skirted causal claims but noted that "Negroes and other nonwhites made up two fifths of the ADC rolls" and comprised "only one tenth of the nation's families."[52]

"Welfare: Has It Become a Scandal?" echoed *Look* magazine in November 1961. In Oklahoma, the article reported, 125 women on the ADC rolls had eight or more illegitimate children. In New York City, a relief recipient reportedly went to collect her check with a hypodermic needle hidden in her brassiere, so that she could promptly spend her payment on drugs. Author Fletcher Knebel used these anecdotes to raise a "puzzle" that had troubled observers since the late 1940s: "in an era of growing abundance," he asked, why were so many more people on the welfare rolls? A rigorous investigation would have interrogated the assumption of growing abundance – an assumption we now know to have been deeply flawed – but Knebel already had his answer: well-intentioned welfare programs were attracting "thousands of the shiftless, cheats and criminals." In many cases, Knebel suggested, these opportunists did not even have to resort to fraud, because overly liberal rules made getting on the rolls so easy: "People of adequate, even affluent, means draw benefits as a matter of 'right' because the rules say so." All the while, "bureaucrats" in Washington were insisting, "All is well." Not so, Knebel claimed: "The house of welfare is in disorder."[53]

Writing for the widely circulated newsmagazine *Reader's Digest*, Charles Stevenson took the argument one step further: the nation's scandalous ADC program remained unchecked because federal bureaucrats actively prevented state and local officials from solving recipients' problems. Reviving old grievances, Stevenson quoted with derision the Bureau of Public Assistance's admonition to state agencies that "assistance comes to needy persons as a right." This "entrenched" bureaucratic position reflected the Depression-era philosophy of "the schools of social work," Stevenson contended, not "common sense." "Why does assistance come to the needy as a right? I have always believed it to be a privilege," one concerned Louisianan wrote his senator after reading the article. "Any aid program should be designed only to help a family subsist," "not to live in luxury."[54]

As these quotations hint, conversations about the "welfare mess" in the fall of 1961 were as much about the solution as the problem. Some articles, like those by caseworker-journalist Edgar May, followed the standard social work line, urging "more and better-trained people" and a deeper commitment to the work of rehabilitation.[55] Many more suggested a return to the golden age of local governance. Freed from Washington's "red tape," local officials could once again take sensible steps, such as issuing relief in kind rather than in cash, or requiring people to work for public aid; they could make sure that families paid "the milk bill ... before the new car installment" – a level of oversight that federal law precluded.[56] These were the very solutions that some local officials in New York proposed in the wake of the Newburgh flare-up. "We went through a very difficult time ... when Social Security came into being," explained Roger Butts, secretary of the New York Public Welfare Association and welfare commissioner of Wayne County, and there were still people who thought that "the old poor master in the 1920s did a better job than the qualified caseworker is doing today."[57] New York's Association of Towns underscored the point: "We feel most strongly," the association averred, "that welfare is a governmental service which should be administered locally to the local citizen by a local welfare officer."[58]

Unfortunately for local officials, their day had passed. Some national politicians would make sympathetic noises, but most were not inclined to restore control to the towns and counties. In other ways, though, the welfare reform measures that President Kennedy delivered to Congress on February 1, 1962, were responsive to critiques. Based in significant part on the recommendations of the Ad Hoc Committee, the Public Welfare Amendments of 1962 promised to do more than ever to rehabilitate public assistance recipients and prevent dependency. The bill included more generous subsidies for social services (matching state spending at a rate of 75 percent, up from 50), and invited states to extend services to former and potential recipients as well as current ones. For child recipients, the bill required that states provide tailored service plans. The bill also outlined the structure for state-administered work training programs, to help parents of dependent children transition to employment as soon as the opportunity arose. And in an (ultimately futile) effort at rebranding, the bill renamed the ADC program Aid to *Families* with Dependent Children (AFDC). (Earlier that year, for similar reasons, HEW had renamed the Bureau of Public Assistance the Bureau of Family Services.)[59]

Other, less publicized measures continued the path of liberal expansion via a gradual but noticeable increase in federal control over poor relief. This was the thrust of the bill's five-year reauthorization of a temporary program called Aid to Dependent Children of Unemployed Parents, or ADC-UP (now AFDC-UP). Back in early 1961, as head of Kennedy's transition team on social policy, Wilbur Cohen had convinced the administration that an appropriate way to alleviate the effects of the 1960 recession was to temporarily extend ADC to children whose fathers were unemployed (up to that point, ADC payments had not been available to children of two-parent households unless the father was demonstrably incapable of working). Enabling legislation was ready by the time Kennedy took office; bundled with other "antirecession" measures, it sailed through Congress in the spring of 1961.[60]

Public welfare experts recognized the reauthorized AFDC-UP benefit, though still temporary, as an unprecedented expansion of the federal government's responsibility. "Employability" had long been one of the main dividing lines in America's complicated system of public welfare provision. Adults who were categorically "unemployable" by reason of old age, disability, or their sole responsibility for a child, were proper subjects of federal beneficence; state and local governments retained responsibility for everyone else, on the theory that they were better qualified to judge need, deservingness, and the amount of pressure necessary to make a capable adult choose work over relief. AFDC-UP blurred this distinction by extending AFDC payments (which, importantly, now supported not just the child but also the caretaker relative) to a subset of the "employable" poor. It also moved the federal government one step closer to abandoning its categorical approach and completely taking over state/local general relief – a shift that the more liberal members of the public welfare community had advocated since the Depression but had never proven politically feasible.[61]

The average congressperson, however, failed to appreciate the potential sea change that AFDC-UP invited. The congressional hearings on the 1962 Public Welfare Amendments included stock critiques of "freeloaders" who "don't want to be rehabilitated," and federal agency "career brains" (perhaps a reference to Wilbur Cohen or his mentor, Arthur Altmeyer) who had "overregulated" traditional poor relief, but overall the bill was not controversial.[62] It aimed to get people off the rolls, it benefited the states financially, and it did not appear to further aggrandize the federal welfare bureaucracy. The bill was ready for the President's signature by July 19, 1962.[63]

Much fanfare accompanied the new law. President Kennedy introduced the bill to Congress with his famous admonishment, "Public welfare must be more than a salvage operation, picking up the wreckage from the debris of human lives." The reforms would be "the most far-reaching revision of our Public Welfare program" since 1935, he promised, and would embody "a new approach." After the bill's passage, Wilbur Cohen and Social Security commissioner Robert Ball (another old hand in Social Security) described the amendments as "the most comprehensive and constructive overhauling of Federal [public assistance] legislation ... that Congress has ever made." Many public welfare professionals embraced the amendments as pragmatic and generally progressive. "Bearing in mind the long-standing unpopularity of public assistance and the recent Newburgh type of hysteria," Arthur Altmeyer wrote Elizabeth Wickenden, the legislation was "a great achievement."[64]

COURTING CONTROVERSY: THE CONFLICT OVER MICHIGAN'S AFDC-UP PROGRAM

Wickenden, as Altmeyer knew, was in fact deeply disappointed by the 1962 Public Welfare Amendments. Rehabilitation was hardly a new idea, nor was it the cure-call that Kennedy suggested. In addition, there were aspects of the 1962 amendments that were not progressive – at least not to those concerned with fair and equitable treatment of the poor. A prime example was the amendment relating to "protective payments": when faced with an AFDC recipient who demonstrated an inability to manage money, a state agency could now direct the recipient's payments to a concerned third party (similar to a guardianship arrangement, but without all the legal process).[65] As Kennedy administration drafters originally conceived that provision, it would have applied to a very small number of "problem families"; indeed, the administration's bill would have explicitly limited such payments to half a percent of the state's total caseload. The protective payments provision that emerged from Congress was much broader. The Committee on Ways and Means not only raised the limit on such payments, to 5 percent of a state's total caseload, but it also added a new provision that allowed states to do essentially the same thing on a bigger scale: section 107(a) provided that whenever a state agency had "reason to believe" that a child's mother (or other caretaker relative) was not using her AFDC payments "in the best interest of the child," the agency had the right to provide the mother with "counseling and guidance," as well as to notify her about the repercussions of "continued misuse of payments." (It had these "rights" in the sense that taking such actions could no longer be the basis for federal defunding.) Additional language made clear that nothing in the federal statute prohibited states from imposing civil and criminal penalties in this situation.[66]

Wickenden found these aspects of the new law troubling. The protective payments provision contradicted the original Social Security Act's money-payment principle. The "best interests of the child" provision gave communities the opportunity to exert the sort of "coercive pressures" that A. D. Smith had long warned about and that the federal agency had often criticized. It also invited local administrators to make "highly variable and subjective judgments" – a direct contradiction of the New Dealers' preference for objective decision making and uniform standards.[67] In other words, the 1962 amendments compromised the very notion that public assistance recipients had rights, just as those rights were gaining a more powerful group of supporters. Although Wickenden endorsed the 1962 amendments before Congress, she privately chastised her friend Wilbur Cohen for "effectively accomplish[ing]" the work of her "adversaries." (Cohen himself would later refer to the 1962 Public Welfare Amendments as his "greatest disappointment.") In the wake of the new law, Wickenden urged her colleagues in the National Social Welfare Assembly to carefully monitor state practices and to identify state bills that could be challenged on constitutional grounds.[68]

For others, however, such as Senator Robert C. Byrd (D., West Virginia), the 1962 amendments did not go far enough in the punitive direction. Byrd had a strong interest in the AFDC program, owing to the many poor mothers in his state, their importance as low-wage laborers, and his own personal history ("I know as much about being a hungry child as anyone in this body," he once declared, in the heat of a Senate welfare debate).[69] As chairman of the Senate Appropriations Subcommittee for the District of Columbia, he held forth on just how much more remained to be done to clean up the "welfare mess." Back in August 1961, in the wake of the Newburgh controversy, Byrd had initiated a thorough review of the district's welfare program. By the following August he had the results: in nearly 60 percent of the ADC cases sampled, recipients were not actually eligible for aid, he reported. (Byrd laid the blame at the feet of Bernard Scholz, a former Bureau of Public Assistance staff member who was now chief of the District of Columbia's public assistance division.)[70] Other findings echoed those that had dogged ADC for years: mothers with multiple illegitimate children and live-in boyfriends; dozens of homes with luxuries such as telephones and televisions.[71] These stories reappeared in newspapers around the nation, where they suggested that readers' tax dollars were allowing "immoral men and women [to live] the life of Riley on relief."[72] Such conclusions made it hard to defend the status quo. Byrd's liberal colleagues may not have agreed with the investigation's methods (early weekend visits to recipients' homes, with one investigator on hand to conduct the interview and another to prevent any "man in the house" from escaping), but no politician wanted to appear to condone fraud or waste.[73] Within days of Byrd's offensive, HEW's leadership had promised a prompt, nationwide study of the ADC program.[74]

HEW was thus in a difficult position by 1963, under pressure from both the left and the right. These dual stresses erupted in the spring, when the agency became embroiled in yet another dustup with a recalcitrant state. The location of the battleground this time – Michigan – is, at first glance, surprising. State officials had responded coolly to federal public assistance grants in the early days, but by the early 1960s Michigan was not among the states that the federal agency considered rebellious or difficult.[75] Politically, the state appeared to be moving in a progressive direction. In 1962 Michiganders revised their outdated constitution, and in doing so, established the nation's first constitutionally mandated civil rights commission.[76] That fall, voters chose as their governor the moderate Republican George Romney, a "self-made" businessman who professed disdain for partisan squabbling and promised to restore power to individual citizens.[77] And yet it was in Michigan that the next flare-up over public welfare occurred.

The new governor may, in fact, have been the spark. Before he even announced his candidacy, Romney captured nationwide interest.[78] He had "magazine ad charm," a picture-perfect family, and an appealing personal story: from an impoverished childhood and two unfinished attempts at college, Romney became the head of a struggling automobile manufacturer and successfully challenged the Motor City's giants. He was white, but as a Mormon he claimed to understand the feelings of persecuted minority groups.[79] He seemed to be a fresh, youthful heir to President Eisenhower's "Modern Republicanism," and at one time he had Ike's blessing. After he won the gubernatorial election (and even before), commentators were confident that he would be in the running for the GOP's 1964 presidential nomination.[80] On this point Romney would not speculate; he concentrated instead on asserting forceful leadership in Michigan and tackling issues that had deadlocked other politicians. AFDC-UP was one such issue. Democratic state legislators had tried in 1961 and again in 1962 to pass legislation allowing Michigan to participate in the program, and both times, conservative Republicans from rural districts blocked them. Romney came into the first session of the legislature with a compromise bill in hand, drafted by veteran state welfare administrator Willard Maxey, and a determination to see it passed.[81]

What opponents feared, Maxey understood, was an open-ended program that would run away with state funds and, more important, capture counties' general relief clients. The significance of general relief was twofold. First, it kept local welfare agencies in business. After the enactment of the Social Security Act in 1935, when most states rushed to claim federal grants, Michigan counties jealously guarded their autonomy. Rather than force local operations to conform to federal standards, the state legislature ultimately created a separate bureaucratic structure to administer the new federally subsidized programs, and that separate structure had endured.[82] Second, general relief preserved local authorities' power over poor, able-bodied residents. AFDC-UP, with its many federal rules and procedural regulations, was a threat to that control. It did, however, offer cash-strapped localities a way to shift their relief costs onto another level of government. By carefully choosing who was eligible for the new program, Maxey believed, he could make all localities see that the fiscal benefits outweighed their traditional concerns.[83]

Maxey's bill threaded the needle by defining "unemployed parent" as a parent who had received or been eligible to receive unemployment benefits after January 1, 1958. This definition would qualify an estimated 10,000 families for AFDC-UP benefits. More important, it excluded some 20,000 other families: those in which the parent did not work in an industry covered by the current unemployment program (farm labor and domestic service, for example, were not covered) and those who moved in and out of the workforce too frequently to qualify.[84] These were the families, not coincidentally, that county welfare authorities were most loath to give up. As a top state welfare administrator later explained, they were "the less educated, the less employable, [and] the less intelligent unemployed." (They were also, research suggests, the nonwhite: compared with white Americans, African Americans were considerably less likely to qualify for unemployment insurance.) If served by a county-level direct relief program, these families would be subject to "certain controls" – most notably, relief in kind rather than cash – that would be unavailable under a federally funded program like AFDC-UP.[85] In other words, the proposed bill was a classic political product (much like the original Social Security Act): it sliced and diced the potentially eligible population until the circle of inclusion was precisely tailored to entrenched interests.

With Maxey's skillful drafting and Romney's backing, the bill moved easily through the state House of Representatives and appeared certain to pass the Senate. Before Romney could claim victory, however, the state welfare department received a disturbing call from its federal regional representative, Phyllis Osborne. Osborne's office had approved the draft bill earlier in the year, but since then, she sheepishly reported, Wilbur Cohen had determined that it did not satisfy federal requirements. To critics, the move was blatantly political: Cohen was a Michigander with strong ties to the Democratic Party, and HEW had raised no objection to similar plans in two other states. But HEW refused to back down: when state officials ignored the federal agency's warnings, HEW secretary Anthony Celebrezze formally announced that Michigan's proposed eligibility restrictions were unreasonably narrow; if the state legislature enacted the bill, no federal funds would follow.[86]

Celebrezze left it to his general counsel, Alanson Willcox – an old New Dealer, restored to power with the Kennedy administration – to explain the technicalities of HEW's objection. Willcox and his colleagues in the 1940s had drawn from the Social Security Act's relatively spare legal requirements a more robust set of principles (see Chapter 3). One principle was "equal protection," which to the lawyers meant more than non-discrimination on the basis of race. It also meant preventing states from drawing distinctions that "really d[id] not matter" among needy individuals. A person's mental competence, her length of residence in the state, the citizenship status or behavior of her relatives – these were no indication of an individual's need for public assistance, federal administrators maintained, and so were not valid bases for distinguishing one potential client from another.[87] Many states and localities never accepted this interpretation, and the lawyers failed in their 1948 bid to have explicit equal protection guarantees added to the Social Security Act. But Willcox and the other lawyers of his era did not change their minds about what the law required. Applying this older interpretation to Michigan's bill, Willcox found it wanting.[88]

In a formal legal memorandum – which Secretary Celebrezze promptly circulated to Governor Romney – Willcox stated the basic rule (which, following Arthur Flemming's example, he was careful to describe as a statutory interpretation rather than an interpretation of the Fourteenth Amendment): if a state's eligibility criteria were narrower than what the Social Security Act explicitly permitted, the agency was authorized to approve federal funds only if the limiting classification was "a rational one in the light of the purposes of the public assistance programs." The purpose of AFDC-UP was to aid a group of needy children who were ineligible for traditional AFDC – namely, needy children of "intact" families with an employable but unemployed breadwinner.[89]

It was true, Willcox continued, that the federal law establishing AFDC-UP allowed states to define "unemployed" (just as the Social Security Act of 1935 allowed states to define "need"), but it did not give states latitude to be "whimsical" (or in this case, unfairly discriminatory) in their choices. "A man losing his employment with a nonprofit university or hospital is just as much (or just as little) 'unemployed' as a person in like circumstance losing his employment with a commercial establishment," Willcox argued. Unemployment compensation laws might draw a "highly artificial" line between these two men, but unemployment compensation had a different purpose. In the context of AFDC-UP, the same line-drawing was irrational and perhaps, Willcox hinted, unconstitutional.[90]

In a move that was becoming increasingly common in state welfare administration, Romney asked his own lawyer, Richard Van Dusen, to review the Willcox memo, and not surprisingly, he received a different interpretation. Willcox's so-called rule was a "bald assertion" with no statutory support, Van Dusen proclaimed. The federal agency lacked the authority to disapprove Michigan's plan on the grounds stated. In fact, Van Dusen contended, federal law obligated HEW to *approve* the plan: Michigan's bill fulfilled all the statutory requirements. With this opinion in his pocket, Romney signed the state's AFDC-UP bill into law. He would not "acced[e] to unauthorized federal dictation" in federal-state sharing programs, he announced. He was prepared to fight for Michigan's rights.[91]

Over the following weeks, Romney attempted to rally support, and succeeded. To members of the House Committee on Ways and Means, the legislators most directly responsible for the federal AFDC-UP requirements, Romney let it be known how HEW had "simply arrogate[d] to [itself]" dictatorial powers over federal funds. To his fellow governors, he sent a letter detailing Michigan's struggle with HEW and asking whether they shared his interest in preserving states' rights vis-à-vis federal agencies. From both quarters, he received encouraging responses. Self-declared "States Righters," such as Texas congressman Bruce Alger and Alabama governor George Wallace, pledged their support. So did Republican governors from the West, where entanglements with federal power were vast and complex: "Welcome to the club!" replied Oregon governor Mark Hatfield, recounting HEW's recent interference with his state's administrative reorganization efforts. Governors George D. Clyde (Utah) and

John A. Love (Colorado) relayed similar stories involving the Labor Department. This was just one more example, Governor Robert E. Smylie (Idaho) noted, of federal administrators "fabricat[ing] requirements and judgments from their individual social philosophies."[92]

Much less encouraging was the response from Michigan attorney general Frank J. Kelley. The "eternal general," as he was later known, was just beginning his record-setting career in office and had yet to develop a warm working relationship with Governor Romney. The two had sparred during Michigan's 1962 constitutional convention, over legislative reapportionment, and again after Romney took office, when Kelley insisted on having a say in the appointment of government attorneys.[93] It was April before Romney asked Kelley's office for a formal opinion on the proposed AFDC-UP plan, and the opinion he got was the opposite of what he wanted. Assuring Romney that he was "concerned only with the law," not with "politics and public relations," Kelley adopted and extended Willcox's reasoning, venturing into the constitutional territory where HEW was increasingly shy to tread. Kelley's April 11 opinion concluded that Michigan's AFDC-UP law denied the people the equal protection of the law, in violation of both the state and U.S. constitutions.[94]

Romney had other powerful antagonists as well, such as Secretary of Labor Willard Wirtz. Unemployment insurance preserved its respectable and nonstigmatizing character precisely because it did not get mixed up in determinations of need, Wirtz noted in a letter to Celebrezze; if states borrowed definitions from unemployment compensation for use in a welfare program, dangerous confusion could result.[95] Elizabeth Wickenden and her NSWA allies also rushed to the agency's defense. In a widely circulated memo, to which she attached the Willcox opinion, Wickenden compared Michigan's actions to Louisiana's and reminded readers that the federal government paid the vast majority of state public assistance costs. In light of this, and of the equal treatment guarantees in both the Social Security Act and the Constitution, the federal agency had ample authority to say no to "arbitrary and discriminatory" treatment, she argued.[96] Privately, Wickenden acknowledged that the Michigan case was "much tougher ... to dramatize than Louisiana," but she believed that the principle was just as important: when states excluded people from federally funded programs, she wrote, "the federal agency has the right and obligation to interpret the federal law and constitution with respect to [those] exclusions."[97]

The dispute seemed to drift inevitably toward adjudication. Some of Romney's constituents had advocated a legal challenge to the 1961

Flemming ruling (Michigan at the time had its own suitable home policy), and they raised the issue again during the AFDC-UP controversy. It was time to stop "bow[ing]" to federal administrators and start "assert[ing] our rights," one local prosecutor urged the governor. Romney also hinted at a judicial resolution. The state attorney general's opinion was "not the final word," he announced, and "the courts may yet be called upon." Other governors agreed, both on the merits and on the basic principle. Not a year earlier, following in the footsteps of New York State's 1952 Kelley Commission and in the wake of the Newburgh controversy, the 1962 Governors' Conference had resolved to seek a means of appealing "the unilateral administrative decisions" of federal bureaucrats. The "rule of men" ought not substitute for "the rule of law," the governors declared.[98]

Ultimately, however, it was not a good time for a "Modern Republican" with presidential aspirations to affiliate so strongly with states' rights, or to appear dismissive of equality concerns. At that very moment, Americans were watching a civil rights debacle unfold in Birmingham, Alabama, where the segregationist police chief Eugene "Bull" Connor was leading merciless attacks on peaceful black protesters. Governor George Wallace warned that resistance would be just as fierce if integration were imposed on the University of Alabama. His ensuing defiance of federal law resulted in a historic display of federal force in Tuscaloosa and a landmark civil rights speech from President Kennedy. But the cycle of vigilante violence, mass demonstrations, and political confrontations showed no signs of abating.[99]

In this heated climate, Romney quietly backed down. As he explained at a July 21 meeting of the Governors' Conference, his interpretation of the federal law was almost certainly correct, but he did not want to waste resources on a court challenge if the court was going to refuse to hear the case. Given the DC Circuit ruling in *Arizona v. Hobby*, the 1953 case involving Arizona's desire to exclude reservation Indians from state aid, the possibility was real. "We may have a right without a remedy," he lamented. Romney urged again that the governors seek explicit congressional recognition of their right to judicial review. With that tool, states would surely win back power from the federal bureaucracy.[100]

THE BIRTH OF POVERTY LAW

Those on the other side of the issue, such as Elizabeth Wickenden, also gestured toward some form of judicial review. Because of her involvement in the Louisiana controversy and her statement on the worrisome implications of the 1962 Public Welfare Amendments, Wickenden had begun to receive correspondence about ground-level rights violations in welfare administration. A confidential letter from Jules Berman, chief of HEW's Division of Welfare Services, informed Wickenden about welfare workers making "sudden midnight and Sunday visits" to ADC recipients' homes, "tailing recipients, and even making women take pregnancy tests." Such methods seemed to infringe on civil liberties, Berman confided. I. Jack Fastau, a federal Bureau of Family Services consultant, funneled similar information to Wickenden in February and March of 1963, describing questionable welfare legislation proposed in Washington and Illinois.[101]

Like many liberals, Wickenden had also eagerly tracked the Warren Court's growing solicitude for the rights and liberties of vulnerable populations. By early 1963 the Court had not only invalidated racial segregation in public schools and public transportation but also vindicated the due process and free speech rights of unpopular groups, entered the "political thicket" of election law, opened the doors to plaintiffs seeking to challenge rights violations by state and local officials, and begun to scrutinize the constitutional dimensions of heavy-handed police and prosecutorial tactics (tactics often deployed in minority communities).[102] In the landmark case *Cooper v. Aaron* (1958), meanwhile, the Court had issued a forceful reminder to states that the Constitution was the law of the land and that it, the Court, was the ultimate arbiter of constitutional meaning.[103]

It was in this context that Wickenden began pondering the use of "test cases" in the welfare field. The seed of this idea had existed in her mind since at least 1954, when in a manual titled *How to Influence Public Policy* she urged public welfare advocates to consider the litigation strategy of the NAACP. Might a welfare recipient, she wondered, contest the outcome of an administrative fair hearing in court as a way of determining the legality of an undesirable state policy?[104] Wickenden edged much closer to the test-case strategy in 1960, when she and her colleagues filed amicus briefs with HEW, although at that time she still seemed to have faith in HEW's ability to enforce the law. Since then, however, she had become increasingly aware of HEW's limitations. As she wrote in a letter to her old friend Abe Fortas – two days after his oral argument before the Supreme Court in the famous right-to-counsel case *Gideon v. Wainright* – public officials persistently attempted to hold the poor to a "different standard of behavior, law enforcement, civil right etc. ... *because*" of their poverty. Without "judicial backing," she maintained, administrators were going to find it harder and harder to keep this illegal tendency in check. With judicial backing, she implied, they might accomplish goals that had long eluded them.[105]

Wickenden expanded this theme in a longer memo titled "Poverty and the Law: The Constitutional Rights of Assistance Recipients," which she had started developing in 1962 and circulated in March 1963 (right before the Michigan controversy exploded). Drawing on evidence from informants around the country, the memo described typical ways in which state and local governments either overpoliced or punished the poor. In New Jersey, mothers of illegitimate children found that applying for aid triggered prosecution under otherwise rarely enforced adultery and fornication laws. In Connecticut, a mother of an illegitimate child who had recently migrated from a southern state faced deportation. And in many jurisdictions, public assistance recipients were subjected to unannounced, late-night searches for the presence of male visitors. Wickenden urged her growing network of policymakers, lawyers, academics, and activists to challenge these abuses via legal proceedings. "The possibilities for legal remedies do exist," she insisted.[106] It was no surprise, then, that Wickenden saw an opportunity in the Michigan welfare battle. She hoped that Romney would take the matter to court, because the result might be a conclusive statement on the authority of the federal agency and the imperative of equal treatment.[107]

Federal officials, too, gestured toward the courts. General Counsel Alanson Willcox certainly did not want to invite interference with HEW's decision making, but he subtly encouraged potential plaintiffs to consider their rights against the states. Should the Michigan AFDC-UP bill become law, his widely distributed memo had noted, a person excluded from the program for failing to meet the state's strict definition of "unemployed" "could make a forceful challenge against the state under the Fourteenth Amendment."[108] With people like Wickenden on the case, and with the federal courts signaling a greater commitment to equal protection, that possibility seemed real.

Willcox had additional reasons for hoping to outsource, in a sense, some of his agency's efforts to police state and local violations of welfare rights. One was HEW's entanglement in the fraught issue of school desegregation. By the early 1960s, HEW administered grants not only for public assistance but also for public education. At that time most of the grants were limited to areas affected by federal governmental activities, such as defense installations. But the expansion of education grants was on the congressional agenda, and even the existing grants presented thorny questions.[109] If public school districts in these areas maintained racial segregation but technically complied with the conditions of grant-authorizing statutes, did HEW have the right – and if so, the responsibility – to withhold federal funds?

HEW secretary Abraham Ribicoff had posed that very question to Willcox in the spring of 1962, as the Kennedy administration contemplated what to do about the South's slow response to *Brown*.[110] Willcox – who in the 1940s had championed the equal treatment principle – responded cautiously. He was "quite prepared to assume," he wrote to Ribicoff, that such school districts were violating the Fourteenth Amendment, irrespective of whether they were under court orders to desegregate, but HEW's role in policing such violations was questionable. In his view, administrative officers were not free "to project" the Supreme Court's school segregation decisions "into areas where [their] applicability is open to serious legal doubt," especially when it meant contravening a statutory mandate. "Federal financial aid of course does strengthen schools that discriminate," Willcox noted, but this "powerful argument" was not HEW's to consider; it ought to be addressed to Congress or the courts.[111] That view was in clear tension with what Willcox himself would do a year later in the Michigan case – a point that underscores the increasingly delicate position that HEW administrators found themselves in.[112]

A second source of pressure on HEW – one that also hindered the agency's ability to police state and local violations of welfare rights – was the continued unpopularity of AFDC, even after the supposedly transformative Public Welfare Amendments of 1962, and notwithstanding the agency's promise of a nationwide review of the program (referred to at HEW as the "eligibility review"). The results of that review, released in August 1963, actually showed far fewer errors and far less intentional fraud than critics suggested. Based on a sampling of cases in every state, HEW estimated that 5.4 percent of the families receiving AFDC were technically ineligible – a far cry from the 60 percent suggested by Senator Byrd's investigation in the District of Columbia. In New York, a supposed hotbed of welfare fraud, the ineligibility rate was 5.5 percent. Eleven states were found to have ineligibility rates of less than 2 percent.[113]

To critics, however, the review only confirmed what they already believed. They noted that in some states, rates were well above 10 percent. (Byrd's home state of West Virginia topped the charts at 17.3 percent, a finding the senator proudly attributed to the six former state troopers whom the state had hired to help ferret out welfare abuse.[114]) Critics also questioned HEW's commitment to reducing errors: Every ineligible case was a waste of taxpayer dollars, and yet HEW seemed pleased with single-digit ineligibility rates.[115] Byrd, for his part, masterfully turned the tables on HEW by calling attention to the dramatic *underpayment* rates in some states. He noted that more than 60 percent of eligible families in North Carolina – the home state of HEW's top welfare administrator, Ellen Winston – received less than their statutory due. "A program to help the needy which is that much out of line in that direction certainly warrants a drastic and quick overhauling," Byrd remarked.[116]

Had Byrd made such an argument in 1940, he would have been a voice in the wilderness, but in 1963, he was not alone in seeing the need for an "overhaul" of public welfare. Thanks to scholar-activists like Michael Harrington, middle- and upper-class Americans had begun to recognize deep trenches of poverty within their seemingly prosperous nation, and they were disturbed. Building on economist John Kenneth Galbraith's *The Affluent Society* (1958), Harrington documented entire communities whose material existence fell far below common standards and who appeared to be locked out of the American dream: towns in the seemingly idyllic Appalachian Mountains where shoes and running water were a rarity; ghettos within great cities, in which children had difficulty finding a good meal, much less a ticket out. Harrington also made visible the millions of Americans who lived among the prosperous but struggled to make ends meet: nonunionized service workers, poor farmers, migrant workers, the elderly. All told, Harrington estimated, about a quarter of the U.S. population was poor. The conclusion was not, however, that the poor were "just like us." To the contrary, Harrington and his peers characterized the poor as "other" – as a nation within a nation, or "internal alien[s]," in Harrington's words, complete with their own culture and creed.[117]

Framed thus, the poverty of the 1960s seemed to call for new solutions, not for a recommitment to New Deal public assistance programs. The existence of mass poverty on the "New Frontier" suggested either that those older programs had not worked or, more charitably, that they had worked as well as they could have, and now a new approach was necessary – something capable of reaching the "hard core" poor and bringing them back into the mainstream. By mid-1963, top officials in the Kennedy administration were developing "a possible Kennedy offensive against poverty," one that rejected income transfers in favor of mobilizing "human capital," especially among the nation's youth. Thus began the hodgepodge of "opportunity"-oriented initiatives that would form the basis for President Johnson's War on Poverty.[118]

Over in HEW, meanwhile, public assistance administrators responded to these pressures by quietly lending their expertise to outside advocates – as in the Louisiana case – and attempting to protect the programs they still controlled. HEW's January 1963 reorganization is relevant here: Social Security and Public Assistance became separate divisions, with separate commissioners; the Bureau of Family Services now fell under the newly created Welfare Administration (along with the Children's Bureau and several smaller offices and programs). One of the Welfare Administration's first innovations was a system that would become known as "quality control": taking systematic samplings of state AFDC cases and carefully calculating error rates. Rates that exceeded a federal "tolerance level" would trigger a response. The concept of quality control arguably vindicated an interest in equal treatment, since reviews could turn up cases in which similarly situated families were receiving different benefit amounts, or in which eligible families were denied aid. The system that evolved, however, focused on erroneous eligibility findings rather than erroneous *in*eligibility findings, and on overpayments rather than underpayments. The reviews also failed to inquire into the number of people who were eligible for aid but chose not to apply.[119]

This version of "quality control" probably did help AFDC weather attacks, but such a crabbed and, indeed, conservative attempt to address welfare's failings also helps explain why 1963 witnessed the emergence of multiple welfare reform efforts that did not rely on federal administrative machinery or target federal legislators. Some of these efforts came from far outside the halls of power, in poor communities in major cities. In Ohio, a Cleveland-based group of welfare mothers, religious leaders, and civil rights activists (Citizens United for Adequate Welfare) came together to protest the inadequacy of local welfare grants; downstate in Columbus, a coalition of social service workers and welfare recipients (South Side Family Council) pursued similar goals. The following year, in Los Angeles, the welfare rights group Aid to Needy Children Mothers Anonymous took shape. Outraged by the local welfare department's oversight of her spending choices and behavior, future national leader Johnnie Tillmon obtained a list of all the ADC recipients living in her public housing project and began knocking on doors; by August 1963, after arousing the interest of hundreds of people, the organization had an office and a staff. Within another year, a similar group called Mothers for

Adequate Welfare would form in Boston's Roxbury neighborhood, after years of informal activism.[120]

At this point, however, the most coherent plan for reform came from elite circles. Between 1963 and the summer of 1964, at least three thousand copies of Elizabeth Wickenden's "Poverty and the Law" memo went into circulation.[121] The memo became a rallying point. In addition to raising awareness among Wickenden's usual crowd of legislators, administrators, and civil rights and public welfare advocates, the memo won attention from lawyers and legal academics. Former HEW administrator Charles Schottland used it in a session with the Ford Foundation, a wealthy backer of liberal reform, and all the law school deans in the Boston area, including Harvard's Erwin Griswold.[122] Copies also reached professors Ralph Fuchs (Indiana University) and Jacobus tenBroek (University of California, Berkeley), two legal academics who had been virtually alone in writing about public welfare administration in the previous two decades but were now part of a widening circle.[123]

Wickenden's most important contact in academia was relatively new to the scene. When Wickenden first consulted Charles Reich, he was just beginning his teaching career at Yale Law School. He had already built impressive credentials, however: as editor in chief of the *Yale Law Journal*, as a clerk for Supreme Court justice Hugo Black, and in a stint at Arnold, Fortas & Porter, a prestigious Washington, DC, law firm built by New Deal lawyers.[124] Most important, Reich was a friend of Wickenden's close collaborator Justine Wise Polier, a New York City family court judge. Reich quickly became Wickenden's "court of last resort on welfare law issues."[125] She corresponded with him in 1962 regarding the constitutionality of Congress's proposed public welfare amendments, and again in March 1963 regarding her "Poverty and the Law" memo (he gave it his stamp of approval).[126] Later that month, she and the Poliers (Justine and her husband, Shad) approached Reich about writing a legal memorandum on the issue of the "midnight raids" conducted on ADC recipients.[127] Reich agreed, and produced a law review article and a companion piece for the *Social Service Review*. Within months, Wickenden and her allies had distributed more than 2,500 reprints of "Midnight Welfare Searches and the Social Security Act" – including to state welfare commissioners – and succeeded in having it included in the *Congressional Record*.[128]

Taken together, these developments were remarkable: in 1960, when Wickenden first entered the fray, the field of poverty law simply did not exist; in less than three years, a legal canon and a set of practitioners had coalesced. In one sense, of course, the fall of 1963 was a time of deep despair – the nation reeled from the assassination of President Kennedy and the loss in Birmingham of four young girls to a white supremacist's bomb – but for Wickenden's growing network of poverty law theorists and activists, the future looked bright indeed.

* * *

Scholars of welfare rights will be familiar with what happened next: building on his "midnight searches" research and his own observations of the coercive side of state power, Charles Reich would go on to write the seminal article of his career, "The New Property" (1964). The article married the plight of welfare recipients to the condition of all Americans who relied on government largesse, whether for a professional license, a job, or a travel document. Reich then suggested how a basic change in the legal conceptualization of public benefits – from gratuity to property – could restore individual liberty and independence.[129] Many of Reich's insights, I have attempted to show, resonated with those of earlier thinkers located inside the federal welfare bureaucracy.[130] To a generation of law students, however, these insights were new and exciting. Inspired by the work of Reich and others, galvanized by the civil rights movement, and supported by a new stream of federal funds (via the War on Poverty's Legal Services Program), an emerging cohort of "poverty lawyers" would fan out around the country to attempt to bring justice to poor communities. Often the lawyers would target those who directly exploited the poor – landlords, lenders, low-wage employers – but they also represented their indigent clients in dealings with state and local government. In both contexts, the lawyers sought to win favorable results for individual clients and also to reform existing legal doctrines and regulations, to the benefit of poor people more generally. By the late 1960s, observers would see a welfare rights "revolution" afoot, both at the ground level, where thousands of poor mothers were making their voices heard, and in the federal courts, where poverty lawyers were scoring unprecedented victories.

This chain of events – which I elaborate on in Chapter 8 – is important, but so are the events described here: between 1960 and 1963, as elite Americans rediscovered issues of mass poverty and existing welfare programs faced sharp criticism in both the North and the South, a network of liberal advocates and policy brokers searched for a way to redeem what they saw as the promise of the New Deal. Like the federal administrators described throughout this book, they sought to establish that the poor were not at the mercy of local communities but were instead rights-bearing citizens of a benign, rational, centralized state. The reformers of the early 1960s were on to a new solution, however. Gathering together the mass of regulatory, statutory, and constitutional provisions that now informed the day-to-day administration of federal-state public assistance grants, the reformers created a field of knowledge that they called "poverty law." And then they went to court.

8

Subjects of the Constitution, Slaves to Statutes

The Judicial Articulation of Welfare Rights

"Of course nobody has a constitutional right to go on the relief rolls," declared U.S. District Court judge Alexander Holtzoff on October 7, 1966. "Relief payments are a gratuity or a grant"; they are "not a debt" owed by the government. Such was one jurist's reaction to a court challenge from the new cohort of poverty lawyers – in this case, an attempt to enjoin the allegedly "harsh, oppressive, illegal and humiliating methods" that public welfare investigators applied to recipients of Aid to Families with Dependent Children in the District of Columbia. In the face of the judge's skepticism, legal aid attorney David Marlin backpedaled, emphasizing the modesty of his clients' position: these poor mothers merely contended that if a woman satisfied the statutory eligibility requirements, she had "a right to welfare" – and thereafter should not be subject to intrusive administrative monitoring. Judge Holtzoff was unmoved. "Welfare is discretionary," he repeated. Eligibility rules existed "to exclude," not to entitle. Case dismissed.[1]

A Truman appointee and a former legal advisor to President Roosevelt's Committee on Economic Security, Holtzoff might have been expected to be more sympathetic, but by 1966, a year away from his retirement from the bench, he was notoriously conservative and acted accordingly. Other federal court judges confronted with welfare rights claims in the late 1960s would take a different approach.[2] Judge Holtzoff's response does, however, highlight the inherent risks of taking such claims to court: doing so raised the prospects of creating unfavorable legal precedents, attracting negative publicity, and making enemies out of the very people who controlled poor claimants' livelihoods. Why, then, is that where welfare rights claims migrated, and what were the consequences?

In tracing the judicial articulation of welfare rights, this chapter begins with the tumultuous stretch between the middle of 1963 and the close of 1965. These were the months when Americans witnessed a historic march on Washington, the launching of a "war on poverty," and the enactment of the most significant civil rights protections since Reconstruction. These were also the months in which scattered interest in the field of poverty law began to translate into actual litigation. From Oakland, California, to upstate New York, a loose network of civil rights advocates, civil libertarians, and public welfare professionals started going to court to contest the restrictive and discriminatory policies that pervaded public assistance administration. Last but not least, these were the months in which administrators in the federal Department of Health, Education, and Welfare shifted decisively over to the margins of welfare rights enforcement, even as many of them remained committed to the project. The AFDC program's continued public image problem helps explain HEW's cautious positioning, but so does the Civil Rights Act of 1964, which embroiled HEW in the poisonous politics of school desegregation and clarified the agency's authority vis-à-vis federal grant-in-aid beneficiaries.

With HEW on the sidelines, it was initially unclear who, if anyone, would lead the legal campaign for welfare rights or which legal issues would come to the fore. But by late 1965, a coherent campaign had taken shape. That effort, directed by federally funded legal-services lawyers, would in some senses affirm the vision of public welfare aficionada and pioneering poverty law theorist Elizabeth Wickenden – a vision that a generation of federal administrators had largely shared. Cases such as *King v. Smith* (1968), *Shapiro v. Thompson* (1969), and *Goldberg v. Kelly* (1970) established that for those who satisfied basic eligibility requirements – requirements that states were not allowed to narrow – welfare benefits were a legal entitlement. These cases also made it clear that poor people were constitutional "persons" rather than "nonpersons," to borrow Justice Abe Fortas's apt turn of phrase. The Fourteenth Amendment protected them, as did the Bill of Rights, and the federal courts were theirs to call upon.[3]

Legal services lawyers also attempted – unsuccessfully – to establish a principle that federal administrators had largely abandoned: that the poor had an enforceable right, existing apart from statutory law, to the basic necessities of life. *Dandridge v. Williams* (1970) dashed that effort, while also diminishing the value of the Fourteenth Amendment to the poor.

Wyman v. James (1971), decided shortly thereafter, made clear that being a rights holder and a constitutional "person" was fully compatible with state surveillance and policing – precisely the sort of surveillance and policing that had long made the receipt of public aid feel like a badge of inferiority.

But whether cast as victories or defeats, these cases were all clarifying. Taken together, they articulated basic principles governing poor peoples' relationship to the polities around them and the states' relationship to their federal benefactor. In this way, they helped settle debates that had raged since the New Deal and that, by the 1960s, had proven irresolvable through other channels. With the ground rules thus established, reformers could once again begin imagining a complete overhaul of American poor relief. What policymakers actually put in place, by 1972, shows how much ground Americans had traveled over in forty years – in the direction of centralization, uniformity, and legalization – but also how far particular groups remained from the type of citizenship that we continue to associate with the modern American state.

SCATTERED EFFORTS TO VINDICATE WELFARE RIGHTS, 1963–1964

As Elizabeth Wickenden worked to develop the field of poverty law in the early 1960s and imagined possibilities for legal reform, she corresponded regularly with top-ranking HEW administrators. She often funneled to them copies of correspondence regarding legal decisions or controversies, in some cases simply to keep them abreast of notable developments and in others to solicit their help.[4] Wickenden also informed her contacts in HEW about situations that seemed to raise "conformity issues," suggesting that she still had some faith in the agency's ability to enforce the law. In June of 1963 she told acting Bureau of Family Services director John Hurley that at least five states were surreptitiously circumventing the 1961 Flemming ruling (prohibiting suitable home rules, where "suitability" turned on a parent's alleged immorality).[5] According to local informants, some agencies had made a practice of discontinuing aid to existing recipients as soon as they became pregnant with an illegitimate child; new applicants in that position were simply turned away, with no record made of their request for benefits.[6] Later in 1963 Wickenden spoke to a regional attorney (likely Bernice Bernstein) and the commissioner of Welfare Administration herself, Ellen Winston, about an Illinois proposal to threaten poor mothers with child neglect proceedings should they attempt to use AFDC to support illegitimate children.[7]

HEW administrators reciprocated, with time and counsel. Starting in November of 1962, the Bureau of Family Services regularly sent Wickenden copies of its own digest of press reports on activities in public welfare.[8] The following November, the agency distributed reprints to all its regional offices of the law review article on "Midnight Searches" (by Charles Reich) that Wickenden had commissioned.[9] Some individual HEW administrators also offered personal assistance. In 1963, at Wickenden's request, HEW assistant secretary Wilbur Cohen used his influence to pressure the Field Foundation to publish a controversial study of suitable home–type practices in AFDC administration. Written by Wickenden's mentee and friend Winifred Bell, with the cooperation of HEW administrators, the study criticized the Flemming ruling and suggested that policymakers consider "federalizing" state public assistance programs.[10] As for Wickenden's own research, such as her "Poverty and the Law" memo, Welfare Administration commissioner Ellen Winston urged its wide circulation, as did HEW general counsel Alanson Willcox.[11]

Willcox also warned Wickenden about HEW's limitations. The agency could not do "much against the present climate of opinion," he wrote her in March 1963, during the agency's acrimonious dispute with Michigan. Litigation, he hinted, would be more productive: He urged her to discuss her "Poverty and the Law" memo with a contact of his at the ACLU, so that "perhaps we could get some test cases." Winston was similarly cautious. "There is no question about what is right here," she reportedly told her staff that spring, when one of Wickenden's concerns came up; the issue was "pick[ing] our battleground."[12]

By the summer of 1964 the nation looked very different: President Kennedy had been assassinated the previous November, placing his administration's most conservative critics on the defensive. Kennedy's successor, Lyndon Johnson, had seized the moment to announce the "War on Poverty," which he framed as a key component of a "Great Society" in the making.[13] And yet top HEW administrators were now even less inclined to choose the battles that Wickenden suggested. The enactment of the Civil Rights Act of 1964, another building block of Johnson's Great Society, had much to do with HEW's reticence. "We are so busy with civil rights these days," Willcox confessed to Wickenden two weeks after Johnson signed the Civil Rights Act into law, "that there's not much time for anything else."[14] Willcox was not exaggerating: Title VI of the new act prohibited racial discrimination in all programs receiving federal financial assistance and authorized the federal agencies that disbursed such funds to enforce the law.[15] Of those agencies, HEW was the most important, both because of its responsibility for education and because of the sheer volume of money it distributed – some $3.7 billion in 1963, to 128 separate programs.[16]

If Title VI gave HEW the responsibility to act, however, it also gave administrators reason to tread cautiously. The previous months of congressional debate had established that some members of Congress mistrusted the agency and intended to keep a close eye on it. HEW secretary Anthony Celebrezze endured intense questioning about how HEW would interpret the Supreme Court's mandate in *Brown* and whether he would cut off funds to a state for failing to adhere to his personal understanding of "racial imbalance." Throughout Celebrezze's testimony in the hearings, representatives from Ohio and Michigan made it clear that they remembered past defunding decisions (dating back to 1936, in the case of Ohio), and that they resented what they saw as unchecked bureaucratic power.[17] The hearings also included animated debates about whether the proposed Title VI was even necessary, with some witnesses arguing that the president already had the power to refuse federal funds to programs that violated the Constitution, and others insisting that he did not.[18] These conversations gave HEW administrators reason to pause before seeking to vindicate any sort of welfare right that was not well established and firmly grounded in the Social Security Act.

As HEW hovered on the sidelines, an assortment of civil libertarians, civil rights advocates, and sympathetic welfare workers continued to raise welfare rights issues, but in a localized, issue-specific manner. In California, liberal Democrats on the state's Social Welfare Board – led by board chairman and welfare rights advocate Jacobus tenBroek and backed by Governor Edmund Brown – took on the practice of conducting mass "midnight raids" on AFDC recipients. In public hearings in February and March of 1963, tenBroek characterized the practice as unconstitutional and inconsistent with state regulations. By July, such raids were officially banned (although as tenBroek regretfully pointed out to Wickenden, unannounced daytime visits remained permitted).[19]

California civil libertarians also got involved that spring, via their advocacy on behalf of a welfare worker named Benny Parrish. Before the ban on midnight raids went into effect, Parrish had been dismissed from his post for refusing to participate in "Operation Bedcheck," a large-scale effort by the Alameda County Board of Supervisors to catch women welfare recipients with men in their homes in the early hours of the morning. These raids "infringe[d] upon the privacy" of their targets, Parrish unabashedly told the *Oakland Tribune*. Lawyer Albert Bendich, former counsel for the Northern California branch of the ACLU, helped Parrish appeal the termination decision, first before the state Civil Service Commission and then in state court. Parrish's case, like the state Social Welfare Board hearings, called attention to the harshness and questionable legality of this common investigatory procedure.[20]

Meanwhile, across the country in the northernmost reaches of upstate New York, civil liberties lawyers publicized the plight of a different set of clients. For several months, including in the depths of winter, Joseph LaFountain, Theodore Perry, Morton Swinyer, Loyal Snyder, and Ambrose Woodard had maintained roads and cemeteries under the direction of local authorities. They did so because they were "able-bodied" and their families were receiving welfare (four of the families received aid via New York's version of AFDC-UP; the fifth, via the state's non–federally funded program of "home relief"). In all of the cases, the county had required the men to work. On the morning of January 30, however, they refused, citing knee-deep snow and near-freezing temperatures. County authorities pressed criminal charges – as a "test," they explained, of the "right" of "this county, this state, or this nation" to condition public aid on work. It was also a test of a speedier disciplinary tool: the normal procedure for sanctioning an uncooperative worker was to terminate his relief payments, but only after discussing the matter with the man, documenting his continued refusal to work, and arranging alternative support for the family. A criminal prosecution allowed the county to send an offender directly to jail. The ACLU saw the matter differently: as the enforcement of involuntary servitude and therefore a violation of the men's rights under the Thirteenth Amendment. (The ACLU lawyers ultimately succeeded in having the indictment reversed, although the constitutional argument went nowhere.)[21]

Similar cases arose around the country in 1964. In Washington, DC, part-time legal aid lawyer Marie Stuart Klooz shone a light on the district's punitive "man in the house" policy when she filed a restraining order on behalf of Marie Simmons, against the devoted father of Simmons's nine children. Caseworkers and welfare investigators had warned her client, Klooz explained, that if the father did not curtail his visits to the children, the money that she used to feed them would be cut off – hence the need to keep this willing patriarch away. The Domestic Relations Court responded with a different sort of restraining order, one directed at the Department of Public Welfare.[22]

Around the same time, in New York City, neighborhood legal aid lawyers used the fair hearing process (a historically neglected tool there) to win back AFDC benefits for Minnie Lee Nixon, who had been removed from the rolls on account of her refusal to go along with attempts to send her back to North Carolina. Nixon's victory meant little for others in her position – she avoided deportation by disputing the factual findings in her case – but like the Simmons case, Nixon's hearing offered evidence of the unfairness of local policy and the arbitrariness of its application. Law professor Charles Reich cited her hearing, for example, in an influential article on "the emerging legal issues" in "individual rights and social welfare."[23]

For all this activity, however, litigation efforts generally remained disconnected. A lawyer in one area displayed little awareness of similar efforts in other jurisdictions. "I would be interested in the basis of your interest [this case]," Elizabeth Wickenden wrote to one such attorney in early 1965. "Are you a Legal Aid lawyer? ACLU? This is coming up also from all sides – how are 'the poor' to get legal representation?"[24]

THE INSTITUTIONALIZATION OF OUTSIDE ADVOCACY

Wickenden herself was not in a position to provide such representation. Her chosen role had always been that of "gadfly," to borrow one colleague's admiring characterization. She was someone who "knew all the rules [and] all the regulations," "knew [when] they weren't being enforced," and made powerful people pay attention. But she was not a lawyer. As she wrote in June 1964 to law professor Charles Ares, she was "highly gratified" by the sudden interest in the field of poverty law, but also "somewhat overwhelmed"; she felt that the field deserved "a degree of help and guidance" that "far exceed[ed] [her] own resources."[25]

In early 1965 Wickenden used her connections at the Field Foundation and in academia to launch an institution that could, at the very least, serve as an information hub: the Project on Social Welfare Law, at New York University (NYU) Law School. Spokes extended to federal administrators in Washington, to sympathetic state and local administrators around the country, to allies in civil rights and civil liberties organizations, and to reform-minded legal practitioners and scholars. NYU law professor Norman Dorsen agreed to direct the project, and a prominent slate of academics and advocates signed on as advisors, including Charles Reich (Yale), Bernice Bernstein (HEW), Marvin Frankel (Columbia University), and Wickenden herself.[26]

From its inception, the Project on Social Welfare Law was "run by lawyers and beamed *toward* lawyers," in Wickenden's words.[27] Lingering over the enterprise, however, was Wickenden's question about the capacity of the legal profession to respond to the project's call: given financial realities and the bar's traditional conservatism, who was going to help the poor assert the claims that Wickenden and her allies believed they had? The answer, as it turned out, would come from the fertile intersection of social-scientific research, philanthropic giving, and urban reform, where another set of legal campaigns on behalf of the poor was developing.

The impetus for federally funded legal services dates at least back to 1961, to one of the Ford Foundation's many efforts to solve the era's social problems via money and social scientific expertise. A relative newcomer on the philanthropy scene, but one with boundless ambition and a vast endowment, the Ford Foundation had begun pouring millions of dollars into decentralized service centers in so-called gray areas: urban neighborhoods that had been stopping points along the European immigrant's path toward assimilation and upward mobility but had since become dead ends for poor migrants from Appalachia, Puerto Rico, and the rural South. The academics and urban planners behind the project believed that by combining theories of social disorganization, lessons from behavioral research, and on-the-ground citizen participation, they could turn these neighborhoods and their new inhabitants into success stories. As part of this effort, the Ford Foundation funded a "Neighborhood Socio-Legal Team" in New Haven and a similar program in Washington, DC, under the auspices of the United Planning Organization. Many of the ideas that informed the gray areas projects also underlay efforts to combat juvenile delinquency – efforts that in turn spurred additional experiments with neighborhood legal services. The most noteworthy example is Mobilization for Youth (MFY), based in Manhattan's Lower East Side and designed by Columbia University social work professors Lloyd Ohlin and Richard Cloward. In November 1963, MFY financed a legal-services unit, using money from the President's Committee on Juvenile Delinquency, the Ford Foundation, and the Vera Foundation (an organization founded just a few years prior, aimed at reforming the nation's unjust bail system). Uniting all of these experiments was a repudiation of the traditional legal aid model, under which bar-sponsored legal aid societies helped deserving clients with discrete legal issues. These new ventures sought to empower entire poor communities by helping them navigate a web of interrelated problems.[28]

Some of the lawyers involved with these projects developed even grander ambitions. The short-lived New Haven experiment (it shuttered after mere weeks, owing to its work on a controversial criminal case) proved especially generative. In 1964, inspired by their experiences working directly with poor clients, as well as by the teachings of Professor Charles Reich, Yale law student Edgar Cahn and recent Yale law graduate Jean Camper Cahn, his wife, published an article outlining a new legal aid philosophy. Titled "The War on Poverty: A Civilian Perspective," the article made a forceful argument for including legal services in President Johnson's recently announced War on Poverty. Community-based legal services, the Cahns suggested, could soften the "military" approach of the poverty program by providing the poor with a voice. Neighborhood law offices could train community residents and cultivate local leadership, while simultaneously offering poor people the legal services most relevant to their needs. Without such a project, the Cahns warned, the War on Poverty could quickly become captive to local service providers and politicians.[29]

The Cahns' article was well timed. Thanks to the Supreme Court's widely publicized decision in *Gideon v. Wainwright* (1963), establishing a government obligation to provide legal counsel to indigent criminal defendants, elite Americans were thinking about access to justice.[30] The Cahns also had the connections to make their vision a reality. Prior to publishing their article, the Cahns showed drafts to friends and coworkers in the U.S. State Department, the National Institute for Mental Health, the U.S. Attorney General's office, and the Washington, DC, public defender's office. They also persuaded Supreme Court justice Arthur Goldberg to write President Johnson about bringing the theme of "justice and the poor" into his poverty program. At first, Johnson apparently said "Hell no," but after the Cahns relocated to Washington (where Edgar and Jean worked for Robert F. Kennedy and the State Department, respectively), their idea grew legs. Within months the Cahns had advisory appointments in the recently created Office of Economic Opportunity and access to some of the millions of dollars appropriated for the War on Poverty's capacious Community Action Program.[31]

Thus began the federal Legal Services Program, which formally went into effect in the fall of 1965. Thanks to the conservative influence of the organized bar, the program would not emphasize some of the ideas that most excited the Cahns, such as group legal services and meaningful community participation. But it would emphasize law reform, saleable to the bar as "orderly social change" and to eager young lawyers as a way to take part in the broader civil rights revolution.[32]

Perhaps the most important of these lawyers was Edward V. Sparer, an institution builder every bit as dedicated as Elizabeth Wickenden and the architect, in many ways, of the subsequent legal campaign for welfare rights. Sparer would also contribute to the erasure from the historical record of New Dealers' influence on that campaign – not because he explicitly denied it, but because he perceived the need for a new narrative, grounded in the inadequacies of the past two decades of federal administrative enforcement.

Sparer's path to the role of "welfare law guru" was an unusual one. As a former labor organizer for the Communist Party, he was an unlikely candidate for successful admittance to the bar in 1959, even though he had by then renounced the party and graduated at the top of his class from Brooklyn Law School. Only after receiving a letter of recommendation from a renowned anticommunist – David Dubinsky of the International Ladies' Garment Workers' Union (ILGWU) – were state judicial officials satisfied that Sparer possessed the requisite "character and fitness" to practice law in New York. That Sparer would make his career as a crusader for the poorest of the poor was also not evident. He spent his first few years in practice working for the ILGWU, and then attempted to transition to teaching law, by assisting Columbia Law School professor Monrad Paulsen with a study of juvenile courts. This work led Sparer not to the classroom, however, but to Mobilization for Youth, for which Paulsen served as an advisor. Sparer became the first director of MFY's groundbreaking legal unit – and ultimately, one of the nation's most recognized authorities on "the law of the poor."[33]

From the beginning, Sparer promoted "law as an instrument of social change" and encouraged his MFY colleagues to adopt the methods of the NAACP and ACLU. He quickly recognized, however, that MFY's small, neighborhood law office was ill equipped to engage in the large-scale strategic litigation that the major civil rights organizations conducted. Sparer used his contacts in the foundation world and academia to create a new outfit, one that would focus exclusively on this missing piece. The Center on Social Welfare Policy and Law opened in late 1965, with a staff of nine lawyers and office space at the Columbia School of Social Work. The center became one of the Legal Services Program's earliest grantees and created a precedent for funding other university-affiliated law reform operations ("back-up centers," in Legal Services' parlance). Within just a few years, the center would become the source of a flood of test-case litigation, including cases that would reach the highest court in the land.[34]

TOWARD STRATEGIC LITIGATION, 1965–1967

First, however, a word about HEW, which had once appeared to be both a valuable source of legal knowledge for outside advocates and a promising avenue for achieving change. One could imagine a legal campaign for welfare rights that focused entirely on the federal agency. But Sparer and many other grantees of the federal Legal Services Program had a different relationship with HEW than Elizabeth Wickenden did. As a former New Deal administrator, Wickenden remembered an earlier era, when liberals of her generation ran the agency and people like A. D. Smith and Jane Hoey advanced bold claims about the government's obligation to people in need. Sparer and his younger colleagues, many of whom came to federally funded legal aid operations straight out of law school, had no such memories. The HEW they knew was timid, ineffectual, and defensive.[35]

The department's responses to the many civil rights complaints it received in the mid-1960s were a case in point. To be clear, HEW had never appeared to be a particularly strong ally of civil rights advocates, despite its support of American Indian claimants in the Southwest and Secretary Flemming's important stance on racially discriminatory suitable home policies. For example, in the spring of 1963, after Mississippi welfare director and ardent segregationist Fred Ross told a large gathering of social welfare workers that integration pressures would lead only to the abolishment of his department and the closure of public schools, federal Welfare Administration commissioner Ellen Winston assured an outraged Medgar Evers (field secretary of the NAACP) that HEW had "regular procedures" for ensuring that "eligible persons are not denied assistance." Winston assured Ross, meanwhile, that HEW had no intention of cutting off Mississippi's federal funds.[36] A month later, Evers would be dead, gunned down in front of his own house for speaking out against white supremacy, and Ross would be accusing black citizens of "getting more for nothing than any minority race in the world."[37]

Welfare applicants and recipients had reason to expect more of HEW in 1964, after the enactment of the Civil Rights Act. But the agency's record did not improve, despite its receipt of hundreds of complaints of discriminatory state and local welfare administration. Civil rights organizations complained of refusals to hire black welfare workers in Oklahoma, segregated caseloads in Maryland, and denials of aid to Mexican American green card holders in California. Others complained about the use of welfare to discipline low-wage workers: the Georgia Council on Human Relations reported that black AFDC recipients were removed from the rolls in order to force their children to work in the fields; Universalist minister Albert Q. Perry sent word that a group of black domestic workers in Alabama lost their AFDC allotments when they collectively sought a pay raise.[38] Numerous individuals complained of having their benefits cut or withdrawn after they housed civil rights workers, enrolled their children in formerly all-white public schools, helped register voters, or themselves attempted to vote.[39] "Mr Martin Luth King" would "want all negro too work for there own children [*sic*]," an applicant in Boligee, Alabama, reported hearing from a white welfare worker.[40]

HEW typically responded to complaints with a gracious letter of acknowledgment and an investigation of the offending local department. Some of the investigations turned up stark evidence of discrimination, such as segregated institutions and steadfast refusals to use courtesy titles for African American clients. Nevertheless, the agency typically gave great weight to the assurances they received from state and local welfare workers. More often than not, HEW concluded that the local department under investigation "was operating with knowledge of and within the State plan for compliance under the Civil Rights Act of 1964." With that, HEW stamped the complaint "closed" and moved on.[41]

HEW administrators gave little indication, meanwhile, that they registered the many other rights violations (aside from overt racial discrimination) that complainants described. The law office of prominent Georgia civil rights attorney C. B. King wrote to inform HEW of a welfare worker who refused to authorize AFDC for the child of a mentally disabled teenage rape victim because, after repeated questioning, the victim's family could not supply the identity of the father. Such tactics were widespread, this letter alleged, and were "calculated to reduce the everyday life of a citizen receiving or applying for welfare to one of apprehension and constant scrutiny in his private affairs." Rosa Britt of Independence, Kansas, seemed to share that sentiment when she complained that her local welfare worker "will hold up your check" if "you don't let the kids daddy visit" (because a woman on welfare was supposed "to put up with [her] husband no matter how bad he treats you") or if "you borrow someone elses car and ... its a late model" (because "it dos'nt look nice" for a welfare recipient to have new things). More than 260

Alabamans signed a letter of complaint after a six-week-old child in their community froze to death because of her mother's unredressed poverty. The mother had been removed from the welfare rolls in July 1964 for having a man in the house and was never reinstated, despite her obvious need.[42] When such allegations were not framed in racial terms, however, or when they implicated policies that were technically race neutral, no meaningful investigation followed.[43] As one HEW investigator explained in response to a North Carolina welfare rights group's charges of inadequate grants and lack of notice of their appeal rights, such complaints did not raise "real issues."[44]

Grassroots welfare rights groups may have lacked sophistication, but poverty lawyers fared no better in their concerted efforts with HEW. A prime example was the February 1966 petition to HEW from the NAACP Legal Defense Fund and Sparer's Center on Social Welfare Policy and Law, asking for a conformity hearing on "substitute father" policies in Arkansas and Georgia. Requesting a conformity hearing had worked well for outside advocates in 1960, when they sought to dismantle Louisiana's suitable-home policy: Louisiana prevailed at the hearing, in the sense that it kept its grant, but the federal agency used the occasion to formally prohibit such policies going forward (the 1961 Flemming ruling). Since then, however, states had used substitute father policies to skirt that very ruling. Under such policies, a woman's boyfriend, rather than her "unfit" home, became grounds for terminating AFDC payments, but the effect was the same: substitute father policies singled out the children of sexually active, unmarried women, and, as administered, disproportionately harmed black Americans.[45] HEW administrators were no fools – they recognized the similarities and had in fact declined to approve the two states' actions – but this was a case of savvy state policymaking. HEW had insisted that eligibility restrictions be grounded in need, not morality, and so it was here, the states' lawyers could argue: where a child had a substitute father, he or she was presumably not in need of public support. Outside advocates saw this logic as clearly flawed, but they could not convince federal administrators to put it to the test.[46]

This is not to say that HEW was completely unresponsive. Several months earlier, HEW had summoned representatives from Alabama for a conformity hearing after that state refused to issue a formal statement of compliance with Title VI (then on the books for more than a year). During the hearing, HEW lawyers goaded Alabama welfare director Ruben King into an impassioned defense of segregated welfare practices. Similarly, in March 1966 HEW took the important step of updating its handbook (the official collection of guidance documents that it issued to state agencies) to make it clear that state policies and procedures for determining eligibility had to be "consistent ... with the constitutional and statutory rights of applicants" and could "not violate ... the individual's privacy or personal dignity." The new guidance was a response, an HEW representative explained to skeptical members of the Senate Appropriations Committee, to the use of early-morning raids, polygraph tests, and over-zealous welfare investigators. In both instances, however, HEW was magnanimous toward the states: the agency delayed its decision on the Alabama case for more than a year and gave states a similarly generous amount of time to comply with the new handbook provision. [47]

This pattern caused people working in the burgeoning field of poverty law to view administrative enforcement as a lost cause. In February 1967, after an advisory committee to the U.S. Commission on Civil Rights heard days of testimony about blatant rights violations committed by Mississippi welfare officials, welfare rights leader George Wiley summed up his feelings thus: "The system is just being run in a totally corrupt manner, and ... the Federal Government is not enforcing the laws." Ed Sparer agreed, pointing out that HEW not only had longtime knowledge of problems (going back at least fifteen years, in Mississippi's case) but also the power to correct them, and yet the day of reckoning never came. HEW's representative at the hearing, Fred Steininger, could hardly deny the charges. "Maybe remedies don't come as fast as people like to have them come," he responded weakly, "but we sure try." [48]

If the federal agency appeared to be a dead end, going through Congress looked like a worse option, especially for AFDC. "The over-riding trend in welfare politics and policy in the late 1960s" was "toward harsher, more restrictive welfare laws," historian Jennifer Mittelstadt has summarized. [49] This orientation stemmed from multiple causes, including growing skepticism about the belief that mothers ought to be kept out of the workforce, anxiety about the persistent rise in the number of AFDC recipients (up to 5 million by June 1967, from 3.5 million at the beginning of 1963), and the continued association of AFDC with black, unmarried women. This was occurring at the same time as a series of violent urban riots and a perceived "degeneration" of the black family – both develop-ments that observers laid at the feet of female heads of household. (A report by Assistant Secretary of Labor Daniel Patrick Moynihan titled "The Negro Family" was particularly influential in developing this line of thought, but Moynihan was by no means alone in his thinking.) Meanwhile, there were few constituencies to speak up in favor of the status quo. To the extent that civil rights groups were concerned with the poor, most preferred to spend their political capital on job creation and training for black men. Welfare rights groups – numerous enough by 1966 to form a national organization – had an interest in the existing system, but they also voiced sharp critiques. And their members, in any case, were precisely the women whom many policymakers found so troubling: "brood mares" and "riffraff," Senator Russell Long (D., Louisiana) famously labeled them; women who could find time during the workday to protest and drink, but could not be bothered "to pick a beer can off the street ... in front of their own house or catch a rat." As for the traditional defenders of public assistance, such as HEW's Wilbur Cohen, they had long ago opened the door to the harsher policies by characterizing welfare recipients as damaged, and by tying recipients' "rehabilitation" to their participation in the workforce.[50]

Whatever the precise causes, the effect on the law was unmistakable. Five years after President Kennedy proclaimed that public welfare "must be more than a salvage operation," the Social Security Amendments of 1967 singled out children who needed AFDC because of the desertion of a parent (that is, illegitimate children and legitimate children whose fathers had absconded) and gave states a strong incentive to get them off the rolls. Effective June 30, 1968, Congress ordered a "freeze" on the percentage of each state's population that could receive AFDC on this basis (states could aid additional children but would not receive federal matching payments). The same set of amendments inaugurated "workfare," a compulsory work and training program for AFDC recipients over the age of sixteen.[51] The freeze, as it turned out, was repeatedly postponed and ultimately repealed, and the work incentive program took years to roll out, but both aspects of the law sent a clear message: the national lawmakers who mattered most were actively hostile toward many welfare recipients.[52]

In the face of these realities, people who cared about the rights of the poor embraced three closely related tactics: (1) they joined welfare recipients in exerting political pressure, via sit-ins, demonstrations, and lobbying; (2) they helped welfare recipients exert financial pressure through vigorous use of the existing welfare system (the so-called "crisis" or "overload" strategy); and (3) they enabled and encouraged welfare recipients to assert their claims in judicial and administrative settings.[53]

We still have much to learn about all of these strands of activism, especially as they played out at the local level, but claims making – specifically, strategic litigation on behalf of poor claimants – is the focus

of the rest of this chapter.[54] Such litigation efforts built on, and in some
ways diverged from, three decades of administrative thinking about the
meaning of the Social Security Act and the constitutional and statutory
rights of public assistance applicants. The resulting court decisions also
clarified, at last, the relationship of the poor to the polities (federal, state,
and local) around them.

WELFARE AND RIGHTS BEFORE THE FEDERAL COURTS, 1967–1971

It would be incorrect to describe the strategic litigation efforts of poverty
lawyers in the late 1960s as coordinated, but they were coherent, especially relative to the disconnected lawsuits of the previous several years.
Federal funds proved crucial: the Office of Economic Opportunity's
National Clearinghouse for Legal Services, launched in 1967, kept poverty lawyers abreast of one another's cases with a monthly newsletter, the
Clearinghouse Review. (The short-lived *Welfare Law Bulletin*, published
by the NYU-based Project on Social Welfare Law, served a similar function.) Ed Sparer and his colleagues at the federally funded Center on Social
Welfare Policy and Law also helped keep lawyers on the same page.
Drawing largely on the writings of Elizabeth Wickenden, Charles Reich,
and Jacobus tenBroek (all of whom had experience with the legal interpretations of federal welfare administrators), Sparer published concrete
agendas for law reform and made clear that his center was available to
assist lawyers who had potentially significant cases on their hands.

   Prime targets for strategic litigation included residency laws (laws
conditioning public benefits on the length of an applicant's residency in
a jurisdiction) and "man in the house" eligibility restrictions. The agenda
also emphasized increasing the procedural protections accorded to welfare recipients and bringing greater uniformity to the landscape of public
welfare, two longtime goals of federal administrators.[55] (Sparer himself
had an additional and more ambitious goal: to establish a constitutional
right to a guaranteed minimum income. But this was not obvious from his
early writings and was not supported by all his colleagues.)[56] Sparer's
center spread this agenda throughout the country through its training for
new legal-services lawyers and its efforts to educate welfare recipients and
social workers. Lawyers from the center also circulated ideas about how
to overcome potential hurdles to judicial review. Sparer never lost sight of
the importance of administrative enforcement, but the poverty lawyers of
his generation had their eyes firmly fixed on the federal courts.[57]

What followed, between 1967 and 1970, was a series of stunning victories for those who had claimed the mantle of poverty law. Most notable were the Supreme Court cases *King v. Smith* (1968), *Shapiro v. Thompson* (1969), and *Goldberg v. Kelly* (1970), decisions that appeared to work a revolution in the law of the poor but were also broadly consistent with the aspirations of New Deal reformers and their vision of modern governance. Sprinkled amid these apparent victories, however, were major defeats, most notably in *Dandridge v. Williams* (1970) and *Wyman v. James* (1971). To observers at the time, these defeats signaled that the apparent welfare rights "revolution" would be fleeting indeed. These were also cases, not coincidentally, in which poverty lawyers pushed for principles that had divided New Deal administrators – such as the government's obligation to meet citizens' basic human needs – and that, by the late 1960s, were not recognized as core components of modern American governance.

King v. Smith, one of the first welfare rights lawsuits to reach the Supreme Court, had its origins in a local administrative decision made in the fall of 1966, when the Alabama Department of Pensions and Security notified Sylvester Smith that her family would no longer receive AFDC payments. Though meager, those payments amounted to more than a quarter of Smith's household income. The problem, Smith's caseworker told her, was that she appeared to have a boyfriend who occasionally visited on the weekends. Under Alabama's substitute father regulation, the agency presumed that the boyfriend supported Smith's children and that they were therefore ineligible for need-based aid. Smith believed a different logic was at work: she was being punished, she felt, for her sexual behavior and her political outspokenness (she had recently written President Johnson to complain about Alabama's welfare program). Smith told her story to civil rights workers in the Selma area, who in turn relayed it to Sparer's Center on Social Welfare Policy.[58]

From Sparer's perspective, Smith was an ideal plaintiff, for at least three reasons. First, her case perfectly implicated one of the center's targets for reform – a target that the center had already attempted (and failed) to address through federal administrative channels. Second, Smith's story suggested racial discrimination, at a time when racial discrimination claims had traction in federal court, especially in the South.[59] Between 1964 and 1966, Alabama's substitute father regulation had resulted in the removal of 15,000 children from the rolls and the rejection of another 6,400 applications; black Americans like Smith comprised an estimated 97 percent of those cases.[60] Third, Alabama's substitute father policy had actually never received a formal stamp of approval from HEW, suggesting that the center could litigate the case without taking on the federal government.[61] Under the center's direction, Smith's case became a class action, brought under 42 U.S.C. § 1983 (a Reconstruction-era civil rights law that provided a federal remedy for rights violations by state and local officials). The complaint alleged that Alabama's substitute father regulation was inconsistent with both the Social Security Act and the Fourteenth Amendment, because it arbitrarily and irrationally classified certain needy dependent children as ineligible for aid.[62]

A three-judge panel of the district court agreed, issuing a decision that embraced the plaintiffs' equal protection argument. Under the Fourteenth Amendment, the court explained, "classifications may only be created which are rationally related to the purpose of the federal and Alabama Aid to Dependent Children statutes." The court deemed Alabama's classification "precisely the type" that the Constitution prohibited: it was aimed primarily at discouraging the immoral conduct of mothers rather than meeting the needs of poor children.[63]

The Supreme Court, to which Alabama turned next, took a different tack but reached the same result – and produced a decision with implications for every federally funded welfare program in the nation. The touchstones of the Social Security Act's public assistance titles, Chief Justice Earl Warren explained, writing for the majority, were need and, in the case of AFDC, a child's lack of parental support. These characteristics defined the population that Congress intended to help. Undeniably, states were free to add eligibility requirements and set their own standards of need – control over those choices was built into the original act – but Alabama was not entitled to impose restrictions that had nothing to do with need and everything to do with discouraging immorality. As for Alabama's argument that when a man cohabited with a woman, the state could presume that her children were not in need, Justice Warren treated it as disingenuous. Adopting Alabama's position, Justice Warren explained, "would require us to assume that Congress, at the same time that it intended to provide programs for the economic security and protection of all children, also intended arbitrarily to leave one class of destitute children entirely without meaningful protection." The Court could not adopt such an "unreasonable" interpretation of congressional intent.[64]

King was a remarkable precedent, for two reasons. First, for decades HEW had battled punitive, moralistic state welfare rules and had faced ever-greater resistance. When the Court at last turned its gaze to federal welfare grants to states, spurred by poverty lawyers and rights-conscious claimants, it achieved what federal administrators had been unable to do: it forced state and local officials to relinquish one of the most powerful tools they had for controlling their citizens. As summarized by one contemporary commentator, "*King* not only prohibits states from withholding AFDC to deter illegitimacy or control sexual conduct, but also precludes *all* eligibility requirements unrelated to need, except those explicitly sanctioned by the statute or its legislative history."[65] This was not what states had bargained for when they had first pursued federal public assistance grants in the 1930s. Three decades later, after becoming utterly dependent on federal aid, it was the bargain they would have to live with.[66]

Second, the *King* decision ignored the question of whether the plaintiff welfare recipients had the right to bring their disputes with state welfare agencies into federal court in the first place. Arguably, welfare recipients already had a means of contesting decisions about their cases: statutorily mandated "fair hearings" before state welfare agencies. Smith had not pursued her claim in an administrative forum before going to court. (Not long before the Supreme Court heard *King*, the Court of Appeals for the DC Circuit had made just this point – known in law as "failure to exhaust administrative remedies" – in ordering the dismissal of a similar case.)[67] It was also unclear that welfare recipients ought to be enforcing federal law against the states. Congress had already charged HEW, after all, with policing states' compliance with federal law.[68] The Court discussed neither of these arguments, a choice that observers interpreted as a welcome mat to plaintiffs like Smith. As one observer explained, *King* held that so long as a state received federal funds, it had to comply with federal conditions; should a state fail to comply, anyone who was adversely affected had the right to seek judicial redress.[69] The Court was similarly silent with regard to the plaintiffs' use of Section 1983 – only recently revived after decades of desuetude. *King* was the first case in which the Court accepted a Section 1983 case seeking to enforce the Social Security Act.[70] These silences were powerful: they signaled that the poor were not at the mercy of state and local governments. Via the judiciary, they enjoyed a direct and meaningful relationship with the federal government.

The next major victory for welfare rights advocates followed quickly on *King*'s heels. *Shapiro v. Thompson* began as multiple lawsuits, none directed by Sparer's center (to his disappointment) but all involving federally funded legal services lawyers. Through those attorneys, plaintiffs in Pennsylvania, Connecticut, and the District of Columbia all contested the residency restrictions, or "waiting periods," that their jurisdictions had attached to federally funded public assistance programs.[71] In each case, federal district courts struck down the residency restriction as unconstitutional. The defendants appealed to the Supreme Court, where other states joined them as amici.[72]

Despite the lower court victories, the outlook for the plaintiffs looked bleak in the spring of 1968. After an unimpressive showing by the plaintiffs' lawyers at the May 1, 1968, oral argument, a majority of the Court, led by Justice Warren, was prepared to uphold the residency restrictions. Fortunately for the plaintiffs, two draft dissents, by Justices William O. Douglas and Abe Fortas, produced a deadlock, and the Court was forced to carry the case over to the next term. At that point, the Center on Social Welfare Policy and Law took over the litigation and secured former solicitor general Archibald Cox to handle the reargument.[73]

A stunning victory followed: the Supreme Court, in a decision by Justice William Brennan, held that the residency restrictions violated the plaintiffs' rights to equal protection of the laws. This result followed from the Court's decision to characterize travel from one state to another as a rare "fundamental right" under the Constitution. Legislative classifications that burdened such rights, the Court explained, would not be tolerated unless necessary to promote a compelling government purpose. In this case, the purpose was not compelling enough: while every state had "a valid interest in preserving the fiscal integrity of its programs," no state was permitted to pursue that purpose via "invidious distinctions between classes of its citizens."[74]

The reaction from poverty lawyers was "euphoric." At the center, attorneys predicted that the decision would have a "profound" impact on the law by opening up many more potential equal protection claims.[75] *Shapiro* was also a victory for the generations of public welfare professionals who had attempted to make poor relief part of a more modern pattern of governance. State-level residency restrictions, these reformers believed, were a vestige of an older way of organizing power and responsibility, under which a person's claims on public resources flowed from localized forms of belonging. (This was the logic of "settlement," one of the most enduring organizing principles of Anglo-American poor law.) *Shapiro* signaled that poor people were citizens of the nation, first and foremost, and that their rights as national citizens could trump the long-standing prerogatives of state and local governments.[76]

The most celebrated welfare rights case, however, was *Goldberg v. Kelly*, a class action that grew out of legal services lawyers' interest in establishing a judicially recognized "right to welfare."[77] Many poverty lawyers were then enamored with Charles Reich's 1964 *Yale Law Journal* article "The New Property," in which Reich – building on his consulting work for Wickenden – argued that welfare and other government benefits, once awarded, should be considered a property right and given all the legal protection traditionally accorded to that sacred category.[78] Poverty lawyers believed that they had the ability to turn Reich's theory into doctrine by bringing to a sympathetic court a case in which a welfare recipient had been deprived of his or her benefits before having any opportunity to contest the decision.[79]

Such a case might have been brought anywhere: states throughout the nation suspended recipients' benefits as soon as local caseworkers determined that the recipients were no longer eligible. But the lawyers in New York City were scouting potential plaintiffs with particular vigilance. MFY's Legal Unit (Sparer's previous outfit) found the first one, John Kelly, in late 1967. After a hit-and-run driver left him disabled in 1966, Kelly had relied on New York's locally administered home relief program to make ends meet – until, that is, he defied his caseworker's request that he move out of the hotel room he had been occupying and into a drug-infested hotel elsewhere in the neighborhood. When Kelly's caseworker discovered his disobedience, she summarily terminated his benefits. Within weeks, a network of legal aid lawyers had found other plaintiffs in New York with similar stories, including a woman with eight children who had been cut off from AFDC. By January 1968, the lawyers had enough to file a class action against state and local welfare officials alleging a violation of the plaintiffs' rights to due process.[80]

In the wake of the filing, state and city officials moved in the direction that poverty lawyers had long hoped, adopting formal notification procedures for benefit terminations and establishing a way for recipients to contest decisions before being formally removed from the rolls. The defendant government officials also conceded that the Due Process Clause applied to welfare benefits – a position that was far from accepted in the broader legal community. And yet the three-judge panel that heard the case at the district court level agreed with the plaintiffs that the Constitution required even more. Nothing short of a full evidentiary hearing before benefit termination would satisfy the Due Process Clause.[81]

To poverty lawyers' delight, the U.S. Supreme Court agreed. In the welfare context, the Court held, only a pretermination evidentiary hearing, not a posttermination hearing, would do. Even more important, the

Court explicitly treated welfare benefits as the sort of interest to which the Due Process Clause applied. (The clause itself was notoriously restrictive, naming only "life," "liberty," and "property" as the sorts of interests it protected, and several lower courts had refused to apply the clause to welfare payments.) "It may be realistic today," reads a celebrated footnote to Justice Brennan's majority opinion, "to regard welfare entitlements as more like 'property' than a 'gratuity.'" Poverty lawyers were not the only ones taken with Reich's "new property" theory.[82]

The decision was not without controversy. Justice Hugo Black, for whom Reich had clerked not long before, issued a strong dissent focused primarily on the majority's capacious interpretation of the Due Process Clause: he accused his brethren of treating that clause as an invitation to forbid "any conduct that a majority of the Court believes 'unfair,' 'indecent,' or 'shocking to their consciences.'" But Black also cited a pragmatic concern, one that reflected his years of experience as a legislator: Fearing an excessive drain on its pocketbook, he warned, the government would eventually respond to the Court's holding by simply resorting to even more exhaustive eligibility investigations before putting applicants on the rolls. Treating welfare benefits as a property right, in other words, would only serve to enhance scrutiny of poor applicants and diminish the number of people who gained access to these vital benefits.[83]

Still, observers saw *Kelly* as a clear victory for welfare rights. The decision gave welfare recipients a "panoply" of "impressive" procedural protections and appeared "finally to inter" the formalistic argument that welfare benefits fell on the "privilege" side of an outdated right/privilege dichotomy. It was even possible to see in *Kelly* hints of a constitutional "right to live" – that is, an affirmative right, grounded perhaps in the Fourteenth Amendment, to a minimum standard of living.[84]

Within days, however, lawyers who held such hopes would be disappointed. *Dandridge v. Williams*, decided two weeks after *Kelly*, began as an effort to check another item off poverty lawyers' reform agenda: the "maximum grant" regulations that some states used to limit their benefit expenditures and discourage existing AFDC recipients from having additional children.[85] The plaintiffs' lawyers in *Dandridge* argued that Maryland's maximum-grant rule, which capped a family's benefits at $250 per month, violated the poor plaintiffs' rights under the Social Security Act and the Fourteenth Amendment's Equal Protection Clause.[86]

This argument was in fact more than a decade old – Pearl Collins's lawyers pioneered it in Iowa in 1955 – but, tellingly, it had never been on the agenda of federal administrators, even after Collins's remarkable victory in state court.[87] Family caps did not come up in administrators' many discussions of the "equal protection principle" in the 1940s and 1950s, nor did administrators characterize the practice as a violation of the Social Security Act. This was likely because federal administrators saw limited state budgets as a fact of life – unfortunate but undeniable. They were accustomed to across-the-board percentage cuts to recipients' grants during years of scarcity, and they had seen many states simply stop accepting new applications when they ran out of money for the year. Family caps were arguably less arbitrary than those tactics. Family caps were also tricky, federal administrators understood, because of what Elizabeth Wickenden called "the loaves and fishes problem": states could in theory be forced to treat people equally, but unlike Jesus, they did not have the ability to turn scarce resources into abundant ones. Faced with an equality mandate, state legislatures would simply give everyone smaller grants. (That is why Wickenden continued to lobby for the broadening of social insurance, even as she pressed for greater recognition of the rights of public assistance recipients.)[88]

The lawyers in *Dandridge* were more optimistic, or perhaps simply more naïve, and their efforts led to a disappointing precedent. Reversing a lower court judgment in favor of the plaintiffs and implicitly overruling several similar lower court decisions, the Supreme Court found that Maryland's maximum grant regulation conflicted with neither the Social Security Act nor the Fourteenth Amendment.[89] The constitutional holding was particularly significant: writing for the majority, Justice Potter Stewart characterized the lower court's equal protection holding as "far too reminiscent" of the infamous *Lochner* era, "when the Court thought the Fourteenth Amendment gave it power to strike down state laws 'because they may be unwise, improvident, or out of harmony with a particular school of thought.'" The Court applied instead its most deferential standard of review, the so-called rational basis test, explaining that this was the general standard for regulations "in the area of economics and social welfare" – even regulations "involv[ing] the most basic economic needs of impoverished human beings."[90]

The holding was a crushing blow to advocates of welfare rights. In the words of dissenting Justice Thurgood Marshall, the Court had "refus[ed] to accord the Equal Protection Clause any role in this entire area of law."[91] The implications were twofold. First, having recognized poor Americans as national citizens who fell within the Constitution's protections (the lesson of *Shapiro*), the Court now signaled that it would give "no scrutiny whatsoever," to borrow the words of legal scholar Julie Nice, to the body of laws that, in practice, set the poor apart from everyone else. Second, the Court made clear that when it came to substantive rights – the actual content of the government's financial commitments to its citizens – federal and state legislatures had nearly unfettered discretion. Unless a legislature discriminated on an explicitly prohibited ground, such as race, or burdened a "fundamental right" (of which the Supreme Court had recognized very few), the Constitution was essentially agnostic about the degree to which the government supported the poor. By implication, the Constitution certainly did not *require* a particular level of income support. In short, welfare benefits may have become something like a property right to those whom legislators favored and administrators recognized, but, as Judge Holtzoff put it back in 1966, "nobody [had] a constitutional right to go on the relief rolls."[92]

The next Supreme Court term brought another significant defeat, in *Wyman v. James*.[93] Inspired by what she read in a newsletter from the National Welfare Rights Organization, AFDC recipient Barbara James refused to let her caseworker into her home for a routine visit. After the local agency warned James that her benefits would be terminated, James presented herself to a New York Legal Aid Society attorney (David Gilman, one of Sparer's close associates) and indicated that she was prepared to litigate the case. The resulting complaint alleged that home visits violated welfare recipients' constitutional and statutory rights. James's strongest argument – the one endorsed by a divided three-judge district court in the Southern District of New York – was that absent an emergency criminal situation, the Fourth Amendment barred warrantless searches of homes; a regulation tying the receipt of welfare benefits to the recipient's waiver of her Fourth Amendment rights was, by implication, also unconstitutional.[94]

Poverty lawyers hoped that the Supreme Court would agree and that future test cases would establish protections for other facets of welfare recipients' privacy.[95] Instead, the Supreme Court reversed the lower court, in a decision that read like a repudiation of Justice Brennan's famous dicta in *Goldberg v. Kelly*. This majority opinion, issued in January 1971 by Justice Harry Blackmun, a Nixon appointee, emphasized instead the rights of the taxpaying public – President Nixon's much-heralded "silent majority." Yes, welfare mothers had a legitimate interest in the privacy of their homes, Justice Blackmun explained, but this interest must be balanced against the *public's* right to know "how [its] charitable funds [were] utilized and put to work." Blackmun saw no problem with the "gentle means, of limited extent and of practical and considerate application," that New York had used to "achiev[e] that assurance." Ignoring the Court's previous recognition of welfare recipients' life-or-death dependency on public benefits, Justice Blackmun went on to characterize James's refusal to consent to a home visit as a "choice," similar to a taxpayer's refusal to show an agent from the Internal Revenue Service proof of a claimed deduction. In neither case was the citizen's action criminalized; he or she stood to lose only money. James's choice was thus "entirely hers, and nothing of constitutional magnitude [was] involved."[96]

Paired with previous cases, *Wyman* showed that even national citizens could be denied their privacy if they happened to be poor. Phrased differently, the statutory right to welfare came with at least one very significant obligation: the obligation to be visible to the state – not merely tallied, or broken down into assets and liabilities, but *seen*, in one's most private spaces. *Wyman* also showed that although the Court had dealt a powerful blow to state and local authority, it had no general objection to the use of government administrative machinery for surveillance and discipline.

THE FUTURE OF PUBLIC WELFARE

Cases like *Dandridge* and *Wyman* left Sparer and his colleagues profoundly demoralized. The welfare recipients' lawyer was once "a grand strategist," Sparer lamented – someone who mobilized "legal process to help change the very nature of the welfare system and, thereby, to change the ground rules of American society." By 1971, Sparer feared that lawyers had become "what the revolutionist has often accused the lawyer of being – a technical aide who smooths the functioning of an inadequate system and thereby helps perpetuate it."[97]

If poverty lawyers had failed to achieve their most ambitious goals, what or who had prevailed? In the next two years, four developments further clarified the kind of state that Americans had built for themselves over the course of the previous decades, and, by extension, the kind of poor-relief system that would be imaginable in the future. The first was the Supreme Court's decision in *Jefferson v. Hackney* (1972), a case that legitimated the now almost complete rift between AFDC recipients and other public assistance clients. The second was the failure of the Nixon administration's Family Assistance Plan (FAP), a proposed overhaul of the categorical programs established under the original Social Security Act. The third and fourth developments were piecemeal reforms that Congress enacted in the FAP's stead: the tightening of "workfare" requirements for adult caregivers receiving AFDC, and the federalization of Old Age Assistance, Aid to the Blind, and Aid to the Permanently and Totally Disabled (commonly referred to as the "adult" programs).

A group of Texas AFDC recipients – including well-known welfare rights activist and community organizer Ruth Jefferson – commenced *Jefferson v. Hackney* in early 1969 in response to scheduled changes in the way the state calculated public assistance payments.[98] Constrained by the state constitution from spending more than $60 million per year on welfare programs, the Texas legislature appropriated fixed amounts for each of the state's public assistance programs. This posed a problem for the Texas Department of Public Welfare: eligibility requirements for each program were firmly in place, as were standards of need (that is, set amounts for clothing, shelter, and so on). Decades earlier, administrators might have stayed within their budget by simply turning away some people who satisfied the requirements, but in the age of welfare rights groups and legal services lawyers, that tactic was no longer realistic. The solution settled upon was a statewide directive reducing the percentage of need that the state committed to "recognize" for each program. Going forward, the department announced in February 1969, AFDC families would receive only 50 percent of their state-determined level of need. In contrast, recipients of OAA, APTD, and AB would receive grants covering 100, 95, and 95 percent, respectively, of their determined need. Through federally funded lawyers, the plaintiffs alleged that this new system deprived them of the equal protection of the law, in two ways. First, the new policy irrationally discriminated between categories of poor citizens. Second, the new policy gave preference to programs that tended to benefit Texas's white population, at the expense of a program that predominantly served people of color. As of March 1, 1969, the plaintiffs noted, 62.5 percent of recipients of OAA were white; 84.6 percent of recipients of AFDC were African American and Latino.[99]

Viewed more broadly, these arguments probed two tenets of modern American governance: uniformity and equal treatment. As we have seen, New Deal state builders imagined a rational, centralized, unified system of governance – one that encompassed thousands of previously autonomous local jurisdictions and that relied for its legitimacy on its commitment to the rule of law. Beyond that, however, there were disagreements, both about what the state ought to do for its citizens and about how much variation – from place to place, from person to person – was allowable. The plaintiffs in *Jefferson v. Hackney* represented one end of the

spectrum: they started from the premise that government had an obligation to meet the basic human needs of its citizens, and they implicitly
questioned whether, in doing so, the state could separate the needy into
discrete categories. At a bare minimum, they insisted, the government had
to accord equal treatment to members of all the concededly needy
categories.

The Supreme Court disagreed. Without commenting on the wisdom of
a completely unified system of poor relief, the majority's May 1972
opinion made clear that there was nothing illegitimate about the categorical approach, even when the states treated similar categories of needy
citizens very differently, and even when that differential treatment tracked
racial lines. "So long as its judgments are rational, and not invidious,"
wrote Justice William Rehnquist, a legislature could "tackle the problems
of the poor" however it pleased.[100] Unstated but implied was a particular
understanding of the sacred ideas of uniformity and equality. Those
principles, Rehnquist suggested, were really about eliminating the parochialism and blatant prejudice of the "old days," not about constraining
rational, centralized problem solving.

The next noteworthy development was the failure of the Nixon administration's Family Assistance Plan, a legislative reform that might have
established the sort of uniform welfare system that poor plaintiffs were
trying, unsuccessfully, to secure via the courts. As outlined in August
1969, the FAP would have provided a minimum income grant of $1,600
($10,321 in 2014 dollars) for a family of four, regardless of where in the
nation they lived. The grant was not "guaranteed," in that it would be
attached to the parents' good-faith efforts to participate in the workforce
(Nixon was always careful to avoid the term "guaranteed minimum
income"), but eligibility requirements would in all other regards be sim-
plified. Crucially, a family's entitlement to support would not turn on a
father's absence from the home, as it did under the existing and much-
criticized AFDC program. The FAP proposal would have similarly
streamlined the so-called adult programs, although it stopped shy of
complete federalization: for AB, OAA, and APTD, national eligibility
and payment standards would replace the complex and highly variable
state standards.[101]

Nixon's reasons for proposing the FAP – a seemingly odd choice for a
conservative politician – have now been extensively documented and
analyzed.[102] More relevant, for our purposes, are the assumptions about
governance that were built into the plan. As Martha Derthick has argued,
the FAP epitomized "moderni[ty]" and "rationality," values that had

grounded progressive "good government" campaigns, that had long animated the field of public administration, and that many Nixon administration policymakers apparently considered uncontroversial in 1969. Existing public assistance programs could be made more modern and rational, the FAP's designers believed, by eliminating state-to-state inequities in payment amounts, correcting perverse incentives (such as the incentive that AFDC created for poor fathers to abandon their children), simplifying eligibility requirements, and automating the delivery of benefits.[103]

A seemingly logical way to accomplish all of these goals was by shifting administrative responsibility from the states to the federal government. Thus, at the very same moment that Nixon and his political advisors courted proponents of states' rights, "Nixon planners operated on the assumption that federal administration was inherently superior to state administration."[104] The FAP's designers acted, in other words, as if the modern American state of scholars' imagination – thoroughly centralized and bureaucratized, insensitive to local preferences and values, committed to universal individual rights – was the state that most Americans had consented to by the late 1960s.

They were wrong. Scholars disagree about the precise reasons for the FAP's defeat, with some emphasizing the strategic choices of key political actors and constituencies and others emphasizing the plan's inconsistency with a deeply ingrained desire to separate the "deserving" from the "undeserving" poor.[105] But the fact is that by October 1972, the FAP was dead (and has never been resurrected). In its stead, Congress enacted two reforms that were much more reflective of the regime of governance that had coalesced during the preceding several decades.

The first reform was a further tightening of the workfare aspect of AFDC. The Talmadge Amendments of 1971 – named for Senator Herman Talmadge (D., Georgia), a leading critic of the FAP – took the discretionary features of the existing work incentive program and made them mandatory on the states. The vast majority of AFDC caregivers (all except for single women with children under the age of six) now had to register for work or work training. This arrangement was far better, in Talmadge's view, than a plan that would support 22 percent of his state's population (at higher benefit levels than ever before) and "make it practically impossible to police [them]."[106] The widely criticized AFDC program thus soldiered on. It remained a state-administered program, funded largely with federal money and subject to federal rules, but those federal rules had taken a decisive turn – away from allowing state-level discretion and toward congressional oversight, away from supporting caregiving and toward labor market discipline. For their part, AFDC recipients could still claim a statutory entitlement to welfare and all the procedural protections that now came with that claim, but the price of the entitlement had gone up. And so long as lawmakers played by the rules, there was nothing to stop the price from rising further.

The second reform – passed with surprisingly little discussion for a change of such magnitude – was the federalization of all the public assistance programs that served unemployable adults. In October 1972 Congress bundled together the state-administered programs for Old Age Assistance, Aid to the Blind, and Aid to the Permanently and Totally Disabled and rolled them into a new, federally funded and administered program called Supplemental Security Income (SSI).[107] Effective January 1, 1974, all the clients of these state-level welfare programs would become clients instead of the federal government. They would enjoy "a federally guaranteed income as a right," freedom from a maze of state-level eligibility restrictions, and relief "from the stigma of going to an office patronized solely by the poor" – just like the honorable retirees on the Social Security rolls.[108]

* * * *

This narrative could easily continue. It could cover the Supreme Court decisions that further defined poor people's legal status, assuring them of the law's protection while giving them nothing more of substance than what the political process willed.[109] It could cover the legislative reforms that made more and more Americans clients of the federal government by virtue of their inability to participate in local labor markets, while using the power of the federal purse to impose ever more stringent discipline on the ostensibly employable. By 1972, however, it was clear where poor Americans stood. Through a series of hard-fought battles, at all levels of government and in both agencies and in courts, they had become subjects of the Constitution – formal, legally recognized citizens of state and nation. But in their daily lives, just as before, their dependency made them less than free. No longer bound to their communities or to a local overseer of the poor, they were instead slaves to statutes – to the legislators who created the welfare laws and the judges and administrators who interpreted them. Going forward, some of the poor, such as the elderly, would feel only minimally constrained, thanks to the generosity of the laws that applied to them. Others, such as unmarried mothers, would feel their unfreedom daily and deeply. Both experiences represent citizenship in the modern American state.

Conclusion

On July 28, 1957, as future "welfare law guru" Ed Sparer was preparing for his second year at Brooklyn Law School, the great social worker Edith Abbott quietly succumbed to pneumonia at her family home in Grand Island, Nebraska. Born more than fifty years apart, the two would appear to have had little in common. Abbott played a significant role in crafting the public assistance titles of the Social Security Act of 1935. Thirty years later, Sparer would attempt to convince courts to rewrite those very titles, hoping to make the law more generous and inclusive than legislators had ever intended. From her post as dean of the University of Chicago School of Social Service Administration, Abbott trained generations of public welfare workers, believing that skilled and professional employees could transform the administration of public assistance from the inside out. Sparer had come to view these same workers as cogs in a wheel: in their day-to-day actions they could be allies or enemies to the poor, but a larger rubric of laws and policies constrained everything they did. Abbott questioned the value of the "legal right to assistance": absent public support (moral and financial), what did it even mean? Sparer made that legal right the focal point of his career.

In doing so, Sparer was convinced that he and his cohort of poverty lawyers were forging a new path – that their work "had no prior history," no "historical precedents."[1] In fact, however, Sparer and Abbott shared a larger project: along with public welfare lobbyist Elizabeth Wickenden, poverty law theorists Jacobus tenBroek and Charles Reich, and a bevy of federal administrators (Jane Hoey, A. D. Smith, and others), they dedicated much of their lives to bringing American poor relief into what they saw as a more modern pattern of governance. They imagined a future in which poor relief was professionally and objectively administered according to only the most rational criteria; in which authority emanated from above the local level and imposed uniformity across jurisdictions; in which the governing laws were firm and fixed, rather than subject to value-laden local interpretations; and in which poor people were tethered to a benign central state, through the powerful and honorable device of rights.

On paper, the task appeared to have been completed long before Sparer's time: the Social Security Act ostensibly modernized traditional poor relief when it offered states generous grants-in-aid to apply toward relieving broad categories of the "unemployable" within their jurisdictions. Along with the grants came the mandate that states centralize, professionalize, and unify their diffuse systems of locally administered poor relief, and that states cement these changes in statutory and administrative law. Desperate for federal funds, states agreed. Virtually overnight, many poor citizens went from the lowly category of paupers – a rights-less and stigmatized class – to the category of claimants, entitled by law to payments from the government.

Yet for pragmatic as well as ideological reasons, many Americans resisted this vision. State officials happily accepted federal money, but many state governments lacked the administrative machinery and the political will to comply with the federal rules. Local officials often clung to their traditional prerogatives, fearing both a loss of power and an irreparable rend in the fabric of their communities. The broader public struggled with the idea that the poorest among them deserved the rights of national citizenship, or that there was such a thing as undue infringement on the liberties of the indigent. For all intents and purposes, poor people still appeared to be subjects of local concern, and local governments therefore thought they ought to be subject to local regulation, surveillance, and discipline. It took work to convince people otherwise.

During the late 1930s and 1940s, much of this work occurred inside the administrative state, via negotiations between federal government officials and their state and local counterparts. Through guidance, vigilance, and the sheer power of money, federal administrators helped states develop sophisticated, centralized administrative structures, staffed with professionals. They demanded the establishment of written rules and policies, operable throughout the state, along with channels for communicating these rules to the local level. They encouraged the supervisors of state and local welfare agencies to see themselves as part of a national community of experts, with a shared sense of public purpose. And they developed and broadcast the notion that poor people had legal claims on government – *rights* – enforceable in administrative hearings if not yet in courts of law. Through the use of rights language, they hoped to mark a clean break between modern, centralized public assistance and the localized, discretionary poor-relief system of generations past.

This agenda was subject to stress, however – both from within and without the federal agency. Over the course of the 1940s, it became clear that the predominantly female social workers inside the federal agency had a different understanding of what government should do for the poor than did the predominantly male agency lawyers. When the social workers spoke of the rights of public assistance claimants, they referred not only to statutory guarantees but also to a general government obligation to meet human need. The modern American state that social workers envisioned made affirmative, substantive commitments to its citizens and, by implication, redistributed resources. Agency lawyers, by contrast, were primarily concerned with fair treatment, rational decision making, and adherence to the rule of law. These commitments, the lawyers believed, were at the core of modern government and were the keys to its legitimacy.

Forces outside the agency shaped the fate of both visions. The gains of the black freedom and civil rights movements and corresponding realignments in the Democratic Party; post–World War II suspicion of active, centralized governance; a growing Aid to Dependent Children population, which for the first time included significant numbers of black, unmarried women; the onset of the Cold War – all combined to limit social workers' hopes of realizing a rights-based, need-fulfilling state. The agency lawyers' vision had greater appeal, at least in Washington. Legalistic values like due process and equal treatment appeared to place limits on government; this, in turn, allowed for active regulation of society and the economy while ostensibly ensuring that U.S. citizens would never experience the coercion associated with the nation's communist enemies. These values also suggested a commitment to justice, while promising little by way of redistribution.

It is difficult to know how the complex designs of legislators and bureaucrats played out in actual communities – I hope that other historians will continue this work – but the scattered records of state-level fair hearings and state court proceedings are a start. They show that after the creation of New Deal public assistance programs, thousands of Americans approached government in the posture of a claimant, entitled by law to more than they were getting. In contesting the decisions of local welfare officials, they also reached for the kind of citizenship that federal administrators envisioned: a citizenship that bypassed local government and connected individuals, through legal guarantees of social and economic security, to a more remote polity. Whether poor claimants felt any different for having mobilized the legal process – whether they in fact wanted *more* from government than they could plausibly claim in these legal settings – is hard to know. At a minimum, however, the records reveal the mark that poor claimants left on the law. Resulting decisions characterized public benefits as legal entitlements rather than charity; focused attention on statutory eligibility criteria rather than community mores; and recognized poor people's right to fair treatment.

Mapatis v. Ewing, the 1948 American Indian welfare rights case filed in federal court, showed how threatening even these seemingly modest principles could seem when applied on a large enough scale and to populations that did not fit conventional notions of deservingness. In this regard, the case serves as a crucial pivot in the book's narrative. Through it, we see how New Deal public assistance programs went beyond simply undermining the traditional system of poor relief and the bonds it created between poor residents and local government and in fact constructed the foundation of something new: a system in which poor people were citizens of state *and nation*, and could wield their rights as national citizens against state officials.

In this new order, the content of national laws – and more important, prevailing *interpretations* of those laws – mattered greatly. That is one of the reasons why state officials began to rebel against federal welfare administrators and advance their own interpretations of federal law (drawing, ironically, on the enhanced state capacities that the New Deal bequeathed them). Resistance cropped up in states as diverse as Indiana, Arizona, and New York in the early 1950s and intensified over the course of the decade as New Deal public assistance programs became further entangled in the public's mind with distant federal bureaucrats, nonwhite, unmarried mothers, and the politics of desegregation. By the end of the decade, the notions that poor relief was a shared federal-state responsibility and that statutory law set the boundaries of acceptable practice – two tenets of "modern" poor relief – were no longer controversial, but state officials had attacked many of the other principles that New Deal administrators had worked hard to advance. Especially contested was the idea of equality – of treating poor people in one jurisdiction the same as those in another, and of recognizing poor people as equal in status to their ostensibly "independent" peers.

This was the context for a general shift toward the federal courts. Starting in the early 1960s, people outside the federal welfare agency who shared its original vision – people such as the formidable New Dealer Elizabeth Wickenden and her diffuse network of lawyers, academics, and public welfare professionals – took up the task of policing state welfare operations and articulating the legal rights of the poor. For a few years, they worked within the administrative state and achieved important but circumventable victories, such as the 1961 prohibition on so-called suitable home policies. Taking cues from the Warren Court and drawing on the resources available through the federal government's War on Poverty, these outside advocates then turned decisively to the courts.

It was there, after a decades-long reform effort, that they delivered the apparent coup de grâce to the old American system of poor relief. In the late 1960s and early 1970s, they won a series of pronouncements from the highest court in the land that poor people were full citizens – of their states and of the nation; that they enjoyed the same constitutional rights as every other citizen; and that federal law, not local mores, governed virtually this entire policy area. But the efforts of outside advocates also produced some legal precedents that were deeply discouraging and that, at the time, seemed to signal the failure of the broader welfare rights movement. The Supreme Court not only rejected the idea that the Constitution included a right to a minimum subsistence income but also signaled that it would give minimal scrutiny to legislative judgments about how and whether to support the poor at all. And in virtually the same breath that they recognized poor people as rights holders, the justices approved of policies that asked the poor to exchange some of those rights, such as the right to privacy, for that which they needed most: money to feed their families.

I hope that, taken together, my narrative and arguments enable readers to think differently about American governance in the late twentieth century and after. Over the course of three and a half decades, culminating with a series of Supreme Court pronouncements in the late 1960s and early 1970s, an identifiably "modern" system of American poor relief came into being – one that reveals basic features of the broader scheme of governance of which it was a part. In contrast to the system of poor relief that had prevailed for much of the nation's history, this modern system embraced centralization and eschewed local variation, favoring instead a uniform, transjurisdictional approach to problem solving. It championed rational, objective decision making, anchored in positive law. And it spoke in the language of individual rights, with a heavy emphasis on the guarantees of due process and equal treatment.

This use of rights is particularly noteworthy: it reminds us that although Americans have often used rights language to make claims on the state (and have been sharply criticized for that tendency), the state has also used rights language to claim people. In the history recounted here, the language of rights articulated both a connection between poor people and centralized government and, by implication, a lack of meaningful connection between the poor and the local communities to which they traditionally belonged.

This history of welfare rights also reveals what, by the early 1970s, the modern American state was *not*. Although it embraced centralization, it recognized both the states and the federal government as valid centers and hence valid administrators – allowing, in effect, for unequal, nonuniform citizen experiences with authority. Although this system demanded rational decision making, it took no firm stance on the rationale for public relief, leaving the poor to fight that important battle in forums where they traditionally lacked power. Similarly, although the modern American state relied on the seemingly value-laden language of legal fairness and equality, it did not take a position on the inherent worth of human life. It was therefore capable of tolerating extraordinary levels of poverty and inequality.

It is hard to imagine that this edifice of contradictions is what progressive and New Deal reformers wanted when they set out to remake the landscape of American poor relief at the beginning of the twentieth century. But this is what they and their antagonists built, with input along the way from the millions of regular people who found themselves entangled in America's complex network of dependencies. This is the house we live in.

Some aspects of this system deserve praise, or at least nods of respect. This is not necessarily a story about the modern American state's "counterfeit" promise for the poor, as historian Christopher Tomlins famously argued regarding the organized labor movement.[2] Government officials today recognize that poor people have constitutional rights: to receive advice from an attorney, in criminal cases; to demand fair treatment at the hands of government officials; to access the electoral process; to migrate between states; to shield some of their choices from public scrutiny.[3] Legalistic appeal procedures, though ineffectual in many regards, continue to provide claimants with opportunities to contest erroneous decisions, confront authority, and propagate "counternarratives."[4] Race-based discrimination – long an uncontroversial feature of American poor relief – is forbidden, in both the giving of public benefits and the hiring and promotion of public servants. And the poor enjoy a freedom of movement that, while still limited, would have been unfathomable in earlier eras.

With geographical mobility comes the possibility of reinvention, of release from the worst forms of ascriptive hierarchy, of a fresh start for the next generation.[5] These changes, though arguably more formalistic than real, are not trivial.

Other aspects of this system deserve criticism. I have long been haunted by a 1967 article by activists and scholars Frances Fox Piven and Richard Cloward, titled "Starving by the Rule Book." The article used testimony from a series of U.S. Commission on Civil Rights hearings in Mississippi to contrast clear welfare eligibility rules, entitling the poor to assistance, with a much bleaker reality: intimidation and harassment of applicants, seemingly arbitrary reductions and denials of benefits, and, at the end of the day, thousands of hungry families. "How is it they don't die?" a hearing examiner reportedly asked. "They do," was the response from a young poverty lawyer – just "slowly."[6]

Much has changed since 1967, and yet the phrase "starving by the rule book" remains apt: a set detailed federal and state laws, administered by a cast of thousands of government employees, ostensibly prevents any American citizen from starving to death. On paper, at least, today's laws guarantee some poor Americans a good deal more. Yet even taking into account the impact of government benefits, 15.5 percent of Americans (48.7 million people) were living below the official poverty line in 2013.[7] And studies are filled with accounts of "bureaucratic disentitlement" – what claimants experience when they lose benefits or go without as they struggle through the maze of highly technical rules and regulations.[8] Other studies document the now paper-thin line between successfully navigating the system and committing a crime, sufficient not only to deprive the offender of benefits but also to enmesh them and their families in the government's robust carceral apparatus.[9] Race remains salient in ways that would have been all too familiar to previous generations of welfare recipients.[10] In short, the rule books have gotten thicker, but citizens are still dying, slowly and unequally, from economic need.

I do not want to end this book, however, with the image of "a big empty building," to borrow the words of an astute reader of an early draft. That reader was not my late mentor, Michael Katz, but it might as well have been. Katz managed to conclude even his darkest assessments of the past with notes of optimism and lessons for would-be reformers. He criticized many historical attempts at "progress," but he never gave up on the word itself. In his spirit, I will close with a more sanguine observation about the contemporary American state and the promise it might still hold for the poor.

Over time, the American state has systematically eroded the concept of citizenship based on personal status and community membership and replaced it with the notion of citizenship we are familiar with today. According to this modern framework, legal historian William Novak explains, "*all* citizens are entitled to the same bundle of state protections and privileges qua national citizens"; "local statuses, social memberships, and public and private personalities" may endure, but they are "subordinate to [the] supreme equalizing political and juridical identity of the national citizen."[11] This state leaves room, I believe, for a reinvigorated *local citizenship* – one that remains subsidiary to national citizenship, and hence cannot impinge on the civil and political rights that flow from that status (that is, it is limited in its ability to exclude), but offers some of the social and economic protections that membership in the nation-state has never adequately secured.

Many contemporary citizenship theorists in fact agree that "there is such a thing as local (or urban) citizenship" – some type of membership that is based not on lineage or birth but simply on the individual's physical presence in a defined space.[12] As for the actual content of local citizenship – what does, or could, flow from it – scholars are vague, probably because financially, legally, and otherwise, most localities no longer possess meaningful autonomy from larger polities. The events of the past dozen years, however, offer at least two concrete example of local citizenship in action.

First, as of October 2015, twenty-six cities and counties, plus the District of Columbia, had passed local minimum wage ordinances, raising the wage floor in their communities above federal and state standards. Whereas the federal minimum wage has remained at $7.25 an hour since 2009, the rate in the Seattle-Tacoma area in Washington is now $15.00; in Oakland, California, it is $12.25; Chicago's is scheduled to reach $13.00 by 2019.[13] Similarly, as of 2012 more than 140 cities, counties, and universities have passed "living wage" ordinances, requiring particular employers (such as private-sector firms holding service contracts with the local entity) to pay workers at a rate that meets the federal floor but is adjusted upward to account for the actual cost of living.[14] For some critics of the existing poor relief system, of course, these ordinances will offer little comfort, for they continue to tie the benefits of citizenship to productivity, and only to the sort of productivity that the labor market rewards. Other critics, however, recognize that in today's climate, "improv[ing] the low-wage labor market" is "the first task" in improving the lives of the poor.[15]

A second example of local citizenship in action is local sanctuary ordinances, which declare a policy of non-involvement with federal immigration enforcement. So-called "sanctuary cities," ranging from Miami to Minneapolis, limit public employees' ability to gather and disseminate information about residents' immigration status.[16] At first glance, such policies seem distinct from local minimum-wage ordinances, in that they do not appear to address the material, or economic, dimension of belonging. Like those wage ordinances, however, they address a deficiency in national citizenship as it currently exists. Today, to be a citizen of the American nation-state – especially a poor one – is to be subject to extensive surveillance, the Fourth Amendment notwithstanding.[17] Sanctuary ordinances create "blind spots" on behalf of local citizens. They represent a willful refusal by nonnational state actors to "see like" (or rather, to "see for") the nation-state when it comes to particularly harsh state practices (detention without due process, deportation) and particularly vulnerable populations.[18] Phrased differently, these ordinances are an example of what legal scholar Heather Gerken calls "dissenting by deciding" – in this case, dissenting from a punitive, border-focused concept of citizenship by deciding to withhold the boots on the ground and ears to the wall needed to effectuate it.[19] A full assessment of these policies is beyond the scope of this book. The point is simply to suggest possibility – to show how the modern American state leaves room for local authorities to infuse an old, place-based notion of belonging with new meanings.

As we wait to see whether a reinvigorated notion of local citizenship holds real promise for the poor, a more general observation does ring true: within human life spans – the life, for example, of an Edith Abbott or an Ed Sparer – the logic and structures of governance can change. And although many factors contribute to the pace and nature of change, humans represent one of them. From presidents and members of Congress to lowly local bureaucrats, neighborhood lawyers, and welfare recipients, people decide every day what is legitimate governance and what is not. In the aggregate, over time, these decisions matter. Something like this process is perhaps what the great policy historian Hugh Heclo had in mind when he cautioned that we should not be so "preoccup[ied] with the 'revolutionary'" as to lose "our sensitivity to change itself."[20] For readers who can imagine a better way, *States of Dependency* offers few lessons for launching a revolution, but it does help identify the everyday opportunities that produce change itself.

Notes

INTRODUCTION

1. John F. Kennedy, "Address of Senator John F. Kennedy Accepting the Democratic Party Nomination for the Presidency of the United States – Memorial Coliseum, Los Angeles," July 15, 1960, in Gerhard Peters and John T. Woolley, *The American Presidency Project*, accessed May 15, 2015, http://www.presidency.ucsb.edu/ws/?pid=25966; Joseph McDowell Mitchell, untitled address, ca. 1961 [hereafter cited as Mitchell address], Box 1, Mss 800, Elizabeth Wickenden Papers, Wisconsin Historical Society, Madison [hereafter cited as EWP]. For the epigraphs, see William E. Royer, Welfare Director, Montgomery County, Maryland, quoted in Henry F. Pringle and Katharine Pringle, "The Case for Federal Relief," *Saturday Evening Post*, July 19, 1952; A. Delafield Smith, "Community Prerogative and the Legal Rights and Freedom of the Individual," *Social Security Bulletin* 9, no. 9 (1946): 6.
2. Mitchell address; Thom Blair, "The Newburgh Story," *New York Amsterdam News*, July 2, 1961; "Newburgh Stirs New Relief Rift," *New York Times* [hereafter cited as *NYT*], May 19, 1961; "Newburgh Welfare Rules," *NYT*, July 16, 1961; "Newburgh Plans More Relief Bars," *NYT*, July 6, 1961.
3. "Famous Overnight," *NYT*, June 24, 1961; "The Dark Ages in Newburgh?" *NYT*, June 29, 1961; Robert M. Busselle, "Applauds Newburgh Action," *NYT*, June 30, 1961; Alan D. Whitney, "Another Revolution?" *Wall Street Journal* [hereafter cited as *WSJ*], July 26, 1961; Douglas Taylor, *NYT*, July 7, 1961; "A Counter-Revolution in Newburgh," *Los Angeles Times* [hereafter cited as *LAT*], July 19, 1961; R. Fiske, "Admires Mayor," *NYT*, July 7, 1961; "Relief Fraud Hit by Oneida County," *NYT*, July 20, 1961; "The Newburgh Battle," *Chicago Tribune* [hereafter cited as *CT*], July 26, 1961; Joseph A. Loftus, "Newburgh Code Stirs Welfare Review," *NYT*, August 6, 1961; "Plan Benefits Seen for Whole Community," *LAT*, August 13, 1961; "Calif. Seeks Data on Newburgh's New Explosive Relief Program," *Chicago Defender* [hereafter cited as *CD*], August 16, 1961; Donald Janson, "Newburgh's

Course Debated," *NYT*, August 20, 1961; "The Storm in Washington," *CD*, October 26, 1961; Arthur Edson, "Work, Not Relief, Now Ribicoff Aim," *LAT*, February 18, 1962; "Helping the Unfortunate," *CD*, March 22, 1962; Marjorie Hunter, "'Welfare Mess' in Capital Spurs National Inquiry," *NYT*, August 19, 1962.

4. Mitchell's subsequent career path suggests how tightly bound were issues of welfare administration, local control, and race: after bribery charges sullied his name, Mitchell returned to Maryland to work for the segregationist Citizens' Councils of America. "All's Same in Newburgh after 'Crackdown' on Welfare Cheats," *CD*, January 7, 1963; "Mitchell Resigning to Take Birch Post," *NYT*, July 9, 1963; "Mitchell, Ex-Newburgh Aide, Organizing Segregation Units," *NYT*, July 25, 1964.

5. For more on this, see Lisa Levenstein, "From Innocent Children to Unwanted Migrants and Unwed Moms: Two Chapters in the Public Discourse on Welfare in the United States, 1960–1961," *Journal of Women's History* 11, no. 4 (2000); Felicia Ann Kornbluh, *The Battle for Welfare Rights: Politics and Poverty in Modern America* (Philadelphia: University of Pennsylvania Press, 2007); Annelise Orleck, *Storming Caesars Palace: How Black Mothers Fought Their Own War on Poverty* (Boston: Beacon Press, 2005); Martha F. Davis, *Brutal Need: Lawyers and the Welfare Rights Movement, 1960–1973* (New Haven, CT: Yale University Press, 1993). The cases alluded to are *Goldberg v. Kelly*, 397 U.S. 254 (1970) [holding that due process required the government to provide a full evidentiary hearing before terminating welfare benefits], and *King v. Smith*, 392 U.S. 309 (1968) [striking down a state law that made discovery of a "man in the house" grounds for terminating welfare benefits].

6. Social Security Act of 1935, Titles I, IV, and X, Pub. L. No. 74–271, 49 Stat. 620 (1935) [hereafter cited as SSA]. These programs still exist, in various guises. In the decades covered here, Aid to Dependent Children (ADC) became controversial and, in many places, reviled. Eventually, the Personal Responsibility and Work Opportunity Reconciliation Act of 1996 "ended welfare as we know it" by replacing ADC with a program called Temporary Assistance for Needy Families (TANF). TANF is funded through flexible block grants rather than federally supervised matching grants, and the benefits it provides to children and their caregivers are time-limited, not open-ended. The so-called "adult" programs – Old Age Assistance, Aid to the Blind, and a 1950 addition to the Social Security Act called Aid to the Permanently and Totally Disabled – also still exist but are now under federal control and have been rolled into one program, Supplemental Security Income. For useful overviews of these changes, see Edward Berkowitz, *America's Welfare State: From Roosevelt to Reagan* (Baltimore: Johns Hopkins University Press, 1991); and Michael B. Katz, *The Price of Citizenship: Redefining the American Welfare State* (Philadelphia: University of Pennsylvania Press, 2008).

7. W. L. White, "'On the County' – Then and Now," *Reader's Digest*, March 1952.

8. "Goldwater Hails Newburgh Plan as Welfare Ideal for All Cities," *NYT*, July 19, 1961.

9. Cecile Goldberg, "Development of Federal Grant Allocations," *Social Security Bulletin* 10, no. 9 (1947): 3–4; George E. Bigge, "Federal Grants-in-Aid: A Bulwark of State Government," *Social Security Bulletin* 13, no. 11 (1950): 3; Governmental Affairs Institute, *A Survey Report on The Impact of Federal Grants-in-Aid on the Structure and Functions of State and Local Governments* (Washington, DC: U.S. Government Printing Office, 1955), 62, 178, 366, 406 (reporting, for example, that for the fiscal year ending June 30, 1953, federal grants accounted for 24.5 percent of state revenue in Colorado; 25.7 percent in Kentucky; 28.8 percent in South Dakota; 20.2 percent in Texas; and 22 percent in Utah). On the significance of the federal income tax, see Ajay K. Mehrotra, *Making the Modern American Fiscal State: Law, Politics, and the Rise of Progressive Taxation, 1877–1929* (Cambridge: Cambridge University Press, 2013).

10. Council of State Governments, *Federal Grants-in-Aid: Report of the Committee on Federal Grants-in-Aid* (Chicago: Council of State Governments, 1949), 80.

11. Similar devices were attached to other types of grants-in-aid, but as of the mid-1950s, it was clear that welfare's "strings" had been particularly significant to the organization and operation of state and local governments. See generally Governmental Affairs Institute, *A Survey Report on the Impact of Federal Grants-in-Aid*.

12. This federal agency underwent significant changes during the period in question. It began as the Social Security Board (SSB), an independent agency headed by a three-member advisory board. In 1939, as part of a broader reorganization of executive agencies, the SSB became part of the Federal Security Agency (FSA), a sub-cabinet-level agency that housed various New Deal and war-related programs. In 1946, the SSB was renamed the Social Security Administration and a single commissioner replaced the board at the top of the hierarchy. In 1953, the FSA became a cabinet-level agency and was renamed the Department of Health, Education, and Welfare (HEW). Social Security Administration, "Organizational History," http://www.ssa.gov/history/orghist.html, accessed May 15, 2015.

13. Barry Goldwater, *The Conscience of a Conservative* (Shepherdsville, KY: Victor Publishing Company, 1960), 26. On the impact of *The Conscience of a Conservative*, see Rick Perlstein, *Before the Storm: Barry Goldwater and the Unmaking of the American Consensus* (New York: Hill and Wang, 2001), 61–68.

14. Alan Brinkley, *Voices of Protest: Huey Long, Father Coughlin, and the Great Depression* (New York: Vintage Books, 1982), 143–68; Mitchell address.

15. The best source on technical changes to federal public assistance law and policy in this period is Blanche D. Coll, *Safety Net: Welfare and Social Security, 1929–1979* (New Brunswick, NJ: Rutgers University Press, 1995). On the merit system requirement, see ibid., 128–31; on social work training, see ibid., 132–33.

16. Mitchell address; "Newburgh to Use 'Thought Control,'" *NYT*, August 4, 1961; "Newburgh Names Head of Welfare," *NYT*, July 29, 1961; William

Henry Chamberlin, "Parasite's Paradise," *WSJ*, July 25, 1961; see also Karl
M. Elish, "Praise for Authorities," *NYT*, July 18, 1961.

17. "New Welfare Aide Named by Newburgh," *NYT*, August 11, 1961; Mitchell
address. The Alfange quote is from Dean Alfange, "My Creed" (also titled
"An American's Creed"), which appeared in multiple popular publications in
the 1950s, including the October 1952 issue of *Reader's Digest*.

18. "Court Move Urged," *NYT*, July 19, 1961; Thomas F. Lewin, "Carrying Out
State Law," *NYT*, July 7, 1961; "Newburgh Plans More Relief Bars," *NYT*,
July 6, 1961; Hailey, "Newburgh Rules Become Effective"; "Newburgh and
the Law," *NYT*, July 11, 1961.

19. Peter Braestrup, "Ribicoff Upholds Work-Relief If U.S. Funds Are Not
Involved," *NYT*, July 20, 1961.

20. Edson, "Work, Not Relief, Now Ribicoff Aim."

21. My claim about boldness is in tension with decades of writing on poverty law
and policy. Disappointed with the treatment of poor women, children, and
racial minorities in the late twentieth century, scholars have tended to emphasize the ways in which New Deal–era interventions perpetuated, rather than
broke from, dark traditions. We have gained much from seeing this continuity, including an appreciation for how poor-relief policies have consistently
regulated the low-wage labor market, policed women's sexuality, and reinforced racial hierarchies. See, generally, Frances Fox Piven and Richard A.
Cloward, *Regulating the Poor: The Functions of Public Welfare* (New York:
Pantheon, 1971); Mimi Abramovitz, *Regulating the Lives of Women: Social
Welfare Policy from Colonial Times to the Present* (Boston: South End Press,
1988); Linda Gordon, "What Does Welfare Regulate?" *Social Research* 55,
no. 4 (1988): 609–30; Robert Lieberman, *Shifting the Color Line: Race and
the American Welfare State* (Cambridge, MA: Harvard University Press,
1998); Cybelle Fox, *Three Worlds of Relief: Race, Immigration, and the
American Welfare State from the Progressive Era to the New Deal*
(Princeton, NJ: Princeton University Press, 2012), 250–80. These gains have
come at a cost, however. First, they have tended to obscure important changes
over time. Contrary to the prevailing narrative among today's poverty law
scholars, the federally funded welfare programs of the twentieth century were
not simply a codification of the Elizabethan Poor Law. That narrative mis-
represents past actors and unduly constricts the imagination of future reformers. Second, an emphasis on sameness tacitly encourages the continued
ghettoization of the study of poverty and the poor. If we imply that nothing
ever really changes for the poor, scholars may safely treat them as outside the
mainstream of American history, relevant only because of the ways in which
they occasionally forced those in power to change tactics.

22. There were exceptions to the exclusivity of this jurisdiction – for veterans, for
example, and for individuals who lacked a legal settlement in any local
jurisdiction. I elaborate on this point in Chapter 1.

23. Austin Sarat, "'... The Law Is All Over': Power, Resistance and the Legal
Consciousness of the Welfare Poor," *Yale Journal of Law & the Humanities*
2, no. 2 (1990): 343.

24. See, for example, Davis, *Brutal Need*; R. Shep Melnick, *Between the Lines: Interpreting Welfare Rights* (Washington, DC: Brookings Institution, 1994); Premilla Nadasen, *Welfare Warriors: The Welfare Rights Movement in the United States* (New York: Routledge, 2005); Orleck, *Storming Caesars Palace*; Kornbluh, *Battle for Welfare Rights*. The Clinton quote is from Katz, *The Price of Citizenship*, 322.

25. See Barbara Nelson, "The Origins of the Two-Channel Welfare State: Workmen's Compensation and Mothers' Aid," in *Women, the State, and Welfare*, ed. Linda Gordon (Madison: University of Wisconsin Press, 1990); Gwendolyn Mink, "The Lady and the Tramp: Gender, Race, and the Origins of the American Welfare State," in *Women, the State, and Welfare*, ed. Linda Gordon (Madison: University of Wisconsin Press, 1990); Linda Gordon, "Social Insurance and Public Assistance: The Influence of Gender in Welfare Thought in the United States, 1890–1935," *American Historical Review* 97, no. 1 (1992); Theda Skocpol, *Protecting Soldiers and Mothers: The Political Origins of Social Policy in the United States* (Cambridge, MA: Belknap Press of Harvard University Press, 1992); Linda Gordon, *Pitied but Not Entitled: Single Mothers and the History of Welfare, 1890–1935* (New York: Free Press, 1994); Suzanne Mettler, *Dividing Citizens: Gender and Federalism in New Deal Public Policy* (Ithaca, NY: Cornell University Press, 1998); Lieberman, *Shifting the Color Line*; Alice Kessler-Harris, "In the Nation's Image: The Gendered Limits of Social Citizenship in the Depression Era," *Journal of American History* 86, no. 3 (1999): 1251–79; Alice Kessler-Harris, *In Pursuit of Equity: Women, Men, and the Quest for Economic Citizenship in 20th-Century America* (New York: Oxford University Press, 2001); Ira Katznelson, *When Affirmative Action Was White: An Untold History of Racial Inequality in Twentieth-Century America* (New York: W. W. Norton, 2005). Scholars have now expanded on and, in some ways, remade this theory. Edwin Amenta has challenged assumptions about how deeply rooted the two-track welfare state is, arguing that it was not entrenched until after the New Deal. Edwin Amenta, *Bold Relief: Institutional Politics and the Origins of Modern American Social Policy* (Princeton, NJ: Princeton University Press, 1998). Others have suggested additional policy tracks: Michael Willrich has described state regulation of "delinquent husbands" as a third policy track; Christopher Howard, among others, has made the same argument for the tax code, a "hidden" means of distributing state beneficence; Michael Katz would have added public education and veterans' benefits. Michael Willrich, "Home Slackers: Men, the State, and Welfare in Modern America," *Journal of American History* 87, no. 2 (2000): 462; Christopher Howard, *The Hidden Welfare State: Tax Expenditures and Social Policy in the United States* (Princeton, NJ: Princeton University Press, 1997); David J. Erickson, *The Housing Policy Revolution: Networks and Neighborhoods* (Washington, DC: Urban Institute, 2009); Michael B. Katz, "The American Welfare State and Social Contract in Hard Times," *Journal of Public History* 22, no. 4 (2010). Still other scholars have departed from the two-track concept by suggesting bigger and more fundamental divisions, such as the division between the "public" welfare state (which would include both social insurance and

public assistance) and the "private" welfare state (employee health and retirement benefits). Edward D. Berkowitz and Kim McQuaid, *Creating the Welfare State: The Political Economy of Twentieth-Century Reform*, rev. ed. (Lawrence: University Press of Kansas, 1992); Andrea Tone, *The Business of Benevolence: Industrial Paternalism in Progressive America* (Ithaca, NY: Cornell University Press, 1997); Jacob S. Hacker, *The Divided Welfare State: The Battle over Public and Private Social Benefits in the United States* (Cambridge: Cambridge University Press, 2002); Jennifer Klein, *For All These Rights: Business, Labor, and the Shaping of America's Public-Private Welfare State* (Princeton, NJ: Princeton University Press, 2003); Katz, *The Price of Citizenship*. None of these revisions, however, challenges the idea that entitlement or right was a fundamental feature of superior social welfare programs, such as old age insurance, and a feature missing from inferior programs, such as public assistance. The only exception worth noting is the recent literature on government support for the blind, which emphasizes blind citizens' long-standing and sometimes successful efforts to characterize their need-based programs as part of the more desirable track. See Felicia Kornbluh, "Disability, Antiprofessionalism, and Civil Rights: The National Federation of the Blind and the 'Right to Organize' in the 1950s," *Journal of American History* 97, no. 4 (2011): 1023–47; Thomas A. Krainz, "Transforming the Progressive Era Welfare State: Activists for the Blind and Blind Benefits," *Journal of Policy History* 15, no. 2 (2003): 223–64.

26. See, for example, Jerry R. Cates, *Insuring Inequality: Administrative Leadership in Social Security, 1935–1954* (Ann Arbor: University of Michigan Press, 1983), 26–31; James T. Patterson, *America's Struggle against Poverty: 1900–1980* (Cambridge, MA: Harvard University Press, 1981), 74–76; Gordon, *Pitied but Not Entitled*, 5; Kessler-Harris, "In the Nation's Image," 1263–65; Molly C. Michelmore, *Tax and Spend: The Welfare State, Tax Politics, and the Limits of American Liberalism* (Philadelphia: University of Pennsylvania Press, 2012), 13.

27. "Welfare" is in quotes because people at the time would not have used this label. As I explain in Chapter 1, federal administrators used the term "public assistance." The broader public tended to know these programs as either "relief" or some type of "pension."

28. Frank Bane to the League of Women Voters, Cincinnati, April 29, 1936, Box 7, Frank Bane Papers, Small Special Collections Library, University of Virginia, Charlottesville [hereafter cited as FBP].

29. My examination of "what happened along the way" is what distinguishes my study of New Deal public welfare and citizenship from Suzanne Mettler's important work on this topic. See Mettler, *Dividing Citizens*. Whereas she has focused on the structure of New Deal social welfare programs, I focus on administration. We both, however, are ultimately interested in how "the governing arrangements for New Deal policies affect[ed] the character and experience of American citizenship." Suzanne Mettler, "Social Citizens of Separate Sovereignties: Governance in the New Deal Welfare State," in *The New Deal and the Triumph of Liberalism*, ed. Sidney M. Milkis and Jerome M. Mileur (Amherst: University of Massachusetts Press, 2002), 232.

30. On how claims to social resources came to be understood as "charity" and why that label was so difficult to change, see Nancy Fraser and Linda Gordon, "Contract versus Charity: Why Is There No Social Citizenship in the United States?" *Socialist Review* 22 (1992): 45–68.

31. For an important exploration of the role of rights in legitimizing the unprecedented government interventions in American life that accompanied World War II, see James Sparrow, *Warfare State: World War II Americans and the Age of Big Government* (New York: Oxford University Press, 2011). This is not simply a World War II story, however. Historian Jeremy Kessler has documented the participatory rights, recognized by the War Department in its treatment of conscientious objectors to World War I, that undergirded Progressives' attempts to build a more centralized, bureaucratized state. Jeremy K. Kessler, "The Administrative Origins of Modern Civil Liberties Law," *Columbia Law Review* 114 (2014): 1083–166. And as historian Laura Edwards has recently argued, the Civil War and Reconstruction deserve credit for both augmenting the power of the centralized government and encouraging people to see themselves as rights-bearing citizens of the nation-state. Laura F. Edwards, *A Legal History of the Civil War and Reconstruction: A Nation of Rights* (New York: Cambridge University Press, 2015).

32. On the perceived connection between taxes and welfare, see Michelmore, *Tax and Spend*. On the perception that welfare motivated African Americans' migration, employment, and reproductive choices, see Winifred Bell, *Aid to Dependent Children* (New York: Columbia University Press, 1965); Ellen Reese, *Backlash against Welfare Mothers: Past and Present* (Berkeley: University of California Press, 2005); Lisa Levenstein, *A Movement without Marches: African American Women and the Politics of Poverty in Postwar Philadelphia* (Chapel Hill: University of North Carolina Press, 2009).

33. See, generally, Kornbluh, *The Battle for Welfare Rights*. The tripartite classification of citizenship rights comes from T. H. Marshall, "Citizenship and Social Class," in *Citizenship and Social Class and Other Essays* (Cambridge: Cambridge University Press, 1950), 1–85.

34. The "out of sight" characterization comes from Brian Balogh, *A Government Out of Sight: The Mystery of National Authority in Nineteenth-Century America* (Cambridge: Cambridge University Press, 2009). On changing understandings of citizenship, see William Novak, "The Legal Transformation of Citizenship in Nineteenth-Century America," in *The Democratic Experiment: New Directions in American Political History*, ed. Meg Jacobs, William J. Novak, and Julian E. Zelizer (Princeton, NJ: Princeton University Press, 2003), 85–119. On the roles of taxation, conscription, political participation, and empire building, see, for example, Mark H. Leff, *The Limits of Symbolic Reform: The New Deal and Taxation, 1933–1939* (Cambridge: Cambridge University Press, 1984); Mehrotra, *Making the Modern American Fiscal State*; Christopher Cappozola, *Uncle Sam Wants You: World War I and the Making of the Modern American Citizen* (New York: Oxford University Press, 2010); Sparrow, *Warfare State*; Suzanne Mettler, *Soldiers to Citizens: The G.I. Bill and the Making of the Greatest Generation* (Oxford: Oxford University Press, 2005); Lizabeth

Cohen, *Making a New Deal: Industrial Workers in Chicago, 1919–1939* (Cambridge: Cambridge University Press, 1990); Alfred W. McCoy and Francisco A. Scarano, eds., *Colonial Crucible: Empire in the Making of the Modern American State* (Madison: University of Wisconsin Press, 2009).

35. I use the term "governance" in the sense that Laura Jensen uses it in her essay "Government, the State, and Governance," *Polity* 40, no. 3 (2008): 379–85. The word "govern*ment*," she explains there, "signifies the structure and function of public institutions, their authority to make binding decisions, and their authoritative implementation of those decisions and allocation of values through politics, policy and administration"; "'govern*ance*,'" by contrast, "embraces all actors, organizations, and institutions, public and non-public, involved in structuring polities and their relationships, whether within sovereign nation-states or without." The latter term "conveys a sense of something happening" – of states "constantly in motion," of "power and resources … being deployed," of "relationships … at work." Ibid., 381 (emphasis added).

36. See, for example, Tracy L. Steffes, *School, Society, and State: A New Education to Govern Modern America, 1890–1940* (Chicago: University of Chicago Press, 2012); Mason B. Williams, *City of Ambition: FDR, LaGuardia, and the Making of Modern New York* (New York: W. W. Norton, 2013); Gail Radford, *The Rise of Public Authority: Statebuilding and Economic Development in Twentieth-Century America* (Chicago: University of Chicago Press, 2013); Douglas S. Reed, *Building the Federal Schoolhouse: Localism and the American Education State* (New York: Oxford University Press, 2014); Philip Bartholomew Rocco, "Reorganizing the Activist State: Conservatives, Commissions, and the Politics of Federalism, 1947–1996," PhD diss., University of California, Berkeley, 2015; Brent Cebul, *Developmental State: Business, Poverty, and Economic Empowerment from the New Deal to the New Democrats* (Philadelphia: University of Pennsylvania Press, forthcoming). For a thoughtful discussion of why this line of research is necessary and important, see Brent Cebul and Mason B. Williams, "Revisiting the Question of Federalism: Intergovernmental State-Building and the New Deal Roots of Urban Liberalism and Sunbelt Conservatism," paper presented at the Beyond the New Deal Order conference, University of California, Santa Barbara, September 26, 2015.

37. Jon C. Teaford, *The Rise of the States: Evolution of American State Government* (Baltimore: Johns Hopkins University Press, 2002), 5; see also Ann O'M. Bowman and Richard C. Kearney, *The Resurgence of the States* (Englewood Cliffs, NJ: Prentice-Hall, 1986). On the rise of state governors, in particular, see Ethan G. Sribnick, ed., *A Legacy of Innovation: Governors and Public Policy* (Philadelphia: University of Pennsylvania Press, 2008).

38. Political scientist Martha Derthick deserves credit for first suggesting the extent to which the Social Security Act transformed state government. Martha Derthick, *The Influence of Federal Grants: Public Assistance in Massachusetts* (Cambridge, MA: Harvard University Press, 1970). She has made a similar argument regarding public education. Martha Derthick,

Keeping the Compound Republic: Essays on American Federalism (Washington, DC: Brookings Institution Press, 2001), 23–29. Scattered state-level accounts of the New Deal have made similar, if subtler, claims. See, for example, William Pickens, "The New Deal in New Mexico," in *The New Deal: The State and Local Levels*, ed. John Braeman, Robert H. Bremner, and David Brody (Columbus: Ohio State University Press, 1975), 331; Douglas Carl Abrams, *Conservative Constraints: North Carolina and the New Deal* (Jackson: University Press of Mississippi, 1992), 157. As Margaret Weir has observed, however, much work remains to be done on the "place of states in the history of twentieth-century state-building and political reform." Margaret Weir, "States, Race, and the Decline of New Deal Liberalism," *Studies in American Political Development* 19 (Fall 2005): 157.

39. One of my aims in advancing this argument is to invite the field of social welfare history to move beyond a framework that has been hugely influential and remains compelling, but now seems unduly simplistic. In *Regulating the Poor*, Frances Fox Piven and Richard Cloward famously argued that from the colonial period onward, public officials, acting in service of the ruling class, have used public welfare programs to control the poor and maintain an adequate supply of low-wage labor. One of the implications of my argument is that different levels of government *competed* to regulate the poor. The history of modern poor relief is not one of single-minded dominance of the poor, but of an ongoing contest between multiple powers, some great and others small, some rising and others in decline, with different relationships to the poor and varying agendas.

40. By the early 1980s, some aspects of this "legalization" – such as its tendency to mire welfare applicants in "red tape" – had become readily apparent to scholars. See, for example, William H. Simon, "Legality, Bureaucracy, and Class in the Welfare System," *Yale Law Journal* 92, no. 7 (1983): 1198–269; Michael Lipsky, "Bureaucratic Disentitlement in Social Welfare Programs," *Social Service Review* 58 (1984): 3–27. These scholars were more focused on critique, however, than on identifying the causes and contours of the trend toward legalization. They were also writing at a moment of *heightened* legalization, in the form of what Charles Epp and others call "legalized accountability": "a law-styled attempt to bring bureaucratic practices into line with emerging legal norms." Charles R. Epp, *Making Rights Real: Activists, Bureaucrats, and the Creation of the Legalistic State* (Chicago: University of Chicago Press, 2009), 2–3. They may thus have perceived a sharp break with the past where it is now possible to see continuity.

41. "Clients Write," *Public Welfare in Indiana* 54, no. 6 (1944): 8.

42. On Americans' commitment to law and legalism during and after World War II, see, generally, Edward A. Purcell, *The Crisis of Democratic Theory: Scientific Naturalism and the Problem of Value* (Lexington: University Press of Kentucky, 1973); William Edward Nelson, *The Legalist Reformation: Law, Politics, and Ideology in New York, 1920–1980* (Chapel Hill: University of North Carolina Press, 2001); Anne M. Kornhauser, *Debating the American State: Liberal Anxieties and the New Leviathan, 1930–1970* (Philadelphia: University of Pennsylvania Press, 2015).

43. Sarat, "'. . . The Law Is All Over,'" 344n2.
44. William E. Leuchtenburg, "The Pertinence of Political History: Reflections on the Significance of the State in America," *Journal of American History* 73, no. 3 (1986): 589; see also Peter B. Evans, Dietrich Rueschemeyer, and Theda Skocpol, eds., *Bringing the State Back In* (Cambridge: Cambridge University Press, 1985). Research flourished despite fundamental disagreements about how to define the state. Bartholomew Sparrow, *From the Outside In: World War II and the American State* (Princeton, NJ: Princeton University Press, 1996), 11–22. Historians, in particular, continue to write about the state without laboring over definitional matters. Margot Canaday's important recent study of state power, for example, defines the state simply as "what officials do" (quoting John R. Commons). Margot Canaday, *The Straight State: Sexuality and Citizenship in Twentieth-Century America* (Princeton, NJ: Princeton University Press, 2009), 5. This approach – focusing on "what [the state] *does*" rather than "the abstract, metaphysical question of what the state *is*" – may well be the right one, as James Sparrow, William Novak, and Stephen Sawyer argue in an important edited collection published just as this book was going to press. See James T. Sparrow, William J. Novak, and Stephen W. Sawyer, eds., *Boundaries of the State in U.S. History* (Chicago: University of Chicago Press, 2015), 5 (emphasis in the original). For readers who would benefit from an attempt at definition, however, I find Alfred Stepan's useful: the state, he argues, is the compilation of "administrative, legal, bureaucratic and coercive systems" that together aim to structure all "relations between civil society and public authority in a polity" as well as "many crucial relations *within* civil society." Alfred C. Stepan, *The State and Society: Peru in Comparative Perspective* (Princeton, NJ: Princeton University Press, 1978), xii, quoted in Sparrow, *From the Outside In*, 14. I would modify this definition, however, to emphasize that the state does not simply act upon a passive civil society but exists in dialogue with it; indeed, as Brian Balogh and others have argued, the state exists *through* the institutions and organizations we often label private or nongovernmental. See, generally, Joel S. Migdal, *State in Society: Studying How States and Societies Transform and Constitute One Another* (New York: Cambridge University Press, 2001); Brian Balogh, *The Associational State: American Governance in the Twentieth Century* (Philadelphia: University of Pennsylvania Press, 2015). This understanding of the state affects my understanding of where to look for it: I agree with William Novak that we can best see the state by examining "the intersection of polity and society and the actual everyday conduct and consequences of government." William J. Novak, *The People's Welfare: Law and Regulation in Nineteenth-Century America* (Chapel Hill: University of North Carolina Press, 1996), 8–9; see also Jensen, "Government, the State, and Governance," 382: "If we are to understand [states] adequately, we can and must study [them] empirically, *through the lens of actual governance* in specific locations at specific times in history" (emphasis in the original).
45. Stephen Skowronek, *Building a New American State: The Expansion of National Administrative Capacities, 1877–1920* (Cambridge: Cambridge University Press, 1982); Skocpol, *Protecting Soldiers and Mothers*.

46. See, for example, Richard Franklin Bensel, *Yankee Leviathan: The Origins of Central State Authority in America, 1859–1877* (Cambridge: Cambridge University Press, 1990); Richard White, *"It's Your Misfortune and None of My Own": A History of the American West* (Norman: University of Oklahoma Press, 1991); Richard R. John, *Spreading the News: The American Postal System from Franklin to Morse* (Cambridge, MA: Harvard University Press, 1995); Elizabeth Sanders, *Roots of Reform: Farmers, Workers, and the American State, 1877–1917* (Chicago: University of Chicago Press, 1999); Karen Merrill, "In Search of the 'Federal Presence' in the American West," *Western Historical Quarterly* 30 (1999): 449–73; Daniel P. Carpenter, *The Forging of Bureaucratic Autonomy: Reputations, Networks, and Policy Innovation in Executive Agencies, 1862–1928* (Princeton, NJ: Princeton University Press, 2001); Laura Jensen, *Patriots, Settlers, and the Origins of American Social Policy* (Cambridge: Cambridge University Press, 2003); Kimberley S. Johnson, *Governing the American State: Congress and the New Federalism, 1877–1929* (Princeton, NJ: Princeton University Press, 2007); Capozzola, *Uncle Sam Wants You*; Nicholas R. Parrillo, *Against the Profit Motive: The Salary Revolution in American Government, 1780–1940* (New Haven, CT: Yale University Press, 2013); Mehrotra, *Making the American Fiscal State*; Kessler, "The Administrative Origins of Modern Civil Liberties Law."

47. See, for example, Sparrow, *From the Outside In*; Marc Allen Eisner, *From Warfare State to Welfare State: World War I, Compensatory State Building, and the Limits of the Modern Order* (University Park: Pennsylvania State University Press, 2000); Julian E. Zelizer, "The Uneasy Relationship: Democracy, Taxation, and State Building since the New Deal," in *The Democratic Experiment: New Directions in American Political History*, ed. Meg Jacobs, William J. Novak, and Julian E. Zelizer (Princeton, NJ: Princeton University Press, 2003), 276–300; Meg Jacobs, *Pocketbook Politics: Economic Citizenship in Twentieth-Century America* (Princeton, NJ: Princeton University Press, 2005); Canaday, *The Straight State*; Sparrow, *Warfare State*; Steffes, *School, Society, and State*; Joanna L. Grisinger, *The Unwieldy American State: Administrative Politics since the New Deal* (New York: Cambridge University Press, 2012); Megan Ming Francis, *Civil Rights and the Making of the Modern American State* (New York: Cambridge University Press, 2014); Daniel R. Ernst, *Tocqueville's Nightmare: The Administrative State Emerges in America, 1900–1940* (New York: Oxford University Press, 2014); Kornhauser, Debating the American State.

48. Novak, *The People's Welfare*, 9–16. Similarly, Laura Edwards has excavated the robust system of localized law that "maintained the social order – the 'peace'" – in North and South Carolina in the decades after the American Revolution. Edwards shows how this regime operated alongside, and often independently of, a set of formal state laws. Laura F. Edwards, *The People and Their Peace: Legal Culture and the Transformation of Inequality in the Post-Revolutionary South* (Chapel Hill: University of North Carolina Press, 2009), 4, 7. On the "statelessness" critique, see William J. Novak, "The Legal

Origins of the Modern American State," in *Looking Back at Law's Century*,
ed. Austin Sarat, Bryan Garth, and Robert A. Kagan (Ithaca, NY: Cornell
University Press, 2002); William J. Novak, "The Myth of the 'Weak'
American State," *American Historical Review* 113, no. 3 (2008): 752–72;
Desmond King and Robert Lieberman, "Finding the American State:
Transcending the 'Statelessness' Account," *Polity* 40, no. 3 (2008): 368–78.

49. Novak, *The People's Welfare*; Novak, "The Legal Origins of the Modern
American State." On New Deal liberalism, see Alan Brinkley, *The End of
Reform: New Deal Liberalism in Recession and War* (New York: Vintage
Books, 1996); Jason Scott Smith, *Building New Deal Liberalism: The
Political Economy of Public Works, 1933–1956* (Cambridge: Cambridge
University Press, 2009).

50. The quote is from Novak, "The Legal Origins of the Modern American
State." Historians have long noted the same general transformation (while
disagreeing about its precise extent and timing). See, for example, Samuel P.
Hays, *The Response to Industrialism, 1885–1914* (Chicago: University of
Chicago Press, 1957); Robert H. Wiebe, *The Search for Order, 1877–1920*
(New York: Hill and Wang, 1967); Morton Keller, *Affairs of State: Public
Life in Late Nineteenth-Century America* (Cambridge, MA: Harvard
University Press, 1977).

51. Derthick, *Keeping the Compound Republic*, 10, 141.

52. Thomas Sugrue, "All Politics Is Local: The Persistence of Localism in
Twentieth-Century America," in *The Democratic Experiment: New
Directions in American Political History*, ed. Meg Jacobs, William J. Novak,
and Julian E. Zelizer (Princeton, NJ: Princeton University Press, 2003), 302.

53. Ibid., 304; Lizabeth Cohen, *A Consumers' Republic: The Politics of Mass
Consumption in Postwar America* (New York: Alfred A. Knopf, 2003),
227–51. On policing, see William J. Stuntz, *The Collapse of American
Criminal Justice* (Cambridge, MA: Belknap Press of Harvard University
Press, 2011), 188, 196–215, 236–41, 254; Lawrence Friedman, *Crime and
Punishment in American History* (New York: Basic Books, 1994), 262. On
education, see Richard Briffault, "The Role of Local Control in School
Finance Reform," *Connecticut Law Review* 24 (1992): 773–812; Steffes,
School, Society, and State; Reed, *Building the Federal Schoolhouse*, although
note Steffes's and Reed's sophisticated arguments about the significant exer-
cises of central-state power that occurred via local public schools. On land use
and land assessment practices, see Richard Briffault, "Our Localism: Part I –
The Structure of Local Government Law," *Columbia Law Review* 90 (1990):
1–115; Richard Briffault, "Our Localism: Part II – Localism and Legal
Theory," *Columbia Law Review* 90 (1990): 346–454; Isaac William
Martin, *The Permanent Tax Revolt: How the Property Tax Transformed
American Politics* (Stanford, CA: Stanford University Press, 2008). On "loc-
alist ideology," see Briffault, "Our Localism: Part I," 113–14; Briffault, "Our
Localism: Part II," 444–54.

54. My thinking here reflects the influence of Karen Orren and Stephen
Skowronek's theory of "intercurrence": the simultaneous existence of "multi-
ple-orders-in-action," some older and some newer, each with a different logic.

The result, they argue, is that "at any given historical juncture," "[c]ontrolling authorities . . . will be . . . a mixed bag of coercive instruments, with future political conflict all but guaranteed given their asymmetries and mutual impingements." Karen Orren and Stephen Skowronek, *The Search for American Political Development* (Cambridge: Cambridge University Press, 2004), 108–18. Morton Keller outlines a similar argument when he describes how the "administrative centralization, increasing professionalism, and new educational goals" of the early twentieth century existed alongside, and in fact gave new life to, the "traditionalism, localism, and group autonomy" characteristic of the nineteenth century. Keller, *Affairs of State*, 486.

55. I am by no means the first to note the proceduralist bent of modern American governance or the inegalitarian consequences of seemingly neutral legal and political processes. See, for example, Ira Katznelson, *Fear Itself: The New Deal and the Origins of Our Time* (New York: W. W. Norton, 2013), 18–19. My contribution is to illuminate the relationship between proceduralism and other trends that scholars associate with the modern American state, such as centralization, bureaucratization, standardization, and a deep commitment to rights.

56. Jeffery A. Jenkins and Eric M. Patashnik, "Living Legislation and American Politics," in *Living Legislation: Durability, Change, and the Politics of American Lawmaking*, ed. Jeffery A. Jenkins and Eric M. Patashnik (Chicago: University of Chicago Press, 2012), 5–6. For a useful model of this approach, see William N. Eskridge Jr. and John Ferejohn, *A Republic of Statutes: The New American Constitution* (New Haven, CT: Yale University Press, 2010).

57. Grant Gilmore, *The Ages of American Law* (New Haven, CT: Yale University Press, 1977), 95. For other works on the importance of statutes in the twentieth century, see Guido Calabresi, *A Common Law for the Age of Statutes* (Cambridge, MA: Harvard University Press, 1982); J. Willard Hurst, *Dealing with Statutes* (New York: Columbia University Press, 1982).

58. Jenkins and Patashnik, "Living Legislation and American Politics," 5–6.

59. Seminal works include James Willard Hurst, *Law and the Conditions of Freedom in the Nineteenth-Century United States* (Madison: University of Wisconsin Press, 1956); and James Willard Hurst, *Law and Economic Growth: The Legal History of the Lumber Industry in Wisconsin, 1836–1915* (Cambridge, MA: Belknap Press of Harvard University Press, 1964). On Hurst and his approaches to history and law, see the collection of essays in *Law and History Review* 18, no. 1 (2000); Harry N. Scheiber, "At the Borderland of Law and Economic History: The Contributions of Willard Hurst," *American Historical Review* 75, no. 3 (1970): 744–56; David H. Flaherty, "An Approach to American History: Willard Hurst as a Legal Historian," *American Journal of Legal History* 14, no. 3 (1970): 222–34; Hendrik Hartog, "Snakes in Ireland: A Conversation with Willard Hurst," *Law and History Review* 12, no. 2 (1994): 370–90.

60. I take inspiration here from Lucy Salyer's pioneering work on the Bureau of Immigration, as well as a spate of more recent work in legal history. See Lucy E. Salyer, *Laws Harsh as Tigers: Chinese Immigrants and the Shaping of*

Modern Immigration Law (Chapel Hill: University of North Carolina Press, 1995); Erika Lee, *At America's Gates: Chinese Immigration during the Exclusion Era, 1882–1943* (Chapel Hill: University of North Carolina Press, 2003); Risa Lauren Goluboff, *The Lost Promise of Civil Rights* (Cambridge, MA: Harvard University Press, 2007); Canaday, *The Straight State*; Peggy Pascoe, *What Comes Naturally: Miscegenation Law and the Making of Race in America* (New York: Oxford University Press, 2010), especially chap. 5; Kristin A. Collins, "Administering Marriage: Marriage-Based Entitlements, Bureaucracy, and the Legal Construction of the Family," *Vanderbilt Law Review* 62 (2009): 1085–167; Mary Farmer-Kaiser, *Freedwomen and the Freedmen's Bureau: Race, Gender, and Public Policy in the Age of Emancipation* (New York: Fordham University Press, 2010); Fox, *Three Worlds of Relief*; Gautham Rao, "Administering Entitlement: Governance, Public Health Care, and the Early American State," *Law & Social Inquiry* 37, no. 3 (2012): 627–56; Parrillo, *Against the Profit Motive*; Sophia Z. Lee, *The Workplace Constitution from the New Deal to the New Right* (New York: Cambridge University Press, 2014); Alexander Gourse, "Restraining the Reagan Revolution: The Lawyers' War on Poverty and the Durable Liberal State, 1964–1989," PhD diss., Northwestern University, 2015; Gautham Rao, *National Duties: Custom Houses and the Making of the American State* (Chicago: University of Chicago Press, forthcoming).

61. For a fuller discussion, see Felicia Kornbluh and Karen Tani, "Siting the Legal History of Poverty: Below, Above, and Amidst," in *The Blackwell Companion to American Legal History*, ed. Alfred Brophy and Sally Hadden (Malden, MA: Wiley-Blackwell 2012), 329–48.

62. Here, I join historian Laura Edwards's call for legal historical research that seeks to illuminate national phenomena without focusing exclusively on the federal level or relying primarily on federal government sources. Edwards, *A Legal History of the Civil War and Reconstruction*, 9–10.

63. On the importance of such actors and institutions to twentieth-century governance, see generally Balogh, *The Associational State*.

I   A NEW DEAL FOR POOR RELIEF?

1. The record does not disclose Mr. Manning's first name, nor does it detail precisely when or how he lost his job. On the likely steps that a family with an unemployed breadwinner would have taken at this time, see Michael B. Katz, *In the Shadow of the Poorhouse: A Social History of Welfare in America*, 10th anniversary ed. (New York: Basic Books, 1996), 217–18; Lizabeth Cohen, *Making a New Deal: Industrial Workers in Chicago, 1919–1939* (Cambridge: Cambridge University Press, 1990), 214–49.

2. The background information on relief programs in Massachusetts comes from Susan Traverso, *Welfare Politics in Boston, 1910–1940* (Amherst and Boston: University of Massachusetts Press, 2003). On the mothers' pension movement, see Theda Skocpol, *Protecting Soldiers and Mothers: The Political Origins of*

Social Policy in the United States (Cambridge, MA: Belknap Press of Harvard University Press, 1992).

3. Rose J. McHugh to A. D. Smith, November 1, 1937, Box 3, Office of the General Counsel, Correspondence on Public Assistance Programs and the Social Security Act, 1935–1961 [hereafter cited as GC Correspondence on PA], Record Group 235, General Records of the Department of Health, Education, and Welfare, National Archives, College Park, Md. [hereafter cited as HEWR]; Rose J. McHugh to A. D. Smith, November 6, 1937, Box 3, GC Correspondence on PA, HEWR; A. D. Smith to Rose J. McHugh, December 3, 1937, Box 3, GC Correspondence on PA, HEWR.

4. By this time, the federal government had funded "pensions" to veterans and widowed mothers, but these payments were ostensibly based on service to the state rather than economic need. Skocpol, *Protecting Soldiers and Mothers*; Megan J. McClintock, "Civil War Pensions and the Reconstruction of Union Families," *Journal of American History* 83, no. 2 (1996): 456–80.

5. William J. Novak, *The People's Welfare: Law and Regulation in Nineteenth-Century America* (Chapel Hill: University of North Carolina Press, 1996), 8–18, 239–41.

6. I borrow the notion of "seeing" from James C. Scott, *Seeing Like a State: How Certain Schemes to Improve the Human Condition Have Failed* (New Haven, CT: Yale University Press, 1998).

7. Jon C. Teaford, *The Rise of the States: Evolution of American State Government* (Baltimore: Johns Hopkins University Press, 2002), 5. The history recounted here also connects to the broader history of what happened to local government across the span of the twentieth century and what difference, specifically, the New Deal made. Here, however, my claims are much more tentative. For an example of how scholars are grappling with this complicated question, see Mason B. Williams, *City of Ambition: FDR, LaGuardia, and the Making of Modern New York* (New York: W. W. Norton, 2013).

8. See, generally, Katz, *In the Shadow of the Poorhouse*, 3–59. On settlement and warning out, see Cornelia H. Dayton and Sharon V. Salinger, *Warning Out: Robert Love's Search for Strangers in Pre-Revolutionary Boston* (Boston: Beacon Press, 2010); Ruth Wallis Herndon, *Unwelcome Americans: Living on the Margin in Early New England* (Philadelphia: University of Pennsylvania Press, 2001). For examples of state statutory schemes and the role of state courts and state attorneys general, see Isabel Campbell Bruce and Edith Eickhoff, *The Michigan Poor Law* (Chicago: University of Chicago Press, 1936); Aileen Elizabeth Kennedy, *The Ohio Poor Law and Its Administration*, ed. Sophonisba P. Breckinridge (Chicago: University of Chicago Press, 1936); Alice Shaffer, Mary Wysor Keeper, and Sophonisba Breckenridge, *The Indiana Poor Law* (Chicago: University of Chicago Press, 1936); Margaret Creech, *Three Centuries of Poor Law Administration: A Study of Legislation in Rhode Island* (Chicago: University of Chicago Press, 1936), 111–34; Kunal M. Parker, "State, Citizenship, and Territory: The Legal Construction of Immigrants in Antebellum Massachusetts," *Law and History Review* 19, no. 3 (2001): 583–643.

9. Here I agree with a host of scholars on the importance of progressive political thought and reform to large-scale transformations in American governance. The caveat I emphasize is that, as of 1929, those transformations were incomplete and contested.

10. James Leiby, "State Welfare Administration in California, 1879–1929," *Pacific Historical Review* 41, no. 2 (1972): 179; William Haber, "The Public Welfare Problem in Massachusetts," *Social Service Review* 12, no. 2 (1938): 202–3; Ellen C. Potter and Blanche L. La Du, "Co-Ordination of State and Local Units for Welfare Administration," *Social Service Review* 7, no. 3 (1933): 390–91; Kennedy, *Ohio Poor Law*, 1; Elna C. Green, *This Business of Relief: Confronting Poverty in a Southern City, 1740–1940* (Athens: University of Georgia Press, 2003), 133–34.

11. Homer Folks, "Making Relief Respectable," *Annals of the American Academy of Political and Social Sciences* 176 (November 1934): 151.

12. Katz, *In the Shadow of the Poorhouse*, 88–113; Josephine Chapin Brown, *Public Relief, 1929–1939* (New York: Henry Holt and Company, 1940), 18–22. One could argue, as Michael Willrich has, that the criminalization of nonsupport was another form of state aid, because it resulted in payments to poor mothers and children, but here, as well, the state's role was indirect and filtered through the machinery of local law enforcement. Michael Willrich, "Home Slackers: Men, the State, and Welfare in Modern America," *Journal of American History* 87, no. 2 (2000): 462.

13. Brown, *Public Relief*, 26–29. On the administration of mothers' pensions, see Emma Octavia Lundberg, "Progress of Mothers' Aid Administration," *Social Service Review* 2, no. 3 (1928): 435–58; James Leiby, "State Welfare Administration in California, 1930–1945," *Southern California Quarterly* 55, no. 3 (1973): 304–5, 310; Susan Stein-Roggenbuck, *Negotiating Relief: The Development of Social Welfare Programs in Depression-Era Michigan, 1930–1940*, 2nd ed. (Columbus: Ohio State University Press, 2008), 28–37; Thomas A. Krainz, *Delivering Aid: Implementing Progressive Era Welfare in the American West* (Albuquerque: University of New Mexico Press, 2005), 147–80; Joanne L. Goodwin, *Gender and the Politics of Welfare Reform: Mothers' Pensions in Chicago, 1911–1929* (Chicago: University of Chicago Press, 1997); Roy Lubove, *The Struggle for Social Security, 1900–1935* (Cambridge, MA: Harvard University Press, 1968), 109–10; Skocpol, *Protecting Soldiers and Mothers*, 465–79. On the administration of old age pensions, which were much less common than mothers' pensions at this juncture, see Abraham Epstein, "The American State Old Age Pension System in Operation," *Annals of the American Academy of Political and Social Science* 170 (November 1933): 107–11; Jill Quadagno, *The Transformation of Old Age Security* (Chicago: University of Chicago Press, 1988). On the administration of pensions for the blind, see Krainz, *Delivering Aid*. On state-level veterans' pensions, see Elna C. Green, "Protecting Confederate Soldiers and Mothers: Pensions, Gender, and the Welfare State in the U.S. South: A Case Study from Florida," *Journal of Social History* 39, no. 4 (2006): 1079–104.

14. Robert W. Kelso, "Recent Advances in the Administration of Poor Relief," *Journal of Social Forces* 1, no. 2 (1923): 92. Historian Thomas Krainz argues that in Colorado, pensions for the blind actually did "significantly change the welfare state." He notes that a statewide agency was in charge, that the law clearly defined who was entitled to aid, and that knowledgeable advocates insisted on differentiating pensions from traditional poor relief. Krainz recognizes, however, that most Progressive Era pension programs did not have this effect. Krainz, *Delivering Aid*, 182–83.

15. Laura M. French, *History of Emporia and Lyon County, Kansas* (Westminster, MD: Heritage Books, 2008), 103; William E. Connelley, *A Standard History of Kansas and Kansans*, vol. 4 (Chicago: Lewis Publishing Company, 1918), 2198; W. L. White, "'On the County' – Then and Now," *Reader's Digest*, March 1952; Randolph's recollection squares with accounts from the time. See "Poor Relief in Kansas," *Social Service Review* 9, no. 3 (1935): 554–55.

16. Michelle Landis Dauber, *The Sympathetic State: Disaster Relief and the Origins of the American Welfare State* (Chicago: University of Chicago Press, 2012); Gautham Rao, "Administering Entitlement: Governance, Public Health Care, and the Early American State," *Law & Social Inquiry* 37, no. 3 (2012): 627–56; Laura Jensen, *Patriots, Settlers, and the Origins of American Social Policy* (Cambridge: Cambridge University Press, 2003); Skocpol, *Protecting Soldiers and Mothers*; McClintock, "Civil War Pensions"; Patrick J. Kelly, *Creating a National Home: Building the Veterans' Welfare State, 1860–1900* (Cambridge, MA: Harvard University Press, 1997); Mary Farmer-Kaiser, *Freedwomen and the Freedmen's Bureau: Race, Gender, and Public Policy in the Age of Emancipation* (New York: Fordham University Press, 2010); Frank M. Loewenberg, "Federal Relief Programs in the 19th Century: A Reassessment," *Journal of Sociology and Social Welfare* 19 (1992): 121–36.

17. Ann Shola Orloff, "The Political Origins of America's Belated Welfare State," in *Welfare and the State: Critical Concepts in Political Science*, ed. Nicholas Deakin, Catherine Jones-Finer, and Bob Matthews (London: Routledge, 2004), 62–63.

18. Katz, *In the Shadow of the Poorhouse*, 216–17. On the transition toward county administration and consolidation, see, for example, B. F. Timmons, "Experience in County Public Welfare Organization and Administration as a Basis for Planning in Illinois," *Social Forces* 15, no. 2 (1936): 248–54; Ellen C. Potter, Mary Ruth Colby, and Alice F. Liveright, "The County as a Public Welfare Unit," *Social Service Review* 6, no. 3 (1932): 452–83; Mary Phlegar Smith, "Trends in Municipal Administration of Public Welfare: 1900–1930," *Social Forces* 10, no. 3 (1932): 371–77. "Little or no official relationship" is from Brown, *Public Relief*, 52.

19. Frank Bane, interview by James R. W. Leiby, January 5, 1965, transcript, Regional Oral History Office, University of California, Berkeley.

20. Brown, *Public Relief*, 16; Morton Keller, *Regulating a New Society: Public Policy and Social Change in America, 1900–1933* (Cambridge, MA: Harvard University Press, 1994), 187–88.

21. Robert Kelso, *The Science of Public Welfare* (New York: H. Holt and Company, 1928), 133. Kelso served as commissioner for public welfare in Massachusetts.
22. Daniel T. Rodgers, *Atlantic Crossings: Social Politics in a Progressive Age* (Cambridge, MA: Belknap Press of Harvard University Press, 1998) (emphasis added).
23. Michael Willrich, "The Case for Courts: Law and Political Development in the Progressive Era," in *The Democratic Experiment: New Directions in American Political History*, ed. Meg Jacobs, William J. Novak, and Julian E. Zelizer (Princeton, NJ: Princeton University Press, 2003), 215.
24. Fred K. Hoehler, "Public Welfare Administration under the Social Security Act," *Law and Contemporary Problems* 3, no. 2 (1936): 279.
25. Edward Ainsworth Williams, *Federal Aid for Relief* (New York: Columbia University Press, 1939), 10; Kelso, *The Science of Public Welfare*, 162–93; Krainz, *Delivering Aid*, 31–101, 212. Ohio's system was particularly complex: whether responsibility belonged to one of the state's eighty-eight counties or, instead, one of its 1,337 townships depended on how the individual in question was categorized ("permanent pauper" or temporary). Kennedy, *Ohio Poor Law*, 2; Wayne McMillen, "Unemployment Relief in Ohio," *Social Service Review* 9, no. 3 (1935): 466.
26. Anna R. Igra, *Wives without Husbands: Marriage, Desertion, and Welfare in New York, 1900–1935* (Chapel Hill: University of North Carolina Press, 2007), 98–117; Eric C. Schneider, *In the Web of Class: Delinquents and Reformers in Boston, 1810s–1930s* (New York: New York University Press, 1992), 2–13; Stein-Roggenbuck, *Negotiating Relief*, 40–43; Krainz, *Delivering Aid*, 103–45.
27. Green, *This Business of Relief*, 132–33. For a more detailed account of local and regional variation, with an emphasis on the importance of race, citizenship status, and labor needs, see Cybelle Fox, *Three Worlds of Relief: Race, Immigration, and the American Welfare State from the Progressive Era to the New Deal* (Princeton, NJ: Princeton University Press, 2012).
28. Katz, *In the Shadow of the Poorhouse*, 220–21; Cohen, *Making a New Deal*, 222–38; William R. Brock, *Welfare, Democracy, and the New Deal* (Cambridge: Cambridge University Press, 1988), 84–126; Brown, *Public Relief*, 64–65. On the associative vision of the state that Herbert Hoover and others of his era pursued, see Ellis Hawley, "Herbert Hoover, the Commerce Secretariat, and the Vision of an 'Associative State,' 1921–1928," *Journal of American History* 61, no. 1 (1974): 116–40. On associative governance more generally, see Brian Balogh, *The Associational State: American Governance in the Twentieth Century* (Philadelphia: University of Pennsylvania Press, 2015).
29. Brock, *Welfare, Democracy, and the New Deal*, 129–37; National Industrial Recovery Act, Pub. L. No. 73-67, 48 Stat. 195 (1933).
30. On federal-state grants-in-aid, see, generally, V. O. Key Jr., *The Administration of Federal Grants to States* (Chicago: Public Administration Service, 1937); Kimberley S. Johnson, *Governing the American State:*

Congress and the New Federalism, 1877–1929 (Princeton, NJ: Princeton University Press, 2007).

31. 262 U.S. 447 (1923) [finding no jurisdiction to review state and taxpayer challenges to the Sheppard-Towner Maternity and Infancy Act].

32. Brock, *Welfare, Democracy, and the New Deal*, 136–39, Williams, *Federal Aid for Relief*, 43–57; Marc Allen Eisner, *From Warfare State to Welfare State: World War I, Compensatory State Building, and the Limits of the Modern Order* (University Park: Pennsylvania State University Press, 2000), 284–90. The act also authorized loans for self-liquidating construction projects and the expenditure of about $322 million for federal public works projects.

33. Elias Huzar, "Federal Unemployment Relief Policies: The First Decade," *Journal of Politics* 2, no. 3 (1940): 321–35, 324.

34. Brock, *Welfare, Democracy, and the New Deal*, 138–61; Brown, *Public Relief*, 126–27, 134, 146–47.

35. Brown, *Public Relief*, 148.

36. Brock, *Welfare, Democracy, and the New Deal*, 174–76.

37. Quoted in June Hopkins, *Harry Hopkins: Sudden Hero, Brash Reformer* (New York: St. Martin's Press, 1999), 158.

38. Brock, *Welfare, Democracy, and the New Deal*, 179–85, 204–48; Cohen, *Making a New Deal*, 268. Note, however, that federal officials trod cautiously around claims of local discrimination, despite forbidding state relief administrations from tolerating such practices. Fox, *Three Worlds of Relief*, 190, 199.

39. Brown, *Public Relief*, 161–62.

40. SSA, Titles I, IV, and X. Other titles provided for old-age insurance (initially called "federal old-age benefits"), unemployment compensation, maternal and child welfare, and public health work. SSA, Titles II, III, V, and VI. At the time of the SSA's enactment, it was common to hyphenate the phrase "old age" in program titles. The hyphen disappeared over time. For consistency, I eliminate it from all future references.

41. Brock, *Welfare, Democracy, and the New Deal*, 257–325. On the fate of work relief programs, see Jason Scott Smith, *Building New Deal Liberalism: The Political Economy of Public Works, 1933–1956* (Cambridge: Cambridge University Press, 2006); Bonnie Fox Schwartz, *The Civil Works Administration, 1933–1934: The Business of Emergency Employment in the New Deal* (Princeton, NJ: Princeton University Press, 1984).

42. This oft-quoted (and oft-misinterpreted) phrase is from President Roosevelt's 1935 message to Congress, in which he stated that "[t]o dole out relief in this way" – i.e., on an emergency basis, without differentiating the employable from the unemployable – was "to administer a narcotic, a subtle destroyer of the human spirit"; it was "inimical to the dictates of sound policy" and "in violation of the traditions of America." He demanded that work, not relief, be given to "able-bodied but destitute workers." Franklin D. Roosevelt, "Annual Message to the Congress" (speech, Washington, DC, January 4, 1935), in *The Public Papers and Addresses of Franklin D. Roosevelt*, ed. Samuel I. Rosenman (New York: Random House, 1938): 4, 19–20.

43. Arthur J. Altmeyer, *The Formative Years of Social Security* (Madison: University of Wisconsin Press, 1966), 16.

44. Michael Katz's work is representative: he has argued that the SSA and other New Deal relief policies "modified but did not erase archaic distinctions between the worthy and unworthy" poor, "reinforced" rather than undermined the stigma attached to welfare, and did nothing to disrupt welfare's role in the regulation of the labor market or the management of social order. Katz, *In the Shadow of the Poorhouse*, 155.

45. On the formation of the CES, see Edwin E. Witte, *The Development of the Social Security Act* (Madison: University of Wisconsin Press, 1962), 3–61. Labor economists were largely responsible for the content of the act's OAA title, which in turn became the model for AB. FERA head Harry Hopkins and members of his staff worked with top administrators in the Children's Bureau (Grace Abbott, Martha Eliot) to design ADC, with input from the upper echelons of the social work and public welfare administration communities (Dorothy Kahn, Elizabeth Wisner, Edith Abbott, Frank Bane, and Fred Hoehler, for example). Arthur Altmeyer, interview by Peter A. Corning, June 29, 1967, transcript, Columbia Center for Oral History, Columbia University, New York; Linda Gordon, "Social Insurance and Public Assistance: The Influence of Gender in Welfare Thought in the United States, 1890–1935," *American Historical Review* 97, no. 1 (1992): 19–54, 48; Robyn Muncy, *Creating a Female Dominion in American Reform, 1890–1935* (New York: Oxford University Press, 1994), 151–52. On the importance of popular alternative plans, such as Townsend's and Long's, see Edwin Amenta, *When Movements Matter: The Townsend Plan and the Rise of Social Security* (Princeton, NJ: Princeton University Press, 2006); Quadagno, *The Transformation of Old Age Security*; Frances Perkins, *The Roosevelt I Knew* (New York: Harper and Row, 1964), 278–79.

46. Eveline M. Burns, interview by Blanche D. Coll, July 1, 1985, transcript, Box 2, M99-098, EWP. For other accounts of the divides among the drafters, see Gordon, "Social Insurance and Public Assistance"; Blanche D. Coll, *Safety Net: Welfare and Social Security, 1929–1979* (New Brunswick, NJ: Rutgers University Press, 1995), 48–49.

47. Rodgers, *Atlantic Crossings*, 12, 25.

48. The idea of states as standard bearers for progressive reform is often associated with lawyer Louis Brandeis, a leading light in reform circles in the first decades of the twentieth century. Later, as a Supreme Court justice, he famously described states as "laborator[ies]" for "social and economic experiment[ation]" within the American federal system. New State Ice Co. v. Liebmann, 285 U.S. 262, 311 (1932) (Brandeis, J., dissenting).

49. James T. Patterson, *The New Deal and the States: Federalism in Transition* (Princeton, NJ: Princeton University Press, 1969), 7; Edgar Kemler, *The Deflation of American Ideals: An Ethical Guide for New Dealers* (Washington, DC: American Council on Public Affairs, 1941); Perkins, *The Roosevelt I Knew*, 287–95; Martha Derthick, *The Influence of Federal Grants: Public Assistance in Massachusetts* (Cambridge, MA: Harvard University Press, 1970), 18–19; Rodgers, *Atlantic Crossings*, 437–46; Bary

D. Karl, *The Uneasy State: The United States from 1915 to 1945* (Chicago: University of Chicago Press, 1983), 154; Orloff, "The Political Origins of America's Belated Welfare State," 70.

50. Examples include Kennedy, *Ohio Poor Law*; Grace A. Browning, *The Development of Poor Relief Legislation in Kansas*, ed. Sophonisba P. Breckinridge (Chicago: University of Chicago Press, 1935); Isobel Campbell Bruce, "The History and Interpretation of Poor Relief Legislation in Michigan," master's thesis, University of Chicago School of Social Service Administration, 1934; Margaret Creech, "Three Centuries of Poor Law Administration: A Study of Legislation in Rhode Island," PhD diss., University of Chicago School of Social Service Administration, 1935; Harriet Louise Tynes, "The History of Poor Relief Legislation in Virginia, 1776 to 1930," master's thesis, University of Chicago School of Social Service Administration, 1932; and Elizabeth Wisner, "Public Welfare Administration in Louisiana, with Special Reference to the Care of the Sick Poor, the Insane and the Adult Offender," PhD diss., University of Chicago School of Social Service Administration, 1929.

51. Edith Abbott, "Abolish the Pauper Laws," *Social Service Review* 8, no. 1 (1934): 1.

52. Folks, "Making Relief Respectable," 155; Abbott, "Abolish the Pauper Laws," 9–10.

53. Committee on Economic Security, *Report to the President of the Committee on Economic Security* (Washington, DC: U.S. Government Printing Office, 1935).

54. Orloff, "Political Origins of America's Belated Welfare State," 71.

55. Frank Bane, interview by James R. W. Leiby, January 13, 1965, transcript, Regional Oral History Office, University of California, Berkeley. On the phenomenon of transatlantic borrowing more generally, see Rodgers, *Atlantic Crossings*.

56. The drafters plucked this language from the Massachusetts and New York old age assistance laws. Witte, *Development of the Social Security Act*, 144.

57. This change cannot be attributed solely to an ideological commitment to "states' rights" vis-à-vis the national government. As political scientist Robert Lieberman notes, states' rights arguments were "striking[ly] absen[t]" from the debates over old age insurance, which entailed a much greater expansion of federal power. Robert Lieberman, *Shifting the Color Line: Race and the American Welfare State* (Cambridge, MA: Harvard University Press, 1998), 48–56. On the power of southern Democrats in Congress during this period, see Ira Katznelson, Kim Geiger, and Daniel Kryder, "Limiting Liberalism: The Southern Veto in Congress, 1933–1950," *Political Science Quarterly* 108 (1993): 283–306; Ira Katznelson, *Fear Itself: The New Deal and the Origins of Our Time* (New York: W. W. Norton, 2013).

58. Coll, *Safety Net*, 22–23.

59. Helen Valeska Bary, interview by Jacqueline K. Parker, January 13, 1973, transcript, Regional Oral History Office, University of California, Berkeley; Harold P. Levy, *A Study in Public Relations: Case History of the Relations of Public Assistance and the People of the State* (New York: Russell Sage

Foundation, 1943), 29; Wilma Van Dusseldorf, "The In-Service Training of Public Welfare Workers," *Social Forces* 17, no. 1 (1938), 61; Brock, *Welfare, Democracy, and the New Deal*, 255–56. For more on the resentment against social workers involved in relief administration, see Key, *Administration of Federal Grants to States*; Albert Henry Aronson, interview by Peter A. Corning, March 23, 1965, transcript, Columbia Center for Oral History, Columbia University, New York; Frank Z. Glick, *The Illinois Emergency Relief Commission: A Study of Administrative and Financial Aspects of Emergency Relief* (Chicago: University of Chicago Press, 1940), 152.

60. SSA, Title I, § 2(a)(5); Title IV, § 402(a)(5); Title X, § 1002(a)(5).

61. For an observer's account of the dramatic impact of FERA's ruling, see Brown, *Public Relief*, 183–90. On how the once powerful network of Catholic charities responded to this "revolution of public welfare administration" (in the words of the influential Reverend John O'Grady), see Dorothy M. Brown and Elizabeth McKeown, *The Poor Belong to Us: Catholic Charities and American Welfare* (Cambridge, MA: Harvard University Press, 1997), 164–70. Under the Sheppard-Towner Maternity and Infancy Act, which made federal funds available to states for maternal and infant health care, states sent their grant applications to the Children's Bureau. The bureaucrats there, largely professionally trained social workers, rejected all requests that called for the involvement of private agencies. Muncy, *Creating a Female Dominion*, 108, 121.

62. Frank Bane, interview by James R. W. Leiby, January 9, 1965, transcript, Regional Oral History Office, University of California, Berkeley.

63. Just a few years prior, for example, these private organizations had played a significant role in distributing the funds issued by President Hoover's Reconstruction Finance Corporation. Arthur Parker Miles, *Federal Aid and Public Assistance in Illinois* (Chicago: University of Chicago Press, 1941), 24.

64. Bane, interview by Leiby, January 9, 1965.

65. SSA, Title I, § 2(a)(3); Title IV, § 402(a)(3); Title X, § 1002(a)(3); Coll, *Safety Net*, 68–69; Hoehler, "Public Welfare Administration under the Social Security Act," 287. The "single state agency" provision also disrupted the existing system of poor relief by disentangling the judiciary from localized webs of social welfare provision. In some jurisdictions, juvenile courts administered mothers' pensions, a vestige of the regime of governance that Stephen Skowronek famously described as a "state of courts and parties." The "single state agency" provision suggested that when it came to federally subsidized public assistance programs, administrative authority would have to reside elsewhere. R. Clyde White, *Administration of Public Welfare* (New York: American Book Company, 1940), 51; Marietta Stevenson, *Public Welfare Administration* (New York: Macmillan, 1938), 116; Stephen Skowronek, *Building a New American State: The Expansion of National Administrative Capacities, 1877–1920* (Cambridge: Cambridge University Press, 1982), 39–46.

66. On the well-understood connection between decentralized administration and Jim Crow, see Lieberman, *Shifting the Color Line*, 52–55.

67. SSA, Title I, § 2(a)(1); Title IV, § 402(a)(1); Title X, § 1002(a)(1).

68. SSA, Title I, § 2(a)(4); Title IV, § 402(a)(4); Title X, § 1002(a)(4). Although the act specifically referenced only the denial of assistance, the SSB interpreted any dissatisfaction regarding the amount of assistance granted as the equivalent of a denial. Robert Lansdale et al., *The Administration of Old Age Assistance* (Chicago: Public Administration Service, 1939), 299n4. The administration of the fair hearing provision is taken up in more detail in Chapters 3 and 4.

69. This logic appears in reforms from previous decades. Rebecca McLennan notes that when New York attempted to create a centralized, statewide prison system, the State Prison Commissioners extended "quasi-legal protections and entitlements to the prisoners" and "independent channels of appeal." The idea, apparently, was to create a mechanism of surveillance over prison keepers and to discourage them from abusing their charges. Rebecca M. McLennan, *The Crisis of Imprisonment: Protest, Politics, and the Making of the American Penal State, 1776–1941* (New York: Cambridge University Press, 2008): 228–29.

70. SSA, §§ 3(a)(1), 1003(a)(1).

71. On the rise and fall of institutionalization, see David L. Rothman, *Conscience and Convenience: The Asylum and Its Alternatives in Progressive America* (Boston: Little, Brown, 1980); Katz, *In the Shadow of the Poorhouse*; Timothy Hacsi, *Second Home: Orphan Asylums and Poor Families in America* (Cambridge, MA: Harvard University Press, 1997).

72. SSA, §§ 6, 406, 1006. In the words of Viviana Zelizer, this provision established the legal basis for a "revolutionary reinterpretation of the consumer sovereignty of poor people." Viviana A. Zelizer, *The Social Meaning of Money* (New York: Basic Books, 1994), 190.

73. Charles Irwin Schottland, interview by Frances Lomas Feldman, January 5, 7, and 8, 1987, transcript, California Social Welfare Archives' Oral History Collection, University of Southern California, Los Angeles; Brown, *Public Relief*, 16.

74. Zelizer, *The Social Meaning of Money*, 143–69, 189–92; see also Joanna Carver Colcord, *Cash Relief* (New York: Russell Sage Foundation, 1936).

75. Dauber, *The Sympathetic State*, 79–125, 185–223; Dorothy C. Kahn, "The Use of Cash, Orders for Goods, or Relief in Kind, in a Mass Program," in *Proceedings of the National Conference of Social Work* (Chicago: University of Chicago Press, 1933), 270–79.

76. Elisa Martia Alvarez Minoff, "Free to Move? The Law and Politics of Internal Migration in Twentieth-Century America," PhD diss., Harvard University, 2013, 29–33; SSA, §§ 2(a), 402(a), 1002(a).

77. See, generally, Katz, *In the Shadow of the Poorhouse*; Gordon, *Pitied but Not Entitled*; Gwendolyn Mink, *The Wages of Motherhood: Inequality in the Welfare State, 1917–1942* (Ithaca, NY: Cornell University Press, 1995); Lieberman, *Shifting the Color Line*; Mettler, *Dividing Citizens*; Michael K. Brown, *Race, Money, and the American Welfare State* (Ithaca, NY: Cornell University Press, 1999); Alice Kessler-Harris, "In the Nation's Image: The Gendered Limits of Social Citizenship in the Depression Era," *Journal of American History* 86, no. 3 (1999): 1251–79; Fox, *Three Worlds of Relief*.

78. Within just a few decades, policy expert Gilbert Steiner could describe the poor as "the personification of the captive group," utterly dependent on government for support. Gilbert Y. Steiner, *Social Insecurity: The Politics of Welfare* (Chicago: Rand McNally & Company, 1966), 3.

79. Frank Bane to the League of Women Voters, Cincinnati, April 29, 1936, Box 7, FBP.

80. Frank Bane, "Administrative Problems and Progress of the Social Security Board," address, Brookings Institution, Washington, DC, April 6, 1937, quoted in Coll, *Safety Net*, 58.

81. In theory, a plan was like a contract between a state and the federal government. In practice, such plans were untidy compilations of all the state laws and regulations relating to public assistance. Derthick, *The Influence of Federal Grants*, 22.

82. SSA, §§ 1, 401, 1001. On the swift increase in federal funding, see Bureau of Research and Statistics and Division of Public Assistance Research, "Sources of Funds Expended for the Special Types of Public Assistance in 1939," *Social Security Bulletin* 3, no. 7 (1940): 45–72, 45 (noting that in 1939, federal expenditures for the three categorical assistance programs amounted to over $243 million).

83. SSA, §§ 4, 404, 1004. This was a departure from the FERA years, when the federal government had the power to instead assume control over state administration. Federal Emergency Relief Act of 1933, Pub. L. No. 15, 48 Stat. 55 (1933), § 3(b); Brown, *Public Relief*, 208–9.

84. This leadership structure lasted for just over a decade. In 1946 the Social Security Board became the Social Security Administration and the powers vested in the three board members were transferred to a single commissioner (Arthur Altmeyer). Reorganization Plan No. 2 of 1946, Pub. L. No. 79-263, 59 Stat. 613 (1946), § 4.

85. Bane, interview by Leiby, January 13, 1965.

86. Linda Gordon, writing about ADC, has characterized the administrators who controlled the program as "social insurance advocates," not professional social workers. She described the Social Security Board as ADC's "wicked stepmother." Gordon, *Pitied but Not Entitled*, 272. To the Roosevelt administration's credit, Labor Secretary Frances Perkins asked Grace Abbott, one of the nation's preeminent social workers, to serve on the board, but she declined. Lela B. Costin, *Two Sisters for Social Justice: A Biography of Grace and Edith Abbott* (Urbana: University of Illinois Press, 1983), 226.

87. Bary, interview by Parker, January 13, 1973.

88. Frank Bane, interview by James R. W. Leiby, January 14, 1965, transcript, Regional Oral History Office, University of California, Berkeley; Albert Henry Aronson, interview by Peter A. Corning, February 18, 1965, transcript, Columbia Center for Oral History, Columbia University, New York; Bary, interview by Parker, January 13, 1973.

89. Daniel P. Carpenter, *The Forging of Bureaucratic Autonomy: Reputations, Networks, and Policy Innovation in Executive Agencies, 1862–1928* (Princeton, NJ: Princeton University Press, 2001), 19–21.

90. Mark P. Hale, "The Process of Developing Policy for a Federal-State Grant-in-Aid Program, as Illustrated by the Work of the Social Security Board, 1935–46," *Social Service Review* 31, no. 3 (1957): 290–310, 293; Social Security Board, *First Annual Report of the Social Security Board* (Washington, DC: U.S. Government Printing Office, 1936), 3–4; Saiyid Zafar Hasan, "Policy Formulation and Development in Public Assistance: A Study of the Role of the Federal Government in the First Five Years of the Social Security Act, 1935–1940," PhD diss., New York School of Social Work, Columbia University, 1958, 107. The BPA's regional representatives were supposed to report to their regional directors, but in practice they often took their concerns directly to the central BPA office in Washington. There was some feeling among the BPA personnel (as well as among the Office of the General Counsel personnel) that the regional directors were "general practitioners" who could not appreciate the technical problems that were apparent to those with more expertise. Bane, interview by Leiby, January 13, 1965.

91. Jane Margueretta Hoey, interview by Peter A. Corning, March 10, 1965, transcript, Columbia Center for Oral History, Columbia University, New York.

92. Bary, interview by Parker, January 13, 1973.

93. Ibid.; Bane, interview by Leiby, January 13, 1965; Charles McKinley and Robert W. Frase, *Launching Social Security: A Capture-and-Record Account, 1935–1937* (Madison: University of Wisconsin Press, 1970), 180–81. The "red-headed blue-eyed" quote is from Maurine Mulliner, interview by Peter A. Corning, April 26, 1967, transcript, Columbia Center for Oral History, Columbia University, New York.

94. Lansdale et al., *Administration of Old Age Assistance*, 16.

95. From 1935 to 1938 the SSB had its own general counsel's office, one of its five service bureaus. When the Federal Security Agency came into being in 1939, that office became GC for the entire FSA. Fowler Harper to Paul V. McNutt, October 10, 1939, Box 12, GC Correspondence on PA, HEWR.

96. McKinley and Frase, *Launching Social Security*, 197–217; Altmeyer, interview by Peter A. Corning, June 29, 1967. The board also initiated official measures to rein in the auditors, such as issuing instructions on "the limitations of their duties." McKinley and Frase, *Launching Social Security*, 216.

97. Ellen Black Winston, interview by Blanche D. Coll, September 13, 1982, transcript, Columbia Center for Oral History, Columbia University, New York.

98. Jane Margueretta Hoey, interview by Peter A. Corning, January 31, 1966, transcript, Columbia Center for Oral History, Columbia University, New York.

99. To give a sense of the scope of this effort, in just one month in 1943 the GC's public assistance duties required attorneys in Washington, DC, to participate in 71 group conferences involving 289 people and 496 oral and telephone conversations; write 26 legal opinions; study and comment on 95 state bills and 196 state laws (submitted to them by the Bureau) and draft 233 responses; review 117 state plan amendments; deal with 27 opinions by state attorneys general; review 30 memos from regional attorneys; and clear

20 submissions to the Board. Jack B. Tate to Paul V. McNutt, June 10, 1943, Box 12, GC Correspondence on PA, HEWR.
100. Thomas H. Eliot, *Recollections of the New Deal: When the People Mattered* (Boston: Northeastern University Press, 1992), 126–28; Jack B. Tate, interview by Peter A. Corning, June 3, 1965, transcript, Columbia Center for Oral History, Columbia University, New York. Altmeyer freely admitted his suspicion of lawyers. Reflecting on his time on the board and later as head of the Social Security Administration, he recalled how he "half-jokingly and half-seriously" had to "take [the lawyers] to task and insist that they stay within their role of adviser not line officer." Altmeyer, interview by Corning, June 29, 1967.
101. Hoey, interview by Corning, January 31, 1966.
102. Clark Bane Hutchinson, interview by Larry DeWitt, July 18, 1997, transcript, Social Security Administration, http://www.socialsecurity.gov/his tory/fbane.html.
103. On colleagues' impressions of Eliot, see Dauber, *Sympathetic State*, 135–36. Jerold Auerbach famously characterized the New Deal as "a lawyers' deal" because "lawyers' skills – drafting, negotiation, compromise – and lawyers' values – process divorced from substance – permitted its achievements, yet set its boundaries." Jerold S. Auerbach, "Lawyers Who Govern," review of *A Question of Judgment: The Fortas Case and the Struggle for the Supreme Court*, by Robert Shogan, and *Kennedy Justice*, by Victor S. Navasky, *Reviews in American History* 1, no. 1 (1973): 146–51; see also Jerold S. Auerbach, *Unequal Justice: Lawyers and Social Change in Modern America* (New York: Oxford University Press, 1976); Peter H. Irons, *New Deal Lawyers* (Princeton, NJ: Princeton University Press, 1982). Ronen Shamir has moved the conversation beyond legal professionals to note how heavily the New Deal relied on law and legal discourse. Ronen Shamir, *Managing Legal Uncertainty: Elite Lawyers in the New Deal* (Durham, NC: Duke University Press, 1995), 2. For a similar argument, tailored to the National Labor Relations Board, see Christopher L. Tomlins, *The State and the Unions: Labor Relations, Law, and the Organized Labor Movement in America, 1880–1960* (Cambridge: Cambridge University Press, 1985). By making the case for lawyers' power within the SSB, I do not mean to imply that the lawyers there were as important as they were in, for example, the Agricultural Adjustment Administration, the National Recovery Administration, or the National Labor Relations Board. The variability of lawyerly dominance across the New Deal merits greater study. I also do not intend to generalize about the "New Deal lawyer." For every high-flying Frankfurter protégé, Michele Landis Dauber has observed, there were hundreds of "older, more anonymous government lawyers" who "treated representing the New Deal as ordinary legal work." This project supports her important revision to the literature. Michele Landis Dauber, "New Deal Lawyers," in *Encyclopedia of the Supreme Court of the United States*, ed. David S. Tanenhaus (New York: Gale Cengage Learning, 2009), 399, 401.
104. Frank Bane, "The Social Security Board and State Organizations," *Annals of the American Academy of Political and Social Science* 202 (March 1939):

137–44, 137–38; Frank E. Horack Jr., "Federal-State Cooperation for Social Security: The Grant-in-Aid," *Illinois Law Review* 30, no. 3 (1935–36): 292–313, 292; see also Jane Perry Clark, *The Rise of a New Federalism: Federal-State Cooperation in the United States* (New York: Columbia University Press, 1939).

105. Arthur Chester Millspaugh, *Public Welfare Organization* (Washington, DC: Brookings Institution, 1935), 131, 145–76.

106. Bary, interview by Parker, January 13, 1973; Bane, interview by Leiby, January 13, 1965. Loula Dunn, who worked for various Alabama public welfare and relief agencies and later became director of the American Public Welfare Association, agreed: "those were the days when it was relatively – as compared to with later days – easy to go in and say, 'The federal government says you must do this in order to get the federal money.'" Loula Dunn, interview by Peter A. Corning, August 3, 1965, transcript, Columbia Center for Oral History, Columbia University, New York. On the specific concerns of state legislatures, see Harry Greenstein, "Problems Confronting State Welfare Administrations in Accepting Grants-in-Aid, " in *Proceedings of the National Conference of Social Work* (Chicago: University of Chicago Press, 1936).

107. McKinley and Frase, *Launching Social Security*, 153–54; Coll, *Safety Net*, 69. In at least one instance, a state secured even more tailored assistance: after a board emissary told the governor of Colorado that the SSB intended to reject his state's plans, he ordered her to sit down with his deputy attorney general and legislative reference counsel, "write laws that you do like," and have them on the desks of Colorado state legislators the following morning. Bary, interview by Parker, January 13, 1973.

108. Brown, *Public Relief*, 408; Coll, *Safety Net*, 69, 73; Bary, interview by Parker, January 13, 1973.

109. By December of 1936 the board had approved forty-two OAA plans, twenty-seven ADC plans, and twenty-eight AB plans. From 1935 through 1940, the board disapproved of only twelve plans, and of these all were eventually approved. Coll, *Safety Net*, 77–78; Hasan, "Policy Formulation and Development in Public Assistance," 146, 148.

110. McKinley and Frase, *Launching Social Security*, 145–47; Hasan, "Policy Formulation and Development in Public Assistance," 100. In 1936 the board rejected Kansas's plans (all three), Colorado's plans (all three), Minnesota's OAA plan and AB plan, Illinois's OAA plan, and California's AB plan. In 1937 and 1938, the board disapproved New Jersey's ADC plan and Pennsylvania's AB plan, respectively. Mark P. Hale, "The Federal Role in Public Assistance," PhD diss., University of Chicago, 1956, 147.

111. Hale, "The Federal Role in Public Assistance," 206–10; Elwood B. Davis, "Family versus Individual Budgeting in Old Age Assistance Grants in Wisconsin," *Social Service Review* 16, no. 2 (1942): 278–308, 281.

112. Hasan, "Policy Formulation and Development in Public Assistance," 121–24.

113. McKinley and Frase, *Launching Social Security*, 174–76.

114. McKinley and Frase, *Launching Social Security*, 169–74; David J. Maurer, "Relief Problems and Politics in Ohio," in *The New Deal*, ed. John Braeman, Robert H. Bremner, and David Brody (Columbus: Ohio State University Press, 1975), 2:92.

115. Pierce Atwater, "The County as a Unit for Co-Ordinate Planning and Service in Public and Private Social Work," in *Proceedings of the National Conference of Social Work* (Chicago: University of Chicago Press, 1937), 369.

116. William Haber, "Problems of State Administration," in *Proceedings of the National Conference of Social Work* (Chicago: University of Chicago Press, 1937); Federal Security Agency, Social Security Administration, Bureau of Public Assistance, "Public Assistance 1941," in *Public Assistance 1941*, Public Assistance Report no. 4 (Washington, DC: U.S. Government Printing Office, 1941), 22. (NB: these figures include expenditures for work relief and subsistence grants, but not care given in institutions). The fact that local contributions remained significant helps explain why FERA preferred to issue funds to state agencies rather than local ones. As one New Deal administrator later explained, direct grants to the local level would have simply made local units more powerful in relation to the states, and thereby further entrenched a system of relief that reformers considered embarrassingly primitive. Elizabeth Wickenden, interview by Blanche D. Coll, May 28, 1986, transcript, Box 2, M99-098, EWP.

117. Stevenson, *Public Welfare Administration*, 90.

118. Bane, "Social Security Board and State Organizations," 140; see also Robert T. Lansdale, "These Public Welfare Boards," *Survey* 73, no. 3 (1937): 67–69, 67.

119. David C. Adie, "Responsibility of the State in the Supervision of Public Welfare Programs," *Social Service Review* 13, no. 4 (1939): 611–25, 618.

120. Potter, Colby, and Liveright, "The County as a Public Welfare Unit," 452.

121. Katz, *In the Shadow of the Poorhouse*, 217. For more on the stunning state-by-state variety of local welfare organizations as of 1934, see Millspaugh, *Public Welfare Organization*, 205–23, 276–300.

122. Wilfred S. Reynolds, "Public Welfare Administration a Patchwork in Illinois," *Social Service Review* 6, no. 1 (1937): 1–8, 6.

123. Glick, *Illinois Emergency Relief Commission*, 11–12. On the gender of the local officials who had been administering poor relief, see Stein-Roggenbuck, *Negotiating Relief*, 120; Traverso, *Welfare Politics in Boston*, 48.

124. Brown, *Public Relief*, 14–15. A 1934 Pennsylvania State Department of Welfare study produced similar findings: almost one-third of the "poor directors" surveyed were farmers; on the side, they administered outdoor relief, supervised almshouses, and admitted almshouse inmates. Levy, *Study in Public Relations*, 23. Similarly, in Rhode Island a study found that the job of overseer of the poor was something that "housewives, farmers, [and] business and professional men" did on a part-time basis. Creech, *Three Centuries of Poor Law Administration*, 240.

125. Brown, *Public Relief*, 14–16; see also Levy, *Study in Public Relations*, 23.

126. Brown, *Public Relief*, 220–21; Dorothy C. Kahn, "Problems in the Administration of Relief," *Annals of the American Academy of Political and Social Science* 176 (November 1934): 40–48, 43.
127. Bane, interview by Leiby, January 9, 1965.
128. Marjorie Anne Merrill, "Lessons Learned in Personnel Selection and Management in Emergency Relief Administration," in *Proceedings of the National Conference of Social Work* (Chicago: University of Chicago Press, 1936); Brown, *Public Relief*, 221, 278.
129. Brown, *Public Relief*, 216. Former FERA administrator Arlien Johnson agreed. Reflecting on her time stationed in Olympia, Washington, she noted "great resistance in the counties, among the county welfare supervisors, to having anything interfere with their own operation of poor relief." Arlien Johnson, interview by Vida S. Grayson, August 18, 1978, transcript, Columbia Center for Oral History, Columbia University, New York.
130. Dunn, interview by Corning, August 3, 1965.
131. Quoted in Stein-Roggenbuck, *Negotiating Relief*, 184.
132. Brock, *Welfare, Democracy, and the New Deal*, 174; Stein-Roggenbuck, *Negotiating Relief*, 120–21, 24.
133. Anonymous to Harry L. Hopkins, September 1935, quoted in *Down & Out in the Great Depression: Letters from the Forgotten Man*, ed. Robert S. McElvaine (Chapel Hill: University of North Carolina Press, 2008), 141. This letter was not exceptional. In another from McElvaine's compilation, the writer complained about the "salaried bunch" running the local relief office: they "brought their friends and their friends from other towns to work in the office," as if "the men and women from town here was dum [*sic*].... [P]lenty of high schooled people in town on relief could been give them Jobs and not been kept on relief." P.W.A. workers to Harry L. Hopkins, December 31, 1935, quoted in ibid., 214.
134. Gertrude Springer and Helen Cody Barker, "Social Workers Grope for Unity," *Survey* 73, no. 6 (1937): 179–91, 185 (quoting William Haber of the Michigan Emergency Relief Commission).
135. Glick, *Illinois Emergency Relief Commission*, 237–38; "The ABC of A.D.C. in Chicago," *Social Service Review* 15, no. 4 (1941): 753–57.
136. Hale, "The Federal Role in Public Assistance," 102; Edith Abbott, "Public Welfare and Politics," *Social Service Review* 10, no. 3 (1936): 395–412, 401.
137. V. O. Key Jr., "State Administration of the Social Security Act," *Annals of the American Academy of Political and Social Science* 202 (March 1939): 153–58, 155. Josephine Brown estimated that in 1939, state and local public assistance divisions employed approximately 60,000 persons, including clerical workers, to administer categorical assistance. Brown, *Public Relief*, 397.
138. Coll, *Safety Net*, 68–69.
139. In terms of the state systems that federal administrators envisioned, there are striking resonances with historian Rebecca McLennan's account of the state-use labor system that New York developed around the turn of the twentieth century: from "a motley collection of old and decaying prisons, each of which had been ... an isolated, autonomous institution subject to

local political patronage practices," reformers attempted to create "a single, centralized, and bureaucratically administered prison system." McLennan, *The Crisis of Imprisonment*, 203. The difficulties that attended prison reform were compounded in the poor relief context, where the impetus for state-level centralization and bureaucratization did not necessarily come from the states themselves, but from the federal level.

140. Coll, *Safety Net*, 71–72; McKinley and Frase, *Launching Social Security*, 158.

141. McKinley and Frase, *Launching Social Security*, 166–68.

142. Derthick, *The Influence of Federal Grants*, 84.

143. Coll, *Safety Net*, 76–77; Stevenson, *Public Welfare Administration*, 193; Hasan, "Policy Formulation and Development in Public Assistance," 311.

144. Teaford, *Rise of the States*, 12.

145. Ibid., 121. Historian Alan Brinkley has advanced a related argument: he notes that by remaining sensitive to local concerns in the short term – for example, by adopting decentralized program structures – New Deal reformers sapped strength in the longer term from those who opposed centralization and bureaucratization. Brinkley, *Voices of Protest*, 248.

146. New State Ice Company, 285 U.S. at 311 (Brandeis, J., dissenting). On Biddle's Department of Justice murals, see Roger G. Kennedy, *When Art Worked: The New Deal, Art, and Democracy* (New York: Rizzoli, 2009).

147. Robert M. Cover, "Violence and the Word," *Yale Law Journal* 95, no. 8 (1986): 1604.

148. This language of puzzling – and the general idea of puzzling as "part of the work" of statecraft – borrows from Margot Canaday, *The Straight State: Sexuality and Citizenship in Twentieth-Century America* (Princeton, NJ: Princeton University Press, 2009), 3; Canaday, in turn, borrows it from Hugh Heclo, *Modern Social Politics in Britain and Sweden: From Relief to Income Maintenance* (New Haven, CT: Yale University Press, 1974), 305.

2   RIGHTS AS AN ADMINISTRATIVE TOOL

1. W. B. Hayes to George V. Gillie, March 12, 1939, Box 26, GC Correspondence, HEWR. On the conjunction of alienage and pauperism in U.S. history, see Kunal M. Parker, "State, Citizenship, and Territory: The Legal Construction of Immigrants in Antebellum Massachusetts," *Law and History Review* 19, no. 3 (2001).

2. George V. Gillie to W. B. Hayes, March 15, 1939, Box 26, GC Correspondence, HEWR.

3. W. B. Hayes to George V. Gillie, February 18, 1940, Box 26, GC Correspondence, HEWR.

4. Federal Security Agency, in collaboration with Bureau of Accounts and Audits and Office of the General Counsel, *Money Payments to Recipients of Old-Age Assistance, Aid to Dependent Children, and Aid to the Blind* (Washington, DC: U.S. Government Printing Office, 1944).

5. Hendrik Hartog, "The Constitution of Aspiration and 'The Rights That Belong to Us All,'" *Journal of American History* 74, no. 3 (1987): 1016–17; see also Daniel T. Rodgers, "Rights Consciousness in American History," in *The Bill of Rights in Modern America after 200 Years*, ed. David J. Bodenhamer and James W. Ely Jr., (Bloomington: Indiana University Press, 1993), 8–24; John P. Reid, *The Constitutional History of the American Revolution*, vol. 1: *The Authority of Rights* (Madison: University of Wisconsin Press, 1986); Elizabeth B. Clark, "'The Sacred Rights of the Weak': Pain, Sympathy, and the Culture of Individual Rights in Antebellum America," *Journal of American History* 82, no. 2 (1995): 463–93; Felicia Kornbluh, "To Fulfill Their 'Rightly Needs': Consumerism and the National Welfare Rights Movement," *Radical History Review* 69 (1997): 76–113; Richard A. Primus, *The American Language of Rights* (Cambridge: Cambridge University Press, 1999); and Laura F. Edwards, *A Legal History of the Civil War and Reconstruction: A Nation of Rights* (New York: Cambridge University Press, 2015).

6. By the early nineteenth century, sociologist T. H. Marshall has explained, the English Poor Law "treated the claims of the poor not as an integral part of the rights of the citizen, but as an alternative to them—as claims which could be met only if the claimants ceased to be citizens in any true sense of the word." T. H. Marshall, "Citizenship and Social Class," in *Citizenship and Social Class and Other Essays*, 1–85 (Cambridge: Cambridge University Press, 1950), 24. Others have extended his insight to the U.S. and into the twentieth century. Frances Fox Piven and Richard Cloward, for example, found that as late as 1934, fourteen states deprived relief recipients of the right to vote or hold office. Frances Fox Piven and Richard A. Cloward, *Regulating the Poor: The Functions of Public Welfare* (New York: Pantheon, 1971), 166; see also Chad Alan Goldberg, *Citizens and Paupers: Relief, Rights, and Race, from the Freedmen's Bureau to Workfare* (Chicago: University of Chicago Press, 2008).

7. Jack B. Tate to Paul V. McNutt, May 12, 1941, Box 12, GC Correspondence on PA, HEWR.

8. For a summary of the "rights talk" literature, see Karen M. Tani, "Welfare and Rights before the Movement: Rights as a Language of the State," *Yale Law Journal* 122 (2012): 369–72. Recent additions to the literature include George I. Lovell, *This Is Not Civil Rights: Discovering Rights Talk in 1939 America* (Chicago: University of Chicago Press, 2012); Emily Zackin, *Looking for Rights in All the Wrong Places: Why State Constitutions Contain America's Positive Rights* (Princeton, NJ: Princeton University Press, 2013); Michael McCann, "The Unbearable Lightness of Rights: On Sociolegal Inquiry in the Global Era," *Law & Society Review* 48, no. 2 (2014): 245–73, and the comments in the same issue; Lee B. Wilson, "A Manifest Violations of the Rights of Englishmen: Rights Talk and the Law of Property in Early Eighteenth-Century Jamaica," *Law and History Review* 33, no. 3 (2015): 543–76.

9. Although some scholars have noted rights language within New Deal public assistance administration, they have neglected to consider the audience that federal administrators targeted and have therefore not made the claim that I advance in this chapter. William Simon's revisionist welfare rights article called attention to the rights language in a number of federal public assistance

communications from the 1940s, but Simon's interest was the value of this rights discourse as "jurisprudence," and specifically as an alternative to the jurisprudence that animated the welfare rights test cases of the late 1960s and 1970s. He was not interested in questions about the nature or function of rights in the New Deal administrative state. William H. Simon, "The Invention and Reinvention of Welfare Rights," *Maryland Law Review* 44, no. 1 (1985): 1–37. Historian Linda Gordon has also noted this administrative "rights talk" (my phrasing, not hers), but has characterized it as a convenient rhetorical mask for the "needs talk" that she believes dominated professional social work (and differentiated predominantly female social workers from the predominantly male advocates of social insurance). Linda Gordon, "Social Insurance and Public Assistance: The Influence of Gender in Welfare Thought in the United States, 1890–1935," *American Historical Review* 97, no. 1 (1992): 33–35. I do not mean to imply, however, that I am alone in writing about administrators' constructions of rights or administrative uses of rights language. The argument I advance here is in productive conversation, for example, with recent work on rights of conscience in selective service administration during World War I. See Jeremy K. Kessler, "The Administrative Origins of Modern Civil Liberties Law," *Columbia Law Review* 114 (2014): 1083–1166. I am also in dialogue with other scholars writing about the role of rights in efforts to undermine or displace more locally oriented legal regimes. See, in particular, Laura F. Edwards, *The People and Their Peace: Legal Culture and the Transformation of Inequality in the Post-Revolutionary South* (Chapel Hill: University of North Carolina Press, 2009).

10. John G. Winant, "An Approach to Social Security," *Atlantic Monthly* 158 (July 1936); Arthur J. Altmeyer, "Speech to Catholic Charities," quoted in Jerry R. Cates, *Insuring Inequality: Administrative Leadership in Social Security, 1935–1954* (Ann Arbor: University of Michigan Press, 1983), 30.

11. Jill Quadagno, *The Transformation of Old Age Security* (Chicago: University of Chicago Press, 1988), 66–72.

12. On the movement for old age pensions, see, generally, Edwin Amenta, *When Movements Matter: The Townsend Plan and the Rise of Social Security* (Princeton, NJ: Princeton University Press, 2006); Alan Brinkley, *Voices of Protest: Huey Long, Father Coughlin, and the Great Depression* (New York: Vintage Books, 1982).

13. Committee on Economic Security, *Report to the President of the Committee on Economic Security* (Washington, DC: U.S. Government Printing Office, 1935), 1330.

14. The precise name for the program from 1935 to 1937 was Federal Old-Age Benefits. The name was changed to Old-Age Insurance in September 1937, and was changed again, to Old-Age and Survivors Insurance, in September 1939, in recognition of Congress's decision to expand coverage to dependents and survivors of covered earners.

15. Edward D. Berkowitz, *America's Welfare State: From Roosevelt to Reagan* (Baltimore: Johns Hopkins University Press, 1991), 29–37; see also Edwin E. Witte, "Old Age Security in the Social Security Act," *Journal of Political Economy* 45, no. 1 (1937): 10, which reported disapprovingly that

"popularly, however, old age assistance is called 'old age pensions,' and there is a widespread notion that everyone who reaches a specified age is entitled to a pension and a still more prevalent notion that all eligible persons should receive the same grants." For an example of confused media coverage, see "How Security Bill Aids Aged and Idle," *NYT*, August 15, 1935.

16. Louis LaCoss, "Missourians Rush for Old-Age Grant," *NYT*, September 8, 1935.

17. "Urges Big Pension Fund," *NYT*, September 8, 1935; "2,000 Townsend Aides Assemble in Chicago," *NYT*, October 24, 1935; George P. West, "Townsend's Plan Widely Supported," *NYT*, November 3, 1935; "Politicians Worry over Townsendism," *NYT*, November 24, 1935.

18. Quoted in Cates, *Insuring Inequality*, 29.

19. For the same reason, the SSB encouraged states to limit OAA to the truly needy and discouraged them from promising assistance grants that were more liberal than the federal government had anticipated. "Obviously," SSB staff member Alvin Roseman explained in 1939, "if liberal old-age assistance payments are made to all persons reaching 65, contributory old-age insurance becomes futile." Alvin Roseman, "Old-Age Assistance," *Annals of the American Academy of Political and Social Science* 202 (1939): 58.

20. For more on the two-track welfare state, see works cited in the section "Welfare, Rights, and the Administrative Reconfiguration of Citizenship" in the Introduction to this volume.

21. See, for example, Henry Edward Manning, "Distress in London: A Note on Outdoor Relief," *Fortnightly Review* 49 (1888).

22. See, for example, John A. Ryan, *A Living Wage: Its Ethical and Economic Aspects* (New York: Macmillan, 1906); John A. Ryan, "A Program of Social Reform by Legislation," *Catholic World* 89 (1909); John A. Ryan, *Distributive Justice: The Right and Wrong of Our Present Distribution of Wealth* (New York: Macmillan, 1916); and William Joseph Kerby, *The Social Mission of Charity* (New York: Macmillan, 1921).

23. Jane M. Hoey, "Social Work Concepts and Methods in the Postwar World," in *National Conference of Social Work* (New York: Columbia University Press, 1944), 36–37.

24. June Hopkins, *Harry Hopkins: Sudden Hero, Brash Reformer* (New York: St. Martin's Press, 1999), 94 (quoting "Report on Outdoor Relief," in *Proceedings of the Conference of Charities*, 1877).

25. Morton Keller, *Affairs of State: Public Life in Late Nineteenth-Century America* (Cambridge, MA: Harvard University Press, 1977), 127.

26. Roy Lubove, *The Struggle for Social Security: 1900–1935* (Cambridge, MA: Harvard University Press, 1968), 101–6; Josephine Chapin Brown, *Public Relief, 1929–1939* (New York: Henry Holt and Company, 1940), 45–48; Brian Gratton, "Social Workers and Old Age Pensions," *Social Service Review* 57, no. 3 (1983): 403–15.

27. Hertha Kraus, "Memorandum regarding Discussion of Social Welfare Programs in the Federal, State, and Local Governments," American Association of Social Workers, Division on Government and Social Work, Committee to Outline a National Social Welfare Program, November 23,

1934, Box 19, National Association of Social Workers and Predecessor Organizations Records, Social Welfare History Archives, University of Minnesota, Minneapolis [hereafter cited as NASWR]. Kraus hailed from Germany, where government income support had wider acceptance. But Kraus's ideas could not have been too far outside the mainstream, for the Roosevelt administration hired her as an early advisor to the Social Security Board. Beate Bussiek, "Hertha Kraus: Quaker Spirit and Competence: Impulses for Professional Social Work in Germany and the United States," in *History of Social Work in Europe (1900–1960): Female Pioneers and Their Influence on the Development of International Social Organization*, ed. Sabine Hering and Berteke Waaldijk (Opladen: Verlag Leske & Budrich, 2003), 53–64. Similar statements issued from home-grown social workers. Writing for the same social work organization the following year, Joanna Colcord urged that the organization "hold [as] self-evident that whenever a citizen is genuinely unable to provide for his own subsistence and that of his dependents through his own efforts, he has a right to look for it to government." Joanna C. Colcord, "The Responsibility of Government for Relief," tentative draft of report from the American Association of Social Workers Committee on Current Relief Program, Division on Government and Social Work, Box 19, NASWR; see also American Association of Social Workers, Division on Government and Social Work, "Outline for a Federal Assistance Program," in *This Business of Relief: Proceedings of the Delegate Conference, American Association of Social Workers, Washington, D.C., February 14–16, 1936* (New York: American Association of Social Workers, 1936).

28. Hopkins, *Harry Hopkins*, 190. Historians of mothers' pensions would disagree with Hopkins's statement. Nonetheless, it survives as an example of how positively federal government social workers viewed social welfare policies that treated recipients as rights holders.

29. Perkins, *The Roosevelt I Knew*, 284.

30. "'Respectable' Base for Relief Urged," *NYT*, May 17, 1935; Gordon Hamilton, "Case-Work Responsibility in the Unemployment Relief Agency," in *National Conference of Social Work* (Chicago: University of Chicago Press, 1934), 393. The statements of New York social workers are particularly relevant because the experts tasked with designing and implementing the New Deal relief programs often came directly from New York–based charities, agencies, and schools, probably because of President and Mrs. Roosevelt's strong political and social ties to New York state.

31. On the differences between the rights talk coming from social workers and that coming from lawyers, see Chapter 3.

32. SSA, §§ 2(a)(4), 402(a)(4), 1002(a)(4).

33. Jules H. Berman, "The Administration of the Appeal Provisions of the Public Assistance Legislation," master's thesis, University of Chicago School of Social Service Administration, 1937, 1; Brown, *Public Relief*, 373.

34. Lochner v. New York, 198 U.S. 45 (1905); Risa Lauren Goluboff, *The Lost Promise of Civil Rights* (Cambridge, MA: Harvard University Press, 2007), 16–24.

35. On those traditional distinctions, see Wesley Newcomb Hohfeld, "Fundamental Legal Conceptions as Applied in Judicial Reasoning," *Yale Law Journal* 23, no. 1 (1913): 30.
36. Emmett Delaney to Thomas Eliot, October 23, 1935, Box 10, GC Correspondence on PA, HEWR. Delaney's confusion was widely shared: the question of whether to characterize government benefits as "a common law right subject to protection through judicial process" or "a legislative interest capable of adjustment by whatever process promoted the general welfare" plagued the U.S. administrative state in the twentieth century. Jerry L. Mashaw, "'Rights' in the Federal Administrative State," *Yale Law Journal* 92, no. 7 (1983): 1163.
37. Sue S. White to Thomas Eliot, November 14, 1935, Box 236, Central File (1935–1947), Record Group 47, Records of the Social Security Administration, National Archives, College Park, Md. [hereafter cited as SSAR].
38. Jack Tate, "Opportunity for a Fair Hearing," April 27, 1936, Box 95, Office of the Commissioner, Chairman's Files, 1935–1942, SSAR. As for why the GC's office decided to take this position, one factor may have been the vulnerability of the Social Security Act to judicial evisceration. When Tate wrote his memo in 1936, the legality of the SSA had not been tested before the Supreme Court, but a court challenge appeared inevitable. (Not until May 1937 would the Court uphold the act's controversial Unemployment Compensation and Old Age Insurance titles.) Conservative critiques from the legal community likely also affected the GC's office. The powerful American Bar Association and the "increasingly dyspeptic" Roscoe Pound, one of the nation's foremost legal scholars, were skeptical about agency decision making and seemed likely to use the Due Process Clause as a weapon—a way of showing how agencies violated citizens' constitutional rights. By interpreting the act as he did, Tate may have been trying to head off such attacks. Historians have found that such thinking motivated other New Deal lawyers. See Christopher L. Tomlins, *The State and the Unions: Labor Relations, Law, and the Organized Labor Movement in America, 1880–1960* (Cambridge: Cambridge University Press, 1985), 154; Joanna L. Grisinger, "Law in Action: The Attorney General's Committee on Administrative Procedure," *Journal of Policy History* 20, no. 3 (2008): 388. On Pound, specifically, see John Fabian Witt, *Patriots and Cosmopolitans: Hidden Histories of American Law* (Cambridge, MA: Harvard University Press, 2007), 231–34. It is also possible that Tate wanted to preserve a space for lawyers within the crowded New Deal bureaucracy. Although there were many terms in the Social Security Act that other experts in the bureaucracy (social workers, accountants) could conceivably interpret, Tate once observed in an address to other federal government lawyers, terms such as "fair hearing" were within the lawyer's exclusive jurisdiction and should be claimed as such. Jack B. Tate, "The Problem of Advice in the Administration of Social Security Laws," *Federal Bar Association Journal* 3, no. 2 (1939): 320.

39. Robert Johnston to A. Delafield Smith, March 28, 1938, Box 8, GC Correspondence on PA, HEWR.
40. Frank Bane, "The Social Security Board and State Organizations," *Annals of the American Academy of Political and Social Science* 202 (March 1939): 144.
41. Jack Charnow and Saul Kaplan, "Public Assistance Personnel, Jan.–June 1943," *Social Security Bulletin* 7, no. 7 (1944): 20. Similar figures were reported the following year. Division of Statistics and Analysis, Bureau of Public Assistance, Social Security Administration, "Personnel in State and Local Public Assistance Agencies, June 1949," *Social Security Bulletin* 13, no. 4 (1950): 7.
42. Jane M. Hoey, "The Federal Government and Desirable Standards of State and Local Administration," in *National Conference of Social Work* (Chicago: University of Chicago Press, 1937), 442; Donald S. Howard, "Who Shall Be Granted Public Aid? How Much? In What Form?" in *The Public Assistance Worker: His Responsibility to the Applicant, the Community, and Himself*, ed. Russell H. Kurtz (New York: Russell Sage Foundation, 1938), 44.
43. Rose J. McHugh to A. D. Smith, November 1, 1937, and November 6, 1937, Box 3, GC Correspondence on PA, HEWR. For similar reports from elsewhere in the country, see Gertrude Springer, "New England Grass Roots," *Public Welfare News* 7, no. 9 (1939): 3; Margaret Leahy, "Intake Practices in Local Public Assistance Agencies," *Social Security Bulletin* 4, no. 10 (1941): 5.
44. Litigation Section to Leonard Calhoun, September 22, 1939, Box 15, GC Correspondence on PA, HEWR. Local resistance could also run the other way, in favor of more generous policies. See Gertrude Springer, "Security Has Its Growing Pains," *Survey* 73, no. 2 (1937): 42–43, reporting on the "devious practices" that one county supervisor used to prevent a state agency from "chiseling" too much off the check of "old Mrs. Biggs."
45. Leahy, "Intake Practices," 3–4; see also Gertrude Springer, "Why Can't They Let Us Alone?" *Survey* 75, no. 11 (1939): 340–41.
46. William Haber, "Problems of State Administration," in *National Conference of Social Work* (Chicago: University of Chicago Press, 1937), 445–46; see also Marjorie Roberts, "County Director's Plaint," *Survey* 76, no. 4 (1940): 132.
47. Fowler V. Harper to Paul V. McNutt, March 11, 1940, Box 12, GC Correspondence on PA, HEWR. County resistance in another instance in California (to a state decision regarding an individual ADC case) was so strong that the same state agency sought a court order compelling the county auditor to pay the claim. Fowler V. Harper to Paul V. McNutt, June 12, 1940, Box 12, GC Correspondence on PA, HEWR. Helen Valeska Bary, who spent 1935 to 1948 representing the federal agency to the western states, first as a field representative and then a regional administrator, confirmed that this was no aberration. The county welfare directors in California were a powerful group well into the 1940s, she observed, and "had a general tendency to resist the state." Helen Valeska Bary, interview by Jacqueline K. Parker, January

13, 1973, transcript, Regional Oral History Office, University of California, Berkeley.

48. For New York, see Richard T. Gilmartin, "An Effective Working Team," *Public Welfare* 2, no. 5 (1944): 118. For Minnesota, see Edward W. Weidner, "State Supervision of Local Government in Minnesota," *Public Administration Review* 4, no. 3 (1944): 229; Ruth Raup, *Intergovernmental Relations in Social Welfare* (Minneapolis: University of Minnesota Press, 1952), 83.

49. Arthur Dimsdale to Martha E. Phillips, November 4, 1946, Box 69, GC Correspondence on PA, HEWR; Max Mangum to Riley Mapes, December 31, 1946, Box 71, GC Correspondence on PA, HEWR; Regional Attorney to Luna B. Brown, September 30, 1944, Box 70, GC Correspondence on PA, HEWR; see also Regional Attorney to Phyllis Osborn, March 22, 1944, Box 70, GC Correspondence on PA, HEWR. Not all state agencies encountered local resistance. According to Joanna Colcord, who surveyed public assistance administration in the West for the Russell Sage Foundation, central state agencies had all but replaced local initiatives in Arkansas, Arizona, and New Mexico by 1937. Joanna Colcord, "The West Is Still Different," *Survey* 73, no. 8 (1937): 243–45.

50. Wilma Van Dusseldorp, "The In-Service Training of Public Welfare Workers," *Social Forces* 17, no. 1 (1938): 62.

51. "Alabama Entertains 'Miss Bailey,'" *Public Welfare News* 7, no. 4 (1940): 2. "Miss Bailey" was a fictional character invented by Gertrude Springer and deployed in monthly columns in the *Survey*, a leading journal for professional social workers and others interested in social welfare reform. Springer based her columns on trips into the field, as well as on her own experience as a welfare worker and her extensive network of professional contacts. This particular column was written by a staff member of the Alabama Department of Welfare on the heels of Springer's visit to the state.

52. Michael Aronson, "The Anonymous Complaint in the Public Relief Agency," *Public Welfare* 4, no. 2 (1946): 36, 39.

53. "Dere Lady," *Public Welfare in Indiana*, XLIX, no. 1 (1939): 15.

54. Leahy, "Intake Practices," 4.

55. Josephine Strode, "The County Worker's Job: Tighten the Corner Where You Are," *Survey* 75, no. 5 (1939): 138; see also C. W. Geile, "County Administrators Discuss Welfare Needs," *Public Welfare News* 7, no. 4 (1939): 2, reporting that when county agencies in Indiana attempted to adhere to the SSB's "money payment" principle, they were criticized "for granting old age assistance to alcoholics, gamblers and spendthrifts"; they quickly rejected the federal guidance.

56. Van Dusseldorp, "The In-Service Training of Public Welfare Workers," 62.

57. William Haber and Herman M. Somers, "The Administration of Public Assistance in Massachusetts," *Social Service Review* 12, no. 3 (1938): 410; see also Glick, *The Illinois Emergency Relief Commission*, 226–27.

58. Jack B. Tate to Paul V. McNutt, May 12, 1941, Box 12, GC Correspondence on PA, HEWR.

59. "Supervision: A Tool of Administration," *Public Welfare News* 7, no. 12 (1939): 8–11; "Local Administrators Meet," *Public Welfare News* 8, no. 6 (1940): 7; Martha A. Chickering and Margaret S. Watkins, "How Do We Know Whether It Is a Good Local Job?" *Public Welfare* 3, no. 4 (1945): 80–85.

60. Frank Bane, interview by James R. W. Leiby, January 13, 1965, transcript, Regional Oral History Office, University of California, Berkeley.

61. Jack B. Tate, interview by Peter A. Corning, June 3, 1965, Columbia Center for Oral History, Columbia University, New York.

62. Richard McEvoy, "State-Federal Public Assistance, 1935–1946," PhD diss., University of Maryland, 1980, 14–51; V. O. Key Jr., "State Administration of the Social Security Act," *Annals of the American Academy of Political and Social Science* 202 (March 1939): 154.

63. William Hodson, "When You Work for the Government," *Survey* 75, no. 11 (1939): 331.

64. Fred K. Hoehler, "Public Welfare Administration under the Social Security Act," *Law and Contemporary Problems* 3, no. 2 (1936): 283; Marietta Stevenson, *Public Welfare Administration* (New York: Macmillan, 1938), 191–94; Elizabeth Wisner, "Training for Public Welfare," *Public Welfare News* 5, no. 11 (1937): 2–3; "Philadelphia and the Merit System," *Public Welfare News* 6, no. 11 (1938); "Civil Service and the Case of Dorothy Kahn," *Social Service Review* 12, no. 4 (1938); Fred Hoehler, "'Be It Enacted' ... Crabwise Goes Progress in State Public Welfare Legislation," *Survey* 73, no. 10 (1937): 246–48.

65. Social Security Act Amendments of 1939, §§ 101, 401, 701, Pub. L. No. 76-379, 53 Stat. 1362 (1939).

66. Stevenson, *Public Welfare Administration*, 191–94.

67. Jack B. Tate to Paul V. McNutt, November 12, 1940, Box 220, Records of the Office of the Commissioner, Executive Director's File, SSAR; "Merit Systems," *Survey* 76, no. 12 (1940): 366.

68. For example, merit system legislation would nominally accord power to the state agency but deny the agency the right to set procedures for the selection of employees, or the ability to control compensation and tenure. Tate to McNutt, November 12, 1940; see also Tate to McNutt, May 12, 1941, reporting that in Georgia, the merit system subjected the tenure of county directors to the will of the governor but not to the state agency; Martha H. Swain, *Ellen S. Woodward: New Deal Advocate for Women* (Jackson: University Press of Mississippi, 1995), 142, discussing state officials' failure to comply with the merit system in Mississippi because of continuing patronage demands.

69. Jack B. Tate to Paul V. McNutt, March 10, 1942, Box 12, GC Correspondence on PA, HEWR; Dorothy Lally, "Staff Training to Meet Personnel Needs of Public Welfare Agencies," *Social Security Bulletin* 6, no. 2 (1943): 3; Charnow and Kaplan, "Public Assistance Personnel, Jan.–June 1943," 20; Stuart K. Jaffary, "The Profession of Social Work in the South," *Social Forces* 17, no. 2 (1938): 230.

70. Public welfare correspondent Gertrude Springer described the welfare worker in a typical New England town as "a young home-state girl who left the state university for a job in the state welfare office and later 'went off' for a few months to a school of social work." Springer, "New England Grass Roots," 4; see also Ellen Forder, "Induction of the New Worker into the Agency," *Public Welfare News* 5, no. 7 (1942): 2, noting that "new visitors do not have enough knowledge of [social work] to carry on any worthwhile discussion."

71. Geraldine Francisco, "It Looks Simple," *Survey* 76, no. 8 (1940): 237.

72. Anna A. Cassatt, "Some Considerations in the Orientation of the Inexperienced Worker Who Is Untrained," *Public Welfare* 2, no. 11 (1944): 265–66.

73. Blanche D. Coll, *Safety Net: Welfare and Social Security, 1929–1979* (New Brunswick, NJ: Rutgers University Press, 1995), 112.

74. Hoey, "The Federal Government and Desirable Standards of State and Local Administration," 440.

75. See, for example, Federal Security Agency, in collaboration with Bureau of Accounts and Audits and Office of the General Counsel, *Money Payments*.

76. Agnes Van Driel, "In-Service Training," in *National Conference of Social Work* (Chicago: University of Chicago Press, 1937), 428.

77. Agnes Van Driel, "Staff Development in the Public Assistance Programs," *Social Service Review* 14, no. 2 (1940): 224–26.

78. *Announcements: The School of Social Service Administration for the Sessions of 1941–1942* 41, no. 13 (May 25, 1941), listing the placements of students who received higher degrees over the past decade, Box 3, University of Chicago School of Social Service Administration Records, Special Collections Research Center, University of Chicago [hereafter cited as CSSAR].

79. This was a practice that the Federal Emergency Relief Administration pioneered. From 1934 to 1935, FERA funds allowed 976 emergency workers to attend schools of social work for one semester or two quarters. Josephine C. Brown, "What We Have Learned about Emergency Training for Public Relief Administration," in *National Conference of Social Work* (Chicago: University of Chicago Press, 1935), 237; Wisner, "Training for Public Welfare," 3. On federal encouragement of social work education, see, for example, Lally, "Staff Training to Meet Personnel Needs of Public Welfare Agencies," 7.

80. Franklin D. Roosevelt, Address to Congress, January 6, 1941, in *The Public Papers and Addresses of Franklin D. Roosevelt*, vol. 1940, ed. Samuel I. Rosenman (New York: Macmillan, 1941), 671–72; Franklin D. Roosevelt, Address to the Commonwealth Club, San Francisco, September 23, 1932, in *The Public Papers and Addresses of Franklin D. Roosevelt*, vol. 1, ed. Samuel I. Rosenman (New York: Random House, 1938), 754; Franklin D. Roosevelt, Message to Congress on the Objectives and Accomplishments of the Administration, June 8, 1934, in *The Public Papers and Addresses of Franklin D. Roosevelt*, vol. 3, ed. Samuel I. Rosenman (New York: Random House, 1938), 292; Franklin D. Roosevelt, Acceptance of the Renomination for the Presidency, Philadelphia, June 27, 1936, in *The*

Public Papers and Addresses of Franklin D. Roosevelt, vol. 5, ed. Samuel I. Rosenman (New York: Random House, 1938), 234. On Roosevelt's "exceptionally well-developed knack for taking the pulse of the people," and the specific ways in which he did so as president, see James Sparrow, *Warfare State: World War II Americans and the Age of Big Government* (New York: Oxford University Press, 2011), 29–47.

81. Mason B. Williams, *City of Ambition: FDR, LaGuardia, and the Making of Modern New York* (New York: W. W. Norton, 2013), 161; Lovell, *This Is Not Civil Rights*, 97–99. Drawing on a sample of letters sent to the Civil Rights Section of the Department of Justice in 1939, Lovell also discusses claims to free speech, fair process, and other perceived entitlements. Lovell, *This Is Not Civil Rights*, 70–106.

82. See, generally, Eric Foner, *Free Soil, Free Labor, Free Men: The Ideology of the Republican Party before the Civil War* (New York: Oxford University Press, 1970); Eric Foner, *Reconstruction: America's Unfinished Revolution, 1863–1877* (New York: HarperCollins, 2002); David R. Roediger, *The Wages of Whiteness: Race and the Making of the American Working Class* (New York: Verso, 1999).

83. *Pine Bluff (AR) Commercial*, n.d., reprinted as "A Nation of Panhandlers," *Chicago Tribune*, April 14, 1940.

84. Robert S. Abbott, "New Deal Proves to Be No Deal for Us, Says Editor Abbott," *CD*, October 6, 1934, 11.

85. Quoted in Harvard Sitkoff, *A New Deal for Blacks: The Emergence of Civil Rights as a National Issue: The Depression Decade* (New York: Oxford University Press, 2009), 238. Historian Lizabeth Cohen has made similar observations: "At the same time that workers projected their old paternalistic expectations of ethnic community and welfare capitalism onto the state, ... they were developing a new and somewhat contradictory notion that they were entitled to benefits from the government. Alongside a pattern of dependence grew a new claim to legitimate rights." Lizabeth Cohen, *Making a New Deal: Industrial Workers in Chicago, 1919–1939* (Cambridge: Cambridge University Press, 1990), 283. This is not to say that all workers or racial minorities thought of government aid in rights terms. As Risa Goluboff has noted, some members of disadvantaged groups continued to invoke the language of patronage rather than the language of rights. Risa L. Goluboff, "'Won't You Please Help Me Get My Son Home': Peonage, Patronage, and Protest in the World War II Urban South," *Law & Social Inquiry* 24, no. 4 (1999).

86. The GC tended to have some attorneys work on particular programs (public assistance, unemployment insurance, old age insurance), while others worked on legal developments in particular branches of government (the litigation section, the legislation section).

87. Jack B. Tate, interview by Peter A. Corning, July 6, 1965, Columbia Center for Oral History, Columbia University, New York.

88. Maurine Mulliner, interview by Peter A. Corning, April 26, 1967, transcript, Columbia Center for Oral History, Columbia University, New York; William

Mitchell, interview by Peter A. Corning, March 24, 1965, Columbia Center for Oral History, Columbia University, New York.

89. Tate, interview by Corning, July 6, 1965, 118.

90. Smith believed that the "principles of law" animating the new public assistance laws could, and must, be stated "in very simple terms." A. Delafield Smith, "Interrelationship of Education and Practice in the Development of a Profession," January 26, 1939, Richard G. Smith family papers, private collection [hereafter cited as RSP], notes on file with author.

91. Smith, "Interrelationship of Education and Practice."

92. A. Delafield Smith, "The Need for Legal Concepts in the Formulation of Administrative Procedures," *Social Service Review* 15, no. 3 (1941); see also A. Delafield Smith, "Judicial Trends in Relation to Public Welfare Administration," *Social Service Review* 15, no. 2 (1941): 242.

93. A. Delafield Smith, "Elements of the Judicial in the Security Program," *Social Service Review* 17, no. 4 (1943): 426.

94. A. D. Smith to Gertrude Gates, July 11, 1940, Box 25, GC Correspondence on PA, HEWR.

95. A. D. Smith to Gertrude Gates, February 14, 1940, Box 25, GC Correspondence on PA, HEWR.

96. A. D. Smith to Jane Hoey, July 6, 1943, Box 25, GC Correspondence on PA, HEWR.

97. Smith, "Interrelationship of Education and Practice"; Smith, "The Need for Legal Concepts"; Smith, "Elements of the Judicial"; A. D. Smith to Mary E. Austin, September 26, 1941, Box 25, GC Correspondence on PA, HEWR.

98. The confidentiality provision was added to the act in 1939, after administrators observed state and local officials using information from public assistance agencies to buy votes, either from poor beneficiaries or from disgruntled taxpayers. See SSA Amendments of 1939, §§ 101, 401(b), 701(b), mandating that state plans "provide safeguards which restrict the use or disclosure of information concerning applicants and recipients to purposes directly connected with the administration of [the assistance] programs." This provision is discussed in greater depth in Chapter 5.

99. Jane M. Hoey, "The Contribution of Social Work to Government," in *National Conference of Social Work* (New York: Columbia University Press, 1941), 13.

100. Leahy, "Intake Practices," 3.

101. Federal Security Agency, in collaboration with Bureau of Accounts and Audits and Office of the General Counsel, *Money Payments*. Hoey published a similar document in the *Social Security Bulletin*, where other public welfare administrators presumably read it. Jane M. Hoey, "The Significance of the Money Payment in Public Assistance," *Social Security Bulletin* 7 (1944): 3–5. On the perception in the 1940s that participation in a mass consumption economy was a crucial facet of modern citizenship, see Lizabeth Cohen, *A Consumers' Republic: The Politics of Mass Consumption in Postwar America* (New York: Alfred A. Knopf, 2003); Meg Jacobs, *Pocketbook Politics: Economic Citizenship in Twentieth-Century America* (Princeton, NJ: Princeton University Press, 2005).

102. Charlotte Towle, *Common Human Needs: An Interpretation for Staff in Public Assistance Agencies*, Public Assistance Report No. 8 (Washington, DC: U.S. Government Printing Office, 1945); Agnes Van Driel to Jane Hoey et al., November 1, 1944, Box 215, Bureau of Public Assistance, Correspondence Relating to Plans and Programs, 1935–1948, SSAR.

103. Wendy B. Posner, "Common Human Needs: A Story from the Prehistory of Government by Special Interest," *Social Service Review* 69, no. 2 (1995): 194.

104. Towle, *Common Human Needs*, vii (emphasis added). Another 1944 report, which the bureau distributed to public assistance agencies in 1946, urged similar views on its readers. In *The Nature of Service in Public Assistance Administration*, author Grace Marcus describes "administering assistance as a right" as the agency's primary responsibility; caseworkers had an obligation "to see that the right to assistance acquires meaning and value to each individual." Grace Marcus, *The Nature of Service in Public Assistance Administration*, Public Assistance Report No. 10 (Washington, DC: U.S. Government Printing Office, 1946), 4–5.

105. Towle, *Common Human Needs*, 23; Posner, "Common Human Needs," 200. Subsequently, the report would gain infamy. See Chapter 3.

106. Leonard Calhoun to Louis Resnick, March 10, 1937, Box 4, GC Correspondence Relating to Old-Age and Survivors' Benefits, 1935–42, HEWR; A. Delafield Smith, "Citizenship and Family Security," *Social Security Bulletin* 3, no. 5 (1940): 8; see also Report of the Regional Attorneys Conference, December 5 to 10, 1938, Box 1, Office of the Administrator, General Counsel, Conferences of Regional Attorneys, HEWR.

107. Arthur J. Altmeyer, "Persistent Problems in Social Security," *Public Welfare* 2, no. 11 (1944): 259. Board member George Bigge made a similar comment in 1944: People found to be in need "have a right to look to the community for assistance." The problem was that existing laws and administrative practices made that right "quite ethereal." George E. Bigge, "Looking Ahead in Public Assistance," *Social Security Bulletin* 7, no. 12 (1944): 4, 8.

108. Lillian L. Poses to Alice Weber, February 15, 1946, Box 68, GC Correspondence on PA, HEWR.

109. Bureau of Public Assistance, Regional Staff Conference, May 12, 1944, "Money Payments," Box 193, Mixed Files, Correspondence Relating to Public Assistance Plans and Programs, 1935–1948, SSAR; see also Edith Foster, "Constructive Federal-State Relationships: II. From the Federal Viewpoint," in *National Conference of Social Work* (New York: Columbia University Press, 1944), 316.

110. Oscar M. Powell, "Social Insurance and Public Assistance in the Long Future," in *National Conference of Social Work: 1947* (New York: Columbia University Press, 1948), 151.

111. McEvoy, "State-Federal Public Assistance," 292–93.

112. Bureau of Public Assistance, Regional Staff Conference, May 13, 1944, "Personnel," Box 193, Mixed Files, Correspondence Relating to Public Assistance Plans and Programs, 1935–1948, SSAR; see also Mary

Overholt Peters, "Talks with Beginning Social Workers: Part I: Gaining Perspective," *Social Casework* 28, no. 6 (1947): 224.

113. Margaret Kincaid Bishop, "County Participation in a Public Assistance Program," *Public Welfare* 3, no. 12 (1945): 274; see also Lorraine D. Walling, "State Leadership in Local Staff Development," *Social Casework* 28, no. 6 (1947): 228–35, describing efforts by the Virginia State Department of Public Welfare to develop staff familiarity with the concept of "the right to assistance."

114. Division of Public Assistance, [Indiana] State Department of Public Welfare, *Just a Moment: A Note from the State Department*, January 6, 1941, on file with the Indiana State Library.

115. Bureau of Public Assistance, Regional Staff Conference, May 12, 1944 (comments of Miss Hastings), Box 193, Mixed Files, Correspondence Relating to Public Assistance Plans and Programs, 1935–1948, SSAR.

116. "The Social Front: The Old South," *Survey* 77, no. 5 (1941): 155; Lavinia Engle, interview by Peter A. Corning, May 18, 1967, transcript, Columbia Center for Oral History, Columbia University, New York. On the implications of public officials' use of courtesy titles, consider their place on the agenda of civil rights activists in the 1960s. See, for example, John Dittmer, *Local People: The Struggle for Civil Rights in Mississippi* (Urbana: University of Illinois Press, 1994), 122, 157; David C. Carter, "The Williamston Freedom Movement: Civil Rights at the Grass Roots in Eastern North Carolina," *North Carolina Historical Review* 76, no. 1 (1999): 23; Constance Baker Motley, "Reflections on Justice before and after *Brown*," *Fordham Urban Law Journal* 22, no. 1 (2004): 104.

117. James C. Scott, *Seeing Like a State: How Certain Schemes to Improve the Human Condition Have Failed* (New Haven, CT: Yale University Press, 1998), 49.

3   RIGHTS AS A "LIVE, MOTIVATING PRINCIPLE"

1. Address of the President to Congress, Recommending Assistance to Greece and Turkey, H.R. Doc. No. 80-171 (1947).

2. Donald S. Howard, "The Changing Role of Public Assistance," in *National Conference of Social Work* (New York: Columbia University Press, 1948), 161–62.

3. Ibid., 160.

4. Jane Hoey to Arthur Altmeyer et al., May 15, 1947, Box 191, Mixed Files, Correspondence Relating to Public Assistance Plans and Programs, 1935–1948, SSAR. Minutes of these meetings, which took place in Washington over a period of five months, were circulated to all the agency's regional directors for use in their own staff development programs. Jane Hoey to Regional Directors, August 25, 1947, Box 191, Mixed Files, Correspondence Relating to Public Assistance Plans and Programs, 1935–1948, SSAR.

5. "The Right to Public Assistance," First Meeting, May 28, 1947, Box 191, Mixed Files, Correspondence Relating to Public Assistance Plans and Programs, 1935–1948, SSAR.

6. Legal scholar William Simon explored some of these differences in his classic article "The Invention and Reinvention of Welfare Rights." The key contrast in his article, however, was between the government social workers of the 1940s and the poverty law theorists of the 1960s, especially Charles Reich. Simon, "The Invention and Reinvention of Welfare Rights," *Maryland Law Review* 44, no. 1 (1985): 1–37.

7. According to sociological and historical research on professions, experts can command authority and extract the concomitant benefits only if they "constantly persuade relevant audiences – clients, legislators, state authorities, and the public – that they own a distinct form of symbolic capital." Professions survive and thrive, theorists have argued, by claiming new capital, new territory. Ronen Shamir, *Managing Legal Uncertainty: Elite Lawyers in the New Deal* (Durham, NC: Duke University Press, 1995), 62–63; Andrew Abbott, *The System of Professions: An Essay on the Division of Expert Labor* (Chicago: University of Chicago Press, 1988), 71.

8. Risa Lauren Goluboff, *The Lost Promise of Civil Rights* (Cambridge, MA: Harvard University Press, 2007), 23–25.

9. See, generally, Peter H. Irons, *New Deal Lawyers* (Princeton, NJ: Princeton University Press, 1982); Jerold S. Auerbach, *Unequal Justice: Lawyers and Social Change in Modern America* (New York: Oxford University Press, 1976).

10. Lela B. Costin, *Two Sisters for Social Justice: A Biography of Grace and Edith Abbott* (Urbana: University of Illinois Press, 1983), 219; Loula Dunn, interview by Peter A. Corning, August 3, 1965, transcript, Columbia Center for Oral History, Columbia University, New York.

11. Jane Margueretta Hoey, interview by Peter A. Corning, March 10, 1965, transcript, Columbia Center for Oral History, Columbia University, New York; Albert Henry Aronson, interview by Peter A. Corning, March 23, 1965, transcript, Columbia Center for Oral History, Columbia University, New York; Charles McKinley and Robert W. Frase, *Launching Social Security: A Capture-and-Record Account, 1935–1937* (Madison: University of Wisconsin Press, 1970), 180–81.

12. Frank Bane, interview by James R. W. Leiby, January 13, 1965, transcript, Regional Oral History Office, University of California, Berkeley.

13. Wilbur J. Cohen and Thomas Eliot, "The Advent of Social Security," in *The Making of the New Deal: The Insiders Speak*, ed. Katie Louchheim (Cambridge, MA: Harvard University Press, 1983), 168.

14. Felice Batlan, *Women and Justice for the Poor: A History of Legal Aid, 1863–1945* (Cambridge: Cambridge University Press, 2015).

15. Joel D. Hunter, "The Field Occupied Jointly by Law and Social Service: A Social Worker Looks at the Field," *Annals of the American Academy of Political and Social Science* 145 (September 1929): 8.

16. Quoted in Costin, *Two Sisters for Social Justice*, 63, 187. On the professionalization of social work, see Roy Lubove, *Professional Altruist: The*

Emergence of Social Work as a Career 1880–1930 (New York: Macmillan, 1969); Robyn Muncy, *Creating a Female Dominion in American Reform, 1890–1935* (New York: Oxford University Press, 1994); Leslie Leighninger, *Creating a New Profession: The Beginning of Social Work Education in the United States* (Alexandria, VA: Council on Social Work Education, 2000).

17. Batlan, *Women and Justice for the Poor*, 123–84; Michael Willrich, *City of Courts: Socializing Justice in Progressive Era Chicago* (Cambridge: Cambridge University Press, 2003), 159–62; see also Robert W. Kelso, "The Historical Steps by Which Law and Social Work Are Coming Together," *Annals of the American Academy of Political and Social Science* 145 (September 1929): 20–21; Sophonisba P. Breckinridge, "Social Workers in the Courts of Cook County," *Social Service Review* 12, no. 2 (1938): 230–50.

18. Bradwell v. Illinois, 83 U.S. 130 (1872).

19. Christopher Tomlins, "Framing the Field of Law's Disciplinary Encounters: A Historical Narrative," *Law & Society Review* 34, no. 4 (2000): 938.

20. Kenneth W. Mack, "A Social History of Everyday Practice: Sadie T. M. Alexander and the Incorporation of Black Women into the American Legal Profession, 1925–1960," *Cornell Law Review* 87 (2002): 1415–16, 1420. For general discussions of gender and the legal profession, see Virginia G. Drachman, *Sisters in Law: Women Lawyers in Modern American History* (Cambridge, MA: Harvard University Press, 1998); Cynthia Fuchs Epstein, *Women in Law*, 2nd ed. (Urbana: University of Illinois Press, 1993); Michael Grossberg, "Institutionalizing Masculinity: The Law as a Masculine Profession," in *Meanings for Manhood: Constructions of Masculinity in Victorian America*, ed. Mark C. Carnes and Clyde Griffin (Chicago: University of Chicago Press, 1990), 133–51; Batlan, *Women and Justice for the Poor*, 171–77.

21. Muncy, *Creating a Female Dominion*, 69–71.

22. Tomlins, "Framing the Field of Law's Disciplinary Encounters," 938; Linda Gordon, "Social Insurance and Public Assistance: The Influence of Gender in Welfare Thought in the United States, 1890–1935," *American Historical Review* 97, no. 1 (1992): 19–54, 24–27; Clarke A. Chambers, "Women in the Creation of the Profession of Social Work," *Social Service Review* 60, no. 1 (1986): 1–31; Daniel J. Walkowitz, "The Making of a Feminine Professional Identity: Social Workers in the 1920s," *American Historical Review* 95, no. 4 (1990): 1051–75.

23. Frank Bane remembered Edith Abbott saying to him, sometime during the FERA years, that her School of Social Service Administration was "getting too many women," and that she wanted "Harry" (Hopkins) to send her more men to train – "*sure enough men.*" Frank Bane, interview by James R. W. Leiby, January 6, 1965, transcript, Regional Oral History Office, University of California, Berkeley (emphasis added); see also Margot Canaday, *The Straight State: Sexuality and Citizenship in Twentieth-Century America* (Princeton, NJ: Princeton University Press, 2009), 114–15, noting that critics accused women social workers of being too "mannish" and their male

colleagues of being "cissies"; Muncy, *Creating a Female Dominion*, 66–92; Gordon, "Social Insurance and Public Assistance," 24.

24. Edith Abbott, "The Pauper Laws Still Go On," *Social Service Review* 9, no. 4 (1935): 731–56; John S. Bradway, "The Social Workers of Philadelphia versus the Dead Hand: A Review of the Ellis College Case," *Social Service Review* 3, no. 3 (1929): 422–47; Sophonisba P. Breckinridge, *Social Work and the Courts: Select Statutes and Judicial Decisions* (Chicago: University of Chicago Press, 1934), 1.

25. Marguerite G. Rosenthal, "The Children's Bureau and the Juvenile Court: Delinquency Policy, 1912–1940," *Social Service Review* 60, no. 2 (1986): 11; see also Grace Abbott, "Case Work Responsibility of Juvenile Courts," *Social Service Review* 3, no. 3 (1929): 395–404.

26. Breckinridge, *Social Work and the Courts*, 2, 7; see also Kenneth L. N. Pray, "The Study of Law in Schools of Social Work," *Annals of the American Academy of Political and Social Science* 145 (September 1929): 121–24.

27. John S. Bradway, "The Legal Approach to the Problem of Juvenile Delinquency," *Southern California Law Review* 2 (1928–29): 129; W. Bruce Cobb, "The Legal-Social Field in Practice: The Field in a Large City," *Annals of the American Academy of Political and Social Science* 145 (September 1929): 133; Ralph Fuchs, review of *The Law of Guardian and Ward* by Hasseltine Byrd Taylor, *Yale Law Journal* 45, no. 6 (1936): 1156. But see Batlan, *Women and Justice for the Poor*, 123–53, describing how elite members of the male-dominated legal profession systematically erased women's role in pioneering legal aid organizations.

28. The sisters grew up in Nebraska but attended graduate school and spent their early careers in Chicago. Edith made her home there, in the School of Social Service Administration. Grace built a career in government service in Washington, DC, but maintained tight ties to Chicago up until her death in 1939. See, generally, Costin, *Two Sisters for Social Justice*.

29. Blanche D. Coll, *Safety Net: Welfare and Social Security, 1929–1979* (New Brunswick, NJ: Rutgers University Press, 1995), 65–66; James Leiby, *A History of Social Welfare and Social Work in the United States, 1815–1972* (New York: Columbia University Press, 1978), 179, 243; John H. Ehrenreich, *Altruistic Imagination: A History of Social Work and Social Policy in the United States* (Ithaca, NY: Cornell University Press, 1985), 110–21; Michael Reisch and Janice Andrews, *The Road Not Taken: A History of Radical Social Work in the United States* (Philadelphia: Brunner-Routledge, 2001), 61–64.

30. Leiby, *A History of Social Welfare and Social Work*, 263; Dorothy C. Kahn, "Conserving Human Values in Public Welfare Programs," in *National Conference of Social Work* (New York: Columbia University Press, 1941), 312; Jane M. Hoey, "The Impact of the War on the Public Assistance Programs," *Social Service Review* 17, no. 4 (1943): 483; Charlotte Towle, *Common Human Needs: An Interpretation for Staff in Public Assistance Agencies*, Public Assistance Report No. 8. (Washington, DC: U.S. Government Printing Office, 1945).

31. For more on this point, see Gordon, "Social Insurance and Public Assistance."

32. Towle, *Common Human Needs*, iii–iv.
33. Ibid., 1, 36; Wendy B. Posner, "Common Human Needs: A Story from the Prehistory of Government by Special Interest," *Social Service Review* 69, no. 2 (1995): 199.
34. "Minutes of Executive Staff Meeting of the Bureau Held November 30, 1944, to Discuss Document on Public Assistance Service by Grace Marcus," December 1, 1944, Box 214, BPA Correspondence Relating to Plans and Programs, 1935–1948, SSAR. The main reason for the halfhearted endorsement was that as Marcus discussed the importance of rights, she downplayed social services. (She described services as but "the instrument through which [an individual's] need may be met as a matter of right" and encouraged social workers not to foist them on people.) Not wanting to provoke those in the social work community who saw services as a necessary complement to money, Hoey distributed Marcus's report with the preface that the analysis "indicated need for further study" and that the report was "not an official publication of the Administration." Grace Marcus, *The Nature of Service in Public Assistance Administration*, Public Assistance Report No. 10 (Washington, DC: U.S. Government Printing Office, 1946), iii, 4–5; Coll, *Safety Net*, 136–38.
35. Edith Abbott, "Is There a Legal Right to Relief?" *Social Service Review* 12, no. 2 (1938): 263, 275.
36. Jane M. Hoey, "Aid to Families with Dependent Children," *Annals of the American Academy of Political and Social Science* 202 (March 1939): 77.
37. Kahn, "Conserving Human Values in Public Welfare Programs," 309.
38. Tom Eliot, the agency's first general counsel, received his undergraduate (1928) and graduate (1932) degrees from Harvard. His successor, Jack B. Tate, graduated from Yale Law School in 1926 – and would later become its dean. The lawyer who worked most closely with the BPA, A. D. Smith, graduated from Princeton (1913) and Harvard Law (1916). The agency's legal staff also included women, in greater numbers than many other New Deal agencies. On their backgrounds, see Karen M. Tani, "Portia's Deal," *Chicago-Kent Law Review* 87, no. 2 (2012): 549–70.
39. See Jack B. Tate, Remarks at the Field Staff Conference Session on Fair Hearings, 1946, Box 75, GC Correspondence on PA, HEWR; A. Delafield Smith, "Citizenship and Family Security," *Social Security Bulletin* 3, no. 5 (1940): 8; A. Delafield Smith, "Interrelationship of Education and Practice in the Development of a Profession," January 26, 1939, RSP; A. Delafield Smith, "Community Prerogative and the Legal Rights and Freedom of the Individual," *Social Security Bulletin* 9, no. 9 (1946): 6.
40. Tate, Remarks at the Field Staff Conference; see also Smith, "Community Prerogative," 6, insisting that "th[e] combination of security and independence and freedom is possible only through the operation of law."
41. They were responding to people like law-professor-turned-administrator James Landis, who claimed that the *soundness* of government policy, not its fidelity to creaky Supreme Court doctrine, was the "ultimate test" of its validity. Landis, *The Administrative Process* (New Haven, CT: Yale University Press, 1938),

quoted in Reuel E. Schiller, "Reining in the Administrative State: World War II and the Decline of Expert Administration," in *Total War and the Law: The American Home Front in World War II*, ed. Daniel R. Ernst and Victor Jew (Westport, CT: Praeger, 2002), 186.

42. Benjamin L. Alpers, *Dictators, Democracy, and American Public Culture: Envisioning the Totalitarian Enemy, 1920s–1950s* (Chapel Hill: University of North Carolina Press, 2003); Les K. Adler and Thomas G. Paterson, "Red Fascism: The Merger of Nazi Germany and Soviet Russia in the American Image of Totalitarianism, 1930's–1950's," *American Historical Review* 75 (1970). Antitotalitarianism would grow even more powerful during the late 1940s and early 1950s, through influential works such as Leland Stowe's *Target: You* (New York: Knopf, 1949), Arthur Schlesinger Jr.'s *The Vital Center: The Politics of Freedom* (Boston: Houghton Mifflin, 1949), and Hannah Arendt's *The Origins of Totalitarianism* (New York: Harcourt, Brace, 1951).

43. This paragraph relies generally on David Ciepley, *Liberalism in the Shadow of Totalitarianism* (Cambridge: Cambridge University Press, 2006), 141–43; Aaron L. Friedberg, *In the Shadow of the Garrison State: America's Anti-Statism and Its Cold War Grand Strategy* (Princeton, NJ: Princeton University Press, 2000), 40–61; Schiller, "Reining in the Administrative State," 188–95.

44. Herman Belz, "Changing Conceptions of Constitutionalism in the Era of World War II and the Cold War," *Journal of American History* 59 (1972): 657, 659; Anne M. Kornhauser, *Debating the American State: Liberal Anxieties and the New Leviathan, 1930–1970* (Philadelphia: University of Pennsylvania Press, 2015), 90–129. On the various meanings of the rule of law, see Christopher L. Tomlins, *Law, Labor, and Ideology in the Early American Republic* (Cambridge: Cambridge University Press, 1993); Richard H. Fallon Jr., "'The Rule of Law' as a Concept in Constitutional Discourse," *Columbia Law Review* 97 (1997): 1–56; Daniel R. Ernst, *Tocqueville's Nightmare: The Administrative State Emerges in America, 1900–1940* (New York: Oxford University Press, 2014), 2–6.

45. Quotes are from Smith, "Interrelationship of Education and Practice."

46. The lawyers seem to have embraced the vision of the administrative state that Germany's great liberal jurists developed at the end of the nineteenth century and that their students imported to the United States: the ideal administrative state, they argued, was not one of unfettered administrative action (*Polizistaat*) or broad judicial control (*Justizstaat*), but one "bound by fixed and certain rules" distinguishing "spheres of legitimate state action" from those of individual liberty (*Rechstsstaat*). Daniel R. Ernst, "Ernst Freund, Felix Frankfurter, and the American Rechtsstaat: A Transatlantic Shipwreck, 1894–1932," *Studies in the American Political Development* 23 (2009): 12.

47. For a reprint of the speech, see A. Delafield Smith, "The Need for Legal Concepts in the Formulation of Administrative Procedures," *Social Service Review* 15, no. 3 (1941): 21–55; see also A. Delafield Smith, "Judicial Trends in Relation to Public Welfare Administration," *Social Service Review* 15, no. 2 (1941): 242.

48. T. H. Marshall, "Citizenship and Social Class," in *Citizenship and Social Class and Other Essays* (Cambridge: Cambridge University Press, 1950), 1–85.
49. Smith, "Interrelationship of Education and Practice," alluding to Acts 2:3–4.
50. SSA, §§ 402(a)(4), 1002(a)(4). For legal scholars of the Warren and Burger Courts, as well as for historians of welfare rights, the phrase "fair hearing" is familiar. Welfare recipients and their allies in law, academia, and social work famously attempted to use administrative fair hearings both to win greater benefits for individuals and to tax the welfare system to the breaking point. Martha F. Davis, *Brutal Need: Lawyers and the Welfare Rights Movement, 1960–1973* (New Haven, CT: Yale University Press, 1993), 47, 81–118; Frances Fox Piven and Richard Cloward, "The Weight of the Poor," *Nation*, May 2, 1966, and "Withdrawal of Public Welfare," *Nation*, April 3, 1967. Despite the abundant literature on the connection between constitutional law and welfare rights in the late 1960s and 1970s, historical writing on fair hearings remains thin. Felicia Kornbluh, "Redistribution, Recognition, and Good China: Administrative Justice for Women Welfare Recipients before *Goldberg v. Kelly*," *Yale Journal of Law and Feminism* 20, no. 1 (2008): 167.
51. Beatrice Ida Vulcan, "Fair Hearings in the Public Assistance Programs of the New York City Department of Welfare," PhD diss., Columbia University, 1972, 44–47; Jules H. Berman, "The Administration of the Appeal Provisions of the Public Assistance Legislation Enacted under the Social Security Act in Illinois and Certain Other States," master's thesis, University of Chicago School of Social Service Administration, 1937, 1.
52. A. Delafield Smith, "Elements of the Judicial in the Security Program," *Social Service Review* 17, no. 4 (1943): 426. Smith exaggerated: appeal procedures existed in some state public assistance statutes before the enactment of the SSA. Berman, "Administration of the Appeal Provisions," 4.
53. A. Delafield Smith, Draft of Proposed Statement on Hearings to Accompany Model Decisions for Use at Regional Representatives Meeting, January 24, 1946, Box 75, GC Correspondence on PA, HEWR. Smith and the lawyers in his office were not alone in associating the fair hearing requirement with a legal right to relief. Welfare administrator and public administration scholar Robert Lansdale noted in 1939 that the fair hearing provision in the SSA "appear[ed] to indicate that the [public assistance] applicant is recognized to have certain rights to relief, since his right to a grant is thereby assumed to be capable of adjudication by the state agency." Robert Lansdale et al., *The Administration of Old Age Assistance* (Chicago: Public Administration Service, 1939), 171n10.
54. Smith, Draft of Proposed Statement on Hearings; Office of the GC to All Regional Attorneys, "Fair Hearing Decisions," October 15, 1940, Box 25, GC Correspondence on PA, HEWR.
55. Vulcan, "Fair Hearings," 47.
56. Saiyid Zafar Hasan, "Policy Formulation and Development in Public Assistance: A Study of the Role of the Federal Government in the First Five Years of the Social Security Act, 1935–1940," PhD diss., New York School of Social Work, Columbia University, 1958, 301–2.

57. Vulcan, "Fair Hearings," 49–50, citing BPA administrators Bernard Scholz and Thomas Lewin.
58. Ibid., 89; McKinley and Frase, *Launching Social Security*, 148.
59. Jack B. Tate to the Social Security Board, April 27, 1936, Box 95, Office of the Commissioner, Chairman's Files, 1935–1942, SSAR. This interpretation is an example of what legal scholars have dubbed "administrative constitutionalism." See Sophia Z. Lee, "Race, Sex, and Rulemaking: Administrative Constitutionalism and the Workplace, 1960 to the Present," *Virginia Law Review* 96 (2010): 799–886; Gillian E. Metzger, "Administrative Constitutionalism," *Texas Law Review* 91 (2013): 1897–1935; Sophia Z. Lee, *The Workplace Constitution from the New Deal to the New Right* (New York: Cambridge University Press, 2014). A topic that merits further exploration is the connection between Tate's interpretation of constitutional due process in this context and his famous 1952 interpretation of the doctrine of sovereign immunity written while serving as legal advisor of the State Department (the "Tate Letter"). On legal realism at Yale, see Laura Kalman, *Legal Realism at Yale 1927–1960* (Chapel Hill: University of North Carolina Press, 1986). On the Tate Letter and the legal-interpretive power that it arrogated to the State Department, see Curtis A. Bradley, *International Law in the U.S. System* (New York: Oxford University Press, 2015), 238.
60. Vulcan, "Fair Hearings," 51–53, citing Bureau of Public Assistance, Division of Policies and Procedures, "Some Factors to Be Considered in Developing Procedures for a Fair Hearing," September 30, 1936. The SSB actually approved a "strictly legal and traditional" interpretation of the essentials of a fair hearing, but did not circulate it to state administrators because the BPA and board member Arthur Altmeyer objected. Altmeyer apparently feared "legalistic distortions of administration." McKinley and Frase, *Launching Social Security*, 148; see also Jack B. Tate to Oscar Powell, April 4, 1940, Box 25, GC Correspondence on PA, HEWR, recalling that the GC recommended "precise and simple standards" in March 1936, but the BPA and SSB did not want to "irritate[]" states with "procedural requirements while they were burdened by the major task of getting their programs into operation," and noting that in May, the SSB reconsidered and accepted the standards but authorized issuance only to states that were known to be out of conformity with the fair hearing requirement; Hasan, "Policy Formulation and Development in Public Assistance," 303–4, providing the text of the form letter that the board approved in May 1936.
61. Ellis Radinsky, "Appeals, Fair Hearings and Reviews," master's thesis, New York School of Social Work, Columbia University, 1941, 74–75. On the diversity of state and local practices, see Berman, "Administration of the Appeal Process."
62. Reba Choate, "Fair Hearing Procedure in Missouri, 1933–1941, with an Analysis of Judicial Decisions Relating to Old Age Assistance," master's thesis, University of Chicago School of Social Service Administration, 1942, 29–34, 43–44.

63. Hasan, "Policy Formulation and Development in Public Assistance," 311–12; see also Wilbur C. Hallwachs, "Fair Hearings in the Administration of Old Age Assistance in Illinois," master's thesis, University of Chicago School of Social Service Administration, 1943, 51, stating that between March 1936 and July 1937, OAA claimants in Cook County filed 421 appeals; of those, 256 were withdrawn without a hearing because the cases were reviewed and the awards increased. Hallwachs also discusses the influence of organized pension unions.

64. Mildred Caroline Tallman and John Arthur Dunn, "An Analysis of the Use of the Fair Hearing Process in the Administration of Public Assistance in Colorado," master's thesis, University of Denver, 1952, 36. Tallman and Dunn report that claimants withdrew "the great majority" of these requests after their county departments either explained the laws to them or revised the original determinations. Ibid.

65. David R. Hunter, "The Courts and Administrative 'Fair Hearings' in Public Assistance Programs," *Social Service Review* 14, no. 3 (1940): 484.

66. Lansdale et al., *The Administration of Old Age Assistance*, 313.

67. Radinsky, "Appeals, Fair Hearings and Reviews," 74–75.

68. David Romeyn Hunter, "Fair Hearings in Public Assistance," master's thesis, University of Chicago School of Social Service Administration, 1940, 39, citing BPA, Division of Policies and Procedures, "Staff Conference," October 11, 1937; see also Lansdale et al., *The Administration of Old Age Assistance*, 30, noting that in one of the twelve states he studied, the procedure followed in appeal cases "consisted almost entirely of a special investigation by a state worker, who visited the complainant and endeavored to settle the matter with him."

69. Louis Resnick to Jane Hoey, March 2, 1938, Box 236, Central File (1935–1947), SSAR; Lansdale et al., *The Administration of Old Age Assistance*, 303.

70. Hunter, "Fair Hearings in Public Assistance," 43. Hunter also found that fourteen states had laws requiring appellants to go through a hearing at the county level before presenting their case to the state agency. Ibid., 90.

71. Jane Perry Clark, "Individual Claims to Social Benefits, I," *American Political Science Review* 35 (August 1941): 675–76. Reba Choate made similar findings in her study of Missouri. She reported that following the flood of old age assistance appeals in 1938, Missouri officials "concentrate[d] upon pre-decision conferences" with all recipients or applicants before deeming any person ineligible. The number of appeals dropped considerably. Choate, "Fair Hearing Procedure in Missouri," 47, 67.

72. Clark, "Individual Claims to Social Benefits, I," 676n38.

73. Pierce Atwater, *Problems of Administration in Social Work* (Minneapolis: University of Minnesota Press, 1940), 219.

74. This was the board's modus operandi in the early days. Hasan, "Policy Formulation and Development in Public Assistance"; Coll, *Safety Net*, 68.

75. A. Delafield Smith to Jane Hoey, October 24, 1939, Box 25, GC Correspondence on PA, HEWR (emphasis added). Smith likely got some of his information from an October 16, 1939, memo from regional attorney

Robert Ayers, who reported that with the possible exception Arizona, none of the states in his region (the Southwest) had met the SSA's fair hearing requirement. Ayers's memo also discussed a case called *Colorado Public Welfare Board v. Viles*, 94 P.2d 713 (Colo. 1939), in which the Supreme Court of Colorado characterized the state welfare agency's hearing as a sham. Harold P. Packer to Jack Tate, March 1, 1940, Box 25, GC Correspondence on PA, HEWR.

76. Jack Tate to Oscar Powell, April 4, 1940, Box 25, GC Correspondence on PA, HEWR.

77. Bureau of Public Assistance, "Standards for Fair-Hearing Procedure in Public-Assistance Administration," December 2, 1940, Box 95, Office of the Commissioner, Chairman's Files, 1935–1942, SSAR.

78. A. Delafield Smith, "Fair Hearings and Standards," July 11, 1940, Box 25, GC Correspondence on PA, HEWR.

79. Office of the GC to All Regional Attorneys, "Fair Hearing Decisions"; Transcript, Regional Attorneys Conference, Public Assistance session, November 8, 1940, Box 242, Records of the Office of the Commissioner, Executive Director's File, SSAR.

80. A. Delafield Smith to Geoffrey May, September 19, 1940, Box 25, GC Correspondence on PA, HEWR.

81. A. Delafield Smith to Jane Hoey, September 5, 1940, Box 25, GC Correspondence on PA, HEWR.

82. Kahn, "Conserving Human Values in Public Welfare Programs," 316.

83. Margaret Kincaid Bishop, "County Participation in a Public Assistance Program," *Public Welfare* 3, no. 12 (1945): 270–74; see also George E. Bigge, "Looking Ahead in Public Assistance," *Social Security Bulletin* 7, no. 12 (1944): 5.

84. SSA, §§ 1, 401, 1001 (emphasis added).

85. "Changes in Public Assistance Programs, 1940–42," *Social Security Bulletin* 5, no. 10 (1942): 51–52. The highest paying states, in contrast, paid an average of $37.03 per month to OAA recipients and $62.58 to families on ADC. Ibid. On wartime inflation, see "Public Assistance Goals: Recommendations of the Social Security Board," *Social Security Bulletin* 7, no. 11 (1944): 3.

86. "Permanent plans for meeting human needs should be developed as quickly as possible after the war," BPA director Jane Hoey emphasized to the National Conference on Social Welfare in 1944, before quoting with approval a recently adopted declaration from a meeting of the International Labor Organization: "The war against want" must "be carried on with unrelenting vigor within each nation." Jane M. Hoey, "Social Work Concepts and Methods in the Postwar World," in *National Conference of Social Work* (New York: Columbia University Press, 1944), 44–45.

87. Charles W. Eliot, "A New Bill of Rights," *Vital Speeches of the Day* 8, no. 18 (1942): 556; National Resources Planning Board, *National Resources Development Report for 1943* (Washington, DC: U.S. Government Printing Office, 1943).

88. Nicholas R. Parrillo, "Leviathan and Interpretive Revolution: The Administrative State, the Judiciary, and the Rise of Legislative History, 1890–1950," *Yale Law Journal* 123, no. 2 (2013): 338.

89. Joanna L. Grisinger, *The Unwieldy American State: Administrative Politics Since the New Deal* (New York: Cambridge University Press, 2012), 109–12.

90. Jennifer Mittelstadt, *From Welfare to Workfare: The Unintended Consequences of Liberal Reform, 1945–1965* (Chapel Hill: University of North Carolina Press, 2005), 25–27; Hoey, "Social Work Concepts and Methods in the Postwar World"; Jane M. Hoey, "Next Steps in Public Assistance," in *National Conference of Social Work* (New York: Columbia University Press, 1945), 153.

91. Mittelstadt, *From Welfare to Workfare*, 29, 34.

92. Another way of taking into account differentials in state financial capacity was a progressive grant formula—i.e., a system of matching that varied according to the state's wealth. Since at least 1939, federal administrators had urged Congress to implement such a formula but had not succeeded. Martha Derthick, *The Influence of Federal Grants: Public Assistance in Massachusetts* (Cambridge, MA: Harvard University Press, 1970), 46.

93. Angela J. Murray, "Social Security Amendments of 1946," *Social Security Bulletin* 9, no. 9 (1946): 4; Wilbur J. Cohen and James L. Calhoon, "Social Security Legislation, January–June 1948: Legislative History and Background," *Social Security Bulletin* 11, no. 7 (1948): 5. In both 1946 and 1948, Congress made similar adjustments to the matching rates and ceilings for OAA and AB.

94. "The Right to Public Assistance," Third Meeting, September 10, 1947, Box 191, Mixed Files, Correspondence Relating to Public Assistance Plans and Programs, 1935–1948, SSAR.

95. Bureau of Public Assistance, "Interpretations of Definitions of 'Dependent Child' in Section 406(a), Title IV of the Social Security Act," November 1944, Box 1, State Letters, Policies, and Regulations Relating to Public Welfare Programs, 1942–1971, SSAR; Bureau of Public Assistance, State Letter no. 46, "'Suitable Home' Provisions of State Plans for Aid to Dependent Children," March 5, 1945, Box 1, State Letters, Policies, and Regulations Relating to Public Welfare Programs, 1942–1971, SSAR; Jane Hoey, "Transmittal of Draft Material on 'State Standards for Measuring the Adequacy of Available Income and Resources to Establish the Amount of Assistance Needed,'" October 18, 1946, Box 38, GC Correspondence on PA, HEWR.

96. Hoey, "Transmittal of Draft Material on 'State Standards for Measuring the Adequacy of Available Income and Resources to Establish the Amount of Assistance Needed.'"

97. Howard, "The Changing Role of Public Assistance," 158; see also Philip Soskis, "The Client Has Rights," *Better Times*, March 21, 1947, arguing that "if the community accepted public assistance as a right," adequate appropriations for assistance would follow.

98. Towle, *Common Human Needs*, vii; Posner, "Common Human Needs," 200; "The Right to Public Assistance," Third Meeting.

99. Smith, "Elements of the Judicial," 425–26; Smith, "Community Prerogative," 6.
100. A. Delafield Smith to Mary E. Austin, September 26, 1941, Box 25, GC Correspondence on PA, HEWR; A. Delafield Smith to Jane Hoey, July 6, 1943, Box 25, GC Correspondence on PA, HEWR; draft letter from A. Delafield Smith to Jane Hoey, April 13, 1944, Box 38, GC Correspondence on PA, HEWR.
101. Edward A. Purcell, *The Crisis of Democratic Theory: Scientific Naturalism and the Problem of Value* (Lexington: University Press of Kentucky, 1973).
102. Ciepley, *Liberalism in the Shadow of Totalitarianism*, 194–200; see also William Edward Nelson, *The Legalist Reformation: Law, Politics, and Ideology in New York, 1920–1980* (Chapel Hill: University of North Carolina Press, 2001), 123, arguing that "the spreading shadow of the swastika ... compelled Americans to articulate [an] emerging legalist reform ideology," which emphasized individual liberties and protection of minority views.
103. This paragraph draws generally on Schiller, "Reining in the Administrative State"; Joanna Grisinger, "Law in Action: The Attorney General's Committee on Administrative Procedure," *Journal of Policy History* 20, no. 3 (2008); Grisinger, *The Unwieldy American State*, 14–108.
104. Smith, "Community Prerogative," 6, 9.
105. Ibid., 6; F. A. Hayek, *The Road to Serfdom* (Chicago: University of Chicago Press, 1944).
106. Richard G. Smith, personal communication with author; Smith, "Community Prerogative," 6.
107. Rose McHugh to the Fair Hearing Committee, "Draft Interpretive Statement," January 1, 1945, Box 217, GC Correspondence on PA, HEWR.
108. Alice Stanton to Rose McHugh, February 2, 1945, Box 217, GC Correspondence on PA, HEWR.
109. Jane Hoey to Edith Abbott, March 10, 1945, Box 217, GC Correspondence on PA, HEWR.
110. See, for example, Max Mangum to Riley Mapes, February 14, 1944, Box 71, GC Correspondence on PA, HEWR; Regional Attorney to Phyllis Osborn, March 22, 1944, Box 70, GC Correspondence on PA, HEWR; Carl Harper to Victor Carlson, November 8, 1944, Box 70, GC Correspondence on PA, HEWR; Carl Harper to Ed Rourke, March 27, 1945, Box 70, GC Correspondence on PA, HEWR; Lillian L. Poses to Alice Webber, April 15, 1946, Box 68, GC Correspondence on PA, HEWR; Regional Attorney to Phyllis Osborn, August 28, 1946, Box 68, GC Correspondence on PA, HEWR; Arthur Dimsdale to Martha E. Phillips, November 4, 1946, Box 69, GC Correspondence on PA, HEWR; Max Mangum to Riley Mapes, December 31, 1946, Box 71, GC Correspondence on PA, HEWR.
111. Alice P. Stanton to Rose McHugh, February 2, 1945, Box 217, GC Correspondence on PA, HEWR.
112. A. Delafield Smith to Kathryn Goodwin, November 2, 1945, Box 38, GC Correspondence on PA, HEWR. BPA personnel came around to Smith's view and Smith did not have to take the issue up with the board, as he had

threatened. Donald Gunter to Kathryn Goodwin, November 6, 1945, Box 38, GC Correspondence on PA, HEWR; Transcript, Jane Hoey and Oscar Powell, August 9, 1945, Box 217, GC Correspondence on PA, HEWR. Just a month later the BPA and the GC's office scuffled again, when the BPA gave a lukewarm response to a proposal to publish and circulate model fair hearing decisions. Kathryn Goodwin to Jane Hoey, September 18, 1945, Box 217, GC Correspondence on PA, HEWR; Transcript, Hoey and Powell, August 9, 1945; A. Delafield Smith to Jane Hoey, January 10, 1946, Box 38, GC Correspondence on PA, HEWR.

113. Carl Harper, "Draft Materials on Considerations on the Writing of Fair Hearing Procedures," May 8, 1944, Box 70, GC Correspondence on PA, HEWR.

114. Jack B. Tate to Watson B. Miller, January 10, 1947, Box 11, GC Correspondence on PA, HEWR; Jane Hoey to All Regional Directors, September 22, 1947, Box 186, Mixed Files, Correspondence Relating to Public Assistance Plans and Programs, 1935–1948, SSAR.

115. J. Sheldon Turner to All Regional Directors, April 1, 1947, Box 75, GC Correspondence on PA, HEWR.

116. Jane Hoey to All Regional Directors, October 30, 1946, Box 38, GC Correspondence on PA, HEWR; see also Eveline Burns, *The American Social Security System* (New York: Houghton Mifflin Company, 1949), 384n1, noting that "the Bureau has placed great emphasis upon the appeals machinery as an implementation of the theory of the 'right to public assistance.'"

117. Federal Security Agency, Social Security Administration, *Bureau of Public Assistance, Hearings in Public Assistance* 1, no. 3 (July 1947): 2.

118. Federal Security Agency, Social Security Administration, Bureau of Public Assistance, *Hearings in Public Assistance* 3, no. 4 (October 1949): 18.

119. Federal Security Agency, Social Security Administration, Bureau of Public Assistance, *Hearings in Public Assistance* 4, no. 1 (January 1950): 29.

120. "Townshend Resident to Speak On 'Upheaval in Public Welfare,'" *Bennington (VT) Banner*, November 16, 1967; Bernard W. Scholz, "Hearings in Public Assistance," *Social Security Bulletin* 11, no. 7 (1948): 11.

121. A. Delafield Smith to Kathryn Goodwin, June 3, 1947, Box 69, GC Correspondence on PA, HEWR.

122. J. Sheldon Turner to Jules Berman et al., December 18, 1947, Box 179, Mixed files, Correspondence Relating to Public Assistance Plans and Programs, 1935–1948, SSAR.

123. Thomas J. Sugrue, *Sweet Land of Liberty: The Forgotten Struggle for Civil Rights in the North* (New York: Random House, 2008), 55–57, 65, 68–70.

124. See, generally, Mary L. Dudziak, *Cold War Civil Rights: Race and the Image of American Democracy* (Princeton, NJ: Princeton University Press, 2000).

125. President's Committee on Civil Rights, *To Secure These Rights: The Report of the President's Committee on Civil Rights* (Washington, DC: U.S. Government Printing Office, 1947).

126. Quoted in Barbara Dianne Savage, *Broadcasting Freedom: Radio, War, and the Politics of Race* (Chapel Hill: University of North Carolina Press, 1999), 224.

127. See Patricia Sullivan, *Days of Hope: Race and Democracy in the New Deal Era* (Chapel Hill: University of North Carolina Press, 1996), 223–24; Harvard Sitkoff, "Harry Truman and the Election of 1948: The Coming of Age of Civil Rights in American Politics," *Journal of Southern History* 37, no. 4 (1971): 597–616.

128. Grovey v. Townsend, 295 U.S. 45 (1935); Smith v. Allwright, 321 U.S. 649 (1944).

129. Shelley v. Kraemer, 344 U.S. 1 (1948). The efficacy of these decisions is a separate question. On restrictive covenants in particular, see Richard W. R. Brooks and Carol M. Rose, *Saving the Neighborhood: Racially Restrictive Covenants, Law, and Social Norms* (Cambridge, MA: Harvard University Press, 2013).

130. Patton v. Mississippi, 332 U.S. 463 (1947); Sipuel v. Bd. of Regents, 332 U.S. 631 (1948); Takahashi v. Fish & Game Commission, 334 U.S. 410 (1948); Korematsu v. United States, 323 U.S. 214 (1944) [upholding Korematsu's conviction for failing to comply with an evacuation order directed exclusively at persons of Japanese descent].

131. A. Delafield Smith to Gertrude Gates, February 14, 1940, Box 25, GC Correspondence on PA, HEWR; see also Smith, "Elements of the Judicial," 425, rooting the equal protection guaranty in the act's requirement of a central state agency, financial participation by the state, and application to all subdivisions. For a fuller discussion of federal welfare administrators' interpretation of the Equal Protection Clause, see Karen M. Tani, "Administrative Equal Protection: Federalism, The Fourteenth Amendment, and the Rights of the Poor," *Cornell Law Review* 100 (2015): 825–99. For a discussion of a similar development inside the National Labor Relations Board around the same time, see Lee, *The Workplace Constitution*, 44–55.

132. Smith, "Judicial Trends," 256–58.

133. Tate, Remarks at the Field Staff Conference; see also Smith, "Community Prerogative," 7, charging that laws denying assistance on account of illegitimacy, or failure to attend school, or display of luxury goods, or residence in an unsuitable home, all violated equal protection; A. Delafield Smith to All Regional Attorneys, April 29, 1948, Box 75, GC Correspondence on PA, HEWR, noting various "problems and oddities in classification" that he observed in public assistance administration, such as refusing assistance to a child on the ground that his parent would not undergo a surgical operation, authorizing payment of a fixed income to better-off blind individuals while giving limited, need-based payments to resourceless blind individuals, and conditioning public assistance on the claimant's institution of a criminal support action against another member of the family. As the quotes suggest, Smith, Tate, and their colleagues denied that equal protection was fundamentally about skin color. Smith "deprecate[d]," he wrote in a 1948 memo, "the common view that equal protection is but another name for anti-discrimination and anti-prejudice." A. Delafield Smith, "Equal Protection of the Laws Principle," April 27, 1948, Box 75, GC Correspondence on PA, HEWR.

134. Tate, Remarks at the Field Staff Conference; see also Smith, "Equal Protection of the Laws Principle."
135. Tate, Remarks at the Field Staff Conference.
136. Altmeyer became commissioner in July 1946, pursuant to a reorganization plan that replaced the SSB with the Social Security Administration. Jack B. Tate to Watson B. Miller, October 8, 1946, Box 11, GC Correspondence on PA, HEWR.
137. For example, in August 1947 agency lawyers objected to a Utah appropriation act that keyed standards of assistance to "the income enjoyed by the occupational group to which the recipient belonged." The lawyers characterized this as "a classification unrelated to need" that "would permit discrimination as between individuals similarly situated." Jack B. Tate to Oscar Ewing, August 10, 1947, Box 11, GC Correspondence on PA, HEWR.
138. Howard Bernard Gundy, "Grants-in-Aid for Public Assistance and New York State-Federal Relationships," PhD diss., Public Administration, Syracuse University, 1961, 187–88, 202.
139. Derthick, *The Influence of Federal Grants*, 72.
140. Jack B. Tate to Watson B. Miller, November 8, 1946, Box 11, GC Correspondence on PA, HEWR; Jane Hoey to Regional Directors, October 11, 1946, Box 30, GC Correspondence on PA, HEWR; A. Delafield Smith to Regional Attorneys, October 30, 1947, Box 75, GC Correspondence on PA, HEWR.
141. A. Delafield Smith to Robert Ayers et al., May 12, 1948, Box 54, GC Correspondence on PA, HEWR; President's Committee on Civil Rights, *To Secure These Rights*, 166. On the 1939 reorganization and the motives behind it, see Mariano-Florentino Cuellar, "'Securing' the Nation: Law, Politics, and Organization at the Federal Security Agency, 1939–1953," *University of Chicago Law Review* 76 (2009): 587–718. Willcox was cut from the same cloth as the lawyers previously mentioned: he graduated from law school (Harvard) in 1926 and joined the New Deal administration in 1934, after a brief stint in private practice.
142. Alanson Willcox to Donald Kingsley, April 9, 1948, Box 48, GC Correspondence on PA, HEWR; Alanson Willcox to Oscar Ewing, March 15, 1948, Box 48, GC Correspondence on PA, HEWR; Alanson Willcox to John L. Thurston, November 5, 1948, Box 48, GC Correspondence on PA, HEWR.
143. Section 1407(a)(8) proposed that "determinations of eligibility for and amounts of assistance or welfare services under the plan shall be made on bases which, within the area served, will assure to every individual the equal protection of the laws." A Bill to Amend the Social Security Act to Enable States to Establish More Adequate Public-Welfare Programs, and for Other Purposes, H.R. 2892, 81st Cong., 1st sess. (1949).
144. Grisinger, *The Unwieldy American State*, 109.
145. A. J. Meyers, Notes from Regional Attorneys' Conference, October 19, 1949, Box 75, GC Correspondence on PA, HEWR.

146. Whittington B. Johnson, "The Vinson Court and Racial Segregation, 1946–1953," *Journal of Negro History* 63, no. 3 (1978): 221–27; Lee J. Alston and Joseph P. Ferrie, *Southern Paternalism and the American Welfare State: Economics, Politics, and Institutions in the South, 1865–1965* (Cambridge: Cambridge University Press, 1999), 45–46.

147. Jane M. Hoey, "The Contribution of Social Work to Government," in *National Conference of Social Work* (New York: Columbia University Press, 1941), 4–5.

148. Universal Declaration on Human Rights, G.A. Res. 217A, U.N. GAOR, 3d Sess., 1st plen. mtg., U.N. Doc. A/810 (December 12, 1948). On the document's influence, see Mary Ann Glendon, *A World Made New: Eleanor Roosevelt and the Universal Declaration of Human Rights* (New York: Random House, 2001).

149. On loyalty-security measures, including those predating the Truman program, see Eleanor Bontecou, *The Federal Loyalty-Security Program* (Ithaca, NY: Cornell University Press, 1953); Stanley I. Kutler, *The American Inquisition: Justice and Injustice in the Cold War* (New York: Hill & Wang, 1982); Richard M. Fried, *Nightmare in Red: The McCarthy Era in Perspective* (New York: Oxford University Press, 1990). On anxieties about gender and sexuality in the postwar period, see Elaine Tyler May, *Homeward Bound: American Families in the Cold War Era* (New York: Basic Books, 1988); Allan Bérubé, *Coming Out under Fire: The History of Gay Men and Women in World War II* (New York: Free Press, 1990); K. A. Cuordileone, *Manhood and American Political Culture in the Cold War* (New York: Routledge, 2005); Canaday, *The Straight State*. On the intersection of loyalty-security programs and concerns about gender, see Landon R. Y. Storrs, *Civilizing Capitalism: The National Consumers' League, Women's Activism, and Labor Standards in the New Deal Era* (Chapel Hill: University of North Carolina Press, 2000); David K. Johnson, *The Lavender Scare: The Cold War Persecution of Gays and Lesbians in the Federal Government* (Chicago: University of Chicago Press, 2004); Andrea Friedman, "The Strange Career of Annie Lee Moss: Rethinking Race, Gender, and McCarthyism," *Journal of American History* 94, no. 2 (2007): 445–68; Landon R. Y. Storrs, *The Second Red Scare and the Unmaking of the New Deal Left* (Princeton, NJ: Princeton University Press, 2012).

150. Daniel J. Walkowitz, *Working with Class: Social Workers and the Politics of Middle-Class Identity* (Chapel Hill: University of North Carolina Press, 1999), 183–99.

151. Benjamin H. Lyndon, "Relief Probes: A Study of Public Welfare Investigations in Baltimore, New York, and Detroit; 1947–1949," PhD diss., University of Chicago School of Social Services Administration, 1953, 13–102. This episode is part of a larger history of anti–New Deal conservatism. See Chapter 5.

152. Walter Troham, "Order Aids to Swell Dole Lists, Pour Out Cash, Staffs Told," *Chicago Tribune*, December 16, 1947; DeWitt Emery, "Now It's Relief for Everyone," *San Marino (CA) Tribune*, February 5, 1948; DeWitt

Emery, "Federal Documents Urge Social State," *Kingsport (TN) News*, January 12, 1948; DeWitt Emery, "Relief for Everyone," *Morning (MD) Herald*, January 15, 1948; "What Are We Paying Them For?" *Logansport (LA) Press*, January 18, 1948.

153. This paragraph draws generally on Posner, "Common Human Needs"; Reisch and Andrews, *The Road Not Taken*, 91–92.

154. Storrs, *The Second Red Scare*, 238.

155. Lizabeth Cohen, *Making a New Deal: Industrial Workers in Chicago, 1919–1939* (Cambridge: Cambridge University Press, 1990), 252–89.

4   CLAIMING WELFARE RIGHTS

1. "Dere Lady," *Public Welfare in Indiana* 51, no. 4 (April 1941), 15.

2. A. Delafield Smith, "Public Assistance as a Social Obligation," *Harvard Law Review* 63, no. 2 (1949): 277; Edward V. Sparer, "Materials on Public Assistance Law," chap. 3, p. 34 (unpublished draft casebook, University of Pennsylvania Law School, Reginald Heber Smith Community Lawyer Fellowship Program, 1969); Charles A. Reich, "The New Property," *Yale Law Journal* 73, no. 5 (1964): 758.

3. Wilkie v. O'Connor, 25 N.Y.S.2d 617 (App. Div. 1941); "Pension Refused Elderly Horseman Living under Barn," *Dunkirk (NY) Evening Observer*, January 8, 1941.

4. *Wilkie*, 25 N.Y.S.2d at 619.

5. Walter Gellhorn, "Poverty and Legality: The Law's Slow Awakening," *Proceedings of the American Philosophical Society* 112, no. 2 (1968): 108–9.

6. "'88 Grad Boosts '47 Education," *Syracuse (NY) Herald Journal*, June 22, 1947; "'Dave' of Seneca Falls Fights for Right to Sleep under Barn," *Syracuse (NY) Herald-American*, May 12, 1940.

7. Newland v. Child, 254 P.2d 1066, 1070 (Idaho 1953). See also Adams v. Ernst, 95 P.2d 799, 804 (Wash. 1939), for substantially similar language.

8. Hardy v. State Soc. Sec. Comm'n, 187 S.W.2d 520 (Mo. Ct. App. 1945).

9. Wherever possible, I refer to indigenous persons by the names of their specific indigenous communities. When referring to indigenous people as a collective, I use the terms "American Indian" and "Indian." I do so because these appellations remain common and because to some readers, the term "Native American" serves to efface an important history of war, colonization, and intragovernmental agreements. David E. Wilkins and Heidi Kiiwetinepinesiik Stark, *American Indian Politics and the American Political System*, 3rd ed. (Plymouth, U.K.: Rowman & Littlefield Publishers, 2011), xvii; Russell Means, "I Am an American Indian, Not a Native American!" (T.R.E.A.T.Y. Productions, 1996), http://compusci.com/indian/, accessed April 25, 2014; Christina Berry, "What's in a Name? Indians and Political Correctness," All Things Cherokee, http://www.allthingscherokee.com/articles_culture_events_070101.html, accessed April 25, 2014.

10. Barbara Young Welke, *Law and the Borders of Belonging in the Long Nineteenth Century United States* (New York: Cambridge University Press, 2010).

11. On the importance of agencies, see Joanna L. Grisinger, *The Unwieldy American State: Administrative Politics Since the New Deal* (New York: Cambridge University Press, 2012); James Sparrow, *Warfare State: World War II Americans and the Age of Big Government* (New York: Oxford University Press, 2011), 6. On rights as an important new form or currency, see Sparrow, *Warfare State*, 260.

12. "Hearings in Public Assistance, January 1945–December 1947," *Social Security Bulletin* 11, no. 9 (September 1948): 18. There were minor variations in the reporting jurisdictions from year to year. For example, the forty-two jurisdictions that reported data for January to June 1945 were the same as the forty-two that reported for July to December 1945, with the exception of Wisconsin and Oregon: Wisconsin reported for the first period but not the second; Oregon reported for the second period but not the first. Similarly, in each six-month period of data collection, most of the jurisdictions that reported sent in data for all of their programs (OAA, ADC, and AB), but there were always exceptions. For example, in the July–December 1945 period, Delaware, New Jersey, and North Carolina reported no data for their AB programs. Bureau of Public Assistance, "Appeals and Fair Hearings in Public Assistance, Statistical Analysis, July–December 1945," Box 79, GC Correspondence on PA, HEWR.

13. On the one hand, state agencies in the 1945–47 period had surely grown more aware of the importance of fair hearings, thanks to signaling from the federal agency (see Chapter 3), so we might expect the number of hearings in this period to be high relative to prior years. There is also evidence that the aberrational number of hearings in a single state – Massachusetts – artificially inflated the 1945–47 numbers for the nation as a whole. Bureau of Public Assistance, "Appeals and Fair Hearings in Public Assistance, Statistical Analysis, July–December 1945," Box 79, GC Correspondence on PA, HEWR, attributing the 3,384 hearings requested in Massachusetts in 1945 to changes in the state standards for clothing and personal needs. On the other hand, some state-level evidence shows that hearing requests fell during the 1940s, suggesting that nationwide figures may in fact have been higher in the late 1930s than in the mid-1940s. Werner W. Boehm, "Fair Hearings in Wisconsin," *Social Service Review* 25, no. 2 (1951): 193.

14. Reba Choate, "Fair Hearing Procedure in Missouri, 1933–1941, with an Analysis of Judicial Decisions Relating to Old Age Assistance," master's thesis, University of Chicago School of Social Service Administration, 1942, 44, 66; Boehm, "Fair Hearings in Wisconsin," 193; Wilbur C. Hallwachs, "Fair Hearings in the Administration of Old Age Assistance in Illinois," master's thesis, University of Chicago School of Social Service Administration, 1943, 65.

15. See Chapter 3, section titled "The Right to a Fair Hearing: Disparate Views"; see also Helen L. Allen, "Application of the Fair Hearing Process," *Public Welfare* 7, no. 4 (1949): 93.

16. Bureau of Public Assistance, "Appeals and Fair Hearings in Public Assistance, Statistical Analysis, July–December 1945"; Bureau of Public Assistance, "Appeals and Fair Hearings in Public Assistance, Statistical Analysis, January–June 1946," Box 79, GC Correspondence on PA, HEWR; Bureau of Public Assistance, "Appeals and Fair Hearings in Public Assistance, Statistical Analysis, July–December 1946," Box 79, GC Correspondence on PA, HEWR; Bureau of Public Assistance, "Appeals and Fair Hearings in Public Assistance, Statistical Analysis, January–June 1947," Box 79, GC Correspondence on PA, HEWR. "Suitable home"-type requirements are discussed more extensively in Chapters 6, 7, and 8.
17. Arthur J. Altmeyer, "The First Decade in Social Security," *Social Security Bulletin* 8, no. 8 (1945): 1; Elizabeth T. Alling, "Trends in Recipient Rates for Aid to Dependent Children," *Social Security Bulletin* 11, no. 11 (1948): 14.
18. Bureau of Public Assistance, "Appeals and Fair Hearings in Public Assistance, Statistical Analysis, July–December 1945"; Bureau of Public Assistance, "Appeals and Fair Hearings in Public Assistance, Statistical Analysis, January–June 1946"; Bureau of Public Assistance, "Appeals and Fair Hearings in Public Assistance, Statistical Analysis, July–December 1946."
19. On the scale and power of the movement for old age pensions, see Edwin Amenta, *When Movements Matter: The Townsend Plan and the Rise of Social Security* (Princeton, NJ: Princeton University Press, 2006). On how some claimants successfully wielded the disaster narrative, see Michelle Landis Dauber, *The Sympathetic State: Disaster Relief and the Origins of the American Welfare State* (Chicago: University of Chicago Press, 2012).
20. Bureau of Public Assistance, Standards and Program Development Division, "Bureau of Public Assistance Informational Report – January 1948," January 30, 1948, Box 188, Mixed Files, Correspondence Relating to Public Assistance Plans and Programs, 1935–1948, SSAR.
21. On this entanglement, see, for example, Eric C. Schneider, *In the Web of Class: Delinquents and Reformers in Boston, 1810s–1930s* (New York: New York University Press, 1992); Linda Gordon, *Heroes of Their Own Lives: The Politics and History of Family Violence* (New York: Viking, 1988); Susan Stein-Roggenbuck, "'Wholly within the Discretion of the Probate Court': Judicial Authority and Mothers' Pensions in Michigan, 1913–1940," *Social Service Review* 79, no. 2 (2005): 294–321.
22. See Chapter 3, section titled "The Right to a Fair Hearing: Disparate Views."
23. Max Mangum to Riley Mapes, December 31, 1946, Box 71, GC Correspondence on PA, HEWR.
24. Peter Langan to Riley Mapes, December 21, 1945, Box 71, GC Correspondence on PA, HEWR. Illinois's Division of Public Assistance seems to have followed a similar course, at least as of 1943. Hallwachs, "Fair Hearings in the Administration of Old Age Assistance in Illinois," 5–6.
25. Max Mangum to Riley Mapes, October 10, 1946, Box 71, GC Correspondence on PA, HEWR.
26. Federal Security Agency, Social Security Administration, Bureau of Public Assistance, *Hearing Decisions in Public Assistance* 3, no. 3 (1949): 15–31. On

consumer entitlement and understandings of citizenship in the 1940s, see Sparrow, *Warfare State*, 100–108; see generally Meg Jacobs, *Pocketbook Politics: Economic Citizenship in Twentieth-Century America* (Princeton, NJ: Princeton University Press, 2005).

27. Federal Security Agency, Social Security Administration, Bureau of Public Assistance, *Hearing Decisions in Public Assistance* 3, no. 3 (1949): 15–31.

28. Legal scholars have drawn similar conclusions about fair hearings in the contemporary context, while also noting barriers to meaningful client participation. Lucie E. White, "Subordination, Rhetorical Survival Skills, and Sunday Shoes: Notes on the Hearing of Mrs. G.," *Buffalo Law Review* 38, no. 1 (1990): 1–58; Vicki Lens, "In the Fair Hearing Room: Resistance and Confrontation in the Welfare Bureaucracy," *Law & Social Inquiry* 32, no. 2 (2007): 309–32.

29. Federal Security Agency, Social Security Administration, Bureau of Public Assistance, *Hearing Decisions in Public Assistance* 2, no. 4 (1948): 6–29. For a rich historical exploration of the care work that adult children performed for their parents and the legal status of that work, see Hendrik Hartog, *Someday All This Will Be Yours: A History of Inheritance and Old Age* (Cambridge, MA: Harvard University Press, 2012).

30. Federal Security Agency, Social Security Administration, Bureau of Public Assistance, *Hearing Decisions in Public Assistance* 2, no. 1 (1948): 12–13.

31. Federal Security Agency, Social Security Administration, Bureau of Public Assistance, *Hearing Decisions in Public Assistance* 1, no. 3 (July 1947): 12–13.

32. "Re: Henrietta Litter, V-3207," May 11, 1945, Box 68, GC Correspondence on PA, HEWR; see also Ellis Radinsky, "Appeals, Fair Hearings and Reviews," master's thesis, New York School of Social Work, Columbia University, 1941, 101, noting that the OAA hearings held in New York were "usually inspired by [the claimants'] children, attorneys, [and] friends, and carried out by those interested parties." On the influence of organized pensions groups, see Hallwachs, "Fair Hearings in the Administration of Old Age Assistance in Illinois," 22, 42–50 (describing the role of the Illinois Old Age Pension Union and the OAA Union of Illinois in encouraging fair hearings in Cook County).

33. This definition is arguably too narrow, because it excludes cases involving state-administered, non–federally funded general relief. At least a handful of cases fall into this category, including the federal court case *Sweeney v. State Board of Public Assistance*, 36 F. Supp. 171 (M.D. Pa. 1940), in which two plaintiffs challenged a regulation of the Pennsylvania State Board of Public Assistance on equal protection grounds. One might also include legal challenges to the deportation of poor benefit seekers, such as the Illinois case *Heyendreich v. Lyons*, 374 Ill. 557 (1940). On this case and others involving poor migrants, see Elisa Martia Alvarez Minoff, "Free to Move? The Law and Politics of Internal Migration in Twentieth-Century America," PhD diss., Harvard University, 2013, 178–223.

34. Joseph L. Gerken, "A Librarian's Guide to Unpublished Judicial Opinions," *Law Library Journal* 96, no. 3 (2004): 479.

2

35. This is true for Alabama, Arkansas, Arizona, Florida (until 1957), Hawaii, Idaho, Iowa, Kentucky, Maine, Massachusetts, Michigan, Minnesota, Mississippi, Montana, Nebraska, Nevada, New Hampshire, New Mexico, North Carolina, North Dakota, Oklahoma, Oregon, Rhode Island, South Carolina, South Dakota, Utah, Vermont, Virginia, Washington, West Virginia, Wisconsin, and Wyoming. Connecticut and Delaware also lacked intermediate appellate courts in this period, but those states reported some decisions of their superior courts. Further complicating matters is the fact that since the nineteenth century state supreme courts have had varying degrees of control over their dockets. During the period under review, some state supreme courts would have been able to decline to hear some or all of the appeals they received ("discretionary jurisdiction"). See Theodore Eisenberg and Geoffrey P. Miller, "Reversal, Dissent, and Variability in State Supreme Courts: The Centrality of Jurisdictional Source," *Boston University Law Review* 89 (2009): 1456–58.
36. Arthur Dimsdale to Fowler V. Harper, March, 25, 1940, Box 15, GC Correspondence on PA, HEWR.
37. Fowler Harper to Paul McNutt, January 8, 1940, Box 12, GC Correspondence on PA, HEWR. I deduced the plaintiff's first name through searches of local newspapers and the 1940 census.
38. Carl K. Schmidt Jr., Illinois Public Aid Commission, "Developments in the Appeal of Eva Roberson," March 3, 1950, Box 69, GC Correspondence on PA, HEWR.
39. See, for example, Jack B. Tate to Regional Director, Boston, January 22, 1938, Box 3, GC Correspondence on PA, HEWR, documenting additional OAA cases in Massachusetts; Arthur Miller to Office of the General Counsel, February 18, 1938, Box 15, GC Correspondence on PA, HEWR, documenting additional OAA cases in Washington; Peter Seitz to Harold Packer, February 15, 1939, Box 25, GC Correspondence on PA, HEWR, documenting an additional case in Washington; Jack Tate to Oscar Powell, March 8, 1939, Box 12, GC Correspondence on PA, HEWR, documenting an additional OAA case in South Carolina; Robert C. Ayers to Harold G. Wilson, September 1, 1939, Box 15, GC Correspondence on PA, HEWR, documenting additional OAA cases in Colorado; Fowler Harper to Paul McNutt, January 8, 1940, Box 12, GC Correspondence on PA, HEWR, documenting an additional ADC case in Kansas; Fowler Harper to Paul McNutt, April 10, 1940, Box 12, GC Correspondence on PA, HEWR, documenting additional cases in Oklahoma and Missouri; Jack Tate to Paul McNutt, November 12, 1941, Box 12, GC Correspondence on PA, HEWR, documenting an additional OAA case in California and a group of cases in Washington; Edward Rourke to Elizabeth Doyle, April 29, 1944, Box 72, GC Correspondence on PA, HEWR, documenting an additional OAA case in Washington; Jack Tate to Paul McNutt, May 10, 1944, Box 11, GC Correspondence on PA, HEWR, documenting an additional case in Texas; Elizabeth Doyle to Edward Rourke, December 28, 1944, Box 72, GC Correspondence on PA, HEWR, documenting two additional OAA cases in Washington; Arthur Miller to GC, July 19, 1946, Box 72, GC Correspondence on PA, HEWR, documenting an

additional OAA case in Washington; Arthur Miller to Regional Director, San Francisco, October 9, 1947, Box 72, GC Correspondence on PA, HEWR, documenting six to eight cases pending before the superior courts in Washington; Arthur Miller to GC, May 6, 1948, Box 72, GC Correspondence on PA, HEWR, documenting two OAA cases appealed to the superior courts in Washington; Laurence Dimsdale to Regional PA Representative, July 19, 1950, Box 69, GC Correspondence on PA, HEWR, documenting an additional ADC case in Illinois; Mildred Caroline Tallman and John Arthur Dunn, "An Analysis of the Use of the Fair Hearing Process in the Administration of Public Assistance in Colorado," master's thesis, University of Denver, 1952, 41–47, documenting additional cases in Colorado.

40. An Act Amending the Jurisdiction of District Courts in Civil Actions with Regard to the Amount in Controversy and Diversity of Citizenship, Pub. L. No. 85-554, 72 Stat. 415 (1958). "Amount in controversy" is the minimum amount of money damages that a claimant must sue for in order for a federal court to hear the case.

41. Civil Rights Act of 1871, Pub. L. No. 42-22, 17 Stat. 13 (1871). The provision cited in the text is now codified at 42 U.S.C. § 1983; the jurisdiction-granting provision is 42 U.S.C. § 1343(3). Thomas J. Klitgaard, "The Civil Rights Act and Mr. Monroe," *California Law Review* 49 (1961): 145.

42. Past or future judges included Missouri's Justin Ruark. Past or future legislators included Missouri's Edward V. Long, W. Randall Smart, David W. Hill, and G. Purd Hays, and Washington's Ralph L. J. Armstrong.

43. Reuel E. Schiller, "The Era of Deference: Courts, Expertise, and the Emergence of New Deal Administrative Law," *Michigan Law Review* 106, no. 3 (2007); Jim Rossi, "Politics, Institutions, and Administrative Procedure: What Exactly Do We Know from the Study of State-Level APAs, and What More Can We Learn?" *Administrative Law Review* 58 (2007): 977–78.

44. Jules H. Berman, "The Administration of the Appeal Provisions of the Public Assistance Legislation Enacted under the Social Security Act in Illinois and Certain Other States," master's thesis, University of Chicago of Social Service Administration, 1937, 16–17. A 1942 dissertation added South Dakota to the list. Choate, "Fair Hearing Procedure in Missouri," 51.

45. Berman, "The Administration of the Appeal Provisions," 16; Schiller, "The Era of Deference," 407–8. On the difficulties with securing a writ of mandamus in the welfare context, see A. Delafield Smith, "Judicial Trends in Relation to Public Welfare Administration," *Social Service Review* 15, no. 2 (1941): 246–49.

46. Berman, "The Administration of the Appeal Provisions," 16. The eighteen states were Alabama, Arizona, Arkansas, Georgia, Idaho, Maryland, New Mexico, North Carolina, Ohio, Oklahoma, Pennsylvania (except for in its Aid to the Blind statute, which made no mention of finality), Rhode Island, South Carolina, Tennessee, Texas, Vermont, Wisconsin, and Wyoming. A subsequent article by a federal agency attorney suggests that Mississippi also belongs on this list. Hubert H. Margolies, "Judicial Review of Public Assistance Determinations," *Indiana Law Journal* 16 (1940–41): 488n1.

47. Charles McKinley and Robert W. Frase, *Launching Social Security: A Capture-and-Record Account, 1935–1937* (Madison: University of Wisconsin Press, 1970), 157; Choate, "Fair Hearing Procedure in Missouri," 28–30; "Many Old Folks Protest Against Being Removed from Pension Roll," *Jefferson City (MO) Post Tribune*, January 26, 1938; "Board Disturbed by Pension Ruling," *Joplin (MO) Globe*, November 3, 1938. On the patronage opportunities that the Pendergast machine gained from New Deal programs and on Governor Stark's campaign to take down the machine, see Lyle W. Dorsett, *The Pendergast Machine* (Lincoln: University of Nebraska Press, 1980), 102–37.

48. Charles F. Ernst, "Clients Aren't What They Used to Be," *Survey* 74, no. 5 (1938): 142.

49. Felicia Kornbluh, "Disability, Antiprofessionalism, and Civil Rights: The National Federation of the Blind and the 'Right to Organize' in the 1950s," *Journal of American History* 97, no. 4 (2011): 1028–29; Thomas A. Krainz, "Transforming the Progressive Era Welfare State: Activists for the Blind and Blind Benefits," *Journal of Policy History* 15, no. 2 (2003): 224.

50. See, for example, Rand E. Rosenblatt, "Legal Entitlements and Welfare Benefits," in *The Politics of Law: A Progressive Critique*, ed. David Kairys (New York: Pantheon, 1982), 263; Lucy A. Williams, "Welfare and Legal Entitlements: The Social Roots of Poverty," in *The Politics of Law: A Progressive Critique*, ed. David Kairys (New York: Basic Books, 1998), 574; Paul K. Legler, "Beyond Legal Rights? The Future of Legal Rights and the Welfare System," *Brigham Young University Journal of Public Law* 6 (1992): 74.

51. Helen Hershkoff, "Rights and Freedoms under the State Constitution: A New Deal for Welfare Rights," *Touro Law Review* 13 (1997): 637, citing Goldberg v. Kelly, 397 U.S. 254, 262 (1970).

52. "Pension Test Case Is Heard at Neosho," *Joplin (MO) Globe*, December 18, 1937; Price v. State Soc. Sec. Comm'n, 121 S.W.2d 298 (Mo. App. 1938); see also Moore v. State Soc. Sec. Comm'n, 122 S.W.2d 391 (Mo. App. 1938).

53. Conant v. State, 84 P.2d 378 (Wash. 1938).

54. The court extended this holding even to the applicant who had since died. Bd. of Soc. Welfare v. Los Angeles Cnty., 162 P.2d 630 (Cal.1945).

55. Creighton v. Pope Cnty., 50 N.E.2d 984 (Ill. App. Ct. 1943).

56. Creighton v. Pope Cnty., 54 N.E.2d 543 (Ill. 1944). These cases appear specific to OAA and AB but they also had relevance for ADC: although eligibility requirements differed from program to program, the legal and administrative structures of all the public assistance programs were substantially similar. It took no leap of logic to apply a judicial decision regarding one program to a dispute involving another. See, for example, Meredith v. Ray, 166 S.W.2d 437 (Ky. Ct. App. 1942) [extending the logic of the AB case Bowman v. Frost, 158 S.W.2d 945 (Ky. Ct. App. 1942), to an ADC case].

57. *Conant*, 84 P.2d 378.

58. Federal Security Agency, Office of the General Counsel, "Annual Report for the Year Ending June 30, 1939," Box 214, Records of the Office of the Commissioner, Executive Director's File, SSAR; "Court Decisions Plague

State Old Age Pensions," *Centralia (WA) Daily Chronicle*, January 11, 1939; Arthur Altmeyer to Clarence D. Martin, January 24, 1939, Box 92, Records of the Office of the Commissioner, Chairman's Files, 1935–1942, SSAR; "May Lose U.S. Aid on Pensions," *Moberly (MO) Monitor Index*, November 17, 1938.

59. Buettner v. State Soc. Sec. Comm'n, 144 S.W.2d 864 (Mo. Ct. App. 1940); Howlett v. Soc. Sec. Comm'n, 149 S.W.2d 806 (Mo. 1941); *Adams*, 95 P.2d 799; Adams v. Ernst, 117 P.2d 755 (Wash. 1941); "Pension Issue Still Unresolved," *Moberly (MO) Monitor-Index and Democrat*, October 7, 1938.

60. Oliver v. State Soc. Sec. Comm'n, 184 S.W.2d 774 (Mo. Ct. App. 1945).

61. Hooks v. State Soc. Sec. Comm'n, 165 S.W.2d 267 (Mo. Ct. App. 1942). See also Parks v. State Soc. Sec. Comm'n, 160 S.W.2d 823 (Mo. Ct. App. 1942).

62. E. Blythe Stason, "'Substantial Evidence' in Administrative Law," *University of Pennsylvania Law Review* 89 (1941): 1026–51. Consistent with legal developments in the federal courts, state court judges signaled that they would decide questions of law for themselves but would accord deference to the factual and discretionary judgments that legislatures had entrusted agencies to make. See, for example, Redmon v. State Soc. Sec. Comm'n, 143 S. W.2d 168 (Mo. Ct. App. 1940) [holding that, under the 1939 amendment to the state OAA law, courts did not have jurisdiction to determine the facts themselves and that decisions of the commission must be upheld if based on substantial evidence]; Schneberger v. State Bd. of Soc. Welfare, 291 N.W. 859 (Iowa 1940) [making clear that a court should overturn the state board of social welfare only in cases of fraud or abuse of discretion]; Application of Rasmussen, 289 N.W. 773, 775 (Minn. 1940) [holding that, in reviewing a decision of the state agency, a district court "may go no further than to find whether the order of the state agency is fraudulent, arbitrary or unreasonable"]; Morgan v. Dept. of Soc. Sec., 127 P.2d 686, 699 (Wash. 1942) ["The courts hesitate to interfere with the action of an administrative department, when definitely taken upon an important phase of the work which the department has been created to perform, unless it appears that in reaching its determination the department has proceeded upon a fundamentally wrong basis, or has acted arbitrarily or capriciously"]. On the Illinois Supreme Court's departure from this trend in 1937 and then prompt about-face, see Smith, "Judicial Trends," 244–46. On federal court trends, see Schiller, "The Era of Deference"; Daniel R. Ernst, *Tocqueville's Nightmare: The Administrative State Emerges in America, 1900–1940* (New York: Oxford University Press, 2014).

63. Nichols v. State Soc. Sec. Comm'n, 156 S.W.2d 760 (Mo. Ct. App. 1941).

64. Nichols v. State Soc. Sec. Comm'n, 164 S.W.2d 278 (Mo. 1942).

65. Ibid.

66. See, e.g., Dunnavant v. State Soc. Sec. Comm'n, 150 S.W.2d 1103 (Mo. Ct. App. 1941); Burgfield v. State Soc. Sec. Comm'n, 155 S.W.2d 273 (Mo. Ct. App. 1941); Chapman v. State Soc. Sec. Comm'n, 147 S.W.2d 157 (Mo. Ct. App. 1941); Smith v. State Soc. Sec. Comm'n, 153 S.W.2d 741 (Mo. Ct. App. 1941); Burley v. State Soc. Sec. Comm'n, 163 S.W.2d 95 (Mo. Ct.

App. 1942); Kelley v. State Soc. Sec. Comm'n, 161 S.W.2d 661 (Mo. Ct. App. 1942); Perkins v. State Soc. Sec. Comm'n, 164 S.W.2d 129 (Mo. Ct. App. 1942); Taylor v. State Soc. Sec. Comm'n, 181 S.W.2d 209 (Mo. Ct. App. 1944); Campbell v. State Soc. Sec. Comm'n, 191 S.W.2d 1015 (Mo. Ct. App. 1945); Doolin v. State Soc. Sec. Comm'n, 187 S.W.2d 467 (Mo. Ct. App. 1945).

67. *Hardy*, 187 S.W.2d 520. Courts did not always take this view. See, for example, Gaeckler v. State Soc. Sec. Comm'n, 155 S.W.2d 544 (Mo. Ct. App. 1941) [treating support from relatives as irrelevant where these relatives "positively . . . refuse(d)" to support the claimant any longer].

68. This argument is reminiscent of Michael Grossberg's in *Governing the Hearth: Law and the Family in Nineteenth-Century America* (Chapel Hill: University of North Carolina Press, 1988): in inviting the state into previously "private" realms, litigants sometimes produced outcomes that undermined the governing logic of those spaces.

69. *Dunnavant*, 150 S.W.2d 1103; *Gaeckler*, 155 S.W.2d 544.

70. Los Angeles Cnty. v. La Fuente, 129 P.2d 378 (Cal. 1942); see also *Newland*, 254 P.2d at 1069 ["The old-age assistance law is to be distinguished from so-called 'poor laws' or 'indigent statutes' in that the old-age assistance act does not require that the recipient be a pauper or absolutely destitute"]; cf. Cohasset v. Scituate, 34 N.E.2d 699, 703 (Mass. 1941) [noting, in the context of a dispute between two towns over which should pay for a poor woman and her family, that ADC is a type of aid "different in scope from and more substantial than that afforded by (the state general relief statute), and without the necessity of accepting general welfare"].

71. Ethel J. Hart, "The Responsibility of Relatives under the State Old Age Assistance Laws," *Social Service Review* 15, no. 1 (1941): 24–54; Stefan A. Riesenfeld and Richard C. Maxwell, *Modern Social Legislation* (Brooklyn, NY: Foundation Press, 1950), 792–94; Daniel R. Mandelker, "Family Responsibility under the American Poor Laws: I," *Michigan Law Review* 54, no. 4 (1956): 497–532; Daniel R. Mandelker, "Family Responsibility under the American Poor Laws: II," *Michigan Law Review* 54, no. 5 (1956): 607–32. For glimpses of how relative-responsibility laws intersected with OAA programs in specific states, see Michael V. Hitrovo, "Responsibility of Relatives in the Old Age Assistance Program in Pennsylvania," *Social Service Review* 18, no. 1 (1944): 67–76; Alton A. Linford, "Responsibility of Children in the Massachusetts Old Age Assistance Program: II. Legislation and Administration, 1936–43," *Social Service Review* 19, no. 2 (1945): 218–34; Sema Levinson, "Support from Relatives to Recipients of Old Age Assistance," master's thesis, University of Chicago School of Social Service Administration, 1941.

72. *Howlett*, 149 S.W.2d at 812.

73. When the elderly individual was not utterly destitute, legal historian Hendrik Hartog has shown, the transition was instead from a private duty to a compensable service. Hartog, *Someday All This Will Be Yours*. On the declining role of children's earnings in supporting households, and the desire, by young and old alike, to shift the burden to the state, see Brian Gratton, "The Creation of

Retirement: Families, Individuals and the Social Security Movement," in *Societal Impact on Aging: Historical Perspectives*, ed. K. Warner Schaie and W. Andrew Achenbaum (New York: Springer, 1993), 45–73.

74. Achor v. State Soc. Sec. Comm'n, 191 S.W.2d 259 (Mo. Ct. App. 1945).

75. For an example of how the Supreme Court grappled with the issue around this time, see *Lynch v. United States*, 292 U.S. 571 (1934) [discussing whether benefits owed under government War Risk Insurance policies were "property" for purposes of the Fifth Amendment's Due Process Clause].

76. Bowen v. Dept. of Soc. Sec., 127 P.2d 682 (Wash. 1942).

77. Oklahoma Pub. Welfare Comm'n v. Thompson, 105 P.2d 547 (Okla. 1940). Appellate courts in New York and Kentucky agreed with the *Thompson* decision. Wilkie v. O'Connor, 25 N.Y.S.2d 617 (App. Div. 1941); Greenwood v. Taylor, 60 N.Y.S.2d 452 (App. Div. 1946); Hawkins v. Dep't of Welfare, 197 S.W.2d 98 (Ky. Ct. App. 1946).

78. *Thompson*, 105 P.2d at 553 (Riley, J., dissenting).

79. Rosebraugh v. State Soc. Sec. Comm'n, 196 S.W.2d 27, 34 (Mo. Ct. App. 1946).

80. Foster v. State Soc. Sec. Comm'n, 187 S.W.2d 870 (Mo. Ct. App. 1945).

81. McBee v. State Soc. Sec. Comm'n, 188 S.W.2d 349 (Mo. Ct. App. 1945); see also Hagy v. Dep't of Welfare, 259 S.W.2d 101 (Mo. Ct. App. 1953).

82. *Meredith*, 197 S.W.2d 98. The 1940 census spells the child's name "Mayme." "United States Census, 1940," *FamilySearch*, accessed May 7, 2015, https://familysearch.org/ark:/61903/1:1:K7RY-CDW. For other examples of equal protection claims in the public assistance context in the 1940s, see *Dimke v. Finke*, 295 N.W. 75 (Minn. 1940), and *Wallberg v. Utah Pub. Welfare Comm'n*, 203 P.2d 935 (Utah 1949), both of which involved challenges to lien laws. Lien laws required OAA beneficiaries who owned real property to give the state a legal interest in that property, so that, on the one hand, they would not have to sell their homes in order to qualify for aid, and, on the other, the state would eventually recover some of what it spent from the beneficiaries' estates. The plaintiffs in these cases objected to the nonuniform imposition of a repayment obligation.

83. Sam V. Stiles, "Willingness to Get Into a Scrape Is a Trait Meredith Acquired When a Boy on His Father's Farm in Warren," *City Daily News* (Bowling Green, KY), February 2, 1955; James C. Klotter, *Kentucky: Portrait in Paradox, 1900–1950* (Lexington: University Press of Kentucky, 1996), 318; *Meredith*, 197 S.W.2d 98.

84. Howard Gillman, *The Constitution Besieged: The Rise and Demise of Lochner Era Police Powers Jurisprudence* (Durham, NC: Duke University Press, 1993); Risa Lauren Goluboff, *The Lost Promise of Civil Rights* (Cambridge, MA: Harvard University Press, 2007); Victoria F. Nourse and Sarah Maguire, "The Lost History of Governance and Equal Protection," *Duke Law Journal* 58, no. 6 (2009): 955–1012.

85. For a fuller account of this history, see Karen M. Tani, "States' Rights, Welfare Rights, and 'The Indian Problem': Negotiating Citizenship and Sovereignty, 1935–1954," *Law and History Review* 33, no. 1 (2015): 1–40. Cases involving the rights of poor migrants raised many of the same issues, as

Elisa Minoff has persuasively argued. If we broaden our understanding of welfare rights to include those cases, the first federal welfare rights case would be *Chirrillo v. Lehman*, 38 F.Supp. 65 (S.D.N.Y. 1940). Minoff, "Free to Move?" 178–233.

86. Gregory Ablavsky, "The Savage Constitution," *Duke Law Journal* 63 (2014): 999–1089.

87. Sidney L. Harring, *Crow Dog's Case: American Indian Sovereignty, Tribal Law, and United States Law in the Nineteenth Century* (New York: Cambridge University Press, 1994).

88. Laura E. Gómez, *Manifest Destinies: The Making of the Mexican American Race* (New York: New York University Press, 2007), 90–98; United States v. Sandoval, 231 U.S. 28 (1913).

89. Lewis Meriam, "State and Local Cooperation with the National Government in Social and Educational Work for Indians: Statement of the Problem," in *National Conference on Social Welfare Proceedings: 1931* (Chicago: University of Chicago Press, 1931), 609–11; Lewis Meriam, *The Problem of Indian Administration* (Baltimore: Johns Hopkins Press, 1928). For earlier invocations of the "Indian problem," see Robert G. Hayes, *A Race at Bay: New York Times Editorials on "The Indian Problem," 1860–1900* (Carbondale: Southern Illinois University Press, 1997).

90. For an overview of the historical literature on Indians' entanglement in federal-state power struggles, see Christian McMillen, "Native Americans," in *The Blackwell Companion to American Legal History*, ed. Alfred Brophy and Sally Hadden(Malden, MA: Wiley-Blackwell, 2012), 127–51. I use the term Bureau of Indian Affairs to refer to the agency that has at other times been known as the Indian Service, the Indian Department, and the Office of Indian Affairs. Originally part of the War Department, the BIA was transferred in 1824 to the Department of the Interior, where it has remained.

91. A. Delafield Smith to Geoffrey May, December 20, 1939, Box 92, Office of the Commissioner, Chairman's Files, SSAR. Labor Secretary Frances Perkins, chair of the committee that drafted the law, reportedly told BIA officials that it was unnecessary to insert language specifically including Indians. Yet at least one senator, Peter Norbeck (R., South Dakota), contended that the draft legislation "entirely overlooked" Indians – and suggested adding an "Indian Pensions" title. Norbeck's proposal disappeared from the record without comment. William Zimmerman Jr. to Frank Bane, January 1, 1936, Box 10, GC Correspondence on PA, HEWR; 74 Cong. Rec. 9437 (daily ed. June 17, 1935); 74 Cong. Rec. 9540–41 (daily ed. June 18, 1935).

92. Sue White to Thomas H. Eliot, February 2, 1936, Box 10, GC Correspondence on PA, HEWR; John Winant to Benjamin Ross, April 3, 1936, Box 92, Office of the Commissioner, Chairman's Files, SSAR; John Winant to William Zimmerman Jr., April 11, 1936, Box 92, Office of the Commissioner, Chairman's Files, SSAR; Frank Bane to Carl Hayden, November 21, 1936, Box 92, Office of the Commissioner, Chairman's Files, SSAR.

93. Nathan R. Margold, memo, April 22, 1938, Box 10, GC Correspondence on PA, HEWR; William Zimmerman Jr. to H. A. Willson, June 23, 1936, Box 10, GC Correspondence on PA, HEWR; John Collier to Royal L. Mann,

May 8, 1936, Box 10, GC Correspondence on PA, HEWR. Unsuccessful lawsuits in two states, Montana and Minnesota, supported the board's position. A. Delafield Smith to Alice P. Stanton, February 3, 1944, Box 53, GC Correspondence on PA, HEWR; Jack Tate to Paul McNutt, January 14, 1941, Box 12, GC Correspondence on PA, HEWR.

94. Frank Bane to Carl Hayden, November 24, 1936, Box 92, Office of the Commissioner, Chairman's Files, SSAR; Sue S. White to Thomas H. Eliot, February 27, 1936, Box 10, GC Correspondence on PA, HEWR. This is not to say that Indian applicants were always treated equally. Federal administrators documented inequities in grant amounts, as well as resistance from some county-level officials. Jane Hoey to Oscar M. Powell, June 1, 1940, Box 92, Office of the Commissioner, Chairman's Files, SSAR.

95. Eric V. Meeks, *Border Citizens: The Making of Indians, Mexicans, and Anglos in Arizona* (Austin: University of Texas Press, 2007), 36–42; Pablo Mitchell, Coyote Nation: Sexuality, Race, and Conquest in Modernizing New Mexico, 1880–1920 (Chicago: University of Chicago Press, 2005), 16–18.

96. U.S. Department of Commerce, *The Indian Population of the United States and Alaska 1930*, vol. 1 (Washington, DC: U.S. Government Printing Office, 1937), 3–5; Lewis Meriam, "The Indian Problem: A Challenge to American Capacity for Social Service," in *National Conference on Social Welfare Proceedings: 1929* (Chicago: University of Chicago Press, 1930), 550.

97. Carl Hayden to Frank Bane, November 20, 1936, Box 92, Office of the Commissioner, Chairman's Files, SSAR.

98. William S. Collins, *The New Deal in Arizona* (Phoenix: Arizona State Parks Board, 1999), 381–82.

99. U.S. Bureau of Indian Affairs, *Statistical Report of Public Assistance to Indians, under the Social Security Act: Old Age Assistance, Aid to Dependent Children, Aid to the Blind, as of October 1, 1939* (Washington, DC: U.S. Government Printing Office, 1939); Jane Hoey to Oscar M. Powell, June 1, 1940, Box 92, Office of the Commissioner, Chairman's Files, SSAR; Alanson W. Willcox to Murray A. Hintz, February 21, 1949, Box 53, GC Correspondence on PA, HEWR.

100. Ruth Falkenburg Kirk, "Indian Welfare: The Navaho," *Public Welfare News* 4 (April 1946): 83; Charles F. Schwartz and Robert E. Graham Jr., "State Income Payments in 1948," *Survey of Current Business* (August 1949): 15.

101. Ira Katznelson, *Fear Itself: The New Deal and the Origins of Our Time* (New York: W. W. Norton, 2013), 168.

102. Carl Hayden to Harry W. Hill, October 23, 1939, Box 699, Carl T. Hayden Papers, MS CM MSS 1, Arizona State University Libraries, Arizona Collection, Tempe [hereafter cited as CHP]; Harry W. Hill to Carl Hayden, May 31, 1940, enclosing letter from H.R. Fryer to Leland D. Carmack, May 22, 1940, Box 699, CHP; Harry W. Hill to Carl Hayden, May 31, 1940, Box 699, CHP; John Collier to Carl Hayden, June 1, 1940, Box 699, CHP; Carl Hayden to Harry W. Hill, June 1, 1940, Box 699, CHP.

103. J. R. McDougall to Carl Hayden, April 30, 1943, Box 36, CHP; John Collier to Floyd G. Brown, June 7, 1943, Box 36, CHP.

104. Meeting Minutes, April 25, 1946, Minutes of the Meetings of the Emergency Relief Administration of Arizona/State Board of Public Welfare, RG 37, SG 1, Arizona State Library, Archives and Public Records, Phoenix [hereafter cited as ABPW Minutes]; Ruth F. Kirk to Margaretta Dietrich, November 17, 1945, Box 9691, Records of the Southwestern Association of Indian Affairs, New Mexico State Records Center and Archives, Santa Fe [hereafter cited as SAIAR].

105. Harry W. Hill to Carl Hayden, May 15, 1946, Box 36, CHP; Jane Hoey to Arthur Altmeyer, September 17, 1947, Box 37, GC Correspondence on PA, HEWR.

106. Thomas W. Cowger, *The National Congress of American Indians: The Founding Years* (Lincoln: University of Nebraska Press, 2001), 37, 41; Arthur Altmeyer to Harry W. Hill, November 7, 1947, Box 40, Papers of Governors Sidney Preston Osborn and Daniel E. Garvey, RG 1, SG 14–15, Arizona State Library, Archives and Public Records, Phoenix [hereafter cited as SO/DG Papers]. For other evidence of federal administrators' complicity, albeit for their own reasons, see Jane Hoey to Arthur Altmeyer, September 17, 1947, Box 37, GC Correspondence on PA, HEWR, reporting that in September, 1947, attorney Royal Marks approached the Bureau of Public Assistance to inquire about the eligibility of his clients, members of the Hualapai tribe, and was advised "to have the Indians make application and to insist upon a fair hearing if application was not taken"; Sara H. James, "Public Responsibility for the American Indian," in *National Conference on Social Welfare Proceedings: 1947* (New York: Columbia University Press, 1948), 182–84, urging welfare administrators to "make known to the Indian his rights" so as to "help him resolve his conflict between wanting to be treated like other people, and yet wanting to hold on to the security of government control."

107. "State Drafts Indian Plan," n.d., Box 36, CHP; Memorandum summarizing conference held at the State Department of Social Security and Welfare, November 6, 1947, Box 40, SO/DG Papers; Ben Avery, "Indian Refusal Cuts U.S. Funds," n.d., *Arizona Republic*, Box 43, SO/DG Papers; "Shameful," *Arizona Times*, October 31, 1947, Box 36, CHP; Ben Avery, "Navajo Ponder Fate of Hunger, Disease," November 5, 1947, *Arizona Republic*, Box 113, Records of the National Congress of American Indians, Accession 1, National Museum of the American Indian, Washington, DC [hereafter cited as NCAIR].

108. Alanson W. Willcox to Oscar Ewing, December 10, 1947, Box 11, GC Correspondence on PA, HEWR; Meeting Minutes, January 29, 1948, ABPW Minutes; New Mexico Department of Public Welfare, *Annual Report, Year Ending June 30, 1950*; Harry Hill to Carl Hayden, February 13, 1948, Box 36, CHP.

109. William E. Warne to Carl Hayden, March 2, 1948, Box 36, CHP; Harry Hill to Carl Hayden, March 29, 1948, Box 36, CHP; Meeting Minutes, June 17, 1948, ABPW Minutes; Felix S. Cohen, "Our Country's Shame,"

Progressive, May 1949, Box 67, Felix S. Cohen Papers, WA MSS S-1325, Beinecke Rare Book and Manuscript Library, Yale University [hereafter cited as FCP]; William Zimmerman Jr. to Julius Krug, September 3, 1948, Box 67, Julius A. Krug Papers, Library of Congress Manuscript Division.

110. On the "Indian New Deal," see generally Graham D. Taylor, *The New Deal and American Indian Tribalism: The Administration of the Indian Reorganization Act, 1934–45* (Lincoln: University of Nebraska Press, 1980); Conserve and Develop Indian Lands and Resources Act, Pub. L. No. 73-383, 48 Stat. 984 (1934). On Cohen's departure from government service, see Landon R. Y. Storrs, *The Second Red Scare and the Unmaking of the New Deal Left* (Princeton, NJ: Princeton University Press, 2012), 223. On Cohen's battles for tribal rights and Indian self-determination, see Christian W. McMillen, *Making Indian Law: The Hualapai Land Case and the Birth of Ethnohistory* (New Haven, CT: Yale University Press, 2007). On Cohen's approach to Indian rights and his understanding of Indians' legal status, see Felix S. Cohen, "The Spanish Origin of Indian Rights in the Law of the United States," *Georgetown Law Journal* 31 (1942): 1–21; Dalia Tsuk Mitchell, *Architect of Justice: Felix S. Cohen and the Founding of American Legal Pluralism* (Ithaca, NY: Cornell University Press, 2007).

111. Willard Hughes Rolling, "Citizenship and Suffrage: The Native American Struggle for Civil Rights in the American West, 1830–1965," *Nevada Law Journal* 5 (2004): 126–40. Only two other states, Utah and Maine, denied Indians the franchise at this time. Ibid., 138.

112. Felix S. Cohen, "Breaking Faith with Our First Americans," *Indian Truth* 4 (March–April 1948): 4; Will Rogers Jr., "Starvation without Representation," *Look* (February 3, 1948): 36.

113. Felix S. Cohen and James E. Curry, Petition to the Social Security Board, July 7, 1948, Box 53, GC Correspondence on PA, HEWR; Sam Ahkeah to Ruth Muskrat Bronson, August 27, 1948, Box 113, NCAIR. In support of their novel request, the lawyers cleverly cited the new Administrative Procedure Act, legislation designed to demonstrate agencies' adherence to the rule of law. Pub. L. No. 79-404, 60 Stat. 237 (1946). The Navajo Tribal Council, despite assisting the NCAI in its investigation, was notably absent from this petition, perhaps because the tribe had recently hired its own attorney, former assistant attorney general Norman Littell.

114. Complaint, Mapatis v. Ewing, Civ. No. 3882–48 (D. D.C. 1948). "Subordinate officers" in the Social Security Board reportedly supported the plaintiffs, as did other Southwestern tribes. James E. Curry to the Convention of the National Congress of American Indians, December 12, 1948, Box 457, NCAIR; Meeting Minutes, October 22, 1948, ABPW Minutes.

115. Complaint, *Mapatis*, Civ. No. 3882–48 (D. D.C. 1948).

116. On the board's earlier legal interpretations, see Smith to May, December 20, 1939, Box 92, GC Correspondence on PA, HEWR; A. Delafield Smith to Jane Hoey, November 21, 1947, Box 7, GC Correspondence on PA, HEWR. On the board's response to the complaint, see Joseph Meyers to Alanson W.

Willcox, October 13, 1948, Box 53, GC Correspondence on PA, HEWR; Felix S. Cohen and James E. Curry, "Washington Report to Indians of New Mexico & Arizona on Social Security," October 29, 1948, Box 401, Harold L. Ickes Papers, Library of Congress Manuscript Division.

117. Kenneth R. Philp, *Termination Revisited: American Indians on the Trail to Self-Determination, 1933–1953* (Lincoln: University of Nebraska Press, 2002), 62; Alanson W. Willcox to Oscar Ewing, March 10, 1949, Box 11, GC Correspondence on PA, HEWR. Board officials denied that the litigation influenced the timing of the hearings. Felix Cohen disagreed. Some evidence suggests that the board scheduled the hearing at the behest of New Mexico officials. Alanson W. Willcox to Roger Baldwin, October 19, 1949, Box 53, GC Correspondence on PA, HEWR; Felix S. Cohen to Roger N. Baldwin, October 26, 1949, Box 53, GC Correspondence on PA, HEWR; Arthur Altmeyer to Carl Hayden, February 4, 1949, Box 36, CHP; Meeting Minutes, February 3, 1949, ABPW Minutes; Murray A. Hintz to Jane Hoey, January 18, 1949, Box 37, GC Correspondence on PA, HEWR.

118. A. J. Altmeyer to Felix Cohen and James Curry, January 28, 1949, Box 53, GC Correspondence on PA, HEWR; Brief for All-Pueblo Council et al. as Amici Curiae, in re Arizona (hearing before the Federal Security Agency), Box 332, AAIA; Brief for the San Carlos Apache Tribe et al. as Amici Curiae, in re New Mexico (hearing before the FSA), Box 332, Association on American Indian Affairs Records, MC 147, Seeley J. Mudd Manuscript Library, Princeton University [hereafter cited as AAIAR]. On the Cohen/Curry feud, see Philp, *Termination Revisited*, 109–10. On the Indian voting rights cases, see Felix S. Cohen, "The Erosion of Indian Rights, 1950–1953: A Case Study in Bureaucracy," *Yale Law Journal* 62 (1953): 350.

119. Murray A. Hintz to A. J. Altmeyer, September 9, 1948, Box 37, GC Correspondence on PA, HEWR; Ruth Kirk to Margaretta Dietrich, May 21, 1947, Box 9691, SAIAR; Bob Ward to Jane Hoey, November 22, 1948, Box 37, GC Correspondence on PA, HEWR.

120. Thomas E. Sheridan, *Arizona: A History* (Tucson: University of Arizona Press, 2012), 226–33, 269–73, 292–99.

121. Harry Hill, "Brief on Reservation Indians," February 23, 1949, ABPW Minutes; Avery, "Indian Refusal," Box 43, SO/DG Papers.

122. Alanson W. Willcox to Murray A. Hintz, February 21, 1949, Box 37, GC Correspondence on PA, HEWR; Avery, "Indian Refusal," Box 43, SO/DG Papers; A Bill to Promote the Rehabilitation of the Navajo and Hopi Tribes of Indians, S. 1407, 81st Cong., 1st sess. (March 25, 1949).

123. Alanson Willcox to Oscar Ewing, May 13, 1949, Box 11, GC Correspondence on PA, HEWR.

124. David A. Johnson Sr. to Ruth M. Bronson, February 5, 1949, Box 120, NCAIR; Felix S. Cohen to unnamed recipients, June 17, 1949, Box 88, FCP; Felix S. Cohen to Roger N. Baldwin, October 26, 1949, Box 53, GC Correspondence on PA, HEWR.

5 STATES' RIGHTS AGAINST FEDERAL ADMINISTRATIVE ENFORCEMENT

1. "Notes from Field Workers," *Public Welfare in Indiana* 48, no. 9 (1938): 9; L. B. Shackelford, "Interpretation Takes to the Road," *Public Welfare News* 6, no. 10 (1938): 2–4.

2. Indiana State Welfare Department, "Newsletter to County Welfare Departments: October 1, 1948," Indiana State Library and Historical Bureau, Indianapolis; see also *Public Welfare in Indiana* 57, no. 7 (1947), an issue devoted entirely to "public relations."

3. The phrase "iron curtain" – often associated with the opening of the Cold War – was the centerpiece of British prime minister Winston Churchill's famous March 5, 1946, speech at Westminster College in Fulton, Missouri. Senator Joseph McCarthy used the phrase in the context of government secrecy in a February 20, 1950, Senate speech regarding the Truman administration's concealment of "loyalty risks" in the U.S. State Department. James T. Patterson, *Grand Expectations: The United States, 1945–1974* (New York: Oxford University Press, 1996), 196.

4. On the augmentation of state over local power – a phenomenon that merits more attention from historians – see the reports collected in Governmental Affairs Institute, *A Survey Report on The Impact of Federal Grants-in-Aid on the Structure and Functions of State and Local Governments* (Washington, DC: U.S. Government Printing Office, 1955).

5. On perceptions of normal time and exceptional time, see Mary L. Dudziak, *War Time: An Idea, Its History, Its Consequences* (New York: Oxford University Press, 2012).

6. Julian E. Zelizer, *On Capitol Hill: The Struggle to Reform Congress and Its Consequences* (New York: Cambridge University Press, 2004), 23.

7. Ira Katznelson, *Fear Itself: The New Deal and the Origins of Our Time* (New York: W. W. Norton, 2013), 281, 175–89, 382–98.

8. Kim Phillips-Fein, *Invisible Hands: The Making of the Conservative Movement from the New Deal to Reagan* (New York: W. W. Norton, 2009), xii.

9. F. A. Hayek, *The Road to Serfdom* (Chicago: University of Chicago Press, 1944). On the popularity of *The Road to Serfdom* in the United States in the late 1940s, see Alan Brinkley, "The Problem of American Conservatism," *American Historical Review* 99, no. 2 (1994): 416–17.

10. Phillips-Fein, *Invisible Hands*, 119.

11. Molly C. Michelmore, *Tax and Spend: The Welfare State, Tax Politics, and the Limits of American Liberalism* (Philadelphia: University of Pennsylvania Press, 2012), 11, 17–46. On the emergence of a "that's my tax dollar" sensibility, see also James Sparrow, *Warfare State: World War II Americans and the Age of Big Government* (New York: Oxford University Press, 2011), 122.

12. Charles Stevenson, "When It Pays to Play Pauper," *Nation's Business* 38, no. 9 (1950): 31; "Reform in the Charity Setup," *LAT*, August 29, 1951; see also Rufus Jarman, "Detroit Cracks Down on Relief Chiselers," *Saturday Evening*

Post, December 10, 1949, complaining about the number of persons allowed relief on the basis of "inconsequential" or unconfirmed physical disabilities.

13. See, for example, W. L. White, "'On the County' – Then and Now," *Reader's Digest*, March 1952; Roma K. McNickle, "Relief Rolls in Prosperity," *Editorial Research Reports* 1951, no. 2 (1951): 532, 544; George C. Stoney, "The Weapon of Shame," *Survey* 87, no. 9 (1951): 391–92; Lawrence E. Davies, "Washington State Battling on Relief," *NYT*, May 14, 1950; "The Profit Can Be Taken Out of Chiseling," *Saturday Evening Post*, October 8, 1955. The statistic on average Old Age Assistance and Old Age Insurance payments is from Blanche D. Coll, *Safety Net: Welfare and Social Security, 1929–1979* (New Brunswick, NJ: Rutgers University Press, 1995), 157.

14. Joint Legislative Committee on Interstate Cooperation, *Report of the Special Committee on Social Welfare and Relief*, No. 54 (Albany: Williams Press, 1950), Box 6, Robert T. Lansdale Collection, SW 169, Social Welfare History Archives, University of Minnesota, Minneapolis [hereafter cited as RLC].

15. "Public Assistance," *Social Security Bulletin* 13, no. 9 (1950): 47.

16. Ellen J. Perkins, "Old-Age Assistance and Aid to Dependent Children, 1940–1950," *Social Security Bulletin* 14, no. 11 (1951): 16–17; Elizabeth Alling and Agnes Leisy, "Aid to Dependent Children in a Postwar Year," *Social Security Bulletin* 13, no. 8 (1950): 3–5; Winifred Bell, *Aid to Dependent Children* (New York: Columbia University Press, 1965), 54–55; Mimi Abramovitz, *Regulating the Lives of Women: Social Welfare Policy from Colonial Times to the Present* (Boston: South End Press, 1988), 320–21; Jennifer Mittelstadt, *From Welfare to Workfare: The Unintended Consequences of Liberal Reform, 1945–1965* (Chapel Hill: University of North Carolina Press, 2005), 44; Nancy K. Cauthen and Edwin Amenta, "Not for Widows Only: Institutional Politics and the Formative Years of Aid to Dependent Children," *American Sociological Review* 60 (1996): 427–48.

17. Bell, *Aid to Dependent Children*, 58, 60–136; Abramovitz, *Regulating the Lives of Women*, 319–29; Rickie Solinger, *Wake Up Little Susie: Single Pregnancy and Race before Roe v. Wade*, 2nd ed. (New York: Routledge, 2000), 45–57; Anders Walker, "Legislating Virtue: How Segregationists Disguised Racial Discrimination as Moral Reform following *Brown v. Board of Education*," *Duke Law Journal* 47 (1997): 420–21; Mittelstadt, *From Welfare to Workfare*, 45–46; Regina G. Kunzel, *Fallen Women, Problem Girls: Unmarried Mothers and the Professionalization of Social Work, 1890–1945* (New Haven, CT: Yale University Press, 1993), 156–57; Ellen Reese, *Backlash against Welfare Mothers: Past and Present* (Berkeley: University of California Press, 2005), 22, 63; Lisa Levenstein, *A Movement without Marches: African American Women and the Politics of Poverty in Postwar Philadelphia* (Chapel Hill: University of North Carolina Press, 2009), 52–59.

18. Though missing from many scholarly accounts, this hardening or bitterness on the part of state officials often surfaces in oral histories with federal and state administrators. See, for example, William Mitchell, interview by Peter A. Corning, July 22, 1965, transcript, Columbia Center for Oral History,

Columbia University, New York, NY; Dunn, interview by Corning, August 3, 1965.

19. Alan Keith-Lucas, *Decisions about People in Need: A Study of Administrative Responsiveness in Public Assistance* (Chapel Hill: University of North Carolina Press, 1957), 88–89; Kan Ori, "Basic Ideas in Federal-State Relations: The Indiana 'Revolt' of 1951," PhD diss., Indiana University, Bloomington, 1961, 27–28.

20. "Welfare Worker Quits over Oath," *Terre Haute [IN] Star*, July 26, 1950. On the Stockholm Peace Petition, see Lawrence S. Wittner, *The Struggle against the Bomb*, vol. 1: *One World or None: A History of the World Nuclear Disarmament through 1953* (Stanford, CA: Stanford University Press, 1993), 183–84, 202–9; Robbie Lieberman, *The Strangest Dream: Communism, Anticommunism, and the U.S. Peace Movement, 1945–1963* (Syracuse, NY: Syracuse University Press, 2000), 81–113.

21. Ray Vicker, "Should Relief Rolls Be Made Public?" *WSJ*, August 21, 1951; American Association of Social Workers, Indiana Chapter, "What Happened in Indiana," *Social Work Journal* 33, no. 1 (1952): 36.

22. "Rip Off Welfare Mask, Bill's Author Demands," *Indianapolis Star*, February 10, 1951; Lester M. Hunt, "Bontrager-Malone Bill Hits Welfare Secrecy," *Indianapolis Star*, January 20, 1951. Such concerns animated an important but little-noticed change at the federal level: in 1950, Congress added a child support amendment to the ADC title of the Social Security Act. To continue receiving federal funding, each state had to "provide for prompt notice to appropriate law-enforcement officials" (NOLEO) whenever the state awarded ADC to a deserted or abandoned child. Social Security Act Amendments of 1950, § 321. Congress thus established a vital link between the public welfare and criminal justice systems, and also began to erode the principle of client confidentiality. To Russell Bontrager, however, the NOLEO requirement did not go far enough in the direction of transparency and public accountability.

23. "Rip Off Welfare Mask, Bill's Author Demands."

24. On concerns about vote solicitation, see Ida C. Merriam, "The Protection and Use of Information Obtained under the Social Security Act," *Social Security Bulletin* 4, no. 5 (1941): 13–19 (Massachusetts); Jane Hoey, "Confidential Character of Public-Assistance Records," March 15, 1939, Box 25, GC Correspondence on PA, HEWR (Ohio, Colorado, Wisconsin, Michigan). On discipline and surveillance, see Daniel I. Cronin, "Impact of Federal Welfare Grants on Municipal Government," *Boston University Law Review* 40 (1960): 535; Charles McKinley and Robert W. Frase, *Launching Social Security: A Capture-and-Record Account, 1935–1937* (Madison: University of Wisconsin Press, 1970), 156.

25. In addition to the examples cited in the text, see Jack B. Tate, "Monthly Report – April, 1941," May 12, 1941, Box 12, GC Correspondence on PA, HEWR; Elizabeth Long, "Confidential Nature of Records – Region XI – Threatened Litigation," March 6, 1942, Box 25, GC Correspondence on PA, HEWR; Louis Schneider, "PA – Minnesota – Confidential Nature of Records – Use of Lists in Hands of Registers of Deeds for Political Purposes," September 21, 1944, GC Correspondence on PA, HEWR,

reporting "flagrant violation[s]" in three counties and little effort by the state to correct the problem; "The Social Front: Among the States," *Survey* 78, no. 5 (1941): 154–55, noting resistance in Kansas, Colorado, Minnesota, Pennsylvania, New England, Vermont, and Georgia; "The Social Front," *Survey* 77, no. 9 (1941): 272, describing a battle with the District of Columbia over the publication of recipient names.

26. David Cohen, "Illinois – Aid to Dependent Children – Confidential Nature of Records," October 10, 1942, Box 28, GC Correspondence on PA, HEWR; Newell George, "PA Missouri – ADC Records – Grand Jury Subpoena," May 9, 1947, GC Correspondence on PA, HEWR; Newell George to Office of the GC, September 19, 1947, Box 70, GC Correspondence on PA, HEWR; Paul Malloy, "Relief Chiselers Are Stealing Us Blind," *Saturday Evening Post*, September 8, 1951.

27. On the use of welfare records in insurance litigation, see Bernice L. Bernstein to Alice J. Webber, July 24, 1950, Box 68, GC Correspondence on PA, HEWR; in workmen's compensation evaluations, see Laurence Dimsdale to George M. Keith, August 31, 1950, Box 69, GC Correspondence on Public Assistance Programs and the Social Security Act, 1935–1961, HEWR; in personal injury disputes, see A. Delafield Smith, "West Virginia – Confidential Nature of Records, Use of in Private Litigation," April 1, 1948, Box 68, GC Correspondence on PA, HEWR; and in rape prosecutions, see Arthur Miller to Office of the General Counsel, November 7, 1949, Box 72, GC Correspondence on PA, HEWR.

28. Joseph Meyers, "Furnishing of State Public Assistance Information to Investigators of the General Accounting Office concerning Assistance Status of Dependent Members of Officers of the Army of the United States Claiming Dependency Allowances," June 15, 1950, Box 69, GC Correspondence on PA, HEWR; Alanson W. Willcox, "Monthly Report – March 1948," April 12, 1948, Box 11, GC Correspondence on PA, HEWR; A. Delafield Smith, "Illinois – PA – Confidential Records," September 6, 1946, Box 69, GC Correspondence on PA, HEWR. The only acknowledged exception was when the recipient or applicant requested disclosure of his or her own records. Laurence Dimsdale to George M. Keith, August 31, 1950, Box 69, GC Correspondence on PA, HEWR.

29. Arthur Altmeyer to Otto F. Walls, January 2, 1947, Box 36, GC Correspondence on PA, HEWR.

30. Federal administrators had long urged state and local welfare departments to take precisely this line. See, for example, A. Delafield Smith, "Illinois – PA – Confidential Records," September 6, 1946, Box 69, GC Correspondence on PA, HEWR.

31. For several decades in the nineteenth century, Indiana's constitution prohibited black migration into the state. For much of the twentieth, the state was a Ku Klux Klan stronghold. Leonard J. Moore, *Citizen Klansmen: The Ku Klux Klan in Indiana, 1921–1928* (Chapel Hill: University of North Carolina Press, 1991).

32. Alling and Leisy, "Aid to Dependent Children in a Postwar Year," 10.

33. "Dere Lady," *Public Welfare in Indiana* 47, no. 4 (1937); see also "Dere Lady," *Public Welfare in Indiana* 49, no. 7 (1939): "I don't seem to get anywhere with this broad here in Terre Haute."
34. Mrs. Willard A. Pleuthner, "We Believe in Social Workers, But ...," *Survey* 76, no. 10 (1940): 318; Katharine Hall Brooks, "A Layman Looks at Social Workers," *Social Work Journal* 35, no. 1 (1954): 23, 24; see also Helen Cody Baker, "A Word to the Wise: An Open Letter to Case Workers," *Survey* 76, no. 12 (1940): 355.
35. John Prins, "Business Men Speak Their Minds," *Survey* 78, no. 11 (1942): 303. Social work was a "complicated business," agreed the politically appointed head of Georgia's welfare department, but only because social workers "made it so." Harold C. Fleming, "Georgia Welfare Wins a Round," *Survey* 87, no. 7 (1951): 328.
36. David R. Mayhew, *Placing Parties in American Politics* (Princeton, NJ: Princeton University Press, 1986), 94–99.
37. Katznelson, *Fear Itself*, 189.
38. See, generally, Daniel J. Walkowitz, *Working with Class: Social Workers and the Politics of Middle-Class Identity* (Chapel Hill: University of North Carolina Press, 1999).
39. See, for example, Pleuthner, "We Believe in Social Workers, But ...," 318; Herbert Emmerich, "Public Welfare Is Not the Welfare State," *Public Welfare* 11, no. 1 (1953): 21; H. Leslie McKenzie, "The Citizen Participates in Public Welfare," *Public Welfare* 11, no. 1 (1953): 25.
40. See, for example, Michael Ross, "The Philadelphia Hearings," *Survey* 78, no. 6 (1942); Jim Rossi, "Philadelphia's Red Scare," *Survey* 77, no. 12 (1941); Fleming, "Georgia Welfare Wins a Round," 327; "The Relief Roll Blackout," *Chicago Tribune*, March 7, 1951.
41. Lester M. Hunt, "Illinois Woman Draws State Welfare Salary," *Indianapolis Star*, Jan. 6, 1951; Lester M. Hunt, "Indiana Welfare Hiring under Fire," *Indianpolis Star*, January 10, 1951; "Welfare Workers Go to School on Tax Funds," *Indianpolis Star*, January 3, 1951; see also Lester M. Hunt, "Relief Probers Charge Flouting of Lien Law," *Indianapolis Star*, October 9, 1951, alleging that the more money welfare workers gave away, the greater their agency's power "to control votes and elect public officials who will compromise with socialism and let it flourish in secrecy until it is strong enough to break into the open and take over our government."
42. Letter to the editor, *Indianapolis Star*, January 15, 1951.
43. Joe Alex Morris, "They Don't Want Uncle's Money," *Saturday Evening Post*, March 22, 1952, 31.
44. Indiana Acts, chap. 377, vol. II (1947), cited in Ori, "Basic Ideas in Federal-State Relations," 21. On the second resolution (proposed but never passed by both houses), see Ori, "Basic Ideas in Federal-State Relations," 12–13.
45. Morris, "They Don't Want Uncle's Money," 30, 141–42; K. Ames Smithers, "Setting an Example? Indiana Crusaders Resist Federal Handouts for Housing, Lunches and Other Local Aid," *WSJ*, July 27, 1954. Objections to federal attempts at "dominance" in these nonwelfare policy areas resurfaced during the confidentiality battle and continued after it ended. See Ori, "Basic

Ideas in Federal-State Relations," 44, 59, 61, referencing contemporaneous objections to federal aid for highways, hospitals, education, agriculture, and construction; Indiana State Chamber of Commerce, *Federal-State Relations: Indiana Facts and Figures in the Fields of Education, Public Health, Conservation, Social Security, Veterans, Transportation* (Indianapolis: Indiana State Chamber of Commerce, 1954).

46. "Welfare Is No Longer Charity," *Indianapolis Star*, February 18, 1951.

47. Ori, "Basic Ideas in Federal-State Relations," 42–70; R. Clyde White, "The Needy Are Scapegoats," *Survey* 88, no. 1 (1952): 21.

48. Letter to the editor, *Indianapolis Star*, May 20, 1951.

49. "This Fight Must Be Won," *Indianapolis News*, August 5, 1951. On how members of a white, advantaged majority came to see violations of their own rights in the government's attempts to advance and protect the rights of the disadvantaged, see, for example, Thomas J. Sugrue, "Crab-grass Roots Politics: Race, Rights, and the Reaction against Liberalism in the Urban North, 1940–1964," *Journal of American History* 82, no. 2 (1995): 551–78; Matthew D. Lassiter, "The Suburban Origins of 'Color-blind' Conservatism: Middle-Class Consciousness in the Charlotte Busing Crisis," *Journal of Urban History* 30, no. 4 (2004): 549–82.

50. "Nauseating Welfare Abuses," *Atlanta Constitution*, February 10, 1951.

51. "The Relief Roll Blackout"; see also "The States Win a Fight," *Chicago Tribune*, October 13, 1951; "Oscar's Boomerang," *Cleveland Plain Dealer*, reprinted in the *LAT*, August 16, 1951.

52. Editorial, "A Victory over Bureaucracy,"*Indianapolis Star*, February 14, 1951.

53. Morris, "They Don't Want Uncle's Money," 144.

54. "A Chapter of Legislative History," *Social Service Review* 26, no. 2 (1952): 230; "Indiana Is Dropped from Federal Aid," *NYT*, August 1, 1951.

55. Stoney, "The Weapon of Shame," 391; "Social Security and Welfare," *State Government* 24, no. 11 (1951): 282; "A Chapter of Legislative History," 230–31.

56. Stoney, "The Weapon of Shame."

57. Joseph Hearst, "Secrecy Clause Called Boon to Relief Cheats," *Chicago Tribune*, September 27, 1951.

58. Paul F. Healy, "The Man the Doctors Hate," *Saturday Evening Post*, July 8, 1950; "Oscar's Boomerang: From the Cleveland Plain Dealer," *LAT*, August 16, 1951.

59. Charles F. Fleming, interview by David F. Tudor, February 28, 1974, transcript, Indiana University Center for the Study of History and Memory, Bloomington; Robert S. Webb, interview by David F. Tudor, June 17, 1973, transcript, Indiana University Center for the Study of History and Memory, Bloomington.

60. "Freedom is the Issue!" *Muncie (IN) Star*, May 17, 1951.

61. Indiana v. Ewing, 99 F. Supp. 734 (D.D.C., 1951); "Court Upholds Ewing in Cutting Off Federal Welfare Aid to Indiana," *WSJ*, September 8, 1951.

62. "A Chapter of Legislative History," 230–31; "Indiana Defies Deadline Set on Federal Aid," *Chicago Tribune*, September 29, 1951; Dennis S. Ippolito,

Deficits, Debt, and the New Politics of Tax Policy (Cambridge: Cambridge University Press, 2012), 57–59.

63. John D. Morris, "Conferees Agree on Tax Bill and Senate Promptly Votes It," *NYT*, October 19, 1951; "A Chapter of Legislative History," 233. Congress's only gesture toward the federal agency's concerns was language stating that if states took advantage of the rider, they had to ensure that no commercial or political use be made of public assistance recipients' information.

64. Revenue Act of 1951, § 613, Pub. L. No. 82-183, 65 Stat. 452 (1951); "A Rare Instance," *Time*, November 5, 1951.

65. "Jenner Amendment Wins; Welfare Secrecy Doomed," *Indianapolis Star*, October 11, 1951; Morris, "They Don't Want Uncle's Money," 144; Arthur Krock, "A Very Important Item of Legislation," *NYT*, October 25, 1951; "A Rare Instance." The quotation is from "The States Win a Fight," *Chicago Tribune*, October 13, 1951.

66. Margaret Greenfield, *Confidentiality of Public Assistance Records* (Berkeley, Bureau of Public Administration: University of California), 26–28.

67. "Round Table Conference," *Public Welfare* 10, no. 1 (1952): 12.

68. Morris, "They Don't Want Uncle's Money," 144; White, "The Needy Are the Scapegoats," 22; Greenfield, *Confidentiality of Public Assistance Records*, 30–39.

69. Jane Hoey to Frank Bane, February 6, 1952, Box 3, FBP; "Indiana Wins a Battle – But Not a War," *Indianapolis Times*, October 14, 1951.

70. Gilbert Y. Steiner, *Social Insecurity: The Politics of Welfare* (Chicago: Rand McNally, 1966), 97.

71. "Editorial Notes," *Social Casework* 32, no. 10 (1951): 436.

72. See, generally, Richard White, *"It's Your Misfortune and None of My Own": A History of the American West* (Norman: University of Oklahoma Press, 1991).

73. Matthew G. McCoy, "Bouncing Checks, Union Bosses, and Newspaper Wars: Arizona's 1958 Gubernatorial Election," *Journal of Arizona History* 52, no. 3 (2011): 271.

74. See Chapter 4; see also Karen M. Tani, "States' Rights, Welfare Rights, and 'The Indian Problem': Negotiating Citizenship and Sovereignty, 1935–1954," *Law and History Review* 33, no. 1 (2015).

75. A Bill to Promote the Rehabilitation of the Navajo and Hopi Tribes of Indians, S. 1407, 81st Cong., 1st sess. (1949).

76. Hearings before a Subcommittee on Indian Affairs of the Committee on Public Lands on H.R. 3476: A Bill to Promote the Rehabilitation of the Navajo and Hopi Indians under a Long-Range Program, 81st Cong., 1 sess., (April-May 1949), at 202–4.

77. As passed by the House, the Fernández Amendment also included a provision requiring reservation schools to follow state curricula. "Citizen Navajo Today Builds Future," *Farmington (NM) Daily Times*, August 20, 1949. On LULAC, see David G. Gutierrez, *Walls and Mirrors: Mexican Americans, Mexican Immigrants, and the Politics of Ethnicity* (Berkeley: University of California Press, 1995), 74–87.

78. Conference Report to Accompany S. 1407, H.R. Rep. No. 81-1338 (September 22, 1949), at 4, 6–8.

79. Bethany R. Berger, "*Williams v. Lee* and the Debate over Indian Equality," *Michigan Law Review* 109 (2011): 1488–94; "Indian Bill Is Opposed," *NYT*, October 9, 1949, 38; Paul C. Rosier, *Serving Their Country: American Indian Politics and Patriotism in the Twentieth Century* (Cambridge, MA: Harvard University Press, 2009), 136–38; President, "Rehabilitation of the Navajo and Hopi Tribes of Indians – Veto Message," 81 Cong., 1st sess., 1949, S. Doc. 119, at 3.

80. New Mexico Department of Public Welfare, *Annual Report, Year Ending June 30, 1952*, New Mexico State Library, Santa Fe.

81. The agency's designation changed from "Board" to "Administration" in 1946.

82. "Arizona Loses Federal Funds for Child Aid," *Arizona Republic*, December 30, 1949, Box 36, CHP; Herb Nelson, "State Indian Welfare Pact Abrogated," *Phoenix Gazette*, June 8, 1950, Box 36, CHP; James F. Cooper, "Governor Calls for Release of State from Federal Bonds" [1951], Box 90, CHP.

83. Dean J. Kotlowski, "Burying Sergeant Rice: Racial Justice and Native American Rights in the Truman Era," *Journal of American Studies* 38, no. 2 (2004): 204; Donald Lee Fixico, *Termination and Relocation: Federal Indian Policy: 1945–1960* (Albuquerque: University of New Mexico Press, 1986), 47.

84. Social Security Act Amendments of 1950, § 351, Pub. L. No. 81-734, 64 Stat. 477 (1950).

85. Meeting Minutes, February 9, 1952, ABPW Minutes; Alanson W. Willcox to Oscar Ewing, August 14, 1951, Box 11, GC Correspondence on PA, HEWR; Arizona Code § 70-607 (Cum. Supp. 1952).

86. Transcript of Oral Argument, Arizona v. Hobby, No. 2008-52 (D. D.C. Feb. 20, 1953), Box 238, AAIAR.

87. Ibid. O'Donoghue's arguments borrowed directly from agency lawyers. Alanson W. Willcox to Oscar Ewing, May 22, 1952, Box 11, GC Correspondence on PA, HEWR.

88. Kenneth R. Philp, *Termination Revisited: American Indians on the Trail to Self-Determination, 1933–1953* (Lincoln: University of Nebraska Press, 2002), 108–24; Anthony Leviero, "Indian War Whoop Marks Hearings," *NYT*, January 4, 1952, 9.

89. Philp, *Termination Revisited*, xii; Felix S. Cohen, "The Erosion of Indian Rights: 1950–53: A Case Study in Bureaucracy," *Yale Law Journal* 62, no. 3 (1953): 376; Paul C. Rosier, "The Association on American Indian Affairs and the Struggle for Native American Rights, 1948–1955," *Princeton University Library Chronicle* 62, no. 2 (2006): 378.

90. Transcript of Oral Argument, Arizona v. Hobby, No. 2008-52 (D. D.C. Feb. 20, 1953). For a sampling of Indian perspectives on this legal question, see Tani, "States' Rights, Welfare Rights, and the 'Indian Problem,'" 35–36.

91. Transcript of Oral Argument, Arizona v. Hobby.

92. Arizona v. Hobby, 221 F.2d 498 (D.C. Cir. 1954). Afterward, Arizona officials continued to complain about the difficulty and unfairness of administering benefits to reservation Indians. Paul R. West, "Problems in Administration

of Public Assistance on Arizona Indian Reservation," *Public Welfare* 17, no. 1 (1959): 37–38.

93. "Neglected Children Add to Court Cases," *NYT*, February 19, 1948.

94. "Family on Relief, Evicted, Lodged in Hotel by City at $500 for Month," *NYT*, May 10, 1947; "37 Relief Families Due to Quit Hotels on Mayor's Orders," *NYT*, May 21, 1947.

95. Frank S. Adams, "Charges of 'Luxury Relief' Denied," *NYT*, May 29, 1947.

96. Howard Bernard Gundy, "Grants-in-Aid for Public Assistance and New York State-Federal Relationships," PhD diss., Public Administration, University of Chicago, 1961, 218.

97. James P. McCaffrey, "Albany Gets Data," *NYT*, May 23, 1947; Paul Crowell, "Rhatigan Resigns City Welfare Post," *NYT*, October 25, 1947; Paul Crowell, "City Report Scores 'Laxity' in Relief," *NYT*, October 27, 1947.

98. "Inquiry Bares Relief Abuse," *New York Sun*, October 29, 1947; William R. Conklin, "Restitution Is Due," *NYT*, October 31, 1947. On Shapiro's employment history, see "Shapiro Is Named to Supervise City Welfare Program for State," *NYT*, March 31, 1970.

99. Conklin, "Restitution Is Due"; William R. Conklin, "Grand Jury to Scan Relief; City Backs the 'Lady in Mink,'" *NYT*, November 1, 1947.

100. Charles Wyer, "State Inquiry Reveals Laxity in Many Welfare Cases Here," *New York Sun*, November 6, 1947; Jerome Edelberg and Erwin Savelson, "City Relief Supervision Is 'Nil,' Says Witness," *New York Mirror*, November 8, 1947; William B. Conklin, "Refusals to Work Do Not Disqualify Relief Recipients," *NYT*, November 9, 1947.

101. "Lansdale Attacks City Relief System," *NYT*, November 12, 1947. As a former federal official (he began his career with the Bureau of Indian Affairs) and an expert on New Deal relief policies, Lansdale was also troubled by another finding: that municipal welfare authorities often failed to channel qualified applicants toward the state's federally subsidized public assistance programs. In New York State, "home relief" (known in other places as "general relief") was jointly financed by the state and local governments. Lansdale was outraged to learn that more than one-fourth of sampled home relief cases could have instead received Aid to Dependent Children, which in turn would have entitled the state to a 25 percent reimbursement from the federal government. Given that the city had more than 45,000 home relief cases at the time, the financial implications were stunning. William R. Conklin, "Welfare Refunds Unclaimed by City," *NYT*, November 25, 1947.

102. Stanley Levey, "Relief Study Held 'Orgy of Publicity,'" *NYT*, November 15, 1947.

103. New York City welfare commissioner Fielding, quoted in William R. Conklin, "Collapse in Relief Charged by State, Shake-up Asked," *NYT*, March 23, 1948.

104. Gundy, "Grants-in-Aid for Public Assistance," 156.

105. "U.S. Spur to Waste in Relief Is Denied," *NYT*, January 21, 1948. On the scandal over *Common Human Needs*, see Chapter 3.

106. State of New York, State Board of Social Welfare, "Report of the Inquiry into the Administration of Public Welfare in New York City," March 17, 1948, Box 6, RLC. On the attitude of state board members, see, for example, "Payment of Relief by Voucher Urged," *NYT*, May 6, 1948, quoting board member and former state judge Paxton Blair as stating that "most people on relief are inclined to be a little improvident," which is why he preferred "voucher relief" to cash payments.
107. Bureau of Public Assistance, "Problems of Public Assistance Administration in the New York City Department of Social Welfare April 1947–March 1950," April 1950, Box 37, GC Correspondence on PA, HEWR; Lucy Freeman, "State Will Review City Relief Set-Up," *NYT*, July 12, 1949.
108. SSA, §§ 2(a)(1), 4022(a)(1), § 1002(a)(1); Martha Derthick, *The Influence of Federal Grants: Public Assistance in Massachusetts* (Cambridge, MA: Harvard University Press, 1970), 72.
109. Gundy, "Grants-in-Aid for Public Assistance," 141, 432–44.
110. Report of the Special Committee on State and Local Relationships, New York Association of Public Welfare Officials (May 1947), Box 1, New York Public Welfare Association Records, APAP-126, M. E. Grenander Department of Special Collections and Archives, University Libraries, University at Albany, State University of New York [hereafter cited as NYPWAR].
111. Coll, *Safety Net*, 128–31; Oscar M. Powell, "Merit Systems in the Social Security Program," *Social Security Bulletin* 8, no. 2 (1945): 10–12.
112. Angus Laird, "The Merit System and Public Welfare Administration," *Public Welfare News* 9, no. 2 (1951): 51–55; Charles Irwin Schottland, interview by Frances Lomas Feldman, January 5, 7, and 8, 1987, transcript, California Social Welfare Archives' Oral History Collection, University of Southern California, Los Angeles; Charles Irwin Schottland, interview by Rosemary Levenson, March 2 and 6, 1972, transcript [pp. 66–67], Regional Oral History Office, Bancroft Library, University of California, Berkeley.
113. "New York State Civil Service Commission Directive to County Welfare Commissioners and Chairmen of Boards of Child Welfare," March 4, 1940, quoted in Gundy, "Grants-in-Aid for Public Assistance," 426–30.
114. Jane M. Hoey, to W. L. Mitchell, January 26, 1951, quoted in Gundy, "Grants-in-Aid for Public Assistance," 445; Gundy, "Grants-in-Aid for Public Assistance," 262–71.
115. Gundy, "Grants-in-Aid for Public Assistance," 171.
116. "Relief Grant Rise of 5% Sought Here," *NYT*, November 27, 1950; Henry Root Stern to Thomas E. Dewey, December 19, 1950, Box 1, NYPWAR.
117. Robert T. Lansdale, "Report to the State Board of Social Welfare on a Mandatory Statewide Assistance Standard Required by the Federal Security Agency," December 18, 1950, Box 37, GC Correspondence on PA, HEWR; Henry Root Stern to Thomas E. Dewey, December 19, 1950, Box 1, NYPWAR; "Ewing Strikes Back at Critics at Albany," *NYT*, January 11, 1951.
118. Lansdale, "Report to the State Board of Social Welfare on a Mandatory Statewide Assistance Standards"; Robert T. Lansdale, "Report to the State

Board of Social Welfare on Changes in the State Civil Service System Needed to Meet Federal Security Agency Requirements," December 18, 1950, Box 1, NYPWAR.

119. Henry F. Pringle and Katharine Pringle, "The Case for Federal Relief," *Saturday Evening Post*, July 19, 1952.

120. Gundy, "Grants-in-Aid for Public Assistance," 213–29; "U.S.-State Truce on Relief Aid Seen," *NYT*, September 23, 1951. Negotiations over details continued into 1951 on the statewide standards issue and into 1954 on the merit system issue. Gundy, "Grants-in-Aid for Public Assistance," 230–78.

121. "U.S. Relief Policies Assailed by Dewey," *NYT*, April 7, 1951; Warren Weaver Jr., "Governor Accuses Ewing of Meddling," *NYT*, December 22, 1950; "Federal-Aid Rift Spurs State Study," *NYT*, February 23, 1951; John Mooney, "Uncle Sam Kicks in Many Millions to Help Finance State Projects," *Albany Knickerbocker News*, February 20, 1951.

122. "Dewey Names Five to Study Welfare," *NYT*, April 13, 1951.

123. Report of the Temporary Commission to Study Federally Aided Welfare Programs, State Legislative Document No. 28, Box 259, Textual Records from the Department of HEW, Office of the Secretary, General Classified Files, 1951–55, HEWR. On the lines of thought that informed the Administrative Procedure Act, see Reuel E. Schiller, "Reining in the Administrative State: World War II and the Decline of Expert Administration," in *Total War and the Law: The American Home Front in World War II*, ed. Daniel R. Ernst and Victor Jew (Westport, CT: Praeger, 2002), 186–206; Joanna L. Grisinger, *The Unwieldy American State: Administrative Politics since the New Deal* (New York: Cambridge University Press, 2012).

124. Schottland, interview by Feldman. Schottland was the director of California's welfare department between 1950 and 1954.

125. Frank J. Lausche, "Progress and Problems of the States," *State Government* 24, no. 1 (1951): 288, 268.

126. Quoted in Governmental Affairs Institute, *A Survey Report on The Impact of Federal Grants-In-Aid on the Structure and Functions of State and Local Governments* (Washington, DC: U.S. Government Printing Office, 1955), 204

127. "The Chips Are Down on Welfare," *Indianapolis Times*, August 2, 1951.

128. White, "'On the County' – Then and Now."

129. See, generally, the correspondence in the folder titled "National Council of State Public Assistance and Welfare Administrators," American Public Welfare Association Files, RG 214000, South Carolina Department of Archives and History, Columbia, documenting an awareness by state administrators of common concerns, vis-à-vis federal administrative edicts, and a desire to collaborate on solutions; see also Schottland, interview by Levenson, explaining that by the early 1950s, the state welfare administrators "all knew each other by first names" and "were all very close"; if the administrators opposed a federal policy, they worked together to lobby their governors.

130. Eveline M. Burns, "Wanted: More Thought about Grants-in-Aid," *Social Work Journal* 35, no. 1 (1954): 13.

6. RIGHTS AGAINST THE STATE(S)

1. Tracy E. K'Meyer, *Civil Rights in the Gateway to the South: Louisville, Kentucky, 1945–1980* (Lexington: University Press of Kentucky, 2009), 45, 61–70; Catherine Fosl, *Subversive Southerner: Anne Braden and the Struggle for Racial Justice in the Cold War South* (New York: Palgrave Macmillan, 2002), 135–64.
2. "Six Are Indicted on Sedition Count: One of Louisville Group Also Accused of Dynamiting Home of a Negro," *NYT*, October 2, 1954; Melville H. Hosch to R. J. Decamp, October 26, 1954, Box 254, Textual Records from the Department of HEW, Office of the Secretary, General Classified Files, 1951–55, HEWR.
3. This controversy is discussed in detail in Chapter 5.
4. See generally Jennifer Mittelstadt, *From Welfare to Workfare: The Unintended Consequences of Liberal Reform, 1945–1965* (Chapel Hill: University of North Carolina Press, 2005); Edward D. Berkowitz and Kim McQuaid, *Creating the Welfare State: The Political Economy of Twentieth-Century Reform*, rev. ed. (Lawrence: University Press of Kansas, 1992).
5. On ADC, see Ellen Reese, *Backlash against Welfare Mothers: Past and Present* (Berkeley: University of California Press, 2005). Scholars have paid much less attention to changes in OAA laws.
6. "New Rash of Public Welfare Investigations," *Survey* 87, no. 5 (1951): 230.
7. Kathryn Close, "Whither Public Welfare," *Survey* 88, no. 1 (1952): 36; "The National Councils," *Public Welfare* 10, no. 1 (1952): 12.
8. Marie Lane to Elizabeth Wickenden, March 22, 1953, Box 12, Mss 800, EWP; see also Elizabeth Wickenden to Fred Hoehler, March 6, 1953, Box 9, FHP. On the movement for comprehensive social welfare, see Mittelstadt, *From Welfare to Workfare*, 21–39.
9. Jane Hoey, interview by Peter A. Corning, January 31, 1966, transcript, Columbia Center for Oral History, Columbia University, New York, NY.
10. Paul Molloy, "The Relief Chiselers Are Stealing Us Blind," *Saturday Evening Post*, September 8, 1951; Henry F. Pringle and Katherine Pringle, "The Case for Federal Relief," *Saturday Evening Post*, July 19, 1952.
11. Eveline M. Burns, "The Role of Government in Social Welfare," *Social Work Journal* 35, no. 3 (1954): 95; see also Fred H. Steininger, "The Local Public Welfare Administrator and the Legislator," *Public Welfare News* 9, no. 7 (1941): 165.
12. Melvin A. Glasser, "Social Welfare in 1954: Potentialities and Pitfalls," *Social Work Journal* 35, no. 3 (1954): 106.
13. Mary M. Lehane, "Is Casework Necessary to the Public Assistance Program?" *Public Welfare News* 9, no. 9 (1941): 213; see also "Assistance and Service Too," *Public Welfare News* 8, no. 10 (1940): 1; Deborah

Mauldin, "'Not By Bread Alone' – Service Must Supplement Assistance," *Public Welfare* 5, no. 11 (1947): 257.

14. On the postwar appeal of psychology, see Ellen Herman, *The Romance of American Psychology: Political Culture in the Age of Experts* (Berkeley: University of California Press, 1995). On psychology and welfare administration, specifically, see Laura Curran, "The Psychology of Poverty: Professional Social Work and Aid to Dependent Children in Postwar America, 1946–1963," *Social Service Review* 76, no. 3 (2002): 379.

15. Letter to the editor, *Indianapolis Star*, January 15, 1951.

16. Herbert Emmerich, "Public Welfare Is Not the Welfare State," *Public Welfare* 11, no. 1 (1953): 23. On this theory of professional behavior, see Andrew Abbott, *The System of Professions: An Essay on the Division of Expert Labor* (Chicago: University of Chicago Press, 1988).

17. See, for example, Close, "Whither Public Welfare," 35. For a fuller discussion of this trend, see Mittelstadt, *From Welfare to Workfare*, 48–68.

18. Federal Security Agency, in collaboration with Bureau of Accounts and Audits and Office of the General Counsel, *Money Payments to Recipients of Old-Age Assistance, Aid to Dependent Children, and Aid to the Blind* (Washington, DC: U.S. Government Printing Office, 1944).

19. Mittelstadt, *From Welfare to Workfare*, 36.

20. The University of Chicago School of Social Service Administration, which placed many students in public agencies, had long devoted less attention to casework than its peer schools, but amid their courses on law, history, and the social sciences, Chicago students still received casework training. Folder 1 (SSA – Announcements and Bulletins, 1940–1945), Box 3, CSSAR; Folder 2 (SSA – Announcements, 1945–55), Box 3, CSSAR.

21. See, for example, J. Sheldon Turner, "Service in Public Assistance Administration – An Interpretation According to Federal Purpose and Policy," May 5, 1944, Box 214, Bureau of Public Assistance, Correspondence Relating to Plans and Programs, 1935–1948, SSAR; Helen Hayden, "Case Work Possibilities in a Public Assistance Program," in *Proceedings of the National Conference of Social Work* (New York: Columbia University Press 1944), 326–34.

22. Mittelstadt, *From Welfare to Workfare*, 36–38; Mauldin, "'Not By Bread Alone,'" 257; Constance N. Swander, "A Study of the Services Needed in a Public Assistance Caseload," *Public Welfare* 5, no. 9 (1947): 194–99, 215.

23. Cohen was one of many mezzo-level bureaucrats who stayed on during the Eisenhower administration. Their deep institutional knowledge made them irreplaceable. Berkowitz and McQuaid, *Creating the Welfare State*, 183; William Mitchell, interview by Peter A. Corning, July 22, 1965, transcript, Columbia Center for Oral History, Columbia University, New York.

24. Mittelstadt, *From Welfare to Workfare*, 36–38; Berkowitz and McQuaid, *Creating the Welfare State*, 173–81.

25. Mitchell, interview by Corning; Charles I. Schottland interview by Peter A. Corning, June 4, 1965, transcript, Columbia Center for Oral History, Columbia University, New York; Loula Dunn, interview by Peter A. Corning, August 3, 1965, transcript, Columbia Center for Oral History,

Columbia University, New York; Roswell B. Perkins, interview by Peter A. Corning, April 2, 1966, transcript, Columbia Center for Oral History, Columbia University, New York; Wilbur Cohen to Elizabeth Wickenden, February 2, 1953, Box 16, Mss 800, EWP.

26. Mittelstadt, *From Welfare to Workfare*, 64–66; Berkowitz and McQuaid, *Creating the Welfare State*, 184. Under normal circumstances, a person who worked in covered employment but prematurely left the workforce risked the loss or diminishment of his or her old-age insurance benefits. Under the new policy, a qualifying worker who stopped work because of long-term or total disability could apply to have his or her status "frozen," thereby preventing the period of nonemployment from affecting his or her postretirement benefit level. Martha Derthick, *Policymaking for Social Security* (Washington, DC: Brookings Institution Press, 1979), 300–304.

27. Mittelstadt, *From Welfare to Workfare*, 64–66, referring to the 1956 amendments to the SSA.

28. Bureau of Public Assistance, State Letter No. 296, April 4, 1957, Box 2, State Letters, Policies, and Regulations Relating to Public Welfare Programs, 1942–1971, SSAR; "Major Problem Areas in Public Assistance Cases," attached to Bureau of Public Assistance, State Letter No. 299, May 10, 1957, Box 2, State Letters, Policies, and Regulations Relating to Public Welfare Programs, 1942–1971, SSAR.

29. "Sessions on Services," *Public Welfare* 16, no. 1 (1958): 42; Hidesuke Uyenoyama, "'??? Besides Money' – An Open House," *Public Welfare* 15, no. 3 (1957): 117; Margaret Barnard, "New Developments in Services to PA Recipients," *Public Welfare* 13, no. 2 (1955): 91.

30. Helen Harris Perlman, "The Caseworker's Use of Collateral Information," *Social Casework* 32, no. 8 (1951): 328; Susanne D. Tollen, "How to Motivate Recipients toward Self-Support and Self-Care," *Public Welfare* 16, no. 4 (1958): 209–10; J. P. Kahn, "Attitudes toward Recipients of Public Assistance," *Social Casework* 36, no. 8 (1955): 362; Gordon Hamilton, "The Role of Social Casework in Social Policy," *Social Casework* 33, no. 8 (1952): 318.

31. Grace F. Marcus, "Problems of Principle in the Determination of the Assistance Grant," March 29, 1944, Box 214, Bureau of Public Assistance, Correspondence Relating to Plans and Programs, 1935–1948, SSAR. "The true test of whether government is protecting [the client's] rights," agreed a high-ranking administrator in the New York City Department of Welfare, "is *how* the public agency discharges its obligations in providing for those in need of its services. Implicit in all these is the client's right to respect as an individual, a respect not lost by virtue of financial dependence." Philip Soskis, "Is There Conflict between the Rights of the Individual and Current Case Work Policies and Practices; from the Viewpoint of the Tax-Supported Agency," *Annual Volume of the New York State Conference on Social Work* (1946), Box 6, RLC.

32. A. Delafield Smith to Jane Hoey, "Should the Profession of Social Work Be Tied to Public Assistance by Statute?" December 5, 1946, Box 79, GC Correspondence on PA, HEWR; A. Delafield Smith, "Public Assistance as a

Social Obligation," *Harvard Law Review* 63, no. 2 (1949): 288; see also A. Delafield Smith, "Charity, Behavior, and Social Security," *Journal of Higher Education* 21, no. 1 (1950): 55.

33. A. Delafield Smith, *The Right to Life* (Chapel Hill: University of North Carolina Press, 1955), 175–90. Distribution information comes from the Richard G. Smith family papers, private collection, notes on file with author. On Smith's influence on welfare rights "guru" Edward Sparer, discussed in Chapter 8, see Martha F. Davis, *Brutal Need: Lawyers and the Welfare Rights Movement, 1960–1973* (New Haven, CT: Yale University Press, 1993), 37. Welfare rights theorist Elizabeth Wickenden, discussed in Chapters 7 and 8, was also familiar with Smith's legal philosophical work. See, for example, Elizabeth Wickenden to Alanson Willcox, October 20, 1966, Box 12, Mss 800, EWP; Elizabeth Wickenden, interview by Blanche D. Coll, May 28, 1986, transcript, Box 2, M99-098, EWP.

34. A. Delafield Smith to Richard G. Smith, April 16, 1947, RSP; Richard G. Smith, interview by author, January 17, 2009, transcript, on file with author; Smith, *The Right to Life*, v.

35. Smith, *The Right to Life*, 10–13, 17, 76, 97, 113, 185–90.

36. Alanson W. Willcox, "Patterns of Social Legislation: Reflections on the Welfare State," *Journal of Public Law* 6 (1957): 7.

37. Ibid.

38. Biographical information is from Frank Kuhn, "A Special Remembrance: Dr. Alan Keith-Lucas," *Refocus* 8 (2002): 9.

39. Alan Keith-Lucas, "The Political Theory Implicit in Social Casework Theory," *American Political Science Review* 47, no. 4 (1953): 1076. Keith-Lucas attributed the notion that the needy were sick to the diagnostic school of thought, then dominant in social work. A minority of social workers, including Grace Marcus, belonged to the competing functional, or Rankian, school. Keith-Lucas described the functional school as more compatible with the views of federal administrators Jane Hoey and A. Delafield Smith. Ibid., 1083, 1088, 1090–91.

40. Alan Keith-Lucas, *Decisions about People in Need: A Study of Administrative Responsiveness in Public Assistance* (Chapel Hill: University of North Carolina Press, 1957), 9–10, 256. The book attracted attention from the disciplines of political science, public administration, sociology, and social work. Allan R. Richards and Frank R. Breul, "Democracy and Rights in Administering Assistance," review of *Decisions about People in Need: A Study of Administrative Responsiveness in Public Assistance*, by Alan Keith-Lucas, *Public Administration Review* 18, no. 3 (1958): 249; Paul J. Piccard, review of *Decisions about People in Need: A Study of Administrative Responsiveness in Public Assistance*, by Alan Keith-Lucas, *Journal of Politics* 20, no. 2 (1958); Thomas Fred Lewin, review of *Decisions about People in Need: A Study of Administrative Responsiveness in Public Assistance*, by Alan Keith-Lucas, *American Journal of Sociology* 64, no. 4 (1959); Wilbur J. Cohen, review of *Decisions about People in Need: A Study of Administrative Responsiveness in Public Assistance*, by Alan Keith-Lucas, *Annals of the American Academy of Political and Social Science*, 315

(1958); Jane M. Hoey, review of *Decisions about People in Need: A Study of Administrative Responsiveness in Public Assistance*, by Alan Keith-Lucas, *Social Service Review* 32, no. 2 (1958): 195, 197.

41. For pronouncements from the federal agency, see, for example, Charlotte Towle, *Common Human Needs: An Interpretation for Staff in Public Assistance Agencies*, Public Assistance Report No. 8 (Washington, DC: U.S. Government Printing Office, 1945); Grace Marcus, *The Nature of Service in Public Assistance Administration*, Public Assistance Report No. 10 (Washington, DC: U.S. Government Printing Office, 1946). For statements from social work educators and leaders, see Ralph H. Blanchard, "Social Work's Real Business," *Survey* 85, no. 7 (1949): 372; Herbert Bisno, *The Philosophy of Social Work* (Washington, DC: Public Affairs Press, 1952), 35. For statements from state and local welfare administrators, see Lorraine D. Walling, "State Leadership in Local Staff Development," *Social Casework* 28, no. 6 (1947): 228–35; Lucy Freeman, "Federal Aid Urged on All Assistance," *NYT*, December 11, 1948.

42. Arthur Altmeyer's 1948 speech to the National Conference on Social Work, for example, characterized as "fundamental" the notion of "public assistance as a matter of right." Quoted in Hearings before a Subcommittee of the Committee on Ways and Means, House of Representatives, 83rd Cong., 1st sess., on Economic Status of the Aged and Public Assistance (November 16–17, 1953), 436. Altmeyer was then commissioner of the Social Security Administration.

43. Mary Overholt Peters, "Talks with Beginning Social Workers, Part I: Gaining Perspective," *Social Casework* 28, no. 6 (1947): 224. For additional evidence, see Mauldin, "'Not By Bread Alone,'" 243; Walling, "State Leadership in Local Staff Development," 231; Lavinia Engle, interview by Peter A. Corning, May 18, 1967, transcript, Columbia Center for Oral History, Columbia University, New York; "The Social Front: The Old South," *Survey* 77, no. 5 (1941): 155.

44. "New Rash of Public Welfare Investigations," *Survey* 87, no. 5 (1951): 230.

45. W. L. White, "'On the County' – Then and Now," *Reader's Digest*, March 1952; see also "Welfare Is No Longer Charity," *Indianapolis Star*, February 18, 1951.

46. Hearings on the Economic Status of the Aged and Public Assistance, 435–36; Hearings before a Subcommittee of the Committee on Ways and Means, House of Representatives, 83rd Cong., 1st sess., on OASI: Coverage, Eligibility, Benefits; and Public Assistance (November 18–20, 1953), 528–30, 602–07; Hearings on the Economic Status of the Aged and Public Assistance, 435–36; Hearings before a Subcommittee of the Committee on Ways and Means, House of Representatives, 83rd Cong., 1st sess., on Public Assistance: OASI Financial Position and Benefits (November 23–25, 1953), 678–79, 681, 733–37, 753–54, 812–16.

47. Hearings on Public Assistance: OASI Financial Position and Benefits, 678–79.

48. Ibid., 812–16.

49. Hearings on the Economic Status of the Aged and Public Assistance, 435–36; Hearings on OASI: Coverage, Eligibility, Benefits; and Public Assistance,

528–30; Hearings on Public Assistance: OASI Financial Position and Benefits, 812–16.

50. Hearings on Public Assistance: OASI Financial Position and Benefits, 733–37.

51. Hearings on OASI: Coverage, Eligibility, Benefits; and Public Assistance, 606–7, 610–11; "Bill Offered to Revamp Social Security Program," *LAT*, January 7, 1954.

52. McCoy v. State Dept. of Pub. Welfare, 271 S.W.2d 788 (MO Ct. App. 1954).

53. On the perspective of the state welfare director, see Verne E. Gleason, interview by James Leiby and Julie Gordon Shearer, June 2, 1981, transcript [p. 14], Regional Oral History Office, Bancroft Library, University of California, Berkeley. On the California State Welfare Board's position, see Bertch v. Social Welfare Dept., 276 P.2d 891 (Cal. App. Ct. 1954).

54. Nancy Barr Mavity, "Adventures of a Newshunter: 'The Voice' and the 'Little Men,'" *Oakland (CA) Tribune*, March 19, 1950; "Probers Sift 'Mankind' Fund," *Oakland (CA) Tribune*, March 24, 1944; "16 Leaders of Mankind United Jailed by U.S.," *San Mateo (CA) Times*, December 18, 1942; "Subversive Acts Probe Is Continued," *Oakland (CA) Tribune*, December 4, 1941; H. T. Dohrman, *California Cult: The Story of Mankind United* (Boston: Beacon Press, 1958).

55. Bertch, 276 P.2d 891; Bertch v. Social Welfare Dept., 45 Cal.2d 524 (1955).

56. Collins v. State Bd. of Soc. Welfare, 81 N.W. 2d 4 (Iowa 1957).

57. Welfare recipients would eventually go to federal court with a similar argument, this time grounded in the Fourteenth Amendment of the U.S. Constitution, but not until the late 1960s. See Dandridge v. Williams, 397 U.S. 471 (1970), discussed in Chapter 8.

58. *Collins*, 81 N.W. 2d at 6.

59. Premilla Nadasen, *Welfare Warriors: The Welfare Rights Movement in the United States* (New York: Routledge, 2005), 19; Lisa Levenstein, *A Movement without Marches: African American Women and the Politics of Poverty in Postwar Philadelphia* (Chapel Hill: University of North Carolina Press, 2009), 83.

60. *Collins*, 81 N.W. 2d at 10 (Garfield, J., dissenting).

61. Scholars have been skeptical of any sustained commitment on the part of public welfare workers in the 1950s to the rights of their poor clients. Ellen Reese, for example, describes federal administrators as complicit in the era's welfare backlash. Ellen Reese, *Backlash against Welfare Mothers: Past and Present* (Berkeley: University of California Press, 2005), 42.

62. Jack B. Tate to Paul V. McNutt, July 12, 1941, Box 12, GC Correspondence on PA, HEWR.

63. Scott J. Shackelford and Lawrence M. Friedman, "Legally Incompetent: A Research Note," *American Journal of Legal History* 49, no. 3 (2007): 322.

64. Jack B. Tate to Paul V. McNutt, March 10, 1941, GC Correspondence on PA, HEWR (Delaware and Indiana); Jack B. Tate to Paul V. McNutt, March 10, 1944, GC Correspondence on PA, HEWR (Nevada and Iowa); Jack B. Tate to Paul V. McNutt, June 10, 1944, Box 11, GC Correspondence on PA, HEWR (Minnesota); Jack B. Tate to Watson Miller, February 10, 1946, Box 11, GC Correspondence on PA, HEWR (Minnesota).

65. SSA, Title I, § 6 ["The term old age assistance means money payments to aged individuals"]; Title IV, § 406(b) ["The term aid to dependent children means money payments with respect to a dependent child or dependent children"]; Title X, § 1006 ["The term aid to the blind means money payments to blind individuals"].

66. Tate to McNutt, March 10, 1941.

67. Ibid.; Tate to Miller, February 10, 1946.

68. Jack B. Tate to Paul V. McNutt, March 10, 1943, Box 12, GC Correspondence on PA, HEWR (Utah); Alanson W. Willcox to Oscar Ewing, January 12, 1948, Box 11, GC Correspondence on PA, HEWR (Missouri): A. D. Smith to Oscar Powell, March 3, 1944, Box 71, GC Correspondence on PA, HEWR (Rhode Island).

69. Tate to McNutt, March 10, 1943; see also Jack B. Tate to Paul V. McNutt, January 10, 1944, Box 11, GC Correspondence on PA, HEWR.

70. Jack B. Tate to Paul V. McNutt, October 10, 1944, Box 11, GC Correspondence on PA, HEWR; Tate to Miller, February 10, 1946; A. Delafield Smith, "Utah Assistance Payments to Striking Coal Miners – War Labor Disputes Act," January 3, 1947, Box 71, GC Correspondence on PA, HEWR. The official guidance that the BPA sent to state agencies incorporated this general argument but placed more emphasis on inefficiency than illegality. See Bureau of Public Assistance, State Letter No. 24, August 10, 1943, Box 1, State Letters, Policies, and Regulations Relating to Public Welfare Programs, 1942–1971, SSAR.

71. Blanche D. Coll, *Safety Net: Welfare and Social Security, 1929–1979* (New Brunswick, NJ: Rutgers University Press, 1995), 186; Winifred Bell, *Aid to Dependent Children* (New York: Columbia University Press, 1965), 29.

72. Tate to McNutt, March 10, 1941; Jack B. Tate to Paul V. McNutt, November 12, 1941, Box 12, GC Correspondence on PA, HEWR; Jack B. Tate to Paul V. McNutt, October 10, 1944, Box 11, GC Correspondence on PA, HEWR. The BPA and the board came to share this view. Bureau of Public Assistance, State Letter No. 46, March 5, 1945, Box 1, State Letters, Policies, and Regulations Relating to Public Welfare Programs, 1942–1971, SSAR, recommending "that the 'suitable home' provision be omitted from the public assistance laws and that the protective purpose of the provisions be incorporated in the protective legislation" instead.

73. Schottland, interview by Corning.

74. Oveta Culp Hobby, "Federal-State Relations and Grants-in-Aid," *Public Health Reports* 69, no. 1 (1954): 89, 91.

75. Bert Spector, "The Great Salk Vaccine Mess," *Antioch Review* 38, no. 3 (1980): 294, 301.

76. Mitchell, interview by Corning.

77. Ibid.

78. Acting Associate GC to GC, March 14, 1959, Box 20, GC Correspondence on PA, HEWR (Montana – allowing appointment of a guardian for an ADC child upon petition of the agency); Acting Associate GC to GC, September 15, 1959, Box 20, GC Correspondence on PA, HEWR (North Carolina – allowing agencies to supervise expenditures in cases in which ADC caretakers were

not using payments for necessities); Office of the Regional Attorney, Region III, to GC, March 4, 1955, Box 73, GC Correspondence on PA, HEWR (North Carolina – appointing guardians for the poor without following generally applicable procedures); Office of the Regional Attorney, Region IV, to GC, November 1956, Box 73, GC Correspondence on PA, HEWR (Alabama – seeking federal matching for payments made to "trustees for [the] inebriate"); Office of the Regional Attorney, Region IX, to GC, "Monthly Report – February 1959," March 3, 1959, Box 74, GC Correspondence on PA, HEWR (Washington); Office of the Regional Attorney, Region II, to GC, December 4, 1958, Box 73, GC Correspondence on PA, HEWR (New York).

79. "Legislative Developments in the States," *Public Welfare* 17, no. 3 (1959): 128 (Washington); "Legislative Developments in the States," *Public Welfare* 13 (October 1955): 192 (Missouri); Loren C. Belknap, "An Analysis and Criticism of the Program of Aid to Dependent Children," *Journal of Public Law* 6 (1957): 39, reporting such policies in thirteen jurisdictions, including Florida, Georgia, New Mexico, South Carolina, Tennessee, Mississippi, and the District of Columbia.

80. Belknap, "An Analysis and Criticism," 39, reporting such policies in eleven jurisdictions, including California, Alabama, Georgia, South Carolina, Tennessee, Washington, and West Virginia.

81. Office of the Regional Attorney, Region VI, to GC, April 1, 1957, Box 74, GC Correspondence on PA, HEWR (Wisconsin); "Legislative Developments in the States," *Public Welfare* 17, no. 3 (1959): 128 (South Dakota); "Legislative Developments in the States," *Public Welfare* 17, no. 4 (1959): 166 (California).

82. Dick Friend, "'Politics' Blocks Dole Reforms," *Los Angeles Mirror*, July 17, 1959.

83. GC to Secretary, November 15, 1957, Box 20, GC Correspondence on PA, HEWR (unnamed state).

84. GC to Secretary, July 15, 1958, Box 20, GC Correspondence on PA, HEWR (Illinois); Office of the Regional Attorney, Region III, to GC, February 5, 1958, Box 73, GC Correspondence on PA, HEWR (Virginia); Office of the Regional Attorney, Region IX, to GC, March 3, 1959, Box 74, GC Correspondence on PA, HEWR (Washington).

85. GC to Secretary, July 15, 1958, Box 20, GC Correspondence on PA, HEWR.

86. GC to Secretary, March 14, 1958, Box 20, GC Correspondence on PA, HEWR (Mississippi); Office of the Regional Attorney, Region IV, to GC, February 4, 1959, Box 73, GC Correspondence on PA, HEWR (Tennessee); Belknap, "An Analysis and Criticism," 42 (Georgia).

87. Office of the Regional Attorney, Region IV, to GC, July 8, 1954, Box 74, GC Correspondence on PA, HEWR (Mississippi); Acting Associate GC to GC, June 12, 1959, Box 73, GC Correspondence on PA, HEWR (Alabama); Associate GC to GC, January 15, 1959, Box 73, GC Correspondence on PA, HEWR (North Carolina); Acting Associate GC to GC, March 13, 1959, Box 73, GC Correspondence on PA, HEWR (South Dakota); Acting Associate GC to GC, October 14, 1959, Box 73, GC Correspondence on PA, HEWR (Florida, Louisiana); Office of the Regional Attorney, Region IV,

to GC, "Monthly Report – February 1957," March 6, 1957, Box 73, GC Correspondence on PA, HEWR (Tennessee); Office of the Regional Attorney, Region VI, to GC, April 4, 1957, Box 73, GC Correspondence on PA, HEWR (Illinois); "Legislative Developments in the States," *Public Welfare* 17, no. 3 (1959): 167, 168 (Texas, Louisiana); "Bill Would Bar Pay Toilets in California," *Baytown (TX) Sun*, February 25, 1955 (Missouri). Bell also found evidence of such proposals from Arkansas, Delaware, Kentucky, Michigan, New Jersey, Oregon, Pennsylvania, South Carolina, Utah, and Virginia. Bell, *Aid to Dependent Children*, 72.

88. GC to Secretary, July 15, 1957, Box 20, GC Correspondence on PA, HEWR (Alabama).
89. GC to Secretary, May 13, 1955, Box 11, GC Correspondence on PA, HEWR (Delaware).
90. Elaine Tyler May, *Homeward Bound: American Families in the Cold War Era* (New York: Basic Books, 1988); Rickie Solinger, *Wake Up Little Susie: Single Pregnancy and Race before Roe v. Wade*, 2nd ed. (New York: Routledge, 2000), 26.
91. Solinger, *Wake Up Little Susie*, 29–30.
92. "House Grants $50,000 College Fund Increase," *Joplin (MO) Globe*, March 5, 1958; "Would Halt Illegitimate Children's Aid," *Mt. Vernon (IL) Register News*, March 12, 1957; Bill Maultsby, "Where's the Answer?" *Kannapolis (NC) Daily Independent*, March 20, 1955.
93. Anders Walker, *The Ghost of Jim Crow: How Southern Moderates Used Brown v. Board of Education to Stall Civil Rights* (New York: Oxford University Press, 2009), 79, 111.
94. Ibid., 41–42.
95. Solinger, *Wake Up Little Susie*, 26–27; Walker, *The Ghost of Jim Crow*, 78–80.
96. Molly C. Michelmore, *Tax and Spend: The Welfare State, Tax Politics, and the Limits of American Liberalism* (Philadelphia: University of Pennsylvania Press, 2012). Suzanne Mettler has advanced a similar argument and carried it forward in time. Suzanne Mettler, *The Submerged State: How Invisible Government Policies Undermine American Democracy* (Chicago: University of Chicago Press, 2011).
97. Dick Friend, "Scandals in $1 Million Daily Public Aid," *Los Angeles Mirror*, July 13, 1959. For examples of similar newspaper coverage in Philadelphia, see Levenstein, *A Movement without Marches*, 54–55.
98. Alanson W. Willcox to Oscar Ewing, May 22, 1951, Box 11, GC Correspondence on PA, HEWR; Bell, *Aid to Dependent Children*, 72.
99. Office of the Regional Attorney, Region IV, to GC, February 4, 1960, Box 73, GC Correspondence on PA, HEWR.
100. Associate GC to GC, January 15, 1959, Box 20, GC Correspondence on PA, HEWR; Walker, *The Ghost of Jim Crow*, 77 and n. 163.
101. On South Dakota, see Acting Associate GC to GC, March 13, 1959, Box 20, GC Correspondence on PA, HEWR (lawyers advised the South Dakota agency that the bill "appears to be discriminatory"); I found no subsequent mentions of the bill in federal agency correspondence or newspaper

searches. On Alabama, see Office of the Regional Attorney, Region IV, to GC, May 9, 1956, Box 73, GC Correspondence on PA, HEWR (lawyers informed Alabama officials about the questions that the social security commissioner raised about Georgia's similar proposal in 1951: "we assume ... that the questions were sufficient to discourage the enactment of the Alabama bill"); "Bolls Flood Legislature on 2nd Day," *Anniston (AL) Star*, May 10, 1957, noting that under Alabama state law, unwed mothers could continue to "draw monthly welfare checks for every illegitimate child, no matter how many." On Delaware, see GC to Secretary, May 13, 1955, Box 11, GC Correspondence on PA, HEWR (lawyers advised Delaware officials that a proposal to limit assistance to two illegitimate children per family unless the mother requested to be sterilized would raise "a serious legal question ... under the equal protection clause of the 14th Amendment, and questions of conformity of the State plan would arise"); "Sterilization Sentiment Focuses on the Poor," *St. Petersburg (FL) Times*, July 21, 1966, noting that the proposal never became law. On Illinois, see "Legislative Developments in the States," *Public Welfare* 15, no. 4 (1957): 152; "Reforming Aid to Dependent Children," *Freeport (IL) Journal Standard*, April 12, 1957, noting that the Illinois bill was defeated.

102. Office of the Regional Attorney, Region IV, to GC, February 1957, Box 73, GC Correspondence on PA, HEWR.

103. Office of the Regional Attorney, Region IV, to GC, March 6, 1957, Box 73, GC Correspondence on PA, HEWR; Office of the Regional Attorney, Region IV, to GC, February 4, 1959, Box 73, GC Correspondence on PA, HEWR.

104. Office of the Regional Attorney, Region IV, to GC, December 3, 1958, Box 73, GC Correspondence on PA, HEWR, reporting that Florida's Legislative Reference Bureau asked exactly how far it could go in declaring homes with illegitimate children ineligible for ADC; Office of the Regional Attorney, Region IV, to GC, February 4, 1959, Box 73, GC Correspondence on PA, HEWR, reporting that the director of Florida's agency asked for a citation to the SSA provision prohibiting a state from denying assistance to illegitimate children.

105. Carl Harper, "Suggestions for Topics to Be Included in the Agenda for the Regional and Assistant Regional Attorneys' Conference in Washington the Week of June 17," May 22, 1957, Box 75, GC Correspondence on PA, HEWR.

106. GC to Secretary, June 14, 1954, Box 11, GC Correspondence on PA, HEWR; Office of the Regional Attorney, Region IV, to GC, July 8, 1954, Box 73, GC Correspondence on PA, HEWR; GC to Secretary, February 14, 1955, Box 11, GC Correspondence on PA, HEWR; GC to Secretary, August 14, 1956, Box 11, GC Correspondence on PA, HEWR; Bell, *Aid to Dependent Children*, 96.

107. Office of the Regional Attorney, Region IV, to GC, June 9, 1954, Box 73, GC Correspondence on PA, HEWR; General Counsel to Secretary, January 15, 1958, Box 20, GC Correspondence on PA, HEWR; General Counsel to Secretary, May 14, 1958, Box 20, GC Correspondence on PA, HEWR.

108. Acting Associate GC to GC, November 16, 1959, Box 20, GC Correspondence on PA, HEWR; Office of the Regional Attorney, Region IV to GC, October 6, 1959, Box 73, GC Correspondence on PA, HEWR; Office of the Regional Attorney, Region IV, to GC, June 11, 1959, Box 2, Bureau of Family Services Regional Subject Files, 1959–63, Record Group 363, Records of the Social and Rehabilitation Service, National Archives, College Park, MD [hereafter cited as SRSR].

109. In addition the examples mentioned above, see Office of the Regional Attorney, Region IV, to GC, March 6, 1957, Box 73, GC Correspondence on PA, HEWR, reporting that federal administrators made "a 'Federal' question" out of a Tennessee bill that deemed unwed parents to be "unsuitable"; Office of the Regional Attorney, Region IV, to GC, April 5, 1957, Box 73, GC Correspondence on PA, HEWR, reporting that the Tennessee legislature nonetheless enacted the bill; it failed to become law only after private welfare organizations lobbied the governor to veto it.

110. Bell, *Aid to Dependent Children*, 93–110, 130–33.

111. Office of the Regional Attorney, Region IV, to GC, April 5, 1959, Box 73, GC Correspondence on PA, HEWR; Office of the Regional Attorney, Region IV, to GC, September 1957, Box 73, GC Correspondence on PA, HEWR.

112. After the regional attorney in Region III talked Virginia officials out of a proposal to deny ADC to illegitimate children unless the mother instituted a nonsupport action against the father, his legal staff helped the state legislature draft alternative amendments that would not raise conformity questions. Office of the Regional Attorney, Region III, to GC, February 5, 1958, Box 73, GC Correspondence on PA, HEWR. Federal attorneys unknowingly provided Mississippi with an even worse "end run" when they objected to a regulation targeting the families of "nonlegal" unions (the state had just amended its law to abolish common-law marriage): under the proposed law, the birth of a subsequent child to a nonlegally married couple disqualified all the couple's children from receiving aid. After the federal lawyers identified an "unreasonable classification" (children of nonprocreating nonlegal unions retained their grants), the Mississippi agency's lawyers advised the state agency to deny aid to *all* children of nonlegal unions. Bell, *Aid to Dependent Children*, 98–99. Regarding one state adopting another state's law: "The Alabama 'suitable home' bill substantially parallels the [approved] Mississippi plan material on this point," explained a regional attorney to his superiors in Washington, making it "awkward" for the federal agency to disapprove of the former. Office of the Regional Attorney, Region IV, to GC, May 7, 1959, Box 73, GC Correspondence on PA, HEWR.

7 WELFARE RIGHTS OUTSIDE THE COURTS

1. Act No. 251, 1960 La. Acts 525, 527 (July 7, 1960); Act No. 306, 1960 La. Acts 634, 635 (July 7, 1960).

2. "Louisiana Drops 23,000 Children on Relief Rolls as Illegitimates," *NYT*, August 28, 1960; Lisa Levenstein, "From Innocent Children to Unwanted Migrants and Unwed Moms: Two Chapters in the Public Discourse on Welfare in the United States, 1960–1961," *Journal of Women's History* 11, no. 4 (2000): 10.

3. Anders Walker, "Legislating Virtue: How Segregationists Disguised Racial Discrimination as Moral Reform following *Brown v. Board of Education*," *Duke Law Journal* 47 (1997): 423–24; Kenneth J. Neubeck and Noel A. Cazenave, *Welfare Racism: Playing the Race Card against America's Poor* (New York: Routledge, 2001), 70–71.

4. Groups working at the local level included the Interdenominational Ministers Alliance, the Family Service Society, and the International Longshoreman's Association chapter; at the national level, the National Social Welfare Assembly, the Child Welfare League of America, the American Public Welfare Association, and the Field Foundation. Taryn Lindhorst and Leslie Leighninger, "'Ending Welfare as We Know It' in 1960: Louisiana's Suitable Home Law," *Social Service Review* 77, no. 4 (2003): 573; Jennifer Mittelstadt, *From Welfare to Workfare: The Unintended Consequences of Liberal Reform, 1945–1965* (Chapel Hill: University of North Carolina Press, 2005), 88–89; Levenstein, "From Innocent Children," 12; "Louisiana Action Hit: Urban League Urges U.S. Aid for Children Off Welfare," *NYT*, August 30, 1960.

5. "League Asks Aid for La. Children," *CD*, September 8, 1960; "Help 300 Each Day in 'Operation Feed Babies,'" *CD*, September 21, 1960; Mittelstadt, *From Welfare to Workfare*, 89; Levenstein, "From Innocent Children," 12; "British Flying Food to Negroes in South," *NYT*, September 14, 1960; "Cry for Food in New Orleans," *CD*, August 29, 1960; "Inhumanity in Louisiana," *CD*, September 14, 1960.

6. Claude Sittons, "Jimmie Davis Wins Louisiana Run-Off," *NYT*, January 10, 1960; "Governor Calls ADC Mothers Prostitutes," *CD*, September 26, 1960; John Corporon, "Louisianans Dispute Effect of Cut in Relief for Unwed Mothers," *Washington Post* [hereafter cited as *WP*], September 29, 1960.

7. "Sins of the Fathers," *NYT*, October 6, 1960; "Louisiana Relief Rolls," *CD*, September 5, 1960; see also "Suffer Little Children," *Nation*, September 24, 1960, 171.

8. Steven M. Teles, *The Rise of the Conservative Legal Movement: The Battle for Control of the Law* (Princeton, NJ: Princeton University Press, 2009), 18–19. Teles derives the "network entrepreneur" idea from organizational sociology.

9. Myron J. Berman to Kathryn Goodwin, August 14, 1959, cited in Frances L. White, "Equitable Treatment under the Public Assistance Titles" (1963), Frances White papers, private collection, on file with author [hereafter cited as FWP]. Berman seems to have been invoking the Supreme Court's 1953 equal protection case *Morey v. Doud*, 354 U.S. 457 (1953), in which the Court "caution[ed] that '[d]iscriminations of an unusual character especially suggest careful consideration to determine whether they are obnoxious to the constitutional provision.'" Ibid., 464, citing Louisville Gas & Electric Co. v. Coleman, 277 U.S. 32, 37–38 (1928). Other, more recent decisions, however,

would have suggested a less stringent form of review. See Williamson v. Lee Optical, Inc., 348 U.S. 483, 489, 491 (1955), [upholding the challenged regulation because it bore a "rational relation" to a legitimate objective; observing that "the prohibition of the Equal Protection Clause goes no further than ... invidious discrimination"].

10. See Chapter 3, in the section titled "The Equal Protection Principle: Toward Uniformity and Equal Treatment," and Chapter 6, under "'Stemming the Tide': Protecting Rights by Policing State Law."

11. Winifred Bell, *Aid to Dependent Children* (New York: Columbia University Press, 1965), 142–43. Eisenhower informed the delegation that he could not interfere with this matter of states' rights. Lindhorst and Leighninger, "Suitable Home Law," 575. On Moore's history of activism, see Erik S. McDuffie, "'I Wanted a Communist Philosophy, but I Wanted Us to Have a Chance to Organize Our People': The Diasporic Radicalism of Queen Mother Audley Moore and the Origins of Black Power," *African and Black Diaspora: An International Journal* 3, no. 2 (2010): 181–95.

12. Gilbert Y. Steiner, *Social Insecurity: The Politics of Welfare* (Chicago: Rand McNally & Company, 1966), 100.

13. Harnett T. Kane, "Louisiana Story: End of a Chapter," *NYT*, September 27, 1959.

14. Loula Dunn to Sidney Hollander, March 18, 1958, Box 12, Mss 800, EWP.

15. "School Desegregation Ordered in New Orleans, Davis Enjoined," *WP*, August 28, 1960. For a full account of the long and acrimonious contest over the desegregation of New Orleans schools, see Liva Baker, *The Second Battle of New Orleans: The Hundred-Year Struggle to Integrate the Schools* (New York: HarperCollins, 1996).

16. Kathryn D. Goodwin to Mary Evelyn Parker, September 1, 1960, Box 53, National Social Work Council, National Social Welfare Assembly, and National Human Services Assembly Records, SW 0004, Supplement 2, Social Welfare History Archives, University of Minnesota, Minneapolis [hereafter cited as NSWAR]; Mary Evelyn Parker to Kathryn D. Goodwin, September 14, 1960, Box 53, NSWAR.

17. Clark W. Blackburn to Arthur Flemming, September 30, 1960, Box 53, NSWAR.

18. Landon R. Y. Storrs, *The Second Red Scare and the Unmaking of the New Deal Left* (Princeton, NJ: Princeton University Press, 2012), 29, 47–49, 245–47. For more on Wickenden's time as a FERA administrator, see Elisa Martia Alvarez Minoff, "Free to Move? The Law and Politics of Internal Migration in Twentieth-Century America," PhD diss., Harvard University, 2013; Margot Canaday, *The Straight State: Sexuality and Citizenship in Twentieth-Century America* (Princeton, NJ: Princeton University Press, 2009), 102–33.

19. Elizabeth Wickenden, interview by Blanche D. Coll, May 28, 1986, transcript, Box 2, M99-098, EWP.

20. Storrs, *The Second Red Scare*, 8–9, 45–50. Wickenden's ability to act on her convictions was constrained during the 1940s and 1950s, after Martin Dies's House Committee on Un-American Activities named her husband a

"crackpot, radical bureaucrat" (for his work in New Deal public works agencies). But by the late 1950s the danger appeared to have passed. Ibid., 244–58.

21. "Residence Laws: National Conference of Social Work," *Public Health Reports* 72, no. 2 (1957): 108. For more on this point, see Minoff, "Free to Move?" 66–100.

22. Bess Furman, "Flemming Calls Aged Plan Sound," NYT, September 23, 1960; "Federal Agents Probe Louisiana Child Aid Cut," WP, October 14, 1960.

23. Elizabeth Wickenden, notes on conversation with Harry Rosenfeld, November 1, 1960, Box 53, NSWAR.

24. Jane Hoey, "Aid to Dependent Children – Title IV, Social Security Act – Louisiana," November 7, 1960, Box 53, NSWAR.

25. Elizabeth Wickenden to Shad Polier, November 4, 1960, Box 53, NSWAR.

26. The other two were Harry Rosenfeld and Leonard Lesser. Wickenden, notes on conversation with Harry Rosenfeld.

27. Wickenden to Polier, November 4, 1960.

28. "Louisiana Rejects U.S. Aid Demands," WP, November 3, 1960; "The South: D-Day in New Orleans," *Time*, November 28, 1960; Bess Furman, "U.S. Seeks to Bar Aid for Louisiana," NYT, November 15, 1960; Eve Edstrom, "Louisiana Aid Rule Attacked," WP, November 15, 1960.

29. Bess Furman, "Louisiana Cites Relief Revisions," NYT, November 16, 1960; Eve Edstrom, "Louisiana Bars to Relief Eased," WP, November 16, 1960.

30. Mittelstadt, *From Welfare to Workfare*, 89–90.

31. U.S. Department of Health, Education, and Welfare, Social Security Administration, "In the Matter of: The Conformity of the Louisiana Plan for Aid to Dependent Children under Title IV of the Social Security Act, Decision of Commissioner of Social Security," January 16, 1961, Box 53, NSWAR; "Louisiana Yields on Children's Aid," NYT, December 2, 1960; Bess Furman, "U.S. to Continue Louisiana Relief as State Alters Child Home Law," NYT, December 16, 1960.

32. Arthur S. Flemming, interview by Harlan Phillips, April 25, 1964, transcript, Columbia Center for Oral History, Columbia University, New York. Banta's private notes suggest that he believed the matter to be one of "fed-state relations," best "handled quietly." Note card on Louisiana public assistance matter, September 1, 1960, Box 2, Miscellaneous Series, Parke M. Banta Papers, Collection no. 3844, State Historical Society of Missouri, Columbia.

33. This paragraph draws generally on Flemming, interview by Phillips. Social Security commissioner William Mitchell remembered events differently, or at least recalled a detail that Flemming omitted. In Mitchell's recollection, he (Mitchell) wanted to find Louisiana out of conformity with the act and Flemming initially disagreed; Flemming warned Mitchell that he would have no choice but to publicly denounce Mitchell if he stuck to his position. Mitchell, interview by Corning. On Flemming's background, see Eric Pace, "Arthur S. Flemming, 91, Dies; Served in Eisenhower Cabinet," NYT, September 9, 1996. On Bernice Bernstein, see Karen M. Tani, "Portia's Deal," *Chicago-Kent Law Review* 87, no. 2 (2012): 564–68.

34. Smith, interview by author.

35. U.S. Department of Health, Education and Welfare, Office of the Secretary, "Memorandum for the Commission of Social Security," January 16, 1961, Box 53, NSWAR [hereafter cited as Flemming ruling] (emphasis added).

36. Rufus Miles to the Secretary, Box 219, Office of the Secretary, Secretary's Subject Correspondence, 1956–1974, HEWR. For more on this point, see Karen M. Tani, "Administrative Equal Protection: Federalism, The Fourteenth Amendment, and the Rights of the Poor," *Cornell Law Review* 100 (2015): 872–73.

37. Flemming ruling. At the time, seven states had policies that clearly violated this ruling: Georgia, Arkansas, Mississippi, Texas, Florida, Virginia, and Michigan. Bell, *Aid to Dependent Children*, 146–47.

38. Aid to Dependent Children of Unemployed Parents Act, Pub. L. No. 87-31, 75 Stat. 77 (May 8, 1961); Wilbur Cohen, interview by James Sargent, March 18, 1974, transcript, Columbia Center for Oral History, Columbia University, New York.

39. News Bureau, Florida State University, untitled press release on Florida suitable-home study, September 25, 1962, Box 2, RLC. The study was published as Robert T. Lansdale, *The Florida Suitable Home Law: A Statistical Analysis of 17,999 Aid to Dependent Children Cases Affected* (Tallahassee: Florida State University, 1962).

40. Elizabeth Wickenden to Wilbur Cohen, July 15, 1959, Box 12, Mss 800, EWP; Elizabeth Wickenden, "The Legal Needs of the Poor from the Point of View of Public Welfare Policy," presentation to the Conference on the Extension of Legal Services to the Poor, Washington, DC, November 12, 1964, Box 20, NSWAR.

41. See, for example, Edgar May, "Storm Center of Relief: Dependent Children's Aid," *Buffalo (NY) Evening News*, June 13, 1960; Edgar May, "Many Families on Relief Permanent Public Wards," *Buffalo (NY) Evening News*, June 9, 1960. These articles and others in the same series won May the Pulitzer Prize for Local Reporting. For more on the emergence of a racialized "notion of a 'culture of welfare dependency'" in the 1950s, see Lisa Levenstein, *A Movement without Marches: African American Women and the Politics of Poverty in Postwar Philadelphia* (Chapel Hill: University of North Carolina Press, 2009), 53–54.

42. May, "Many Families on Relief Permanent Public Wards."

43. Contra Costa County v. Social Welfare Bd., 229 Cal. App. 2d 762 (1964). Poor mothers who were clients of non–federally funded programs of general relief also seemed to be stirring. In Connecticut, the Hartford Legal Aid Society reportedly helped a poor, twenty-one-year-old mother named Ida English bring a lawsuit in federal court to challenge the state's attempt to deport her to her to South Carolina, her previous place of residence. The case was dismissed after authorities transferred English to the state's ADC program. National Social Welfare Assembly, "1961 Residence Roundup," April 1961, Box 55, NSWAR; Dan Gottlieb, "Constitutionality Test Unlikely as City Drops 'Deporting' Fight," *Hartford (CT) Times*, October 25, 1960.

44. Brief for Petitioners, Monroe v. Pape, 365 U.S. 167 (1961) (No. 39), 1960 WL 98617; Monroe v. Pape, 365 U.S. 167 (1961). The fact that the Monroe family received ADC comes from *Monroe v. Pape*, 221 F.Supp. 635 (N.D. Ill. 1963).
45. Dick Friend, "Hordes of Cheap Chiselers Burden Taxpayers of County," *Los Angeles Mirror*, July 14, 1959.
46. Premilla Nadasen, *Welfare Warriors: The Welfare Rights Movement in the United States* (New York: Routledge, 2005), 18–20.
47. "Newburgh Welfare Rules," *NYT*, June 24, 1961.
48. Edgar May, "A Way Out of the Welfare Mess," *Harper's Magazine*, October 1961.
49. John H. Averill, "Newburgh Aid Program Raises Political Storm," *LAT*, August 10, 1961; "Obligation and Abuse," *WSJ*, June 26, 1961; William Henry Chamberlin, "Parasite's Paradise," *WSJ*, July 25, 1961.
50. Peter Braestrup, "Ribicoff Upholds Work-Relief If U.S. Funds Are Not Involved," *NYT*, July 20, 1961.
51. Shaffer, "Public Welfare Policy," *Editorial Research Reports* 2 (1961), accessed September 7, 2011, http://library.cqpress.com/cqresearcher/cqresrr e1961100400, quoting Ribicoff's May 14, 1961, address to the National Conference on Social Welfare; Mittelstadt, *From Welfare to Workfare*, 115; Steiner, *Social Insecurity*, 37.
52. "The Growing Scandal in Relief," *U.S. News & World Report*, September 11, 1961. On the use of the term "welfare mess," see, for example, May, "A Way Out of the Welfare Mess"; "Ribicoff Hints He Wants Tightening of Relief Rolls, Cost Reductions," *WSJ*, August 25, 1961; Duane Dewel, "What's Wrong about This? *Washington [IA] Evening Journal*, September 8, 1961;
53. Fletcher Knebel, "Welfare: Has It Become a Scandal?" *Look* 25, no. 23 (November 7, 1961). For another high-profile example, see May, "A Way Out of the Welfare Mess." On the mistaken assumption of prosperity and abundance, see Thomas J. Sugrue, *The Origins of the Urban Crisis: Race and Inequality in Postwar Detroit* (Princeton: Princeton University Press, 1996).
54. Charles Stevenson, "Children without Fathers: The Shocking Truth about the Dependent Children Welfare Program," *Reader's Digest*, November 1961, 72–73, 79–80; John C. O'Connor Jr. to Senator Russell Long, November 6, 1961, Box 6, Family Services Bureau, Master Subject Files, 1963–65, SRSR.
55. May, "A Way Out of the Welfare Mess."
56. See, for example, "The Growing Scandal in Relief," *U.S. News & World Report*; Knebel, "Welfare: Has It Become a Scandal?"; Charles Stevenson, "Must We Have Relief Programs That Make Chronic Dependents?" *Reader's Digest*, December 1961. The "milk bill" quote is from Friend, "Hordes of Cheap Chiselers."
57. State of New York Moreland Commission on Welfare, *Public Welfare in the State of New York: Moreland Commission Report*, January 15, 1963, Box 1, New York (State) Moreland Commission on Welfare Correspondence and subject files, 1961–63, Record Series 10991-12, New York State Archives, Albany.

58. State of New York Moreland Commission on Welfare, Special Hearings, September 11–13, 1962, Statements, Box 2, New York State Moreland Commission on Welfare Special Hearing, New York, NY, September 11, 1962, Record Series 10991-83, New York State Archives, Albany.

59. Public Welfare Amendments of 1962, §104(a), Pub. L. No. 87-543, 76 Stat. 172 (1962) (emphasis added); Blanche D. Coll, *Safety Net: Welfare and Social Security, 1929–1979* (New Brunswick, NJ: Rutgers University Press, 1995), 222.

60. Mittelstadt, *From Welfare to Workfare*, 109–12; Aid to Dependent Children of Unemployed Parents Act, Pub. L. No. 87-31, 75 Stat. 77 (1961).

61. Mittelstadt, *From Welfare to Workfare*, 112–13.

62. Hearings before the Committee on Ways and Means of the House of Representatives, 87th Cong, 2d. sess., on H.R. 10032, A Bill to Extend and Improve the Public Assistance and Child Welfare Services Programs of the Social Security Act, and for Other Purposes (February 7, 9, and 13, 1962) (statement of Hon. Neal Smith); ibid. (statement of Henry A. Wise, New York state senator).

63. See, generally, Charles E. Gilbert, "Policy-Making in Public Welfare: The 1962 Amendments," *Political Science Quarterly* 81, no. 2 (1966): 196–224.

64. John F. Kennedy, *Message from the President of the United States relative to a Public Assistance and Welfare Program*, 87th Cong., 1st sess., February 1, 1962 (H.R. Doc. No. 325); John F. Kennedy, "Statement by the President upon Approving the Public Welfare Amendments Bill," July 26, 1962, in John Woolley and Gerhard Peters, *The American Presidency Project*, accessed May 20, 2015, http://www.presidency.ucsb.edu/; Wilbur J. Cohen and Robert M. Ball, "Public Welfare Amendments of 1962 and Proposals for Health Insurance for the Aged," *Social Security Bulletin* 25, no. 3 (1962): 3; Arthur Altmeyer to Elizabeth Wickenden, September 10, 1962, Box 1, Mss 800, EWP.

65. Public Welfare Amendments of 1962, § 108. Technically, a state could issue protective payments prior to the amendment; state officials simply could not ask the federal government to subsidize those payments. Ruth M. Wilson, "Strengthening Services through Money Management Counseling," *Public Welfare* 20, no. 2 (1962): 98.

66. Public Welfare Amendments of 1962, §107(a); Cohen and Ball, "Public Welfare Amendments of 1962."

67. Elizabeth Wickenden, "Draft National Social Welfare Assembly Statement on the Public Welfare Amendments of 1962, Memo #2: The Issue of the Civil Rights of Assistance Recipients," August 17, 1962, Box 1, Mss 800, EWP; see also National Social Welfare Assembly, "Public Welfare Amendments of 1962 (H.R. 10606), Memo #1: The Issue of Restricted Payments," April 18, 1962, Box 1, Mss 800, EWP. As Elisa Minoff has demonstrated, Wickenden's skepticism of potentially coercive poor relief policies dates back to the early 1930s. Minoff, "Free to Move?" 82. In retrospect, the "waiver" provision of the 1962 amendments should also have raised red flags: it authorized the secretary of HEW to waive the normal requirements for state plans to allow states to pursue experimental projects. By the 1990s, many states had used

waivers to implement more punitive and restrictive programs than would otherwise have been allowed. Susan Bennett and Kathleen A. Sullivan, "Disentitling the Poor: Waivers and Welfare 'Reform,'" *University of Michigan Journal of Law Reform* 26 (1993): 2157–212.

68. Steiner, *Social Insecurity*, 40; Storrs, *The Second Red Scare*, 248; Wilbur J. Cohen, interview by Blanche D. Coll, 1985, transcript, Box 2, M99-098, EWP; Wickenden, "Draft National Social Welfare Assembly Statement on the Public Welfare Amendments of 1962, Memo #2."

69. Elsie Carper, "Senate Votes D.C. Fund of $319 Million," WP, November 19, 1963.

70. John J. Lindsay, "$22 Million for Welfare Sent Back," WP, August 17, 1961; Eve Edstrom, "19 of 21 Not Eligible For Relief, Says Byrd," WP, August 3, 1962.

71. Marjorie Hunter, "'Welfare Mess' in Capital Spurs National Inquiry," NYT, August 19, 1962.

72. Eve Edstrom, "Relief Scandal Here Provokes Remote Echoes," NYT, Aug. 26, 1962.

73. Coll, *Safety Net*, 227.

74. Steiner, *Social Insecurity*, 64–65; Hunter, "'Welfare Mess.'"

75. See, generally, Susan Stein-Roggenbuck, *Negotiating Relief: The Development of Social Welfare Programs in Depression-Era Michigan, 1930–1940*, 2nd ed. (Columbus: Ohio State University Press, 2008).

76. Sidney Fine, *"Expanding the Frontiers of Civil Rights": Michigan, 1948–1968* (Detroit: Wayne State University Press, 2000), 191–227.

77. Robert D. Novak, "Rambling Romneyism," WSJ, October 15, 1962.

78. See, for example, Chesly Manly, "George Romney: A New Star in Political Skies," *Chicago Tribune*, February 5, 1962; A. F. Mahan, "Political Highway Now Beckoning to Romney," LAT, February 4, 1962.

79. Marquis Childs, "Romney's Backers Look to the Future," WP, March 25, 1963; Fine, *"Expanding the Frontiers of Civil Rights,"* 207. For more on Romney's biography as it would have been known to the public in the early 1960s, see Tom Mahoney, *The Story of George Romney* (New York: Harper & Brother, 1960).

80. James T. Patterson, *Grand Expectations: The United States, 1945–1974* (New York: Oxford University Press, 1996), 271; "Ike Likes Romney, GOP Politicians Told," WSJ, January 15, 1962; Roscoe Drummond, "Romney's Chances," WP, January 13, 1962; Manly, "George Romney"; Childs, "Romney's Backers Look to the Future"; James Reston, "Romney Only Figure Filling GOP White House Formula," LAT, February 4, 1962.

81. "Three for '64: G.O.P. Hopefuls Make Plans," NYT, February 18, 1963; John Millhone, "Romney Tangles Political Lines," *Detroit Free Press*, February 3, 1963; Steiner, *Social Insecurity*, 102.

82. Herbert Rubinstein, "Issues in Michigan Public Welfare," September 12, 1963, Box 23, Papers of George Romney, 852178 Aa 2, Bentley Historical Library, University of Michigan, Ann Arbor [hereafter cited as GRP]; Lynn Kellogg to George Romney, April 17, 1963, Box 57, NSWAR.

83. Kellogg to Romney, April 17, 1963.

84. Persons who worked in a workplace with less than four employees were not eligible for unemployment compensation under Michigan law. Steiner, *Social Insecurity*, 101.

85. Kellogg to Romney, April 17, 1963; Lynn Kellogg to Frank Kelley, April 5, 1963, Box 57, NSWAR; Peter B. Fletcher to George Romney, June 25, 1963, Box 23, GRP; Richard Van Dusen to Peter B. Fletcher, July 11, 1963, Box 23, GRP. On the racial consequences of federal-state Unemployment Insurance rules, see Robert Lieberman, *Shifting the Color Line: Race and the American Welfare State* (Cambridge, MA: Harvard University Press, 1998), 177–215.

86. Steiner, *Social Insecurity*, 102–6; Transcript of conversation between Phyllis Osborne and Lynn Kellogg, March 8, 1963, Box 23, GRP; John J. Hurley to Lynn Kellogg, April 17, 1963, Box 4, Office of the Commissioner General Subject Files, 1963–65, SRSR; Anthony Celebrezze, statement on Michigan's ADC-UP plan, March 26, 1963, Box 7, Mss 800, EWP.

87. Alanson W. Willcox, "Civil Rights in Social Legislation," November 5, 1948, Box 48, GC Correspondence on PA, HEWR; see also A. Delafield Smith, "Equal Protection of the Laws," April 29, 1948, Box 75, GC Correspondence on PA, HEWR.

88. As I have argued elsewhere, this is an example of the phenomenon that legal scholars call "administrative constitutionalism." Tani, "Administrative Equal Protection," 875–76.

89. Alanson Willcox, "Memorandum concerning Authority of the Secretary under Title IV of the Social Security Act, to Disapprove Michigan House Bill 145 on the Ground of its Limitations on Eligibility," March 25, 1963 [hereafter cited as Willcox Memo on Michigan House Bill 145], Box 7, Mss 800, EWP.

90. Ibid.

91. Richard Van Dusen to George W. Romney, March 27, 1963, Box 4, Office of the Commissioner General Subject Files, 1963–65, SRSR; George W. Romney, public statement, March 27, 1963, Box 4, Office of the Commissioner General Subject Files, 1963–65, SRSR.

92. George W. Romney to members of the House Committee on Ways and Means, April 10, 1963, Box 23, GRP; Bruce Alger to George Romney, May 14, 1963, Box 23, GRP; George C. Wallace to George Romney, May 6, 1963, Box 23, GRP; Mark O. Hatfield to George Romney, April 25, 1963, Box 23, GRP; George D. Clyde to George W. Romney, May 2, 1963, Box 23, GRP; John A. Love to George Romney, April 16, 1963, Box 23, GRP; Robert E. Smylie to George Romney, April 17, 1963, Box 23, GRP.

93. On Kelley's biography, see Elmer E. White, "Frank J. Kelley: The Eternal General," *Michigan Bar Journal* (June 2000): 688; John Minnis, "The Eternal General: State Legend Still Offers His Share of Opinions," *Detroit Legal News*, January 14, 2011, accessed September 7, 2011, http://www.legal news.com/detroit/1004433. Anticipating the Supreme Court's holding in *Reynolds v. Sims*, 377 U.S. 533, 558 (1964) [holding that state senators must be elected on the basis of "one person, one vote"], Kelley had urged the constitutional convention delegates to tread cautiously as they considered legislative reapportionment. Romney, the convention vice president, ignored

his warnings. The apportionment feud continued into 1963. "Decision May Affect State," *Ironwood [MI] Daily Globe*, April 5, 1962; "Governor, Attorney General Stand Ground on Their Fight," *Holland [MI] Evening Sentinel*, April 11, 1963; Glenn Engle, "Feud Sparks Reports: Kelley-Romney Race Eyed in '64," *Detroit Free Press*, March 29, 1963.

94. Frank J. Kelley to George Romney, April 8, 1963, Box 228, GRP; Opinion No. 4156, April 11, 1963, Box 57, NSWAR.

95. W. Willard Wirtz to Anthony Celebrezze, April 23, 1963, Box 4, Office of the Commissioner General Subject Files, 1963–65, SRSR.

96. Elizabeth Wickenden, "The Issues in the Michigan Welfare Controversy Relating to Extension of AFDC to Children of the Unemployed," March 28, 1963, Box 7, Mss 800, EWP. Wickenden sent this memo to the Senate Finance Committee, the House Ways and Means Committee, Michigan senators Patrick McNamara and Phil Hart, the National Urban League, all state welfare commissioners, all regional HEW officers, and many of her public welfare friends and acquaintances.

97. Wickenden to Nelson H. Cruikshank, April 9, 1963, Box 57, NSWAR; Wickenden to Anthony Celebrezze, April 10, 1963, Box 57, NSWAR.

98. Leo Farhat to George Romney, April 16, 1963, Box 23, GRP; George W. Romney, statement on AFDC-UP, April 12, 1963, Box 57, NSWAR; Smylie to Romney, April 17, 1963; George W. Romney, presentation to Committee on Federal-State Relations, Governors' Conference, July 21, 1963, Box 228, GRP.

99. See, generally, Taylor Branch, *Parting the Waters: America in the King Years 1954–63* (New York: Simon and Schuster, 1988), 673–845.

100. Romney, presentation to Committee on Federal-State Relations. On *Arizona v. Hobby*, see Chapter 5.

101. Jules H. Berman to Elizabeth Wickenden, October 9, 1962, Box 1, Mss 800, EWP; I. Jack Fastau to Elizabeth Wickenden, February 21, 1963, Box 7, Mss 800, EWP; I. Jack Fastau to Elizabeth Wickenden, March 21, 1963, Box 7, Mss 800, EWP.

102. On racial segregation, see, for example, Brown v. Board of Education, 347 U.S. 483 (1954); Bolling v. Sharpe, 347 U.S. 497 (1954); Boynton v. Virginia, 364 U.S. 454 (1960). On due process and free speech rights of unpopular groups, see, for example, NAACP v. Alabama, 357 U.S. 449 (1958); Speiser v. Randall, 357 U.S. 513 (1958). On election law, see, for example, Gomillion v. Lightfoot, 364 U.S. 339 (1960); Baker v. Carr, 369 U.S. 186 (1962). On rights violations by state and local officials, including police officers, see, for example, Monroe v. Pape, 365 U.S. 167, and Mapp v. Ohio, 367 U.S. 643 (1961).

103. 358 U.S. 1 (1958).

104. Elizabeth Wickenden, *How to Influence Public Policy: A Short Manual on Social Action* (New York: American Association of Social Workers, 1954), 34.

105. Elizabeth Wickenden to Abe Fortas, January 17, 1963, Box 16, Mss 800, EWP (emphasis in original). Wickenden said as much to fellow social welfare activist Sidney Hollander in early 1964: "One of the reasons that you

sense a certain amount of caution [about prohibiting midnight raids] on the part of Ellen Winston [HEW's head of Welfare Administration] and others in Washington is that the lawyers there do not feel too sure of their ground in the light of existing court decisions. This is why it is so extremely important to get a test case in the courts." Elizabeth Wickenden to Sidney Hollander, January 10, 1964, Box 1, Mss 800, EWP.

106. Elizabeth Wickenden, "Poverty and the Law: The Constitutional Rights of Assistance Recipients," March 25, 1963, Box 52, NSWAR.
107. Elizabeth Wickenden to Arthur Flemming, April 16, 1963, Box 57, NSWAR.
108. Willcox Memo on Michigan House Bill 145.
109. See School Construction in Areas Affected by Federal Activities, Pub. L. No. 81-815, 64 Stat. 967 (1950) and Pub. L. No. 81-874, 64 Stat. 1100 (1950) [repealed and eventually reauthorized and codified as part of Title VIII of the Elementary and Secondary Education Act, 20 U.S.C. § 7701, et seq.].
110. Alanson W. Willcox to Abraham Ribicoff, April 25, 1962, FWP. Congress had also expressed interest in the issue. Only two months prior, the House Committee on Labor and Education had summoned Ribicoff to give testimony about "integration in public education programs" and had grilled him about his agency's basis for continuing to issue federal funds to segregated school districts. Stephen C. Halpern, *On the Limits of the Law: The Ironic Legacy of Title VI of the 1964 Civil Rights Act* (Baltimore: Johns Hopkins University Press, 1995), 27.
111. Willcox to Ribicoff, April 25, 1962. Around this time, the United States Department of Justice (DOJ) did try to bring this argument before the courts, by seeking to enjoin certain public schools from racially segregating the children of U.S. military personnel and other federal government employees. DOJ lawyers advanced a "contractual obligation" theory, arguing that when local schools used federal grant monies for construction of their facilities, they had to comply with *Brown*'s desegregation mandate. The strategy produced underwhelming results. Tani, "Administrative Equal Protection," 879n278.
112. The GC's office attempted to resolve this tension in the fall of 1963 by tasking new recruit Frances White, fresh out of Yale Law School, with analyzing the legal basis for HEW's equal treatment principle. After spending weeks sifting through agency records, White concluded that "Federal administrators ha[d] always required State plans to satisfy" an equal treatment condition – one "not explicitly contained in the statute." She also found evidence that administrators believed they were giving life to the Constitution's equal protection mandate. If the agency were to take that stance in late 1963, however, it would lead to an "inevitable" – and unpalatable – conclusion: "that all State programs which were receiving Federal aid could be forced to satisfy the requirements of the equal protection clause." White's solution to this dilemma was to urge her colleagues to think more carefully about how the Social Security Act, rather than the Constitution, could support the agency's goals. A statutory-based approach to equal protection, she explained, would not be "readily transferable" to

other programs and hence would allow the agency to avoid the desegregation landmine. White, "Equitable Treatment." Going forward, HEW lawyers would follow her advice. Tani, "Administrative Equal Protection,"
887–89.

113. "National Survey Shows 5.4% of Recipients of Aid for Children Ineligible,"
WSJ, August 2, 1963; "94.5% Eligibility Found in Aid to Dependent
Children," *Buffalo (NY) Evening News*, August 3, 1963.

114. Morris Cunningham, "Byrd Urges Cleanup Action on National Welfare
Abuses," *Commercial Appeal* (Memphis), August 7, 1963.

115. See, for example, "Looking Cheerfully on Evidences of Connecticut Welfare
Fakery," *New Haven (CT) Register*, August 4, 1963; "Our Welfare
Cheaters," *Ocala (FL) Star-Banner*, August 4, 1963; "Reforming the
ADC," *Commercial Appeal* (Memphis), August 4, 1963.

116. Brandt Ayers, "N.C. Accused of Leading Nation," *News & Observer*
(Raleigh, NC), August 7, 1963.

117. John Kenneth Galbraith, *The Affluent Society* (New York: Houghton
Mifflin, 1958); Michael Harrington, *The Other America: Poverty in the
United States* (New York: Macmillan, 1962).

118. Carl M. Brauer, "Kennedy, Johnson, and the War on Poverty," *Journal of
American History* 69, no. 1 (1982): 105–8.

119. Coll, *Safety Net*, 234–35; Jerry L. Mashaw, "The Management Side of Due
Process: Some Theoretical and Litigation Notes on the Assurance of
Accuracy, Fairness and Timeliness in the Adjudication of Social Welfare
Claims," *Cornell Law Review* 59 (1974): 808–9.

120. Nadasen, Welfare Warriors, 18–20; Thomas J. Sugrue, *Sweet Land of
Liberty: The Forgotten Struggle for Civil Rights in the North* (New York:
Random House, 2008), 386–87; Felicia Ann Kornbluh, *The Battle for
Welfare Rights: Politics and Poverty in Modern America* (Philadelphia:
University of Pennsylvania Press, 2007), 28–29.

121. Elizabeth Wickenden, Draft "memorandum relating to developments in the
area of extending legal services to welfare recipients," June 2, 1964, Box 7,
Mss 800, EWP. A later document estimates that four thousand copies were
distributed. "Project on Social Welfare Law: Historical Chronology," n.d.
(ca. summer 1965), Box 7, Mss 800, EWP. For a sense of the specific
individuals and groups that received the memo, see Folders 1 and 7, Box
2, Mss 800, EWP.

122. Charles I. Schottland to Wickenden, March 15, 1963, Box 2, Mss 800, EWP.

123. Ralph F. Fuchs to Wickenden, March 19, 1963, Box 2, Mss 800, EWP;
Jacobus tenBroek to Elizabeth Wickenden, March 5, 1963, Box 2, Mss 800,
EWP. Professor tenBroek was not on the law faculty at Berkeley but was
trained as a lawyer and often published in law reviews. See, for example, his
magisterial series of articles on "California's Dual System of Family Law,"
published in volumes 16 and 17 of the *Stanford Law Review* (1964–65), and
his pathbreaking article on the rights of the disabled, "The Right to Live in
the World: The Disabled in the Law of Torts," *California Law Review* 54,
no. 2 (1966): 841–919.

124. Roger D. Citron, "Charles Reich's Journey From the Yale Law Journal to the New York Times Best-Seller List: The Personal History of *The Greening of America*," *New York Law School Review* 52, no. 3 (2007–8): 391–95.
125. Elizabeth Wickenden to Charles Reich, October 13, 1964, Box 57, NSWAR.
126. Charles A. Reich to Wickenden, August 30, 1962, Box 1, Mss 800, EWP; Charles A. Reich to Elizabeth Wickenden, March 4, 1963, Box 2, Mss 800, EWP.
127. For Reich's troubles, they secured an honorarium from the Field Foundation. Shad Polier to Elizabeth Wickenden, March 26, 1963, Box 2, Mss 800, EWP.
128. Charles A. Reich, "Midnight Welfare Searches and the Social Security Act," *Yale Law Journal* 72, no. 7 (1963): 1347–60; Charles A. Reich, "Searching Homes of Public Assistance Recipients: The Issues under the Social Security Act," *Social Service Review* 37, no. 3 (1963): 328–39; Wickenden, Draft "memorandum relating to developments in the area of extending legal services to welfare recipients"; Elizabeth Wickenden to Charles Reich, September 25, 1963, Box 57, NSWAR. For a sense of the specific individuals and groups that received the memo, see Folder 1, Box 2, Mss 800, EWP.
129. Charles A. Reich, "The New Property," *Yale Law Journal* 73, no. 5 (1964); Karen M. Tani, "*Flemming v. Nestor*: Anticommunism, the Welfare State, and the Making of 'New Property,'" *Law and History Review* 26, no. 2 (2008): 379–414.
130. The parallels to the writings of A. D. Smith are striking. See also Alanson Willcox's 1957 essay "Patterns of Social Legislation: Reflections on the Welfare State," *Journal of Public Law* 6 (1957): 3–24, which Reich quotes extensively in the first footnote of his article "Individual Rights and Social Welfare: The Emerging Issues," *Yale Law Journal* 74 (965): 1244.

8 SUBJECTS OF THE CONSTITUTION, SLAVES TO STATUTES

1. Excerpt from the transcript of Smith v. Board of Commissioners, docket no. 1447-66, hearing in the U.S. District Court for the District of Columbia, October 7, 1966, reprinted in 112 Cong. Rec. 28457 (daily ed. October 21, 1966); Smith v. Bd. of Comm'rs, 259 F. Supp. 423, 424 (D.D.C. 1966).
2. On Holtzoff, see "Judge Holtzoff Retires," WP, November 29, 1967; Carl Bernstein, "Judge Alexander Holtzoff Dies; Controversial U.S. Court Figure," WP, September 7, 1969.
3. Abe Fortas, *New York Law Journal*, April 5, 1967, 4.
4. Elizabeth Wickenden to Ellen Winston, September 18, 1963, Box 57, NSWAR; Elizabeth Wickenden to Genevieve Carter, September 20, 1963, Box 57, NSWAR; Elizabeth Wickenden to Alanson Willcox, June 16, 1964, Box 57, NSWAR; Elizabeth Wickenden to Alanson Willcox, November 17, 1964, Box 57, NSWAR.
5. The Bureau of Public Assistance was renamed the Bureau of Family Services in January 1962.

6. Elizabeth Wickenden to John Hurley, June 17, 1963, Box 57, NSWAR; Elizabeth Wickenden to Ellen Winston, October 4, 1963, Box 7, Mss 800, EWP.
7. Elizabeth Wickenden to Maxwell Hahn, October 8, 1963, Box 57, NSWAR. Such correspondence continued over the following years, even as federal administrators ceded more and more of their enforcement work to outside advocates. See, for example, Elizabeth Wickenden to Ellen Winston, June 8, 1965, Box 57, NSWAR.
8. See Folder 30, Box 1, Mss 800, EWP.
9. Folder 30, Box 1, Mss 800, EWP; "Items Discussed at OC Staff Meeting, November 8, 1963," Box 16, Records of the Welfare Commissioner, Minutes of Staff Meetings, 1963–1967, SSAR.
10. Elizabeth Wickenden to Wilbur Cohen, July 13, 1963, Box 1, Mss 800, EWP; Wilbur Cohen to Max Hahn, July 16, 1963, Box 1, Mss 800, EWP. The study was ultimately published by Columbia University Press, but the Field Foundation supported Bell financially. Winifred Bell, *Aid to Dependent Children* (New York: Columbia University Press, 1965).
11. Ellen Winston to Elizabeth Wickenden, March 7, 1963, Box 2, Mss 800, EWP; Alanson Willcox to Elizabeth Wickenden, March 5, 1963, Box 2, Mss 800, EWP.
12. Willcox to Wickenden, March 5, 1963; "Items Discussed at OC Staff Meeting, March 28, 1963," Box 16, Records of the Welfare Commissioner, Minutes of Staff Meetings, 1963–1967, SSAR.
13. Lyndon B. Johnson, "Annual Message to the Congress on the State of the Union," January 8, 1964, online in Gerhard Peters and John T. Woolley, *The American Presidency Project*, accessed May 15, 2015, http://www.presidency.ucsb.edu/ws/?pid=26787; Lyndon B. Johnson, "Remarks at the University of Michigan," May 22, 1964, Ibid., accessed May 15, 2015, http://www.presidency.ucsb.edu/ws/?pid=26262. On the effect of Kennedy's assassination on politics, see Rick Perlstein, *Before the Storm: Barry Goldwater and the Unmaking of the American Consensus* (New York: Hill and Wang, 2001), 247–49.
14. Alanson Willcox to Elizabeth Wickenden, July 14, 1964, Box 7, Mss 800, EWP.
15. *Civil Rights Act of 1964*, Pub. L. 88-352, 78 Stat. 241 (1964). On the enactment and enforcement of Title VI, see Stephen C. Halpern, *On the Limits of the Law: The Ironic Legacy of Title VI of the 1964 Civil Rights Act* (Baltimore: Johns Hopkins University Press, 1995).
16. Hearings before Subcommittee No. 5 of the Committee on the Judiciary House of Representatives on Miscellaneous Proposals Regarding the Civil Rights of Persons within the Jurisdiction of the United States, 88th Cong., 1st sess. (May–August 1963) [hereafter cited as Hearings before Subcommittee No. 5], Serial No. 4, Part II, 1531.
17. Ibid., 1473, 1515–48.
18. Hearings before the Subcommittee on Constitutional Rights, Committee on the Judiciary, U.S. Senate, on S. 1117 and S. 1219, Bills Relating to Extension of the Civil Rights Commission, 88th Cong., 1st sess. (May–June 1963),

22–23, 31; Hearings before Subcommittee No. 5, Serial No. 4, Part III, 2093–94, 1890–91.

19. Elizabeth H. Pleck, *Not Just Roommates: Cohabitation after the Sexual Revolution* (Chicago: University of Chicago Press, 2012), 53; "Night Raids on Welfare Homes Hit," *LAT*, February 22, 1963; Jerry Gillam, "Welfare Board Bans Mass Raids," *LAT*, July 27, 1963; Jacobus tenBroek to Elizabeth Wickenden, August 19, 1963, Box 57, NSWAR.

20. "County to Push Surprise Welfare Visits Despite Revolt," *Oakland (CA) Tribune*, January 12, 1963; "4th Session for Appeal by Parrish," *Hayward (CA) Daily Review*, February 22, 1963; "Court OKs Welfare Dismissal," *Oakland (CA) Tribune*, December 5, 1963; Jacobus tenBroek to Elizabeth Wickenden, March 5, 1963, Box 2, Mss 800, EWP. Correspondence suggests that ACLU lawyers were preparing to make similar arguments in Baltimore, another jurisdiction known for its midnight raids. See Irving Murray to Alvin Thalheimer, December 23, 1963, Box 7, Mss 800, EWP. For more on the Alameda County raids and the Parrish case, see Alexander Gourse, "Restraining the Reagan Revolution: The Lawyers' War on Poverty and the Durable Liberal State, 1964–1989," PhD diss., Northwestern University, 2015, 113–17; Felicia Ann Kornbluh, *The Battle for Welfare Rights: Politics and Poverty in Modern America* (Philadelphia: University of Pennsylvania Press, 2007), 29–30.

21. "Canton Trial to Test Welfare Work Law," *Syracuse (NY) Post-Standard*, August 3, 1963; "Work-Relief Refusal Nets Jail Terms," *Syracuse Post-Standard*, August 20, 1963; Betty Mandell, "The Crime of Poverty," *Social Work* 11, no. 1 (1966): 11–15. On how this interpretation of the Thirteenth Amendment became imaginable, see Risa L. Goluboff, "The Thirteenth Amendment and the Lost Origins of Civil Rights," *Duke Law Journal* 50 (2001): 1609–85. At least one civil rights group, the National Urban League, also expressed interest in welfare rights litigation in 1963. See Whitney Young to Elizabeth Wickenden, March 14, 1963, Box 2, Mss 800, EWP. But to my knowledge, none actually pursued test cases. As historian Jennifer Mittelstadt and others have observed, welfare was a fraught issue for civil rights organizations. Welfare recipients, especially single mothers, were not a sympathetic face for the movement. Indeed, some civil rights leaders agreed with the critiques leveled against welfare programs and their clients. Civil rights organizations certainly concerned themselves with poverty, but often they focused their resources on securing better employment opportunities for black men. Jennifer Mittelstadt, *From Welfare to Workfare: The Unintended Consequences of Liberal Reform, 1945–1965* (Chapel Hill: University of North Carolina Press, 2005), 98–99; Lisa Levenstein, *A Movement without Marches: African American Women and the Politics of Poverty in Postwar Philadelphia* (Chapel Hill: University of North Carolina Press, 2009), 56–57.

22. Jack C. Landau, "Father's Visit Held No Bar to Child Aid," *WP*, May 29, 1964; Ramon Geremia, "Court Bars Ending Aid to Mother Mate Visits," *WP*, June 9, 1964; "Appeals Court Gets Man-in-House Welfare Case," *WP*, November 10, 1964. Klooz is an interesting figure, both because she was significantly older than most of the poverty lawyers of her era and because she

came to law relatively late, after working in a Chicago settlement house and several federal government departments. Elizabeth Farquhar, Bar Association of Montgomery County, Maryland, "Marie S. Klooz," accessed May 15, 2015, http://www.barmont.org/general/custom.asp?page=326.

23. Matter of Nixon, New York Dept. of Social Welfare Fair Hearing Decision, December 1, 1964, in Edward V. Sparer, "Materials on Public Assistance Law" (unpublished draft casebook, University of Pennsylvania Law School, Reginald Heber Smith Community Lawyer Fellowship Program, 1969), chap. 18, 10–13; Charles A. Reich, "Individual Rights and Social Welfare: The Emerging Legal Issues," *Yale Law Journal* 74, no. 7 (1965): 1249. Poverty lawyers eventually challenged these policies in court, in *Gaddis v. Wyman*, 304 F. Supp. 713 (S.D.N.Y. 1969). On welfare clients' historically spare use of fair hearings in New York City, see Walter Gellhorn, *When Americans Complain: Governmental Grievance Procedures* (Cambridge, MA: Harvard University Press, 1966), 198.

24. Elizabeth Wickenden to Peter Franck, January 25, 1965, Box 57, NSWAR.

25. Edgar Cahn, interview by Alan Houseman, July 3, 2002, transcript, Oral History Collection, National Equal Justice Library, Georgetown Law Library, Washington, DC; Elizabeth Wickenden to Charles E. Ares, June 23, 1964, Box 57, NSWAR.

26. Elizabeth Wickenden to Alanson Willcox, April 20, 1965, Box 57, NSWAR. The other members of the Advisory Committee were Charles Ares (New York University Law School), Robert Carter (NAACP), Vern Countryman (Harvard Law School), Fidele Fauri (University of Michigan School of Social Work); Leonard Lesser (AFL-CIO), Howard Lesnick (University of Pennsylvania Law School), Justine Wise Polier (New York City Family Court), Shad Polier (American Jewish Congress), Ed Sparer (transitioning at that time from Mobilization for Youth to the Center for Social Welfare Policy and Law), Arnold Trebach (Howard University School of Law), and Melvin Wulf (ACLU). "Arthur Garfield Hays Civil Liberties Center Project on Social Welfare Law," May 1965, Box 20, NSWAR. By September, the Advisory Committee had expanded further, to include representatives from the United Planning Organization, the National Urban League, the organized bar, and a handful of other law schools. "Arthur Garfield Hays Civil Liberties Center Project on Social Welfare Law," ca. September 1965, Box 20, NSWAR.

27. Elizabeth Wickenden to Max Doverman, December 16, 1965, Box 7, Mss 800, EWP (emphasis in original).

28. Alice O'Connor, "Community Action, Urban Reform, and the Fight against Poverty: The Ford Foundation's Gray Areas Program," *Journal of Urban History* 22, no. 5 (1996): 586–87; Earl Johnson Jr., *Justice and Reform: The Formative Years of the American Legal Services Program* (New York: Russell Sage Foundation, 1974), 21–32; Peter Marris and Martin Rein, *The Dilemmas of Social Reform: Poverty and Community Action in the United States*, 2nd ed. (Chicago: Aldine Publishing Company, 1973), 14–32, 171–77. On the Ford Foundation, see generally Olivier Zunz, *Philanthropy in America: A History* (Princeton, NJ: Princeton University Press, 2012); Karen Ferguson, *Top Down: The Ford Foundation, Black Power, and the*

Reinvention of Racial Liberalism (Philadelphia: University of Pennsylvania Press, 2013). On the Vera Foundation, Lee S. Friedman, "The Evolution of Bail Reform," *Policy Sciences* 7 (1976): 285–86.

29. Edgar S. Cahn and Jean C. Cahn, "The War on Poverty: A Civilian Perspective," *Yale Law Journal* 73, no. 8 (1964): 1317–52. The Cahns' article also shows the influence of Edgar's father, Edmond Cahn, who taught law at NYU. One of the senior Cahn's well-known legal insights from this period was that courts no longer accepted the "imperial or official perspective" of the law; increasingly, they considered the perspective of the law's "consumer." All such consumers, he argued, needed "processors of law who will consider the people's needs more significant than administrative convenience." Edmond Cahn, "Law in the Consumer Perspective," *University of Pennsylvania Law Review* 112 (1963): 13. There is some debate about how "new" the Cahns' legal aid philosophy was. Jerold Auerbach calls the Cahns' plan "an amalgam of rather shopworn ideas." Richard Pious notes that neither the traditional legal aid movement nor its new counterpart emphasized redistributing resources or fundamentally changing local decision-making structures. Jerold S. Auerbach, *Unequal Justice: Lawyers and Social Change in Modern America* (New York: Oxford University Press, 1976), 200; Richard M. Pious, "Policy and Public Administration: The Legal Services Program in the War on Poverty," *Politics and Society* 1 (May 1971): 388.

30. 372 U.S. 335 (1963). Journalist Anthony Lewis attracted wide attention to the decision via his book *Gideon's Trumpet* (New York: Vintage Books/ Random House, 1964).

31. Cahn, interview by Houseman; Michael L. Gillette, *Launching the War on Poverty: An Oral History* (New York: Oxford University Press, 2010), 295–96, citing an interview that the author conducted with the Cahns in 1980; Auerbach, *Unequal Justice*, 269.

32. E. Clinton Bamberger, "The Legal Services Program of the Office of Economic Opportunity," *Notre Dame Lawyer* 41 (1966): 850.

33. Martha F. Davis, *Brutal Need: Lawyers and the Welfare Rights Movement, 1960–1973* (New Haven, CT: Yale University Press, 1993), 22–29.

34. Ibid., 28–35.

35. Here I hope to add to a growing body of research on how and why civil rights advocates (and opponents) toggled between agencies and courts over the course of the twentieth century. See, especially, Sophia Z. Lee, *The Workplace Constitution: From the New Deal to the New Right* (New York: Cambridge University Press, 2014).

36. "Two Extreme Views on Race Issue," *Greenville Delta (MS) Democrat Times*, April 17, 1963; Medgar Evers to Department of Health, Education, and Welfare, April 17, 1963, Box 2, Office of the Commissioner General Subject Files, 1963–65, SRSR; Ellen Winston to Medgar Evers, May 3, 1963, Box 2, Office of the Commissioner General Subject Files, 1963–65, SRSR; Ellen Winston to Fred Ross, May 10, 1963, Box 2, Office of the Commissioner General Subject Files, 1963–65, SRSR.

37. "Claims Reds behind Race Drive," *Greenville Delta (MS) Democrat Times*, June 16, 1963; "If Only Laughs, We're Lucky," *Greenville Delta (MS) Democrat Times*, June 19, 1963.

38. Rev. J. H. Chapman to Civil Rights Commission, January 7, 1965, Box 13, Office of the Commissioner General Subject Files, 1963–65, SRSR; Frances Pauley to Ellen Winston, March 17, 1965, Box 13, Office of the Commissioner General Subject Files, 1963–65, SRSR; Charles Guzzetta to Philip Schafer, October 6, 1967, Box 9, General Subject Files, 1966–67, SRSR; Frances Pauley to Sam Simmons, July 26, 1966, Box 9, General Subject Files, 1966–67, SRSR; Albert Q. Perry to Arthur Chapin, February 18, 1966, Box 9, General Subject Files, 1966–67, SRSR; Michael Tabor to James M. Quigley, July 13, 1965, Box 9, General Subject Files, 1966–67, SRSR; Aaron E. Henry to John Gardner et al., August 15, 1966, Box 9, General Subject Files, 1966–67, SRSR.

39. See, for example, Mrs. Hursey Mae Smith to President Johnson, November 11, 1965, Box 9, General Subject Files, 1966–67, SRSR; Susie Walker to President Johnson, n.d., Box 9, General Subject Files, 1966–67, SRSR; Edwards McKentire to Bobby D. Doctor, March 2, 1967, Box 9, General Subject Files, 1966–67, SRSR; Elizabeth Hunter to Samuel Younger, February 20, 1967, Box 9, General Subject Files, 1966–1967, SRSR; F. D. Reese to Orriville Freeman, May 18, 1965, Box 9, General Subject Files, 1966–67, SRSR; Rufus A. Lewis to Moreland Smith, October 4, 1965, Box 9, General Subject Files, 1966–67, SRSR; James L. Draper to Dick Thornell, March 11, 1966, Box 9, General Subject Files, 1966–67, SRSR.

40. Wynette Belle to Sharon R. Gore, n.d., Box 9, General Subject Files, 1966–67, SRSR.

41. See, for example, Report of an Investigation of Compliance with Title VI of the Civil Rights Act of 1964 – WA Docket No. 22 – Monroe County Welfare Department, Aberdeen, Mississippi, May 25, 1966, Box 9, General Subject Files, 1966–67, SRSR; Report of an Investigation of Compliance with Title VI of the Civil Rights Act of 1964, Quitman County Welfare Department, Marks, Mississippi, February 28 and March 1, 1966, Box 9, General Subject Files, 1966–1967, SRSR.

42. Peter Haberfeld and Charles Radford Lawrence III to Mrs. Bruce Schaefer, August 13, 1966, Box 9, General Subject Files, 1966–67, SRSR; Rosa Britt to Civil Rights Compliance VI, Department of Health, Education, and Welfare, May 20, 1966, Box 9, General Subject Files, 1966–67, SRSR; Orzell Billingsley Jr. to Samuel J. Simmons, March 7, 1966, Box 9, General Subject Files, 1966–67, SRSR.

43. A notable exception was HEW's response to NAACP complaints about police harassment and other discourteous treatment of AFDC recipients in Springfield, Massachusetts, the site of a major school desegregation battle and a race riot in the previous months. HEW officials investigated those complaints thoroughly. The case did not result in formal sanctions, however. It was marked "resolved" after HEW facilitated a dialogue between NAACP representatives and state and local welfare authorities. Whitney C. Jansen to Margaret A. Emery, June 14, 1966, Box 9, General Subject Files, 1966–67,

SRSR; Neil P. Fallon to Chief, Division of Program Operations, Bureau of Family Services, June 1, 1966, Box 9, General Subject Files, 1966–67, SRSR; Neil P. Fallon to Chief, Division of Program Operations, Bureau of Family Services, May 19, 1966, Box 9, General Subject Files, 1966–67, SRSR.

44. Report on Investigation of North Carolina Civil Rights Complaint #WA-152, Tyrrell County Welfare Department, October 24, 1967, Box 10, General Subject Files, 1966–67, SRSR.

45. Bell, *Aid to Dependent Children*, 76–92.

46. Sparer, "Materials on Public Assistance Law," chap. 5, 20–34; "Rights Legal Fund Says Gardner Lags on Aid Complaints," *NYT*, January 14, 1967.

47. On the Alabama hearing, see Gardner v. Alabama, 385 F.2d 804, 808–10 (5th Cir. 1967); Eve Edstrom, "Alabama Chief Defies U.S. on Welfare Funds," *WP*, October 22, 1965. On the handbook revision, see "Statement for the Record of Hearings Held August 19, 1967, before the Senate Appropriations Committee," August 30, 1967, Box 1, Records of Deputy Administrator, Joseph Meyers, Correspondence and Reports on State Programs, 1965–69, SRSR; Fred H. Steininger to State Agencies Administering Approved Public Assistance Plans, March 18, 1966, Box 20, NSWAR. Hostility from powerful members of Congress gave HEW officials reason to enforce their decisions with a light touch. On the reaction in the Senate to the Alabama funds cutoff, see Hearings before the Committee on Finance, U.S. Senate, 90th Cong., 1st sess., on Proposed Cutoff of Welfare Funds to the State of Alabama (January 25 and February 23, 1967). On hostility in the Senate to the handbook provision, see 112 Cong. Rec. 28543–28458 (daily ed., October 21, 1966) [statement of Senator Byrd].

48. Meeting of Mississippi Advisory Committee (Commission on Civil Rights), February 18, 1967, Jackson, Transcript, pp. 481, 485–86, 504–5, Box 1, Records of Assistant Administrator for Federal-State Relations Fred Steininger, Advisory Council Files, 1964–68, SRSR. On HEW's perceived inefficacy, see also Walter Gellhorn, "Poverty and Legality: The Law's Slow Awakening," *Proceedings of the American Philosophical Society* 112, no. 2 (1968): 113–14. The disillusionment described here appears to have been part of a broader phenomenon. Writing in 1967, political scientist James Wilson observed that, in general, those on the Left had become concerned about federal bureaucracy's role in "working a conservative reaction"; centrists, meanwhile, "fear[ed] that the bureaucracy [wa]sn't working at all." James Q. Wilson, "The Bureaucracy Problem," *Public Interest* 6 (Winter 1967): 3.

49. Mittelstadt, *From Welfare to Workfare*, 168.

50. Ibid., 41–153; Marisa Chappell, *The War on Welfare: Family, Poverty, and Politics in Modern America* (Philadelphia: University of Pennsylvania Press, 2011), 35–58; Steven M. Teles, *Whose Welfare? AFDC and Elite Politics* (Lawrence: University Press of Kansas, 1996). The numbers for AFDC recipients are from Gilbert Y. Steiner, *The State of Welfare* (Washington, DC: Brookings Institution Press, 1971), 41. Steiner also notes that the racial composition of AFDC cases had, in fact, changed little in the past six years, and that, as of 1967, a majority of AFDC payees were white. Ibid. On the formation of the National Welfare Rights Organization and its critiques of

the welfare system in the late 1960s, see Premilla Nadasen, *Welfare Warriors: The Welfare Rights Movement in the United States* (New York: Routledge, 2005), 38–77. The Long quotes are from Chappell, *The War on Welfare*, 52–53.

51. *Social Security Act Amendments of 1967,* Pub. L. No. 90-248, 81 Stat. 821 (1968).

52. Kornbluh, *The Battle for Welfare Rights,* 95–100; Steiner, *The State of Welfare,* 40–74.

53. On the "overload" strategy, see Frances Fox Piven and Richard Cloward, "The Weight of the Poor," *The Nation,* May 2, 1966.

54. For important work on local welfare rights activism, see Anne M. Valk, "'Mother Power': The Movement for Welfare Rights in Washington, D.C., 1966–1972," *Journal of Women's History* 11, no. 4 (2000): 34–58; Rhonda Y. Williams, *The Politics of Public Housing: Black Women's Struggles against Urban Inequality* (New York: Oxford University Press, 2004); Annelise Orleck, *Storming Caesars Palace: How Black Mothers Fought Their Own War on Poverty* (Boston: Beacon Press, 2005); Kornbluh, *The Battle for Welfare Rights;* Kent B. Germany, *New Orleans after the Promises: Poverty, Citizenship, and the Search for the Great Society* (Athens: University of Georgia Press, 2007), especially Chapter 11. On local litigation efforts, see Kris Shepard, *Rationing Justice: Poverty Lawyers and Poor People in the Deep South* (Baton Rouge: Louisiana State University Press, 2009); Gourse, "Restraining the Reagan Revolution."

55. Davis, *Brutal Need,* 36; Edward V. Sparer, "The Role of the Welfare Client's Lawyer," *UCLA Law Review* 12 (1965): 361–80; Edward V. Sparer, "Social Welfare Law Testing," *Practical Lawyer* (April 1966): 13–31.

56. Davis, *Brutal Need,* 37, 104–5; Edward V. Sparer, "The Right to Welfare," in *The Rights of Americans,* ed. Norman Dorsen (New York: Pantheon, 1971), 65–93.

57. Davis, *Brutal Need,* 56–60; Robert M. Cover, note, "Federal Judicial Review of State Welfare Practices," *Columbia Law Review* 67 (1967): 84–129.

58. Davis, *Brutal Need,* 60; Walter Goodman, "The Case of Mrs. Sylvester Smith: A Victory for 400,000 Children," *New York Times Magazine,* August 25, 1968.

59. Davis, *Brutal Need,* 56–69. On the openness of federal courts in the South to claims of racial discrimination, see Jack Bass, *Unlikely Heroes* (Tuscaloosa: University Alabama Press, 1990).

60. Goodman, "The Case of Mrs. Sylvester Smith."

61. King v. Smith, 392 U.S. 309, 326 n23 (1968) [chronicling the battle between Alabama and federal authorities over the state's suitable home and substitute father policies from 1959 to 1962].

62. Brief for Appellees at 9, King v. Smith, 392 U.S. 309 (1968) (No. 949), 1968 WL 112516, at *9.

63. Smith v. King, 277 F. Supp. 31, 38–40 (M.D. Ala. 1967). At the time, federal law required a three-judge court to hear any case seeking an injunction restraining the enforcement, operation, or execution of any act of Congress

on grounds of unconstitutionality. 28 U.S.C. § 2282. Repealed. Pub. L. No. 94-381, 90 Stat. 1119 (1976).

64 *King*, 392 U.S. at 317-18, 325-26, 329-30. This statutory interpretation read much like a constitutional equal protection interpretation and indeed accomplished similar ends. As I have argued elsewhere, HEW pioneered this very move in the early 1960s, when its administrative interpretations of the Fourteenth Amendment came to seem too dangerous. Karen M. Tani, "Administrative Equal Protection: Federalism, The Fourteenth Amendment, and the Rights of the Poor," *Cornell Law Review* 100 (2015): 870–81.

65. Roger E. Kohn, "AFDC Eligibility Requirements Unrelated to Need: The Impact of *King v. Smith*," *University of Pennsylvania Law Review* 118, no. 9 (1970): 1250.

66. R. Shep Melnick, *Between the Lines: Interpreting Welfare Rights* (Washington, DC: Brookings Institution, 1994), 69, 84.

67. Davis, *Brutal Need*, 64, citing Smith v. Bd. of Comm'rs, 380 F.2d 632 (D.C. Cir. 1967).

68. On the uncertainty regarding jurisdiction, see Cover, "Federal Judicial Review. "

69. Joseph L. Askew, "Analysis of Cases Arising under the Public Assistance Titles of the Social Security Act and Decided by the Supreme Court Since 1960," *North Carolina Central Law Journal* 3 (1971–72): 83.

70. Mark Neal Aaronson, "Representing the Poor: Legal Advocacy and Welfare Reform during Reagan's Gubernatorial Years," *Hastings Law Journal* 64 (2013): 993. After *King*, poverty lawyers flooded the federal courts with suits. Between 1968 and 1975, the Supreme Court alone decided eighteen AFDC cases. Melnick, *Between the Lines*, 83.

71. Harrell v. Tobriner, 279 F. Supp. 22 (D.D.C. 1967); Thompson v. Shapiro, 270 F. Supp. 331 (D. Conn. 1967); Smith v. Reynolds, 277 F. Supp. 65 (E.D. Pa. 1967).

72. Shapiro v. Thompson, 394 U.S. 618 (1969).

73. Davis, *Brutal Need*, 76–79.

74. *Shapiro*, 394 U.S. at 629, 634–38, 642.

75. Davis, *Brutal Need*, 80.

76. For a more detailed account of the *Shapiro* litigation and a similar interpretation of its significance, see Elisa Martia Alvarez Minoff, "Free to Move? The Law and Politics of Internal Migration in Twentieth-Century America," PhD diss., Harvard University, 2013, 447–59.

77. 397 U.S. 254 (1970).

78. As William H. Simon and others have noted, "The New Property" was in some ways a poor basis for claiming a "right to welfare," because Reich himself stopped short of arguing that the government owed citizens a decent existence. William Simon, "The Invention and Reinvention of Welfare Rights," *Maryland Law Review* 44, no. 1 (1985): 23–28. Reich's deepest concern – one grounded not in economic need but in his friendships with persecuted political radicals and in his own anxieties as a closeted gay man – was that Americans' growing dependency on government enabled government coercion. In the era of what he called the "public interest state," many

Americans had no alternative *but* to accept government largesse, Reich noted. He was troubled by the price that government officials had often asked in return, in the form of restrictions on speech, association, privacy, and other constitutional rights. Reich believed that if courts treated government-issued licenses, jobs, and other benefits like private property, state power would be appropriately constrained. Charles A. Reich, "The New Property," *Yale Law Journal* 73, no. 5 (1964): 733–87; Karen M. Tani, "*Flemming v. Nestor*: Anticommunism, the Welfare State, and the Making of 'New Property,'" *Law and History Review* 26, no. 2 (2008).

79. Davis, *Brutal Need*, 86.
80. Ibid., 87–90; Kelly v. Wyman, 294 F. Supp. 893, 895 (S.D.N.Y. 1968). The three-judge district court consolidated two cases to make one case with eight plaintiffs (six from one case, two from the other), and twelve plaintiffs later intervened. Davis, *Brutal Need*, 895–96.
81. *Goldberg*, 397 U.S. at 257; Davis, *Brutal Need*, 93; *Kelly*, 294 F. Supp. at 908.
82. *Goldberg*, 397 U.S. at 262–63. For examples of lower court decisions that applied the Due Process Clause more restrictively, see *Williams v. Shapiro*, 23 A.2d 376 (Conn. Cir. Ct. 1967), and *McCullough v. Terzian*, 80 Cal. Rptr. 283 (Ca. Ct. App. 1969). On Brennan's familiarity with Reich's work, see Davis, *Brutal Need*, 111.
83. *Goldberg*, 397 U.S. at 276, 279 (Black, J., dissenting); Davis, *Brutal Need*, 114–16.
84. Craig W. Christensen, "Of Prior Hearings and Welfare as 'New Property,'" *Clearinghouse Review* 3, no. 12 (1970): 333–34. On the right/privilege dichotomy and its decline over time, see William W. Van Alstyne, "The Demise of the Right-Privilege Distinction in Constitutional Law," *Harvard Law Review* 81 (1968): 1439–64.
85. 397 U.S. 471 (1970).
86. Williams v. Dandridge, 297 F. Supp. 450, 453 (D. Md. 1968). Sparer's center joined the litigation effort in an amicus capacity. Davis, *Brutal Need*, 130.
87. See Chapter 6, in "The Endurance of Claims Making."
88. Elizabeth Wickenden to J. M. Wedemeyer, December 9, 1965, Box 12, Mss 800, EWP.
89. *Dandridge*, 397 U.S. at 478, 486–87. The other lower court decisions were *Dews v. Henry*, 297 F. Supp. 587 (D. Ariz. 1969), *Westberry v. Fisher*, 297 F. Supp. 1109 (D. Me. 1969), and *Lindsey v. Smith*, 303 F. Supp. 1203 (W.D. Wash. 1969).
90. *Dandridge*, 397 U.S. at 484–85 (citations omitted). The Court distinguished its previous poverty-related equal protection cases by suggesting that these involved infringements of interests protected by the Bill of Rights.
91. Ibid. at 509 (Marshall, J., dissenting).
92. Julie A. Nice, "No Scrutiny Whatsoever: Deconstitutionalization of Poverty Law, Dual Rules of Law, and Dialogic Default," *Fordham Urban Law Journal* 35 (2008): 629–70. On the significance of *Dandridge*, see Samuel Krislov, "The OEO Lawyers Fail to Constitutionalize a Right to Welfare: A Study in the Uses and Limits of the Judicial Process," *Minnesota Law Review* 58 (1973): 211–45; C. Thomas Dienes, "To Feed the Hungry: Judicial

Retrenchment in Welfare Adjudication," *California Law Review* 58, no. 3 (May 1970): 555–627; Christopher N. May, "Supreme Court Approves Maximum Grants; Holds § 402(a)(23) Permits Welfare Cuts," *Clearinghouse Review* 3, no. 12 (April 1970).

93. 400 U.S. 309 (1971).
94. Davis, *Brutal Need*, 133–34; *Wyman*, 400 U.S. at 314; Brief for Appellees at 7, 11, 14, Wyman v. James, 400 U.S. 309 (1971) (No. 69), 1970 WL 136367, at *7, 11, 14.
95. "Center on Social Welfare Policy and Law: Director's Column," *Clearinghouse Review* 4, no. 3 (1970–71): 131.
96. *Wyman*, 400 U.S. at 319, 324. On Nixon and the silent majority, see Dan T. Carter, *From George Wallace to Newt Gingrich: Race in the Conservative Counterrevolution, 1963–1994* (Baton Rouge: Louisiana State University Press, 1996); Matthew D. Lassiter, *The Silent Majority: Suburban Politics in the Sunbelt South* (Princeton, NJ: Princeton University Press, 2006).
97. Sparer, "The Right to Welfare," 84.
98. The case began as two suits: one by Ruth Jefferson, Emma Gipson, and Jose Apalinor Vasquez and the other by Maria T. Davila and Jo Ann Guttierez. By the time the case reached a three-judge panel of the district court, the cases had been combined and Ed Sparer had assumed the role of lead attorney. Jefferson v. Hackney, 304 F. Supp. 1332 (N.D. Tex. 1969). On Ruth Jefferson and her history of activism, see "Welfare Demonstrators Planning Holiday Dinner," *Paris (TX) News*, November 28, 1968; Dennis Hoover, "Welfare Skimpy in Texas," *Robstown (TX) Record*, February 20, 1969; "Co-Op Plans to Remedy Work Lack," *Lubbock (TX) Avalanche Journal*, March 10, 1969; Ken Siner, "State's Poor Children Winners of Election," *Odessa (TX) American*, August 6, 1969.
99. Brief for Appellants, Jefferson v. Hackney, 406 U.S. 535 (1972) (No. 70-5064), 1971 WL 133434.
100. Jefferson v. Hackney, 406 U.S. 535, 546 (1972).
101. Richard Nixon, "Special Message to the Congress on Reform of the Nation's Welfare System," August 11, 1969, Peters and Woolley, *The American Presidency Project*, accessed May 20, 2015, http://www.presidency.ucsb.edu/ws/?pid=2194.
102. Essentially the proposal grew out of broad dissatisfaction with the AFDC program, including, especially, concerns about the incentives it created for the breakup of black families and for migration from the rural South to the more generous urban North; Nixon's desire to offer government support to white, working-class voters who felt alienated by the Great Society; and years of spadework inside HEW during previous administrations. See Daniel Patrick Moynihan, *The Politics of Guaranteed Income: The Nixon Administration and the Family Assistance Plan* (New York: Random House, 1973); Brian Steensland, *The Failed Welfare Revolution: America's Struggle over Guaranteed Income Policy* (Princeton, NJ: Princeton University Press, 2007); Chappell, *The War on Welfare*, 65–105; Kornbluh, *The Battle for Welfare Rights*, 137–48; Nadasen, *Welfare Warriors*, 158–70; Scott J. Spitzer, "Nixon's New Deal: Welfare Reform

for the Silent Majority," *Presidential Studies Quarterly* 42, no. 3 (2012): 455–81; Minoff, "Free to Move?" 462–65.

103. Martha Derthick, *Agency under Stress: The Social Security Administration in American Government* (Washington, DC: Brookings Institution Press, 1990), 54–59.

104. Ibid., 58.

105. For explanations that stress politics, albeit with different emphases, see, for example, Moynihan, *The Politics of Guaranteed Income*, focusing on lack of support from welfare rights organizations and liberals; Kornbluh, *The Battle for Welfare Rights*, 148–60, shifting the blame from welfare rights advocates to White House officials and members of Congress, Republicans and Democrats; Chappell, *The War on Welfare*, 79–105, attributing the FAP's fate to politicized disagreements about how best to shore up the family wage model and who ought to have access to it. For an account that stresses the role of ideas, see Steensland, *The Failed Welfare Revolution*.

106. Mittelstadt, *From Welfare to Workfare*, 168–69; Tom Herman, "Welfare Reform: The Southern View," *WSJ*, December 15, 1970. For more on Talmadge's views on welfare, see "Guaranteed Income Pitfalls Cited," *WP*, February 9, 1967.

107. See, generally, Derthick, *Agency under Stress;* Social Security Act Amendments of 1972, Pub. L. No. 92–603, 86 Stat. 1329 (1972).

108. Derthick, *Agency under Stress*, 98.

109. See, for example, Matthews v. Eldridge, 424 U.S. 319 (1976) [holding that in cases involving government benefits, due process is a "flexible" requirement]; San Antonio Indep. School Dist. v. Rodriguez, 411 U.S. 1 (1973) [refusing to accord greater judicial scrutiny to classifications based on wealth].

CONCLUSION

1. Edward V. Sparer, "The Right to Welfare," in *The Rights of Americans*, ed. Norman Dorsen (New York: Pantheon, 1971), 65–93.

2. Christopher L. Tomlins, *The State and the Unions: Labor Relations, Law, and the Organized Labor Movement in America, 1880–1960* (Cambridge: Cambridge University Press, 1985), 326–28.

3. *Gideon v. Wainwright*, 372 U.S. 335 (1963) and *Harper v. Virginia State Board of Elections*, 383 U.S. 663 (1966), for example, remain good law. Recent cases affirming the constitutional rights of the poor include *Weston v. Cassata*, 37 P.3d 469 (Colo. App. 2001) [holding that plaintiffs' "property" interests in their Temporary Assistance for Needy Families benefits merited constitutional protection, and that county-issued sanction notices deprived plaintiffs of due process]; *Halbert v. Michigan*, 545 U.S. 605 (2005) [holding that an indigent criminal defendant who pled nolo contendere still had a right to appointed counsel at the Michigan Court of Appeals]; *Lebron v. Secretary of Florida Department of Children and Families* (4th Cir. 2014) [finding that Florida's statute mandating suspicionless drug testing of all TANF applicants violated the plaintiff's Fourth Amendment right against unreasonable searches

and seizures]; and *Veasey v. Perry*, Civ. Action No. 13-CV-00193, 2014 WL 5090258 (S.D. Texas, October 9, 2014) [holding that a Texas voter identification law placed an unconstitutional burden on the right to vote because of its disproportionate impact on African Americans, Hispanics, and the poor].

4. Vicki Lens, "Confronting Government after Welfare Reform: Moralists, Reformers, and Narratives of (Ir)responsibility at Administrative Fair Hearings," *Law and Society Review* 43, no. 3 (2009): 563–92. For a more pessimistic view of fair hearings after welfare reform, see Jason Parkin, "Adaptable Due Process," *University of Pennsylvania Law Review* 160, no. 5 (2014): 1336–58.

5. The groundbreaking "right to travel" case *Shapiro v. Thompson*, 394 U.S. 618 (1969), remains good law and its holding has in fact been extended. See Graham v. Richardson, 403 U.S. 365 (1971) [finding that state statutes that denied welfare benefits to resident aliens who have not resided in the United States for a specified number of years violated the Fourteenth Amendment]; Memorial Hospital v. Maricopa County, 415 U.S. 250 (1974) [striking down an Arizona statute that required a year's residence in a county before an indigent could receive nonemergency hospitalization or medical care, because it created an "invidious classification" that violated the Fourteenth Amendment]; Saenz v. Roe, 526 U.S. 489 (1999) [holding that California's statute imposing durational residency requirements, which limited TANF benefits through the recipient's first year of residency, violated the Fourteenth Amendment]. On the relationship between geographic mobility and intergenerational economic mobility, see Raj Chetty and Nathaniel Hendren, "The Impact of Neighborhoods on Intergenerational Mobility: Childhood Exposure Effects and County-Level Estimates," Executive Summary, April 2015, accessed May 20, 2015, http://www.equality-of-opportunity.org/images/nbh ds_exec_summary.pdf.

6. Richard A. Cloward and Frances Fox Piven, "Starving by the Rule Book," *Nation*, April 3, 1967, 429–31.

7. Carmen DeNavas-Walt and Bernadette D. Proctor, U.S. Census Bureau, *Income and Poverty in the United States: 2013* (Washington, DC: U.S. Government Printing Office, 2014).

8. Inside the welfare bureaucracies, Matthew Diller argues, these rules and regulations have now been paired with "private sector management techniques" –"funding incentives, training, and performance-based evaluation" – that tend to exacerbate bureaucratic disentitlement. Matthew Diller, "The Revolution in Welfare Administration: Rules, Discretion, and Entrepreneurial Government," *New York University Law Review* 75, No. 5 (2000): 1126–29. On the phenomenon of bureaucratic disentitlement, see Michael Lipsky, "Bureaucratic Disentitlement in Social Welfare Programs," *Social Service Review* 3 (1983): 3–27; Timothy J. Casey and Mary R. Mannix, "Quality Control in Public Assistance: Victimizing the Poor through One-Sided Accountability," *Clearinghouse Review* 22, no. 11 (1989): 1381–89; Susan D. Bennett, "'No Relief but upon the Terms of Coming into the House': Controlled Spaces, Disentitlements, and Homelessness in an Urban Shelter System," *Yale Law Journal* 104, no. 8 (1995): 2157–212; John Gilliom,

Overseers of the Poor: Surveillance, Resistance, and the Limits of Privacy (Chicago: University of Chicago Press, 2001); Amy Mulzer, "The Doorkeeper and the Grand Inquisitor: The Central Role of Verification Procedures in Means-Tested Welfare Programs," *Columbia Human Rights Law Review* 36, no. 3 (2005): 663–712.

9. Kaaryn Gustafson, "The Criminalization of Poverty," *Journal of Criminal Law and Criminology* 99, no. 3 (2009): 643–716; Kaaryn S. Gustafson, *Cheating Welfare: Public Assistance and the Criminalization of Poverty* (New York: New York University Press, 2011). On the dire implications of gaining a criminal record, see Michelle Alexander, *The New Jim Crow: Mass Incarceration in the Age of Colorblindness* (New York: The New Press, 2012). Unfreedom of another sort is built into today's welfare state, Viviana Zelizer has pointed out. Since the late 1960s, policymakers have increasingly chosen to meet the needs of the poor via benefits "in kind" (food stamps, housing vouchers, and so on) rather than through unrestricted cash transfers. Viviana A. Zelizer, *The Social Meaning of Money* (New York: Basic Books, 1994), 195.

10. For example, studies have shown that race affects the quality of client-staff interactions and correlates with the likelihood of being "sanctioned" (disciplined for failing to comply with eligibility requirements). See Susan T. Gooden, "All Things Not Being Equal: Differences in Caseworker Support toward Black and White Welfare Clients," *Harvard Journal of African American Public Policy* 4 (1998): 23–33; Lael R. Keiser, Peter R. Mueser, and Seung-Whan Choi, "Race, Bureaucratic Discretion, and the Implementation of Welfare Reform," *American Journal of Political Science* 48, no. 2 (2004): 314–27; Ariel Kalil, Kristin S. Seefeldt, and Hui-Chen Wang, "Sanctions and Material Hardship under TANF," *Social Service Review* 76, no. 4 (2002): 642–62; Celeste Watkins-Hayes, "Race-ing the Bootstrap Climb: Black and Latino Bureaucrats in Post-Reform Welfare Offices," *Social Problems* 56, no. 2 (2009): 285–310; Shannon M. Monnat, "The Color of Welfare Sanctioning: Exploring the Individual and Contextual Roles of Race on TANF Case Closures and Benefit Reductions," *Sociological Quarterly* 51, no. 4 (2010): 678–707; Joe Soss, Richard C. Fording, and Sanford F. Schram, *Disciplining the Poor: Neoliberal Paternalism and the Persistent Power of Race* (Chicago: University of Chicago Press, 2011); Rose Ernst, Linda Nguyen, and Kamilah C. Taylor, "Citizen Control: Race at the Welfare Office," *Social Science Quarterly* 94, no. 5 (2013): 1283–307.

11. William Novak, "The Legal Transformation of Citizenship in Nineteenth-Century America," in *The Democratic Experiment: New Directions in American Political History*, ed. Meg Jacobs, William J. Novak, and Julian E. Zelizer (Princeton, NJ: Princeton University Press, 2003), 86.

12. Yishai Blank, "Spheres of Citizenship," *Theoretical Inquiries in Law* 8 (2007): 421. On the "denationalization" of citizenship more generally, see Linda Bosniak, "Citizenship Denationalized," *Indiana Journal of Global Legal Studies* 7 (1999): 447–509.

13. National Employment Law Project, Economic Policy Institute, "It's Time To Raise the Minimum Wage," April 23, 2015, accessed May 20, 2015, https://www.nelp.org/publication/time-raise-minimum-wage/; National Employment Law Project, "City Minimum Wage Laws: Recent Trends and Economic Evidence," September 2015, accessed October 14, 2015, http://www.nelp.org/content/uploads/City-Minimum-Wage-Recent-Trends-Economic-Evidence.pdf.

14. Stephanie Luce, "Living Wage Policies and Campaigns: Lessons from the United States," *International Journal of Labour Research* 4, no. 1 (2012): 12–14.

15. Joel F. Handler and Yeheskel Hasenfeld, *Blame Welfare: Ignore Poverty and Inequality* (Cambridge: Cambridge University Press, 2007), 325; see also Greg Kaufmann, "Poor People Need a Higher Wage, Not a Lesson in Morality," *Nation*, April 22, 2015, accessed May 20, 2015, http://www.thenation.com/article/205153/poor-people-need-higher-wage-not-lesson-morality.

16. Rose Cuison Villazor, "'Sanctuary Cities' and Local Citizenship," *Fordham Urban Law Journal* 37 (2010): 573–98; Cristina M. Rodriguez, "The Significance of the Local in Immigration Regulation," *Michigan Law Review* 106, no. 4 (2008): 600–605.

17. On the importance of local surveillance to the enforcement of immigration laws, see Anil Kalhan, "Immigration Surveillance," *Maryland Law Review* 74, no. 1 (2014): 1–78. For a historical examination of this topic, focusing on local welfare authorities, see Cybelle Fox, *Three Worlds of Relief: Race, Immigration, and the American Welfare State from the Progressive Era to the New Deal* (Princeton, NJ: Princeton University Press, 2012), 124–87. On surveillance of the poor, see Gilliom, *Overseers of the Poor*. On surveillance of U.S. residents more generally, see Robert O'Harrow Jr., *No Place to Hide* (New York: Simon and Schuster, 2006); Laura K. Donohue, "Anglo-American Privacy and Surveillance," *Journal of Criminal Law & Criminology* 96, no. 3 (2006): 1072–151.

18. The allusion is to James C. Scott, *Seeing Like a State: How Certain Schemes to Improve the Human Condition Have Failed* (New Haven, CT: Yale University Press, 1998).

19. Heather K. Gerken, "Dissenting by Deciding," *Stanford Law Review* 56 (2005): 1745–806.

20. Hugh Heclo, *Modern Social Politics in Britain and Sweden: From Relief to Income Maintenance* (New Haven, CT: Yale University Press, 1974), 1.

Selected Bibliography of Primary Sources

ARCHIVAL COLLECTIONS

These sources are also cited in full in their first appearance in the endnotes. Subsequent references in the notes employ the abbreviations listed here.

Arizona State Library, Archives and Public Records, Phoenix
> Minutes of the Meetings of the Emergency Relief Administration of Arizona/
> State Board of Public Welfare, RG 37, SG 1 (ABPW Minutes)
> Papers of Governors Sidney Preston Osborn and Daniel E. Garvey, RG 1, SG
> 14–15 (SO/DG Papers)
> Public and Personal Papers of Ernest McFarland, 1894–1985, MG 98
Arizona State University Libraries, Arizona Collection, Tempe
> Carl T. Hayden Papers, 1851–1979, MS CM MSS 1 (CHP)
Beinecke Rare Book and Manuscript Library, Yale University, New Haven, CT
> Felix S. Cohen Papers, WA MSS S-1325 (FCP)
Bentley Historical Library, University of Michigan, Ann Arbor
> Papers of George Romney, 852178 Aa 2 (GRP)
Frances White papers, private collection, on file with author (FWP)
Indiana State Library and Historical Bureau, Indianapolis
Library of Congress Manuscript Division, Washington, DC
> Harold L. Ickes Papers
> Julius A. Krug Papers
M. E. Grenander Department of Special Collections and Archives, University
> Libraries, University at Albany, State University of New York, Albany
> New York Public Welfare Association Records, APAP-126 (NYPWAR)
National Archives, College Park, MD
> Records of the Department of Health, Education, and Welfare and the
> Federal Security Agency, RG 235 (HEWR)
> Records of the Social and Rehabilitation Service, RG 363 (SRSR)
> Records of the Social Security Administration, RG 47 (SSAR)
National Museum of the American Indian, Washington, DC
> Records of the National Congress of American Indians, Accession 1 (NCAIR)

New Mexico State Library, Santa Fe
New Mexico State Records Center and Archives, Santa Fe
    New Mexico Supreme Court Law Library State Agency Collection
    Records of the Health and Social Services Department
    Records of the Southwestern Association of Indian Affairs (SAIAR)
New York State Archives, Albany
    New York (State) Moreland Commission on Welfare, Record Series 10991
Richard G. Smith family papers, private collection, notes on file with author
    (RSP)
Seeley J. Mudd Manuscript Library, Princeton University, Princeton, NJ
    Association on American Indian Affairs Records, MC 147 (AAIAR)
Social Welfare History Archives, University of Minnesota, Minneapolis
    National Association of Social Workers and Predecessor Organizations
        Records, SW 1000 (NASWR)
    National Social Work Council, National Social Welfare Assembly, and
        National Human Services Assembly Records, SW 0004 (NSWAR)
    Robert T. Lansdale Collection, SW 169 (RLC)
Small Special Collections Library, University of Virginia, Charlottesville
    Papers of Frank Bane, Accession no. 7280-a (FBP)
South Carolina Department of Archives and History, Columbia
    American Public Welfare Association Files, RG 214000
Special Collections Research Center, University of Chicago, Chicago
    University of Chicago School of Social Service Administration Records
        (CSSAR)
The State Historical Society of Missouri, Columbia
    Parke M. Banta Papers, Collection no. 3844
Wisconsin Historical Society, Madison
    Papers of Elizabeth Wickenden, Mss 800, M99-098 (EWP)

ORAL HISTORY COLLECTIONS

California Social Welfare Archives' Oral History Collection, University of
    Southern California, Los Angeles
Columbia Center for Oral History, Columbia University, New York
Indiana University Center for the Study of History and Memory, Bloomington
National Equal Justice Library Oral History Collection, Georgetown Law
    Library, Washington, DC
Regional Oral History Office, Bancroft Library, University of California, Berkeley

SELECTED STATUTES AND LEGISLATIVE DOCUMENTS

Administrative Procedure Act, Pub. L. No. 79-404, 60 Stat. 237 (1946)
Aid to Dependent Children of Unemployed Parents Act, Pub. L. No. 87-31, 75 Stat. 77
    (1961)

An Act Amending the Jurisdiction of District Courts in Civil Actions with Regard to the Amount in Controversy and Diversity of Citizenship, Pub. L. No. 85-554, 72 Stat. 415 (1958)

A Bill to Amend the Social Security Act to Enable States to Establish More Adequate Public-Welfare Programs, and for Other Purposes, H.R. 2892, 81st Cong., 1st sess. (1949)

A Bill to Promote the Rehabilitation of the Navajo and Hopi Tribes of Indians, S. 1407, 81st Cong., 1st sess. (1949)

Civil Rights Act of 1871, Pub. L. No. 42-22, 17 Stat. 13 (1871)

Civil Rights Act of 1964, Pub. L. 88-352, 78 Stat. 241 (1964)

Conference Report to Accompany S. 1407, H.R. Rep. No. 81-1338 (September 22, 1949)

Conserve and Develop Indian Lands and Resources Act, Pub. L. No. 73-383, 48 Stat. 984 (1934)

Federal Emergency Relief Act of 1933, Pub. L. No. 15, 48 Stat. 55 (1933)

Hearings before the Committee on Finance, U.S. Senate, 90th Cong., 1st sess., on Proposed Cutoff of Welfare Funds to the State of Alabama (January 25 and February 23, 1967)

Hearings before the Committee on Ways and Means, House of Representatives, 87th Cong, 2d sess., on H.R. 10032, A Bill to Extend and Improve the Public Assistance and Child Welfare Services Programs of the Social Security Act, and for Other Purposes (February 7, 9, and 13, 1962)

Hearings before Subcommittee No. 5 of the Committee on the Judiciary, House of Representatives, on Miscellaneous Proposals regarding the Civil Rights of Persons within the Jurisdiction of the United States. 88th Cong., 1st sess. (May–August, 1963)

Hearings before a Subcommittee of the Committee on Ways and Means, House of Representatives, 83d Cong., 1st sess., on Economic Status of the Aged and Public Assistance (November 16–17, 1953)

Hearings before a Subcommittee of the Committee on Ways and Means, House of Representatives, 83d Cong., 1st sess., on OASI: Coverage, Eligibility, Benefits; and Public Assistance (November 18–20, 1953)

Hearings before a Subcommittee of the Committee on Ways and Means, House of Representatives, 83d Cong., 1st session, on Public Assistance: OASI Financial Position and Benefits (November 23–25, 1953)

Hearings before a Subcommittee on Indian Affairs of the Committee on Public Lands, on H.R. 3476: A Bill to Promote the Rehabilitation of the Navajo and Hopi Indians under a Long-range Program, 81st Cong., 1st sess. (April–May, 1949)

Hearings before the Subcommittee on Constitutional Rights, Committee on the Judiciary, on S. 1117 and S. 1219 Bills Relating to Extension of the Civil Rights Commission, 88th Cong., 1st sess. (May–June, 1963)

Indian Citizenship Act, Pub. L. No. 68-175, 43 Stat. 253 (1924)

National Industrial Recovery Act, Pub. L. No. 73-67, 48 Stat. 195 (1933)

Old-Age, Survivors, and Disability Insurance Amendments of 1965, Social Security Amendments of 1965, Pub. L. No. 89-97, 79 Stat. 286 (1965).

Public Law 280, Pub. L. No. 83-280, 67 Stat. 588 (1953)

Public Welfare Amendments of 1962, Pub. L. No. 87-543, 76 Stat. 172 (1962)

Reorganization Plan No. 2 of 1946, Pub. L. No. 79-263, 59 Stat. 613 (1946)
Revenue Act of 1951, Pub. L. No. 82-183, 65 Stat. 452 (1951)
School Construction in Areas Affected by Federal Activities, Pub. L. No. 81-815, 64
  Stat. 967 (1950) and Pub. L. No. 81-874, 64 Stat. 1100 (1950)
Social Security Act of 1935, Pub. L. No. 74-271, 49 Stat. 620 (1935)
Social Security Act Amendments of 1939, Pub. L. No. 76-379, 53 Stat. 1362 (1939)
Social Security Act Amendments of 1950, Pub. L. No. 81-734, 64 Stat. 477 (1950)
Social Security Act Amendments of 1967, Pub. L. No. 90-248, 81 Stat. 821 (1968)
Social Security Act Amendments of 1972, Pub. L. No. 92-603, 86 Stat. 1329 (1972)

LEGAL OPINIONS

Achor v. State Social Security Commission, 191 S.W.2d 259 (Mo. Ct. App. 1945)
Adams v. Ernst, 95 P.2d 799 (Wash. 1939)
Adams v. Ernst, 117 P.2d 755 (Wash. 1941)
Anderson v. Burson, 300 F. sup. 401 (N.D. Ga. 1968)
Application of Rasmussen, 289 N.W. 773 (Minn. 1940)
Arizona State Department of Public Welfare v. Department of Health, Education and
  Welfare, 449 F.2d 456 (9th Cir. 1971)
Arizona v. Hobby, 221 F.2d 498 (D.C. Cir. 1954)
Baker v. Carr, 369 U.S. 186 (1962)
Bertch v. Social Welfare Department, 276 P.2d 891 (Cal. App. Ct. 1954)
Bertch v. Social Welfare Department, 45 Cal.2d 524 (1955)
Board of Social Welfare v. Los Angeles County, 162 P.2d 630 (Cal. 1945)
Bolling v. Sharpe, 347 U.S. 497 (1954)
Borreson v. Department of Public Welfare, 14 N.E.2d 485 (Ill. 1938)
Bowen v. Department of Social Security, 127 P.2d 682 (Wash. 1942)
Boynton v. Virginia, 364 U.S. 454 (1960)
Bradwell v. Illinois, 83 U.S. 130 (1872)
Brown v. Board of Education, 347 U.S. 483 (1954)
Buettner v. State Social Security Commission, 144 S.W.2d 864 (Mo. Ct. App. 1940)
Burgfield v. State Social Security Commission, 155 S.W.2d 273 (Mo. Ct. App. 1941)
Burley v. State Social Security Commission, 163 S.W.2d 95 (Mo. Ct. App. 1942)
Campbell v. State Social Security Commission, 191 S.W.2d 1015 (Mo. Ct. App. 1945)
Carmichael v. Southern Coal & Coke Company, 301 U.S. 619 (1937)
Chapman v. State Social Security Commission, 147 S.W.2d 157 (Mo. Ct. App. 1941)
Chirrillo v. Lehman, 38 F.Supp. 65 (S.D.N.Y. 1940)
Cohasset v. Scituate, 34 N.E.2d 699 (Mass. 1941)
Collins v. State Board of Social Welfare, 81 N.W.2d 4 (Iowa 1957)
Colorado Public Welfare Board v. Viles, 94 P.2d 713 (Colo. 1939)
Conant v. State, 84 P.2d 378 (Wash. 1938)
Contra Costa County v. Social Welfare Board, 229 Cal. App. 2d 762 (1964)
Cooper v. Aaron, 358 U.S. 1 (1958)
Creighton v. Pope County, 50 N.E.2d 984 (Ill. App. Ct. 1943)
Creighton v. Pope County, 54 N.E.2d 543 (Ill. 1944)
Dandridge v. Williams, 397 U.S. 471 (1970)

Dews v. Henry, 297 F. Supp. 587 (D. Ariz. 1969)

Dimke v. Finke, 295 N.W. 75 (Minn. 1940)

Doolin v. State Social Security Commission, 187 S.W.2d 467 (Mo. Ct. App. 1945)

Dunnavant v. State Social Security Commission, 150 S.W.2d 1103 (Mo. Ct. App. 1941)

Escalera v. New York City Housing Authority, 425 F.2d 853 (2d Cir. 1970)

Flemming v. Nestor, 363 U.S. 603 (1960)

Foster v. State Social Security Commission, 187 S.W.2d 870 (Mo. Ct. App. 1945)

Gaddis v. Wyman, 304 F. Supp. 713 (S.D.N.Y. 1969)

Gaeckler v. State Social Security Commission, 155 S.W.2d 544 (Mo. Ct. App. 1941)

Gardner v. Alabama, 385 F.2d 804 (5th Cir. 1967)

Gideon v. Wainwright, 372 U.S. 335 (1963)

Goldberg v. Kelly, 397 U.S. 254 (1970)

Gomillion v. Lightfoot, 364 U.S. 339 (1960)

Graham v. Richardson, 403 U.S. 365 (1971)

Greenwood v. Taylor, 60 N.Y.S.2d 452 (App. Div. 1946)

Grovey v. Townsend, 295 U.S. 45 (1935)

Hagy v. Department of Welfare, 259 S.W.2d 101 (Mo. Ct. App. 1953)

Halbert v. Michigan, 545 U.S. 605 (2005)

Hardy v. State Social Security Commission, 187 S.W.2d 520 (Mo. Ct. App. 1945)

Harper v. Virginia State Board of Elections, 383 U.S. 663 (1966)

Harrell v. Tobriner, 279 F. Supp. 22 (D.D.C. 1967)

Hawkins v. Department of Welfare, 197 S.W.2d 98 (Ky. Ct. App. 1946)

Helvering v. Davis, 301 U.S. 548 (1937)

Heyendreich v. Lyons, 374 Ill. 557 (1940)

Hooks v. State Social Security Commission, 165 S.W.2d 267 (Mo. Ct. App. 1942)

Howlett v. Social Security Commission, 149 S.W.2d 806 (Mo. 1941)

Hughes v. State Social Security Commission, 128 SW.2d 671 (Mo. 1939)

Indiana v. Ewing, 99 F. Supp. 734 (D.D.C. 1951)

Jefferson v. Hackney, 304 F. Supp. 1332 (N.D. Tex. 1969)

Jefferson v. Hackney, 406 U.S. 535 (1972)

The Kansas Indians, 72 U.S. (5 Wall) 737 (1866)

Kelley v. State Social Security Commission, 161 S.W.2d 661 (Mo. Ct. App. 1942)

Kelly v. Wyman, 294 F. Supp. 893 (S.D.N.Y. 1968)

King v. Smith, 392 U.S. 309 (1968)

Korematsu v. United States, 323 U.S. 214 (1944)

Lebron v. Secretary of Florida Department of Children and Families (4th Cir. 2014)

Lindsey v. Smith, 303 F. Supp. 1203 (W.D. Wash. 1969)

Lochner v. New York, 198 U.S. 45 (1905)

Los Angeles County v. La Fuente, 129 P.2d 378 (Cal. 1942)

Louisville Gas & Electric Co. v. Coleman, 277 U.S. 32 (1928)

Lynch v. United States, 292 U.S. 571 (1934)

Mapp v. Ohio, 367 U.S. 643 (1961)

Massachusetts v. Mellon, 262 U.S. 447 (1923)

Matthews v. Eldridge, 424 U.S. 319 (1976)

McBee v. State Social Security Commission, 188 S.W.2d 349 (Mo. Ct. App. 1945)

McCoy v. State Department of Public Welfare, 271 S.W.2d 788 (Mo. Ct. App. 1954)

McCullough v. Terzian, 80 Cal. Rptr. 283 (Ca. Ct. App. 1969)
Memorial Hospital v. Maricopa County, 415 U.S. 250 (1974)
Meredith v. Ray, 166 S.W.2d 437 (Ky. Ct. App. 1942)
Monroe v. Pape, 365 U.S. 167 (1961)
Monroe v. Pape, 221 F. Supp. 635 (N.D. Ill. 1963)
Moore v. State Social Securities Commission, 122 S.W.2d 391 (Mo. App. 1938)
Morey v. Doud, 354 U.S. 457 (1953)
Morgan v. Department of Social Security, 127 P.2d 686 (Wash. 1942)
Morton v. Mancari, 417 U.S. 535 (1974)
NAACP v. Alabama, 357 U.S. 449 (1958)
Newland v. Child, 254 P.2d 1066 (Idaho 1953)
New State Ice Company v. Liebmann, 285 U.S. 262 (1932)
Nichols v. State Social Security Commission, 156 S.W.2d 760 (Mo. Ct. App. 1941)
Nichols v. State Social Security Commission, 164 S.W.2d 278 (Mo. 1942)
Oklahoma Public Welfare Commission v. Thompson, 105 P.2d 547 (Okla. 1940)
Oliver v. State Social Security Commission, 184 S.W.2d 774 (Mo. Ct. App. 1945)
Parks v. State Social Security Commission, 160 S.W.2d 823 (Mo. Ct. App. 1942)
Patton v. Mississippi, 332 U.S. 463 (1947)
Pease v. Hansen, 404 U.S. 70 (1971)
Perkins v. State Social Security Commission, 164 S.W.2d 129 (Mo. Ct. App. 1942)
Price v. State Social Security Commission, 121 S.W.2d 298 (Mo. App. 1938)
Redgate v. Walcott, 3 A.2d 852 (Sup. Ct. of Errors of Conn., 1939)
Redmon v. State Social Security Commission, 143 S.W.2d 168 (Mo. Ct. App. 1940)
Reynolds v. Sims, 377 U.S. 533 (1964)
Rosado v. Wyman, 397 U.S. 397 (1970)
Rosebraugh v. State Social Security Commission, 196 S.W.2d 27 (Mo. Ct. App. 1946)
Saenz v. Roe, 526 U.S. 489 (1999)
San Antonio Independent School District v. Rodriguez, 411 U.S. 1 (1973)
Schneberger v. State Board of Social Welfare, 291 N.W. 859 (Iowa 1940)
Shapiro v. Thompson, 394 U.S. 618 (1969)
Shelley v. Kraemer, 344 U.S. 1 (1948)
Sipuel v. Board of Regents, 332 U.S. 631 (1948)
Smith v. Allwright, 321 U.S. 649 (1944)
Smith v. Board of Commissioners, 259 F. Supp. 423 (D.D.C. 1966)
Smith v. King, 277 F. Supp. 31 (M.D. Ala. 1967)
Smith v. Reynolds, 277 F. Supp. 65 (E.D. Pa. 1967)
Smith v. State Social Security Commission, 153 S.W.2d 741 (Mo. Ct. App. 1941)
Speiser v. Randall, 357 U.S. 513 (1958)
State v. Katz, 40 N.W. 2d 41 (Iowa 1949)
Steward Machine Company v. Davis, 301 U.S. 495 (1937)
Takahashi v. Fish & Game Commission, 334 U.S. 410 (1948)
Taylor v. State Social Security Commission, 181 S.W.2d 209 (Mo. Ct. App. 1944)
Thompson v. Shapiro, 270 F. Supp. 331 (D. Conn. 1967)
Wallberg v. Utah Public Welfare Commission, 203 P.2d 935 (Utah 1949)
Westberry v. Fisher, 297 F. Supp. 1109 (D. Me. 1969)
Weston v. Cassata, 37 P.3d 469 (Colo. App. 2001)
Wheeler v. Montgomery, 296 F. Supp. 138 (N.D. Cal. 1968)

Wilkie v. O'Connor, 25 N.Y.S.2d 617 (App. Div. 1941)
Williams v. Dandridge, 297 F. Supp. 450 (D. Md. 1968)
Williams v. Lee, 358 U.S. 217 (1959)
Williamson v. Lee Optical, Inc., 348 U.S. 483 (1955)
Worcester v. Georgia, 31 U.S. (6 Pet.) 515 (1832)
Wyman v. James, 400 U.S. 309 (1971)
United States v. Sandoval, 231 U.S. 28 (1913)
Veasey v. Perry, Civ. Action No. 13-CV-00193, 2014 WL 5090258 (S.D. Texas, Oct. 9, 2014)

SELECTED AGENCY REPORTS AND PUBLICATIONS

Committee on Economic Security. *Report to the President of the Committee on Economic Security.* Washington, DC: U.S. Government Printing Office, 1935.
Federal Security Agency, in collaboration with Bureau of Accounts and Audits and Office of the General Counsel. *Money Payments to Recipients of Old-Age Assistance, Aid to Dependent Children, and Aid to the Blind.* Washington, DC: U.S. Government Printing Office, 1944.
Federal Security Agency, Social Security Administration, Bureau of Public Assistance. *Hearing Decisions in Public Assistance*, vols. 1–4 (1947–49).
Public Assistance 1941. Public Assistance Report No. 4. Washington, DC: U.S. Government Printing Office, 1941.
Marcus, Grace F. *The Nature of Service in Public Assistance Administration.* Public Assistance Report No. 10. Washington, DC: U.S. Government Printing Office, 1946.
National Resources Planning Board. *National Resources Development Report for 1943.* Washington, DC: U.S. Government Printing Office, 1936.
President's Committee on Civil Rights. *To Secure These Rights: The Report of the President's Committee on Civil Rights.* Washington, DC: U.S. Government Printing Office, 1947.
Social Security Board. *First Annual Report of the Social Security Board.* Washington, DC: U.S. Government Printing Office, 1936.
Towle, Charlotte. *Common Human Needs: An Interpretation for Staff in Public Assistance Agencies.* Public Assistance Report No. 8. Washington, DC: U.S. Government Printing Office, 1945.
U.S. Bureau of Indian Affairs. *Statistical Report of Public Assistance to Indians, under the Social Security Act: Old Age Assistance, Aid to Dependent Children, Aid to the Blind, as of October 1, 1939.* Washington, DC: U.S. Government Printing Office, 1939.
U.S. Bureau of the Census. *Fifteenth Decennial Census of the United States, 1930.* Washington, DC: U.S. Government Printing Office, 1932.
U.S. Bureau of the Census. *Sixteenth Decennial Census of the United States, 1940.* Washington, DC: U.S. Government Printing Office, 1943.

U.S. Commission on Organization of the Executive Branch of Government and Council of State Governments. *Federal-State Relations*. Washington, DC: U.S. Government Printing Office, 1949.

U.S. Department of Agriculture. Federal-State Relations Committee, *Agricultural Planning and Federal-State Relations*. Washington, DC: U.S. Government Printing Office, 1938.

U.S. Department of Commerce. *The Indian Population of the United States and Alaska 1930*. Washington, DC: U.S. Government Printing Office, 1937.

Index